nicholas of cusa's dialectical mysticism

OTHER BOOKS BY THE SAME AUTHOR

A Companion to the Study of St. Anselm
(Minneapolis, 1972)

*Anselm of Canterbury: Volume Four: Hermeneutical
and Textual Problems in the Complete Treatises of St. Anselm*
(New York, 1976)

A Concise Introduction to the Philosophy of Nicholas of Cusa
(Minneapolis, 1978; 2nd ed. 1980; 3rd ed. 1986)

*Nicholas of Cusa on God as Not-other:
A Translation and an Appraisal of De Li Non Aliud*
(Minneapolis, 1979; 2nd ed. 1983; 3rd ed. 1987)

*Nicholas of Cusa on Learned Ignorance:
A Translation and an Appraisal of De Docta Ignorantia*
(Minneapolis, 1981; 2nd ed. 1985)

*Nicholas of Cusa's Debate with John Wenck:
A Translation and an Appraisal of
De Ignota Litteratura and Apologia Doctae Ignorantiae*
(Minneapolis, 1981; 2nd ed. 1984; 3rd ed. 1988)

Nicholas of Cusa's Metaphysic of Contraction
(Minneapolis, 1983)

*A New, Interpretive Translation
of St. Anselm's Monologion and Proslogion*
(Minneapolis, 1986)

nicholas of cusa's dialectical mysticism

text, translation, and interpretive study of de visione dei

second edition

by jasper hopkins

the arthur j. banning press
minneapolis

Herrn Prof. Dr. Rudolf Haubst und allen Mitgliedern
des Instituts für Cusanus-Forschung gewidmet

Second edition 1988
(First edition published 1985)

Library of Congress Catalog Card Number 84-71736

ISBN 0-938060-39-2

Printed in the United States of America

pReface

Within the tradition of late medieval mysticism Nicholas of Cusa's *De Visione Dei* (*On the Vision of God*), composed in 1453, commands a place of central importance. In this speculative work, instinct with a spirit of devotion, Nicholas meditates both upon the philosophical theme of God's infinity and upon the theological theme of God the Son's absolute mediatorship. For he recognizes that the Divine Being is not only *deus absconditus* but also *deus revelatus.* Because Nicholas emphatically develops, along paradoxical lines, such contrasting notions as *absconditus/revelatus, absolutus/contractus, infinitus/finitus, aeternalis/temporalis, perfectus/imperfectus,* and *exemplaris/participalis,* his speculative mysticism, like Meister Eckhart's, is highly dialectical.[1] Thus, Nicholas is not reporting actual mystical experiences but is reflecting dialectically upon the relationship between God's vision of man and man's vision of God. The former vision is necessarily exact, because God observes, so to speak, "from every possible angle." The latter vision is inevitably inexact, because the relationship between the finite and the Infinite is noncomparative, thus rendering man's positive conception of God, whether in this life or the next, only symbolical.

Given the magnificent intellectual and spiritual richness of *De Visione Dei,* the work itself (in translation) should appeal to a broad range of discerning readers. By contrast, the study that precedes the translation envisions as its audience a much narrower spectrum of students and specialists. The method of the study is *literarhistorisch,* not *problemgeschichtlich.* Indeed, the dangers of the latter method, when not subordinated to the former, are amply illustrated by Hans Blumenberg's unscholarly interpretation of Cusanus in his major book, *Die Legitimität der Neuzeit.* I set forth Blumenberg's mistakes in detail. For were I not to do so, no one would believe my mere assertion that his interpretation collapses. And in that case Nicholas's role at the end of the Middle Ages and the beginning of the Renaissance would, because of Blumenberg's preponderant influence, continue to be misjudged.[2]

In preparing the present edition of the Latin text, I not only worked from photographs and photocopies but also made on-site inspections of all the manuscripts. All told, I went over each of the manuscripts three times; and three times I proofread the final printed collation. Whatever errors may remain do so in defiance of my best efforts.

v

Preface

This project was begun while I was an exchange professor (1981-82) at the *Philosophisches Institut* of the University of Graz, Austria. It was completed during a sabbatical year (1983-84), while I was a fellow at the National Humanities Center, in Research Triangle Park, North Carolina. I am grateful to my colleagues at Graz for their generosity in arranging my teaching schedule. I likewise express appreciation to the University of Minnesota for granting the sabbatical leave, and to the directors and staff at the National Humanities Center for providing assistance in many forms, one of the most needed being the expert library service afforded by Alan Tuttle, Rebecca Sutton, and Jean Houston. At other libraries, in Europe and North America, I was kindly assisted by the following individuals, whose distinguished identifying-titles I here leave aside: Bernd Bader, Universitätsbibliothek, Giessen; Elisabeth Beare, Stadtbibliothek, Nürnberg; G. Franz, Stadtbibliothek, Trier; Hermann Hauke, Bayerische Staatsbibliothek, Munich; Otto Hunold, Cusanusstift, Bernkastel-Kues; Walter Neuhauser, Universitätsbibliothek, Innsbruck; Helga Ornig and Christl Unterrainer, Universitätsbibliothek, Salzburg; Beda Paluzzi, Biblioteca del Monumento Nazionale, Monastero di S. Scolastica, Subiaco; Julian Plante, Hill Monastic Library, St. John's College, Collegeville, Minnesota; Ivo Pomper, Stiftsbibliothek, Kloster Sankt Peter, Salzburg; Konrad von Rabenau, Evangelische Kirche der Union, Berlin (DDR); Hans-Erich Teitge and Ursula Winter, Deutsche Staatsbibliothek, Berlin (DDR); Brooke Whiting and James Davis, University Research Library, University of California at Los Angeles; Hans Zotter, Universitätsbibliothek, Graz. In addition, I owe special thanks to Otto Reberschak, of the University of Graz, who developed photographs for me, and to Pauline O'Connor, of Minneapolis, who assisted in other technical ways.

Finally, in dedicating the present volume to Rudolf Haubst and his associates at the *Institut für Cusanus-Forschung*, I do so in tribute to those whom I regard as among the finest exemplifiers of German historical scholarship.

Jasper Hopkins
Professor of Philosophy
University of Minnesota

PREFACE TO THE SECOND EDITION

Since the publication of the first edition, which took account of twenty-three manuscripts of *De Visione Dei*, two additional ones have come to my attention: Latin Codex 19 - 26 at the Cathedral Library in Toledo, Spain and Latin Codex 99 at the Staats- und Stadtbibliothek in Augsburg, Germany. The latter of these is a valuable copy which was transcribed, onto paper, in 1472 and which was previously located in Augsburg at the Benedictine monastery of St. Ulrich and Afra. *De Visione Dei*, found on folios 167^r - 227^r, is the only Cusan work in the manuscript. I am grateful to Gertraud Weinzierl of the Staats- und Stadtbibliothek for her kind reception and assistance on the occasion of my visit to the library.

By contrast with the Augsburg codex, Latin Codex Toledo 19 - 26, which was also transcribed during the second half of the fifteenth century, is of no value apropos of *De Visione Dei*. Its readings are much too erratic and impressionistic to be reliable; and its scribe seems to have had only a meager knowledge of Latin. My examination of it in Toledo confirmed my decision to exclude it from the list of manuscripts here being compared. Thus, in Appendix III only the variant readings for Augsburg 99 are given.

contents

nicholas of cusa's dialectical mysticism

part 1: interpretive study

NICHOLAS OF CUSA'S DIALECTICAL MYSTICISM
Part I: Interpretive Study

1. *Preliminary Observations.* 1.1. When Pope Nicholas V elevated Nicholas of Cusa to the office of cardinal on December 20, 1448, he did so partly in recognition of Nicholas's service as papal envoy and apostolic legate to the German peoples. For Nicholas's multiple missions between 1438 and 1448 were perceived in Rome as having helped persuade both clergy and nobility that the authority of the papacy exceeded the authority of the Council of Basel. The success of the papal initiatives can be seen in the fact that on February 17, 1448 Frederick III, King of Germany and Archduke of Austria, signed the Concordat of Vienna, therewith acknowledging the supremacy of the Holy See in religious matters.

On January 3, 1449 Nicholas was assigned titular headship of the Church of St. Peter in Chains, at Rome. And on April 26, 1450 he was consecrated Bishop of Brixen,[1] in Tirol. But before assuming vigorous administration of the bishopric, by taking up personal residence there two years later, he once again accepted the role of apostolic legate to the German nation—this time with the commission to renew spiritually the German church. His journey during 1451 and the first quarter of 1452 led him to visit such centers of spirituality as the Benedictine monasteries at Melk and Salzburg, the religious congregations at Deventer, Diepenveen, and Windesheim—in addition to visiting such centers of episcopal power as Trier, Mainz, Cologne, and Aachen. We have no reason to believe that this journey of reform led him, when en route from Salzburg to Munich, to make a detour to the Benedictine abbey at Tegernsee. The Abbey's records[2] inform us only of a subsequent sojourn, between May 31 and June 2, 1452. With the Tegernsee monks, and in particular with their abbot, Caspar Ayndorffer, Nicholas enjoyed exceptionally cordial relations. He not only valued their counsel[3] but even expressed the desire to have a cell prepared for him, since he longed for sacred leisure (*otium sacrum*) amid their company.[4] The Tegernsee monks, for their part, avidly solicited new works from Nicholas—works which they diligently copied and intently studied. Through their abbot and their prior they posed such questions as "whether apart from intellectual knowledge, and even apart from prevenient or accompanying knowledge—whether only by means of affection or of the highest capability of the mind (a capability which many call *synderesis*)—the devout soul can attain unto God . . . ."[5] This question was crucial to the concerns of the Tegernsee community because, quintessentially, it was a question about the proper understanding of *theologia mystica* and of the pathway toward union with God. The soul that truly loves God desires to be united with Him. And mystical theology, as derived from Pseudo-Dionysius,[6] taught that mystical union occurs not merely through the will's loving God but also through the intellect's seeing God. Yet, this seeing is likewise a not-seeing, since that which is beheld is too resplendent to be observed. One beholds the place where God dwells but does not behold God in Himself.[7]

By the middle of the fifteenth century there was still no agreement regarding just what mystical theology was, though usually it was thought to consist of a configuration of some of the following tenets, variously interpreted: (1) In man the highest degree of perfection is in the spirit, or mind, or intellect (*spiritus vel mens vel intelligentia*). (2) God is approached by the cognitive power of the intellect most truly when He is approached *via negationis*. For since God is not, except in a symbolic sense, *like* anything whose nature the intellect can conceive, the intellect can more truly ascertain what God is not than it can descry what He is; but because He is not like *anything* the intellect either knows or conceives, He seems closer to nothing than to something. (3) Just as in accordance with the *via negationis* the intellect must become released from all imaginative and conceptual restraints, so in accordance with the *via devotionis* it must become released from the distorting strictures of sin. (4) This latter form of purification is communicated through divine grace, which enables the human response of faith and love, so that the greater the faith and love, the closer the soul approaches unto God. (5) When the soul, thus enabled, ascends beyond all that is sensible, rational, and intelligible, it enters into the darkness of unknowability and inconceivability—a darkness that Dionysius alluded to as *irrationalis et amens*.[8] (6) Herein it awaits, with keen expectancy and ardent longing, the vision of the glorious God, whose superbrilliance incomparably exceeds the splendor of the sun. And just as no sensible eyes can peer directly into the blinding sun, so, a fortiori, no intellectual eyes can behold

God as He is in Himself: the beblinding Divine Light is seen only unseeably. (7) This vision occurs in rapture (*raptus*), accompanied by ecstasy (*extasis*). (8) These, together, conduce unto happiness (*felicitas*) and rest (*quietas*). (9) And happiness and rest are more fully attained the more fully the soul is united with God. (10) Momentary mystical union in this lifetime is but a foretaste of the fuller beatific union in the heavenly state—a union so close that it can be spoken of as a transformation, an absorption, a deification, even though it falls short of an identity.

1.2. John Gerson,[9] in his *De Mystica Theologia*, cites a number of alternative descriptions of mystical theology:[10]

- Mystical theology is the soul's stretching forth unto God through loving desire.
- Mystical theology is anagogic movement (i.e., upward movement leading unto God) through fervent and pure love.
- Mystical theology is experiential knowledge-of-God acquired through the embrace of uniting love.
- Mystical theology is wisdom, i.e., appetizing knowledge of God, acquired when through love the highest summit of the affective power of the rational [soul] is united unto God.[11]
- Mystical theology is experiential knowledge-of-God acquired through a union-of-spiritual-affection with God.[12]

Gerson also includes the well-known formula: "*Theologia mistica est irrationalis et amens, et stulta sapientia . . . .*"[13] Obviously, all of the foregoing descriptions, which Gerson regards as mutually compatible, require explication. What is meant, after all, by "*stulta sapientia*"? Just how closely uniting is the embrace of uniting love (*amoris unitivi complexus*)? And is the *supremus apex potentiae rationalis* to be identified with what Meister Eckhart and others had referred to as the *scintilla animae*? Gerson, to his lasting credit, attempted to answer such questions by distinguishing different forms of love and different kinds of knowing,[14] by sketching different theories regarding the *transformatio animae in deum*.[15] Gerson was intent upon drawing a clear distinction between *theologia mystica* and *theologia speculativa*. The latter, he said, originates from the intellectual power of the rational soul, whereas the former arises out of the rational soul's affective power. The latter takes as its object what is true, the former what is good.[16] Speculative theology makes use of rational considerations that conform to philosophical studies such as physics, metaphysics, logic, and grammar, and therefore it requires scholastic training; mystical theology, by contrast, requires only that the soul acquire moral virtue and that it be perfected in its love for the good.[17] Therefore, mystical theology, though involving some kind of knowledge, does not require formal training and study; hence, it is accessible to believers who are unschooled as well as to those who are erudite. Indeed, through faith, hope, and love, thinks Gerson, the unschooled can arrive at mystical union more quickly than can the scholastic theologians.[18] Moreover, scholastic, or speculative, theology cannot be perfected in anyone apart from mystical theology, though someone's being perfected in mystical theology does not require his being perfected in speculative theology as well.[19]

One kind of knowledge *is*, however, requisite to mystical theology:[20] viz., the knowledge that God is totally lovable—a knowledge that can be obtained from faith and revelation.[21] Gerson cites approvingly Augustine's words "*invisa diligere possumus, incognita nequaquam*": "We are able to love things that are unseen, but we cannot at all love things that are unknown."[22] When Gerson goes as far as to speak of mystical theology as "*suprema atque perfectissima notitia*" ("supreme and most perfect knowledge"),[23] he has in mind the kind of acquainting knowledge that derives from religious experience.[24] And experiential knowledge of God, he believes, is attained more by means of penitent love than by means of intellectual ferreting.[25] Through love the rational soul is united with God—a union that Gerson is willing to call "*experimentalis Dei cognitio seu notitia vel perceptio*," and even "*theologia mystica.*"[26] Mystical theology, then, is not theology in the sense of being a series, or a system, of theological propositions. Rather, for Gerson, it is theology in a twofold sense: primarily in the sense of being a knowledge of God, where the word "knowledge" has reference to the soul's *experiencing* the unitive embrace of the one whom it *recognizes* to be incomparably desirable—and secondarily in the sense of being instruction about what this experience of God is[27] and about how it is attainable. Gerson's descriptions of *theologia mystica* reflect these two senses. For sometimes he speaks of "the loving union, of which mystical theology is seen to consist" ("*per predictam amorosam unionem, in qua mistica theologia consistere videtur . . .* "),[28] and sometimes he speaks of "the loving union of the mind with God—a union which occurs through mystical theology" ("*amorosa unio mentis cum Deo, que fit per theologiam misticam . . .* ").[29] If mystical theology is *theology* because it is an experiential knowledge of God through a loving union, then it is *mystical* because this union is a transforming spiritual union[30] in which the soul, having become cognitively and affectionally detached from the world, is longingly and lovingly conscious only of God.[31]

Gerson depicts two routes toward mystical union of the human soul with God: the *via purae intelligentiae* and the *via devotionis*.[32] Regarding the first route, Gerson's statements are not fully consistent (though interpreters[33] sometimes talk as if they were). In the latter part of his *De Mystica Theologia* he writes: "Mystical theology is ecstatic love which is subsequent to our spirit's understanding—an understanding which, to be sure, is free of images, which becloud. Accordingly, whoever wills to devote himself to mystical theology must endeavor to attain unto this pure understanding. Otherwise, how would he attain unto the [state of] love that follows thereupon?"[34] But in his later work *Collectorium super Magnificat* he takes an altogether different position: "experiential perception of God does not require either a preceding or a succeeding acquaintance in terms of pure understanding."[35] Aside from this discrepancy, together with other attending ones, Gerson's views appear not unharmonious.[36] Three things, he himself seems to believe,[37] are conditions of the soul's mystical union with God, whether this union be sought *via purae intelligentiae* or whether it be sought *via devotionis*: there must be (1) longing for God, (2) removal of hindrances to union, and (3) earnest solicitation of God's good pleasure. The soul's longing is to be stimulated through heightened recognition of God's beauty and value; hindrances are to be removed through the soul's confessing its failing and torpor; and solicitation is to be made through importunate and ardent prayer.

To be sure, such longing, such arousal of the soul, such ardent prayer is possible only for believers. And yet, reminds Gerson: during their lifetimes on earth believers will not attain unto a union which is so close that it will be an immediate and, as it were, face-to-face experiencing of God; for this state of knowing is reserved for the future life.[38] Moreover, in the present lifetime only a relatively small number of believers will be able to follow the *via purae intelligentiae* and to motivate their longing by contemplating the fact that God transcends not only all the beauty of all finite things but also all other characteristics of these things as well. Intrinsic to this kind of contemplation is a mode of *negatio*, or *abnegatio*,[39] that involves an intellectual turning away from created things in order to be directed more fully toward the Creator Himself. To this end the mind must abandon, or transcend, its sensible and intellectual operations; but it must ascend even higher by abandoning, or transcending, its very self.[40] The mind begins to detach itself from *its sensible operation* by recognizing that God is not like any actual material object. It begins to abandon *its intellectual operation* by recognizing that God is not like any conceivable finite being, whether this conceivable being is actually existent or is nonexistent. Finally, the mind begins to abandon *its very self* by detaching itself, insofar as possible,[41] from the awareness of everything except God.[42] Metaphorically speaking, the soul at this point will have entered into divine darkness—the darkness wherein dwells *deus absconditus*. Insofar as humanly possible the soul will have directed its thought and its affections[43] away from the world, away from itself, and upward toward God. At this point it will be dead to the world, which will hold no attraction, no value for it; it will be alive only unto the Creator,[44] whose unitive embrace it will expectantly and contemplatively be awaiting. In accordance with God's good pleasure, the deeply yearning, upward-mounting, silently imploring soul may be rewarded with the ecstatic experience of superinfused love and of rapturous union.[45] And yet, this union will not be of such intimacy that the soul will see God clearly and unveiledly, since God does not choose to present Himself directly and immediately to rapt believers in this lifetime.[46]

During the moment of ecstatic union the mind will be aware of the unitive bond between itself and God—will be aware of itself only in relation to God. Without this awareness, or knowledge, the mystical encounter could not rightly be called an experience.[47] When in *De Mystica Theologia* and *Super Magnificat* Gerson asserts that experiential knowledge of God does not occur through negation and remotion alone, that the *via superexcellentiae* is also required,[48] he does so in order to preserve the legitimacy of the soul's belief that God is more excellent than—not less excellent than—our highest conceptions of goodness, love, beauty, and whatever else is valuable. For it is precisely this belief which motivates the soul in its desire to be united with God. The state of pure, or purified, understanding (*pura intelligentia*)—the state that characterizes the highest stage of the *via abnegationis* when the intellect is free from images and concepts of everything creaturely, prior to the soul's experience of ecstatic unitive love—is not attainable by the simple and unlearned (*simplici et rustici*), who are incapable of the abstractive contemplation that is required. And yet, these simple believers are not excluded from mystical theology, which, as Dionysius himself had said, is common to Christians.[49] In order to take account of this group, who also are required to believe with most devout faith that there exists a Good than which a greater cannot be *thought* (where *thinking* is construed as encompassing *sensing, imagining, inferring,* and *understanding*),[50] Gerson introduces his second route, the *via devotionis*.[51] Through faith and love, he explains, the soul of the simple, fervent believer can attain unto the same heights as the soul of the erudite— i.e., can attain unto ecstasy and can do so without the precondition of intellectual detachment. For through the edifying quality of his devout love the simple believer can become released from attachment to the world in order to soar upward unto the Beauty of the Lord. Thus, the *via devotionis* has its own mode of *abnegatio*—of dying to the world and to the self.

According to Gerson both the *via devotionis* and the *via purae intelligentiae* require love for God,[52] just as both require some positive conception of God, whether obtained from Scripture or from a combining, philosophically, of the *via abnegationis* and the *via superexcellentiae*.[53] Through the presence of love both routes lead to the possibility of the rapture which Gerson terms *extasis*.[54] But— keeps insisting Gerson—the *via devotionis* more readily leads to mystical union than does any pathway that requires an initial erudition.[55] His example of a typical ascent by faith is instructive. The simple believer may begin by considering the sacrament of the Eucharist and by believing through faith that during the celebration thereof the true and living Body of Christ is present. He can then proceed from this belief to meditating upon the deeds performed by Christ during His earthly ministry. This meditating can conduce to even greater devotion by stimulating holy and humble affection. Moreover, the power of the Holy Spirit can purify the believer's devotional affection by turning it at that time toward loving no object the love of which would interfere with loving God. Thereafter, the believer can turn toward a holy and faith-filled consideration of the mystical Body of Christ, i.e., of the redeemed souls in Paradise and of those other souls which are yet to be redeemed. Finally, he can elevate his meditative devotion unto God alone, separating off every created lovable thing—separating them off not by means of reason or of understanding but by means of sincere love and by means of the mystery of devout faith, by which he believes the following: that his God is that than which nothing greater or more noble can be conceived or loved—that his God is all-desirable.[56] Gerson admits that the erudite can know all of these points more clearly than can the simple believer; but he denies that the erudite can know them more truly and more sublimely.[57] Furthermore, he denies that they can know them in such way as to be elevated more readily unto mystical union or in such way as to dispense with the precondition of love.

All in all, then, Gerson's conception of *theologia mystica* attempts to harmonize the two motifs of love and knowledge. For on the one hand, his conception includes the view that love is the root of all the affections,[58] together with including the view that it is more perfect than faith.[59] And on the other hand, his conception embraces the doctrine that mystical union-of-love does not occur apart from some kind of prevening and accompanying knowledge, as well as embracing the doctrine that, in general, the *via purae intelligentiae* must be supplemented by the *via superexcellentiae*. Both during and after his lifetime Gerson was accused of not having done justice either to the motif of love or to the motif of knowledge. The followers of Ruysbroeck were convinced that Gerson had never experienced ecstatic love, so that his teachings thereabout were bound to be misguided—a judgment confirmed, in their minds, by his attack upon their master. Perhaps it was with these disciples in mind that Gerson defended his authority to write about *experimentalis cognitio dei* even in the absence of an experience of mystical union.[60] Yet, perhaps it was the absence of such an experience that led him to take account, theologically, of the "inner experience . . . of blessed union" ("*experientia intrinseca . . . beatae unionis*"),[61] where the experience of union with God was now understood as nonecstatic experience fostered through the more usual pathways of faith-filled devotion.

If Gerson gave offense with his statement that oftentimes affection is greater where knowledge is minimal and that therefore no special knowledge other than the "knowledge of faith" is needed for mystical theology,[62] he was nonetheless not dismissive of erudition. Indeed, he argued that the doctrinal tradition of mystical theology (*doctrinalis traditio theologiae mysticae*) intersects with Scholastic theology and is not different or separate from it, as it is also not different or separate from true philosophy.[63] And yet, he was attacked on the alleged ground that he himself had betrayed the doctrinal tradition of mystical theology by veering from the teachings of the Great Dionysius.[64] One of the most instructive of such attacks came years after his death and is an indirect tribute to his great stature, as well as being a sign of his continuing influence. For the critic, Vincent of Aggsbach, one-time prior of the Carthusian Monastery at Aggsbach, Austria, did not hesitate to admit: "Gerson has a name next to the names of the great men on earth. And he has written many things which are transmitted everywhere. To these places faith is brought because of his celebrated reputation, especially among the learned."[65]

1.3. In 1453 Vincent wrote a treatise in which he roundly denounced Gerson's treatment of mystical theology.[66] He admitted to having previously held Gerson's writings in esteem and to having transcribed many of them. But after having studied these works more carefully, he found them objectionable. To begin with, he objects to Gerson's definitions of *mystical theology*, all of which he regards as too general and too vague—as leaving aside much that is essential.[67] Accordingly, infers Vincent, they do not clarify the practice of mystical theology but serve only to obfuscate it. Equally problematical in Vincent's eyes are other of Gerson's statements which, though not definitions, also display ignorance of what mystical theology is. Gerson states, for example, that love and mystical theology and perfect prayer either are the same thing or else presuppose one another.[68] But he seems to understand "perfect prayer" in the sense of verbal or mental or intellectual prayer—none of which modes, indicates Vincent, are identical with mystical theology. For these modes do not transcend all conceptualizing of God, whereas mystical theology teaches that just such transcendence is required. Hence, mystical theology could rightly be called prayer only in the sense of being nonintellectual, or *superintellectual*, prayer—something which would better be termed *adoratio*.[69]

Vincent's first complaint overlaps with his second: Gerson goes wrong by teaching that an intellectual knowledge of God must guide and accompany the devout love that attains unto mystical union.[70] By contrast, continues Vincent, Dionysius and such true followers of his as Hugh of Balma taught that the soul is to elevate itself upward toward God through the power of love, assisted by the intellect's becoming ignorant, by its ceasing to conceptualize not only creatures (a point Gerson concedes) but also God or any of His persons (a point Gerson does not concede). For whoever conceptualizes God cannot do so otherwise than in terms of goodness, truth, being oneness, and eternity. He thus thinks of Him delimitedly, as being *this* rather than *that*.[71] (Precisely because every positive conception is delimiting, Dionysius taught that God is to be approached beyond all intellectual understanding.[72]) "And although this practice [of mystical theology] is difficult for many people (and, indeed, impossible for some), it is, in my opinion, very easy for a mind that is disposed thereto. If I had love (which, alas, I do not experience myself to have), then I would be sweetly and fervently aglow. I would hope that the breaking free from, or the abandoning of, images and concepts, etc., would not prove a great hindrance to me. But this art requires men of temperate passion, men of tranquil and modest spirit, men aglow with sweet love. It does not admit men who are involved in many tasks, men who are concerned with fleshly desires, men who are proud, ambitious, insincere, hypocritical, curious (who attempt to approach [solely] for the sake of the experience) . . . ."[73] From Vincent's point of view the *via devotionis* becomes vitalized when it is taken in conjunction with the *via purae intelligentiae*. Gerson emphasized the independence of the two because of his fears regarding the capability of the simple religious believer. But in order to accommodate the simple believer he ends up with what Vincent regards as a distorted account of mystical theology.

Furthermore, Gerson makes a third mistake, thinks Vincent. By refusing to acknowledge that the *via purae intelligentiae* is essential to mystical theology—by insisting that some positive conception of God must accompany the soul's detachment from the world and from its own self—Gerson associates himself with Scholastic theology, which looked askance at Dionysius's talk about the need to approach God *irrationaliter et amentaliter.* Indeed, Gerson keeps trying, though in vain, to harmonize mystical theology with Scholastic theology and philosophy:

> The same reverend doctor [i.e., Gerson], with much concern and with many words, endeavored, in different works, to harmonize mystical theology with Scholastic theology and with the philosophers. I believe that this harmony is scarcely more useful than if the same thing were made by a cobbler and by a painter (the former making a shoe of leather and the latter making it of colors) and the agreement and differences between these objects were cleverly sought. Scholastic theology is the reading, study, and understanding of Sacred Scripture—of both the Old and the New Testaments. Mystical theology is a form, or an act, of devotion or is a unique mode of the mind's extension unto God . . . .[74]

Vincent sees Gerson as undermining the Dionysian tradition by attempting to *de-radicalize* it, to *de-mystify* it. Symptomatic of this attempt is Gerson's misconstrual of Dionysius's reference to "the unlearned" ("*indocti*"). For although Gerson takes this to indicate those who live evilly, clearly Dionysius was referring to those who " 'are attached to existing things, who believe that there is not anything supersubstantially above existing things, and who suppose themselves to know, by means of the knowledge that conforms to themselves, Him who has made darkness His hiding place.' "[75] Because of Gerson's predilection for Scholasticism, his theology—unlike Hugh of Balma's—is mixed with curious, subtle, and irrelevant considerations, accuses Vincent. It draws, for example, upon Aristotle's doctrine of the potencies of the soul. But, assails Vincent, the whole of *De Anima*—indeed, the whole of philosophy—has little importance for mystical theology; otherwise—and here Vincent turns Gerson's argument back upon itself—simple believers would not be capable of attaining unto mystical theology.[76]

A fourth accusation charges Gerson with contradicting himself[77] when in *Super Magnificat* he writes that mystical union presupposes *charitas* but in *Elucidatio Scolastica Mysticae Theologiae* states that superinfused love remains without *charitas*.[78] In other instances, admits

Vincent, Gerson may simply be changing his mind rather than contradicting himself. Thus, whereas in *De 12 Industriis* he seems to
hold the opinion that mystical theology does not preclude an intellectual knowledge of God,[79] in *Anagogicum de Verbo et Hymno Gloriae* he rejects this opinion.[80] However, in both of these instances,
charges Vincent, Gerson opposes himself to the "expositors of Blessed
Dionysius," thereby not only breaking with the tradition but, in one
of the cases, even miscasting it through false interpretation.[81]

Finally, Vincent purports to come to the source of Gerson's
errors:[82] viz., his mistaken identification of mystical theology with
contemplation[83]—an identification even more patently erroneous than
the identification with prayer. Contemplation, after all, takes its name
from contemplating, or seeing; but mystical theology is called mystical because it has to do with hiddenness.[84] And between sight and
concealment (i.e., between seeing and not-seeing) there is no identity.
Moreover, the activity of the advance stages of contemplation requires a
union of an intellectual component and an affective component. By
contrast, the exercise of mystical theology is said by Vincent to consist only of affection. Gerson himself, argues Vincent, concedes that
there are many differences between contemplation and mystical theology, for in *De 12 Industriis* he acknowledges that through love the
believer who is little trained in metaphysics can successfully turn
away from images.[85] In the end, Vincent reaffirms the radical character of mystical theology: unlike contemplation—which is the elevation of the mind unto God, an elevation guided and accompanied by
reflection—mystical theology is a *bedarkened* elevation of the mind
unto God, *without any guiding or accompanying reflections.*[86]

Vincent's critique serves to exhibit the context within which the
controversy over mystical theology had developed. The monks at
Aggsbach, Salzburg, Melk, Tegernsee, and other affiliate monasteries
were puzzled over how rightly to construe the relationship between
love and knowledge, over whether an immediate, "face-to-face"
vision of God was possible during their lifetimes, over what steps
were prerequisite to this vision. What was meant by the soul's "transcending itself"? What was meant by "superintellectual prayer," by "pure
understanding," "pure devotion," "experiential knowledge of God,"
"entering into darkness with Moses," "being raptured unto the third
heaven with Paul"? To monastic communities these were questions
that seemed to be vital.

1.4. When Nicholas of Cusa assumed active administration of the diocese of Brixen in April 1452, he was already esteemed as cardinal and reformer—but also as the author of some eighteen treatises and dialogues, not to mention an even larger number of sermons. His masterly and powerful *De Docta Ignorantia* (1440) had firmly secured his reputation as an important thinker—though a controversial one. John Wenck, of course, had denounced the treatise of 1440 as heretical and had labelled Nicholas a pseudo-prophet,[87] just as Vincent of Aggsbach later accused him of resisting the Holy Spirit and of teaching a strange, new doctrine.[88] Vincent grouped Nicholas with Gerson and Marquard Sprenger and impugned all three collectively. Each member of this erring trinity, he maintained, taught the same grave falsehood: viz., that acquainting knowledge of God *preceded* rather than *succeeded* the experience of loving union.[89] And yet, Vincent still esteemed Nicholas highly enough to refer to him as "a man great in body, great in mind, great in knowledge, great in eloquence, great in benefices, great in wealth, elevated in honors"[90]— as someone whose work[91] was of value for the *via illuminativa*, even if not for the *via unitiva*.[92] That such a man as Nicholas would be consulted by the monks of Tegernsee seems only natural—especially given his vigorous rebuttal of Wenck in *Apologia Doctae Ignorantiae* (1449) and his exultation of unschooled wisdom in *Idiota de Sapientia* (1450). His tribute to this kind of wisdom seems to have something in common with Gerson's respect for the simple religious believer. And we know, in fact, that Nicholas was acquainted both with Gerson's *Theologia Mystica Speculativa* and with his *Theologia Mystica Practica*.[93]

In two letters to the abbot and monks at Tegernsee—the two that sought to answer queries about the teachings of Dionysius—Nicholas displays agreement with ideas from Gerson and with ideas from Dionysius.[94] Mystical theology, he explains in the later of these two letters and in the fashion of Dionysius, must go beyond not only the *via positiva* but also the *via negativa*.[95] It goes beyond the former by realizing that the soul's encounter with any positively conceived being would be an encounter, at best, with only a semblance of God— perhaps even with the angel Satan, who can transform himself into an angel of light.[96] It goes beyond the latter by realizing that what is altogether unknown is neither loved nor discovered—and that even if such an unknown thing *were* "discovered," i.e., encountered, it would not be recognized.[97] According to mystical theology, maintains Nicholas, the soul rises upward unto God not by altogether suspending the operation of the intellect (*non linquendo intellectum*), as Vincent would have us believe; rather, the intellect itself must discern that the soul is entering into the density and darkness where contradictions coincide. In the letter written a year earlier[98] Nicholas gave a different answer to a different question—a question about the relationship between mystical theology, love, and knowledge. In mystical theology, he answered in a manner reminiscent of Gerson, knowledge must accompany love. For whatever is loved is loved under the aspect of the good—i.e., is loved as being a good. So if the soul did not deem God to be a good, it would not love Him; and if it loves Him, it deems Him a good. This judging, or deeming, is the intellectual, or "cognitive," component that is necessary for love. And yet, though the loving soul apprehends God to be a good, it understands the nature of this good only *aenigmatice*, and not as it is in itself.[99] Like Gerson, Nicholas sometimes, as here, uses the word "knowledge" ("*cognitio*") where what he means in the context is "conception" ("*conceptio*").[100] In accordance with this broad usage of "*cognitio*" and in agreement with his teaching in *De Docta Ignorantia*, he is claiming, unlike Gerson, that our concept of good has only a *symbolic* meaning insofar as it is used to refer to God.

The foregoing two letters of September 22, 1452 and September 14, 1453 testify to the fact that Nicholas's reflections on mystical theology were an extension of his doctrine of learned ignorance.[101] In the second of these letters he discloses his intention to expand a section of *De Theologiis Complementis* (i.e., *Complementum Theologicum*) into a separate treatise that deals with mystical theology and that makes use of an omnivoyant portrait. This separate work could only have been *De Visione Dei*. Three considerations warrant the presumption that it was finished before the end of the year: (1) In the letter of September 14, 1453 Nicholas indicates that he is eager to complete it—a statement which suggests that completion is not far off.[102] (2) Codex Latinus Gissensis 695 contains as *explicit* the words "*Finivit Brixne 1453. 8 Novembris. Nycolaus cardinalis*".[103] And (3) Letter 8, from Abbot Caspar of Tegernsee, indicates that he, Caspar, has received a copy of *De Visione Dei*. Although we do not know the exact date of Caspar's letter, we know that it must have been written a considerable time before February 12, 1454—the date of Nicholas's reply thereto.[104] Given the usual intervals required for the exchange of correspondence, we may judge reliably that Nicholas was finished with *De Visione Dei* by the end of 1453. And taking seriously the *explicit* of Giessen 695, we may infer that Nicholas completed it before November 8. Indeed, it was probably among the "*aliqua*" to which he referred in a letter dated October 23, 1453: "Regarding the items about which I wrote on a previous occasion: you will have some of them (*aliqua*) soon. I was planning to send them now, but they have not yet been copied."[105]

The title *De Visione Dei* (*The Vision of God*) has a deliberately twofold meaning, corresponding, respectively, to the subjective and the objective construal of the genitive case of "*Deus*." On the first construal the vision is *God's vision* of creatures; on the second, it is *creatures' vision* of God. The titles of Chapters 4 and 8 illustrate the first construal; the title of Chapter 9 contains an instance of the second. And a sentence in Chapter 10 combines both ideas: "In that You see all creatures You are seen by all creatures."[106] Insofar as vision-of-God is *God's* vision, Nicholas compares it with an eye: "O Lord, You see and You have eyes. Therefore, You are an eye, because Your having is being."[107] The eye is like a living mirror, mirroring the visible forms of all that it sees. In the case of human beings whatever is seen is seen from a given angle, or perspective. Consequently, many things whose forms are mirrored in the human eye remain unobserved because the eye cannot attend to all these images at once.

> But since Your sight *is* an eye, i.e., a living mirror, it sees within itself all things. Indeed, because it is the Cause of all visible things, it embraces and sees all things in the Cause and Rational Principle of all things, viz., in itself. Your eye, O Lord, proceeds to all things without turning. The reason our eye turns toward an object is that our sight sees from an angle of a certain magnitude. But the angle of Your eye, O God, is not of a certain magnitude but is infinite. Moreover, the angle of Your eye is a circle—or better, an infinite sphere—because Your sight is an eye of sphericity and of infinite perfection. Therefore, Your sight sees—roundabout and above and below—all things at once.[108]

The angle of God's eye is an infinite sphere inasmuch as God's infinite sight sees all things from all perspectives. God—as all-seeing Subject who views, at once, all things "roundabout and above and below"—has, so to speak, the center of His perception everywhere and its delimiting circumference, or circumscribing bound, nowhere.[109] The identity of divine seeing and divine being, maintains Nicholas, is adumbrated in the Greek word for God, viz., "*theos*"—a word that is cognate with "*theōrō*,"[110] as in Latin "*visus*" is cognate with "*video*." "Therefore, the sages say that God sees Himself and all things by means of one indescribable viewing, because He is the Vision of visions."[111]

Nicholas illustrates God's all-encompassing vision by means of the portrait, or icon, of a face that appears to be omnivoyant: from whatever perspective anyone looks at it he has the impression that its eyes are upon him alone; but by inquiring of someone else, he can ascertain that its gaze is also directed, as it were, completely at the other. If one observer moves while the other remains stationary, the icon's eyes seem for the one who moves to be moved with him and for the one who is unmoving to be fixed unmovedly upon him himself. But if both observers move, in such way that they approach each other from opposite directions while looking toward the icon, the icon's eyes are experienced by each as wholly following his own motion; and yet, the eyes are inferred to be following opposite motions at the same time. Like the omnivoyant figure, God's eyes "run to and fro throughout the whole earth,"[112] so that at once He beholds all things, for the angle of His eye is infinite. "Whither shall I flee from thy face?" asks the Psalmist.

> If I ascend into heaven, thou art there: if I descend into hell, thou art present. If I take my wings early in the morning, and dwell in the uttermost parts of the sea: Even there also shall thy hand lead me: and thy right hand shall hold me.[113]

The divine eye never forsakes us, never turns away. But when we turn our gaze away from God, fixing it upon worldly goods which we prefer to the Supreme Good, the eye of God looks upon us no longer with graciousness but now with condemnation.[114]

Because of Nicholas's use of an illustrative icon, his work was sometimes referred to by the alternative title "*De Icona*."[115] Indeed, in *De Possest* 58:20-21 he himself refers to it in this way. Like the

face of the icon, God's Face looks upon us; and we, for our part—
and here occurs the objective construal of the genitive in "*visio
dei*"—look unto God as we would look unto the face of the icon.
But our mental eye, says Nicholas, is "cloaked with contraction and
affection," so that the mind, in looking unto God, sees Him according to its own affections, inclinations, and propensities. Whoever
looks lovingly unto God will see God as looking back lovingly upon
him; whoever looks angrily unto God will see God as looking back
with wrath. Thus, the divine eye mirrors back unto us our own propensities, just as when we look eastward toward the icon, it seems to
look back at us from the east, and when we are positioned so that we
look westward toward it, it looks back at us from the west, as it
were. We mentally behold God, then, not as He is in Himself but
only in accordance with the conditioning nature of our finitude. For
the mind's eye can never escape from its contractedness in order to
behold God from all angles, as it were—behold Him as He beholds
and knows Himself.[116] Nor can the mind rid itself of its affectional
nature, though this nature can be transformed through spiritual
regeneration wrought by the Holy Spirit in cooperation with a man's
faith.[117]

2. *Our Knowledge of God.* 2.1. The soul that looks believingly unto
God may begin to contemplate, as did the Psalmist, "the beauty of
the Lord."[118] Nicholas himself, from out of his own contemplation,
exclaims: "O Face exceedingly lovely! All the things which have
received the gift of looking thereupon do not suffice for admiring its
beauty."[119] In the Neoplatonic tradition within which Nicholas is situated, beauty is regarded as guiding and edifying the soul. Through
the vision of beauty the soul's love can become intensified and
ennobled, until, finally, the soul gazes upon Beauty itself. Though
this traditional view has its origins in Plato's *Symposium*, it is
mediated to Nicholas through Dionysius's writings.[120] (Gerson, too,
as we have seen, incorporates the theme of beauty into his conception
of mystical theology.) Nicholas follows Dionysius in allowing that
God's beauty is "seeable" by the mind *only insofar as the mind
transcends itself.* That is, God's beauty is not mentally seeable, is not
conceivable; it is seeable only in the sense that it is seen to be inconceivable: "Therefore, as regards whoever sets out to see Your Face: as

long as he conceives of something, he is far removed from Your Face. For every concept of face is less than Your Face, O Lord; and all beauty that can be conceived is less than the beauty of Your Face."[121] God, says Nicholas, is Absolute Beauty, the Form that gives being to all beautiful forms.[122]

It may seem strange that Nicholas speaks of our seeing God's beauty, while at the same time telling us that in Himself God is not beautiful and that His nature is inconceivable by all except Himself.[123] So although Nicholas calls God "Absolute Beauty" and uses the predicate "beautiful" of Him, these expressions must be taken symbolically. For what Nicholas says of goodness applies equally to beauty: "infinite goodness is not goodness but is Infinity."[124] However, just as Nicholas continues to call God good, so he continues to call Him beautiful. In all beautiful objects, he declares, God's beauty is seen symbolically and beveiledly (*velate et in aenigmate*).[125] And during the present lifetime it can be seen unveiledly (*revelate*) in one and only one manner: by way of mystical theology. The seeker of God's Face must enter into darkness, or ignorance, by passing beyond all knowledge and all conception of every kind of face and every kind of beauty. This is the familiar route of the *via purae intelligentiae*; and it draws upon the comparison with the light of the sun:

> When our eye seeks to see the sun's light, which is the sun's face, it first looks at it in a veiled manner in the stars and in colors and in all participants in the sun's light. But when our eye strives to view the sun's light in an unveiled manner, it passes beyond all visible light, because all such light is less than the light it seeks. But since it seeks to see a light which it cannot see, it knows that as long as it sees something, this is not the thing it is seeking.[126]

Nicholas adds the crucial words: "*In this way and in no other* the inaccessible light and beauty and splendor of Your Face can be approached *unveiledly*."[127] In this lifetime God's light and beauty are "seen unveiledly" only insofar as the darkness in the eye of the intellect becomes more dense and forbidding—i.e., only insofar as the intellect becomes more and more cognisant of its necessary ignorance.

Gerson made a different use of a related example. He likened man's vision of God to an observer situated atop a high mountain. Beneath him are dark clouds that shut him off visually from the world below; between him and the sun there is another set of dark clouds that block his direct vision of the sun but that display diffusedly and obliquely some small measure of sunlight, so that the darkness is not pitch black.[128] In the contrast between this illustration and Nicholas's illustration rests an essential difference between Cusanus and Gerson: it is the difference between ascending into pitch darkness and ascending into an obscuring darkness *that can be seen*.[129] According to Nicholas, that is, there is an infinite disproportion between any finite concept of God and God's undifferentiated being,[130] which only God Himself can truly conceive. According to Gerson, on the other hand, the *via superexcellentiae* legitimates some measure of real analogy and proportion between the divine nature and the human conception thereof, so that the *via negativa*, by itself, is not adequate for mystical theology. Now, Nicholas himself subscribes to the *via superexcellentiae*, as we recognize from *De Possest* 56:15-17; but, unlike Gerson, he uses it to establish the fact of God's incomprehensibility.[131] For though we affirm that God is supergood, superbeautiful—indeed, supersensible, superimaginable, superintelligible—what we mean is that He infinitely surpasses every characteristic that any finite thing has and every characteristic that any finite thing does not have but could have. When God is encountered mystically, He is encountered as transcending *per infinitum* all differentiation—encountered as beyond the coincidence of contradictories such as good and not-good, being and not-being.[132] (This encounter, repeats Nicholas, occurs in darkness, where *deus absconditus* is concealed from the eyes of all the wise.)[133] Thus, Nicholas can claim that God is encountered beyond the *via positiva* and the *via negativa*,[134] beyond the distinction between "is an *x*" and "is not an *x*." Gerson, too, seems to acknowledge this point when he endorses Dionysius's statement that the rational soul, as it follows the *via theologiae mysticae*, must suspend its intellectual operation with respect to all created or creatable being and not-being.[135] But, as we have seen, Gerson, unlike Nicholas, defines *mystical theology* in such way that it allows another pathway unto God: viz., the pathway of negation qua negation-of-affection. This route has little to do with the *via purae intelligentiae*, which is not attainable by the simple religious believer, thinks Gerson. Nicholas, however, interprets *mystical theology* in such way that the *via purae intelligentiae* is a necessary condition of approaching God *mystically*,[136] though God may be approached other than mystically, as when He is entreated in public prayer or worshipped in the privacy of the monastic cell.

By now it has become apparent that in *De Visione Dei* Nicholas uses diversely the expression "*videre deum*"—an expression which corresponds to the objective-genitive construal of "*visio dei.*" The sense we have just been exploring is the one related to the possibility of *mystical* union in this lifetime. Prerequisite to this union, we have noted, is the recognition that *what God is*[137] is unknowable and inconceivable by us, except symbolically. "When I see You to be Absolute Infinity . . . ," remarks Nicholas, "then I begin to behold You unveiledly and to enter unto the source of delights."[138] This beholding is a mental viewing which is to be accomplished as a precondition of the possibility of rapture. It is part of what is meant by "entering into darkness with Moses." And it is associated with the doctrines of learned ignorance and of the coincidence of contradictories. For to see that God is Absolute Infinity is to recognize that He is beyond all differentiation, that every finite mind is, therefore, necessarily ignorant of His nature. Accordingly, Nicholas avows: "I see You in the garden of Paradise, and I do not know what I see, because I see no visible thing. I know only the following: viz., that I know that I do not know—and never can know—what I see."[139] Here, as so often, Nicholas speaks paradoxically: "I see . . . no visible thing." Indeed, to see the Unseeable God is, for Nicholas, one kind of seeing: viz., the seeing *that* God is unseeable.

Nicholas continues in this same paradoxical vein by reasoning: (1) There are finite beings. (2) If there is an end of the finite, then there is the Infinite. (3) But there is an end of the finite. (4) Therefore, there is the Infinite.[140] This argument is too imprecise to qualify as an attempt to establish God's existence. Nor is Nicholas making such an attempt, for nowhere in *De Visione Dei* does he ever call into question the existence of God, so that a proof would become desirable. He is simply contemplating God's being the End of all creation[141]—an End that is without an end, because it is an Infinite End. Such paradoxical speculation, he believes, is helpful for introducing the intellect to a knowledge both of its own ignorance and of the coincidence of contradictories:

> Because, O Lord, You are the End that delimits all things, You are an End
> of which there is no end; and thus You are an End without an end—i.e., an
> Infinite End. This [fact] escapes all reasoning, for it implies a contradiction.[142]

God delimits the universe, and each thing in it, in that He is the
center and the circumference of the world and of all things in the
world.[143] For the infinity of His perspectives completely encompasses
and defines each and every thing. And yet, puzzles Nicholas, how
can God *be* the definition, the limitation, the end of everything if He
Himself is without definition, limitation, and end?[144] For an Infinite
End is no more an end than infinite goodness is goodness.[145] Taken
literally, the words "Infinite End" seem to Nicholas to form a phrase
whose meaning is contradictory; but interpreted figuratively, as when
Nicholas says in *De Docta Ignorantia* that God is the *circumference*
of the world, the words neither have a contradictory meaning nor are
in danger of being meaningless. For God is Infinite End in that He is
the circumference of the world and each thing in it; and He is the
circumference, Nicholas has said, in that at once He beholds the
world and all its objects from every possible perspective. Yet, Nicholas does not suppose that we can imagine or conceive what such
infinite perception is like, since it is not at all like anything we could
ever experience. But, as Nicholas understands the matter: when God
is compared, metaphorically, to an all-seeing eye, He is *not being
signified as* resembling any kind of eye or any kind of seeing that we
can imagine or can form a conceptual likeness of. Rather, He *is
being signified as* seeing in a way which does not resemble anything
we can imagine or can form a conceptual likeness of.[146] And just as it
makes some sense to assert that God is undifferentiated being, even
though we cannot imagine or (positively) conceive of undifferentiated
being, so it makes some sense to speak of Him as "perceiving" in a
way that necessarily eludes our power to imagine or to conceive a
likeness thereof. Nicholas never abandons his point that Infinite Sight
is not sight but is Infinity. But he does not consider this point to
preclude the legitimacy of speaking of God *as if* He perceived in a
way analogous to our mental insight and *as if* His perceiving eye
were an infinite sphere that "sees—roundabout and above and below—all
things at once."[147]

But how, we might wonder, does Nicholas legitimate the use of some symbolisms and the repudiation of others? The correct answer, it seems clear, is that he does so by appeal both to revelation and to the principle of supereminence. According to the latter appeal God may not fittingly be symbolized as less than the summit of all perfection; rather, He must be affirmed to be *incomparably more perfect* than any compatible set of perfections that is humanly conceivable.[148] According to the former appeal we learn from the life and teaching of Jesus, "the sole Revealer of His own Father,"[149] which symbolisms most befit God. Thus, even though infinite goodness is not goodness, still Nicholas purports to learn through Christ's ministry, doctrine, and sacrificial death about the kind of goodness that God requires of us and that makes us more and more Godlike, as it were. "If by every possible means I make myself like unto Your goodness," he declares regarding Christ, "then according to my degree of likeness thereto I will be capable of receiving truth."[150] To become "like unto Your goodness" is to become "more conformed, and similar, to the Word."[151] Becoming conformed to the Word—through faith, love, and good works—is the spiritual prerequisite to any kind of union with God, and therefore, to *mystical* union in particular.[152]

On the basis of such spiritual conformity of soul, the intellect of the mystical theologian can mount upward unto the wall of absurdity that surrounds Paradise, wherein dwells Inaccessible Divine Light. The wall of absurdity is the wall of the coincidence of contradictories— of goodness and not-goodness, mercifulness and not-mercifulness, creator and not-creator, oneness and not-oneness, etc.—beyond which *deus absconditus* makes His abode. In rising up mystically, the soul, we have noted, must recognize that the goodness-of-God as seen in Christ does not and cannot characterize Infinity itself in itself. This recognition, together with spiritual conformity to Christ, is a precondition of the intellect's experiencing God—i.e., of the intellect's being caught up beyond its own powers and operations unto experiencing as darkness the superbrillant Divine Light. This experience of darkness will not be dreadful or frightening. For the darkness will be experienced as intimate, beshielding warmth that befits joyous and loving union. Such union can be accomplished only insofar as the soul is united to God through Christ, the Son of God.[153] And it may be preceded by a lesser state of mental rapture accompanying the discernment—prior to entering into intellectual darkness—that Christ is Absolute Mediator.[154]

2.2. A second sense of *"videre deum"* is related to the notion of sonship (*filiatio*).

2.2.1. Nicholas takes this notion from John 1:12: "But as many as received him, he gave them power to be made the sons of God, to them that believe in his name."[155] In *De Visione Dei* 18 (83) sonship is alluded to in the following words: "A man who receives You, His receivable God, passes over into a union which, because of its closeness, can be given the name *sonship.*" Nicholas does not develop the notion any further here because he has already explored it at length in *De Filiatione Dei* (1445), where he identified sonship with deification and with the intuitive vision of God.[156] This intuitive vision is said to be an apprehension of Truth[157] and to be a participation in the divine power.[158] Accordingly, sonship is the ultimate perfecting of the intellect; it is the intellect's attaining not merely unto truth insofar as it is befigured in symbolisms drawn from the sensible world but even unto Truth insofar as it is intellectually seeable apart from symbolisms. Though this seeing will occur without any symbolisms from the sensible world, it will not occur apart from the modalities of seeing and knowing that characterize the future life.[159] Sonship, which Nicholas affirms to be attainable by faith, begins in this lifetime but is brought to perfection only in the future, resurrected state, where Truth is seen as it is. Qua commencing in this lifetime, it precedes the possibility of mystical theology; qua brought to perfection in the future life, it excels the results of mystical theology, for it is a higher state of ascent. In becoming sons of God believers do not become something other than they now are, states Nicholas; rather, what they now are they shall then be in another manner.[160] Thus, their transformation—their becoming ever more like Christ—will not be a transformation of their essence into the divine essence. Only Christ Himself, the only-begotten Son of God, is so perfectly Son that His (divine) nature is identical with the Father's. Through participation, by faith, in Christ's Superabsolute Sonship all believers obtain their own sonship.[161] The highest stages of this participatory union with Christ and—through Christ—with the Father take place in the future life and are referred to as seeing Truth itself, which is the Word of God.[162]

In the eschaton[163]—Nicholas has told us (in accordance with I John 3:1-2)—Christ will be seen *as He is* and God will be seen in Christ; but though in Christ God will be intellectually seen apart from any sensory image or symbolism, He will not be seen *as He is in Himself*.[164] This *intellectualis visio Christi*, apart from symbolisms, is that which the practicer of mystical theology is ultimately seeking:

> Accordingly, this name ["*possest*"] leads the one-who-is-speculating beyond all the senses, all reason, and all intellect unto a mystical vision, where there is an end to the ascent of all cognitive power and where there is the beginning of the revelation of the unknown God. For, having left all things behind, the seeker-after-truth ascends beyond himself and discerns that he still does not have any greater access to the invisible God, who remains invisible to him. (For God is not seen by means of any light from the seeker's own reason.) At this point the seeker awaits, with most devout longing, the omnipotent Sun—expecting that when darkness is banished by its rising, he will be illuminated, so that he will see the invisible [God] to the extent that God will manifest Himself.[165]

The prospective banishing of darkness will be the seeing of God in Christ. For Christ is the sole Revealer of the Father not only during the present era but also during the eschatological age. The believer, in being united to Christ through his intellectual nature, may be said to see the Face of God. This union will be so close that in Christ the human intellect will see itself as it is. Nicholas illustrates this point[166] by likening Christ, who is the supreme Reflection of God, unto a completely perfect and completely straight Mirror in which God appears. He calls this Mirror the Mirror-of-truth, because in it all creatures—whom he likens unto mirrors that are variously contracted and curved—are reflected *as they are*. In turn, the Mirror-of-truth is reflected in these contracted mirrors not as it is but with a degree of variation that accords with the degree of curvature of the respective mirror. Now, if any given *intellectual* creature—i.e., intellectual, living "mirror"—were brought into position in front of the Mirror-of-truth, in which all creaturely mirrors are reflected, then into this given mirror the Mirror-of-truth would infuse itself; and the given mirror would receive this infused ray in which would be contained the true images of all the other mirrors. Thus, at one and the same instant this given mirror (1) would see itself, as it is, in the Mirror-of-truth and (2) would see, in the mirror which it itself is, all other objects. But the objects would be seen not as they are in themselves but as they are conditioned by the degree of curvature of the given receiving mirror. Thus, the more nearly straight and the more perfectly clean this mirror is, the more truly and clearly it will see in itself both God's glory and all other objects. In this way, then, the mirror in question becomes a possessor of God—becomes, as it were, a son of God, so that all things are in it and so that in it they *are* it.

The foregoing illustration, believes Nicholas, displays how in accordance with faith, love, and righteous deeds the human intellect will be elevated in the future life unto very close union with God-in-Christ. In this union the intellect will embrace Christ, who is all in all.[167] In becoming one with Christ—one through union, not through identity—it will receive the likenesses of all things at the moment when "in it all things are it."[168] Even though Nicholas does not mean to imply that this union of the human intellect with the Word of God will be an identity, he opens the door to misunderstanding when he goes as far as to write: "God will not be, for this [intellectual] spirit, *other* than it or different or distinct from it; nor will the Divine Form (i.e., the Word of God) or the Spirit of God be *other* than it. For all otherness and difference are far beneath sonship itself. For a most pure intellect makes to be intellect all that is understandable, since in this intellect all that which is understandable is the intellect itself."[169] In attaining unto the highest stage of sonship, the intellect can be said to have become deified, notes Nicholas,[170] and to have transcended all comparative relationships and all rational considerations.[171]

> But since the intellect is a living intellectual likeness of God: when it knows itself, it knows in its own oneness all things. Now, it knows itself when it beholds itself in God as it is. But this is when in the intellect God is the intellect. Therefore, knowing all things is nothing other than seeing oneself as a likeness of God—[a vision] which is sonship.[172]

At this point the intellect will have become the intellectual universality (*intellectualis universitas*) of all things; for it will be the discrete notion of all things, since it will have become like all that it has understood.[173] This Cusan doctrine is also found in *De Possest*, where the intellect is said to be able to attain unto complete knowledge when it attains unto a future knowledge of God's Word:

> For the highest degree of happiness—viz., the intellectual vision of the Almighty—is the fulfillment of that desire of ours whereby we all desire to

know. Therefore, unless we arrive at the knowledge of God—viz., the knowledge by which He created the world—our mind (*spiritus*) will not be at rest. For as long as the mind does not attain to this knowledge, it will not attain to complete knowledge (*scientia scientiarum*). This knowledge is the knowledge of God's Word; for the Word of God is the Concept both of itself and of the universe. Indeed, anyone who does not arrive at this Concept will not attain to a knowledge of God and will not know himself. For what is caused cannot know itself if its Cause remains unknown.[174]

Nicholas's exuberance in *De Filiatione Dei* and in *De Possest* is an echo of his earlier exuberance in *De Docta Ignorantia* III, where he spoke of the believer's ascending upward unto the point where he would be *absorbed* into Christ: "Be aware that as someone's flesh is progressively and gradually mortified by faith, he progressively ascends to oneness with Christ, so that he is absorbed into Christ by a deep union—to the extent that this is possible on [this pilgrim's] pathway."[175] Similarly, Nicholas's talk about the believer's *arising as Christ*,[176] about his being *transformed into Jesus*,[177] and about his *existing in Christ Jesus as Christ*[178] was highly misleading. For it suggested a union so close that it passed over into an identity. Given the controversy that had been occasioned by Meister Eckhart's declaration that the man who loves to suffer for God's sake is "*in deum transformatus*"—a phrase that was condemned as heretical—even someone such as John Gerson exercised caution in his use of the word "*transformatio*."[179] Though Nicholas himself was incautious, a careful reading of *De Docta Ignorantia*, like a careful reading of *De Filiatione Dei*, discloses that he is teaching nothing unorthodox. For when he speaks more precisely, he speaks of being "transformed into Christ's *image*."[180] And though he mentions that believers shall arise as Christ and be transformed into adopted sons,[181] he additionally states that each believer's own being will be preserved.[182] Likewise, in *De Filiatione Dei* he declares that the intellect is the *likeness* of God,[183] but not a likeness which is an identity of nature.[184] To be sure, sonship is said to be a knowledge of God and of the Word (*notitia dei et verbi*)[185] and is said to transcend all comparative relation (*per transcensum omnium proportionum . . . ad puram intellectualem vitam*);[186] but it is a knowledge of God only as He is revealed in the Word;[187] and the pure intellectual life transcends all comparative relationships only in that it encounters a God who is ineffable and inconceivable.[188]

2.2.2. Nicholas's theme of sonship and deification is borrowed not only from Dionysius but also from Meister Eckhart. We know from *Apologia Doctae Ignorantiae* that Nicholas was familiar with many of Eckhart's works and that he regarded them as orthodox.[189] Moreover, traces of Eckhart's views can be located in Nicholas's own writings.[190] A good example of such a trace occurs in *De Ludo Globi*:

> Cardinalis: Esto igitur ens esse omnium existentium complicationem. Tunc cum nullum ens sit, nisi in ipso sit entitas, certissimum esse vides deum eo ipso quod entitas est in ente, esse in omnibus. Et licet ens ipsum in omnibus quae sunt videatur, non est tamen nisi unum ens, sicut de uno et puncto dictum est. Nec est aliud dicere deum esse in omnibus, quam quod entitas est in ente omnia complicante. Sic optime ille vidit qui dixit: quia deus est, omnia sunt.[191]

In general, an interpreter must be cautious in linking Eckhart and Cusanus. For even when Nicholas borrows certain of Eckhart's themes, he develops them in ways that differ significantly from their development within Eckhart's framework. Regarding sonship, for example, Nicholas develops this theme without recourse to such Eckhartian declarations as the following: (1) that in the "spark" of the devout believer's soul, as truly as in Himself, God begets His only-begotten Son,[192] (2) that God begets the devout believer as His only-begotten Son, [193] (3) that the power in the soul of the devout believer co-begets the Son—co-begets Him in the power of the Father,[194] (4) that the devout believer is so one with God that He has power over God and can command God,[195] and (5) that God's love for the devout believer is necessitated by the divine nature.[196]

Nonetheless, in *De Filiatione Dei* Nicholas's entire account of sonship is inspired by Eckhart's teachings.[197] This same theme of sonship recurs in *De Visione Dei*, where Eckhart's influence is also detectable. In *De Visione Dei* 7, for instance, Nicholas introduces the example of a tree, whose seminal power is ultimately produced by the Divine Power, which is Absolute Power, or Absolute Cause. As the tree and its seminal power exist in their Cause they are this Cause. And, hence, in this Cause, i.e., in God, they are the cause of themselves.[198] This line of thinking, in *De Visione Dei* 7, is reminiscent of Meister Eckhart's: "And hence, in accordance with my being, which is eternal, I am cause of myself—but not in accordance with my becoming, which is temporal."[199] But though Nicholas agrees with Eckhart that in God everything is God, he avoids the radicalness of Eckhart's further statement: "That God is 'God,' of that I am the cause."[200] So, in last analysis, even though Nicholas moderates Eckhart's extreme tone, traces of Eckhart's thought are still evident in his writings. Three last examples of such traces may be mentioned. First, the metaphor of God-as-infinite-sphere, a metaphor which plays a special role in *De Visione Dei* 8, was mediated to Nicholas through Eckhart.[201] (Indeed, the theme of God's vision looms large in Eckhart's works.) Secondly, Nicholas's distinction, in *De Filiatione Dei* 3 (63:4-9), between God as He is in Himself and God insofar as He is Truth, reflects Eckhart's distinction between *deitas* and *deus*.[202] For Nicholas states that *"veritas ipsa non est deus ut in se triumphat, sed est modus quidem dei . . . "*: "Truth itself is not God as He is triumphant in Himself but is a mode of God . . . ."[203] And, thirdly, the contrasting themes of *image* and *exemplar* loom so large in Eckhart's works that Nicholas's own development of these themes could not fail to owe much of its motivation to Eckhart.[204]

2.3. Nicholas's third sense of *"videre deum"* has to do with a creature's *existing*. For in *De Visione Dei* 10 Nicholas interprets a creature's seeing God as its receiving existence from God's sight. Since God's seeing is not other than His hearing, says Nicholas, His gaze may be said to speak, just as it may also be said to create. And the creature's coming into existence is its hearing the voice of God, its seeing God:

> By Your Word You speak to all existing things, and You summon into being nonexisting things. Therefore, You summon them in order that they may hear You; and when they hear You, they exist. Therefore, when You speak, You speak to all; and all the things to which You speak hear You. You speak to the earth, and You summon it to [become] human nature; and the earth hears You, and its hearing is its becoming man.[205]

2.4. A final sense of *"videre deum"* concerns the speculative approach to God whereby one comes to discern that He is Absolute Power, Absolute Cause, Absolute Being—even though one cannot descry any positive, nonsymbolic content to these notions. In *De Visione Dei* 7, where Nicholas introduces the example of the nut tree, he does so in order to illustrate how he *sees* "Your Absolute Face to be (1) the natural Face of every nature, (2) the Face which is the Absolute

Being of all being, (3) the Art and Knowledge of everything knowable." In this chapter he speculates upon how the nut tree is an unfolding of a seed's power and upon how the seed is an unfolding of Omnipotent Power. The tree was enfolded in the power of the seed as an effect is present in its cause. Likewise, the seminal power is enfolded in God, who is its Cause.

> This Beginning and Cause has within itself—qua Cause, and in an absolute and enfolded manner—whatever it gives to the effect. In this way I see that this Power is the Face, or Exemplar, of every arboreal species and of each tree. In this [Power] I see this nut tree not as in its own contracted seminal potency but as in the Cause and Maker of that seminal power. And so, I see that this tree is a certain unfolding of the seed's power and that the seed is a certain unfolding of Omnipotent Power.[206]

Nicholas is thus inviting us to view each thing as *created*, as pointing to a Maker, upon whom our intellect may reflect but into whose secret abode it may never enter. [207]

3. *Christology.* 3.1. If God can be known only in the manner in which He reveals Himself, and if He reveals Himself most fully in Christ, then Christ is the Supreme Mediator between God and man. But since Nicholas also believes that Christ is God Himself, he must explain how it is that Christ can rightly be said to *mediate*. His explanation remains orthodox, even though his theory is innovative and his terminology in many respects misleading. For example, his language sounds Nestorian when he writes: "I see that Blessed Jesus, the son of man, was most closely united to Your Son and that only by the mediation of Your Son, who is Absolute Mediator, could the son of man be united to You who are God the Father."[208] This statement sounds as if Nicholas meant the following: viz., that Jesus, who consisted of a human nature and a human person, was united to the divine person and nature of the second member of the Trinity, so that in Christ there are not only two natures—a divine and a human—but also two persons.[209] However, a careful reading of *De Visione Dei* shows that Nicholas's terminology, though misleading, does not commit him to any form of Nestorianism; for he nowhere—even outside of *De Visione Dei*—deviates from the view that in Christ there are two natures united in the one person of God the Son.[210] Moreover, in *Cribratio Alkoran* he suggests that Mohammed

was once converted to Nestorianism—a doctrine from which he, Nicholas, disassociates himself.[211] Another misleading statement is the following statement about Jesus: "*Verbum enim dei es humanatum, et homo es deificatus.*"[212] One way of translating this statement (viz., "For You are the Word of God made human; and You are a man made divine") makes it sound as if the *homo*, or man, which was made divine were both a person and a nature.[213] And yet, the subsequent sentences in the passage attest that the reason Jesus is a deified man, or a humanified God, is that in Him a human nature and a divine nature (not a human person and a divine person) are united inexplicably. (Thus, the Latin statement is better rendered as "For You are the humanified Word of God; and You are the deified man.")[214] To this extent Nicholas's view is compatible with his earlier discussion in *De Docta Ignorantia* III and with his later statements in *Cribratio Alkoran*.

3.2. Prima facie, Nicholas's Christology seems to be stated more consistently in *De Visione Dei* than in *De Docta Ignorantia*. For in *De Docta Ignorantia* III, 7 Nicholas spoke of Jesus's human nature as both absolute and contracted—as a medium between what is purely absolute and what is purely contracted: "As united with the divinity, [the humanity] is fully absolute; [but] as it is considered to be that true man Christ, [the humanity] is contracted, so that Christ is a man through the humanity. And so, Jesus's humanity is as a medium between what is purely absolute and what is purely contracted." This doctrine casts a strain upon the logic of the argument in *De Docta Ignorantia*;[215] and so, the fact that the doctrine does not reoccur in *De Visione Dei* or elsewhere seems to take on special importance. In *De Visione Dei* Nicholas speaks only of *God the Son* as Medium—as Absolute Medium.[216] In this way he seems to extricate himself from a set of conceptual problems. However, closer analysis will show that his extrication is only apparent. For according to *De Visione Dei* Jesus's human nature is united *maximally* to God the Son—i.e., is united so closely that no closer union, short of identity, is possible: "The human nature that is most closely united to You |who are Father| . . . cannot be more closely united to the Medium than it is. For it cannot be immediately united to You. Therefore, it is maximally united to the Medium and yet does not become the Medium. Hence, although the human nature cannot become the Medium (since it cannot be immediately united to You), nevertheless it is joined to the Absolute Medium in such way that nothing can mediate between the human nature and Your Son, who is the Absolute Medium. For if something could mediate between the human nature and the Absolute Medium, then the human nature would not be most closely united to You."[217]

Let us try to understand Nicholas's view more clearly, so that subsequently we may better discern the difficulties that beset it. Nicholas regards the second member of the Trinity, viz., God the Son, as having assumed a human nature into a personal union with His divine nature. As thus humanified, God the Son is the man Jesus, who may be called the deified man—the most highly deified of all sons of God, for He is Son through eternal begottenness, not through adoption. Moreover, Jesus is *son of man* (his body having been formed from the fertile purity of the Virgin Mother) in such way that He is also *Son of God* (having received His divinity from the Father). Since in Jesus the human nature is united to the divine nature, it is also united to God the Father, who is one nature with the Son. In Jesus the human nature and the divine nature are united in such way that the former may be said to exist in the latter and to be inseparable from it; for only such a union is a union so close that no closer union is either possible or conceivable.[218] Now, in this doctrine of hypostatic union, as Nicholas conceives it, a number of points are included. First of all, between the human nature and the divine nature in Jesus *there is no medium*.[219] These two natures are said to be united apart from any medium. In other words, the medium that Nicholas speaks of is a medium, not between the natures but between the human nature of Jesus and the person of the Father. In still other words, God the Son is the Medium between the assumed human nature and God the Father. In this sense God the Son is called *Absolute Mediator*; and this is the only sense of *Absolute Mediator* and *Absolute Medium* that Nicholas allows in *De Visione Dei*.

Secondly, Jesus's human nature is said to exist in His divine nature in such way that the human intellect is united to the divine intellect.[220] And since Jesus's human intellect understands all things and is the likeness of all things, all things—through their likenesses in Jesus's human intellect—are united to the divine intellect.[221] Thirdly, the humanity of each man is united to God the Father through being united to Jesus's humanity.[222] But though each man is one in species with the man Jesus, not each is one in spirit, notes Nicholas.[223] Only those who are spiritually united with God the Father will merit the happiness of eternal life.[224] Fourthly, Nicholas maintains that just as Jesus is son of man and Son of God, so the human sonship is the closest image of the Divine Sonship.[225]

> Therefore, just as an image between which and its exemplar a more perfect image cannot mediate exists most closely in the truth of which it is the image, so Your human nature, I see, exists in the divine nature. Therefore, in Your human nature I see whatever I also see in Your divine nature. But all this, which in the divine nature is the Divine Truth, I see to be in the human nature in a human way. Whatever I see to exist in a human way in You, Jesus, is a likeness of the divine nature. But the likeness is joined to its Exemplar without a medium, so that there can neither be nor be thought to be a greater likeness.[226]

Fifthly, the union between the two natures in Jesus, though a maximal union, is not an unqualifiedly maximal union, we are told. Only the Union between God the Father and God the Son—the Union which the Holy Spirit is—is an infinite and unqualifiedly maximum Union, for it is a Union qua essential identity, i.e., qua an identity of nature. By contrast, the union of a human nature with the Son of God does not involve an identity of natures, for neither nature is transformed into the other. So although this union is maximal in the sense that no closer union is possible apart from there being an essential identity, it is not an absolute union, even though the Son of God is the Absolute Medium. Sixthly and finally, Nicholas teaches, along with Meister Eckhart, that the union of the two natures in Christ transcends all temporality, so that in the order of eternity the human nature—which consists of a body and a soul and which, in the order of time, was assumed by God the Son—is never separate from God the Son.[227]

3.3. Nicholas's terminology and distinctions are no doubt initially confusing; and yet, if the intelligibility of traditional orthodox Christology be granted, then in the context of Nicholas's metaphysic of contraction his articulation of a Christology is not unintelligible. Still, it is not perfectly consistent with this metaphysic. For two metaphysical theses are among Nicholas's fundamental tenets: viz., that "there is no comparative relation of the infinite to the finite"[228] and that "except for the Maximal Image (which is, in oneness of nature, the very thing which its Exemplar is) no image is so similar or equal to its exemplar that it cannot be infinitely more similar and equal."[229] Given these theses and given Nicholas's view that Jesus's humanity is finite—because no created nature, but only the divine nature, is infinite—then since the Maximal Image is the Son of God qua second member of the Trinity,[230] Jesus's human nature and whatever is in it in a human way cannot literally be called a likeness of the divine nature and cannot properly be called a likeness than which a greater likeness can neither *be* nor be conceived.[231] For Jesus's human nature, Nicholas has asserted, is united to the divine nature in such way that it is not essentially identical to the divine nature—i.e., in such way that it is not the Maximal Image. In accordance with thesis two, therefore, neither the human nature nor the human intellect can be a likeness than which no closer likeness to the divine nature or intellect is possible. Moreover, since in accordance with thesis one neither the human nature nor the human intellect bears a comparative relation to the divine nature, neither of them can rightly be called a *likeness* of the divine nature in any sense other than the sense of *symbolic likeness*. But if the likeness in question is only a symbolic likeness, then once again the conclusion follows that a closer likeness is possible; for a very close "literal likeness" between a finite image and a finite exemplar would be a closer likeness than the remote "symbolic likeness" between a finite image (viz., human nature and the things in it in a human way) and the Infinite Exemplar (viz., the divine nature). Nicholas, it might seem, could escape this incoherence only by arguing, as he did in *De Docta Ignorantia* III, 7, that Jesus's human nature is *plurimum absoluta*, as well as being *contracta*, so that it "is as a medium between what is purely absolute and what is purely contracted." But for him to argue in this way would expose him to the charge of introducing into *De Visione Dei* the analogous incoherence of *De Docta Ignorantia* III.[232]

4. *Paradox and Dialectic.* 4.1. Whatever incoherence may beset Nicholas's line of reasoning about Christ's two natures, this incoherence, unrecognized by Nicholas, should not be confused with the paradoxes that he deliberately propounds. That is, the paradoxical

articulations should not be dismissed as inconsistent deliberations or utterances. For such a dismissive judgment would fail to take into consideration the crucial interrelationship between paradox and dialectic. An example of paradoxical discourse occurs at the end of *De Visione Dei* 21: "Every happy spirit sees the invisible God and is united, in You, Jesus, to the unapproachable and immortal God. And thus, in You, the finite is united to the Infinite and Ununitable; and the Incomprehensible is apprehended with eternal enjoyment, which is a most joyous and ever-inexhaustible happiness." We have already noted some of the senses in which the invisible God is seen—and, thus, in which the unapproachable God is approached and the incomprehensible God apprehended. When Nicholas says that to the Ununitable God the finite is united, he is not contradicting himself. Rather, he is deliberately expressing himself in an unqualified way when what he means can be reexpressed nonparadoxically by adding qualifications. In the present instance what he means is what he stated earlier: Jesus's human nature, and through this nature whatever is finite, *is united* to God the Son; but it *is not united* to Him in an identity of nature, for whatever is finite cannot become essentially identical with God.

In assessing Nicholas's use of paradox, perhaps we may be helped by comparison with a statement from one of Dickens' novels: "It was the best of times, it was the worst of times . . . ." This statement is far more striking than would be its expansion: 'It was in some respects the best of times; it was in other respects the worst of times.' Dickens expresses himself as he does in order to capture the attention and the imagination of the reader—in order to create a more vivid and provocative impression. Similarly, Nicholas's statement that "the finite is united to the Infinite and Ununitable" conjoins two prima facie inconsistent conceptions. And it conjoins them for two reasons: to foster in the reader's mind a sense of amazement and inquiry and to "summarize pithily," as it were, an elaborate series of nonparadoxical propositions. Accordingly, the given paradoxical expression is not beyond all understanding even though some of the propositions "summarized" by it may be beyond understanding, as Nicholas acknowledges when he writes: "I see You, Lord Jesus, to be, beyond all understanding, one person (*suppositum*), because You are one Christ."[233] Here Nicholas purports to understand *that* Jesus is one person with two natures, but he admits to not understanding, because it is *super omnem intellectum, how* this union of natures in the divine person is possible.[234]

A further example may be taken from *Apologia Doctae Ignorantiae* 31-32, where Nicholas is responding to a criticism by John Wenck, Professor of theology at the University of Heidelberg: " 'The Adversary [i.e., Wenck] does not understand what theology is or what he is attacking or what he is saying. For example, because it is stated in *Learned Ignorance* that "God is not this thing and is not any other thing, but is all things and is not any of all things (which are the words of Holy Dionysius)," he says that the [expression] "is all things and is not any of all things" is self-contradictory; and he does not understand that in the mode of enfolding [God] is all things but that in the mode of unfolding He is not any of these things.' " Hereby Nicholas shows that the paradoxical expression in question was meant to be understood as tacitly accompanied by qualifiers. Moreover, he regards Wenck as someone who should have known, from a complete reading of *De Docta Ignorantia* and from familiarity with the writings of Dionysius, just what these qualifiers were. And he reproaches Wenck for his utter lack of comprehension. Nicholas's use of paradoxical expression is motivated not only by Dionysius but also by Anselm[235] and by Eckhart.[236] Like Eckhart, Nicholas, in *De Visione Dei*, works certain of these expressions into a dialectical line of reasoning, i.e., into a line of reasoning that draws its main impetus from the conceptual opposition that underlies the paradoxical expression. In *De Visione Dei* the primary oppositions are between the finite and the infinite, the temporal and the eternal, the imaging and the exemplifying, the creatable and the uncreatable, the unequal and the nonequal, the immanent and the transcendent, the seeable and the unseeable, the revealable and the unrevealable, the contractible and the uncontractible, the mutable and the immutable, that which is able to satisfy and that which is not able to satisfy.

4.2. Perhaps the most highly dialectical chapter in *De Visione Dei* is Chapter 15. Here Nicholas pursues further the illustrative likening of the face of the icon to the Face of God. The icon's gaze is not confined to one perspective but is "infinite" in that it is not restricted to beholding a single onlooker, for it beholds all onlookers at once. And yet, to each onlooker the icon's gaze seems concentrated upon him alone, as if it were limited by him, as if its direction were determined by his position. In accordance with the illustration of the icon, Nicholas had earlier inferred about God:

> Your Face is turned toward every face that looks unto You. Your gaze, O Lord, is Your Face. Accordingly, whoever looks unto You with a loving face will find only Your Face looking lovingly upon him. And the greater his endeavor to look more lovingly unto You, the more loving he will likewise find Your Face to be. Whoever looks angrily unto You will find Your Face likewise to display anger. Whoever looks unto You joyfully will find Your Face likewise to be joyous, just as is the face of him who is looking unto You.[237]

Along similar lines, Nicholas now infers from the illustration that, as it were, the onlooker bestows form upon the Face of God—a Face whose features seem to be determined by the onlooker himself, who seems to see himself mirrored in God's Face. Here Nicholas draws upon his metaphor that the Divine Eye is a Mirror in which the images of all things are present; but now he adds that in this Divine Mirror the onlooker sees his own form.

> And he judges the form seen in the Mirror to be the image of his own form, because such would be the case with regard to a polished material mirror. However, the contrary thereof is true, because in the Mirror of eternity that which he sees is not an image but is the Truth, of which the beholder is the image. Therefore, in You, my God, the image is the Truth and Exemplar of each and every thing that exists or can exist.[238]

Nicholas's line of reasoning plays upon the contrast between image and exemplar: what at first seems to be the image is really the exemplar; and what at first seems to be the exemplar, or original, is seen to be really the image. Thus, the one who looks unto God is said by Nicholas to come to see himself in God when he recognizes and contemplates the fact that he has received his form of being from God, the Form of forms. Thus, the form of his being is present in God as what is caused is present in its cause.[239] Accordingly, whoever speculatively beholds himself in God may perhaps behold what he initially takes to be the *image* of himself. But through further contemplation he can come to see that this image is really the truth, or exemplar, of which he the viewer is the image: "In You, my God, the image is the Truth and Exemplar of each and every thing that exists or can exist." For in God the image is not an image but is God Himself;[240] and, qua God, this "image," so to speak, is the Cause of itself and all other things.[241]

Nicholas's dialectic now becomes heightened: "You, O God, worthy of admiration by every mind, You who are Light sometimes seem as if You were a shadow. For when I see that in accordance with my changing, Your icon's gaze seems to be changed and that Your countenance seems to be changed because I am changed, You seem to me as if You were a shadow which follows the changing of the one who is walking. But because I am a living shadow and You are the Truth, I judge from the changing of the shadow that the Truth is changed. Therefore, O my God, You are shadow in such way that You are Truth; You are the image of me and of each one in such way that You are Exemplar."[242] The last sentence is deliberately expressed in a paradoxical manner, for Nicholas does not repeat the word "*quasi*" ("as if") from the opening sentence. Nonetheless, he intends that this word be understood as tacitly present. God is not at all *shadow*, for in Him there is no darkness (I John 1:5). Yet, he sometimes *seems as if* He were a shadow insofar as His gaze does not desert the one who looks unto Him but rather follows him as closely as does his shadow. Indeed, says Nicholas, the man himself is a kind of living and moving shadow that sometimes judges Truth itself to be changed. But then, subsequently,

> You show me, O Lord, that with respect to the changing of my face Your Face is changed and unchanged, alike: it is changed because it does not desert the truth of my face; it is unchanged because it does not follow the changing of the image. Hence, just as Your Face does not desert the truth of my face, so also it does not follow the changing of the changeable image. For Absolute Truth is Unchangeability. The truth of my face is mutable, because it is truth in such way that it is image; but [the Truth of] Your [Face] is immutable, because it is image in such way that it is Truth. Absolute Truth cannot desert the truth of my face. For if Absolute Truth deserted it, then my face, which is a mutable truth, could not continue to exist. Thus, O God, on account of Your infinite goodness You seem to be mutable, because You do not desert mutable creatures; but because You are Absolute Goodness, You are not mutable, since You do not follow mutability.[243]

So Nicholas concludes that God is not mutable even though He sometimes appears to us to be a mutable shadow: "You seem (*videris*) to be mutable . . . but . . . You are not mutable." In his dialectical style Nicholas sometimes avoids repeating the key words "*quasi*" and "*videris*" in order to heighten the effect of the interplay between the motifs of mutability and immutability, image and exemplar, shadow and truth; yet, these keywords are meant to be understood as operative throughout Chapter 15.[244] Similarly, for stylistic reasons, he does not keep repeating the qualifications which he expects the reader to supply. When he exclaims "O my God, deepest Depth, You who do not desert creatures and, at the same time, do not follow them!"[245] his words have an impact that is achieved by their *not* being explicitly unpacked. For the reader himself has already been told enough to supply an answer to the engendered question: 'How is it possible that God does not desert and yet does not follow? How does He follow without following?'

The speculation in Chapter 15 now moves to its finale. Just as the one who looks unto God seems to see himself in God, and therefore to bestow form upon God, so he seems to bestow (facial) being, so that God, with respect to His (facial) being, is the created likeness of man. Previously, Nicholas remarked in Chapter 6: "A man can judge only in a human way. For example, when a man ascribes a face to You, he does not seek it outside the human species; for his judgment is contracted within human nature and does not, in judging, go beyond the affection that belongs to this contractedness. Similarly, if a lion were to ascribe to You a face, he would judge it to be only lionlike; an ox [would judge it to be only] oxlike; and an eagle [would judge it to be only] eaglelike."[246] In Chapter 15 this idea is developed further. In seeing our own image in God, we see God as formed in our image, see Him as our creaturely likeness. Moreover, God lends Himself to this imagery, says Nicholas, in order that we may love Him by loving our image in Him, since we cannot hate ourselves. At this point Nicholas's line of reasoning reflexes: "the likeness which seems to be created by me is the Truth which creates me," so that God is seen *not to be my* image but I am seen to be *His* image. But if I love God when He seems to be an image-of-me that I have begotten, then I should love Him all the more when I see myself to be an image-of-Him that He has begotten.

4.3. Nowhere in *De Visione Dei* does Nicholas use the word "*paradoxa*"; and yet, *De Visione Dei* is replete with paradoxical expressions. God is infinite; and infinite goodness is not goodness, he asserts.[247] Nonetheless, he continues to refer to God as maximal goodness,[248] as infinite good,[249] as goodness itself.[250] God is goodness which is not goodness: i.e., He is symbolized as if He were goodness in some sense analogous to our conception of it. Elsewhere Nicholas speaks of God as both moved and stationary—and as neither moved nor stationary.[251] Or again, God seems to create Himself, even as He sees Himself, since His seeing is creating; thus, He is both creator and creatable.[252] Yet, He neither creates nor is creatable, although all things are that which they are because He exists.[253] His infinite Equality is equal to all things in such way that it is equal to none.[254] His trinity is a plurality without plural number.[255] He is the revealed but unrevealable vision.[256]

Each of the foregoing statements, like the ones mentioned still earlier, is equivalently translatable into a conjunction of nonparadoxical propositions. Moreover, like the earlier paradoxical utterances these too are non-self-contradictory: they merely have a surface appearance of self-contradictoriness because of their syntactical form. Even when Nicholas speaks of God as surrounded by the coincidence of contradictories,[257] he does not mean that God acts in ways that defy all intelligibility or that He is rightly conceivable in accordance with an inconsistent description. Rather, the expression indicates that God's being is uniquely beyond all actual and conceptual differentiation, so that it cannot be truly and nonmetaphorically characterized by any predicate whose meaning is drawn from human experience.[258] At times Nicholas makes this same point in reverse fashion—i.e., by asserting that *all* terms are predicable of God. In *De Possest* 12, for example, Bernard remarks: "Beware lest you contradict yourself. For a moment ago you denied that God is sun; and now you are asserting that He is all things." And Nicholas replies:

> On the contrary! I affirmed that God is sun—though [He is] not [sun] in the same way as is the visible sun, which is not what it is able to be. For, assuredly, He who is what (He) is able to be does not fail to have solar being; rather, He has it in a better way, because [He has it] in a divine and most perfect way.[259]

Even in *De Visione Dei* 13 (54), where Nicholas indicates that a contradiction is implied by the claim that God is an End without an end, i.e., is an Infinite End, he is talking about contradiction in the context of the coincidence-of-contradictories. And his point, therefore, is not that the statement "God is an Infinite End" is self-contradictory. Rather, he is maintaining that we cannot conceive pos-

itively of God's infinity, in which contradictories coincide.[260] Though
we can conceive *that God is Infinity*, we cannot conceive of Infinity
as it is in itself.[261] "Infinite End" implies a contradiction insofar as
Infinity cannot be "ended." But Nicholas leaps beyond this surface
contradiction to the deeper point about coincidence and inconceivability. Accordingly, though he says "You are an End without an
end—i.e., an Infinite End" and then adds "This [fact] escapes all
reasoning, for it implies a contradiction," his addition must be
construed as only a preliminary step of dialectic. This step is tacitly
meant to be surpassed in the course of the speculation, so that the
one speculating will say what Nicholas already said in Chapter 12
regarding a preliminary apparent contradiction:

> Although the wall of absurdity (viz., the wall of the coincidence of creating
> with being created) stands in the way, as if creating could not possibly coin-
> cide with being created (since to admit this coinciding would seemingly be to
> affirm that something exists before it exists; for when it creates, it *is*—and yet
> *is not*, because it is created), nevertheless *this wall is not an obstacle*.[262]

Subsequent to the words above, Nicholas goes on to explain why no
genuine contradiction occurs. Similarly, the wall of the absurdity of
an Infinite End *is not an obstacle*. But Nicholas leaves it to the
reader to work out the details of the explanation as to why not.

4.4. At times the form of a given paradoxical statement of Nicholas's does *not* have the appearance, syntactically, of a self-contradiction.
Instead, the paradoxicality arises from the statement in relation to
the immediate context within which it is embedded—as when Nicholas asks, "How will You give Yourself to me unless You also give me
to myself?"[263] It seems strange that God's giving Himself to me
should require His giving me to myself—stranger still that in some
way I *could be* given to myself. And yet, in the present instance
Nicholas explains that God gives me to myself—grants me the power
of self-possession—when he assists my reason in governing my
senses. At a later period in the history of theology Sören Kierkegaard came to formulate explicitly an elaborate doctrine of paradox—
distinguishing, for example, the absolute paradox and the divine
paradox. But even Kierkegaard retained a Cusanlike notion of con-
textual paradox, as is made evident by a single example from *Fear
and Trembling*: In the reconstructed narrative of the Old Testament
account of Abraham and Isaac, Kierkegaard puts into Abraham's

mouth the words "All is lost but God is love." Neither the syntactical form nor the semantical interpretation of the sentence constitutes a self-inconsistency. And yet, the utterance is paradoxical in that it evinces a theological tension between two motifs. For how can God be love if all is lost? Or how can all be lost if God is love? Kierkegaard does not seek immediately to escape the dialectical tension between the motif of divine love and the motif of human despair. Rather, he accentuates the tension: Abraham believes simultaneously that all is lost and, yet, that God is love.[264] Just as Kierkegaard's conception of faith is more radical than Nicholas's in that it encompasses the notions of risk and of doubt, so his use of paradoxical expression is both more radical and more dramatic. Nonetheless, there are certain parallels between the two thinkers. When in the *Sickness unto Death* Kierkegaard asks whether despair is an advantage or a drawback, he answers that dialectically speaking it is both. This response constitutes a prima facie inconsistency, which is removed by the introduction of different respects: despair is an advantage insofar as the capability of despair marks human beings as superior to the brute animals; despair is a disadvantage in that it is a sickness that is symptomatic of spiritual death. This way of reasoning resembles Nicholas's own recourse to paradoxical language that is translatable into different respects.[265]

Dialectical reasoning, as it is present in *De Visione Dei*, is proleptic more of Kierkegaard than of Hegel.[266] For Nicholas's use of opposition does not proceed linearly from a most general category to progressively more specific categories. Nor is it interrelated as a series of triads: thesis-antithesis-synthesis (the synthesis becoming a new thesis). True, Nicholas and Eckhart foreshadow certain of Hegel's major tenets, as when they teach that the Infinite is manifested in and through the finite. Still, Nicholas takes these points from Dionysius and makes of them something quite different from their use within the Hegelian context of *Aufhebung*. Nicholas's dialectical reasoning, as evidenced from *De Visione Dei* 15, progresses programmatically and topically, not systematically. That is, Nicholas advances considerations that cohere with his overall viewpoint in *De Visione Dei*, but these considerations do not connect into a chain in which each link of reasoning is presumed to depend necessarily upon the preceding links. Rather, just as Dionysius had earlier proceeded by

tersely playing off opposing motifs and just as Kierkegaard was later
to proceed in the same manner, only more starkly and more narra-
tively, so Nicholas, being partly influenced by Eckhart, sets opposites
in opposition. Still, he does not think of the opposition as altogether
unmediated, since there is an Absolute Mediator who unites the
finite to the Infinite, the temporal to the Eternal, the image to the
Exemplar, the contractible to the Uncontractible. Sometimes Nicholas's propensity for paradoxical terminology misleads, as when he
uses the expressions "Uncontractible Contraction,"[267] "Uncontracted
Humanity,"[268] and "Human Nature per se"[269] to refer to God, who
is—as Nicholas himself states—not contractible to anything.[270] Likewise, the phrase "Contradiction without contradiction"[271] might seem
gratuitously perplexing. And yet, these locutions besuit Nicholas's
style in *De Visione Dei*, for their prima facie obscurity serves to
accentuate the hiddenness that is presumed to accompany mystical
theology.

4.5. The beauty of Nicholas's style does not arise from elegance of
expression in Latin, though the charming simplicity of his sentences
in *De Visione Dei* contrasts strikingly with the cumbersome expressions of *De Docta Ignorantia* and with the aridness of *De Coniecturis*.
The stylistic beauty of *De Visione Dei* arises from the effective use
of simile and metaphor. The comparison between the face of the icon
and the Face of God is pleasingly ingenious—as is the address: "O
good Jesus, You are the Tree of Life in the Paradise of delights. For
no one can be nourished by the desirable Life except from Your fruit.
You, O Jesus, are the food forbidden to all the sons of Adam, who,
expelled from Paradise, seek in the earth, wherein they labor, their
means of life."[272] Just as, subsequent to their sin, Adam and Eve
were expelled from the Garden of Eden and prevented from partak-
ing of the Tree of Life, so those of their descendants who remain
unrepentant are also not allowed to partake of the Tree of Life, now
identified by Nicholas with Christ. Other of Nicholas's comparisons
are no less vivid: his metaphor of the wall of absurdity, his likening
of God to an uncountable treasure, to an Infinite Eye, to the Mirror-
of-eternity. *De Visione Dei* is Nicholas's sole literary masterpiece. It
stands as an illustrious witness to the fact that philosophical content
can best be communicated when it affiliates itself with a conducive
literary style.

5. *Textual and Translation Considerations.* 5.1. The present volume contains a new edition of the Latin text of *De Visione Dei*. This edition was prepared from the eighteen manuscripts cited in the accompanying critical apparatus. Together, these manuscripts furnish the basis for a reliable reconstruction of Nicholas's work, even in the absence of other copies that are known to be missing. Four additional manuscripts—Magdeburg 166, Minneapolis Z193N519/OD, Graz 910, and Vatican City 11520—were examined; but because of their inferior quality, their variant readings were not included in the line notes to the Latin text.[273] Within the eighteen manuscripts compared, the hands of the various redactors have been distinguished insofar as possible.[274] (For example, in Eisleben 960, the hands of E^2, E^3 and E^4 are distinguished from the hand of the main copyist E.) Such redactors do not in every case improve the quality of the manuscript by their corrections—not even if one of the redactors should turn out to be the author himself.[275] In Codex Cusanus 219, for example, C^2 corrects a subsequently illegible word in the text to "*domine*", when the right word is "*omnem*" (at 24:1). Similarly, at 47:4 C^2 corrects "*futili*" to "*futilis*", when the right word is "*fictilis*". By contrast, other emendations, though not obviously wrong, represent a departure from the original. Thus, between the end of 1:15 and the beginning of 2:1 C^3 inserts the title "*Prefacio*"[276]. And at 63:1, where C had "*esse infinitas*", C^2 deletes "*esse*" instead of changing "*infinitas*" to "*infinitatis*".

The present edition, on the basis of the manuscripts compared, makes such important determinations as the following: (1) At 24:16 the preferable reading is "*speciei*" (not "*faciei*"). (2) At 25:7 the correct punctuation is " . . . *exemplar sui ipsius. Et arboris et seminis tu, deus,* . . . " (instead of " . . . *exemplar sui ipsius et arboris et seminis. Tu, deus,* . . . "). (3) At 40:7-8 "*Et quia synonima sunt videre tuum et loqui tuum*" should be included in the text, even though these words are deleted by C^2. (4) At 79:12 the correct reading is "*pluralitas*" (not "*unitas*"). Although this list could be extended, these few examples will suffice to show why a critical edition is required—why, for instance, a mere transcription of C or of p would be less than fully desirable. Of the eighteen manuscripts compared, no single one is of overriding authority. Even C, though it is a copy that was commissioned and checked by Nicholas himself, contains a modest number of errors.[277] Likewise, even though the copy of *De Visione Dei* contained in *G* (=Giessen 695) may be the earliest extant transscription,[278] overriding weight cannot be assigned to it. For we have no evidence that *G* was transcribed directly from the autograph, which has not survived. Given the large number, and the diverse ranges, of the variant readings in the eighteen manuscripts, it is not possible to construct a *memoria libelli* without introducing unreliable conjectures.[279] Because no single one of the manuscripts is of pre-emptive authority, no set of rigid a priori rules for determining the critical text can be acceptable.[280] The only mandatory a priori rule is the following editorial rule-of-thumb: be prepared to justify, with regard to the edition of the Latin text of *De Visione Dei*, all readings that deviate from the text in *C*. These justifications, if solicited, will have to draw upon considerations which will not be universally and uniformly applicable but which will tend to vary from case to case. For example, the considerations that justify an editor's inserting the Latin word "*imagine*" into the text at 2:3 will be different from the considerations that justify his rejection of the division title "*Praefatio*" between 1:15 and 2:1 or his choice of "*quin*" (instead of "*quae . . . non*") at 10:12 or his selection of "*ibi amor ubi oculus*" (instead of "*ibi oculus ubi amor*") at 11:3.

5.2. Besides determining which readings to accept for the edition he is preparing, an editor must also determine just what words are contained in each manuscript and how these words are to be grouped into sentences. The accuracy of these determinations is endangered by four conditions that characterize many medieval manuscripts: (1) the letters *n* and *u*, *c* and *e*, *f* and *s* are not clearly and distinctly formed; (2) the letter *i* is not everywhere dotted; (3) no space is left between a preposition and the noun it governs; (4) no punctuation within the manuscript indicates the end of one sentence and the beginning of another. Even experienced editors must guard against misreading "*nos*" as "*vos*", "*nostri*" as "*vostri*", "*in eo*" as "*meo*", "*in te*" as "*vite*", "*sit*" as "*sic*", "*a deo*" as "*adeo*", "*ex eo*" as "*exeo*", "*quem*" as "*que in*", "*meus*" as "*mens*", "*huic*" as "*hinc*", "*per te*" as "*parce*", "*sint*" as "*fuit*", "*in deo*" as "*video*", "*movet*" as "*monet*", "*una in*" as "*unam*", etc. Moreover, many *abbreviations* are looka-likes when handwritten: *s̄u/s̄n (sum/sine), n̄o/v̄o (nomen/verbo), sp̄m/sp̄ui (spiritum/spiritui), c̄u/ēu (cum/eum), qūi/qm̄ (quin/quo-*

niam), o̅m̅s̅/o̅n̅i̅s̅ *(omnes/omnis)*, o̅e̅/e̅e̅ *(omne/esse)*. Even the medieval copyists themselves often mistook one another's handwriting, thereby introducing new errors into their transcriptions. By not insisting upon unambigous letter formation, word spacing, and sentence punctuation, the medieval grammarians, together with the directors of the medieval scriptoria, condemned the scholarly world to unnecessary misapprehensions. Sometimes these misapprehensions are relatively harmless, as when the scribe of Ms. *O* writes "*ut*" in place of "*et*" (29:6) or "*carpere*" in place of "*capere*" (64:1) or "*enim*" in place of "*etiam*" (98:12). At other times they are more grave, as when he writes "*non*" in place of "*hoc*" (36:4) or "*mocione*" in place of "*monicione*" (16:13).[281]

5.3. The earlier English translation of *De Visione Dei* made by Emma G. Salter[282] and published in 1928 in New York and London is not without merit. (It is superior to the one made by Giles Randall and published in 1646.) Yet, it suffers from four deficiencies. First of all, it contains all the inadequacies which any translation based upon the Basel edition of 1565 is destined to have.[283] For example, in Chapter 11 Salter's translation of 47:15-16 reads:[284] "For the creature, to go forth from Thee is to enter into the creature, and to unfold is to enfold." But the Basel edition, like the Paris edition which it follows, omits the words "*in te*". When these words are restored, the translation changes significantly: "For creation's going out from You is creation's going in unto You; and unfolding is enfolding." Or again, in Chapter 21 (94:14-15) Salter's translation, in correspondence with the Basel edition, reads: "None of the blessed can see the Father in Paradise save with Thee, Jesu." However, a critical edition should exclude the word "*patrem*", which is present in the Basel and the Paris editions, and should have "*felicem*" instead of "*foelix*", or "*felix*", so that a correspondingly correct translation would be: "No one can see anyone happy, except inside Paradise with You, Jesus." Or again, in Chapter 6, at 19:16-17, the Paris and the Basel editions omit the words "*quacumque facie. Ideo aequalis omnibus et singulis, quia nec maior nec minor*", with the result that no translation thereof occurs in Salter's work.[285] At 44:4-6 (Chapter 10) the words "*ille non est omnipotens conceptus—sicut ille oculus qui prius unum videt et postea aliud*" are missing from the Paris edition and, hence, also from the Basel edition; accordingly, not only were these words not translated by Salter but even the defective Latin sentence that *was* correctly translated, wrongly presents Nicholas's thought. At 47:8-9 (Chapter 11) the important sentence "*Cum te reperio virtutem complicantem omnia, intro*" is also not translated, for it too is missing from the Basel edition, though not from the Paris edition.

Secondly, Salter's translation neglects to render into English certain Latin words and phrases that are not omitted in the Basel edition. At 13:6-7 (Chapter 4), for example, "*non . . . nisi . . . nisi*" should be translated by the English words "only": "And Your seeing is only Your enlivening, only Your continually instilling . . . ."[286] In the same chapter, at 12:15-16, a decision must be made about the Latin syntax—about how to understand the grammatical construction governed by "*non nisi*".[287] (From *De Docta Ignorantia* we know that Nicholas is not careful regarding his use of this construction.)[288] Yet, Salter ignores the words "*non nisi*" with her rendition (p. 17) " . . . when all my endeavour is turned toward Thee because all Thy endeavour is turned toward me . . . ." Or again, at 47:7 of Chapter 11 Salter ignores the important word "*simul*"—thereby writing (on p. 53) " . . . and as I go in and go out by this door of Thy word . . . , " instead of " . . . and when at one and the same time I go in and out through the door of Your Word . . . ."

Salter's translation also suffers in a third respect: viz., it often fails to make clear the logical connection between Nicholas's thoughts. Thus, at the beginning of Chapter 14 her translation omits the word "therefore", which corresponds to "*igitur*", the logical connective between the first and the second Latin sentence. Likewise, at 56:4-6, in Chapter 13, Salter neglects the transition words "*enim*" and "*ideo*", so that her translation reads "Absolute infinity includeth and containeth all things. If infinity could ever exist . . . " instead of reading "For Absolute Infinity includes and encompasses all things. And so, if there were 'Infinity' . . . ." At 65:21-22 (Chapter 15) Salter translates the adversative word "*sed*" by the causal word "for," thereby altering the logical relationship between two independent clauses.[289]

Finally, Salter's translation contains certain outright errors that are of sizable import to Nicholas's Christology and trinitarianism. The title of Chapter 17, mispunctuated in the Basel edition ("*Quod Deus, non nisi unitrinus, videri perfecte potest*"), should be rendered not as "How God, unless He were one and Three, could not be perfectly seen" but as (something like) "God can be seen perfectly only as triune." At 77:12-13 of this same chapter the Salter translation has "Thus the essence is triune, and yet there are not three essences therein, since it is most simple."[290] However, the word "triune" should be changed to "trine"; and "essences" should be changed to the more general term "things", for "*tria*", which is neuter plural, does not allude to "*essentiae*". At 77:17 Salter has "There is no numerical distinction between the three, for plural number is essential to distinction . . . ";[291] but she ought rather to have (something like) "Therefore,[292] there is not a numerical distinction of the three, because a numerical distinction would be an essential distinction . . . ." The opening sentence[293] of Chapter 20, "Thou showest me, O Light unfailing, that the perfect union whereby human nature is united through my Jesus with Thy divine nature is not in any wise like unto infinite union", would be more accurately translated if "perfect union" were changed to "maximum union", if "human nature" were changed to "the human nature", and if "through my Jesus" were changed to "in my Jesus". Nicholas does not assert, but rather denies, that *through Jesus* (the) human nature is united to the divine nature: "O most sweet Jesus, You cannot be said, either, to be the uniting medium between the divine nature and the human nature, since between the two natures there cannot be posited a middle nature that participates in both."[294] At 88:15-16 of Chapter 20 Salter's translation takes no account of the immensely important word "*eius*," so that it reads "This union, then, of human nature, as such, with the divine is the greatest"[295] instead of reading "Therefore, the union of His [i.e., Jesus'] human nature, qua human, to the divine nature is maximal . . . ." Thus, her translation fosters the misimpression that in Jesus human nature qua unindividuated species is united to God. This misimpression is further fostered by the translation of "*Verbum enim Dei es, humanatum, et homo es, deificatus*" as "For Thou art the Word of God humanified, and Thou art man deified"[296] instead of as "For You are the humanified Word of God; and You are the deified man."

At 90:7-8 of Chapter 20 the translation should not be "A stone existeth not in human understanding as in its proper cause or nature, but as in its specific idea and likeness"[297] but rather (something like) "A stone is not present in the human intellect as it is present in its cause or its own rational principle but as it is present in its image and likeness." Similarly, in the sentences that immediately follow the foregoing one the Latin word *"species"* should be rendered not by the English word "species" but rather by "image". Accordingly, Salter's translation "So[298] in Thee, Jesu, Master of masters, I see that the absolute idea of all things, and with it what resembles it in species, are united in the highest degree"[299] should instead be (something like) " . . . in You, Jesus, Master of masters, I see that the Absolute Idea of all things and the resembling image of these things are likewise most closely united."[300] For nothing resembles the Absolute Idea (i.e., the Word of God) in species, since the Absolute Idea infinitely transcends all species. Toward the beginning of Chapter 23 the following translation by Salter does not accurately convey Nicholas's argument: "Nor can any nature by reason of its union with the divine pass over into another nature: as is illustrated in the case of the image, when united unto its truth. For an image cannot be said to become other when thus united, but rather to withdraw itself from otherness, because it is united unto its own truth, which is unchangeableness itself."[301] But what Nicholas means is something significantly different: "Nor would any nature on account of its union to the divine nature pass over into *another* nature (as when an image is united to its truth). For in the case of that passing over, the nature could [rightly be said] to recede from otherness but could not [rightly] be said to be altered, because it would be united to its own Truth, which is Unalterability itself." Thus, Nicholas does not make a *general* point about the relationship between images and their respective exemplars. Indeed, the point he makes entails a proposition which is opposed to the meaning that is found in Salter's translation; for it entails that ordinary kinds of images *would* rightly be said to be altered if they could somehow become transformed into their respective exemplars.

So the immediately foregoing examples show that Nicholas's Christology and trinitarianism are not accurately captured by Salter's translation of *De Visione Dei*.[302] And when taken all together, the four objections to her translation evidence amply the need for a new English version based upon a critical edition of the Latin text.

6. *Nicholas of Cusa and the Modern Age*. 6.1. Frederick Copleston, in Volume III of his well-known *History of Philosophy*, writes:

"Nicholas of Cusa is not an easy figure to classify. . . . But it seems to me preferable to see in him a transition-thinker, a philosopher of the Renaissance, who combined the old with the new."[303] This statement witnesses to the difficulty of determining Nicholas's place within the course of Western thought. For Nicholas is indeed a transitional figure, whose thought belongs to the larger cluster of intellectual boundary points that marks the end of the Middle Ages and the beginning of Modernity. Some interpreters, such as Heinrich Rombach, view his thought as so epoch-making that he deserves to be called "the Aristotle of Modern Thought."[304] Others, such as Hans Blumenberg, detect in his writings primarily a concern for the continuance of the medieval epoch.[305] Blumenberg concedes that Nicholas does not explicitly articulate this concern; he insists, however, that the unity of Nicholas's thought can be understood only on the basis of such a concern.[306] Blumenberg recognizes, on the one hand, that Nicholas does not want to restore the world of Scholasticism, and, on the other, that Nicholas's writings contain a newness and a vividness, as indicated by their many neologisms. But Nicholas's constructive effort, thinks Blumenberg, does not minimize the fundamental conservatism of his central undertaking: viz., the saving of the Middle Ages.[307]

6.2. Though certain of Blumenberg's instincts seem right, his overall picture of Cusanus is wrong. (This wrongness does not, however, entail that Rombach's picture is correct.)[308] The many reasons supporting this judgment are now worth marshalling, since Blumenberg's massive work *Die Legitimität der Neuzeit* has now been published in English translation (*The Legitimacy of the Modern Age*)[309] and is bound to have wide influence in British and North American academic circles. The translation was not made from the 1966 edition of the German text but rather from a revision thereof that was published as three paperback volumes.[310] Let us concentrate, for our present purposes, upon Part IV, Chapter 2 of the English translation—a section which corresponds to Part II of the third paperback volume. In general, the quality of the English translation is high, given Blumenberg's convoluted style. Still, there are crucial slips. On pp. 490-491, for example, the following translation is erroneous: "The curvature of the circle (which decreases as the radius increases) approaches identity with the curvature of a straight line, so that the circle's radius and its circumference coincide." But, of course, a straight line has no curvature (both according to Nicholas and according to common-sense), so that the doctrine of *coincidentia oppositorum* becomes distorted by the translation. The translator, has construed *"der Geraden"* as a genitive instead of, correctly, as a dative. Another faulty rendering occurs on p. 489: "Anselm conceals this dilemma in his *Proslogion*, in whose first chapter he offers his much disputed[311] proof . . . ." Here the translator has not recognized that the word for "chapter" is plural (*"in dessen ersten Kapiteln"*). Thus, he saddles Blumenberg with an error. For although Anselm's argument appears in the first chapters of the *Proslogion*, it does not appear in Chapter 1 but in Chapter 2 and following. Likewise, the first sentence of the first new paragraph on p. 501 should be changed to something like: "In the following respect faith and conjecture, *fides* and *coniectura*, are shown to be functionally equivalent: they provide reason with the presuppositions it needs in order to arrive at conclusions within the total system." On p. 514, lines 11-12, the verb "to experience" should be replaced by "to detect" (*"spüren"*); for Blumenberg does not make the unintelligible claim that, according to Nicholas, man can *experience* the infinity of the finite. Or again, the words "motive" and "motives" on p. 484 (lines 22 and 31) should be changed to "motif" and "motifs".

On p. 514 the Latin passage[312] is mistranslated as: "And so you understand that the world, than which no magnitude can be greater, is contained in a point, than which nothing can be smaller, and that its center and circumference cannot be seen." The two occurrences of "can be" should be changed to "is", for Nicholas does *not* teach that no magnitude can be greater than the world. Rather, he teaches in *De Docta Ignorantia* that although God could not have created *this* world, with *its* possibility, to be greater than it is, he could nonetheless have created a greater world than this one.[313] Similarly, no physical point, he believes, is ever so small that there could not be one still smaller. On p. 531 the translation of *"Sicut voluisti, fecisti"* as "Just as He wanted it, He made it" is mistaken, though without grave consequence. Also without serious consequence is the faulty translation of *"vero"* as "truly," instead of as "but", on p. 499. The title *"De ignota litteratura"*, on p. 494, should be rendered as *"On Unknown Learning"* instead of as *"On Ignorant Erudition"*; this fact becomes clear when one reads the treatise itself, where John Wenck explains his title. Likewise the title "*On God's Vision*", on p. 538, would more correctly be rendered as "*On the Vision of God*"; for Nicholas intends the Latin title ("*De Visione Dei*") to indicate not only God's vision of man but also man's vision of God. An acceptable translation, therefore, will retain the ambiguity of the Latin, as does the German translation "*Vom Sehen Gottes*". On p. 500 the title "*De coniecturis*" is translated by the singular "*On Conjecture*". By contrast, it appears on p. 533 in the plural "*On Conjectures*". And on p. 526 it is written as "*On conjectures*". Similarly, on p. 507 the Latin title of Nicholas's major work of 1440 is translated as "*Of Learned Ignorance*"; but on p. 543 the same reoccurring German translation of the same reoccurring Latin title is translated into English as "*On Knowing Ignorance*". Moreover, there are difficulties of style—as evidenced by the following opaque renderings:[314] "This sort of transcendence is thus an intrahistorical reservation . . . " (p. 486).[315] "In this passage, a Platonizing exemplarism conflicts with the absolutism of will that is supposedly owed to the sovereignty of the Divinity . . . " (p. 520).[316] "Precisely because and if it was the case that God indulged in this self-referential behavior, His work had in the highest degree to give to each being what belonged to it" (p. 516).[317] Finally, and of no small importance, Blumenberg's references are mistranslated where they make use of the abbreviation "p."—as in "Wenck, De ignota litteratura, p. 35." The English translator does not realize that "p." here stands for the Latin word "*pagina*" (i.e., "page"), and so he everywhere misrenders it by the English abbreviation "par." (i.e., "paragraph").

In spite of these and other mistakes and infelicities the quality of Robert Wallace's translation is reasonably high. Indeed, only someone unfamiliar with the many problems and pitfalls of the art of translating could judge otherwise. All translations of lengthy and weighty philosophical works inevitably contain mistakes. These can be eliminated only over a long period of time by the collective efforts of many different scholars, each spotting some things that the other misses (and missing some things that the other spots).

6.3. Yet, even apart from the considerations of English translation, Blumenberg's work is beset by problems that are the author's own. Let us look briefly at some of the *scholarly* problems before turning to assess Blumenberg's analysis of Nicholas's cosmology, anthropology, and Christology. To begin with, Blumenberg has certain mistranslations of his own. On p. 92 of Vol. III of the German paperback edition (*Aspekten der Epochenschwelle: Cusaner und Nolaner*) he both misstates and mistranslates the Latin text cited from *De Coniecturis* II, 14. For his excerpt "*omnia ex se explicare intra regionis suae circulum, omnia de potentia centri exercere*" contains the word "*exercere*" instead of the correct word "*exerere*" (or "*exserere*"); and, in addition, he takes "*intra regionis suae circulum*" to mean "*in den Kreis seines Lebensbereiches hinein*" instead of "*innerhalb des Umkreises seines Lebensbereiches*".[318] On p. 97 of the German volume, which corresponds to p. 537 of the English, Blumenberg once again misunderstands the Latin, for he writes: "*In der ersten der beiden Frühschriften* [i.e., De docta ignorantia] *ist das Thema der methodischen Verwendbarkeit ausdrücklich gestellt: die Mathematik verhilft uns am ehesten zum Erfassen der Andersartigkeit des Göttlichen.* (*Quod mathematica nos iuvet plurimum in diversorum divinorum apprehensione.*)" But the Latin title here in parentheses is taken from *De Docta Ignorantia* I, 11 and speaks not of the *Erfassen der Andersartigkeit des Göttlichen* but rather of the *Erfassen verschiedener Bereiche des Göttlichen*, as the very contents of I, 11 attest. Or again, Blumenberg's translation on p. 100 (corresponding to p. 540 of the English edition) goes astray: indeed, the sentences "*Du nötigst insofern meine Freiheit, als du nicht mein Eigentum sein kannst, wenn ich mir nicht selbst zu eigen bin. Du nötigst mich nicht, insofern du dies meiner Freiheit anheimgegeben hast, sondern du erwartest, dass ich selbst mich dafür entscheide, mir zu eigen zu sein*" do not capture Nicholas's meaning at the end of *De Visione Dei* 7. Blumenberg has not understood Nicholas's argument, and hence he mistranslates "*cum*" as "*insofern . . . als*" and mistranslates "*quia*" as "*insofern*".[319]

6.4. In another vein, both Blumenberg's use of Latin editions and his system of referencing is most unscholarly. He appears to use the Paris edition (1514) of the Latin text of *De Docta Ignorantia*, even though the critical edition by Hoffmann and Klibansky (1932) was available to him. In note 71, line 1, p. 169 of the German paperback (corresponding to p. 656, line 1 of n. 50 in the English edition) the Paris edition's "*sic quaelibet*" is misprinted as "*sic qualibet*" and is at odds with Hoffmann and Klibansky's *"sicut quaelibet"*. In line 1 of note 81 on p. 171 (corresponding to line 1 of n. 60 on p. 657 of the English edition) the verb *"sit"* is excised without any ellipsis marks to indicate an elision. As for other of Nicholas's texts: the Paris edition is also used for many of these in spite of the fact that the critical editions of the Heidelberg Academy were available. Indeed, Blumenberg has recourse to the Paris edition of *Apologia Doctae Ignorantiae* in apparent disregard of the fact that it deviates so extensively from the best manuscript tradition as it is recorded in Klibansky's critical edition. Thus, on p. 53 (English p. 500) he puts " . . . *quis credit se scire, quod scire nequit* . . . " where the critical edition has " . . . *quis credit se scire, quod sciri nequit"*. This difference is serious, because there is a vast discrepancy between asserting that a given human being cannot know something and asserting that no human being can know it.

At other times a reader is uncertain about just what edition Blumenberg is using, since most of Blumenberg's notes do not indicate the edition being referred to, so that the reader is left to draw his own conclusions. Note 27 on p. 166 (=n. 6 on p. 652 of the English text) seems to have reference to the Latin-German edition of *De Venatione Sapientiae* published by Felix Meiner Verlag in 1964, for the reference in the note reads "De venatione sapientiae XIV 41"; and "41", which does not appear in the Paris edition, is presumably the margin number in the 1964 publication. Yet, when we compare with this publication the Latin citation that is given by Blumenberg, we find the addition of the word *"sint"* in line 1; i.e., this word does not appear either in the Meiner edition or in the Paris edition. Blumenberg seems simply to have supplied it on his own without giving any indication of this fact. On the other hand, citations from *De Beryllo* seem to be drawn from the Paris edition. And yet, this observation is rendered uncertain by note 89 on pp. 171-172 (=n. 68 on pp. 657-658 of the English edition). Moreover, this note in the German volume differs from the corresponding note in the English volume. But no indication of this difference is anywhere indicated by the English translator-editor.[320] A reader is simply left to hazard his own explanatory surmises, just as he is left to figure out which Latin edition is being cited. Since the German edition's citation of the Latin text omits 13 words that are incorporated into the English edition's citation, the following surmise seems plausible: viz., that Blumenberg revised the Latin quotation for the English edition. Now, the words added are "*scilicet cur caelum caelum et terra terra et homo homo, nulla est ratio* . . . ." The very first word, "*scilicet*", is not found in the Paris edition, which has "*sed*", but *is* present in the text of Leo Gabriel's edition, published in 1967 in Vienna. Might Blumenberg have been using this text? We cannot be certain, since in line 4 on p. 172 (=line 5, n. 68, p. 657 of the English edition), Blumenberg has "*qui*" instead of "*quod*", the word found in both Gabriel's edition and the Paris edition. Moreover, in line 1 of the same page (=line 3 of n. 68 in the English edition) Blumenberg has "*qua*" instead of "*quia*", the word found in the Paris edition, the Heidelberg Academy edition prepared by Ludwig Baur, the Latin-German edition prepared by Karl Bormann, and the text contained in the Gabriel edition. Surely a reader cannot be expected to trace through edition after edition in order to determine which edition Blumenberg is borrowing from and to what extent alterations have been made without being signaled or else the edition has been misquoted.

Other indications of Blumenberg's unscholarliness abound. Note 68 on p. 169 (=n. 47 on p. 655 of the English edition) consists of the reference "De ludo globi I". Besides there being no indication of the edition from which the Latin text is taken, the directions for locating the Latin passage are frustratingly vague. For *De Ludo Globi* I runs from folio 152^r to folio 159^v in Volume I of the Paris edition. This amounts to 16 pages—14 of which are each the equivalent of 2 ordinary-size printed pages. Equally vague is note 87 on p. 171 (=n. 66, p. 657 of the English edition), which gives as a reference "De ludo globi II". No less than the former reference, this one too retards a reader's attempt to locate the Latin passage that is being documented; for in the Paris edition *De Ludo Globi* II extends from folio 160^v to folio 168^v—the equivalent of 33 ordinary-size printed pages. Similarly frustrating are such impoverished references as "Excitationes I" (n. 86, p. 171 = n. 65, p. 657 of the English edition, which adds the words "Paris ed.") or "Excitationes IX" (n. 48, p. 168 = n. 27, p. 654 of the English edition, which also adds "Paris ed."). In the latter instance, the word "*igitur*" is missing from the first line of the body of the note, and the subsequent ellipsis between "*forma*" and "*Credit*" eliminates a portion of Nicholas's text that is essential for understanding the remainder of the quotation in the note. In the end, Blumenberg seems altogether unfamiliar with standard scholarly documentation requirements. It seems never to have dawned upon him that his reference in note 89 (=n. 68 of the English edition) to "De beryllo 29" needs to specify the edition if only because Chapter 29 in one edition might some day become Chapter 30 in another.[321]

6.5. The undisciplined character of Blumenberg's documentary procedures is paralled by imprecisions in his historical judgments.[322]

6.5.1. Symptomatic of these imprecisions are the misprinting of Nicholas's dates as 1410-1464,[323] the unqualified claim that Nicholas attended the school of the Brethren of the Common Life at Deventer,[324] and the vagueness of the ascription "his [i.e., Nicholas's] fundamentally Scholastic realism regarding universals"[325]—as if "Scholastic realism" signified some uniquely identifiable position rather than being a rubric for cognate but incompatible theories. With regard to Anselm of Canterbury, Blumenberg asserts that in *Proslogion* 15 Anselm "speaks of two concepts of God, a rational one defined by the intensification of what is thinkable to the point of insurpassability and a transcendent one requiring one to go beyond the limits of what is thinkable. Transcendence withdraws the concept from definability."[326] But here again Blumenberg is imprecise. For in *Proslogion* 15 Anselm speaks only of *one* concept of God—the same concept that he advanced in *Proslogion* 2, viz., the concept of God as that than which a greater cannot be thought. And just as he pointed out in *Proslogion* 7 that such a being is omnipotent and in *Proslogion* 13 that it is unlimited and eternal, so in *Proslogion* 15 he points out that such a being is also greater than can be thought. Thus, in Chapter 15 he is continuing to unpack the concept of that than which a greater cannot be thought; he is not setting a second concept antithetically along side it. Indeed, in affirming that God is greater than can be thought, he does not mean that God is beyond all positive conception but simply that God is beyond comprehension. In other words, according to Anselm's *Proslogion*, God is reliably conceivable by us, but He is not perfectly conceivable by us; He is apprehensible, without being fully comprehensible.[327] Anselm later elucidates this point in response to Gaunilo's charge that God is altogether inconceivable *secundum rem*;[328] and in doing so, Anselm shows that he adheres to the method of *analogia*. So Blumenberg is wrong to suggest that

Anselm himself speaks of *two* concepts in Chapter 15—one that admits of definability and one that withdraws from definability; and a fortiori he is wrong in regarding these allegedly *two* concepts as constituting an *antinomy* for Anselm. Indeed, of no passage in the *Proslogion* is it true to say, as Blumenberg says, that "the medieval inventor of the [ontological] argument himself distinguishes between the God of his proof, than Whom nothing greater can be thought, and the God of his revealed faith, Who is greater than anything that can ever be thought."[329]

Secondly, just as Blumenberg is wrong about Anselm's distinction between the God of his proof and the God of his faith, so he is also mistaken in judging that Anselm can eliminate the resulting discrepancy only by "an 'ex post facto' reinterpretation of the concept [of God], a projection of rationality into transcendence . . . ."[330] Thirdly, Blumenberg is wrong in implying that, for Anselm, the concept of God in *Proslogion* 2 is *definitional* of God.[331] Nowhere does Anselm call the expression "God is that than which a greater cannot be thought" a *definition*. Indeed, in *Reply to Gaunilo* 7 he shows clearly that he regards the expression as nondefinitional. For were the expression intended by Anselm to be definitional, he would not have allowed the possibility that someone could in some respect understand the expression while in no respect understanding the meaning (*sensus*) of the term "God."

Fourthly, when Blumenberg bespeaks his own philosophical viewpoint, he often does so with statements of dubious merit—as on pp. 488-489, where he writes:

> Anselm of Canterbury's (1033-1109) 'ontological proof' of God's existence from His concept already makes the antinomy manifest, since the concept of a highest being must be definable from positive predicates only, but the idea of transcendence precisely denies and excludes such predicates.

But here Blumenberg fails to distinguish the concept of a highest being from the concept of a highest *conceivable* being. Moreover, it is false that the concept of a supreme being must be definable solely from positive predicates. A supreme being might be definable in such way that among the defining predicates were "timeless." But what would be the positive conceptual content signified by this predicate? On the other hand, it is also false that the idea of transcendence denies and excludes all positive predicates. The concept of God could, for example, be defined in such way that the (positive) predicate "omnipotent"[332] was consistently included along with the (transcendence-indicating) predicate "timeless." The foregoing quotation from Blumenberg shows that, in a way, he has missed the ingeniousness of Anselm's reasoning in the *Proslogion*. For Anselm does not attempt to *define* the concept of God—does not attempt to determine a precise set of necessary properties that suffice to describe the Divine Being. His formula "*id quo maius cogitari nequit*" is more like a definite description. And Anselm regards it as entailing that God is whatever it is better to be than not to be—where "what it is better to be" is only partially unpacked in the *Proslogion*, and where there is included in this unpacking the further formula "*quiddam maius quam cogitari potest*." Finally, Blumenberg does not understand Anselm's *overall aim* in the *Proslogion*; for if he did, he would not allude to "Anselm's substitution of the highest thinkable thing for something beyond thought."[333] For Anselm does not *substitute* the former for the latter (or, more precisely, does not substitute the description of the former for the description of the latter). Nor can Anselm rightly be said anywhere to *replace* the concept of *quiddam maius quam cogitari potest* by the concept of *aliquid quo maius cogitari nequit*.

These five failings invalidate Blumenberg's interpretation of Anselm's *Proslogion*, thereby disqualifying his comparison between Anselm of Canterbury and Nicholas of Cusa.[334] Moreover, they lead to a sixth shortcoming: viz., the error of claiming that in the sermon "*Dies Sanctificatus*" Nicholas introduces a *transformation* of Anselm's ontological argument[335] when he, Nicholas, infers the existence of God, who is Truth, from the truth of any true proposition. In his footnote Blumenberg attenuates this claim, for no longer does he speak of Nicholas's reasoning as a *transformation* of Anselm's ontological argument; instead, he now says that it is "only *modeled on* the ontological proof that proceeds from the mere concept of God . . . ."[336] However, the argument in Nicholas's sermon cannot be *modeled on* Anselm's argument for God's existence in the *Proslogion*, because the argument in the *Proslogion*—but not the argument in the sermon—has the structure of a *reductio ad absurdum*. Surprisingly, Blumenberg fails altogether to draw the comparison with Anselm's reasoning in *Monologion* 18—reasoning repeated in *De Veritate* 1.

6.5.2. In a related vein, Blumenberg's criticism of Martin Grabmann is faulty:

> At bottom, in spite of Grabmann's two-volume and incomplete work [*Die Geschichte der scholastischen Methode*], there never was such a thing as *a Scholastic method*. The transposition of the modern concept of method to the Middle Ages belongs among the supposedly justifying deobscurifications of the Middle Ages that were long held to be necessary. What was called the Scholastic method consists simply of formal prescriptions for disputation and the composition of treatises. It is not an epistemological method.[337]

Hereby Blumenberg shows, once again, that he does not understand the thought of the "Father of Scholasticism," Anselm of Canterbury. For, assuredly, Anselm has *a Scholastic method*. This method consists of the attempt to justify on an independent rational basis—i.e., to establish *sola ratione* and *rationibus necessariis* and *Christo remoto*—various truths of Scripture that are initially accepted on faith. The method is employed in the *Monologion*, the *Proslogion*, and the *Cur Deus Homo*. Naturally, what Anselm means by *ratio* must be carefully specified, since it does not coincide exactly with the contemporary notions of *ratio*. But even when we allow for the differences, we are not entitled to deny that he has a distinctive programmatic method that can rightly be called *Scholastic*. Of course, his method is associated with different styles of presentation and with various strategies of reasoning. The *Monologion* is a soliloquy, the *Proslogion* a prayerful address to God, the *Cur Deus Homo* a dialogue. Yet, Anselm regards each as proceeding *sola ratione* toward confirming the truths of faith.[338] Indeed, can anyone really not see the difference between Anselm's method in the *Cur Deus Homo* and Nicholas of Cusa's method in Book III of *De Docta Ignorantia* or Augustine's method in *De Trinitate* or Erigena's method in *De Divisione Naturae*? That Anselm's *programmatic method* is not reducible to *a particular method of arguing*, e.g., the method of *reductio ad absurdum*, does not entail that it is not a method and, a fortiori, not a Scholastic method or not an epistemological method.

6.5.3. The foregoing clarifications are essential to a correct historical understanding of St. Anselm's thought. Anyone who misapprehends the structure of his ontological argument and the overall aim of the *Proslogion*, anyone who neglects *Monologion* 18 and *De*

Veritate 1, anyone who fails to see that Anselm is proposing an epistemological method and not just offering "formal prescriptions for disputation and the composition of treatises"[339] will inevitably miscast the comparison between Anselm and Cusanus.

Having detected the looseness of certain of Blumenberg's textual and historical judgments, we may well wonder whether a similar looseness carries over into his treatment of Nicholas's cosmology, anthropology, and Christology. And the answer is clearly affirmative.

6.6. *Nicholas's Cosmology.* 6.6.1. To begin with, the very title of Chapter 2 of Part IV, viz., "The Cusan: The World as God's Self-Restriction"[340] is erroneous; and this error pervades the entire chapter. For Nicholas teaches that God is not at all contracted[341] and cannot become so; by contrast, everything other than God *is* contracted and cannot lose its contractibility.[342] Perhaps Blumenberg is being misled by the title of *De Docta Ignorantia* III, 1: "*Maximum ad hoc vel illud contractum, quo maius esse nequeat, esse sine absoluto non posse*" ("A maximum which is contracted to this or that and than which there cannot be a greater cannot exist apart from the Absolute [Maximum].") This title, rather than referring to the universe, refers to a maximum contracted to a species; but even so, the *divine nature* is never thought by Nicholas to be contracted. On p. 508 Blumenberg interprets Nicholas as maintaining that creation is "an act in which the essence of its Author must unavoidably be invested . . . ." But "invested" ("*investiert*") is entirely the wrong word, because Nicholas maintains that the essence of God cannot become mingled with His creation: the absolutely Maximum is "*incommunicabile, immersibile et incontrahibile ad hoc vel illud . . . .*"[343] The world, therefore, is not God in a contracted state.[344]

6.6.2. Blumenberg's misinterpretation is linked with his imprecisions about Nicholas's conception of the universe as privatively infinite:

> It is true that for Nicholas of Cusa the new cosmology was nothing but the consequence, thought through to the end, of the old idea of creation. But what happened to man while the cosmos grew into the infinite with its Author? The step in metaphysical speculation by which finitude was suspended had as its consequence . . . that from then on the world was, as it were, 'on the point of' itself becoming divine . . . . [345]

This is exegetical nonsense—at least vis-à-vis Nicholas of Cusa, for whom the universe does not "grow into the infinite with its Author"

and for whom it was not the case either that "finitude was suspended" or that "the world was, as it were, 'on the point of' itself
becoming divine." Nowhere does Blumenberg make unequivocally
clear—as he ought to—that for Nicholas, both in *De Docta Ignorantia* and elsewhere, the universe is *finite*, though unbounded. Nicholas
calls the universe privatively infinite because it is unbounded, not
because it is not finite. Again and again Blumenberg slurs over this
distinction, as if not rightly discerning it.[346] Further confusion and
obfuscation occur on p. 531, where he ascribes to Nicholas the view
that "will is the world aspect of the infinite . . . , "[347] as if God had
some world aspect or as if the expression "world aspect of the infinite" did not border upon the opaque. On p. 523 Blumenberg speaks
imprecisely when he maintains that, for Nicholas, "the 'natures' of
which the world is composed are in turn foldings together of the
infinity of characteristics that are realized in the individuals of a
kind."[348] For he should here indicate that the infinity of characteristics which he mentions can be only a potential infinity, not an actual
infinity, according to Cusanus.[349] Yet, the words "are realized" give
the impression that an actual infinity is meant. A further imprecision
appears on p. 509, where Blumenberg remarks: "For the Cusan, without his admitting it, *complicatio* and *explicatio* stand in a relation of
equivalence, in fact an equivalence of interiority, of emanation from a
center from which everything real unfolds itself." However, according
to Nicholas, *complicatio* and *explicatio* are decidedly *not* equivalent.
For all that is unfolded from God is enfolded in God, but not all that
is enfolded in God is unfolded from God.[350]

6.6.3. Blumenberg blunders historically when he asserts: "The conception of transcendence deriving from Platonism can be traced back
to a *spatial* schema in which the primary assertion about the Ideas is
that they are nothing in or of this world but rather are located outside and apart from it . . . ."[351] Hereby Blumenberg shows that he
does not understand the doctrine of *chorismos eidōn* either as it
derives from Plato or as it becomes transformed by Plotinus and
passes into medieval Christian theology. For the Platonic Forms—
such as the Form of Justice and the Form of the Good—are *not*
spatial; they are not *located* in a domain beyond the earthly domain.
Rather, they are altogether spaceless and immaterial, just as they are
altogether timeless. They are beyond the world and separate from the

world but are not *spatially* beyond or *spatially* separate. Nor are they *represented* in spatial terms.

6.6.4. Blumenberg's statements on p. 520 constitute *un fatras d'idées mal comprises.*

6.6.4.1. On p. 520 he cites *De Venatione Sapientiae* 27 (81), where Nicholas, mentioning Dionysius, speaks of exemplars in the mind of God. But he fails to cite *De Venatione Sapientiae* 28, which indicates that there is only one Eternal Form (*aeterna ratio*), in which the specific forms (*rationes seu exemplaria*) of all other things participate.[352] He shows no signs of realizing that when Nicholas follows Dionysius in speaking of exemplars in the Divine Mind, the use of the plural is a *modus loquendi*. For Nicholas believes that the Mind of God is Absolute Oneness, enfolding all things absolutely. This belief does not, however, prevent him from speaking, plurally, of *things* enfolded in God and does not prevent him from *naming* them by their unfolded names. What occurs in *De Venatione Sapientiae* 27-28 is the same thing that occurs in *De Mente* 2-3. In *De Mente* 2 (67:4-7) Nicholas states unequivocally that

> infinita forma est solum una et simplicissima, quae in omnibus rebus resplendet tamquam omnium et singulorum formabilium adaequatissimum exemplar. Unde verissimum erit non esse multa separata exemplaria ac multas rerum ideas.

But this denial of a plurality of exemplars, or ideas, does not prevent him from stating in the very next chapter—i.e., in Chapter 3 (73:1)—that "*omnia in Deo sunt, sed ibi rerum exemplaria . . .* ": "all things are present in God, but in God they are the exemplars of things . . . ." Nicholas is not being inconsistent in these two chapters; he is simply speaking of the things that are enfolded in God *as if* they were manifold forms. These facts about Nicholas's view are already clear in *De Docta Ignorantia*. For in Book I, Chapter 24 he writes:

> Who could understand the infinite Oneness which infinitely precedes all opposition?—where all things are incompositely enfolded in simplicity of Oneness, where there is neither anything which is other nor anything which is different, where a man does not differ from a lion, and the sky does not differ from the earth. Nevertheless, in the Maximum they are most truly the Maximum, [though] not in accordance with their finitude; rather, [they are] Maximum Oneness in an enfolded way.[353]

And this passage accords with *De Docta Ignorantia* II, 9 (148-150), where he makes such statements as the following: "the forms of things are not distinct except as they exist contractedly; as they exist absolutely they are one, indistinct [Form], which is the Word in God."³⁵⁴ "Therefore, when it is said that God created man by means of one essence and created stone by means of another, this is true with respect to things but not true with respect to the Creator . . . ."³⁵⁵ Just why Nicholas should on occasion speak plurally of exemplars in the Mind of God becomes more evident from a passage in *De Docta Ignorantia* II, 3: "Just as number arises from our mind by virtue of the fact that we understand what is commonly one as individually many: so the plurality of things [arises] from the Divine Mind (in which the many are present without plurality, because they are present in Enfolding Oneness). For in accordance with the fact that things cannot participate equally in the Equality of Being: God, in eternity, understood one thing in one way and another thing in another way. Herefrom arose plurality, which in God is oneness."³⁵⁶ Here Nicholas's statement that God understood one thing in one way and another in another way is the equivalent of his elsewhere sometimes saying that exemplars are present in the Divine Mind—even though these so-called exemplars are really only one Exemplar, viz., the Word of God.

    6.6.4.2. Blumenberg mentions none of the foregoing clarifications. Instead, he simply cites from *De Venatione Sapientiae* 27 Nicholas's mention of *exemplars*, in the plural, and judges it to be a remnant of Platonism that conflicts with the doctrine of God's absolute will. But then Blumenberg proceeds to make a *second* mistake—i.e., not only the mistake of "finding" the immediately preceding conflict (which is not actually present in Nicholas's texts) but also the mistake of "finding" a further conflict: viz., an inconsistency within Nicholas's doctrine of creation. In particular, Blumenberg judges the account in *De Venatione Sapientiae* to be in at least one important respect incompatible with the account in *De Docta Ignorantia*: "The Cusan's path," he notes, "from the *Docta ignorantia* to the *Venatio sapientiae*, over almost a quarter of a century, is not consistent. It begins with a God Who, as *the* [absolute] maximum [*der Grösste*], could produce likewise only a work of His order of magnitude, *the* [restricted] maximum [*das Grösste*]. This God is replaced by a God of complicated formulas, for Whom the world that He was actually to create had no precedence over any other entirely heterogeneous—to us, admittedly, inconceivable—possible world contents." In this passage (p. 520) Blumenberg is comparing *De Docta Ignorantia* III, 3 (201:10)[357] with *De Venatione Sapientiae* 27. But, contrary to what he contends, there is no inconsistency between these two passages. In *De Venatione Sapientiae* Nicholas speaks of God as free to create or not to create one world or another in accordance with His will. This point is not at all incompatible with anything propounded in *De Docta Ignorantia*, where God's creating act is also regarded as free. In *De Docta Ignorantia* II, 4 (116:11) Nicholas remarks that "all things sprang into existence from God's design"—a statement which implies, by virtue of the word "design" ("*intentio*"), the freedom of the creative act. This freedom is also implied by the statement in *De Docta Ignorantia* I, 22 (69:9) that God "was able to foresee even the opposite of that which He did foresee." This point is related to the point made in *De Possest* 8:14-15: "God's creative power is not exhausted in His creation." In *De Docta Ignorantia* II, 1 (96:18-21) Nicholas writes: "There is not positable anything which would limit the Divine Power. Therefore, the Divine Power can posit a greater and a lesser than any given thing, unless this given thing is also the Absolute Maximum . . . ."[358] Blumenberg seems to labor under the misimpression that according to *De Docta Ignorantia* there is only one unique maximal universe that God could have created if He was to create a maximal universe; and this misimpression seems to be connected with his misconception about Nicholas's notion of "infinite universe." At any rate, Nicholas maintains in *De Docta Ignorantia* that God created the present universe to be maximal in the sense that it is as great as it can be, in relation to its created possibilities; but God could have created another maximal universe with even greater possibilities.[359]

6.6.4.3. Thirdly, in the passage under discussion—viz., p. 520 of Blumenberg's book—Blumenberg alleges that according to *De Venatione Sapientiae* the world that God was actually to create "*had no precedence over any other entirely heterogeneous . . . possible world contents.*"[360] If Blumenberg is suggesting—as he seems to be—that according to *De Venatione Sapientiae* 27 God might have created a world that was not as great or as perfect as *it* could be, then this suggestion need not be taken seriously. For *De Venatione Sapientiae* 27 does not so much as hint at this view. Nicholas says only that ontologically prior to anything's having been created, one thing was as creatable as another and that God, in creating, selected between alternative possible worlds. But from this statement it does not follow that God might possibly have chosen to create an imperfect world— that perfect worlds did not take precedence over imperfect worlds. Blumenberg apparently believes that in *De Venatione Sapientiae* Nicholas returned to a view that he had held *prior to* his view in *De Docta Ignorantia*. That is, he apparently believes—though his own text is not fully clear here—that at the time of composing the sermon "*Dies Sanctificatus*" Nicholas held the view that creation was a free choice of the Divine Will between alternative possible worlds. This is the view that Nicholas is said by Blumenberg to have abandoned in *De Docta Ignorantia* and to have come back to in *De Venatione Sapientiae*: "The later Nicholas of Cusa *returns* to the intradivine volitional decision, which is indeed asserted to be rational but is not accessible as such, and which *ordains* this world like a *decree.*"[361] However, Blumenberg's interpretation is defeated by the fact that we find written in *De Docta Ignorantia* II, 13 (178):

> Who would not admire this Artisan, who with regard to the spheres, the stars, and the regions of the stars used such skill that there is—though without complete precision—both a harmony of all things and a diversity of all things? [This Artisan] *considered in advance* the sizes, the placing, and the motion of the stars in the one world; and He *ordained* the distances of the stars in such way that unless each region were as it is, it could neither exist nor exist in such a place and with such an order—nor could the universe exist. Moreover, He *bestowed* on all stars a differing brightness, influence, shape, color, and heat . . . . And He *established* the interrelationship of parts so proportionally that in each thing the motion of the parts is oriented toward the whole.[362]

There is no justification for Blumenberg's belief that in *De Docta Ignorantia* creation is not presented by Nicholas as an act of Divine Will.[363] Moreover, Blumenberg, in the revised German text of 1976, should no longer have held—if indeed this was his view—that the sermon "*Dies Sanctificatus*" was written before *De Docta Ignorantia*. For long before 1976 Rudolf Haubst established the correct date of this sermon as Christmas, 1440, a date subsequent to the completion of *De Docta Ignorantia*.

6.6.4.4. Finally, still with respect to p. 520, Blumenberg misleadingly insinuates that at one time or another, or in one place or another, Nicholas propounded his doctrine of *coincidentia oppositorum* "only to bring about mystical obscurification." To be sure, Nicholas's doctrine is related to his teachings about *visio dei*. But only someone who did not discern, within the Cusan system, the utterly pivotal position of the doctrine of coincidence could suppose that it was ever envisaged by Nicholas as serving only to bring about mystical obscurification.

6.6.5. Many of Blumenberg's statements are either overstatements or half-truths. A prime example of a half-truth is found on p. 513:

> The ancient/medieval world picture was geocentric in not only its static but also its dynamic structure. The earth not only 'stood' in the center but it was also the ultimate pole of reference of all cosmic influences, which always passed from 'above' to 'below.' The God of High Scholasticism still made use, for the exercise of His world regime, of mediating agencies, secondary causalities, and thus adhered to the very schema on which the continuing acceptance of astrological ideas also depended. *The Cusan breaks with this schema*; the heavenly powers no longer flow only in one direction, from above to below, from the sublime spheres to the purely receptive and thus all too 'earthly' earth. That old idea now proves to be dependent on the cosmological illusion of the central position of the earth, toward which the directions of influence of the universe appear to converge . . . . The ancient and medieval *hierarchical cosmos has lost its reality*, and indeed precisely because its mediating function between God and man has been eliminated.[364]

Blumenberg creates the false impression that Nicholas breaks with the picture of a universe that is hierarchically arranged and that has mediating features, secondary causes, astrological ideas. But when we turn to *De Docta Ignorantia*, and even to later works, we find Nicholas's thought allowing for the very items that Blumenberg claims to have been rejected. In *De Docta Ignorantia* II, 12 (172:13), for example, Nicholas speaks of causal relations (*proportiones influentiales*) between all the individual stars; and what are these causal relations if not secondary causes? Likewise, his conception of the universe is in many respects hierarchical. This fact is evident from *De Docta Ignorantia* III, 1 (184-188), where he makes statements such as the following: "Among genera, which contract the one universe, there is such a union of a lower [genus] and a higher [genus] that the two coincide in a third [genus] in between. And among the different species there is such an order of combination that the highest species of the one genus coincides with the lowest [species] of the immediately higher [genus], so that there is one continous and perfect universe."365 And he adds: "It is evident that species are like a number series which progresses sequentially and which, necessarily, is finite, so that there is order, harmony, and proportion in diversity . . . ."366 Similarly, in *De Docta Ignorantia* III, 3 he speaks of higher and lower natures—the human order being created lower than the angelic order.367 In *De Docta Ignorantia* II, 12 (172:6-7) he refers to "the one universal world" which is contracted "in terms of its own fourfold descending progression . . . ." Even in *De Coniecturis* he retains a *hierarchical* conception of the four onenesses (God, intellect, soul, the corporeal).368 Likewise, in *De Visione Dei* 24 he subscribes to a hierarchy of powers: Divine, intellectual, rational, imaginative, sensitive, vegetative. And he posits movers for the heavenly orbits. And when stating in *De Docta Ignorantia* II, 12 that the inhabitants of other stars bear no comparative relationship to the inhabitants of the earth, he adds the qualifier: this is true "even if, with respect to the goal of the universe, that entire region bears to this entire region a certain comparative relationship which is hidden to us—so that in this way the inhabitants of this earth or region bear, through the medium of the whole region, a certain mutual relationship to those other inhabitants."369 Not only does Nicholas retain a medieval conception of the relation of whole to parts, he also retains, as was already briefly noted, a medieval conception of gradation: "When I say 'God exists,' this sentence proceeds by means of a certain motion but in such an order that I first articulate the letters, then the syllables, then the words, and then, last of all, the sentence—although the sense of hearing does not discern this order by stages. In like manner, motion descends by stages from the universal [*universum*] unto the particular, where it is contracted by the temporal or natural order. But this motion, or spirit, descends from the Divine Spirit, which moves all things by this motion."370 Furthermore, Nicholas continues to conceive created things in terms of actuality and potentiality,371 form and matter,372 substance and accident.373 Even the alleged inhabitants of the sun and the moon and the known inhabitants of the earth are described in terms of actuality and potentiality.374 And even the Aristotelian medieval belief that heavy things move "downward" toward the center and light things "upward" away from the center is not excluded from Nicholas's system.[375] Finally, Nicholas leaves open the possibility of astrology when he introduces the speculation that on earth there are as many species of things as there are stars and that "the earth contracts to distinct species the influence of all the stars . . . ."[376] Instead of condemning the astrologers in *De Possest* 23, he makes a special point of alluding to their knowledge.

So Blumenberg speaks a half-truth when he asserts flatly that Nicholas breaks with the Scholastic conception of the universe and that, for Nicholas, the ancient and medieval hierarchical cosmos has lost its reality. Ironically, Blumenberg supports these half-truths by appealing to still other half-truths—and even to falsehoods. Thus, on p. 514 he alludes to "the transfer of the mystical formula . . . of the intelligible sphere, whose center is everywhere and circumference nowhere, from the Divinity (for whose mystical representation it had originally been invented) to the universe . . . ." But contrary to Blumenberg's comment, this formula is *not* transferred *from* the Divinity *to* the universe (whether in *De Docta Ignorantia* II, 12 or elsewhere in the Cusanus corpus). For to the universe Nicholas applies not the formula "the intelligible sphere, whose center is everywhere and circumference nowhere" but rather the formula 'God, who is everywhere and nowhere, is the circumference and the center of the world, so that the world has its center everywhere and its circumference nowhere, so to speak.'[377] This difference is critical, since it evidences that Nicholas at no point transfers the formula *away from the Divinity*, because the formula that is applied to the universe includes, in an essential way, reference to the Divinity.

A second example of a half-truth by Blumenberg is displayed on p. 516, where we read:

> In general the Cusan has an aversion to teleological interpretations in his cosmology; teleology appears to him as compensation for a deficiency in creatures such that the latter are supposed to find in the preparation of their world circumstances what is denied to their self-realization . . . . The stars shine in order not[378] to give light to man or to other beings but rather to fulfill their own nature. Light shines by virtue of its nature—that its light[379] also allows one to see is not its primary definition but rather a secondary process of putting it to work—a process that is based on the activity of the seer, that is, on what he makes of the world.

Blumenberg is here misinterpreting *De Docta Ignorantia* II, 12 (166), which does *not* manifest on Nicholas's part an aversion to teleological interpretations in his cosmology. A foot exists, says Nicholas, for walking; an eye exists for seeing. "A similar thing," he continues, "holds true regarding the parts of the world." A star exists in order to gleam with a certain degree of brightness, to be moved in a certain orbit, and to produce its own degree of heat. Moreover, each thing desires to conserve its own existence. Here Nicholas's explanation is *already* teleological. It becomes more so when he adds that God created each thing "in such way that when each thing desires to conserve its own existence as a divine work, it conserves it in communion with others."[380] So although the foot exists for walking, it serves the other parts of the body; for God has coordinated each part of the body in such way that in fulfilling its own nature it conduces to the functioning of the entire bodily system. A similar fact holds true, teaches Nicholas, concerning the earth and the other planets within the "region" of the earth;[381] "the mutual relationship of influence is such that one influence cannot exist without the other."[382] And with regard to the different regions God "ordained the distances of the stars in such way that unless each region were as it is, it could neither exist nor exist in such a place and with such an order—nor could the universe exist."[383] Moreover, since "the Perfect God created all things for Himself,"[384] "all existing things endeavor, as best they can, to participate in His 'brightness and blazing splendor,' so to speak,"[385] so that "He alone is sought in all things."[386] Nicholas speaks, too, of the "goal of the universe."[387] Thus, far from having an aversion to teleological interpretations within his cosmology, he himself promotes these interpretations. Blumenberg remarks that, according to Nicholas, "light shines by virtue of its nature" and that light's also allowing someone to see "is not its primary definition but rather a secondary process of putting it to work." Blumenberg fails to realize that a cosmology or a philosophy of nature can be teleological even when denying that the primary definition of "light" is in terms of enabling perceivers to see. Such a philosophy need only admit that one of the purposes of the *source* of light is to furnish light and that within the total system of things light aids the proper functioning of some other part or parts.

6.6.6. Nicholas's conception of *providentia* (foresight, providence) is also misinterpreted by Blumenberg: "If God is the enfolding of everything—even, then, of contradictories—nothing remains that could escape His foresight (*Vorsehung*). This universality can be neither increased nor decreased—not even had it foreseen something other than, in fact, it did foresee or will foresee, and not even though it did foresee much that it did not need to foresee."[388] Herefrom, together with an accompanying example, Blumenberg concludes: "Thus, already in Cusa's early work *providentia* is related to the concept of possibility, so that it [i.e., God's foresight] would remain unchanged even if something were to occur that in fact will not occur. But this means that the individual cannot find in the concept of *providentia* a justification of his existence."[389] Blumenberg's premise is partially inaccurate as an interpretation of *De Docta Ignorantia* I, 22; and his conclusion is wholly a non sequitur. In the premise, the expression "though it did foresee much that it did not need to foresee"[390] is objectionable. Nicholas's Latin reads: " . . . [*quamvis deus*] *multa etiam providit, quae potuit non providere . . . .*"[391] And this clause in no way contains the idea that God foresaw much that He *did not need to foresee*. Instead, it indicates that God foresaw many things which He was *able not to foresee*. This difference is pivotal to Nicholas's line of reasoning, which becomes incoherent on Blumenberg's construal.

Little wonder, then, that Blumenberg's conclusion is a non sequitur. But what, exactly, are we to make of his conclusion?—a conclusion that is as bizarre as it is illogical: "This means that the individual cannot find in the concept of *providentia* [foresight, providence] a justification of his existence." First of all, let us realize that no one at all—under any conceivable circumstances—could ever find in the *concept* of divine foresight a *justification* of his existence. For concepts cannot intelligibly be said to justify anyone's existence. Someone's discovery, or formulation, of an important concept, formula, model, schema, or logical connection might intelligibly be said to provide—in some sense of "justifying"—a justifying ground for that person's life. So too might his belief in the truth of the applicability of some concept. But what sense would it make to say, flatly, that some person's life is justified by a concept? Not in the *concept of divine foresight* but rather in the *reality of divine foresight* might someone find a transcendent meaning or a theological justification of his life.

Accordingly, let us assume that this latter is the expression that Blumenberg really meant to employ. Even so, his conclusion remains a non sequitur that results from his failure to recognize a central historical fact: viz., that according to Nicholas of Cusa's belief—even at the time he wrote *De Docta Ignorantia*—God's foreknowledge is logically dependent upon His foreordination.[392] Thus, when Nicholas says that "although God could have foreseen many things which He did not foresee and will not foresee and although He foresaw many things which He was able not to foresee, nevertheless nothing can be added to or subtracted from divine foresight,"[393] he implies that God could have ordained many things which He does not ordain and that, likewise, He ordains many things which He was able not to ordain. And if this *implicatum* is true, then someone might well find, in the reality that accords with this truth, a theological justification of his human condition. For he would then be entitled to believe that God ordained not out of necessity but in accordance with perfect wisdom (*sapientia* and *providentia* being conceptually distinguishable).

6.7. *Nicholas's Anthropology.* 6.7.1. Just as Blumenberg's documentation is imprecise, as is also his discussion of Nicholas's cosmology, so too is his representation of Nicholas's philosophical anthropology. Many of his claims are vague and unsupported—as if the mere assertion of them should suffice:

> From the urgency of the foregoing starting point one can develop Cusa's intellectual accomplishment: (1) his maintenance, indeed intensification, of the factor of divine transcendence, but at the same time the advancement both of man and the cosmos toward the qualities of this transcendence; (2) his holding fast to the triumph over Aristotelian epistemology with its idea of a conceptuality 'taken from' the objects themselves (that is, his holding fast to the critical achievements of nominalism as he had probably become acquainted with them in the school of the Brethren of the Common Life at Deventer), but at the same time his conducting of this new theory-of-concepts away from functioning merely as an economical expedient unto its becoming the acknowledgement of the authentic and specific dignity of human systematic comprehension of reality.[394]

Almost everything about this passage is problematical. The opening point tacitly attributes to Nicholas's thought an antinomy: Nicholas is said to attempt, on the one hand, to intensify the factor of divine transcendence and, on the other, to formulate a picture of man and the cosmos that advances them toward the qualities (*Qualitäten*) of this transcendence. Now, insofar as God is transcendent He has no *qualities* (both according to Nicholas of Cusa and in accordance with the ordinary theological understanding of the concept *divine transcendence*).[395] Hence, if the factor of transcendence is intensified, then the notion of divine qualities ("the qualities of this transcendence") becomes so diminished that man cannot at all be understood to be advanced toward any such qualities. By contrast, if human beings and the cosmos *are* intelligibly said to be advanced "toward the qualities of this transcendence," then the notion of transcendence will have to be so reduced that the entire program of *docta ignorantia*—and with it the doctrine of divine simplicity—will collapse. Since Nicholas himself, however, nowhere entertains either the concept or the expression *the qualities of this transcendence*, it is difficult to see how he could be developing a viewpoint in which man and the cosmos are "advanced" toward such qualities.

6.7.2. The foregoing passage also represents Nicholas as "holding fast to the critical achievements of nominalism," even though Blumenberg never makes an attempt to articulate just what these achievements are and though his statement seems inconsistent with his equally vague claim on p. 523 that Nicholas is fundamentally a Scholastic realist regarding universals. Rather than facing up to his own inconsistency of exposition, Blumenberg prefers to avoid serious analysis of Nicholas's epistemology by levelling a sweeping indictment against it: "I will not make what I believe would have to be a futile attempt at a unitary interpretation of the Cusan's theory of knowledge. Here in particular the inner consistency of his philosophical accomplishment is doubtful. The reason for this can be specified: It lies, again, in the inability to deal with or successfully to evade the consequences of nominalism."[396] Yet, Blumenberg nowhere manages to show any such inconsistency on Nicholas's part, and thus his own evasion of a careful exposition of Nicholas's epistemology remains without any apparent foundation. By making such sweeping claims as that Nicholas holds fast to the triumph over Aristotelian epistemology, Blumenberg places himself under a special obligation to provide this foundation. However, his attitude is so dismissive that he does not even bother to mention—let alone discuss—Nicholas's acceptance of the Aristotelian-Thomistic doctrine that "there cannot be in the intellect anything which is such that it was not first in the senses."[397]

Moreover, certain passages mentioned by Blumenberg are expounded misleadingly. His discussion of Nicholas's illustration of the map-maker[398] furnishes a prime instance. Nicholas uses the illustration as a means for directing our contemplation unto the Maker of ourselves and our world. Within ourselves, he says, the intellect resembles a mapmaker who resides within an enclosed city that has five gates, analogous to the five senses. Through these gates messengers are received from all parts of the sensible world, bringing with them reports, or sensations. Those messengers who bring news regarding light and color must enter through the gate of sight; those who bring news of sounds and voices must enter through the gate of hearing; and so on. The cosmographer takes cognizance of these reports. And he strives to keep all five gates open, so that he may continually receive reports from new messengers and thus make for himself a description-of-the-sensible-world that is progressively more accurate. Had one of these gates always remained shut—e.g., the gate of sight—the cosmographer would have had no information about the sun or the stars or about any object in the sensible world insofar as that object is visible. At length, having made an overall determination of the sensible world, beyond the domain of the gates, he reduces it to a well-ordered and proportionally measured map. Thereafter, he sends away the messengers and closes the gates. And he transfers his inner gaze to the Creator of the sensible world—a Creator who is none of all the things of which he has learned through the messengers, but who is rather the Cause of all these things. And he reflects upon how it is that, in an antecedent way, the Creator bears to the whole world a relationship that is like his own relationship to his map. And just as truth about the sensible world shines forth in his map, so truth about the Maker of the whole world shines forth in himself qua mapmaker.

Nicholas's purpose in proposing the foregoing illustration is to indicate how we may formulate, if only symbolically,[399] an acceptable concept of God as Creator. The illustration does not aim at addressing the issue of how exactly the map is related to the sensible world. It does not seek to illuminate the dispute between epistemological realists and epistemological idealists or conventionalists. In an implicit manner, however, the illustration does show that Nicholas regards the map as a true representation of the sensible world—a true representation that can in principle always be made progressively more accurate.[400] The cosmographer, in reducing to a map the determinations-of-the-sensible-world that he has attained through the reports of the messengers, preserves both the order of the sensible world and, proportionally, the distances between objects. The cosmographer shuts the gates of the senses only after gathering information and making an accurate—though not perfectly accurate—map. He wants the map in order not to forget the determinations that he has been making; and he shuts the gates in order to be able to contemplate in quietude the Cause of the sensible world. Nicholas implies that the cosmographer can at any time thereafter reopen the gates, receive more messengers, and check the accuracy of his map.

Blumenberg seems to suppose—though his discussion is unduly vague—that the illustration is a step in Nicholas's path toward overcoming Aristotelian epistemology, for he writes:

> The world map which the cosmographer makes is, for Cusanus, an especially typical illustration: the map does indeed have a likeness to the world that is represented, but it is anything other than a [mere] combination of the images of the things it represents. It is a reconstruction; and it resembles a conjecture in the following way: though it is a "participation" insofar as it represents, it is nonetheless a participation in otherness. The cosmographer gives a representation of the entire sensibly apprehensible world. He does so, to be sure, by working upon, ordering, and reducing to a common scale the data and information that are brought to him from without—but nonetheless by remaining at home, closing the doors, and turning his gaze inward toward the World Ground which is present within him and which first provides him with the unifying principle for all the facts brought in from without.[401]

Here Blumenberg's emphasis upon reconstruction (*Nachkonstruktion*), upon conjecture, upon the cosmographer's staying within the city, closing the gates, turning inward to find the unifying principle of the data from without—these emphases, as presented by Blumenberg, suggest that Nicholas is here "holding fast to the critical achievements of nominalism."[402] If this is what Blumenberg is aiming to say, then he is surely mistaken. For, as we have seen, in the illustration Nicholas indicates that (1) the cosmographer receives reports that enable him to make a true—but not perfectly true—description of the world and that (2) the cosmographer reduces this description to a rightly ordered and proportionally measured map (*"in mappam redigit bene ordinatam et proportionabiliter mensuratam . . . "*). Blumenberg calls attention to the mapmaker's not leaving the city and not keeping the gates open. But who would expect the mapmaker to leave the city?—something comparable to obtaining a direct, intuitive (i.e., non-sensible) vision of the world. Such a summons to cognize the world directly and independently of the five senses was never a part of the fourteenth- and fifteenth-century epistemological realist's platform. Moreover, Blumenberg, fails to mention that (1) the gates are closed only *after* the map has been made and that (2) the Creator who is thereafter contemplatively sought is not sought in order to acquire some further knowledge about things in the sensible world, nor even in order to unify the knowledge-of-the-world that has already been attained.

6.7.3. Blumenberg's use of the word "conjecture" as it relates to Nicholas needs the following kind of clarification:

> We generally contrast what is conjectured with what is known. And Nicholas sometimes does so too—but not routinely. In *De coniecturis* a "conjecture" is construed as a judgment (about reality) which does not attain unto maximal precision. Since only God, who is *mens infinita*, has absolutely precise knowledge, all human knowledge is said to be a mode of "conjecture." But this statement does not mean that *"coniectura"* is not also oftentimes a mode of knowledge, in our sense of "knowledge." Accordingly, Nicholas regards a *coniectura* as participating in the truth, as being partly (but never precisely) true [*De coniecturis* I, 11 (57:10-11)]. This fact explains why he can use the expression *"coniecturalis cognitio"* ("conjectural knowledge") at the beginning of *De coniecturis* II, 17 and why in II, 16 (157) he can indicate that, with the cooperation of the intellect, the sense of sight attains unto what is visible (e.g., a human passer-by). Again and again, as in II, 15 (148), he makes clear that what cannot be attained by us except *in coniectura* is the *precise* truth (*praecisio veritatis*).[403]

Such a clarification is never forthcoming in Blumenberg's book. Indeed, from other mistakes that Blumenberg makes, we may infer that he does not really understand Nicholas's notion of *coniectura*. For if he did, he would not interpret Nicholas's doctrine of *image* along the following lines: "The truth is by no means present in the image unless the image is always immediately suspended as such. For while each image does represent the truth, at the same time, as an image, it has already fallen away and is hopelessly distant from it."[404]

Blumenberg misreads *Apologia Doctae Ignorantiae*, which he cites in support of his assertion. For there is nothing in *Apologia* 11—or even in *Apologia* 30—that warrants the foregoing interpretation. In these passages, together with the parts of *De Docta Ignorantia* to which they allude, Nicholas teaches (1) that "God shines forth in creatures as the truth [i.e., as an original, or an exemplar,] shines forth in an image";[405] (2) that "every image, in that it is an image, falls short of the truth of its exemplar,"[406] so that a potentially infinite number of ever-closer approximations of image to exemplar remain;[407] (3) that, thus, "in an image the truth cannot at all be seen as it is [in itself]";[408] (4) that, nonetheless, some degree of truth is seen in the image, insofar as the image is an image of an exemplar [i.e., of a real object],[409] so that through the image the exemplar is seen; (5) that in the case of God what is seen from the image, or creature, is that God, the Creator, is unknowable.[410] Blumenberg, however, insinuates that, according to *De Docta Ignorantia* and the *Apologia*, the relationship of *all* exemplifying images to their respective exemplar is such that the exemplar is incomprehensible on the basis of the image. This insinuation is present in the tendentiously elided footnote[411] with which he supports his claim on pp. 498-499. And it is even more strongly present in his words "hopelessly distant" ("*hoffnungslos entfernt*"): an image—any image—is alleged to be hopelessly distant from its truth.

In fact, Blumenberg does not understand even the broad outlines of Nicholas's program of learned ignorance. Otherwise, he would never assert, on p. 487: "He [viz., Nicholas] opposes to *and* superimposes upon the plunge into the all-extinguishing obscurity of the mystical experience of God the 'method' of *docta ignorantia* . . . ." If *opposition* and *superimposition* were not incompatible notions, so that Blumenberg's assertion were not unintelligible, then the assertion would be false. For Nicholas nowhere *opposes* learned ignorance and mystical experience but instead interrelates them, as has already been shown.[412]

6.7.4. We may return now to the quotation with which this present subsection (viz., *6.7*) on anthropology began—viz., the passage (from pp. 35-36 of the German edition) out of which arose the topic of nominalism. At the end of this passage Blumenberg repeats, uncritically, the legend about Nicholas's having been a schoolboy amongst the Brothers of the Common Life at Deventer, in Holland.[413] Then he goes on to remark: Nicholas leads the nominalistic theory of concepts "away from functioning merely as an economical expedient [*ökonomische Notlösung*] unto its becoming the acknowledgement of the authentic and specific dignity of human systematic comprehension of reality." But to regard fourteenth-century nominalistic concept theory as a *Notlösung* is to misconceive the intellectual situation— and, therefore, to misconceive the *Fragestellung*—that occasioned the development of nominalism. And, in any event, since Nicholas is not a nominalist—either in *De Docta Ignorantia, De Coniecturis, De Mente*, the *Compendium*,[414] or anywhere else—he cannot rightly be said to conduct this "new theory-of-concepts" anywhere.

6.7.5. In interpreting Nicholas's conception of faith Blumenberg fares no better than in interpreting other of his doctrines.

6.7.5.1. Oftentimes, he reads Nicholas's texts only cursorily, analyzing them only superficially as he rushes headlong toward making some sweeping claim or other. This indictment holds true regarding the following passage:

> The Cusan presses the functionalization of faith a step further in the treatise *De genesi* [*On Genesis*].[415] He recommends that one should accept the declarations of *theological authority as though they were made known by divine revelation*, and only then should one attempt to grasp intellectually what one has at first assumed. He explicitly grounds this recommendation on his own experience. Here faith has drawn quite near to conjecture. They have in common the hypothetical function that has to prove itself by experience.[416]

This passage is a *Fehldeutung*, because in *De Genesi* 5 (175:7-12)— the Cusan text to which Blumenberg refers—Nicholas is not speaking of *theological* authority; nor is he speaking of the declarations of theological authority *as though* they were made known by divine revelation. Rather, he is dealing with *Biblical* authority and with declarations which *are*, on his view, divine revelation. For what is under discussion is the interpretation of Psalms 32:6 (33:6). And the general context deals with the issue of interpreting correctly the book of Genesis and the words of Moses. Nicholas would not have the same opinion about ecclesiastical authority or about theological authority, so-called. Certainly he does not hold that the theological authority of someone such as St. Augustine is equal to the authority of Scripture: indeed, Augustine's opinions need not be received on the basis of faith.

But in Blumenberg's exegesis there is a second error. "Here," he says, "faith has drawn quite near to conjecture. They have in common the hypothetical function that has to prove itself by experience." But in *De Genesi* 5 (175:7-12)—the referent of "here"—Nicholas is making no claim about *proving by experience*. He is dealing with the meaning of Psalms 32:6 (33:6): "By the word of the Lord the heavens were established; and all the power of them by the spirit of his mouth . . . ."[417] And is there anything that is a less likely candidate for proof by experience than is the proposition "By the word of the Lord the heavens were established . . . "'? Blumenberg's exegesis of Nicholas's text is altogether undisciplined. Let us concede that in Nicholas's works there *are* places—not mentioned by Blumenberg—where Nicholas likens faith to conjecture, in some sense of "conjecture," and to hypothesis, in some sense of "hypothesis." If an interpreter is to avoid exegetical falsity, he must take the trouble to place proper restrictions upon the use of the words "conjecture" and "hypothesis"; for faith, as depicted by Nicholas, is not like speculative conjecture or like scientific hypothesis. In *De Visione Dei* 21 Nicholas declares: "If anyone believes and accepts, he will most truly find that You descended from Heaven and that You alone are the Teacher of truth."[418] Here he *does* consider faith to carry with it a promissory note about future findings. But faith is not here understood as being tested—in the manner in which a scientific hypothesis is tested—so that it may be either *confirmed or disconfirmed*. 'Most truly finding that the Son of God descended from Heaven' is only in a metaphorical sense like finding a treasure.[419]

In *De Visione Dei* Nicholas does not envision the possibility of faith's being disconfirmed. His instructions are not: 'Do this, viz., believe, and such and such can be expected to occur; however, if it does not occur, then this nonoccurrence will count against the truth of the proposition that is, or was, believed.' The statement from *De Visione Dei* 21 is not intended to make a straightforward empirical claim. For the kind of finding that Nicholas has in mind is a finding that can take place only if preceded by devout faith, which dare not be equated with hypothesizing belief. By comparison, the Biblical statement "And we know that to them that love God all things work together unto good"[420] is not a proposition whose putative truth is treated by St. Paul as reformulable into an hypothesis that is empirically confirmable or disconfirmable in the course of this lifetime. Rather, it expresses St. Paul's hope and conviction; moreover, it contains an implicit recommendation to the believer to view his suffering as serving some good end—good even for himself, the sufferer. Similarly, Nicholas's statement about finding that the Son of God descended from Heaven expresses his hope and conviction; and it contains an implicit recommendation that accords with the teaching of Jesus: "Seek, and you shall find."[421] Nicholas would not suppose that anyone who does not "find" thereby casts doubt upon the "validity" of the injunction; instead, he would regard such a person as not seeking with all his heart.[422]

In *De Docta Ignorantia* III, 11 (244:3-9) Nicholas remarks, from his standpoint within Christianity: "All our forefathers unanimously maintain that faith is the beginning of understanding. For in every branch of study certain things are presupposed as first principles. They are grasped by faith alone, and from them is elicited an understanding of the matters to be treated. For everyone who wills to ascend to learning must believe those things without which he cannot ascend. For Isaiah says 'Unless you believe, you will not understand.' " Perhaps this is the passage that Blumenberg has in mind when he observes that, for Nicholas, *fides* and *coniectura* are functionally equivalent in that "they provide reason with the presuppositions it needs in order to arrive at conclusions within the total system."[423] At least, this passage will help to illuminate Blumenberg's interpretation. But it must be brought into relationship with other texts which show that *religious* faith is depicted differently from the foregoing kind of faith. Indeed, from the viewpoint of Christianity religious faith is the gift of God, says Nicholas.[424] It is faith-in-Christ, faith in-formed by love, faith that makes a man Christlike, faith that has the power to move mountains, faith that wills to be elevated to a level of indubitable certainty. Such faith is not functionally equivalent to *coniectura*; consequently, Blumenberg has once again furnished us with only a vague half-truth.

6.7.5.2. But let us turn to a second instance of misinterpreting what Nicholas says about faith. "Now one sees," notes Blumenberg, "as soon as one investigates the Cusan's descriptions of the act of faith, that Wenck's opposition to the effacement of the distinction between the status of knowledge in this world and in the next was not groundless. The antithesis of earthly faith to the *visio* [vision] in the world to come disappears when faith itself is defined as *coincidentia visibilis et invisibilis* [coincidence of the visible and the invisible] and the intellect takes the content of revelation *in certitudine, ac si vidisset* [for certainty, as though it had seen it]."[425] But, once again, almost everything about this interpretation is erroneous. First of all, Wenck's opposition *is* groundless, because Nicholas does not so much as *tend toward* effacing the distinction between the status of understanding (*intellectus, Erkenntnis*) in this world and in the next.[426] Secondly, Nicholas does not cause to disappear the opposition between present faith and future vision.[427] Thirdly, he does not *define* faith as *coincidentia visibilis et invisibilis*; and, fourthly, the intellect does not *unqualifiedly* take the content of revelation for a certainty. These third and fourth assertions by Blumenberg result from his faulty exegesis of Nicholas's sermon "*Sic currite ut compraehendatis.*"[428] What Nicholas says in the relevant section of this sermon is the following:

> Therefore, the ability to believe is the greatest power of our soul. It exceeds all intellectual power; for it pertains to the things which the soul wills, since it proceeds from freedom of will. For the rational soul can believe or not believe depending upon whether it wills [to believe] or does not will [to believe]; and this is the greatest gift of God. Similarly, the spirit, or free will, through the faith which it adopts, governs the intellect and in-forms it with its own form. For it commands the intellect. And certain individuals were accustomed to say that in the speculative intellect faith is under the command of the will, because the will does not allow the intellect to discern unless the intellect is habituated by faith. But the intellect readily receives the faith which it does not understand—[receives it] when the will announces to it, through faith, the items-to-be-believed which we hear; for they have been revealed to us by the Son of God, i.e., through the Word of God [i.e., through Scripture]. For the will is the soul's "hearing," as it were; and the intellect is its "sight," so to speak. And so, the things which a soul that is zealous for the good has heard, it announces to the intellect, so that the intellect may know itself. For the things which the will reports are such that they cannot be seen. The intellect believes that true things have been reported to it, and it accepts them as if they were seen—i.e., [it accepts them] in certitude, as if it had seen. Thus, faith, as it concerns the intellect, is present in a coincidence of the visible and the invisible.

Obviously, Nicholas is not here *defining* the concept of faith, and a fortiori he is not defining it as *coincidentia visibilis et invisibilis*.

Moreover, the *visibilis* that he alludes to has been clearly stated to be
as if visible. Hence, the coincidence here posited does not destroy,
but rather reinforces, the distinction between earthly faith and future
vision. Blumenberg should emphasize that the "certitude of faith" is
significantly different from theoretical certitude. Instead, he wrongly
emphasizes the opposite: "This mediation between faith and knowledge [*Wissen*] seems at first to tend, entirely in the framework of the
medieval, toward positing faith as absolute; but faith can now equally
well stand in the service of knowledge [*Wissen*], in that it postulates
freedom for playing through new possibilities of knowledge [*Erkenntnis*]."[429] Yet, in the passage from the sermon Nicholas is not making
faith stand in the service of *Wissen*; nor is he mediating *Glaube* and
Wissen. Since the truths of faith are accepted by the believer's intellect as if they were seen, i.e., as if they were known, it follows that
they are not known in any ordinary sense of "known" and do not
have the kind of certainty that accompanies sight. Accordingly, in
De Docta Ignorantia III, 11 Nicholas has no hesitancy about writing: "But soundest faith-in-Christ, made steadfastly firm in simplicity, can, in accordance with previously given instruction in ignorance,
be increased and unfolded in ascending degrees. For although hidden
from the wise, the very great and very deep mysteries of God are
revealed, through faith in Jesus, to the small and humble inhabitants
of the world. For Jesus is the one in whom all the treasures of wisdom and knowledge are hidden, and without Him no one can do
anything . . . . Since God is not knowable in this world (where by
reason and by opinion or by doctrine we are led, with symbols,
through the more known to the unknown), *He is apprehended only
where persuasive considerations cease and faith appears*."[430]

In the sermon "*Sic currite ut compraehendatis*" Nicholas is dealing
not with faith in Christ (viz., saving faith) but with faith (i.e., propo-
sitional faith) by which a mortal man believes that he can attain unto
immortality. Nevertheless, even in this regard Nicholas affirms that
faith must vanquish reason, just as Abraham's faith vanquished reason when Abraham believed that which reason judged to be impossible—
viz., that he would become the father of many nations. By comparison, since we have no experience of immortality, says Nicholas, and
since reason even opposes belief in immortality, a man who accepts
this doctrine on the basis of faith in the Word of God must triumph

over reason. So Nicholas's view of the relationship between faith and reason—as this view is presented in the sermon—does not support Blumenberg's assertion that here there is a mediation (*Vermittlung*) between faith and knowledge (*Wissen*) or that faith can now equally well stand *im Dienste des Wissens*, i.e., in the service of knowledge.

6.7.5.3. Instead of pointing out the complexity of Nicholas's notion (or notions) of faith, Blumenberg selects a passage here and there and, without examining its fuller context, interprets it to fit his preconceptions and earlier misconceptions. In the present instance his misfocusing of Nicholas's notion of faith is influenced by his misconception regarding *docta ignorantia*, wherein he sees signs of an ambivalence, on Nicholas's part, between "skeptical resignation and encouragement of theory . . . ."[431] Nonetheless, as described by Nicholas himself the concept of *docta ignorantia* neither includes nor implies skeptical resignation. In the program of *docta ignorantia* the intellect neither aims at, nor terminates in, skeptical resignation; instead, it aims at *quies, pax, fruitio, gaudio*.[432] Even when in mystical ascent the intellect seeks to transcend itself,[433] it does not aim at skeptical resignation but at approaching nearer unto God.[434]

6.7.6. Just as Blumenberg does not understand Nicholas's conception of man's relationship to God through faith, so he does not understand Nicholas's conception of God. This fact is already evident from our previous examination of his statements about Nicholas's cosmology; but it surfaces again in his statements about Nicholas's philosophical anthropology. In particular, we may look at his treatment of Nicholas's illustration, in *De Visione Dei*, of the omnivoyant icon. According to Blumenberg "everyone who raises his gaze to the picture is regarded; but he is regarded only when and because he, for his part, looks toward the picture. The plurality and individuality of the viewers are not opposed to the identity of the picture; rather they are the partnership appropriate to it that for the first time unfolds its mysterious potentiality."[435] Yet, according to Nicholas, it is not the case that the icon's gaze—which symbolizes the divine gaze—looks upon the beholder "only when and because he, for his part, looks toward the picture." For Nicholas says unequivocally: "By means of this icon of You, O Lord, I see how favorably disposed You are to show Your face to all who seek You. For You never close Your eyes; You never turn [them] away. And although I turn away from You when I completely turn to something else, You do not on this account change Your eyes or Your gaze."[436] Indeed, remarks Nicholas, "since Your seeing is Your being, I exist because You look upon me. And if You were to withdraw Your countenance from me, I would not at all continue to exist."[437] The angle of God's eye is an infinite sphere, asserts Nicholas, so that it sees all things at once,[438] so that it cannot fail to see every existent thing from every possible perspective. Blumenberg has failed to recognize Nicholas's dialectical approach.[439] For what Nicholas means is not that when I cease looking unto God (symbolized by the icon), God ceases looking upon me. He means that at this moment God ceases to look upon me *oculo gratiae*—with an eye of grace[440]—and now looks upon me with an eye of judgment.[441]

The second part of Blumenberg's assertion is equally wrong. For there is no *partnership* (*Partnerschaft*) between the icon and the beholder, i.e., between God and the beholder. Because Blumenberg thinks that God beholds me "only when and because" I look unto Him, he concludes that there is this partnership. His mistake about the former point leads to his mistake about the latter. But by means of the symbolism of the icon, Nicholas himself sees in his relationship to God not partnership but "companionship for my journey."[442] The term "partnership" might be unobjectionable were Blumenberg to understand it differently from the way he does—were he not to construe it in such way that the plurality and individuality of the beholders are the partnership that for the first time unfolds the icon's (and, thus, God's) mysterious potentiality.[443] Blumenberg's understanding, however, is foreign to Nicholas's teachings. For though Nicholas allows that created things are "unfolded" from God, he disallows that they serve in partnership with God to unfold His potentiality. And, in any event, the word "potentiality" ("*Potentialität*") is misleading. For Nicholas considers God to be *Actualized*-possibility;[444] but the word "potentiality" suggests that not all the possibilities of His nature were always actualized.

6.7.7. Finally, Blumenberg distorts Nicholas's understanding of human freedom. To be sure, his discussion of this topic goes astray from the very outset, when he mistranslates *De Visione Dei* 7 (26:14 - 27:5) as:

When I thus come to rest in the silence of contemplation, You answer me, Lord, in my own breast, saying: "Be your own and I will be yours." You, Lord, have placed within my freedom my belonging to myself, if I but will to. If I have not become my own, then You too are not mine. With respect to the fact that You cannot be my possession unless I am my own, You coerce my freedom. With respect to the fact that You have placed this matter within my freedom, You do not coerce me but await my choosing to be my own.[445]

Now, in translating *"necessitares enim libertatem"* as *"Du nötigst . . . meine Freiheit"* ("You coerce my freedom"), Blumenberg takes no account of the fact that *"necessitares"* is an imperfect subjunctive, not a present indicative. Moreover, in translating *"cum tu non possis esse meus nisi . . ."* as *"insofern . . . als du nicht mein Eigentum sein kannst, wenn . . . nicht . . . , "* he misconstrues the meaning of *"cum"*. In the end, he miscasts the argument that Nicholas is making in the passage.[446] And, in fact, his not having grasped the structure of the argument is what led to his mistranslating the passage. For *"necessitares enim libertatem"* can only be rightly translated if the argument in which it is embedded is rightly discerned.

How far Blumenberg remains from correctly comprehending the foregoing argument is displayed by the implications that he draws from it: "According to Cusanus God wills that man himself take over the Creator's original right-of-ownership to His creature and exercise it over himself. The theological concept of release [*Freisprechung*] liberates from guilt; the philosophical [concept of release liberates] from dependency on the ownership which God, as Author of man's existence, exercises over man."[447] This interpretation of Cusanus is nonsense.[448] Nowhere does Nicholas allow that man takes over from God the original right of ownership of himself. On the contrary, he maintains—in *De Visione Dei* itself—that "in the case of the intellectual nature Your Spirit has reserved exclusively for itself the governance and ordering."[449] Moreover, in *De Visione Dei* 7 he indicates clearly what he means by "Be your own." And it has nothing to do with taking over from the Creator the right of ownership to ourselves: "Yet, how will I be my own unless You, O Lord, teach me how? But You teach me that the senses should obey reason and that reason should govern.[450] Therefore, when the senses serve reason, I am my own. But reason has no one to direct it except You, O Lord, who are the Word and the Rational Principle (*ratio*) of rational principles. Hence, I now see the following: if I hearken unto Your Word, which does not cease to speak within me and which continually shines forth in my reason, I shall be my own—free and not a servant of sin—and You will be mine and will grant me to see Your Face and then I shall be saved."[451] Here Nicholas speaks again of God's governance of man's reason and of the need for man to be obedient to God's Word. Nothing is said about man's autonomous governing of himself or about his taking over rights from the Creator. Blumenberg recognizes Nicholas's emphasis on obedience. But he distorts Nicholas's view of the relationship between freedom and obedience when he writes: "Cusanus understood setting-free as an act-of-releasing-oneself which is likewise the epitome of obedience and which does not dissolve the 'family bond' but rather is grounded in God's self-surrender to free-men."[452] But in *De Visione Dei* Nicholas neither states nor implies that man liberates himself through some act of self-release, or *self-emancipation*. Rather, he maintains that man becomes free and no longer a servant of sin through faith and through *self-possession*—a notion which, for Nicholas, signifies not a surrendering of rights by God or an acquiring of them by man but the governance of man's senses by his reason. And his reason is to be directed by God, whose Word is to shine forth in it.

6.8. *Nicholas's Christology.* Various difficulties beset Blumenberg's all-too-brief account of Nicholas's Christology.

6.8.1. Blumenberg views Nicholas as caught in an antinomy which he, Nicholas, then resolves by appeal to the doctrine of Incarnation. The antinomy is allegedly the following: "on the one hand, the creation must possess the highest possible perfection but, on the other hand, must not reach the limit of what is possible in its Beginning [i.e., in its Creator]."[453] Now, this may be an antinomy that is present in some philosopher's work, but it is not present in Nicholas's work—certainly not in *De Docta Ignorantia* or in "*Dies Sanctificatus.*" For Nicholas never claims that creation must possess the highest possible perfection. (Indeed, only God is perfect in this sense.) His point in *De Docta Ignorantia* II, 2 (104) is that in the original creation every creature was as perfect as *it* could be,[454] even though its degree of perfection differed from the degree of perfection of every other created thing. Similarly, in *De Docta Ignorantia* II, 1

(97) he indicates that the totality of things—the universe—exists "in the best way in which the condition of its nature allows."[455] God had the power to create a greater and a more perfect universe; yet, God created *this* universe, with its possibilities, to be as great and as perfect as it could be.[456] In this sense, it approaches as closely as possible to the maximum.[457] In *De Docta Ignorantia* III, 1 (185) Nicholas reaffirms that the universe does not exhaust or delimit the power of God. So in *De Docta Ignorantia* there is no antinomy, because Nicholas does not subscribe unqualifiedly to what Blumenberg ascribes to him as "on the one hand." Moreover, Nicholas has not changed his position in the sermon "*Dies Sanctificatus*," preached on Christmas Day, 1440 (and, therefore, subsequently to the completion of *De Docta Ignorantia*).[458] For even in the sermon Nicholas is not advancing a view different from the view that God created a world which was the most perfect it could be. And as in *De Docta Ignorantia*, so too in the sermon he appeals to the doctrine of Incarnation not in order to resolve an antinomy but in order to explain how all the things which went out from God, their Beginning, will also return unto God, their End.

6.8.2. In delineating the structure of Nicholas's reasoning in *De Docta Ignorantia* III, 2-3, Blumenberg does not represent this structure altogether accurately. "Among the actual objects of the world, among the totality of contracted things," writes Blumenberg, "there must be an actual thing that exhausts the possibility of the species in which it exists."[459] This statement of Blumenberg's is incompatible with his immediately succeeding quotation from Nicholas's text. That is, Nicholas does not say "there *must* be . . . "; he says "if a maximum which is contracted to a species could be posited as actually existing, then . . . ."[460] Blumenberg himself proceeds to acknowledge the hypothetical character of Nicholas's argument. And he recognizes that Nicholas's later [461] assertion that there is such a maximum, viz., Christ, is an assertion that Nicholas regards as confirmed by *historical* considerations more than by *rationibus necessariis*. But Blumenberg still needs to make clear the following important difference between the reasoning in *De Docta Ignorantia* III and that of the sermon "*Dies Sanctificatus*": although the latter explicitly and emphatically affirms that unless God had assumed a human nature the universe could not have been perfect (indeed, could not at all have existed), the former contains this point only as a tacit implication. For in *De Docta Ignorantia* III, 3 (202:14-17)[462] we read that "all things—through most absolute God and by the mediation of the universal contraction, viz., the humanity [of Christ]—go forth into contracted being so that they may be that-which-they-are in the best order and manner possible." Presumably, then: unless Christ were God and man, i.e., unless the Son of God assumed a human nature, all things could not have gone forth into contracted being in the best order possible (and thus could not have gone forth at all, since God would not create that which is less perfect than it could be).

6.8.3. Blumenberg's treatment of Cusanus draws toward an end,[463] with an observation that needs further precision: "Nowhere [in *De Docta Ignorantia*] is there talk of the fact that man's sin compelled God to sacrifice His son. The Creation, not sin, the deficiency of nature, not that of man, presses toward this consequence."[464] But this claim is a conjunction of two false disjunctions: (1) Either creation or sin, but not both, presses toward the consequence of Christ's sacrificial death and (2) either the deficiency of nature or the deficiency of man, but not both, presses toward this same consequence. Yet, within the framework of *De Docta Ignorantia* all four disjuncts are true: both the creation and sin, both the deficiency of nature and the deficiency of man press toward the consequence of Christ's sacrificial death. Let us focus primarily upon the themes of sin and the "deficiency" of man, since these are the themes that Blumenberg purports to be unfindable in *De Docta Ignorantia*—at least unfindable insofar as there follows from them the theme of Christ's sacrificial death. Now, in Chapter 7 of Book III Nicholas reasons:

> Since it was not fitting for human nature to be led to the triumph of immortality otherwise than through victory over death, [Christ] underwent death in order that human nature would rise again with Him to eternal life and that the animal, mortal body would become spiritual and incorruptible. [Christ] was able to be a true man only if He was mortal; and He was able to lead mortal [human] nature to immortality only if through death human nature became stripped of mortality.[465]

Unlike Anselm of Canterbury,[466] Nicholas seems to regard mortality as an essential condition of the natural (i.e., the unsupernaturally transformed) human body, even though immortality is the natural condition of the human intellect.[467] According to the foregoing quotation from Nicholas: when human beings are resurrected, their bodies will be transformed into an incorruptible state.[468] Human nature, which is the actually highest species within the genus *animal*, is a middle nature between the higher purely intellectual beings (viz., angels) and the lower nonintellectual, corporeal beings. Mortality of body belonged to the original degree of perfection of human nature (to which immortality of body would have been given as a reward, had Adam not sinned). Accordingly, Nicholas states that Christ "was able to be a true man only if He was mortal . . . ."[469] Through the resurrection of Christ, in which all men are to participate, each individual human nature will be transformed in such way that each respective human body will become immortal. This transformation will be a supernatural elevation of human nature beyond its natural state: "All of us, whether good or evil, shall arise; but not all of us shall be changed through a glory which transforms us—through Christ, the Son of God—into adopted sons. Therefore, all shall arise through Christ, but not all shall arise as Christ and in Christ through union; rather, only those who are Christ's through faith, hope, and love [shall so arise]."[470] In this elevation human nature will not be changed into another kind of thing, though it will exist in another manner.[471] Those human beings who have chosen to be united with God will receive the fulfillment of their intellectual desires.[472] Those who have rejected God will, though resurrected, be separated from God and hurled into the chaos of confusion, maintains Nicholas.[473]

So in *De Docta Ignorantia* Nicholas teaches that one reason Christ died was in order to lead human nature to victory over death. But in Chapter 6 of Book III he offers another reason as well—a more properly theological reason: Christ died in order to purge all the sins of human nature.[474] His voluntary death, proclaims Nicholas, was "the deletion and purgation of, and the satisfaction for, all the carnal desires of human nature."[475] Here the word "satisfaction" is important, because it shows that Nicholas is addressing himself to the theological theme of atonement. Earlier, using theological language, he stated that in Christ we have redemption and remission of sins.[476] In Chapter 6 this theme is again touched upon. We are justified only by faith in Christ, he declares.[477] Moreover, whatever Christ *merited* by His suffering He merited for those who are one with Him.[478] Indeed, since Christ delivered Himself unto death even on behalf of

His enemies, His humanity "made up for all the defects of all men,"[479] though, of course, His merit must be appropriated by each believer, according to his degree of faith. So in *De Docta Ignorantia* III Nicholas does address himself to the themes of sin and the deficiency of man.[480] And thus he gives a theological as well as a philosophical account of the purpose of Christ's death.[481] If he does not dwell upon the topic of man's sinfulness and the need for atonement through the death of Christ, it is not because he considers the topic inessential to his line of reasoning but because here he has no new contribution to make.[482]

6.9. Given the many misconceptions, half-truths, and imprecisions in Blumenberg's interpretation of Nicholas's cosmology, philosophical anthropology, and Christology, it would be almost a miracle if his overall interpretation of Nicholas's role in Western intellectual history were correct. Blumenberg sees Nicholas as concerned for "the continuance of the medieval world,"[483] as acutely concerned "regarding the disintegration of the Middle Ages,"[484] as attempting "to save the Middle Ages,"[485] as exhibiting a conservative tendency.[486] In reaching this assessment, he affirms that Nicholas's works contain no "explicit evidence of his knowledge of the critical situation of the epoch to which he still wholly belongs."[487] That is, Nicholas did not explicitly formulate questions regarding the viability of the Middle Ages, did not explicitly formulate a policy to prevent, or at least to retard, the disintegration of the Middle Ages. In short, contends Blumenberg, Cusanus "did not *formulate* his concern for the continuance of the age. *But the unity of his thought can be understood precisely and only on the basis of such a concern.*"[488] And so, Blumenberg, adhering to this judgment about unity, sets out to *project back* behind Nicholas's thought questions which Nicholas himself did not formulate—questions which, Blumenberg admits, Nicholas *could not* have formulated.[489] Blumenberg posits as his own hermeneutical task: to take Nicholas's statements, doctrines, dogmas, speculations, and postulates—insofar as they are documented—and to work them into answers to the projected questions, i.e., answers to the questions the author himself did not and could not formulate.[490] Nowhere does Blumenberg make an effort to justify what he is blissful merely to assert: viz., that the unity of Nicholas's thought can be understood only by ascribing to Nicholas a concern for preserving the medieval world.

Nowhere does Blumenberg show an interest in eliciting from Nicholas's texts themselves questions for which there is some evidence that they were the author's. Much of his misidentification of Nicholas's doctrines—e.g., the doctrines of freedom, of cognition, of conjecture, of providence, of perfection, of exemplars, of creation, of teleology, of faith, of the need for Christ's death—results from his having projected his own questions behind Nicholas's thought before first eliciting *Nicholas's* questions from out of Nicholas's own *problématique*. To be sure, there is a place, hermeneutically, for an interpreter's bringing to bear upon an author's works questions which the author himself did not ask—questions which, perhaps, the author was not in a position even to formulate. At times such questions will assist in identifying what the author's doctrines are; at other times they will help in understanding the historical significance or historical influence of the author's doctrines. The problem with Blumenberg's self-imposed hermeneutical task, then, is not that it projects back questions which Nicholas himself did not ask or could not even formulate. The main problem is that it does this projecting before—and even in place of—conducting a serious investigation of what Nicholas's doctrines are and of what Nicholas's own questions were. And the absence of such a primary investigation results in Blumenberg's wrongly identifying Nicholas's doctrines and, consequently, wrongly taking these misidentifications to be answers to the questions that Nicholas could not formulate but which Blumenberg formulates for him and projects back behind the misidentifications.

As a result of the inaccurate identifications Blumenberg projects back the wrong questions. Moreover, by making the misidentifications into answers to these questions he further distorts the already-misidentified doctrines. Earlier we caught a glimpse of a prime instance of this further distortion when we observed Blumenberg's judgment about Nicholas's "holding fast to the critical achievements of nominalism."[491] Instead of seriously endeavoring to answer the primary question 'How did Nicholas view the relationship between concepts and reality?' Blumenberg skips lightly over this question[492] and seems[493] to press toward tacitly asking a secondary one: 'How is Nicholas showing his concern to save the Middle Ages?' When the misidentified doctrine about Nicholas's holding fast to the critical achievements of nominalism is taken as one answer to this secondary question, Nicholas's position become further distorted, so that Blumenberg comes to speak of Nicholas's "inability to deal with or successfully to evade the consequences of nominalism"[494]—as if Nicholas had worked himself into an intellectual impasse.

That Blumenberg has little conception either of textual interpretation or of historical method is confirmed by the fact that he makes little or nothing of the texts which show that Nicholas was *not* straining to hold together a world he considered to be disintegrating. Now, the only work where Nicholas might plausibly be suspected of making such an effort is *De Docta Ignorantia*. But even *there* Nicholas is not exercised about holding together something regarded as crumbling: he is concerned with saying what is new, even if it is not altogether new. In the prologue to Book I he alludes to his work as setting forth unusual things, though not things hitherto completely unknown.[495] Likewise, at the outset of Book II, Chapter 11 he intimates: "Now that learned ignorance has shown these previously unheard of [doctrines] to be true, perhaps there will be amazement on the part of those who read them." This idea is later repeated: "Book Two elicits a few [teachings] about the universe—[teachings which go] beyond the usual approach of the philosophers and [which will seem] unusual to many."[496] In the *Apologia* the approach taken in *De Docta Ignorantia* is said to differ from other approaches "as much as sight differs from hearing."[497] Furthermore, the *Apologia* also affirms of *De Docta Ignorantia*: "This speculation will surely conquer all the modes of reasoning of all the philosophers, although it is difficult to leave behind things to which we are accustomed."[498]

So Nicholas is not striving to hold onto the old: he is striving to present that which is new, viz., the method of learned ignorance and the central truths that he deems derivable by means of it. Of course, he points out that the method of learned ignorance is as old as Socrates and that it is acknowledged by Dionysius and by Augustine. But the fact remains that he envisions his use of the method as yielding truths whereof Socrates, Dionysius, and Augustine did not themselves know. He makes no attempt to hold together the medieval intellectual world, since he does not see it as intellectually endangered.[499] And the reason he does not perceive it as threatened is that he is too centrally a part of it. He can be intent upon presenting *nouveautés* precisely because they seem to him to be *unendangering*.

Even the newness that pervades his Christology and that Wenck judged heretical is regarded by him as altogether unproblematical and as according with Scripture.[500] He seeks to expand the horizons of the medieval world, to penetrate beyond its confines by drawing the consistent consequences of the premises that God is Infinity itself, that man cannot intellectually transcend the condition of learned ignorance, that Aristotelian logic, though valid for the domain of human experience, cannot, cooperatively with experience, ascertain the nature of God. This first modern philosopher neither breaks with the medieval world nor attempts to save it. Rather, he opens the door to Modernity by developing concepts and motifs which, had they been carried further, had they been more influential, had they been detached from their traditional associations, would have ushered in the Modern Age, instead of simply signaling its possibility. Accordingly, the first modern philosopher precedes the main advent of the Modern Age and is not himself "the Father of modern philosophy," an ascription still rightly reserved for Descartes. Finally, his concern with the new and his reinterpretation of the old—whether in *De Docta Ignorantia, De Coniecturis,* the *Idiota* dialogues, the mathematical treatises, or wherever—does not so strain the unity of his thought that we can understand this unity *only* by ascribing to him a concern to continue the Middle Ages.

In the end, what Blumenberg is doing is not *describing* for us how Nicholas himself viewed his intellectual situation or what Nicholas's real concerns within that situation were: he is *recommending* that we picture Nicholas *as if* he had viewed his situation in a certain way and *as if* he had exhibited such and such a concern. And this recommendation Blumenberg passes off as historical interpretation, even though it runs counter to the historical evidence.

7. *Conclusion.* We have seen that just as the unity of Nicholas's thought can be understood otherwise than on the basis of a "concern for the continuance"[501] of the Middle Ages, so the unity that is called *coincidentia oppositorum* was at no time intended "*only* to bring about mystical obscurification."[502] We have seen, too, that the unity sought by Nicholas above all else is the unity of sonship.[503] This relationship is attained through faith and love; and it is brought to fulfillment in the next life.

7.1. But on his pilgrim's pathway Nicholas seeks a foretaste of that future blissful union. In *De Visione Dei* he looks for this foretaste in and through mystical encounter; and he intimates that such savoring has not yet been granted to him.[504] Thus, in *De Visione Dei* he is not writing about actual mystical encounters of God on his own part. There is nothing that resembles the intimatelike accounts of St. Teresa of Avila. One reason why interpreters of *De Visione Dei* have labelled Nicholas's approach *speculative* mysticism has been to mark it off from these other accounts—as well as to call attention to its self-consciously metaphysical and theological orientation. For Nicholas is pointing the way, by means of reflective meditation, to the place where mystical encounter is possible—a place "beyond all sensible, rational, and intellectual sight."[505] But what, then, are we to make of his exclamation?: "Lord, my God, I see You by means of a certain mental rapture."[506] And what is to be said regarding his further statements?:

> Through a foretaste of the sweetness of a glorious life You draw [me unto Yourself], so that I may love You, who are infinite good. You enrapture me, in order that I may transcend myself and foresee the glorious place to which You invite me. You show me many exceedingly appetizing repasts that attract me by their most appealing aroma. You permit [me] to see the treasure of riches, of life, of joy, and of beauty.[507]

With these utterances Nicholas is not making implicit claims to have been mystically raptured or to have mystically partaken of Divine Beauty. Rather, in a metaphorical way he is applying the language of mystical encounter to nonmystical intellectual recognition. Just as someone's mystical vision of God in Christ is different from his non-mystical intellectual recognition that God is encounterable "only where persuasive considerations cease and faith appears,"[508] so his enrapturement beyond all intellect is different from the mental enrapturement which accompanies the recognition that God, because He is Infinity itself, is unseeable as He is in Himself. So too, the foretasting that occurs *in visione mystica* differs from the mental foretasting whereby the Gospel is believed to be food from Heaven and Jesus to be the Tree of Life.[509] At times, so we have seen, Nicholas alludes to religious experience in only a broad sense that is presumed to need no explication: "if anyone believes and accepts, he will most truly find that You descended from Heaven and that You alone are the

Teacher of truth."[510] But in *De Visione Dei* he aims primarily at leading the monks of Tegernsee into darkness with Moses, so that they may be raptured with Paul.[511] This guidance is given by means of the symbolism of the icon, though elsewhere it is provided through the symbolic name "*possest*,"[512] and even through the names "*idem*,"[513] "*non-aliud*,"[514] and "*posse*."[515]

7.2. When Nicholas assumed active administration of the diocese of Brixen in the spring of 1452, he must have suspected that his efforts to set in order its spiritual and financial affairs would provoke immediate resistance. But he had not reckoned with the prolong and intense dispute that would erupt with Duke Sigismund. Little wonder that already in February of 1454 he expressed to the abbot of the monastery at Tegernsee the wish to have a cell prepared for him: "*Retrahor tamen plurimum ab hijs altissimis per huius mundi occupaciones; propterea fratribus dixi michi cellam parari. Utinam concederetur michi sacro ocio frui inter fratres, qui vacant et vident quoniam suavis est dominus.*"[516] If mystical theology requires withdrawal and detachment,[517] it also leads to rest and silence.[518] But it leads likewise to joy, because it is the fulfillment of love. "Fire does not cease from its flame and neither does the burning love which is directed toward You, O God. You are the Form of everything desirable . . . ."[519] The discernment that God is unknowable as He is in Himself moves Nicholas not to resignation or despair but to the following conclusion: "that the reason You, O God, are unknown to all creatures is so that amid this most sacred ignorance creatures may be more content, as if [they were situated] amid a countless and inexhaustible treasure. For one who finds a treasure of such kind that he knows it to be altogether uncountable and infinite is filled with much greater joy than is one who finds a countable and finite treasure."[520] Under Nicholas's tutelage, the monks of Tegernsee seem to have come to this same recognition. Certainly their prior, Bernard of Waging, was one of Nicholas's staunchest defenders. Neither Nicholas nor Bernard interpreted what had come to be called the *via purae intelligentiae* as excluding all cognition. For during the first stages of mystical ascent into darkness the intellect, whose impetus comes from love of the Good, must be aware that it is ascending amid an obscuring mist[521] and must believe that it is ascending toward the Good.[522] But, concomitantly, it must be aware that the Infinite Good which it seeks transcends every finite good that it can conceive—aware that Infinite Goodness is not goodness but is Infinity.[523] Thus, the intellect ascends unto that which it judges to be the Perfection of everything perfectible;[524] and yet, though the intellect can conceive that there is such a Perfection, it cannot conceive of the nature of this Perfection—cannot conceive of it, that is, other than by way of symbols whose significations fall infinitely short of the reality. The intellect's knowing that it cannot know *what* God is—any more than it can know what pure being is—constitutes its state of learned ignorance. And this state is a necessary condition of the intellect's transcending its own operation, in order to encounter the Unknown unknowingly.

Among the Tegernsee monks there may well have been those who identified themselves more closely with Gerson's emphasis upon the *via devotionis* than with Nicholas's emphasis upon *docta ignorantia*. Some may even have shunned Nicholas's interpretation of mystical theology on the grounds that Nicholas, under the influence of Gerson, had deviated from the true teachings of Dionysius; in so doing, they would have been setting themselves in agreement with Vincent, Prior of the Carthusian monastery at Aggsbach. Whatever the diverse reactions of the Tegernsee community may possibly have been with regard to *De Visione Dei*, the reaction of record is Caspar Ayndorffer's: "O happy compendium, through which the Blessed End desired by all is so easily and quickly attained . . . !"[525] Nicholas had indeed meant to point toward the Blessed End, as well as toward the preconditions thereunto: "O Christ, our Savior, You taught only two things: faith and love. Through faith the intellect approaches unto the Word; through love it is united therewith."[526] *Fides formata charitate*[527] is prerequisite to *visio dei* and to the final attainment of *perfectio*. Nicholas is aware that the notions of *fides* and *perfectio* require a deeper philosophical analysis than he anywhere provides. But he is content to leave the task of this analysis to others. His own mission he sees as furnishing *Hinweise*—pointers, indicators. What else are his discussions of learned ignorance, coincidence of opposites, infinite disproportionality, *universum infinitum privative*, God as the universe's center and circumference? And what else is furnished by his dialectic and paradox?

In opening the door to Modernity, Nicholas does not surrender his pre-Modern standpoint: viz., the conception of a hierarchical world, containing a gradation of more and less perfect genera-and-species contracted to individual objects which in varying degrees of perfection[528] fulfill their respective genus and species (with the human species being an intellectual nature than which there is no more perfect intellectual nature on any of the other "stars")[529]—in short, a world wherein "all existing things endeavor, as best they can, to participate in God's 'brightness and blazing splendor,' so to speak."[530] Only when the intellect transforms the philosophical mode-of-reflecting into a contemplative mode that suspends all activity of the senses and all mental analysis—only then can the soul, in proportion to its faith and love, draw mystically near unto Him who is beyond the distinction between modern and premodern, unto Him whom Augustine apostrophized as "Beauty so ancient and so new."[531] Nicholas of Cusa's *theologia mystica* teaches that the devout believer may possibly attain unto a vision of this Beauty in the present lifetime if he figuratively enters into the seclusion of the monk's cell, cognitively and affectionally abandoning the outside world during the contemplative ascent. Gerson thought that any necessity for cognitive abandonment would exclude simple believers from the *via mystica*, since many such believers would be incapable of attaining the state of *pura intelligentia*.[532] Thus, Gerson accommodated his version of *theologia mystica* to the *via devotionis*, thereby so attenuating it that it seemed to many to lack both depth and power.[533] By contrast, Nicholas shows no signs of supposing that the pathway of mystical theology is available to all believers. Indeed, his conclusion in *De Visione Dei* is not an exhortation, generally, to the brothers of the Tegernsee community. It is rather a query to himself ("Why, then, do I delay? . . . What holds me back?") conjoined with a prayer regarding himself: "Draw me, O Lord, because no one can come unto You unless he be drawn by You. [Draw me] so that, being drawn, I may be freed from this world and be joined unto You, the Absolute God, in an eternity of glorious life. Amen."

nicholas of cusa's dialectical mysticism

part ii: text and translation

A   Salzburg b.IV.11, fol. 1^r- 31^v.
Location: St. Peter Archabbey, Salzburg, Austria.
Date *DVD* was copied: 2nd half of 15th c.
Described: Catalog of Manuscripts in Stift St. Peter, Salzburg,
Austria. Vol. 3 (Xerox—at Hill Monastic Library, St. John's
University, Collegeville, Minnesota—of the catalogue in the
St. Peter Archabbey).

C   Cusanus 219, fol. 1^r- 24^r.
Location: Cusanusstift, Bernkastel-Kues, Germany.
Date *DVD* was copied: ca. 1460 in Rome, at the request of
Nicholas himself.
Described: *Nicolai de Cusa Opera Omnia*, Vol. VII (1959); Vol.
XII (1982). J. Marx, *Verzeichnis der Handschriften-Sammlung
des Hospitals zu Cues bei Bernkastel a./Mosel.* Trier, 1905
(reprinted Frankfurt: Minerva GmbH, 1966).

E   Eisleben 960, fol. 10a^v- 28^v.
Location: Turmbibliothek St. Andreas, Eisleben, Germany (DDR).
Previous location: Carthusian Monastery on Erlöserberg, near
Erfurt, Germany (DDR).
Date *DVD* was copied: 1461.
Described: *Nicolai de Cusa Opera Omnia*, Vol. I (1932). More
fully described in *Mittelalterliche Bibliotheks-Kataloge Deutsch-
lands und der Schweiz*, Vol. II, p. 308; and in Paul Wilpert,
"Die Entstehung einer Miscellanhandschrift des 15. Jahr-
hunderts," *Mittellateinisches Jahrbuch* 1 (1964), 34-47.

G   Giessen 695, fol. 136^r- 236^v.
Location: Universitätsbibliothek, Giessen, Germany.
Previous location: Maulbronn, Germany.
Date *DVD* was copied: 1453.
Described: J. V. Adrian, *Catalogus codicum manuscriptorum
Bibliothecae Academicae Gissensis* (Frankfurt, Germany, 1840),
p. 212. (Adrian's dating of the ms. is incorrect.)

I   Innsbruck 444, fol. 108^v - 131^r.
        Location: Universitätsbibliothek, Innsbruck, Austria.
        Previous location: Carthusian Monastery at Snals (near Bres-
        sanone, Italy).
        Date *DVD* was copied: ca. 1461.
        Described: *Nicolai de Cusa Opera Omnia*, Vol. I (1932) and
        Vol. IV, *Opuscula I* (1959).

J   Subiaco 148, fol. 11^v - 44^v.
        Location: St. Scolastica Monastery (Benedictine), Subiaco, Italy.
        Date *DVD* was copied: ca. 1460.
        Described: *Nicolai de Cusa Opera Omnia*, Vol. IV, *Opuscula I*
        (1959).

L   Munich 24862, fol. 46^r - 73^v.
        Location: Bayerische Staatsbibliothek, Munich, Germany.
        Previous location: unknown.
        Date *DVD* was copied: 2nd half of 15th c.
        Described: *Catalogus codicum manu scriptorum Bibliothecae
        Regiae Monacensis. Codices Latini* (Series reprinted in Wies-
        baden, Germany by Otto Harrassowitz Book Dealers).

M   Munich 18570, fol. 1^r - 26^r. (Chapter titles precede 1^r on the verso
        of the previous page.)
        Location: Bayerische Staatsbibliothek, Munich, Germany.
        Previous location: Benedictine Monastery in Tegernsee, Germany.
        Date *DVD* was copied: 1454.
        Described: *Nicolai de Cusa Opera Omnia*, Vol. VII (1959).

N   Nürnberg V 72, fol. 1^r - 21^v.
        Location: Stadtbibliothek, Nürnberg, Germany.
        Previous location: Nürnberg Predigerkloster.
        Date *DVD* was copied: 1463.
        Described: *Nicolai de Cusa Opera Omnia*, Vol. II (1932). Vol.
        IV, *Opuscula I* (1959).

O   Munich 18592, fol. 99^v - 124^v.
        Location: Bayerische Staatsbibliothek, Munich, Germany.
        Previous location: Benedictine Monastery in Tegernsee, Germany.
        Date *DVD* was copied: 1455.
        Described: *Catalogus codicum manu scriptorum Bibliothecae
        Regiae Monacensis. Codices Latini*.

P   Munich 17247, fol. 106^v - 123^v.
Location: Bayerische Staatsbibliothek, Munich, Germany.
Previous location: Schäftlarn Monastery, Bayern, Germany.
Date *DVD* was copied: 2nd half of 15th c.
Described: *Catalogus codicum manu scriptorum Bibliothecae Regiae Monacensis. Codices Latini.*

Pa   Munich 17247, fol. 124^r - 140^v.
Location: same as *P*.
Previous location: same as *P*.
Date *DVD* was copied: 2nd half of 15th c.
Described: *Catalogus codicum manu scriptorum Bibliothecae Regiae Monacensis. Codices Latini.*

Q   Munich 5606, fol. 154^r - 167^r.
Location: Bayerische Staatsbibliothek, Munich, Germany.
Previous location: Benedictine Monastery of the Virgin Mary in Diessen, Germany.
Date *DVD* was copied: 2nd half of 15th c.
Described: *Catalogus codicum manu scriptorum Bibliothecae Regiae Monacensis. Codices Latini.*

R   Munich 14213, fol. 125^r - 140^r.
Location: Bayerische Staatsbibliothek, Munich, Germany.
Previous location: St. Emmeram Benedictine Monastery, Regensburg, Germany.
Date *DVD* was copied: 2nd half of 15th c.
Described: *Nicolai de Cusa Opera Omnia*, Vol. I (1932) and Vol. IV, *Opuscula I* (1959).

S   Salzburg MI 397 (previously V.4.H164), fol. 116^r - 167^r.
Location: Universitätsbibliothek, Salzburg, Austria.
Previous location: Chiemsee diocesan library.
Date *DVD* was copied: 2nd half of 15th c.
Described: *Nicolai de Cusa Opera Omnia*, Vol. IV, *Opuscula I* (1959).

T   Trier 683/245 8^0, fol. 60^r - 93^r.
Location: Stadtbibliothek, Trier, Germany.
Date *DVD* was copied: 2nd half of 15th c.
Described: *Beschreibendes Verzeichnis der Handschriften der Stadtbibliothek zu Trier*, ed. Max Keuffer. Heft 6: Ascetische Schriften, 2. Abteilung. Nachträge, by G. Kentenich (Trier, 1910).

V   Vatican City 9425, fol. 1^r - 18^r.
        Location: Biblioteca Apostolica.
        Date *DVD* was copied: 2nd half of 15th c.
        Described: *Nicolai de Cusa Opera Omnia*, Vol. VII (1959).

Z   Los Angeles 170/21, fol. 1^r - 113^r.
        Location: University Research Library, University of California
        at Los Angeles.
        Previous location: Carthusian monastery in Buxheim, Germany.
        Date *DVD* was copied: 2nd half of 15th c.
        Described: C. U. Faye and W. H. Bond, eds., *Supplement to
        the Census of Medieval and Renaissance Manuscripts in the
        United States and Canada* (New York, 1962), p. 539. Also
        described: University of California at Los Angeles, Catalogue
        for the Department of Special Collections.

OTHER MANUSCRIPTS

(examined but not compared in the notes to the Latin text)

B   Magdeburg 166, fol. 451^r - 484^v.
        Location: Deutsche Staatsbibliothek, Berlin, Germany (DDR).
        Previous location: Domgymnasium, Magdeburg, Germany (DDR).
        Date *DVD* was copied: not before 1464.
        Described: *Nicolai de Cusa Opera Omnia*, Vol. IV, *Opuscula I*
        (1959); Vol. XI/3, (1982).

D   Minneapolis Z193N519/OD, frontpiece plus 87 pp.
        Location: Department of Special Collections, Wilson Library,
        University of Minnesota.
        Previous location: Ecole Sainte-Geneviève, Paris.
        Date *DVD* was copied: end of 17th c.
        Described: Contains only *DVD*. Printed frontpiece, with printed
        words "De Icona sev Visione Dei". Pp. 1-87 handwritten.
        Copied from the Basel edition (1565), though with occasional
        minor changes of word order and spelling. Of no value for
        establishing a critical edition. Title on p. 1, "De Visione Dei,
        Sive de Icona Liber", is followed by "Praefatio". Text begins
        with "Si vos humaniter . . .", ends with "iungar tibi deo
        absoluto in aeternitate vitae gloriosae. Amen", and adds
        "Finis. Ad maiorem Dei et Virginis Mariae Matris Jesu
        gloriam". Text written between lined margins of 5.1 x 9.5 cm.,
        29 lines per page. No abbreviations. Chapter 24 misnumbered
        as 23.

F   Graz 910, fol. 8ʳ - 29ʳ.
  Location: Universitätsbibliothek, Graz, Austria.
  Previous location: Carthusian Monastery at Seitz (today Žiča, Yugoslavia).
  Date *DVD* was copied: 2nd half of 15th c.
  Described: *Die Handschriften der Universitätsbibliothek Graz.* Vol. II, edited by Anton Kern (Vienna: Staatsdruckerei, 1956), p. 124.

W   Vatican City 11520, fol. 1ʳ - 39ʳ.
  Location: Biblioteca Apostolica.
  Date *DVD* was copied: ca. 1460.
  Described: *Nicolai de Cusa Opera Omnia*, Vol. VII (1959).

PRINTED EDITION COMPARED

p   Paris edition, 1514.
  Described: *Nicolai de Cusa Opera Omnia*, Vol. I (1932).

MANUSCRIPTS LOST OR DESTROYED

Copy at the Carthusian monastery at Aggsbach, Austria. Listed on p. 567, lines 1-2, of *Mittelalterliche Bibliothekskataloge Österreichs,* ed. Theodor Gottlieb (Vienna: A. Holzhausen, 1915).

Copy at the Bibliothèque-Médiathèque of Metz, France (manuscript number 355). Listed in *Catalogue général des manuscrits des bibliothèques publiques de France,* Vol. LIII: "Manuscrits des bibliothèques sinistrées de 1940 à 1944."

ABBREVIATIONS IN THE LATIN NOTES

add.	*addit; addunt*
cf.	*confer*
coni.	*conicit*
corr.	*corrigit; corrigunt*
del.	*delet; delent*
in marg.	*in margine*
lin.	*linea; lineam*
om.	*omittit; omittunt*

1. In the text: spelling, capitalization, and punctuation are editorialized.

2. In the variant readings: capitalization, though *not* spelling (except for u=v and terminal y=ii), is editorialized; and, as a rule, punctuation is eliminated. Except in the case of proper nouns, and a few common nouns, variant spellings are not given special notice. Where such differences as the following are noted, they are noted only incidentally: eciam/etiam; conplicat/complicat; assis/adsis; hiis/his; desiisse/desisse; quicquid/quitquid/quidquid; arcam/archam; spera/sphera; ymago/imago; nunccius/nunctius/nuntius; locuntur/loquuntur; fantasma/phantasma; michi/mihi; ycona/eicona; ydemptitas/identitas; tue/tuae; estimatione/aestimatione; cepi/coepi; katholica/catolica/catholica; adtractum/attractum; sicud/sicut; apperio/aperio; congnitum/cognitum; perhennare/perennare; sew/seu; wlt/vult; thezaurus/thesaurus; horologii/horalogii; Cristi/Christi; tuipsius/tui ipsius.

3. In the notes the sign "[-]" indicates that a word or a portion of a word was excised from the manuscript margin (presumably at the time of binding). All other instances of brackets indicate that the editor has supplied bracketed letters or words—except that in the notes for 98:7 the brackets indicate an erasure.

4. In the notes the words "*ut semper*"—wherever they have reference to a Latin word and not to a Latin abbreviation—are a shorthand for "*ut semper quando non abbreviatum.*"

5. Where redactors other than the scribe have made emendations in a manuscript, the redactors are indicated by superscripts (e.g., *E²*, *E³*, *E⁴*). In a few instances, where there is difficulty in systematically distinguishing the different hands, the superscript "n" is used. It indicates, unspecifiedly, someone other than the original scribe.

6. Corrections by a scribe or a redactor are to be understood as having been made *in linea aut supra lineam*, in the absence of specific indication.

7. For the most part, words that scribes have written in the manuscripts and have then deleted are indicated to be such. Ordinarily, however, incomplete words or illegible crossed-out words are not signaled.

de visione dei

(the vision of god)

CAPITULA

CHAPTER TITLES

1. The perfection of the appearance is predicated truly of the most perfect God.
2. Absolute Sight encompasses all modes |of seeing|.
3. Things predicated of God do not differ really.
4. God's vision is said to be providence, grace, and eternal life.
5. |God's| seeing is His tasting, seeking, showing mercy, and working.
6. |Our| vision of |God's| Face.
7. What the fruit of |our| vision of |God's| Face is, and how this fruit will be obtained.
8. God's vision is loving, causing, reading, and the having within itself of all things.
9. |God's vision| is both universal and particular; and what the way to seeing God is.
10. God is seen beyond the coincidence of contradictories, and His seeing is His being.
11. In God we see succession without succession.
12. Where the invisible is seen the uncreated is created.
13. God is seen to be Absolute Infinity.
14. God enfolds, without otherness, all things.
15. Actual Infinity is a oneness in which image is Truth.
16. Unless God were infinite, He would not be the End of desire.
17. God can be seen perfectly only as triune.
18. Unless God were trine, there would not be happiness.
19. Jesus is the union of God and man.
20. How Jesus is understood to be the uniting of the divine nature and the human nature.
21. Without Jesus happiness is not possible.
22. How Jesus sees and how He worked.
23. How Jesus died even though His union with life remained.
24. Jesus is the Word of Life.
25. Jesus is the Consummation.

109

DE VISIONE DEI

Pandam nunc quae vobis dilectissimis fratribus ante promiseram,
circa facilitatem mysticae theologiae. Arbitror enim vos, quos scio
zelo dei duci, dignos quibus hic thesaurus aperiatur utique pretiosus
5 valde et maxime fecundus, orans imprimis mihi dari verbum super-
num et sermonem omnipotentem, qui solum se ipsum pandere potest,
ut pro captu vestro enarrare queam mirabilia, quae supra omnem

1　1　*A*: Tractatus reverendissimi in Christo patris domini Nicolai cardinalis tituli
sancti Petri ad vincula necnon Brixnensis episcopi ad venerabilem patrem dominum Caspar abbatem et fratres in Tegernsee de visione dei. *Capitulorum tituli in
tractatu distribuuntur. Capitulorum numeri omittuntur. Multae abbreviationes
non proprie scriptae sunt, quia litterae finales non elevatae sunt; post capitulum
VI non semper haec verba noto.* *C*: De visione dei. Tractatus reverendissimi in
Christo patris et domini domini Nicolai tituli sancti Petri ad vincula presbyteri
cardinalis episcopi Brixinensis ad abbatem et fratres in Tegernsee de visione dei.
Capitulorum tituli et numeri in tractatu distribuuntur. *E*: Tituli capitulorum
libelli de visione dei *E²*. *Tituli et numeri sequuntur (E³) et etiam in tractatus
margine distribuuntur (E³ vel E⁴).* Tractatus de visione dei domini Nicolai de
Cusa cardinalis episcopi Brixinensis. Ad devotos fratres abbatem et fratres in
Tegerensee.　*G*: Incipit tractatus de visione dei reverendissimi in Christo patris et
domini domini Nycolay de Cusa cardinalis sancti Petri ad vincula ad abbatem et
fratres in Tegernsee ordinis sancti Benedicti. Prologus. *Capitulorum tituli et
numeri in tractatu distribuuntur.* *I*: Incipit tractatus Nicolai de Cusa cardinalis
sancti Petri ad vincula de mistica theologia utilis valde per contemplatione quem
fecit fratribus in Tegernnsee. *Capitulorum tituli et numeri, sed non divisiones,
omittuntur.* *J*: Alius tractatus eiusdem de visione dei. *Capitulorum tituli et
numeri in tractatu distribuuntur.* *L*: Tractatus de visione dei incipit feliciter.
Capitulorum tituli et numeri in tractatu distribuuntur. *M*: Tractatus reverendissimi in Christo patris domini Nicolai cardinalis tituli sancti Petri ad vincula necnon Brixinensis episcopi ad venerabilem patrem dominum Caspar abbatem et fratres in Tegernsee de visione dei. Apparencia qua vos fratres amantissimos per
quandam praxim devocionis in misticam propono elevare theologiam premittendo
tria ad hoc oportuna. *Capitulorum tituli et numeri sequuntur (M). Tituli, sed non
numeri, etiam in tractatu distribuuntur (M³).* *N*: Tractatus domini Nicolay de
Cusa cardinalis, et cetera, de visione dei. *Capitulorum tituli et numeri, sed non
divisiones, omittuntur. Non semper est possibile distinguere* omnes (o̅m̅s) *et* omnis
(o̅n̅i̅s) *in textu.* *O*: Tractatus reverendissimi in Christo patris domini Nicolai cardinalis tituli sancti Petri ad vincula necnon Brixinensis episcopi ad venerabilem

THE VISION OF GOD

I will now make known the things I previously promised you, most beloved brothers, regarding the ready accessibility of mystical theology. For I esteem you, whom I know to be motivated by a zeal for God, to be worthy of having disclosed to you this assuredly most precious and most abundant treasure. First of all, I pray the Heavenly Word and Omnipotent Expression, who alone can make Himself known, that I be given the ability to explain—in proportion to your ability to comprehend—the wonders which are revealed beyond

patrem dominum Caspar abbatem et fratres in Tegernsee de visione dei. Apparencia qua vos fratres amantissimos per quandam praxim devocionis in misticam propono elevare theologiam premittendo tria ad hoc oportuna. *Capitulorum tituli et numeri sequuntur. Tituli in tractatu et numeri in margine etiam distribuuntur.*   *P*: Tractatus reverendissimi in Christo patris domini Nicolai cardinalis tituli sancti Petri ad vincula necnon Brixinensis episcopi ad venerabilem patrem dominum Caspar abbatem et fratres in Tegernnsee de visione dei. Apparencia qua vos fratres amantissimos per quandam praxim devocionis in misticam propono elevare theologiam premittendo tria ad hoc oportuna. *Capitulorum tituli sequuntur (P). Tituli etiam in tractatu distribuuntur (P³). Capitulorum numeri omittuntur.*   *Pa*: Tractatus reverendissimi in Christo patris et domini domini Nicolai tituli sancti Petri ad vincula presbyteri cardinalis ac episcopi Brixinensis ad abbatem et fratres in Tegerzee de visione dei incipit feliciter *(Pa³). Capitulorum tituli in tractatu distribuuntur. Capitula non numerantur (praeter primum) et manu Pa³ scribuntur. (Vide notam pro 7:2.)*   *Q*: Tractatus reverendissimi in Christo patris domini Nicolai cardinalis tituli sancti Petri ad vincula necnon Brixinensis episcopi ad venerabilem patrem dominum Caspar abbatem et fratres in Tegernsee de visione dei et cetera. *(Q²) Capitulorum tituli (Q) sequuntur (titulus capituli 24 omittitur) et etiam in tractatu (Q²) distribuuntur. Capitulorum numeri omittuntur.*   *R*: Incipiunt capitula in tractatum eiusdem de visione dei ad venerabilem dominum abbatem et fratres monasterii Tegernnsee in quo comprehendit sub compendio omnes modos et genera omnium graduum contemplationum. *Capitulorum tituli et numeri sequuntur. Tituli et numeri etiam in tractatu distribuuntur.* Finiunt capitula. Incipit prologus in tractatum de eykona dei cuncta videntis.   *S: Titulus tractatus atque numeri et tituli capitulorum, sed non divisiones, omittuntur.*   *T*: Tractatus reverendissimi in Christo patris [et domini *supra lin. add. T*] domini Nycolai de Cusa cardinalis ad abbatem et fratres in Tegernsee ordinis sancti Benedicti de visione dei incipit prologus. *Capitulorum tituli et numeri in tractatu distribuuntur.*   *V*: Tractatus reverendissimi in Christo patris et domini domini Nicolai tituli

sensibilem, rationalem, et intellectualem visum revelantur. Conabor
autem simplicissimo atque communissimo modo vos experimental-
10 iter in sacratissimam obscuritatem manuducere. Ubi dum eritis, inaccessibilem lucem adesse sentientes, quisque ex se tentabit, modo quo
sibi a deo concedetur, continue propius accedere et hic praegustare,
quodam suavissimo libamine, cenam illam aeternae felicitatis, ad
quam vocati sumus in verbo vitae per evangelium Christi semper
15 benedicti.

2   Si vos humaniter ad divina vehere contendo, similitudine quadam
hoc fieri oportet. Sed inter humana opera non repperi imaginem
[imagine] omnia videntis proposito nostro convenientiorem, ita quod
facies subtili arte pictoria ita se habeat quasi cuncta circumspiciat.
5 Harum etsi multae reperiantur optime pictae (uti illa sagittarii in
foro Nurembergensi, et Bruxellis Rogeri maximi pictoris in pretiosissima tabula, quae in praetorio habetur, et Confluentiae in capella
mea Veronicae, et Brixinae in castro angeli arma ecclesiae tenentis, et
multae aliae undique), ne tamen deficiatis in praxi, quae sensibilem
10 talem exigit figuram, quam habere potui charitati vestrae mitto tabel-

---

sancti Petri ad vincula presbyteri cardinalis episcopi Brixinensis ad abbatem et
fratres in Tegersee de visione dei. Rubrica (*V²*). *Capitulorum tituli et numeri in
tractatu distribuuntur (V²).* Z: *Sine titulo.* Cartusianorum in Buxheim *manu alia
scribitur.* 1456 *manu alia² (scilicet, moderna) scribitur.* Capita 25 (*ex 24 correctum) manu alia³ scribitur. Capitulorum tituli et numeri hic ponuntur et etiam in
tractatu distribuuntur.* Finis capitulorum. Incipit prologus. *p:* Reverendissimi in
christo patris et domini, domini Nicolai de Cusa tituli sancti Petri ad vincula presbyteri Cardinalis Episcopi Brixinensis, ad abbatem et fratres Tegernenses de visione
dei sive de icona liber.

   1 2 pandam: *Litteram initialem magnam ornatam semper om. PPaV* tandem *S*
nunc: *abbreviationem in marg. explicat T⁴*   quae . . . fratribus: vobis dilectissimis
fratribus que vobis *R*   3 facilitatem mysticae theologiae: theologie mistice
facilitatem *V*   theologiae: theologice *S*   vos: dignos *post* vos, *et non post* duci
(1:4), ponit R   4 thesaurus: theuzaurus *Z*   5 fecundus: facundus *V*   mihi
dari: omnipotentem ut mihi det *p*   mihi dari verbum: verbum michi dari *Q*   dari:
dare *G*   6 et: atque *p*   omnipotentem: *hic om., et post* imprimis *(1:5) posuit, p*
solum se ipsum: se ipsum solum *ad* solum se ipsum *transponit O*   7 vestro:
om. Pa   supra: *non proprie abbreviat Pa*   8 rationalem: rationem *I*   racionem
JPa   conabor: conabar *V*   9 autem: *bis E* (autem¹ *del. E)*   9-10 experimen-
taliter: exprimentaliter *PaV*   11 lucem: lumen *S*   adesse sentientes: sencientes
adesse *ad* adesse sencientes *transponit T*   quisque: quisquis *A*   tentabit: tempera-

Cf. De docta Ignorantia

all sensible, rational, and intellectual sight. But I will attempt to lead you—by way of experiencing and through a very simple and very common means—into most sacred darkness. Upon arriving there and sensing the presence of Inaccessible Light, each of you—of yourself and in the manner granted you by God—will endeavor to approach ever nearer. And |you will seek| to acquire in this lifetime, through a most pleasant savoring, a foretaste of that meal of eternal happiness to which we are called in the Word of Life by the Gospel of the Ever-blessed Christ.

2   If I strive to convey you by human means unto divine things, then I must do this through a likeness. Now, among human works I have not found an image more suitable to our purpose than the image of someone omnivoyant, so that his face, through subtle pictorial artistry, is such that it seems to behold everything around it. There are in existence many of these excellently depicted faces—e.g., the one of the archer in the forum at Nuremberg, the one |depicted| by the preeminent painter Rogier[1] in his priceless painting in the city hall at Brussels, the one of Veronica in my chapel at Coblenz, the one, in the castle at Bressanone, of the angel holding the emblems of the church, and many others here and there. Nevertheless, so that you not be lacking in practical experience, which requires such a sensible figure, I am sending to **Your Love** a painting that I was able to

---

bit *T* (temptabit *in marg. coni. T²*)   13 quodam: *ex quo corr. G*   libamine: labamine *N*   14 in: *om. R*   Christi: *ante* Cristi *abbreviationem pro* Cristi *scribit et del. Pa*   15 benedicti: sequitur *in litteris rubris add. A*   et cetera *add. PQ*

  2 1 *ante* si: Prefacio *add. C³p* (Praefatio *p*)   Prefacio *non habent ACE (in 1:1 ut titulum capituli primi* prologus *habet E³) GIJLMNOPPaQRSTVZ (divisionem novam faciunt ACGIJLMOPPaQRSTVZ)* quod perfectio apparencie verificatur de deo perfectissimo. capitulum primum *G*   prohemium *R*   capitulum primum *T* (*titulum capituli om. T*)   similitudine: similitudo *G*   quadam: *om. N* quandam *Pa*   2 non repperi: *om. V*   imaginem: ymagiem *A* ymagine *JLMOPPaV* imaginem imagine *p*   3 imagine: *addidi cum p*   convenientiorem: convenciorem *V* ita: itaque *Q*   ita quod: uti est *E* (uti est *del., et in marg.* ita quod *scribit, Eⁿ*) *N* 4 habeat: *ex* habebat *corr. A*   circumspiciat: conspiciat *A*   5 sagitarii: sagittarie *C* sagitarii *N* sagictarie *V* sagittariae *p*   6 Nurembergensi: Nurenbergensi *CENQSV* Norenbergensi *GT* Nuerenbergensi *I* Nurmbergensi *RZ*   Bruxellis: Bruccellis *GT* Brixellis *J* Brurellis *L*   Rogeri: Rogori *G* (et *post* Rogori *scribit et del. G*) Rogerii *IN* Rugeri *R*   6-7 in pretiosissima tabula: *om. R*   8 Brixinae: Brixne *EGNT* Bririne *L*   10 talem: *bis V*   mitto: tam *post* mitto *scribit et*

lam, figuram cuncta videntis tenentem, quam eiconam dei appello.

3 Hanc aliquo in loco, puta in septentrionali muro, affigetis circumstabitisque vos fratres parum distanter ab ipsa intuebiminique ipsam. Et quisque vestrum experietur, ex quocumque loco eandem inspexerit, se quasi solum per eam videri. Videbiturque fratri qui in oriente
5 positus fuerit, faciem illam orientaliter respicere, et qui in meridie meridionaliter, et qui in occidente occidentaliter. Primum igitur admirabimini quomodo hoc fieri possit, quod omnes et singulos simul respiciat. Nam imaginatio stantis in oriente nequaquam capit visum eiconae ad aliam plagam versum, scilicet occasum vel meridiem.
10 Deinde frater, qui fuit in oriente, se locet in occasu, et experietur visum in eo figi in occasu, quemadmodum prius in oriente. Et quoniam scit eiconam fixam et immutatam, admirabitur mutationem immutabilis visus.

4 Et si figendo obtutum in eiconam ambulabit de occasu ad orientem, comperiet continue visum eiconae secum pergere; et si de oriente revertetur ad occasum, similiter eum non deseret. Et admirabitur quomodo immobiliter moveatur. Neque poterit imaginatio capere,
5 quod cum aliquo alio sibi contrario motu obviante similiter moveatur. Et dum hoc experiri volens fecerit confratrem, intuendo eiconam, transire de oriente ad occasum, quando ipse de occasu pergit ad orientem, et interrogaverit obviantem si continue secum visus eiconae vol-

del. A 11 cuncta: cuncti *EN* habentis *post* cuncta *scribit et del. L* tenentis *post* cuncta *scribit et del. Pa* tenentem: habentem *R* quam: qua *Pa*
3 1 aliquo in: in omni *E* (in *del. E²*) in aliquo *GT* omni *N* septentrionali: *om. T* septentrionali muro: muro septemtrionali *G* septentrionali muro affigetis: muro affigetis septentrionali *E* muro affigetis septemtrionali *N* 2 fratres: pariter *add. Z* distanter: distantes *S* intuebiminique: intuebitisque *ACE (ad* intuebiminique *corr. E²) GIJLMNOPPaQSTVZ* ipsam: illam *p* 3 quisque: quisquis *AT* ex: ut *L* 4 videbiturque: videbitque *E (ex* videbiturque *corr. E) N* fratri: frater *EGNT* qui in oriente: in oriente qui *ad* qui in oriente *transponit A* 5 positus: est *post* positus *scribit et del. E* 6 igitur: ergo *EN* 7 omnes: simul *post* omnes *scribit et del. L* et singulos: singulos et *V* 8 simul: *om. N* simul respiciat: respiciat simul *Z* oriente: origente *J* nequaquam: neququam *L* 9 versum: versu *ex* versum *(?) corr. P* versus *Z* scilicet: *om. LOPZ* 10 se locet: locet se *N* occasu: quemadmodum prius in oriente et quoniam scit *post* occasu *scribit et del. A* 11 visum: usum *S* occasu: occasum *V* prius: *om. EN* 12 et: *om. A* admirabitur: admiretur *EN* admirabiliter *V* mutationem: in *add. Z* 13 visus: usus *S*

acquire. It contains the figure of an omnivoyant |individual|; and I call it the "icon of God."

3   Hang this icon somewhere, e.g., on the north wall; and you brothers stand around it, at a short distance from it, and observe it. Regardless of the place from which each of you looks at it, each will have the impression that he alone is being looked at by it. To the brother who is situated in the east it will seem that the face is looking toward the east; to the brother in the south, that the face is looking toward the south; to the brother in the west, that it is looking westward. First of all, then, marvel at how it is possible that |the face| behold each and every one of you at once. For the imagination of the brother who is standing in the east does not at all apprehend the icon's gaze that is being directed toward a different region, viz., toward the west or the south. Next, let the brother who was in the east situate himself in the west, and he will experience the |icon's| gaze as fixed on him in the west, just as it previously was in the east. But since he knows that the icon is stationary and unchanged, he will marvel at the changing of the unchangeable gaze.

4   Moreover, if while fixing his sight upon the icon he walks from west to east, he will find that the icon's gaze proceeds continually with him; and if he returns from east to west, the gaze will likewise not desert him. He will marvel at how the icon's gaze is moved unmovably. And his imagination will be unable to apprehend that the gaze is also moved in accompaniment with someone else who is coming toward him from the opposite direction. Now, |suppose that,| wanting to experience this |phenomenon|, he has a fellow-monk, while beholding the icon, cross from east to west at the same time that he himself proceeds from west to east. And |suppose| he asks the approaching brother whether the icon's gaze moves continually with

---

4 1 et si: etsi *p*   in: *om. S*   ad: in *IR*   2 et si: etsi *p*   2-3 comperiet . . . oriente: *om. V*   3 oriente: origente *T*   revertetur: revertatur *R* vertetur *S* et: *om. V*   3-4 admirabitur: admiretur *EN*   4 quomodo: eum *add. A*   moveatur: movebatur *CVp*   6 dum: cum *AI*   hoc: *om. LOPZ*   fecerit: *hic om., et post* transire *(4:7) scribunt, EN* fecit *I* ferat *R*   fecerit confratrem: confratrem fecerit *Z*   intuendo eiconam: *om. T*   7 quando: quomodo *J* (*ad* quando *in marg. corr. J^n*) *V*   8 interrogaverit: interroget sibi *EN*   obviantem: ambulantem *Q* 8-9 eiconae volvatur: volvatur eicone *ad* eicone volvatur *transponit L*   volvatur:

vatur, et audierit similiter opposito modo moveri, credet ei; et nisi
10 crederet, non caperet hoc possibile. Et ita revelatione relatoris perveniet ut sciat faciem illam omnes, etiam contrariis motibus, incedentes
non deserere. Experietur igitur immobilem faciem moveri ita orientaliter quod et movetur simul occidentaliter, et ita septentrionaliter
quod et meridionaliter, et ita ad unum locum quod etiam ad omnia
15 simul, et ita ad unum respicere motum quod ad omnes simul. Et
dum attenderit quomodo visus ille nullum deserit, videt quod ita dili-
genter curam agit cuiuslibet, quasi de solo eo, qui experitur se videri,
et nullo alio curet, adeo quod etiam concipi nequeat per unum, quem
respicit, quod curam alterius agat. Videbit etiam quod ita habet dili-
20 gentissimam curam minimae creaturae quasi maximae et totius
universi.
5   Ex hac tali sensibili apparentia, vos fratres amantissimos per quandam praxim devotionis in mysticam propono elevare theologiam,
praemittendo tria ad hoc opportuna.

litteras non proprie format P   9 modo: videri *post* modo *scribit et del.* S   credet: credit *T*   et[2]: *bis* G   10 crederet: credent *N*   caperet: *non proprie abbreviat Pa*   revelatione: relevacione *A*   relacione *EN*   10-11 perveniet: perveniat *TV*
proveniet *Z*   11 sciat: *ex* sciet *corr.* G   sciet *S*   incedentes: incidenter *S* in-
tendentes *T*   12 igitur: *om.* S   ita: septentrionaliter *post* ita *scribit et del.* Q
13 movetur: moveatur *EGNT*   simul: *om.* R   occidentaliter: orientaliter *V*   13-
14 septentrionaliter . . . ita: *om.* A   14 et[1]: *supra lin.* M   15 ad unum respicere:
respicere ad unum *ad* ad unum respicere *transponit Pa aut Pa²* respicere ad
unum *Z*   quod: et *add.* I   ad[2]: et *GT*   16 quomodo: quo *OP* quando *Q*
17 curam: *om.* G   eo: *om.* I   experitur: *ex* ? *corr.* P   18 et: de *add.* GT
quod etiam: eciam quod *EN*   concipi: concepi *Q*   nequeat: nequeant *I*   quem:
concipi *post* quem *scribit et del.* V   19 respicit: *ex* despicit *corr.* L   alterius:
alcius *L*   20 et totius: *bis* C (et tocius[1] *del.* C aut C²)
    5 1 ex: et *R*   apparentia: primo conabor vos amantissimos fratres per quan-
dam praxim in misticam theologiam elevare ubi contemplacionem altissimam subintrabitis. Secundo loco aliquas scripturarum latebras et doctorum enodare. Tercio
et ultimo loco si que ex his que ante hec scripsi obscura videntur ut facilia ac clariora fiant laborabo *add. EN* (hiis *pro* his *habet N*) primo conabor *add.* G   vos:
ante vos *in marg.* capitulum secundum *et titulum scribit E³*   amantissimos: ama-
tissimos *S*   1-2 quandam: quondam *Q*   2 praxim: praximi *S*   devotionis:
om. G   propono: *om.* G   elevare: *om. Pa* (*in marg. add. Pa²*) evolare *Q*   theologiam: ubi contemplacionem altissimam subintrabitis; secundo loco aliquas scripturarum et doctorum latebras enodabo. Tercio et ultimo loco, si que ex hiis que
ante hec scripsi obscura videntur, ut facilia et clariora fiant laborabo, *add.* G
3 praemittendo: promittendo *A*   hoc: hec *RZ*   opportuna: optima *G*

him. Thereupon he will be told that the gaze is also moved in this opposite manner; and he will believe his fellow-monk. And unless he believed, he would not apprehend that this |simultaneous opposition of motion| was possible. And so, through the disclosure of the respondent he will come to know that that face does not desert anyone who is moving—not even those who are moving in opposite directions. Therefore, he will experience that the unmovable face is moved toward the east in such way that it is also moved at the same time toward the west, that it is moved toward the north in such way that it is also moved |at the same time| toward the south, that it is moved toward one place in such way that it is also moved at the same time toward all other places, and that it observes one movement in such way that it observes all other movements at the same time. And while he considers that this gaze does not desert anyone, he sees how diligently it is concerned for each one, as if it were concerned for no one else, but only for him who experiences that he is seen |by it. This impression| is so strong that the one who is being looked upon cannot even imagine that |the icon| is concerned for another. |The one who is pondering all this| will also notice that |the image| is most diligently concerned for the least of creatures, just as for the greatest of creatures and for the whole universe.

5   On the basis of such a sensible appearance as this, I propose to elevate you very beloved brothers, through a devotional exercise, unto mystical theology. To this end I will |now| present three useful |considerations|.[2]

6 CAPITULUM I

QUOD PERFECTIO APPARENTIAE VERIFICATUR DE DEO PERFECTISSIMO

Primo loco praesupponendum esse censeo, nihil posse apparere circa visum eiconae dei, quin verius sit in vero visu dei. Deus etenim,
5 qui est summitas ipsa omnis perfectionis et maior quam cogitari possit, "theos" ob hoc dicitur, quia omnia intuetur. Quare, si visus pictus apparere potest in imagine simul omnia et singula inspiciens, cum hoc sit perfectionis visus, non poterit veritati minus convenire veraciter, quam eiconae seu apparentiae apparenter. Si enim visus unus est
10 acutior alio in nobis, et unus vix propinqua alius vero distantiora discernit, et alius tarde alius citius attingit obiectum, nihil haesitationis est absolutum visum, a quo omnis visus videntium, excellere omnem acutiem, omnem celeritatem et virtutem omnem omnium videntium actu et qui videntes fieri possunt. Si enim inspexero ad
15 abstractum visum, quem mente absolvi ab omnibus oculis et organis, atque consideravero quomodo ille visus abstractus in contracto esse suo, prout videntes per ipsum visum vident, est ad tempus et plagas mundi, ad obiecta singularia, et ceteras conditiones tales contractus, ac quod abstractus visus ab his est conditionibus similiter abstractus
20 et absolutus, bene capio de essentia visus non esse ut plus unum quam aliud respiciat obiectum, licet comitetur visum in contracto esse quod, dum respicit unum, non possit respicere aliud aut absolute omnia.

7 Deus autem, ut est verus incontractus visus, non est minor quam

---

6 1-2 *hic nullam divisionem faciunt EGNT (Vide notas pro 2:1 et 5:1)* 2 apparentiae: *om. V* perfectissimo: perfectissime *ALM³OP³Q² (in 1:1 perfectissimo habent MOPQ) RV²* (rubrica *add. V²*) *Z* 3 praesupponendum: supponendum *G* presupponenda *N* esse: *om. Pa* censeo: censio *G* 4 dei¹: quando *post* dei¹ *scribit et del. M* quin: quando *N* sit: *om. OP* 5 est: es *S* ipsa: *om. N* 6 ob: ab *GRV* ob *ex* ab *corr. P* quare: *non proprie abbreviat Q* 8 sit: *om. Q* veritati: *ex* veritatis *corr. N* 9 quam: *om. V* seu: sew *P (cf. 24:15)* 10 acutior: aucucior *S* nobis: vobis *T* 11 alius¹: unus *EN* alius²: vero *add. R* 12 visum: usum *S* a: *lacuna hic in codice V* 12-13 excellere omnem: omnem excellere *Z* 13 omnem³: *om. EN* 14 actu: *ex* actum *corr. P* videntes: *in abbreviatione* s *plus elevare debet A* enim: *om. Q* 16 atque: itaque *V* 17 vident: videntem *N* et: ad *add. Z* 18 singularia: singlaria *T* et ceteras: caeteras et *p* tales: talis

CHAPTER ONE

THE PERFECTION OF THE APPEARANCE IS PREDICATED TRULY OF THE MOST PERFECT GOD

In the first place, I think we must presuppose the following: whatever is *apparent* with regard to the icon-of-God's sight is *truer* with regard to God's true sight.[3] For, indeed, God, who is the summit of all perfection and who is greater than can be thought,[4] is called *"theos"* by virtue of the fact that He observes all things.[5] Therefore, if in the image the depicted gaze can appear to be beholding each and every thing at once, then since this |capability| belongs to sight's perfection, it cannot truly befit the Truth *less* than it apparently befits the icon, or appearance. For if one person's sight is more acute than another's, if one person's sight scarcely discerns nearby objects but another's discerns more distant objects, if one person's sight reaches its object slowly but another's arrives more quickly, then without doubt ⟨Absolute Sight⟩ from which comes the entire sight of those who have sight, excels all the acuity, swiftness, and power both of all those who actually have sight and of all those who can be given it. For suppose I view abstract sight, which mentally I have freed from all eyes and organs. And suppose I consider (1) the fact that this abstract sight—in its own contracted being, according as those who see see by means of sight—is contracted to time, to the regions of the world, to individual objects, and to other such conditions and (2) the fact that, likewise, abstract sight is free[6] from these conditions. Thereupon, I rightly grasp that it is not of the essence of sight that sight beholds one object more than another—even though the fact that while sight inspects one object it cannot |at the same time| inspect either another object or all other objects whatsoever characterizes sight in its contracted being.

7 But God, insofar as He is true Uncontracted Sight, is not sight

ENQ 19 ac: ad *V* quod: si *R* visus: est *add. V* his: aliis *S* iis *p* 20 bene: optime *p* 21 quam . . . obiectum: respiciat quam aliud obiectum *Pa* (*ad* obiectum respiciat quam aliud *corr. Pa aut Pa²*) visum: *bis O* (visum¹ *del. O*) 22 quod: et *R* ut *p* unum: non respicit aliud seu *add. T* respicere: aspicere *EN* 7 1 autem: omnia *post* autem *scribit et del. G* verus: unus *A* et *add. R*

de abstracto visu per intellectum concipi potest, sed improportionaliter perfectior. Quare apparentia visus eiconae minus potest accedere
ad summitatem excellentiae visus absoluti quam conceptus. Id igitur
5 quod in imagine illa apparet, excellenter in visu esse absoluto non est
haesitandum.

8   CAPITULUM II

VISUS ABSOLUTUS COMPLECTITUR OMNES MODOS

Advertas, post haec, visum variari in videntibus ex varietate contractionis eius. Nam sequitur visus noster organi et animi passiones.
5 Unde iam videt aliquis amorose et laete, post dolorose et iracunde,
iam pueriliter post viriliter, deinde seriose et seniliter. Visus autem
absolutus ab omni contractione simul et semel omnes et singulos
videndi modos complectitur, quasi adaequatissima visuum omnium
mensura et exemplar verissimum. Sine enim absoluto visu non potest
10 esse visus contractus. Complectitur autem in se omnes videndi
modos, et ita omnes quod singulos, et manet ab omni varietate penitus absolutus. Sunt enim in absoluto visu omnes contractionum modi
videndi incontracte. Omnis enim contractio est in absoluto, quia
absoluta visio est contractio contractionum. Contractio enim est
15 incontrahibilis. Coincidit igitur simplicissima contractio cum absoluto. Sine autem contractione nihil contrahitur. Sic absoluta visio in
omni visu est, quia per ipsam est omnis contracta visio et sine ea
penitus esse nequit.

---

2 intellectum: intellctum *Pa (ut saepissime; quod non nisi hic et in 74:5 notavi;
saepissime scribit Pa etiam* intellctus *et* intellctu*)*   2-3 improportionaliter: impro-
porcionabiliter *C* inproporcionabiliter *EGJNPaQRSTVZ* inproportionabiliter *I*
improportionabiliter *p*   3 quare: quam est *Q* visus: *om. ENR*   5 in¹: *in
marg. Q* excellenter: *om. A* esse: *om. N* esse absoluto: absoluto esse *A*
6 haesitandum: et cetera *add. P*
   8 1 capitulum II: capitulum 3ᵐ *E³*   2 visus: quod visus *E³ (in 1:1* quod *om.*
E³) GPa³Tp omnes: videndi *add. R (in 1:1* videndi *non habet R* modos:
rubrica *add. V²*   3 variari: vadari *Q* varietate: veritate *S*   4 noster: *om. R* et
animi: *in marg. R* passiones: affectiones *p*   8 visuum: visum *Pa*   9 mensura:
mensuram *Q* verissimum: virissimum *G* absoluto visu: visu absoluto *EN* visu:

that is *less* than the intellect can conceive abstract sight to be; rather, He is incomparably more perfect Sight.[7] Hence, the appearance of the icon's gaze is less able to approximate the supreme excellence of Absolute Sight than is conception. Therefore, that which is apparent in the case of that image must undoubtedly be present in an excellent way in Absolute Sight.

8

CHAPTER TWO

ABSOLUTE SIGHT ENCOMPASSES ALL MODES |OF SEEING|

Notice, next, that in those who have sight sight varies as a result of the variety of its contractedness. For our sight is conditioned by the affections of the organ |i.e., of the eye| and of the mind. Hence, a given individual looks |upon a given thing| now lovingly and gladly, later sadly and angrily, now as does a child, later as does an adult, and, still later, gravely and as does someone elderly. But Sight that is free from all contractedness—as being the most adequate Measure, and the most true Exemplar, of all acts of seeing[8]—encompasses at one and the same time each and every mode of seeing. For without Absolute Sight there cannot be contracted sight. But Absolute Sight encompasses all modes of seeing—encompasses all modes in such way that it encompasses each mode. And it remains altogether free from all variation. For in Absolute Sight every contracted mode of seeing is present uncontractedly. For all contraction |of sight| is present in Absolute |Sight|, because Absolute Sight is the Contraction of contractions. For it is Uncontractible Contraction.[9] Therefore, most simple Contraction coincides with Absolute |Sight|. Now, without contraction nothing is contracted. Thus, Absolute Sight is present in all seeing, since all contracted sight exists through Absolute Sight and cannot at all exist without it.

ex visum *corr. Pa aut Pa*[2]   10 visus: *om. Q*   11 omnes: *om. S*   quod: et *Q* varietate: veritate *C* (*ad* varietate *corr. C*[2])   12 enim: ab *post* enim *scribit et del. P* contractionum: contracti omnium *L*   12-13 modi videndi: videndi modo *N* 13 incontracte: *ex* contracte *corr. A*   incontracti *G*   contracte *R*   14 enim: *om.* *IJPa*   enim est: est enim *ALMOPRSV*   est enim *ad* enim est *transponit C aut C*[2] enim est *ad* est enim *transponit Q*   15 incontrahibilis: *ex ? in marg. corr. P* incontractibilis *Pa*   15-16 absoluto: absoluta *Q*

De Visione Dei

9

CAPITULUM III

QUOD QUAE DE DEO DICUNTUR REALITER NON DIFFERUNT

Consequenter attendas, omnia quae de deo dicuntur, realiter ob summam dei simplicitatem non posse differre, licet nos secundum
5 alias et alias rationes, alia et alia vocabula deo attribuamus. Deus autem, cum sit ratio absoluta omnium formabilium rationum, in se omnium rationes complicat. Unde quamvis deo visum, auditum, gustum, odoratum, tactum, sensum, rationem, et intellectum, et talia attribuamus secundum alias et alias cuiuslibet vocabuli significatio-
10 num rationes, tamen in ipso videre non est aliud ab audire et gustare et odorare et tangere et sentire et intelligere. Et ita tota theologia in circulo posita dicitur, quia unum attributorum affirmatur de alio. Et habere dei est esse eius, et movere est stare, et currere est quiescere, et ita de reliquis attributis. Sic licet nos alia ratione attribuamus ei
15 movere et alia stare, tamen quia ipse est absoluta ratio, in qua omnis alteritas est unitas et omnis diversitas identitas, tunc rationum diversitas, quae non est identitas ipsa, prout nos diversitatem concipimus, in deo esse nequit.

10

CAPITULUM IV

QUOD VISIO DEI PROVIDENTIA, GRATIA, ET VITA DICITUR AETERNA

Accede nunc tu, frater contemplator, ad dei eiconam, et primum te

---

9 1 capitulum III: capitulum 4^tum *E³   numerus capituli in marg.* M³ *rubrica post* capitulum tercium *add.* V²   2 quod: *om.* CE³GJPa³TV²Z *(in 1:1* quod nec habent *MOPQR)*   realiter: dicuntur *post* realiter *scribit et del.* C   differunt: defferunt J   **9** 3 - **10** 2 *manu alia scriptum est* J   **9** 3 ob: ad A   4 summam dei: dei summam EN   5 alias¹: raciones *add.* S   rationes: tamen in ipso videre non est aliud *post* raciones *scribit et del.* A   attribuamus: attribuimus G   6 absoluta omnium: omnium absoluta *ad* absoluta omnium *transponit* R   formabilium: formalium *ex* formabilium (?) *corr.* Z   formalium *p*   7 omnium: omnes PaSp   rationes: racionum L   complicat: *ex* complicas *corr.* G   implicat OP   conplicatur Q   7-8 gustum: *non proprie scribit* Q   8 odoratum: adoratum G   talia: alia V   8-9 et talia attribuamus: *om.* T   9 secundum: secum *p*   10 rationes: attribuimus

9   CHAPTER THREE

THINGS PREDICATED OF GOD DO NOT DIFFER REALLY

Observe, next, that because of God's supreme simplicity whatever things are predicated of Him cannot differ really, even though we apply different words to God in accordance with different forms. But since God is the Absolute Form of all formable forms,[10] He enfolds in Himself the forms of all things. Hence, although we ascribe to God sight, hearing, taste, smell, touch, sense, reason, understanding, and other such things, in accordance with the different forms of signification of each word, nevertheless in Him seeing is not *other* than hearing, tasting, smelling, touching, perceiving, and understanding. And so, the whole of theology is said to be circular,[11] because |any| one of the attributes is affirmed of |any| other. And God's having is His being, His moving is His remaining at rest, His running is His being still—and so on regarding the other attributes. So although on the basis of one form we ascribe to Him moving and on the basis of another form we ascribe to Him remaining-at-rest, nevertheless because He is Absolute Form in which all otherness is oneness and all diversity is identity, there cannot be in Him a diversity of forms; for this diversity, as we conceive it, is not identity.

10   CHAPTER FOUR

GOD'S VISION IS SAID TO BE PROVIDENCE, GRACE, AND ETERNAL LIFE

Now, O brother contemplative, draw near to the icon of God and

in marg. add. T²   aliud: quam add. RT   ab: scribit et del. T   et: om. Q
11 et¹: om. Q   odorare: adorare AGP   tangere: tange G   12 dicitur: d non
clare scribit E   attributorum: non proprie scribit V   affirmatur de alio: affluatur
de alio ante affirmatur de alio scribit et del. M   alio: ex aliquo corr. I   13 esse:
unius add. V   est²: et Q   currere: curare S   14 ratione: recte A   15 ipse:
ipsa PaV   qua: quo G   16 est: et Q   16-17 rationum diversitas: diversitas
racionum ad racionum diversitas transponit Q   17 ipsa: om. V

10 1 capitulum IV: capitulum 5ᵗᵘᵐ E³   2 dicitur aeterna: eterna dicitur Q² (*in*
1:1 dicitur eterna habet Q) R (*in 1:1* quod providentia dei gratia et vita dicitur
eterna *habet R*) V²   3 *divisionem non facit N*   ad dei: dei ad *ad* ad dei *trans-*

loces ad orientem, deinde ad meridiem ac ultimo ad occasum. Et
5 quia visus eiconae te aeque undique respicit et non deserit quocumque pergas, in te excitabitur speculatio, provocaberisque et dices:
Domine, nunc in hac tua imagine providentiam tuam quadam sensibili experientia intueor. Nam si me non deseris, qui sum vilissimus
omnium, nusquam cuiquam deeris. Sic quidem ades omnibus et sin
10 gulis, sicut ipsis omnibus et singulis adest esse, sine quo non possunt
esse. Ita enim tu, absolutum esse omnium, ades cunctis, quasi non sit
tibi cura de quocumque alio. Et ob hoc evenit quod nulla res est quin
esse suum praeferat cunctis et modum essendi suum omnibus aliorum essendi modis. Et ita esse suum tuetur quod omnium aliorum
15 esse potius sinat in perditionem ire quam suum. Ita enim tu, domine,
intueris quodlibet quod est ut non possit concipi per omne id quod
est, te aliam curam habere, quam ut id solum sit meliori modo quo
esse potest atque quod omnia alia quae sunt ad hoc solum sint, ut
serviant ad id, quod illud sit optime quod tu respicis.

11   Nequaquam, domine, me concipere sinis quacumque imaginatione
quod tu, domine, aliud a me plus me diligas, cum me solum visus
tuus non deserat. Et quoniam ibi amor ubi oculus, tunc te me diligere
experior, quia oculi tui sunt super me servulum tuum attentissime.
5 Domine, videre tuum est amare; et sicut visus tuus adeo attente me
prospicit quod numquam se a me avertit, sic et amor tuus. Et quo-

---

ponit T aut T², etiam T³   4 deinde: te *add. V*   ac: nec et *G*   et *Q*   5 aeque
undique: undique eque *EN*   undique eque *ad* eque undique *transponit R*   6 provocaberisque: provocabisque *A*   7 tua imagine: imagine tua *E* ymagine tua *N*
quadam: quodam *CV* quadam *om. I*   8 intueor: *ex* intuor *corr. Z*   non: de
post non *scribit et del. J*   9 deeris: diceris *A* dederis *V*   sic: si *V*   10 sicut
. . . singulis: *om. V*   ipsis: et *post* ipsis *scribit et del. I*   et *add. S*   ipsis omnibus:
omnibus ipsis *EN*   et: *bis E supra lin. S*   et singulis: *om. Q*   11 tu: *om. ENT*
ex tuum *(?) corr. P*   ades: *ex* adest *in marg. corr. P*   sit: sic *J*   11-12 non sit
tibi: tibi non sit *Z*   12 tibi: *om. S*   quocumque: quoquam *CEGJNPaSTVp*   ob:
om. p   quod: quia *p*   est: *om. M (supra lin. add. M²)*   quin: qui *C (ad* que
corr. C²) quin *M² (abbreviationem del., et in marg. ut* quin *explicat, M²)* quando
N quae *p*   13 suum¹: non *post* suum¹ *add. C² (supra lin.) et p*   omnibus:
omnium *R*   14 essendi: essendi *ex* esse *corr. T (pocius post* esse *scribit et del. T,
etiam del. T³)* suum: *om. T*   tuetur: tenetur *Q*   16 intueris: tueris *N*   quodlibet quod: quidlibet quid *A*   possit: possis *R*   quod²: quoddam *J*   17 quam:
id solum *post* quam *scribit, del. et post* ut *rescribit, O* ut: *om. Pa*   id: quod
post id *scribit et del. A*   meliori: optimo *p*   18 esse: *om. V*   esse potest:
potest esse *p*   19 illud: *om. A*

situate yourself first in the east, then in the south, and finally in the west. The icon's gaze looks at you in equal measure in every region and does not desert you no matter where you go. Therefore, a speculative consideration will be occasioned in you, and you will be aroused and will say: O Lord, by a certain sense-experience I now behold, in this image of You, Your providence. For if You do not desert me, who am the least of all men, then You will never desert anyone. You are present to each and every thing—just as *being*, without which things cannot exist, is present to each and every thing. For You who are the Absolute Being of all things[12] are present to each thing as if You were concerned about no other thing at all. (Consequently, there is no thing which does not prefer its own being to everything else and does not prefer its own mode of being to all the modes of being of other things;[13] and each thing so cherishes its own being that it would let the being of all other things perish rather than its own.) For You, O Lord, behold each existing thing in such way that no existing thing can conceive that You have any other concern than (1) that this very thing exist in the best manner it can and (2) that all other existing things exist only in order to serve the following end: viz., that this thing upon which you are looking exist in the best way.

11   You, O Lord, do not at all allow me to conceive, by any stretch of the imagination, that You, Lord, love anything other than me more than me, for it is me alone whom Your gaze does not desert. And since where Your eye is present Your love is also present, I experience that You love me, because Your eyes are most attentively upon me, Your lowly servant. O Lord, Your seeing is loving; and just as Your gaze regards me so attentively that it never turns away from me, so

---

11 1 me: *om. ALMOPQRZ (in marg. add. Z²)*   sinis: si vis *V*   2 quod: quam *V*   aliud a me: a me aliud *R*   plus: de *add. A*   me²: *om. Q*   3 non: me *post* non *scribit et del. C*   deserat: deseras *N*   desiderat *S*   ibi amor ubi oculus: ibi oculus ubi amor *CEGIJNPaSTVp*   ibi oculus ubi oculus *M* (oculus¹ *ad* amor *in marg. corr. M²*)   ibi amor ubi oculus *ALO* (ubi *ex* ibi *in marg. corr. O*) *PQRZ* (*ad* ibi oculus ubi amor *corr. Z²*)   te: de *N*   me: *om. I*   4 oculi: celi *L*   oculi ... tuum: supra me servulum tuum oculi tui sunt *p*   servulum: servum *V*   attentissime: attentissimi *AGIJLMOPPaQRSVZ*   attentissime *ex* attentissimi *corr. C*   attendissimi *T*   5 visus: est *post* visus *scribit et del. N*   6 prospicit: respicit *R*   numquam: nunque *I*   avertit: convertit *ex* convertat *corr. L*   sic et: et sic *CV*

niam amor tuus semper mecum est, et non est aliud amor tuus, domine, quam tu ipse qui amas me, hinc tu semper mecum es, domine.
Non me deseris, domine; undique me custodis, quia curam mei agis
10 diligentissimam. Esse tuum, domine, non derelinquit esse meum.
Intantum enim sum, inquantum tu mecum es. Et cum videre tuum sit
esse tuum, ideo ego sum quia tu me respicis. Et si a me vultum tuum
subtraxeris, nequaquam subsistam.

12 Sed scio quod visus tuus est bonitas illa maxima quae se ipsam
non potest non communicare omni capaci. Tu igitur numquam poteris me derelinquere, quamdiu ego tui capax fuero. Ad me igitur
spectat ut, quantum possum, efficiar continue plus capax tui. Scio
5 autem quod capacitas quae unionem praestat, non est nisi similitudo;
incapacitas autem ex dissimilitudine. Si igitur ego me reddidero omni
possibili modo bonitati tuae similem, secundum gradus similitudinis
ero capax veritatis. Dedisti mihi, domine, esse, et id ipsum tale quod
se potest gratiae et bonitatis tuae continue magis capax reddere. Et
10 haec vis, quam a te habeo, in qua virtutis omnipotentiae tuae vivam
imaginem teneo, est libera voluntas, per quam possum aut ampliare
aut restringere capacitatem gratiae tuae—ampliare quidem per con-
formitatem, quando nitor esse bonus quia tu bonus, quando nitor esse
iustus quia tu iustus, quando nitor esse misericors quia tu misericors,
15 quando non nisi omnis conatus meus est ad te conversus quia omnis
conatus tuus est ad me conversus, quando solum ad te attentissime
respicio et numquam oculos mentis averto, quia tu me continua visione amplecteris, quando amorem meum ad te solum converto quia
tu, qui charitas, ad me solum es conversus.

6-7 et². . . tuus²: *in marg.* P   7-8 domine: *om.* EN   8 qui: quia A   semper
mecum: mecum semper *ad* semper mecum *transponit* M *aut* M²   9 mei: me G
10 meum: mecum N ([-]eum *in marg. coni.* N²)   11 tu: *om.* G *ex* tue *corr.* L
   12 1 quod: quod (?) G   quia Q   bonitas: tua *add.* R   se ipsam: ipsum se *ad*
se ipsum *transponit* G   2 non¹: *in marg.* A   non²: *supra lin.* Q   communicare:
communicari Q   omni: non S   numquam: numque I   2-3 poteris me: me
poteris AEGIJLMNOPPaST   3 ego: *om.* V   4 plus: plux J   tui: tui *ante*
efficiar *ponit, et post* capax *om.,* EN *om.* T   5 praestat: prestet J   6 dissimilitudine: similitudine J (dis *in marg. add.* J *aut* Jⁿ)   ego: *om.* JQV   ego me: me
ego *ad* ego me *transponit* M *aut* M²   me reddidero: reddi me deo A   reddidero:
tradidero T   7 tuae: tui GL   8 id: ad V   9 bonitatis: *ad* bonitati *corr.* I   hones-
tatis V   tuae: que S (*ad* tue *corr.* S²)   et²: *om.* T   10 vis: *supra lin.* P   virtutis:
virtute R   tuae: tuam I   11 teneo est: tene et S   est: *ex* in (?) *corr.* A   possum:

neither does Your love. And since Your love is always with me and is nothing other, Lord, than You Yourself, who love me, You Yourself are always with me, O Lord. You do not desert me, Lord; You safeguard me on all sides because You most carefully watch over me. Your Being, O Lord, does not forsake my being, for I exist insofar as You are with me. And since Your seeing is Your being, I exist because You look upon me. And if You were to withdraw Your countenance from me, I would not at all continue to exist.

12   But I know that Your gaze is that maximal goodness which cannot fail to impart itself to whatever is capable of receiving it. Therefore, You can never forsake me,[14] as long as I am capable of receiving You. Hence, I must see to it that, as best I can, I be made more and more capable of receiving You. But I know that the capability which conduces to union is only likeness; but incapability results from unlikeness. Therefore, if by every possible means I make myself like unto Your goodness, then according to my degree of likeness thereto I will be capable of receiving truth. O Lord, You have given me being; and my being is such that it can make itself more and more capable of receiving Your grace and goodness. And this power, which I have from You and by virtue of which I possess a living image of Your omnipotent power, is free will. Through free will I can either increase or decrease my capability for receiving Your grace. I can increase it through conformity, when I endeavor to be good because You are good, when I endeavor to be just because You are just, when I endeavor to be merciful because You are merciful, when my every endeavor is turned only toward You because Your every endeavor is turned toward me, when I look most attentively only unto You (never turning the eyes of my mind away) because You embrace me with a steadfast look, and when I turn my love only toward You because You, who are Love,[15] are turned only toward me.

possunt *S*   aut: *om. T*   13 quia tu bonus: *in marg. I*   15 non . . . est: omnis conatus meus non est nisi *p*   est ad te: ad te est *L*   quia: quando *Q* (solum ad te *post* quando *scribit et del. Q*)   15-16 quia . . . conversus: *om. Pa (in marg. add. Pa²) TV*   16 conatus: est *post* conatus *scribit et del. S*   me: *ex* te *corr. L*   quando: *ex* quomodo *(?) corr. J*   17 respicio et: respicior *V*   oculos: oculus *N*   mentis: a te *add. L*   18 converto: *ex* convertem *corr. E*   19 charitas: es *add. C²T (in marg. T) p*   ad me solum: solum ad me *EN*   ad me solum es: solum es ad me *Z*   es conversus: conversus es *p*

13   Et quid est, domine, vita mea nisi amplexus ille, quo tua dulcedo dilectionis me adeo amorose amplectitur? Diligo supreme vitam meam quia tu es dulcedo vitae meae. Contemplor nunc in speculo, in eicona, in aenigmate vitam aeternam, quia non est nisi visio beata, 5 qua quidem visione tu me amorosissime usque ad intima animae meae numquam videre dimittis. Et non est videre tuum nisi vivificare, nisi dulcissimum amorem tui continue immittere, me ad tui amorem per immissionem amoris inflammare, et inflammando pascere, et pascendo desideria ignire, et igniendo rore laetitiae potare, et potando 10 fontem vitae immittere, et immittendo augere et perennare, et tuam immortalitatem communicare, caelestis et altissimi atque maximi regni gloriam immarcessibilem condonare, hereditatis illius quae solius filii est participem facere, et aeternae felicitatis possessorem constituere, ubi est ortus deliciarum omnium quae desiderari pot-15 erunt, quo nihil melius non solum per omnem hominem aut angelum excogitari, sed nec omni essendi modo esse potest. Nam est ipsa absoluta maximitas omnis desiderii rationalis, quae maior esse nequit.

14   CAPITULUM V

QUOD VIDERE SIT GUSTARE, QUAERERE, MISERERI, ET OPERARI

O quam magna multitudo dulcedinis tuae, quam abscondisti timentibus te. Nam est thesaurus inexplicabilis gaudiosissimae laetitiae.

---

13 1 quo: quem *I* qui *NPa*   dulcedo: tue *add. Q*   2 dilectionis: tue *add. R* supreme: sum me (=summe) *S*   super me *T* (*ad* supreme *corr. T²*)   2-3 diligo . . . meae: *om. A*   3 tu: *ex* tue *corr. L*   speculo: seculo *S*   4 aenigmate: enigmate *V* (e¹ *non proprie scribit V; cf. 22:1*)   aeternam: eterna *N*   nisi: michi *O*   mihi *P* 5 quidem: quidam *V*   amorosissime: amorissime *NS*   intima: intimam *S*   6 numquam: nuquam *NPa*   dimittis: desinis *p*   7 dulcissimum: *in abbreviatione* m² *plus elevare debet P*   tui¹: *ex* tuum *corr. EL* tuum *IJPaRZ om. Q*   immittere: mittere *N*   ad: *ex* per *corr. L*   8 immissionem: divisionem *V*   9 igniendo: desideria *add. A* ignendo *G*   potare: *ex* portare *corr. S*   10 fontem: fonte *Q* immitendo: inmittenda *S*   augere: *non proprie scribit R*   et³: in *Pa* (*ad* et *corr.*

13   And what is my life, O Lord, except that embrace by which the
sweetness of Your love embraces me so lovingly? I love my life
supremely because You are the sweetness thereof. I presently contemplate eternal life in a mirror, an icon, a symbolism,[16] because eternal
life is only Your blessed gaze, by which You never cease looking
upon me most lovingly—even to the point of beholding the intimate
recesses of my soul. And Your seeing is only Your enlivening, only
Your continually instilling Your most sweet love and, by instilling,
inflaming me with love for You. In inflaming me You feed me, and
in feeding me You intensify my desires. In intensifying my desires
You give me to drink of the dew of joy, and in giving me to drink
You cause a fountain of life to well up in me. In so causing, You
cause to increase and to be preserved. You impart Your immortality.
You offer the unfading glory of Your celestial, most lofty, and most
great kingdom. You make me a partaker of that heritage which is the
Son's alone, and You bestow upon me eternal happiness. |Your seeing
is all of the foregoing,| wherein is the source of whatever delights can
be desired. Not only can nothing better than this be imagined by any
man or angel but also nothing better can exist by any mode of being.
For this source is the absolute maximality (which cannot be greater)
of all rational desire.

14   CHAPTER FIVE

|GOD'S| SEEING IS HIS TASTING, SEEKING, SHOWING MERCY, AND WORKING

    O how greatly manifold is that sweetness of Yours which You have
reserved for those who fear You![17] For it is an uncountable treasure

Pa²)   11 caelestis: celestisque *G*   atque: ac *p*   12 immarcessibilem: *scribit, et
litteras si clarius supra lin. rescribit, O om. T*   illius: *ex* illis *corr. I*   13 solius:
socius *V*   est: *om. S*   14 deliciarum: omnia *post* deliciarum *scribit et del. J*
omnium quae: omniumque *N*   desiderari: desiderare *AJS*   14-15 poterunt: potu-
erunt *V*   15 nihil melius: melius nichil *V*   omnem hominem: hominem omnem
ad omnem hominem *transponit E*   16 nec: c *non proprie format R*   est: *supra
lin. L*   etiam *S*   17 nequit: et cetera *add. IP*
    14 1 *numerum capituli om. CJ*   capitulum V: capitulum 6^{tum} *E³*   2 quod
. . . operari: *titulum capituli IV hic repetit p*   misereri: *om. R (sed in 1:1* misereri
habet R)   3 *divisionem non facit N*   3-4 timentibus: timetibus *Pa*   4 nam

5 Gustare enim ipsam dulcedinem tuam est apprehendere, experimen-
tali contactu, suavitatem omnium delectabilium in suo principio; est
rationem omnium desiderabilium attingere in tua sapientia. Videre
igitur rationem absolutam, quae est omnium ratio, non est aliud
quam mente te deum gustare, quoniam es ipsa suavitas esse, vitae, et
10 intellectus.

15   Quid aliud, domine, est videre tuum, quando me pietatis oculo
respicis, quam a me videri? Videndo me das te a me videri, qui es
deus absconditus. Nemo te videre potest nisi inquantum tu das ut
videaris. Nec est aliud te videre quam quod tu videas videntem te.
5 Video in hac imagine tua quam pronus es, domine, ut faciem tuam
ostendas omnibus quaerentibus te. Nam numquam claudis oculos;
numquam aliorsum vertis. Et licet ego me a te avertam, quando ad
aliud me penitus converto, tu tamen ob hoc non mutas oculos nec
visum. Si me non respicis oculo gratiae, causa est mea, quia divisus
10 sum a te per aversionem et conversionem ad aliud, quod tibi
praefero. Non tamen adhuc avertis te penitus, sed misericordia tua
sequitur me, an aliquando velim reverti ad te, ut sim capax gratiae
tuae. Quod enim me non respicis, est quia te non respicio, sed respuo
et contemno.

16   O pietas infinita, quam infelix est omnis peccator qui te, venam
vitae, derelinquit et quaerit te non in te, sed in eo quod in se nihil est
et nihil mansisset, si tu non vocasses ipsum de nihilo. Quam fatuus
est qui te quaerit, qui es bonitas, et dum te quaerit, a te recedit et
5 oculos avertit. Quaerit igitur omnis quaerens non nisi bonum, et
omnis qui quaerit bonum et a te recedit, ab eo recedit quod quaerit.
Omnis igitur peccator a te errat et longius abit. Quando autem ad te

est: nan et *S*   est: et *I*   inexplicabilis: in ep explicabilis (ep *deletum*) *scribit S*
gaudiosissimae: gadiosissime *P*   plenissimae gaudio *p*   6 contactu: contractu *CM*
(ad contactu *corr. M²) V*   suavitatem: summitatem *G*   7 tua: *ex* sua *in marg.*
corr. P   7-8 desiderabilium . . . rationem: *om. I*   8 rationem: omnium *post*
racionem *scribit et del. E*   9 quam: quem,*Q*   es: est *P*
   15 2 quam: quasi *L   non proprie abbreviat V*   te *add. p*   videndo . . . videri:
om. J (videndo me das t[e] a me videri *in marg. add. Jⁿ*)   *om. T* (videndo me das te
a me videre *in marg. add. T²)*   a²: *ex* ad *corr. C aut C²* ad *V*   3 ut: *om. I*
4 videre: videri *p*   videas: vides *G*   5 in: *om. R*   7 vertis: vertas *S*   8 ob:
ab *V*   9 respicis: oculos *add. S*   est mea: mea est *AENp*   11 adhuc: non
add. C   avertis: avertas *V*   12 aliquando: aliqui (?) *V*   velim: *bis S*   ad: a *S*

of most joyous joy. For to taste of Your sweetness is to apprehend the sweetness of all delights—to apprehend it in its own Beginning and by experiential contact. It is to attain, in Your wisdom, to the Form of all desirable things. Therefore, to see Absolute Form, which is the Form of all |forms|, is no other than mentally to taste of You, who are God; for You are the Sweetness of being and of life and of understanding.

15   O Lord, when You look upon me with an eye of graciousness, what is Your seeing, other than Your being seen by me? In seeing me, You who are *deus absconditus*[18] give Yourself to be seen by me. No one can see You except insofar as You grant that You be seen. To see You is not other than that You see the one who sees You. By means of this icon of You, O Lord, I see how favorably disposed You are to show Your face to all who seek You. For You never close Your eyes; You never turn |them| away. And although I turn away from You when I completely turn to something else, You do not on this account change Your eyes or Your gaze. If You do not look upon me with an eye of grace, it is my fault, because I am separated from You through my turning away and through my turning toward something else, which I prefer to You. Notwithstanding, You still do not turn altogether away from me, but Your mercy follows me in case at some time I might wish to turn back to You in order to be capable of receiving Your grace. For the reason that You do not look upon me is that I do not look unto You but reject and despise You.

16   O Infinite Graciousness, how unhappy is every sinner who forsakes You, the Stream of life, and seeks You not in Yourself but in that which in itself is nothing and would have remained nothing had You not called it forth from nothing. How foolish is he who seeks You, who are Goodness, and while seeking You departs from You and turns away his eyes. For everyone who seeks seeks only the good, and everyone who seeks the good and departs from You departs from that which he seeks.[19] Therefore, every sinner strays from You and goes farther away. But when he turns back to You,

ut sim: sim ut *ad* ut sim *transponit T aut T², etiam T³*   13 tuae: *om. CVp* sed: *om. Q*

    16 2 derelinquit: dereliquit *A*   3 fatuus: futuus *P* insanus *p*   5 quaerit: queitur *A*   quaerens: bonum *post* querens *scribit et del. E*   5-6 quaerens . . . omnis: *om. V*   6 et: *supra lin. T*   7 ad: a *M (*ad *in marg. coni. M²)* ad *ex* a *corr. S*

revertitur, sine mora tu ei occurris; et antequam te respiciat, tu
paterno affectu in eum oculos misericordiae inicis. Nec est aliud
10 tuum misereri quam tuum videre. Subsequitur igitur omnem hominem misericordia tua quamdiu vivit, quocumque pergat, sicut nec
visus tuus quemquam deserit. Quamdiu igitur homo vivit, non cessas
eum subsequi et dulci atque interna monitione incitare, ut ab errore
cesset et convertatur ad te, ut feliciter vivat.

17 Tu, domine, es socius peregrinationis meae; quocumque pergo,
oculi tui super me sunt semper. Videre autem tuum est movere tuum.
Moveris igitur mecum, et non cessas umquam a motu quamdiu
moveor. Si quiesco et tu mecum es; si ascendero ascendis; si descen-
5 dero descendis; quocumque me verto ades. Nec me deseris in tempore tribulationis. Quotiens te invoco prope es. Nam invocare te est
me convertere ad te. Non potes illi deesse, qui se ad te convertit. Nec
potest quis ad te converti, nisi adsis prius. Ades antequam ad te convertar. Nisi enim adesses et sollicitares me, te penitus ignorarem. Et
10 ad te, quem ignorarem, quomodo converterer?

18 Tu igitur es deus meus, qui omnia vides, et videre tuum est operari.
Omnia igitur operaris. Non nobis igitur, domine, non nobis sed
nomini tuo magno, quod est "theos," gloriam cano sempiternam.
Nihil enim habeo quod tu non das, nec tenerem id quod dedisti, nisi
5 tu ipse conservares. Tu igitur ministras mihi omnia; tu es dominus
potens et pius qui omnia donas; tu es minister qui omnia ministras;
tu es provisor et curam habens atque conservator. Et haec omnia uno
simplicissimo intuitu tuo operaris, qui es in saecula benedictus.

---

9 inicis: vertis *I*   10 misereri: miserere *AEJMNOPPaQV ex* miserere *corr. CI*
misere *S*   11 quamdiu: quoniam diu *L*   quamdiu vivit: quamdiuvivit *p*   12 quemquam: quemque *A ex* quamquam *corr. T*   13 monitione: mocione *AGIJLMPPa
RSZ (*mocione *ad* moicione *corr. Z²) motione *O*   14 cesset: cessat *G ex* cessat
corr. Pa   convertatur: convertetur *Z*   feliciter: foeliciter *Pp (ut paene semper p)*
    17 1 socius: comes *p*   2 tui: *om. I*   super me sunt: sunt super me *N*   est:
videre *post* est *scribit et del. R*   movere tuum: tuum movere *ad* movere tuum
transponit R   3 cessas: a motu *add. EN*   umquam a motu: umquam a motu *E*
(a motu *del. E²*)   4 et: *om. EN*   4-5 si³. . . descendis: *om. Q*   descendero:
om. A   5 verto: vertero *EN*   6 quotiens: quoties *p*   invoco: in tempore *post*
invoco *scribit et del. I*   ades vel *supra lin. add. L*   7 potes: potest *P*   ad te²:
ex a te *corr. Pa*   nec: *non proprie abbreviat M*   8 ad¹: *ex* a *corr. S*   adsis:
*habet M (*assis *supra lin. scribit M²)*   8-9 convertar: convertor *AILMOQRZ*

You straightway come forth to meet him; and, before he beholds You, You cast Your eyes of mercy upon him with fatherly affection. Your showing mercy is nothing other than Your seeing. Hence, wherever any man goes Your mercy follows him for as long as he is alive, just as Your gaze, too, does not desert anyone. Therefore, as long as a man lives You do not cease to follow him and to urge him, with sweet and inward admonition, to cease from error and to turn unto You in order to live happily.

17 You, O Lord, are the companion for my journey; wherever I go Your eyes are always upon me. But Your seeing is Your moving. Therefore, You are moved with me; and You never cease moving as long as I am moved. If I am stationary, You are with me; if I ascend, You ascend; if I descend, You descend; in whatever direction I turn, You are present. And You do not desert me in time of tribulation. As often as I call upon You, You are nearby; for to call upon You is to turn toward You. You cannot be absent from him who turns toward You, nor can anyone turn toward You unless first You are present. You are present before I turn toward You; for unless You were present and unless You aroused me, I would be altogether ignorant of You. And how would I turn toward You, of whom I would be ignorant?

18 You, then, are my God, who sees all things; and Your seeing is Your working. Therefore, You work all things. Not, then, to us, O Lord, do I sing everlasting glory—not to us but to Your great name,[20] which is *Theos*.[21] For I have nothing which You do not give me; and I could not retain that which You have given unless You conserved it. Hence, You supply me with all things; You are the mighty and gracious Lord, who gives all things; You are the Minister, who supplies all things; You are the one who provides, the one who cares, the one who conserves. And by means of Your one most simple viewing You, who are blessed forever, work all these things.

---

9 et: in *Pa* (*ad* et *corr. Pa²*)   tunc *S*   10 converterer: converterem *G*
18 2 domine: *om. R*   4 tenerem id quod dedisti: id quod dedisti tenerem *GT*
5 conservares: *ex* conservarvares *corr. C aut C²*   6 et: *ex* ac *corr. M*   *? post* et
scribit et del. P   qui²: quia *A EIJLMOPPaRTVZ*   qui² *ex* quia *corr. C*   7 et¹:
ex quia *corr. L*   8 in saecula benedictus: benedictus in secula. Amen *R*   benedictus: amen *add. A EN*   et cetera *add. PV*

19 CAPITULUM VI

DE FACIALI VISIONE

Quanto ego, domine deus meus, diutius intueor vultum tuum, tanto mihi apparet quod acutius in me inicias aciem oculorum tuo-
5 rum. Agit autem intuitus tuus, ut considerem quomodo haec imago faciei tuae eapropter est sic sensibiliter depicta, quia depingi non potuit facies sine colore, nec color sine quantitate existit. Sed video non oculis carneis, qui hanc eiconam tuam inspiciunt, sed mentalibus et intellectualibus oculis veritatem faciei tuae invisibilem, quae in
10 umbra hic contracta significatur. Quae quidem facies tua vera est ab omni contractione absoluta. Neque enim ipsa est quanta, neque qualis, neque temporalis, neque localis. Ipsa enim est absoluta forma, quae et facies facierum. Quando igitur attendo, quomodo facies illa est veritas et mensura adaequatissima omnium facierum, ducor in
15 stuporem. Non est enim facies illa, quae est veritas omnium facierum, quanta; quare nec maior nec minor quacumque facie. Ideo aequalis omnibus et singulis, quia nec maior nec minor; nec tamen est aequalis cuiquam, quia non est quanta sed absoluta et superexaltata. Est igitur veritas, quae est aequalitas, ab omni quantitate abso-
20 luta. Sic igitur deprehendo vultum tuum, domine, antecedere omnem faciem formabilem et esse exemplar ac veritatem omnium facierum, et omnes facies esse imagines faciei tuae incontrahibilis et imparticipabilis. Omnis igitur facies quae in tuam potest intueri faciem, nihil videt aliud aut diversum a se, quia videt veritatem suam. Veritas
25 autem exemplaris non potest esse alia et diversa, sed illa accidunt

---

19 1 *numerum capituli om. CJ* capitulum VI: capitulum 7 *E⁴* 2 faciali visione: fatrali visione *A* visione faciali *CJV²p* faciali visione dei *E³G* facili visione *Pa³ et in 1:1 Q* 3 ego: ergo *LR* tempore *V* 4 tanto: tantum *P* in me inicias: inicias in me *Q* 6 tuae: tui *T* eapropter: hec *add. S* sic: *om. R* 8 carneis: *ex carnis corr. Q* inspiciunt: aspicio *G* aspiciunt *T* 10 hic contracta: contracta hic *A* vera: *om. EN* 11 omni: *om. T* contractione: contricione *A* incontractione *GT* ipsa est: est ipsa *R* neque²: *ex nequam corr. I* vel *Pa* 12 enim est: est enim *LZ* 13 et: est *AIOPPa (ad et corr. Pa²) Qp* quomodo: quoniam *A* illa: que *add. EN* 13-16 quando . . . facierum: *om. Pa* (*in marg.* quando . . . quanta *add. Pa²;* quanta *in lin. del. Pa²; pro* adaequatissima omnium facierum *habet Pa²* omnium facierum adequatissima) 14 adaequatissima omnium facierum: omnium facierum adequatissima *IJPa²* facierum: facieris *N*

19 CHAPTER SIX

|OUR| VISION OF |GOD'S| FACE

O Lord my God, the longer I behold Your Face, the more acutely You seem to me to cast the acute gaze of Your eyes upon me. Now, Your gaze causes me to reflect upon the following: that the reason this image of Your Face is depicted in the foregoing perceptible way is that a face could not have been painted without color and that color does not exist apart from quantity. But the invisible Truth of Your Face I see not with the bodily eyes which look at this icon of You but with mental and intellectual eyes. This Truth is signified by this contracted shadow-like image.[22] But Your true Face is free of all contraction. For it is neither quantitative nor qualitative nor temporal nor spatial. For it is Absolute Form, which is also the Face of faces. Therefore, when I consider that this Face is the Truth of, and the most adequate Measure of, all faces[23] I become astounded. For the Face which is the Truth of all faces is not quantitative; hence, it is not greater or lesser than any face. Because it is neither greater nor lesser, it is equal to each and every face; and yet, it is not equal to any face, because it is not quantitative but is absolute and superexalted. It is, therefore, Truth, or Equality, that is free from all quantity. In this way, then, O Lord, I apprehend that Your Face precedes every formable face and is the Exemplar and Truth of all faces—and that all faces are images of Your Face, which cannot be contracted and cannot be participated in. Therefore, every face that can look at Your Face sees nothing that is *other* than itself or *different* from itself, because it sees its own Truth. But Exemplar-Truth cannot be other or different; instead, these characteristics befall the image, by virtue

---

15 est enim: enim est *ad* est enim *transponit M aut M²* quae: *ex* quem *corr. Pa²* 16 quare: *non proprie abbreviat G* nec²: *non proprie scribit N* 16-17 quacumque . . . minor: *om. CENQVp* 17 tamen: tantum *V* 19 veritas: *in abbreviatione* s *plus elevare debet A* ab omni *add. E et del. E²* aequalitas: *ut equalis* (s *non elevatum est) scribit A* omni: *non clare scribit A* 20 deprehendo: compraehendo *p* 21 ac: et *Q* 22 et²: *bis L* 22-23 imparticipabilis: inconparticipabilis *N* 23 quae in: *om. A* in . . . intueri: potest in tuam intuere *EN* tuam: tuum *IJPa* intueri: intuere *AGIJLMOPPaQSTVZ* 24 aliud . . . videt: *om. V* suam: *om. L* 25 exemplaris: et exemplar *EGIJNPaT* esse: *om. M (in marg.*

imagini ex eo quia non est ipsum exemplar.

20   Sicut igitur dum hanc faciem pictam orientaliter inspicio, similiter apparet quod sic ipsa me respiciat, et dum occidentaliter aut meridionaliter, ipsa pariformiter, sic qualitercumque faciem meam muto, videtur facies ad me conversa. Ita est facies tua ad omnes facies te
5 intuentes conversa. Visus tuus, domine, est facies tua. Qui igitur amorosa facie te intuetur, non reperiet nisi faciem tuam se amorose intuentem. Et quanto studebit te amorosius inspicere, tanto reperiet similiter faciem tuam amorosiorem. Qui te indignanter inspicit, reperiet similiter faciem tuam talem. Qui te laete intuetur, sic reperiet
10 laetam tuam faciem, quemadmodum est ipsius te videntis. Sicut enim oculus iste carneus, per vitrum rubeum intuens, omnia quae videt rubea iudicat, et si per vitrum viride omnia viridia, sic quisque oculus mentis, obvolutus contractione et passione, iudicat te, qui es mentis obiectum, secundum naturam contractionis et passionis. Homo non
15 potest iudicare nisi humaniter. Quando enim homo tibi faciem attribuit, extra humanam speciem illam non quaerit, quia iudicium suum est infra naturam humanam contractum et huius contractionis passionem in iudicando non exit. Sic si leo faciem tibi attribueret, non nisi leoninam iudicaret, et bos bovinam et aquila aquilinam.

21   O domine, quam admirabilis est facies tua, quam si iuvenis concipere vellet, iuvenilem fingeret et vir virilem et senex senilem! Quis hoc unicum exemplar verissimum et adaequatissimum omnium facierum, ita omnium quod et singulorum, et ita perfectissime cuiuslibet

add. M²)   et: aut *p*   26 imagini: quia non *post* imagini *scribit, del., et post* eo *rescribit, E*   quia: quod *S*

20 1 pictam: *in marg. Pa*   orientaliter: origentaliter *J*   2 aut: et *A*   3 faciem meam: meam faciem *GIJT*   faciem meam *ad* meam faciem *transponit Pa aut Pa²* muto: mitto *AL*   4 facies¹: me *post* facies¹ *scribit, del., et post* ad¹ *rescribit, L* om. *Pa (supra lin. add. Pa²)*   ita est facies: *om. V*   est: es *Q*   5 intuentes: *in abbreviatione* s *plus elevare debet A*   conversa: converta *L*   tua: *om. Pa*   qui: que *V*   5-6 amorosa . . . se: *om. I*   6 nisi: *om. N* (n[-] *in marg. add. N²)*   se: te *V*   7 quanto: quando *V*   7-8 reperiet similiter: similiter reperiet *Z*   8 inspicit: respicit *GT*   8-9 amorosiorem . . . tuam: *om. ALMOPQRVZ*   10 tuam faciem: faciem tuam *ENQ*   11 iste: *in abbreviatione* t *plus elevare debet (cf. 39:8) A* rubeum: rubrum *p*   12 rubea: rubeat *S*   rubra *p*   viride: *ex* videre *corr. P* viridia: virida *NQ*   viridia *ex* virida *corr. O*   13 iudicat: iudica *T (ad iudicat corr. T³)*   15 homo tibi: tibi homo *Z*   tibi faciem: faciem tibi *ENQ*   16 illam: illud *L*   suum: eius *p*   17 naturam humanam: humanam naturam *PRp*   con-

of the fact that it is not the Exemplar.

20   Therefore, just as while I look from the east at this depicted face it seems likewise to look eastwardly at me, and just as while |I look at it| from the west or from the south it |seems| likewise |to look west-wardly or southwardly at me|, so the |depicted| face seems turned toward me regardless of how I change my face. In a similar way, Your Face is turned toward every face that looks unto You. Your gaze, O Lord, is Your Face. Accordingly, whoever looks unto You with a loving face will find only Your Face looking lovingly upon him. And the greater his endeavor to look more lovingly unto You, the more loving he will likewise find Your Face to be. Whoever looks angrily unto You will find Your Face likewise to display anger. Whoever looks unto You joyfully will find Your Face likewise to be joyous, just as is the face of him who is looking unto You. For just as the bodily eye, in looking through a red glass, judges as red what-ever it sees, and as green whatever it sees if looking through a green glass, so each mental eye, cloaked with contraction and passion, judges You who are the object of the mind, according to the nature of the contraction and the passion. A man can judge only in a human way. For example, when a man ascribes a face to You, he does not seek it outside the human species; for his judgment is contracted within human nature and does not, in judging, go beyond the passion that belongs to this contractedness. Similarly, if a lion were to ascribe to You a face, he would judge it to be only lionlike; an ox |would judge it to be only| oxlike; and an eagle |would judge it to be only| eaglelike.

21   O Lord, how admirable is Your Face! If a youth wished to con-ceive it, he would envision it as youthful; if an adult |wished to con-ceive it, he would envision it as| adult; and someone elderly |would envision it as| elderly. Who could conceive of this unique, most true, and most adequate Exemplar of all faces?—the Exemplar of each and every face and, yet, so perfectly the Exemplar of each that, as it

tractum: contracti *A*   18 in iudicando: *om. EN*   iudicando: iudicado *Pa*   leo: tibi *add. A*   faciem tibi: tibi faciem *QT*   tibi: tuam *S*

21 1 quam¹: quem *S*   tua: *om. T*   si: invenis *post* si *scribit et del. M*   2 et vir virilem: *om. S*   quis: per *add. Q*   3 unicum: unitum *J*   exemplar: exemplum *R*   verissimum: virissimum *G*   3-4 facierum: facieris *N*   4 quod: *om. CV*   et¹:

5 quasi nullius alterius, concipere posset? Oporteret illum omnium
formabilium facierum formas transilire et omnes figuras. Et quomodo conciperet faciem, quando transcenderet omnes facies et omnes
omnium facierum similitudines et figuras et omnes conceptus qui de
facie fieri possunt et omnem omnium facierum colorem et ornatum
10 et pulchritudinem? Qui igitur ad videndum faciem tuam pergit:
quamdiu aliquid concipit, longe a facie tua abest. Omnis enim conceptus de facie minor est facie tua, domine; et omnis pulchritudo
quae concipi potest, minor est pulchritudine faciei tuae. Omnes facies
pulchritudinem habent et non sunt ipsa pulchritudo. Tua autem
15 facies, domine, habet pulchritudinem, et hoc habere est esse. Est
igitur ipsa pulchritudo absoluta, quae est forma dans esse omni formae pulchrae. O facies decora nimis, cuius pulchritudinem admirari
non sufficiunt omnia quibus datur ipsam intueri.

22   In omnibus faciebus videtur facies facierum velate et in aenigmate.
Revelate autem non videtur, quamdiu super omnes facies non intratur
in quoddam secretum et occultum silentium ubi nihil est de scientia
et conceptu faciei. Haec enim caligo, nebula, tenebra, seu ignorantia
5 in quam faciem tuam quaerens subintrat, quando omnem scientiam et
conceptum transilit, est infra quam non potest facies tua nisi velate
reperiri. Ipsa autem caligo revelat ibi esse faciem supra omnia vela-
menta. Sicuti dum oculus noster lucem solis, quae est facies eius,
quaerit videre, primo ipsam velate respicit in stellis et coloribus et
10 omnibus lucem eius participantibus. Quando autem revelate intueri
ipsam contendit, omnem visibilem lucem transilit, quia omnis talis
minor est illa quam quaerit. Sed quia quaerit videre lucem quam
videre non potest, hoc scit quod quamdiu aliquid videt, non esse id

est *EN*   *ex* est *corr. L   om. p*   et[2] . . . cuiuslibet: *om. Q*   5 oporteret: oportet
LR   illum: eum *A*   6 facierum: *om. GT*   transilire: transilere *V*   7 conciperet:
non proprie scribit Pa   transcenderet: trancenderet *C* (*ad* transcenderet *corr.* *C*[2])
omnes[1]: omnis *S*   8 facierum: ita omnium quod et *add. I*   9 possunt: possent (?) *A*
omnem: *bis E* (omnem[1] *del. E*[2])   facierum: *bis V*   10 videndum: videndam *p*
11 concipit: concipitur *Q*   enim: etiam *A*   11-12 enim conceptus: conceptus enim
ad enim conceptus *transponit M aut M*[2]   12 est: conceptu *post* est *scribit et del. L*
13 concipi: *ex* concipit (?) *corr. M*   concipit *T* (*ad* concipi *corr.* *T*[2] *et T*[3])   tuae: tempore *A* (*cf. 23:15 et 31:16*)   14 pulchritudinem: pulchritudines *Q*   non: *om. R*
15 facies domine: domine facies *R*   domine: *om. Q*   habet: *ex* habent *corr. Q*
et: ob *add. S*   17-18 admirari non sufficiunt: non sufficiunt admirari *EN*
   22 4 tenebra: senebra *S*   tenebrae *p*   6 est: est *E* (*ad* et *corr. E*[n]) *et INQ*   est

were, it is not the Exemplar of any other. He would have to pass beyond all the forms and figures of all formable faces. And how could he conceive it to be a *face*, when he would transcend all faces and all likenesses and figures of all faces, as well as all concepts which can be made of a face and all color, adornment, and beauty of all faces? Therefore, as regards whoever sets out to see Your Face: as long as he conceives of something, he is far removed from Your Face. For every concept of face is less than Your Face, O Lord; and all beauty that can be conceived is less than the beauty of Your Face. All faces *have* beauty; but they are not beauty itself. But Your Face, O Lord, has beauty, and this having is being. Hence, Your Face is Absolute Beauty, which is the Form that gives being to every beautiful form. O Face exceedingly lovely! All the things which have received the gift of looking thereupon do not suffice for admiring its beauty.

22   In all faces the Face of faces is seen in a veiled and symbolic manner. But it is not seen in an unveiled manner as long as the seeker does not enter, above all faces, into a certain secret and hidden silence wherein there is no knowledge or concept of a face. For this obscuring-mist, haze, darkness, or ignorance into which the one seeking Your Face enters when he passes beyond all knowledge and conception is that beneath which Your Face can be found only in a veiled manner.[24] Yet, the obscuring mist reveals that Your Face is there, above everything beveiling. By comparison, when our eye seeks to see the sun's light, which is the sun's face, it first looks at it in a veiled manner in the stars and in colors and in all participants in the sun's light. But when our eye strives to view the sun's light in an unveiled manner, it passes beyond all visible light, because all such light is less than the light it seeks.[25] But since it seeks to see a light which it cannot see, it knows that as long as it sees something, this is

ex esse *corr. P*   infra: in qua fra (qua *deletum*) *scribit S*   7 reperiri: *ex* reperire *corr. G*   ibi: sibi *V*   supra: super *EGN*   8 sicuti: sicut *RZ*   dum: cum *R* eius: *om. Q*   9 velate: reperiri ipsa autem caligo revelat *post* velate *scribit et del. A* respicit: inspicit *CVp*   9-10 ipsam . . . eius: *om. S*   10 lucem eius: eius lucem *Z* eius: eis *N*   10-11 intueri ipsam: ipsam intueri *Zp*   11 contendit: ostendit *R* contendit *bis V*   talis: illa *R*   11-14 transilit . . . lucem: *om. I*   12 quaerit[1]: oportet igitur omnem visibilem lucem transilire *post* quaerit[1] *scribit et del. A* videre lucem: lucem videre *EN*   13 quamdiu: cum diu *Q*   id: *om. OP*   illud *Q*

quod quaerit. Oportet igitur omnem visibilem lucem transilire. Qui
15 igitur transilire debet omnem lucem, necesse est quod id quod subintrat careat visibili luce, et ita est oculo tenebra. Et cum est in tenebra
illa, quae est caligo, tunc si scit se in caligine esse, scit se ad faciem
solis accessisse. Oritur enim ex excellentia lucis solis illa caligo in
oculo. Quanto igitur scit caliginem maiorem, tanto verius attingit in
20 caligine invisibilem lucem. Video, domine, sic et non aliter inaccessibilem lucem et pulchritudinem et splendorem faciei tuae revelate
accedi posse.

23   CAPITULUM VII

QUIS FRUCTUS FACIALIS VISIONIS ET QUOMODO HABEBITUR

   Tanta est dulcedo illa qua nunc, domine, pascis animam meam, ut
se qualitercumque iuvet cum his quae experitur in hoc mundo et per
5 eas, quas tu inspiras, similitudines gratissimas! Nam cum tu sis vis
illa, domine, seu principium ex quo omnia, et facies tua sit vis illa et
principium ex quo omnes facies id sunt quod sunt, tunc me converto
ad hanc arborem nucum magnam et excelsam, cuius quaero videre
principium. Et video ipsam oculo sensibili magnam, extensam, coloratam,
10 oneratam ramis, foliis, et nucibus. Video deinde oculo mentis arborem illam fuisse in semine, non modo quo eam hic inspicio, sed vir-

14 transilire: oportet *in marg. add. I*   qui: quod *L*   15 igitur: autem vult *E*
(vult *del. E²*) autem *GIJNPaT*   quod¹: *scribit, del., et abbreviationem alio modo
supra lin. rescribit, O*   ut *p*   quod id quod: quod illud quod *Q (abbreviationes
pro* quod *transponit Q)*   id: illud *Q*   15-16 subintrat: *ex* subintrant *corr. C aut C²*
16 oculo: ut sic dicam *add. p*   tenebra¹: *ex* tenebrossa (?) *corr. J*   tenebrae *p*
cum: dum *R*   16-17 tenebra illa: tenebris illis *p*   17 est: sunt *p*   esse: *om. S*
ad: *om. Q*   18 ex: *om. AIJR*   lucis: *om. EN*   19 oculo: *ex* oculos *corr. G*
quanto . . . maiorem: *om. V*   20 caligine: *ex* caliginem *corr. I*   22 accedi:
accede *Q*   posse: et cetera *add. P*

not the thing it is seeking. Therefore, it must pass beyond all visible light. So if one has to pass beyond all light, the place into which he enters will have to be devoid of visible light; and so, for the eye, it will be darkness. Now, while he is amid that darkness, which is an obscuring mist: if he knows that he is within an obscuring mist, he knows that he has approached unto the face of the sun. For that obscuring mist arises in his eye as a result of the excellence of the light of the sun. Therefore, the more dense he knows the obscuring mist to be, the more truly he attains, within that mist, unto the invisible light. I see, O Lord, that in this way and in no other the inaccessible light and beauty and splendor of Your Face can be approached unveiledly.

23 CHAPTER SEVEN

WHAT THE FRUIT OF |OUR| VISION OF |GOD'S| FACE IS,
AND HOW THIS FRUIT WILL BE OBTAINED

O Lord, that sweetness by which You now feed my soul is so great that |my soul| is somehow aided by means of what it experiences in this world and by means of those most agreeable likenesses which You inspire. For example, since You, O Lord, are the Power, or Beginning, from which all things derive and since Your Face is the Power and Beginning from which all faces are that which they are, I turn toward this large and tall nut tree, whose Beginning I seek to see. And with the sensible eye I see that it is large, spacious, colored, laden with branches, with leaves, and with nuts. Then with the mind's eye I see that this tree existed in its seed not in the manner in

23 1 *numerum capituli om. CJ* capitulum VII: capitulum 8^{vum} *E⁴* 2 facialis: fatralis *A* 3 domine pascis: pascis domine *J* 4 iuvet: vivet *S* his: iis *p* quae: qui *JN* hoc: *om. EN* 5 tu²: *om. p* 6 sit: illa *post* sit *scribit et del. S* vis illa: illa vis *EN* 6-7 omnia . . . quo: *om. L* et principium: *om. A* 7 id sunt: sunt id *ENR* 8 magnam: extensam coloratam *post* magnam *scribit et del. S* quaero videre: videre quero *Z* 9 video: eam *post* video *scribit et del. E* videam *V* oculo sensibili: sensibili oculo *ad* oculo sensibili *transponit Pa aut Pa²* magnam: et *add. p* extensam: excelsam *J (ad* extensa *in marg. corr. Jⁿ)* 10 oneratam: onoratam *A* ramis: et *add. JS* deinde: inde *CVp* oculo: oculis *p* 11 illam:

tualiter. Attente adverto illius seminis admirabilem virtutem, in qua arbor tota ista et omnes nuces et omnis vis seminis nucum et omnes arbores in virtute seminum nucum fuerunt. Et video quomodo vis illa
15 non est ullo umquam tempore, motu caeli, ad plenum explicabilis. Sed vis illa seminis, quamquam inexplicabilis, est tamen contracta, quia non nisi in hac specie nucum virtutem habet. Quare, licet in semine videam arborem, non tamen nisi in contracta virtute.

24 Considero deinde omnem omnium arborum diversarum specierum seminariam virtutem contractam ad cuiuslibet speciem, et in ipsis seminibus video arbores in virtute. Si igitur omnium virtutum seminum talium virtutem volo videre absolutam, quae sit virtus quae et
5 principium dans virtutem omnibus seminibus, necesse est me transire omnem seminalem virtutem quae sciri et concipi potest, et subintrare ignorantiam illam in qua nihil penitus maneat virtutis aut vigoris seminalis. Et tunc in caligine reperio stupidissimam virtutem, nulla virtute quae cogitari potest accessibilem, quae est principium
10 dans esse omni virtuti seminali et non seminali. Quae quidem virtus absoluta et superexaltata, cum det cuilibet virtuti seminali virtutem talem in qua complicat virtualiter arborem, cum omnibus quae ad arborem sensibilem requiruntur et esse arboris consequuntur, tunc principium illud et causa in se habet complicite et absolute, ut causa, quid-
15 quid dat effectui. Et sic video virtutem illam esse faciem seu exemplar omnis speciei arboreae et cuiuslibet arboris, ubi video arborem illam nucum non ut in contracta virtute sua seminali, sed ut in causa et conditrice illius virtutis seminalis. Et ideo video arborem illam quandam explicationem virtutis seminalis, et semen quandam explicatio-
20 nem omnipotentis virtutis.

illa *N*   modo: modo *scribit, et? supra lin. rescribit,* L   hic: nunc *LZ*   12 attente: attendte (d *deletum*) *scribit S*   13 tota ista: ista tota *Q*   vis: *ex* visus *corr. P* nucum: inicium *EN*   14 quomodo: quoniam *R*   15 tempore: *non proprie abbreviat Pa*   16 sed . . . inexplicabilis: *om. J (in marg. add. J^n)*   seminis: nucum *add. et del. S*   inexplicabilis: explicabilis *A*   sit *add. EN*   18 contracta: *ex* contractam *corr. O*

24 1 omnem: *(cf. lineam 6)* domine *ex? corr. C²*   omnia *S*   domine *p*   diversarum: adversarum *V*   2 cuiuslibet: cuiusque *p*   4 virtutem: *om. A*   sit: est *R*   quae²: *bis Q   om. R*   5 me: *om. ALMOPQRZ*   5-6 transilire: transire *p* 6 et²: ut *J*   7 illam: illa *Q*   nihil penitus: penitus nihil *p*   7-8 vigoris: racionis *T* 8 stupidissimam: stupendissimam *Qp*   9 cogitari: cogitare *Q*   10 virtuti: *ad* virtute *corr. E ex* virtute *corr. GI*   virtute *JNPa*   quidem: quidam *V*   11 cui-

which I here behold it but potentially. I consider attentively this seed's admirable power, wherein were present the whole of this tree, all its nuts, the entire seminal power of the nuts, and, in the seminal power of the nuts, all |the derivative| trees. And I discern that this power is never at any time fully unfoldable by the motion of the heavens. Yet, the seed's power, though not |fully| unfoldable, is nevertheless contracted, because |the seed| has power only with respect to *this* species of nuts. Hence, although in the seed I see the tree, nevertheless |I see it| only in a contracted power.

24   Next, I reflect upon the entire seminal power of all the trees of various species—a power that is contracted to each species. And in the seeds I see the trees in potency. If, then, I wish to see the Absolute Power of all the powers of such seeds (this Absolute Power is the Power that is also the Beginning and that gives power to all seeds), I must pass beyond all seminal power that can be known and conceived and must enter into that ignorance wherein remains no seminal power or seminal force at all. Thereupon I will find amid obscuring mist a most stupendous Power, accessible by no conceivable power. It is the Beginning, which gives being to every power, whether seminal or nonseminal. This absolute and superexalted Power gives to each seminal power the power whereby it enfolds a tree potentially, together with |enfolding| all that is required for a sensible tree and all that follows from the being of a tree. Accordingly, this Beginning and Cause has within itself—qua Cause, and in an absolute and enfolded manner—whatever it gives to the effect. In this way I see that this Power is the Face, or Exemplar, of every arboreal species and of each tree. In this |Power| I see this nut tree not as in its own contracted seminal potency but as in the Cause and Maker of that seminal power. And so, I see that this tree is a certain unfolding of the seed's power and that the seed is a certain unfolding of Omnipotent Power.

libet: cuiuslibet *Pa*   virtuti: virtute *Pa*   12 in qua complicat: complicat in qua *I*   14 et[1]: est *Pa (ad* et *supra lin. corr. Pa*[2]*)*   ut: et *I*   causa[2]: cause *N*   14-15 quid- quid: quodquod *MOPRS*   15 effectui: *ex* effectum *corr. A*   effectum *GT*   affectui *PaS*   16 speciei: faciei *Cp*   saciei *V*   video: *om. Q*   videro *S*   illam: illum *IJPa*   17 sua: sew (=seu) *Q*   et: in *add. G*   vi *add. p   om. N*   18 conditrice: condit rite *S*   ideo: ita *EGNT*   18-19 et . . . seminalis: *om. A*   19 explicationem: ex- plicativam *IJPa*   seminalis: habere *add. E (et del. E*[2]*) N*   et: *om. L*   19-20 vir- tutis . . . explicationem: *om. G*

25   Et video quod, sicut arbor in semine non est arbor sed vis seminis, et vis illa seminis est ex qua explicatur arbor, ita quod nihil est reperibile in arbore quod non procedat ex virtute seminis, ita virtus seminalis in causa sua, quae est virtus virtutum, non est virtus seminalis, 5 sed virtus absoluta. Et ita arbor est in te deo meo tu ipse deus meus; et in te est veritas et exemplar sui ipsius. Similiter et semen arboris in te est veritas et exemplar sui ipsius. Et arboris et seminis tu, deus, es veritas et exemplar. Et vis illa seminis, quae est contracta, est vis naturae speciei, quae est ad speciem contracta, et ei inest tamquam 10 contractum principium. Sed tu, deus meus, es vis absoluta et ob hoc natura naturarum omnium.

26   O deus, quorsum me perduxisti, ut videam faciem tuam absolutam esse faciem naturalem omnis naturae, esse faciem quae est absoluta entitas omnis esse, esse artem et scientiam omnis scibilis. Qui igitur faciem tuam videre meretur, omnia aperte videt, et nihil sibi manet 5 occultum. Omnia hic scit, omnia habet, domine, qui te habet. Omnia habet qui te videt; nemo enim te videt nisi qui te habet. Nemo potest te accedere, quia inaccessibilis. Nemo igitur te capiet nisi tu te dones ei. Quomodo habebo te, domine, qui non sum dignus ut compaream in conspectu tuo? Quomodo ad te perveniet oratio mea, qui es omni 10 modo inaccessibilis? Quomodo petam te? Nam quid absurdius quam petere, ut tu te dones mihi, qui es omnia in omnibus? Et quomodo dabis tu te mihi, si non pariter dederis mihi caelum et terram et omnia quae in eis sunt? Immo quomodo dabis tu te mihi, si etiam me ipsum non dederis mihi? Et cum sic in silentio contemplationis

---

25 1 est: *supra lin. M*   2 est[1]: *om. I*   ex: *om. T*   explicatur: u *non proprie format I ex* explicit *corr. S*   3 virtus: virtutus *V*   4 est[2]: *om. R*   5 et ita: ita et *Q*   arbor: *om. R*   arbor est: est arbor *p*   est: *om. Pa (supra lin. add. Pa[2])* 6 est: *om. V*   veritas: *ex* virtus *corr. I*   virtus *QR*   exemplar: et vis illa seminis que est contracta est vis nature speciei que est *post* exemplar *scribit et del. A* ipsius: *non plene legibile J*   7 et[3]: est *Pa*   7-8 tu . . . seminis: *om. QS*   deus es: es es *V*   8 est[2]: et *I*   10 es: *non proprie scribit (cf. 51:6) L*

26 1 perduxisti: produxisti *V*   ut: quod *GT*   videam faciem tuam: faciem tuam videam *V*   faciem: *om. I*   2 naturae: creature *J (ad* nature *corr. J")* nature *Pa (abbreviationem del., et in marg. explanat, Pa[2])*   3 esse[2]: $\overline{\overline{e}}$ *Z*   4 tuam: *om. I*   sibi manet: manet ei *p*   5 domine: hic *om., et post* te habet *scribunt, EN* habet[2]: qui te *post* habet[2] *scribit et del. S   om. V*   6 habet[1]: videt *I*   te[1]: habet *post* te[1] *scribit et del. J   om. N*   videt[1]: et cetera *post* videt[1] *scribit et del. P*

25   Moreover, I see that in the seed the tree is not a tree but is the seminal power, and the seminal power is that from which the tree is unfolded, so that in the tree there can be present only what proceeds from the seed's power. Similarly, in its own Cause, which is the Power of powers, the seminal power is not seminal power but is Absolute Power. And so, in You my God the tree is You Yourself my God; and in You it is the Truth and Exemplar of itself. Likewise, too, in You the seed of the tree is the Truth and Exemplar of itself. Of both the tree and the seed You, O God, are the Truth and Exemplar. And that seminal power, which is contracted, is the natural power of the species; it is contracted to the species and is present in the species as a contracted beginning. But You, my God, are Absolute Power and, hence, the Nature of all natures.

26   O God, You have led me to the place where I see Your Absolute Face to be (1) the natural Face of every nature, (2) the Face which is the Absolute Being of all being, (3) the Art and Knowledge of everything knowable. So whoever merits to see Your Face sees all things plainly, and nothing remains hidden from him. He who has You, O Lord, knows and has all things. He who sees You has all things, for no one sees You except him who has You. No one can approach unto You, because You are unapproachable. Therefore, no one will apprehend You unless You give Yourself to Him. How will I have You, O Lord?—I who am not worthy to appear in Your presence. How will my prayer reach You who are altogether unapproachable? How will I entreat You? For what is more absurd than to ask that You, who are all in all, give Yourself to me? How will You give Yourself to me unless You likewise give to me the sky and the earth and everything in them? Indeed, how will You give Yourself to me unless You also give me to myself? And while I am quietly reflecting in this manner,

7 te¹: *supra lin. Pa om. T*   accedere: accidere *P*   quia: *ex* qui *corr. R*   inaccessibilis: es *add. p*   tu: deus *post* tu *scribit et del. O*   te³: *om. R*   7-8 dones ei: ei dones *Q*   8 quomodo: quo modo *p*   habebo: habeo *CIVp*   compaream: compariam *G*   appaream *L*   9 quomodo: quo modo *p*   ad te perveniet: perveniet ad te *R*   perveniet: perveniat *LS*   veniet *N* (p.?[-] *in marg. add N²)*   preveniet *O*   pervenit *Qp*   mea: meo *Q*   9-10 omni modo: omnino *IL*   11 petere: *om. L*   es: *bis A*   12 dabis tu: tu dabis *V*   dabis tu te: tu te dabis *Pa*   pariter dederis mihi: dederis michi pariter *R*   mihi²: *om. L*   13 dabis tu te: tu te dabis *PaV*   13-14 si . . . mihi: *om. Q*   me ipsum: memetipsum *R*   14 cum: dum *R*   15 qui-

15 quiesco, tu, domine, intra praecordia mea respondes dicens: "Sis tu tuus et ego ero tuus."

27 O domine, suavitas omnis dulcedinis, posuisti in libertate mea ut sim, si voluero, mei ipsius. Hinc nisi sim mei ipsius, tu non es meus; necessitares enim libertatem, cum tu non possis esse meus nisi et ego sim mei ipsius. Et quia hoc posuisti in libertate mea, non me necessi-
5 tas, sed expectas ut ego eligam mei ipsius esse. Per me igitur stat, non per te, domine, qui non contrahis bonitatem tuam maximam, sed largissime effundis in omnes capaces. Tu autem, domine, es bonitas tua.

28 Quomodo autem ero mei ipsius nisi tu, domine, docueris me? Hoc autem tu me doces, ut sensus oboediat rationi et ratio dominetur. Quando igitur sensus servit rationi, sum mei ipsius. Sed non habet ratio unde dirigatur nisi per te, domine, qui es verbum et ratio ratio-
5 num. Unde, nunc video, si audiero verbum tuum, quod in me loqui non cessat et continue lucet in ratione, ero mei ipsius—liber et non servus peccati—et tu eris meus et dabis mihi videre faciem tuam, et tunc salvus ero. Benedictus sis igitur, deus, in donis tuis, qui solus potens es consolari animam meam et erigere, ut speret te ipsum as-
10 sequi et te frui uti suo proprio dono et omnium desiderabilium thesauro infinito.

---

esco: michi *add. EGNT*   intra: inter *L*   sis: eris *S*   16 ego: *ex* ergo *corr. I*

27 1 suavitas: *ut* suavis (=suavi^s) *scribit A*   2 mei ipsius^1: meipsius *C (hic et alias ad* meiipsius *corr. C^2)*   mei ipsius *ex* meis ipsius *corr. G*   ipsius^1: tu non es meus necessitares enim libertatem cum tu non possis esse meus nisi ego sim mei ipsius *post* ipsius^1 *scribit et del. P*   hinc nisi sim mei ipsius: *om. I*   nisi: ut *L* *abbreviationem non proprie format Q*   3 et: *om. N*   4 mei ipsius: meiipsius *ex* meipsius *corr. Pa*   mea: *confuse abbreviat Pa*   5 ego: *om. R*   7 effundis: effundes *R*

28 1 autem: *om. Pa (supra lin. add. Pa^2)*   3 quando: quomodo *JV*   4 unde: dominetur *post* unde *scribit et del. E*   domine: *om. R*   6 mei ipsius: mei met ipsius *Q*   7 servus: servitus *A*   tu: *ex* tue *corr. L*   mihi: *om. CVp*   8 sis igitur: igitur sis *G*   9 es: et *S*   consolari: consalari *Q*   ipsum: ipsam *S*   10 omnium: *non proprie scribit V*   desiderabilium: causare *add. A*

You, O Lord, answer me in my heart with the words: "Be your own and I will be yours."

27   O Lord, Sweet Agreeableness of all sweetness, You have placed within my freedom my being my own if I will to. Hence, unless I am my own You are not mine. For |if You were mine when I did not will to be my own| You would be coercing my freedom, since You can be mine only if I too am mine. And because You have placed this matter within my freedom, You do not coerce me; rather, You await my choosing to be my own. This matter is up to me, then, not up to You, O Lord, who do not constrict Your maximum goodness but most generously shed it on all who are able to receive it. But You, O Lord, *are* Your goodness.

28   Yet, how will I be my own unless You, O Lord, teach me how? But You teach me that the senses should obey reason and that reason should govern. Therefore, when the senses serve reason, I am my own. But reason has no one to direct it except You, O Lord, who are the Word and the Rational Principle (*ratio*) of rational principles. Hence, I now see the following: if I hearken unto Your Word, which does not cease to speak within me and which continually shines forth in my reason, I shall be my own—free and not a servant of sin—and You will be mine and will grant me to see Your Face and then I shall be saved.[26] May You, therefore, be blessed in Your gifts, O God— You, who alone are able to comfort and encourage my soul, so that it may hope to attain unto You and to enjoy You as being its own gift and as being the infinite treasure of all delights.

29

CAPITULUM VIII

QUOMODO VISIO DEI EST AMARE, CAUSARE, LEGERE, ET IN SE OMNIA HABERE

Non quiescit cor meum, domine, quia amor tuus ipsum inflam-
5 mavit desiderio tali, quod non nisi in te solo quiescere potest. Incepi
orare dominicam orationem, et tu inspirasti mihi, ut attenderem quomodo tu es pater noster. Amare tuum est videre tuum. Paternitas tua
est visio quae nos omnes amplectitur paterne; dicimus enim "pater
noster." Es enim universalis pater pariter et singularis. Quisque enim
10 dicit quia tu es pater noster. Paternus amor omnes et singulos filios
comprehendit. Ita enim diligit omnes pater quod singulos, quia ita
omnium pater quod singulorum. Ita unumquemque filium diligit
quod quisque filiorum se omnibus praeferri concipit.

30 Si igitur tu es pater et noster pater, nos igitur tui filii. Praevenit
autem paterna dilectio filialem. Quamdiu nos tui filii te ut filii intu-
emur, tu non cessas nos paterne respicere. Eris igitur provisor noster
paternus, curam de nobis habens paternam. Visio tua providentia est.
5 Quod si nos filii tui abdicamus te patrem, desinimus esse filii. Nec
sumus tunc liberi filii in nostra potestate, sed imus in regionem lon-
ginquam, separantes nos a te; et tunc subimus servitutem gravem sub
principe, qui tibi deo adversatur. Sed tu, pater, qui (ob concessam
nobis libertatem quia filii tui sumus, qui es ipsa libertas) quamquam

---

29 1 capitulum VIII: capitulum nonum E^4 2 quomodo: quod E^3 causare:
causare E^3 *(in 1:1 ad* cantare *corr. E^3)*   2-3 causare . . . habere: causare creare
legere et omnia in se habere *A*   creare legere et omnia in se habere Q^2 *(in 1:1* causare
legere et in se omnia habere *habet Q)*   3 in se omnia: omnia in se AE^3LM^3O
P^3Q^2R *(in 1:1* in se omnia *habent MOPQR)*   habere: tenere *Cp*   4 *divisionem
non facit N*   non quiescit: conquiescit *S*   ipsum: ipsam *J*   5 desiderio tali: tali
desiderio *Q*   6 et: ut *LOP*   tu: *om. Q*   inspirasti: inspirirasti *V*   ut attenderem:
in marg. P   6-7 quomodo: quoniam *I*   qui *V*   quo modo *p*   8 visio: tua *add. p*
nos omnes: omnes nos *Z*   omnes: *om. T*   9 es:est *I*   pariter: *om. p*   quisque:
quisquis *AL*   10 quia tu es: *om. EN*   12 omnium pater: pater omnium *EN*
pater quod: paterque *J*   filium: filiorum *p*   diligit: *om. I*   13 se omnibus: pre
omnibus se *Z*   praeferri: preferre *I*   concipit: accipit *Q*
30 1 et: *om. I*   nos: *om. I*   tui filii: filii tui *EZ*   filii tuo *N*   2 autem: igi-

29 CHAPTER EIGHT

GOD'S VISION IS LOVING, CAUSING, READING, AND
THE HAVING WITHIN ITSELF OF ALL THINGS

My heart is not at rest, O Lord, because Your love has inflamed it
with such desire that only in You alone can it find rest.[27] I began to
pray the Lord's Prayer, and You inspired me to attend to how it is
that You are our father. Your loving is Your seeing. Your paternity is
the seeing which paternally embraces us all, for we say "Our Father."
For You are father of each and all alike. For |in praying the prayer|
each confesses that You are "Our Father." Your paternal love com-
prehends each and every son. For the Father loves all sons in such
way that He loves each son, because He is father of all in such way
that He is father of each. He loves each son in such way that each
son conceives himself to be preferred over all others.

30 If, then, You are father and are our father, we are, accordingly,
Your sons. But paternal love precedes filial love. As long as we, Your
sons, look unto You as sons, You do not cease to look upon us as
father. Thus, You will be our paternal provider, showing paternal
concern for us. Your seeing is Your providence. But if we, Your sons,
renounce You who are our father, we cease being Your sons. And in
that case we are not sons who are free and who are under our own
power, but we depart to a distant region, separating ourselves from
You; and thereupon we undergo harsh servitude to a ruler who is an
adversary to You our God. But You, Father, who allow us (on
account of the freedom conceded to us because we are the sons of
You who are freedom itself) to depart and to waste our freedom and

tur Z   filialem: *non proprie scribit Pa*   tui filii: filii tui *Q* (tuo *post* filii *scribit et
del. Q*)   3 non: *ex* nos *corr. R*   nos: *om. Q*   respicere: inspicere *GIJNPaT*
noster: curam *post* noster *scribit E et del. E²*   4 de nobis habens: habens de
nobis *Q*   providentia est: est providencia *Q*   est: *om. V*   5 abdicamus: ob-
dicamus *Pa*   adicamus *T* (ab *pro* a¹ *in marg. scribit T²*)   8 tibi: *om. L*   deo:
contrariatur et *add. Q*   sed: si *T*   ob: *om. Q*   9 ipsa libertas: libertas ipsa *I*

10 sinas nos abire et libertatem et substantiam optimam consumere secundum sensuum corrupta desideria, tamen non penitus nos deseris. Sed, continue sollicitando, ades et in nobis loqueris et nos revocas ut ad te redeamus, paratus semper respicere nos priori paterno oculo, si reversi et ad te conversi fuerimus. O pie deus, respice in me,
15 qui, compunctus, de misero servitio lubricae foeditatis porcorum, ubi fame defeci, nunc revertor, ut in domo tua qualitercumque pasci queam. Pasce me visu tuo, domine; et doce quomodo visus tuus videt omnem visum videntem et omne visibile et omnem actum visionis, et omnem virtutem videntem et omnem virtutem visibilem et omne ex
20 ipsis exsurgens videre. Quia videre tuum est causare, omnia vides qui omnia causas.

31   Doce me, domine, quomodo unico intuitu omnia simul et singulariter discernas. Cum aperio librum ad legendum, video confuse totam chartam. Et si volo discernere singulas litteras, syllabas, et dictiones, necesse est ut me singulariter ad singula seriatim convertam. Et non
5 possum nisi successive unam post aliam litteram legere et unam dictionem post aliam et passum post passum. Sed tu, domine, simul totam chartam respicis, et legis sine mora temporis. Et si duo nostrum legunt idem, unus citius alius tardius, cum utroque legis; et videris in tempore legere, quia legis cum legentibus. Et supra tem-
10 pus omnia vides et legis simul; videre enim tuum est legere tuum. Omnes libros scriptos, et qui scribi possunt, simul et semel supra moram temporis ab aeterno vidisti, et legisti simul; et cum hoc cum omnibus legentibus eosdem legis seriatim. Nec aliud legis in aeternitate et aliud in tempore cum legentibus, sed idem—eodem te modo

10 nos: non *N*   12 continue: continuo *Q*   nos: non *Pa (ad* nos *supra lin. corr. Pa²)*   12-13 revocas: *non proprie scribit L*   13 respicere nos: nos respicere *ENQ*   14 et: *om. CVp*   fuerimus: fuerius *Pa*   15 servitio: sed vicio *I*   16 revertor: revertar *AGZ*   ut: *om. N*   domo: doma *N*   17 visu: *ex* visa *corr. S*   doce: me *add. ALNQR*   videt: *bis L*   18 videntem: viventem *R*   omne . . . et³: *om. I*   18-19 et¹. . . videntem: *om. S*   19 ex: ex eis *ante* ex *scribit et del. S*   20 exsurgens: exurgens *AC (ad* exsurgens *corr. C²) EGIJLMNOPPaQRTZp*   qui: quia *NR*
31 1 doce: do te *G*   quomodo: quoniam *S*   unico: et *post* unico *scribit et del. E*   unico intuitu omnia: omnia et singula uno intuitu *R*   omnia: *om. CVp*
2 ad legendum: *om. V*   confuse: omnem *post* confuse *scribit et del. A*   2-3 totam chartam: cartam totam *ad* totam cartam *transponit A*   cartam totam *I*   3 si: *om. G*   volo: voluero *I*   et²: *om. R*   4 me: *om. EN*   singulariter: discernas *add. et*

our best substance in accordance with the corrupt desires of the senses: You do not, for all that, altogether desert us. Rather, continually showing concern for us, You are present to us, and You speak within us and call upon us to return unto You. And You are always ready to look upon us with Your earlier paternal eye if we turn back and turn unto You. O gracious God, look upon me, who, remorseful, now turn back from wretched servitude—swinelike in its slimy filth, and in which servitude I was famishing—in order somehow to be fed in Your house.[28] Feed me by Your gaze, O Lord. And teach me how it is that Your gaze sees all sight that sees, every object that can be seen, and every act of seeing, as well as all power to see, all power to be seen, and every actual seeing that arises from both. Since Your seeing is causing, You who cause all things see all things.

31　　Teach me, O Lord, how it is that by a single viewing You discern all things individually and at once. When I open a book, for reading, I see the whole page confusedly. And if I want to discern the individual letters, syllables, and words, I have to turn to each individually and successively. And only successively can I read one letter after another, one word after another, |one| passage after another. But You, O Lord, behold at once the entire page, and You read it without taking any time. Now, if two of us men read the same thing, one more quickly and the other more slowly, You read with both of us; and You seem to read in time, because You read with us who are reading. But above time You see and read all things at once; for Your seeing is Your reading. Simultaneously—from eternity and beyond all passing of time—You have viewed all books that have been written and that can be written, and You have read them at once; but You also now read them successively, in accompaniment of all who are reading them. You do not read one thing in eternity and another thing in time, in accompaniment of those who are reading. Rather,

del. I　singulariter ad singula: ad singula singulariter *ad* singulariter ad singula *transponit R*　singula: *ex* singulariter *corr. I*　seriatim: sereatim *Pa*　6 et: *om. EN*　passum[1]: et *add. S*　simul: domine *post* simul *scribit et del. J*　6-7 simul totam chartam: totam cartam simul *V*　8 legunt: unum *post* legunt *scribit et del. Q* alius: unus *OP*　alter *p*　9 videris: cum et *add. R*　tempore: *non proprie abbreviat Pa*　10 videre enim: enim videre *V*　tuum[1]: *om. S*　11 qui: que *Q* 11-12 simul . . . simul: *om. J (in marg. add. J″; et post* semel *add. J″)*　14 tempore: *non proprie abbreviat Pa*　cum legentibus: *om. EN*　sed: sit *I*　te modo: modo

15 habens, quia non es mutabilis, cum sis fixa aeternitas. Aeternitas autem, quia non deserit tempus, cum tempore moveri videtur, licet motus in aeternitate sit quies.

32   Domine, tu vides et habes oculos. Es igitur oculus, quia habere tuum est esse. Ob hoc in te ipso omnia specularis. Nam si in me visus esset oculus, sicut in te deo meo, tunc in me omnia viderem, cum oculus sit specularis; et speculum quantumcumque parvum in se 5 figurative recipiat montem magnum et cuncta quae in eius montis superficie existunt. Et sic omnium species sunt in oculo speculari. Tamen quia visus noster non videt per medium oculi specularis, nisi id particulariter ad quod se convertit, quia vis eius non potest nisi particulariter determinari per obiectum, ideo non videt omnia quae in 10 speculo oculi capiuntur. Sed visus tuus, cum sit oculus seu speculum vivum, in se omnia videt. Immo quia causa omnium visibilium, hinc omnia in causa et ratione omnium, hoc est in se ipso, complectitur et videt. Oculus tuus, domine, sine flexione ad omnia pergit. Quod enim oculus noster se ad obiectum flectit, ex eo est quia visus noster 15 per angulum quantum videt. Angulus autem oculi tui, deus, non est quantus, sed est infinitus, qui est et circulus, immo et sphaera infinita, quia visus est oculus sphaericitatis et perfectionis infinitae. Omnia igitur in circuitu et sursum et deorsum simul videt.

33   O quam admirandus est visus tuus, qui est theos, deus, omnibus ipsum perscrutantibus! Quam pulcher et amabilis est omnibus te diligentibus! Quam terribilis est omnibus qui dereliquerunt te, domine

---

te *AVZ* modo te *ad* te modo *transponit R*   15 quia: et *L*   16 non: *ex* nos *corr. L*   tempore: *non proprie abbreviat Pa*   17 quies: quatenus *N (*qu[-] *in marg. coni. N²)*

   32 1 et: *om. S*   oculus: *ex* oculos *corr. L*   2 esse: tuum *post* esse *scribit et del. I*   tuum *add. R*   ob hoc: *ex* o hoc *corr. Q*   ipso: *om. Q*   3 esset: *bis E* (esset¹ *del. E²) bis N*   sicut . . . tunc: *hic om. E (in marg. add. E³*; sicut in te deo meo [*et rasura*] *post* viderem *ponit E)*   sicut . . . viderem: in me omnia viderem sicut in te deo meo. Tunc *N*   in²: te *post* in² *scribit et del. O*   4 quantumcumque: quantumqcumque (q² *deletum) scribit S*   parvum: sit *add. R*   5 figurative: *ex* figurativum *corr. G*   recipiat: recipit *Z* respiciat *p*   montis: *om. EN* monte *Q* 6 sic: sicut *IP*   7 tamen quia: tamenque *A*   oculi specularis: specularis oculi *E* (oculi *ex* oculis *corr. E) N*   8 id: *om. Q*   quod: o *non proprie format G* potest: *non clare scribit L*   8-9 ad . . . . particulariter: *om. J* (ad quod se convertit [-] vis eius non potest [-] particulariter deter[-] *in marg. add. Jⁿ)*   9 ideo: igitur *A*

You read |one and| the same thing—doing so in |one and| the same manner, because You are not mutable, since You are fixed eternity. But since eternity does not desert time, it seems to be moved with time, even though in eternity motion is rest.[29]

32   O Lord, You see and You have eyes. Therefore, You are an eye, because Your having is being. Accordingly, You behold within Yourself all things. For if in *me* sight were the eye—as is the case with You my God—then I would view within myself all things. For the eye is like a mirror; and a mirror, however small, figuratively receives into itself a large mountain and all that is on the surface of the mountain. And in this way the visible forms of all things are mirrored in the eye. Nevertheless, by means of the mirroring eye our sight sees only and particularly that to which it turns; for the power of the eye can be determined by the object only in a particular way. Consequently, it does not see all the things which are captured in the mirror of the eye. But since Your sight *is* an eye, i.e., a living mirror, it sees within itself all things. Indeed, because it is the Cause of all visible things, it embraces and sees all things in the Cause and Rational Principle of all things, viz., in itself. Your eye, O Lord, proceeds to all things without turning. The reason our eye turns toward an object is that our sight sees from an angle of a certain magnitude. But the angle of Your eye, O God, is not of a certain magnitude but is infinite. Moreover, the angle of Your eye is a circle—or better, an infinite sphere—because Your sight is an eye of sphericity and of infinite perfection.[30] Therefore, Your sight sees—roundabout and above and below—all things at once.

33   To all who examine it, my God, how admirable is Your sight, which is *theos*![31] How beautiful and lovable it is to all who love You! How terrifying it is to all who forsake You, O Lord my God! For by

10 tuus: domine *add. IJPa*   seu: se *I*   12 omnia: *ex* omnium *corr. I   om. N* in[1]: *supra lin. I*   ipso: ipsa *EN*   14 quia: quod *CVp*   15 angulum: angelum *S* angulus: angelus *S*   oculi tui: tui oculi *R*   16 est[1]: *om. EN*   et[1]: *om. p*   circulus: oculus *IJPa*   immo: *om. T*   17 visus: tuus *add. p*   18 sursum: *non proprie abbreviat M*   simul videt: videt simul *EJN*

33 1 est[1]: *om. T*   est[2]: es *EGIJT*   est *Pa (ad* es *corr. Pa[2])*   est theos deus: es deus theos deus *N*   2 et: est *V*   est: es *EN*   3 quam: quia *V*   est: es *EN* dereliquerunt: derelinquunt *Q*   derelinquerunt *SV*   dereliquerunt te: te derelin-

deus meus! Visu enim vivificas, domine, omnem spiritum et laetificas
5 omnem beatum et fugas omnem maestitiam. Respice igitur in me
misericorditer, et salva facta est anima mea.

34   CAPITULUM IX

QUOMODO EST UNIVERSALIS PARITER ET PARTICULARIS,
ET QUAE VIA AD VISIONEM DEI

   Admiror, domine, postquam tu simul omnes et singulos respicis,
5 uti haec etiam picta figurat imago quam intueor, quomodo coincidat
in virtute tua visiva universale cum singulari. Sed attendo quod propterea non capit imaginatio mea quomodo hoc fiat, quia quaero in
virtute visiva mea visionem tuam, quae cum non sit ad organum sensibile contracta, sicut mea, ideo decipior in iudicio.
35   Visus tuus, domine, est essentia tua. Si igitur ad humanitatem,
quae est simplex et una in omnibus hominibus, respexero, reperio
ipsam in omnibus et singulis hominibus. Et quamvis in se non sit nec
orientalis nec occidentalis nec meridionalis nec septentrionalis, tamen
5 in hominibus orientalibus est in oriente et in occidentalibus in occidente. Et sic, quamvis de essentia humanitatis non sit motus nec
quies, movetur tamen cum moventibus hominibus et quiescit cum
quiescentibus et stat cum stantibus, simul et semel pro eodem nunc,
quia non deserit homines humanitas, sive moveantur sive non movean-
10 tur sive dormiant sive quiescant. Unde haec natura humanitatis, quae
est contracta et non reperitur extra homines, si illa sic se habet quod

---

quunt *A*   te dereliquerunt *N*   4 spiritum: speciem *G*   5 maestitiam: *non proprie
scribit Pa*   in: *om. N*   6 mea: et cetera *add. P*
   34 1 capitulum IX: capitulum X *E³*   3 et . . . dei: *om. Q²* (*in 1:1* et . . . dei
habet Q)   4 *divisionem non facit N*   admiror: adiutor *aut* adnitor *L*   postquam: post *V*   simul: *om. RV*   singulos: singulas *Q*   5 uti: ut *G*   haec etiam:
etiam hec *R*   eciam hec *V*   figurat: figurat *ex* figatur (*?*) *corr. C*   figatur *M*
(figurat *in marg. coni. M²*) figant *Q*   figura *ex* figuratur *corr. S*   figura *V*
6 tua: *om. I*   visiva: *ex ? sub lin. corr. Q*   cum *post* visiva *scribit et del. T*
singulari: *ex* singulare *corr. G*   7 imaginatio mea: mea imaginacio *Q*   8 sit:
om. E (add. E²) N   organum: ordanum *L*   9 contracta: contractum *EN*
   35 1 igitur: igitus *S*   2 una: unam *V*   in: *om. V*   reperio: *om. Pa* (*in
marg. add. Pa²*) reperior *Q*   2-3 hominibus . . . omnibus: *om. OP*   3 quamvis:

Your vision, O Lord, You enliven every spirit, You gladden all who are made glad, and You dispel all sorrow. Look, then, mercifully upon me, and my soul shall be saved.

34   CHAPTER NINE

|GOD'S VISION| IS BOTH UNIVERSAL AND PARTICULAR;
AND WHAT THE WAY TO SEEING GOD IS

Since You behold at once each and every one |of us|—even as is befigured by this painted image that I look upon—I am amazed, O Lord, at how in Your visual power the universal coincides with the singular. But I take note of the following: that because I seek |to understand| Your vision in terms of my own visual power, my imagination does not grasp how this |coincidence| can occur; since Your vision is not contracted to a sensible organ, as is mine, I am deceived in my judgment.

35   Your sight, O Lord, is Your essence. If, then, I consider human nature, which is simple and singular in all men, I find it in each and every man. And although in itself it is not in the east or the west or the south or the north, nevertheless in men who are in the east it is in the east, and in men who are in the west it is in the west. And likewise: although neither motion nor rest belong to the essence of humanity, nevertheless at one and the same time humanity is moved with men who move, it rests with men who are resting, and it remains stationary with men who are stationary. For humanity does not desert men, whether they are moved or are not moved, whether they are sleeping or resting. Hence, human nature, which is contracted and which does not exist apart from human beings,[32] is such that it is present to one man as much as to another; yet, it is so

quam *OP*   nec: *om. EN*   neque *V*   4 nec¹: et *EN*   neque *V*   meridionalis: merioda *L*   5 occidentalibus: occidente talibus *A*   est *post* occidentalibus *add. CVp et add. et del. P*   5-6 occidente: et cetera *add. EN*   7 movetur: *ex* moventur *corr. I*   8 nunc: numeri *V*   9 homines: hominis *C (ad* homines *corr. C²*)   homines *bis M* (homines¹ *del. Mⁿ*)   humanitas: humanitatis *V*   moveantur: moveatur *OP*   9-10 moveantur: moveatur *OP*   10 quiescant: requiescant *I*   humanitatis: est *post* humanitatis *scribit et del. Q*   11 si: sicut *I*   sic *JPa*   habet:

non plus uni homini adest quam alteri, et ita perfecte uni quasi nulli
alteri, multo altius humanitas incontracta, quae est exemplar et idea
istius contractae naturae et quae est ut forma et veritas istius formae
15 humanitatis contractae. Nam humanitatem contractam in individuis
numquam deserere potest. Est enim forma dans esse ipsi naturae
formali. Non igitur sine ipsa esse potest specifica forma, cum per se
non habeat esse. Est enim ab illa quae per se est, ante quam non est
alia. Forma igitur illa quae dat esse speciei est absoluta forma; et tu
20 es illa, deus, qui es formator caeli et terrae et omnium.

36   Quando igitur respicio ad humanitatem contractam et per illam ad
absolutam—scilicet videndo in contracto absolutum, ut in effectu
causam et in imagine veritatem et exemplar—occurris tu mihi, deus
meus, quasi exemplar omnium hominum et homo per se, hoc est
5 absolutus. Quando autem similiter in cunctis speciebus me ad formam formarum converto, in omnibus tu mihi ut idea et exemplar
occurris. Et quia tu es absolutum exemplar et simplicissimum, non es
compositus ex pluribus exemplaribus, sed es unum exemplar simplicissimum infinitum, ita quod omnium et singulorum, quae formari
10 possunt, es verissimum et adaequatissimum exemplar. Es igitur essentia essentiarum, dans contractis essentiis ut id sint quod sunt. Extra
igitur te, domine, nihil esse potest.

37   Si igitur essentia tua penetrat omnia, igitur et visus tuus, qui est
essentia tua. Sicut igitur nihil omnium quae sunt potest fugere ab
esse suo proprio, ita nec ab essentia tua, quae dat esse essentiae
omnibus; quare nec visum tuum. Omnia igitur et singula simul tu,
5 domine, vides. Et cum omnibus quae moventur moveris, et cum stan-

---

habent *T*   12 homini: hominum *V*   perfecte: perfecta *EN*   quasi: quam *I*
quem *V*   13 multo: multa *S*   altius: alcius *habet A (cf. in A alias abbreviationes
quoad lineas 100:13, 104:9, 104:10, 109:12-13)*   14 istius¹: illius *I*   formae:
forme *Pa (abbreviationem del., et in marg. explanat, Pa²)*   14-15 et¹. . .
contractae: *om. S*   17 esse potest: potest esse *EN*   specifica: specifoca *P*
19 igitur: *bis R* (igitur² *del. R*)   20 deus: meus *add. EN*   es²: est *S*   formator:
fomator *A*

36 1 contractam: et contractam *add. E (et del. E²) N*   2 effectu: effctu *Pa*
4 meus: *om. Q*   omnium hominum: *ad* omni homini *corr. G*   hoc: non *OP*
5 similiter: *ex* simpliciter *corr. O*   speciebus: *om. I*   me: *om. G*   5-6 formam:
*bis C (*formam² *del. C aut C²)*   7 absolutum: abtum (=abᵗᵘᵐ=absolutum *hic et
alias) A*   es²: *ex* est *corr. J*   est *S*   8 ex: *supra lin. I*   pluribus: *om. I*
8-9 simplicissimum: non es compositus *post* simplicissimum *scribit et del. M* et
add. Z   9 singulorum quae: singulorumque *N*   12 igitur te: te igitur *CENVp*

completely present to one man that, as it were, it is not present to any other. If so, then in a much higher way |the case is parallel regarding| Uncontracted Humanity,[33] which is the Exemplar and Idea of the contracted human nature and which exists as the Form of, and Truth of, the form of the contracted humanity. For Uncontracted Humanity can never desert the humanity that is contracted in individual human beings. For it is the Form which gives being to that formal nature |viz., to contracted humanity|. Without this Form, then, the specific form cannot exist, since it does not exist through itself. For the specific form derives from the Form which exists through itself and prior to which there is no other form. Therefore, that Form which gives specific being is Absolute Form; and You are this Form, O God—You, who are Former of heaven and earth and all things.[34]

36   Therefore, when I view contracted humanity and, by means of it, view Absolute Humanity (viz., by seeing in the contracted the Absolute, as in an effect the cause is seen and in an image the truth and exemplar is seen), You appear to me, my God, as the Exemplar of all men and as Human Nature per se, i.e., as Absolute Human Nature. But likewise, when with regard to all species I turn to |consider| the Form of forms: in all these species You appear to me as the Idea and Exemplar. And because You are the absolute and most simple Exemplar, You are not composed of many exemplars, but You are one most simple infinite Exemplar, so that You are the truest and most adequate Exemplar of each and every thing that can be formed.[35] Therefore, You are the Essence of essences,[36] giving to contracted essences that they be that which they are. Apart from You, then, O Lord, nothing can exist.[37]

37   If, then, Your essence penetrates all things, then so too does Your sight, which is Your essence. Therefore, just as none of all existing things can escape from its own being, so neither |can it escape| from Your essence, which gives to all things their essential being. Consequently, no |existing thing can escape from| Your sight, either. Thus, You see each and every thing at once, O Lord. And You are moved with all that is moved, and You remain stationary with all that is

te: *supra lin. scribit C aut C²*   domine . . . potest: nichil esse potest domine *A*

37 2 nihil omnium: omnium nichil *A*   2-3 ab . . . tua: esse suum proprium ita nec essentiam tuam *p*   3 suo proprio: proprio suo *Q*   ab essentia: absencia *J* essentiae: essenciis *EN*   4 quare: *non proprie scribit Pa*   simul: *om. EN*   tu:

tibus stas. Et quia reperiuntur quae aliis stantibus moventur, tunc tu, domine, stas simul et moveris, progrederis simul et quiescis. Si enim moveri reperitur simul tempore cum quiescere in diversis contracte et nihil extra te esse potest, nec motus extra te est nec quies; omnibus 10 illis simul et semel et cuilibet totus ades, domine. Nec tamen moveris nec quiescis, quia es superexaltatus et absolutus ab omnibus illis, quae concipi aut nominari possunt. Stas igitur et progrederis, et neque stas neque progrederis, simul. Facies haec depicta mihi ostendit idipsum. Nam si moveor, apparet visus eius moveri quia me non 15 deserit. Si, me movente, alius qui faciem intuetur stat, similiter eum visus non deserit, sed stat cum stante. Tamen proprie non potest faciei absolutae ab his respectibus convenire quod stet et moveatur, quia est supra omnem stationem et motum in simplicissima et absolutissima infinitate. Post quam quidem infinitatem est motus et quies 20 et oppositio et quidquid dici aut concipi potest.

38   Unde experior quomodo necesse est me intrare caliginem et admittere coincidentiam oppositorum super omnem capacitatem rationis et quaerere ibi veritatem ubi occurrit impossibilitas. Et supra illam, omnem etiam intellectualem altissimum ascensum, quando pervenero 5 ad id quod omni intellectui est incognitum et quod omnis intellectus iudicat remotissimum a veritate, ibi es tu, deus meus, qui es absoluta necessitas. Et quanto impossibilitas illa caliginosa cognoscitur magis obscura et impossibilis, tanto verius necessitas relucet et minus velate adest et appropinquat.

tue *L*   6 quae: qui *ACLMOPQRSVZp*   7 moveris: et *add. G*   progrederis: progredieris *Pa*   8 moveri: movere *P*   tempore: *non proprie abbreviat Pa*   contracte: contractum *CVp*   9 potest: *ex* possunt *corr. P*   te²: *om. I*   9-10 omnibus illis: illis omnibus *V*   10 et²: ac *V*   cuilibet: *ex* cuiuslibet *corr. Pa*   totus ades: ades totus *A*   11 quia: qui *T*   superexaltatus et absolutus: absolutus et superexaltatus *Z*   ab: ob *p*   12 aut nominari possunt: possunt aut nominari *ENR* progrederis: progredieris *V*   13 neque²: nec *IQ* et *S*   13-14 mihi ostendit: ostendit michi *EN*   14 idipsum: idipsum *habet Pa (abbreviationem del., et in marg. explanat, Pa²)*   ad ipsum *V*   15 faciem intuetur: intuetur faciem *Z* (meam *post* faciem *scribit Z et del. Z aut Z²*)   eum: *non proprie scribit S* eum (?) *V* 15-16 si . . . deserit: *om. G*   eum visus: visus eum *NR*   16 visus: usus *Pa*   tamen: cum *J*   17 absolutae: ab te (=absolute) *A*   his: aliis *IJPa*   convenire: convertere *V*   et: aut *p*   moveatur: *non plene legibile, causa lacunae, in codice V* 18 est: *ex* et *corr. I*   supra: super *J*   et motum: *in marg. T*   in: et *A*   18-19 et absolutissima: *om. S*   absolutissima: in *add. Q*   19 quam: videret *post* quam *scribit et del. G*   20 aut: vel *EGIJNPaT*

stationary.[38] And because there are some things which are moved while others remain stationary, You O Lord, at once, are both moved and stationary; at once You both advance and are at rest. For if, in different things, being moved and being-at-rest occur contractedly and at the same time, and if nothing can exist apart from You, then neither motion nor rest exists apart from You. O Lord, You are present at one and the same time to all these things, and You are present as a whole to each |of them|.[39] Nevertheless, You are not moved and You are not at rest, because You are superexalted and are free from all these things, which can be conceived or named. Therefore, You are stationary and You advance, and likewise You are neither stationary nor do You advance. This very point is illustrated for me by this painted face. For if I am moved, its gaze appears to be moved, since it does not desert me. If, while I am moving, someone else who is looking at the face remains stationary, then the |face's| gaze does not desert him either but remains stationary with him. However, a Face that is free from these conditions cannot properly be characterized as stationary and as moved; for |such a Face| exists beyond all rest and motion, in most simple and most absolute Infinity. Indeed, motion and rest and opposition and whatever can be spoken of or conceived are subsequent to this Infinity.

38   Hence, I experience the necessity for me to enter into obscuring mist and to admit the coincidence of opposites,[40] beyond all capacity of reason, and to seek truth where impossibility appears. And when—beyond that |rational capacity| and beyond every most lofty intellectual ascent, as well—I come to that which is unknown to every intellect and which every intellect judges to be very far removed from the truth, *there* You are present, my God, You who are Absolute Necessity. And the darker and more impossible that obscuring haze of impossibility is known to be, the more truly the Necessity shines forth and the less veiledly it draws near and is present.

---

38 1 quomodo: quoniam *R*   quando *V*   necesse: sit *post* necesse *scribit et del. E*   intrare: religionem *post* intrare *scribit et del. V*   1-2 admittere: dimittere *Pa (ad* admittere *corr. Pa²)*   2 super: supra *Z*   3 veritatem: veritatem habet *M* (necessitatem *in marg. coni. M²*)   occurrit: occurrat *AMOPQRZ* occurrit *non proprie scribit L*   impossibilitas: *non proprie scribit N*   supra: super *Q*   4 etiam: *om. V*   5 est . . . intellectus: *om. G*   6 absoluta: absoluto *N* 7 cognoscitur magis: *ex* magis cognoscitur *corr. E*   8 verius: magis *Q*   relucet: relucetur *Q*

39   Quapropter tibi gratias ago, deus meus, quia patefacis mihi quod
non est via alia ad te accedendi, nisi illa quae omnibus hominibus,
etiam doctissimis philosophis, videtur penitus inaccessibilis et impossibilis, quoniam tu mihi ostendisti, te non posse alibi videri quam ubi
5 impossibilitas occurrit et obviat. Et animasti me, domine, qui es
cibus grandium, ut vim mihi ipsi faciam, quia impossibilitas coincidet cum necessitate. Et repperi locum, in quo revelate reperieris,
cinctum contradictoriorum coincidentia. Et iste est murus paradisi in
quo habitas, cuius portam custodit spiritus altissimus rationis, qui
10 nisi vincatur, non patebit ingressus. Ultra igitur coincidentiam contradictoriorum videri poteris et nequaquam citra. Si igitur impossibilitas est necessitas in visu tuo, domine, nihil est quod visus tuus
non videat.

40   CAPITULUM X

QUOMODO VIDETUR DEUS ULTRA COINCIDENTIAM
CONTRADICTORIORUM, ET QUOMODO VIDERE EST ESSE

Sto coram imagine faciei tuae, deus meus, quam oculis sensibilibus
5 respicio; et nitor oculis interioribus intueri veritatem, quae in pictura
signatur. Et occurrit mihi, domine, quod visus tuus loquatur; nam
non est aliud loqui tuum quam videre tuum. Et quia synonima sunt

---

39 1 quia: qui *Q*   patefacis: patefacias *S*   quod: quia *Z*   2 via alia: alia
via *Q*   3 inaccessibilis: inaccessabilis *C*   3-4 et impossibilis: *om. T*   4 videri:
videre *N*   ubi: *om. E (in marg. add. E³)*   5 obviat: obviet *GT*   animasti:
amasti *PaS* animasti (?) *V*   es: es *ex* est *corr. T (rasura)*   6 grandium: gaudium *LN* (g[-] *in marg. scribit N²*)   ut: et *I*   vim: *om. V*   ipsi: *om. S*   impossibilitas: occurrit et obviat *post* impossibilitas *scribit et del. J*   possibilitas *L*
6-7 coincidet: coincidit *Np ex* concidet *corr. Q*   coincidat *R*   7 revelate: reperire
post revelate *scribit et del. E*   8 cinctum: in ictu *EN*   auctum *I*   tinttum (?) *V*
contradictoriorum: contradictorium *Q*   coincidentia: coincidencium *EN* coincidencia *ex* coincidenciam *corr. L*   iste: *om. R*   iste est: est iste *IJPa*   paradisi:
paradisii (*ut saepe*) *N*   9 custodit spiritus altissimus: spiritus altissimus cus-

39   I thank You, my God, for disclosing to me that there is no other way of approaching You than this way which seems to all men, including the most learned philosophers, altogether inaccessible and impossible.[41] For You have shown me that You cannot be seen elsewhere than where impossibility appears and stands in the way. And You, O Lord, who are the Nourishment of the full-grown,[42] have encouraged me to do violence to myself, because impossibility coincides with necessity. And I have found the abode wherein You dwell unveiledly—an abode surrounded by the coincidence of contradictories. And |this coincidence| is the wall of Paradise, wherein You dwell. The gate of this wall is guarded by a most lofty rational spirit; unless this spirit is vanquished the entrance will not be accessible. Therefore, on the *other* side of the coincidence of contradictories You can be seen—but not at all on this side. If, then, O Lord, in Your sight impossibility is necessity, then there is nothing which Your sight does not see.

40   CHAPTER TEN

GOD IS SEEN BEYOND THE COINCIDENCE OF CONTRADICTORIES,
AND HIS SEEING IS HIS BEING

I stand before the image of Your Face, my God—an image which I behold with sensible eyes. And I attempt to view with inner eyes the truth which is pointed to by the painting. And it occurs to me, O Lord, that Your gaze speaks; for Your speaking is none other than Your seeing. And because Your seeing and Your speaking are

todit *GT*   spiritus: sanctus *post* spiritus *scribit et del. E*   10 patebit: patebitur *Q*
12 necessitas: *om. S*   tuo: tu *S*   nihil: michi *M* (nichil *in marg. coni. M²*)
tuus: *om. GQ*   13 videat: domine *post* videat *scribit et del. E*
    40 1 capitulum X: capitulum XI *E⁴*   2 deus: *in 1:1* ad *add. P*   4 sto: esto *Q²*
(es *pro* s *scribit Q²*)   tuae: domine *add. V*   5 intueri: *om. E (supra lin. add.
E²) N*   pictura: figuratur *add. Q*   7-8 et . . . loqui tuum: *om. GJTVp del. C²*
sinonima *pro* synonima *scribunt CIP*   synonima *ad* sinonima *corr. M²*   symonia
scribit Pa (in marg. ad synonima *corr. Pa²)*   sinonoma *R*   synonoma *Z*   et quia
synonima sunt loqui tuum et videre tuum *L*   et quia videre tuum est loqui tuum *S*

videre tuum et loqui tuum—cum non differant realiter in te, qui es
ipsa simplicitas absoluta—tunc clare experior quod tu simul omnia
10 vides et singula, quia ego simul et semel, dum praedico, ecclesiae
loquor congregatae et singulis in ecclesia existentibus. Unum verbum
loquor, et in illo unico singulis loquor. Id quod mihi est ecclesia, hoc
tibi, domine, est totus hic mundus et singulae creaturae, quae sunt
aut esse possunt. Sic igitur singulis loqueris et ea, quibus loqueris,
15 vides. Domine, qui es summa consolatio in te sperantium, inspiras ut
te laudem ex me. Nam dedisti mihi faciem unam sicut voluisti, et illa
per omnes quibus praedico singulariter et simul videtur. Videtur
itaque facies mea unica per singulos, et sermo simplex meus integre
a singulis auditur. Ego autem non possum simul omnes loquentes
20 discrete audire, sed unum post unum, neque omnes simul discrete
videre, sed unum post unum. Sed si in me esset tanta vis quod audiri
cum audire coincideret, sic et videri et videre, sic et loqui et audire
uti in te, domine, qui es summa virtus, tunc omnes et singulos simul
audirem et viderem. Et sicut singulis simul loquerer, ita etiam in
25 eodem tunc, quando loquerer, omnium et singulorum responsa viderem et audirem.

41   Unde in ostio coincidentiae oppositorum, quod angelus custodit in
ingressu paradisi constitutus, te, domine, videre incipio. Nam ibi es
ubi loqui, videre, audire, gustare, tangere, ratiocinari, scire, et intelligere sunt idem et ubi videre coincidit cum videri, et audire cum
5 audiri, et gustare cum gustari, et tangere cum tangi, et loqui cum
audire, et creare cum loqui. Si ego viderem sicut visibilis sum, non

---

8 cum: *om. S*   differant: differunt *RS*   9 ipsa: *om. Q*   absoluta: *om. I*   tu:
ex ? corr. T   simul omnia: omnia simul *V*   10 quia: que *V*   ego: ergo *I*   11 ecclesia: ecclesiis *N*   11-12 congregatae . . . loquor[1]: *om. QS*   12 et: *om. V*   in:
om. EN   unico: *om. I*   loquor *post* unico *add. et del. Pa*   est: in *add. J*
13 tibi: *? Pa (ad* tibi *in marg. corr. Pa*[2]*)*   domine: *om. S*   totus hic: hic totus *Pa*
hic: *om. R*   hic mundus: mundus hic *I*   14 loqueris[1]: e *clarius supra lin.*
rescribit G   ea: *om. T*   16 laudem: laudent *I*   unam: tuam *S*   18 unica: *om. G*
integre: integer *Z*   18-19 simplex . . . singulis: meus simplex a singulis integre *EN*
19 simul omnes loquentes: omnes loquentes simul *EN*   omnes loquentes: loquentes
omnes *T*   20 sed . . . unum[2]: *om. EN*   post: alium *post* post *scribit et del. M*
simul: *om. Z (supra lin. add. Z*[2]*)*   20-21 neque . . . unum[2]: *om. LP (in marg.*
add. P[2]*) QRV*   21 unum[2]: neque *post* unum[2] *scribit et del. I*   in me esset: esset
in me *R*   22 coincideret: coinciderent *CVp*   coincederent *G*   et[1]: *supra lin. Pa*

synonymous—since they do not differ really in You, who are Absolute Simplicity—I experience clearly that You see each and every thing at once. For when I preach, I speak at one and the same time to the church assembled as a congregation and to each individual present in the church. I speak one word, and in this one word I speak to each individual. That which the church is to me, this the whole world and each creature that exists or can exist is to You, O Lord. In like manner, then, You speak to each thing, and You see the things to which You speak. O Lord, who are the supreme consolation of those who place their hope in You, You inspire me to praise You on the basis of |an illustration regarding| myself. For You have given me one face, just as You willed to, and it is seen singularly and at once by all to whom I preach. And so, my one face is seen by each individual, and my simple sermon is wholly heard by each. But |only| successively and not at once can I individually hear all who speak. Nor can I see all individually at once, but |only| successively. Yet, if in me there were such great power that being heard coincided with hearing, and likewise being seen coincided with seeing, and speaking with hearing—as is the case with You, O Lord, who are supreme power—then I would hear and see each and every one at once. And just as I would speak to each at once, so also in the same moment when I would be speaking, I would be seeing and hearing the responses of each and all.

41 Hence, at the door of the coincidence of opposites, guarded by the angel stationed at the entrance of Paradise,[43] I begin to see You, O Lord. For You are present where speaking, seeing, hearing, tasting, touching, reasoning, knowing, and understanding are the same and where seeing coincides with being seen, hearing with being heard, tasting with being tasted, touching with being touched, speaking with hearing, and creating with speaking. If I were to see just as I am

note of utilization of all senses

videri: *ex* videre *corr. S*   videri et videre: videre et videri *I*   23 es: est *Pa* 24 simul: *om. Z (sub lin. add. Z²)*   simul loquerer: et loquerer simul *A*   25 omnium: oportet *Q   non proprie scribit V*

41 1 ostio: hostio *ACIJMOPPaQRSV*   angelus: angulus *V*   in²: *om. NPa* 3 loqui videre: videre loqui *ad* loqui videre *transponit R*   videre: et *add. GT* videre audire: audire videre *A*   ratiocinari: raciocinari *ex* raciocinare *corr. G*   racionare *N*   raciocionari *Z*   scire: sciri *N*   4 audire: audirem *N*   6 sicut: ego

essem creatura. Et si tu, deus, non videres sicut visibilis es, non esses deus omnipotens. Ab omnibus creaturis es visibilis, et omnes vides. In eo enim quod omnes vides, videris ab omnibus. Aliter enim esse
10 non possunt creaturae, quia visione tua sunt. Quod si te non viderent videntem, a te non caperent esse. Esse creaturae est videre tuum pariter et videri.

42 Loqueris verbo tuo omnibus quae sunt, et vocas ad esse quae non sunt. Vocas igitur ut te audiant, et quando audiunt te tunc sunt. Quando igitur loqueris, omnibus loqueris; et omnia te audiunt quibus loqueris. Loqueris terrae et vocas eam ad humanam naturam; et audit
5 te terra, et hoc audire eius est fieri hominem. Loqueris nihilo quasi sit aliquid, et vocas nihil ad aliquid; et audit te nihil, quia fit aliquid quod fuit nihil. O vis infinita, concipere tuum est loqui. Concipis caelum et est uti concipis. Concipis terram et est ut concipis. Dum concipis, vides et loqueris et operaris et quidquid dici potest.

43 Sed admirabilis es, deus meus! Semel loqueris, semel concipis. Quomodo ergo non sunt omnia simul, sed successive multa? Quomodo tot sunt diversa ex unico conceptu? Tu me in limine ostii constitutum illustras, quia conceptus tuus est ipsa aeternitas simplicis-
5 sima. Nihil est autem possibile fieri post aeternitatem simplicissimam. Ambit igitur infinita duratio, quae est ipsa aeternitas, omnem successionem. Omne igitur quod nobis in successione apparet, nequaquam est post tuum conceptum, qui est aeternitas. Unicus enim conceptus tuus, qui est et verbum tuum, omnia et singula complicat. Verbum
10 tuum aeternum non potest esse multiplex nec diversum nec variabile nec mutabile, quia simplex aeternitas. Sic video, domine, post tuum

---

add. Z 7 si: deus *post* si *scribit et del. E* non[1]: *om. Pa (supra lin. add. Pa²)*
8 omnipotens: et *add. N* es: *ex* est *corr. E* et: es *Z (ad* et *supra lin. corr. Z²)*
9 in: *bis p* vides: videns *Z (ad* vides *supra lin. corr. Z²)* 10 possunt: possent *A*
te: *om. EN* 11 videntem: et viderentur *EN* creaturae: tue *add. N* est: esse
post est *scribit et del. R* videre tuum: tuum videre *ad* videre tuum *transponit R*
42 2 audiunt te: te audiunt *p* te[2]: *om. TZ (ante* audiunt *supra lin. add. Z²)*
3 audiunt: *non clare scribit L (*u[1] *supra lin. explanat L)* 6 aliquid[1]: aliquod *J*
aliquid[2]: aliquod *JL* quia: et *(ex* qui *corr.) I* aliquid[3]: aliquod *J confuse
abbreviat V (cf.* quicquid *42: 9 in V)* 8 caelum et est uti concipis: *bis Q (*est *post*
celum[2] *scribit, del., et post* et[2] *rescribit Q)* terram: *om. Q* est[2]: et *Q* ut: uti *IR*
8-9 dum concipis: *om. I* 9 et[3]: *om. AEN*
43 1 admirabilis: mirabilis *EN* 2 successive: successiva *L* multa: multas *A*
3 conceptu: concepto *G* ostii: hostii *ACIJLMOPPaQRSV* 4 illustras: illlustras-

seeable, I would not be a creature. And if You, O God, were not to see just as You are seeable, You would not be God Almighty. You are seeable by all creatures,⁴⁴ and You see all creatures. For in that You see all creatures You are seen by all creatures. For otherwise creatures could not exist, since they exist by means of Your seeing. But if they were not to see You, who see |them|, they would not receive being from You. The being of a creature is, alike, Your seeing and Your being seen.

42   By Your Word You speak to all existing things, and You summon into being nonexisting things. Therefore, You summon them in order that they may hear You; and when they hear You, they exist. Therefore, when You speak, You speak to all; and all the things to which You speak hear You. You speak to the earth, and You summon it to |become| human nature; and the earth hears You, and its hearing is its becoming man. You speak to *nothing* as if it were something, and You summon nothing to |become| something; and nothing hears You, because that which was nothing becomes something. O Infinite Power, Your conceiving is Your speaking. You conceive the sky and the sky is as You conceive it. You conceive the earth and the earth is as You conceive it. While You conceive, You see and speak and work and whatever else can be said.

43   But You are wonderful, my God! You speak once, and You conceive once. How is it, then, that all things do not exist at the same time but that many exist successively? How is it that from the one Concept there are so many different things? You enlighten me, who am situated at the threshhold of the door; for Your Concept is most simple eternity itself. Now, *posterior* to most simple eternity no thing can possibly be made. Therefore, infinite duration, which is eternity itself, encompasses all succession. Therefore, everything which appears to us in a succession is not at all posterior to Your Concept, which is eternity. For Your one Concept, which is also Your Word, enfolds each and every thing. Your eternal Word cannot be multiple or different or variable or changeable, because it is simple eternity. In

tras *p*   tuus: *in marg. scribit J om. Pa*   5 est autem: autem est *EN*   autem: *ex ? corr. T*   7 successione: successionem *SV*   8 qui: que *JQ*   aeternitas: eternitas *ut* eternis *scribit A*   unicus: est *post* unicus *scribit et del. G*   9 qui: que *J*   et¹: *om. GT*   10 multiplex: simplex *G*   11 aeternitas: eternitas *ut* eternis

conceptum nihil esse, sed sunt omnia quia concipis. Concipis autem in aeternitate. Successio autem in aeternitate est sine successione ipsa aeternitas, ipsum tuum verbum, domine deus. Rem aliquam quae
15 nobis temporaliter apparet, non prius concepisti quam est. In aeternitate enim, in qua concipis, omnis successio temporalis in eodem nunc aeternitatis coincidit. Nihil igitur praeteritum vel futurum, ubi futurum et praeteritum coincidunt cum praesenti.

44 Sed quod res in hoc mundo secundum prius et posterius existunt, est quia tu prius res tales ut essent non concepisti. Si enim prius concepisses, prius fuissent. Sed in cuius conceptu potest cadere prius et posterius, ut prius unum concipiat et postea aliud, ille non est
5 omnipotens conceptus—sicut ille oculus qui prius unum videt et postea aliud, non est omnipotens. Ita quia tu es deus omnipotens, es intra murum in paradiso. Murus autem est coincidentia illa, ubi posterius coincidit cum priore, ubi finis coincidit cum principio, ubi alpha et o sunt idem. Semper igitur res sunt, quia tu dicis ut sint; et
10 non sunt prius, quia non dicis prius. Et quando ego lego Adam ante tot annos fuisse et hodie talem natum, videtur impossibile quod Adam tunc fuit, quia tunc voluisti, et similiter hodie natus, quia nunc voluisti, et quod tamen non prius voluisti Adam esse quam hodie natum. Sed illud quod videtur impossibile est ipsa necessitas. Nam
15 nunc et tunc sunt post verbum tuum. Et ideo accendenti ad te occurrunt in muro, qui circumdat locum ubi habitas, in coincidentia. Coincidit enim nunc et tunc in circulo muri paradisi. Tu vero, deus meus, ultra nunc et tunc existis et loqueris, qui es aeternitas absoluta.

scribit A tuum: *bis L* 12 sunt omnia: omnia sunt *EN* quia: que *Q* 14 tuum verbum: verbum tuum *Qp* 16 in[1]: *supra lin. A* qua: est *add. et del. E* omnis: *bis S* (omnis[2] *del. S*) 17 aeternitatis: eternitas *S* 17-18 futurum et praeteritum: preteritum et futurum *EN* 18 coincidunt: coincidit *OP*

44 1 existunt: existut *Pa* 2 ut: *ex* non *corr. Pa* concepisti: enim *post* concepisti *scribit et del. N* (vaca[t] *in marg. N*[2]) enim: *om. CVp* 3 sed: *om. S* potest cadere: *bis P* (potest cadere[1] *del. P*) cadere: caderet *L* 4-6 ille . . . aliud: *om. CVp* 5 qui: *om. E (supra lin. add. E*[2]*) N* et: *om. Z* 6 es[2]: *om. V* 7 intra: in terra *G* paradiso: paradiiso *(ut saepe) S* coincidentia illa: illa coincidencia *EN* illa: *om. I* 8 priore: *ex* priori *corr. E* ubi[2]: *om. V* 9 o: *non proprie format Q* omega habet *p* 10 quia: tu *post* quia *scribit et del. P* 11 talem: *in marg. E* natum: sed illud quod *post* natum *scribit et del. O* 12 natus quia: natus *del., et* quia *supra lin. scribit, A* 12-13 et . . . voluisti[1]: *in marg. P* 13 quod: tu *add. A* non prius: prius non *V* prius voluisti: voluisti prius *ad*

this way I see, O Lord, that posterior to Your Concept there is not anything; rather, all things exist because You conceive |them|. Now, You conceive in eternity. But in eternity succession is—without succession—eternity itself, i.e., Your Word itself, O Lord God. Any given thing that appears to us in time was not conceived by You *before* it existed. For in eternity, in which You conceive, all temporal succession coincides in |one and| the same *now* of eternity. Therefore, where the future and the past coincide with the present, nothing is past or future.

44   But the reason that |only| in this world |do| things exist according to earlier and later is that You did not conceive mundane things *before* they existed. For if You had earlier conceived them, they would have existed earlier. Now, if *earlier* and *later* can occur in someone's concept, so that he conceives first one thing and then another, this concept is not omnipotent. (By comparison, that eye which sees first one thing and then another is not omnipotent.) So because You are God Almighty, You dwell on the inner side of the wall of Paradise. But the wall is the coincidence where *later* coincides with *earlier*, where *end* coincides with *beginning*, where *alpha* and *omega* are the same. Therefore, things exist always, because You command that they exist; but they do not exist earlier, because You do not command earlier. Now, when I read that Adam existed so many years ago and that a man like Adam was born today, the following seems impossible: (1) that Adam existed then because then You willed |his existence|; (2) that, likewise, |the other man| was born today because now You willed |his birth|; and (3) that, nevertheless, You did not will Adam to exist before |You willed the existence of| the man born today. But that which seems impossible is necessity itself. For *now* and *then* are posterior to Your Word. And so, to one who approaches unto You, *now* and *then* appear in coincidence in the wall which surrounds the place where You dwell. For *now* and *then* coincide in the circle of the wall of Paradise. But You, my God, who are Absolute Eternity, exist and speak beyond *now* and *then*.

prius voluisti *transponit R*   14 illud: id *A*   15 ideo: *om. OP*   accedenti: accidenti *J*   accedente *N*   ad: *ex a corr. G*   15-16 occurrunt: *? post* occurrunt *scribit et del. L*   16 circumdat: circumdant *S*   habitas: habilitas *V*   17 coincidit: coincidunt *R*   18 es: est *P*   aeternitas: eternitas *ut* eternis *scribit A*   absoluta: et cetera *add. V*

45 ## CAPITULUM XI

QUOMODO VIDETUR IN DEO SUCCESSIO SINE SUCCESSIONE

Experior bonitatem tuam, deus meus, quae me miserum pecca-
torem non solum non spernit sed quodam desiderio dulciter pascit.
5 Inspirasti similitudinem mihi gratam circa unitatem verbi mentalis
seu conceptus tui et varietatem eiusdem in successive apparentibus.
Nam simplex conceptus horologii perfectissimi me ducit, ut sapidius
rapiar ad visionem conceptus et verbi tui. Conceptus enim simplex
horologii complicat omnem successionem temporalem. Et esto quod
10 horologium sit conceptus. Tunc licet prius audiamus sonum sextae
horae quam septimae, non tamen auditur septima nisi quando iubet
conceptus. Neque sexta est prius in conceptu quam septima aut
octava; sed in unico conceptu horologii, nulla hora est prior aut posterior alia, quamvis horologium numquam horam sonet nisi quando
15 conceptus iubet. Et verum est dicere, quando audimus sextam sonare,
quod tunc sex sonat quia conceptus magistri sic vult.

46 Et quia horologium in conceptu dei est conceptus, tunc aliquantu-
lum videtur quomodo successio in horologio est sine successione in
verbo seu conceptu; et quod in simplicissimo illo conceptu complicantur omnes motus et soni et quidquid in successione experimur; et
5 quod omne illud quod successive evenit non exit quovismodo conceptum sed est explicatio conceptus, ita quod conceptus dat esse cuilibet; et quod propterea nihil prius fuit quam eveniat, quia prius non

---

45 1 capitulum XI: capitulum 12 *E⁴*   3 experior: ego *add. R*   quae: que *ex*
quem *corr. C*   qui *LV*   4 spernit: sprevit *T*   quodam: quod *E (ad* quodam *in*
marg. corr. E²) N   pascit: poscit *L*   5 gratam: grata *Pa*   verbi: *ex* verbis *corr. I*
6 varietatem: veritatem *I*   successive: successione *T (ad* successive *corr. T²)*   apparentibus: *non proprie scribit A*   7 nam: luna *T*   perfectissimi: perfectissime *EN*
sapidius: *ex* sapius *corr. C aut C²*   sapidus *I*   8 et: *om. LZ (supra lin. add. Z²)*
9 omnem: omnium *R*   11 horae quam septimae: quam septime hore *R*   quando:
quomodo *J*   12 prius in conceptu: in conceptu prius *Z*   in conceptu: *om. N*
([-] conceptu *in marg. add. N²)*   aut: vel *R*   13 hora est: est hora *T*   14 numquam: numque *A*   15 audimus: dicere *add. V*   16 tunc: tantum *V*   sex: sexta *p*
magistri: *om. R*   sic vult: wlt sic *Q*   vult: *litteram* w *in* wlt *non clare scribit A;*
cf. 114:5 in A

45 CHAPTER ELEVEN

IN GOD WE SEE SUCCESSION WITHOUT SUCCESSION

I experience Your goodness, my God. Not only does it not spurn me, a wretched sinner, but it even nourishes me sweetly with a certain longing. With regard to Your mental Word or Concept's oneness and its variation, successively, in appearances, You have inspired a likeness that is pleasing to me. For the simple concept of a most perfect clock guides me, so that I may more wisely be caught up unto a vision of Your Concept and Word. For the simple concept of a clock enfolds all temporal succession. Now, let it be that the clock *is* the concept. Then, although we hear the sounding of the sixth hour before that of the seventh, nevertheless the |sounding of the| seventh is heard only when the concept gives the command. And in the concept the sixth hour does not occur before the seventh or the eight; rather, in the unitary concept of the clock no hour is earlier or later than another, although the clock never sounds the hour except when the concept gives the command. And when we hear the sounding of the sixth hour, it is true to say that six sounds at that moment because the master's concept so wills it.

46 Now, because in God's Concept the clock is the Concept, we see to some small extent how the following are true: (1) that succession is present in the clock without there being succession in the Word, or Concept; (2) that in this most simple Concept are enfolded all movements and sounds and whatever we experience as in succession; (3) that whatever occurs successively does not in any way pass outside the Concept but is the unfolding of the Concept, so that the Concept gives being to each |successive thing|; (4) that the reason |each event| was nothing before it occurred is that it was not conceived *before* it

---

46 1 dei: *om. EN*   conceptus: et *add. EN*   2 sine: in *A*   3 verbo: vel *post* verbo *scribit et del. E*   seu: in *add. A*   conceptu[1]: concepto *Z*   3-4 complicantur: *bis L* (complicantur[2] *del. L*)   4 omnes: omnis *I*   successione: successionem *V* experimur: exprimitur *Pa*   5 illud: *om. EN*   evenit: eveniet *AEG* (e[1] *in marg. G*) *IJLMNOPPaQRSTZ* (ad evenit *supra lin. corr.* Z[2])   exit: erit *L*   6 est: *om. S* ita quod conceptus: *om. V*   6-7 cuilibet: *bis T* (cuilibet[2] *del.* T[2] *et* T[3])   7 propterea:

fuit conceptum ut esset. Sit igitur conceptus horologii quasi ipsa aeternitas; tunc motus in horologio est successio. Complicat igitur
10 aeternitas successionem et explicat; nam conceptus horologii, qui est aeternitas, complicat pariter et explicat omnia.

47   Benedictus sis, domine deus meus, qui me lacte similitudinum pascis et nutris, quousque solidiorem tribuas cibum. Deduc me, domine deus, per has semitas ad te, quia, nisi duxeris, subsistere in via nequeo propter fragilitatem naturae corruptibilis et fictilis vasis quod
5 circumfero. Redeo iterum confisus adiutorio tuo, domine, ut te ultra murum coincidentiae complicationis et explicationis reperiam. Et cum per hoc ostium verbi et conceptus tui intro et exeo simul, pascua reperio dulcissima. Cum te reperio virtutem complicantem omnia, intro. Cum te reperio virtutem explicantem, exeo. Cum te reperio
10 virtutem complicantem pariter et explicantem, intro pariter et exeo. Intro de creaturis ad te creatorem, de effectibus ad causam. Exeo de te creatore, de causa ad effectus. Intro et exeo simul, quando video quomodo exire est intrare et intrare exire simul—sicut qui numerat, explicat pariter et complicat: explicat virtutem unitatis et complicat
15 numerum in unitatem. Exire enim creaturae a te est creaturam in te intrare, et explicare est complicare. Et quando video te deum in paradiso, quem hic murus coincidentiae oppositorum cingit, video te nec complicare nec explicare disiunctive vel copulative. Disiunctio enim

---

preterea *EN*   prius[1]: *om. R*   prius fuit: fuit prius *Z*   eveniat: eveniet *EN*   8 sit: si *G*   sic IJNS   horologii: horalogii *ex* horalorii *corr Pa*   9 horologio: horalogio *ex* horalogii *corr. L*   10 qui: q *Z (ad* qui *corr. Z²)*

47 1 benedictus: igitur *add. p*   sis: es *I*   similitudinum: *ex* similitudinem *corr. L*   1-2 lacte . . . solidiorem: *in marg. P*   2 solidiorem: solidorem *C (ad* solidiorem *corr. C²)*   tribuas: mihi *add. p*   me: *om. AC (add. C²) JLM (in marg. add. M²) OPPaSTZ*   2-3 deduc me domine deus: deduc domine deus me (me *supra lin.) I*   3 deus: meus *add. AENQ*   nisi: me *add. p*   4 fictilis: fictilis *ex* futili *aut* fictili *corr. M aut M²* futili *C (ad* futilis *corr. C²) JPaSV* fictili *EG NQT* lutei *I* futilis *LPp* fulitis *O* (fictilis *in marg. coni. O²)*   5 circumfero: circumfers *S*   redeo: *cum* redeo *divisio nova incipit in EN*   confisus: de *supra lin. add. I*   6 et explicationis: *om. J* (et explicationi[-] *in marg. add. J^n)* bis *T* (et explicationis[1], *non proprie scriptum, del. T et T³)*   reperiam: repeream *G*   7 ostium: hostium *ACIJLMOPPaQRSV*   et[2]: vel *Pa*   8 dulcissima: dulcessima *P* et *add. Z*   complicantem: explicantem *J (ad* complicantem *corr. J^n)*   8-10 omnia . . . pariter[1]: *in marg. R* (et cetera *post* pariter *add. R*; pariter *etiam in corpore*

existed. So, let the concept of a clock be, as it were, eternity itself. Then, in the clock, movement is succession. Therefore, eternity enfolds and unfolds succession; for the Concept of a clock—a Concept which *is* eternity—both enfolds and unfolds all things.

47 Blessed be You, O Lord my God, who feed and nurture me with the milk of likenesses, until such time as You grant more solid food.[45] O Lord God, guide me unto Yourself by these pathways. For unless You guide, I cannot stay on the pathway—on account of the frailty both of my corruptible nature and of the earthen vessel that I carry about.[46] Trusting in Your help, O Lord, I turn once again in order to find You beyond the wall of the coincidence of enfolding and unfolding. And when at one and the same time I go in and out through the door of Your Word and Concept, I find most sweet nourishment. When I find You to be a power that enfolds all things, I go in. When I find You to be a power that unfolds, I go out. When I find You to be a power that both enfolds and unfolds, I both go in and go out. From creatures I go in unto You, who are Creator—go in from the effects unto the Cause. I go out from You, who are Creator—go out from the Cause unto the effects. I both go in and go out when I see that going out is going in and that, likewise, going in is going out. (By comparison, he who counts unfolds and enfolds, alike: he unfolds the power of oneness, and he enfolds number in oneness.) For creation's going out from You is creation's going in unto You; and unfolding is enfolding. And when I see You-who-are-God in Paradise,[47] which this wall of the coincidence of opposites surrounds, I see that You neither enfold nor unfold—whether separ-

---

textus scriptum est) 9 explicantem: omnia *post* explicantem *scribit et del.* L 9-10 cum². . . explicantem: *om. OP* 11 creatorem: et *add.* Z effectibus: effctibus *Pa non proprie abbreviat T* ad²: *om. N* 11-12 de². . . creatore: *om. V* 12 te: *om. EJNPaS* creatore: ad creaturas *add. AEN* ad creaturam *in marg. add. I et in marg. add. R* ad creaturam *add. p* effectus: effectos G 13 quomodo: ad quando *corr. J aut Jⁿ* intrare²: et *add. et del. A* et *add. Pa* intrare² *om. R* est *post* intrare² *scribit et del. S* sicut: nunc L 14 virtutem: numerum *EN* 15 unitatem: unitate Q creaturae: creare C *(ad* creature *in marg. corr. C²)* V creaturam: creatura *Pa* in te: *del.* C aut C² *om. Gp* 16 et¹: *om. N* ex R est: et *Pa* video te: te video *ad* video te *transponit J aut Jⁿ* 16-17 deum . . . te: *bis* V 17 hic: illic *p* cingit: tingit N 18 complicare: plicare A copulative: coplative *APPa* coniunctive R enim: *non proprie*

pariter et coniunctio est murus coincidentiae ultra quem existis, abso-
20 lutus ab omni eo quod aut dici aut cogitari potest.

48 CAPITULUM XII

QUOD UBI INVISIBILIS VIDETUR, INCREATUS CREATUR

Apparuisti mihi, domine, aliquando ut invisibilis ab omni creatura
quia es deus absconditus infinitus. Infinitas autem est incomprehen-
5 sibilis omni modo comprehendendi. Apparuisti deinde mihi ut ab
omnibus visibilis quia intantum res est, inquantum tu eam vides, et
ipsa non esset actu nisi te videret. Visio enim praestat esse, quia est
essentia tua. Sic, deus meus, es invisibilis pariter et visibilis: invisibilis es uti tu es; visibilis es uti creatura est, quae intantum est, inquan-
10 tum te videt. Tu igitur, deus meus invisibilis, ab omnibus videris. Et
in omni visu videris per omnem videntem; in omni visibili et omni
actu visionis videris, qui es invisibilis et absolutus ab omni tali et
superexaltatus in infinitum.

49 Oportet igitur me, domine, murum illum invisibilis visionis transilire, ubi tu reperieris. Est autem murus omnia et nihil simul. Tu
enim, qui occurris quasi sis omnia et nihil omnium simul, habitas
intra murum illum excelsum, quem nullum ingenium sua virtute
5 scandere potest. Occurris mihi aliquando, ut cogitem te videre in te
omnia quasi speculum vivum in quo omnia relucent. Et quia videre
tuum est scire, tunc occurrit mihi te non videre in te omnia uti speculum vivum, quia sic scientia tua oriretur a rebus. Deinde occurris

scribit P 19 coincidentiae: coindencie *M*
48 1 *numerum capituli om. C* capitulum XII: capitulum 13 *E³* 2 ubi: verbi *T* invisibilis: *non proprie scribit E³* videtur: et *add. R* creatur: creator
E³TZ 4 infinitas: *ex* infinititas *corr. E* infinita *Pa (ad* infinitas *corr. Pa²)*
5 deinde mihi: michi deinde *ad* deinde michi *transponit R* michi deinde *Z* 6 visibilis: *ex* visibilibus *corr. E* est: *om. Pa (supra lin. add. Pa²)* 7 quia: non *post*
quia *scribit et del. G* (non *ad* est *in marg. corr. G)* 8 es: est *T (ad* es *in marg.*
corr. T³) invisibilis pariter et visibilis: visibilis pariter et invisibilis *R* 8-12 pariter . . . invisibilis: *in marg. P* 9 es¹: tu *add. V* tu es: tu deus *Z* (es *post* tu *in*
marg. scribit Z²) es²: deus *L* uti²: ut *T* intantum: inquantum *T* 11 et: in

ately or collectively. For both separating and conjoining are the wall of coincidence, beyond which You dwell, free from whatever can be either spoken of or thought of.

48   CHAPTER TWELVE

WHERE THE INVISIBLE IS SEEN THE UNCREATED IS CREATED

Earlier,[48] O Lord, You appeared to me as invisible by every crea-ture since You are an infinite and hidden God. Infinity, however, is incomprehensible by every mode of comprehending. Later,[49] You appeared to me as visible by all |creatures| because a thing exists insofar as You see it, and it would not exist actually unless it saw You. For Your seeing gives being, because |Your seeing| is Your essence. Thus, my God, You are both invisible and visible: You are invisible as You are |in Yourself|; You are visible in accordance with the existence of creatures, which exist insofar as they see You. You, then, my invisible God, are seen by all |creatures|. In all sight You are seen by every perceiver. You who are invisible, who are free from everything visible, and who are superexalted unto infinity are seen in everything visible and in every act of seeing.

49   I must, then, O Lord, pass beyond the wall of invisible seeing, on the inner side of which You dwell. But |this| wall is both everything and nothing. For You, who seem as if You were both all things and nothing of all things, dwell on the inner side of that high wall, which no intelligence can scale by its own power. At times, You appear to me |in such way| that I think You see all things in Yourself as would a living mirror in which all things shined forth. But because Your seeing is knowing, it occurs to me that You do not see all things in Yourself as would a living mirror; for, if You did, Your knowledge would derive from things. Hereupon, You appear to me to see all

add. AGT
   49 2 reperieris: reperireris *S*   3 qui: *in marg. A*   4 quem: *non proprie ab-breviat L*   ingenium: *non proprie scribit J*   virtute: laudare *add. et del. A*
5 scandere potest: potest scandere *A*   te¹: et *add. S*   videre: *ex* viderem *corr. M*
6 quasi: in *add. A*   quo: *litteram* o *non proprie format L*   7 mihi te: te mihi *P*
8 tua: *om. EN ex* tuam *corr. V*   oriretur: orietur *C (ad* oriretur *corr. C²) V*

mihi ut videas in te omnia quasi virtus se intuendo. Uti virtus seminis
10 arboris, si se intueretur, in se arborem videret in virtute, quia virtus
seminis est arbor virtualiter. Et post hoc occurrit mihi quod non
videas te et in te omnia uti virtus. Nam videre arborem in potentia
virtutis refert a visione qua arbor videtur in actu. Et tunc reperio
quomodo virtus tua infinita est ultra specularem et seminalem, et
15 coincidentiam radiationis et reflexionis, causae et causati pariter; et
quod illa absoluta virtus est visio absoluta, quae est ipsa perfectio et
est super omnes videndi modos. Omnes enim modi, qui perfectionem
visionis explanant, sine modo sunt visio tua, quae est essentia tua,
deus meus.

50   Sed sine, domine piissime, ut adhuc vilis factura loquatur ad te. Si
videre tuum est creare tuum et non vides aliud a te, sed tu ipse es
obiectum tui ipsius—es enim videns et visibile atque videre—quomodo tunc creas res alias a te? Videris enim creare te ipsum, sicut
5 vides te ipsum. Sed consolaris me, vita spiritus mei, quoniam etsi
occurrat murus absurditatis, qui est coincidentiae ipsius creare cum
creari, quasi impossibile sit quod creare coincidat cum creari (videtur
enim quod hoc admittere sit affirmare rem esse antequam sit; quando
enim creat: est, et non est, quia creatur), tamen non obstat. Creare
10 enim tuum est esse tuum. Nec est aliud creare pariter et creari quam
esse tuum omnibus communicare, ut sis omnia in omnibus et ab
omnibus tamen maneas absolutus. Vocare enim ad esse quae non
sunt, est communicare esse nihilo. Sic vocare est creare; communicare est creari. Et ultra hanc coincidentiam creare cum creari es tu,

---

oritur *IJPa*   9 in te omnia: omnia in te *EN*   10 intueretur: intueret *GI* intuetur
V   arborem videret: videret arborem *p*   videret: *ex* viderent *corr. Q*   intueretur *R*
11 et: est *L*   13 refert: refert *Z (ad* differt *corr. Z*[2]*)*   differt *p*   reperio: experior *R*
14 quomodo: vides *post* quomodo *scribit et del. R*   virtus tua: tua virtus *ad* virtus
tua *transponit R*   seminalem: *non proprie scribit S*   16 quod: *ex* quia *corr. P*
quae est: quem et *Q*   17 est: igitur *L*   super: supra *PZ*   18 est: sunt *A*
     50 1 ut: et *V*   vilis: videlicet *A*   factura: tua *add. R*   si: ad *add. V*   2 vi-
dere tuum: tuum videre *V*   creare: causare *A*   tuum[2]: *om. I*   es: est *A*   3 tui:
tu *N*   et: *supra lin. E*   atque: et *EN*   4 tunc: tu *OPQ*   res alias: alias res *P*
ipsum: et si occurrat murus *post* ipsum *scribit et del. P*   4-5 sicut vides te ipsum:
om. T   5 vides te ipsum: te ipsum vides *N*   sed: si *L* *bis V*   consolaris: con-
suluerus *V*   etsi: et si *p*   6 occurrat: *om. Q*   absurditatis: absorditatis *G*   est:
es *J*   creare: creature *A*   7 creari[2]: creare *A*   9 quia: *bis S*   10 est[1]: *om. N*

things in Yourself as would a power in viewing itself. For example, if the power of the seed of a tree were to view itself, it would see within itself a tree in potency; for the power of the seed is potentially a tree. But then it occurs to me that You do not see Yourself and—in Yourself—all things as would a power. For to see a tree in the potency of a power is different from the seeing by which the tree is seen in actuality. And then I find that Your infinite power is beyond the power of a mirror and of a seed and is beyond the coincidence of radiating and reflecting and, likewise, of causing and being caused. |And I find| that Your absolute power is absolute seeing, which is perfection itself and is above every mode of seeing. For Your seeing, which is Your essence, my God, is, without modality, all |these| modes, which display the perfection of sight.[50]

50 But grant, most gracious Lord, that a lowly creature continue to speak to You. Your seeing is Your creating; and You do not see anything other than Yourself but are Your own object, for You are (1) the perceiver, (2) that which is perceived, and (3) the act of perceiving. If so, then how is it that You create things that are other than Yourself? For You seem to create Yourself, even as You see Yourself. But You comfort me, Life of my spirit. For although the wall of absurdity (viz., the wall of the coincidence of creating with being created) stands in the way, as if creating could not possibly coincide with being created (since to admit this coinciding would seemingly be to affirm that something exists before it exists; for when it creates, it *is*—and yet *is not*, because it is created), nevertheless this wall is not an obstacle. For Your creating is Your being. Moreover, Your creating and, likewise, being created are not other than Your imparting Your being to all things, so that in all things You are all things,[51] while nevertheless remaining free of them all. For to summon nonexisting things into being is to impart being to nothing. Hence, Your summoning is creating, and Your imparting is being created. And beyond this coincidence of creating with being created You, O abso-

creare pariter: pariter creare *A*   12 tamen: *om. R*   tamen maneas: maneas tamen *GT*   ad: ab *p*   esse: se *S*   quae: qui *Q*   14 creari[1]: *ad* creare *corr. E* et: ut *V*   et . . . creari: *om. S*   ultra hanc: ut trahant *G*   coincidentiam:

15 deus absolutus et infinitus, neque creans neque creabilis, licet omnia
id sint quod sunt quia tu es.

51 O altitudo divitiarum, quam incomprehensibilis es! Quamdiu concipio creatorem creantem, adhuc sum citra murum paradisi. Sic
quamdiu concipio creatorem creabilem, nondum intravi, sed sum in
muro. Sed absolutam cum te video infinitatem, cui nec nomen crea-
5 toris creantis nec creatoris creabilis competit, tunc revelate te inspicere incipio et intrare ortum deliciarum, quia nequaquam es aliquid
tale quod dici aut concipi potest, sed in infinitum super omnia talia
absolute superexaltatus. Non es igitur creator sed plus quam creator
in infinitum, licet sine te nihil fiat aut fieri possit. Tibi laus et gloria
10 per saecula infinita.

52 CAPITULUM XIII

QUOD DEUS VIDETUR ABSOLUTA INFINITAS

Domine deus, adiutor te quaerentium, video te in horto paradisi et
nescio quid video, quia nihil visibilium video. Et hoc scio solum,
5 quia scio me nescire quid video et numquam scire posse. Et nescio te
nominare, quia nescio quid sis. Et si quis mihi dixerit, quod nomin-
eris hoc vel illo nomine, eo ipso quod nominat scio quia non est
nomen tuum. Terminus enim omnis modi significandi nominum est
murus ultra quem te video. Et si quis expresserit conceptum aliquem,
10 quo modo concipi possis, scio illum conceptum non esse conceptum

coincidencia *Pa*   16 id: *om. T*   id sint: sint id *R*

51 1 altitudo: dulcedo *I*   es: *om. Q*   2 sic: sit *V*   3 quamdiu: quam *T (ad
quamdiu corr. T³)*   creatorem: creaturam *N*   creabilem: creabilis *LMOPQZ (ad
creabilem in marg. corr. Z²)*   nondum: nundum *ex* mundum *corr. C et J aut Jⁿ*
nundum *V*   mundum *IM (nondum in marg. coni. M²) Pa*   4 sed: cum vim *in
marg. add. I*   cum te: tecum *I*   infinitatem: infinitam *I*   5 creantis: creantem *N*
revelate: *om. T*   te: revelate *add. G*   6 intrare: intro *R*   es: *ex* est *corr. E*
aliquid: aliquod *AEJLMNOPPaQRTZ*   aliquld *p*   7 in: *om. C (supra lin. add.
C²) Q*   super: supra *P*   8 absolute: es *add. I*   quam: *om. M (supra lin. add. M²)*
9 in: *supra lin. T*   fiat: fiet *P*   10 infinita: amen *add. AQp*   et cetera *add. P*

lute and infinite God, are neither creating nor creatable, although all things are that which they are because You exist.

51   O Depth of riches, how incomprehensible You are![52] As long as I conceive of a creating creator, I am still on this side of the wall of Paradise. Similarly, as long as I conceive of a creatable creator, I have not yet entered in but am at the wall. But when I see You to be Absolute Infinity, to which belongs neither the name "creating creator" nor the name "creatable creator," then I begin to behold You unveiledly and to enter unto the source[53] of delights. For You are not at all something such that it can be spoken of or conceived but are absolutely and infinitely exalted above all such things. Therefore, although without You nothing is made or can be made, You are not creator but are infinitely more than creator.[54] To You be praise and glory forever and ever.

52

CHAPTER THIRTEEN

GOD IS SEEN TO BE ABSOLUTE INFINITY

O Lord God, Helper of those who seek You, I see You in the garden[55] of Paradise, and I do not know what I see, because I see no visible thing. I know only the following: viz., that I know that I do not know—and never can know—what I see. Moreover, I do not know how to name You, because I do not know what You are. And if someone tells me that You are named by this or that name, then by virtue of the fact that he names, I know that |this| is not Your name. For the limit of every mode of signification that belongs to names is the wall beyond which I see You. And if anyone expresses any concept whereby |allegedly| You can be conceived, I know that this con-

52 1 *numerum capituli om.* C   capitulum XIII: capitulum 14 *E⁴*   2 *titulum capituli in marg. scribit Pa³*   3 te²: *om.* Pa   horto: ortu *p*   orto *habent omnes codices; ad* horto *mutavi*   4 hoc: *om. OP*   5 quid: quod *L*   6 sis: scis *V*   7 illo: illius *Q*   eo ipso: *in marg.* P   quia: quod *CIQSVp*   quia *Z (ad* quod *supra lin. corr. Z²)*   8 significandi: est murum *post* significandi *scribit et del.* S   significationis *p*   10 quo modo: quomodo *Z (ad* quo *supra lin. corr. Z²)*   quo *p*   10-11 conceptum tuum: tuum conceptum *ad* conceptum tuum *transponit* E   tuum

tuum. Omnis enim conceptus terminatur in muro paradisi. Et si quis expresserit aliquam similitudinem et dixerit secundum illam te concipiendum, scio similiter illam similitudinem non esse tuam. Sic si intellectum tui quis enarraverit, volens modum dare ut intelligaris, hic

15 longe adhuc a te abest. Separaris enim per altissimum murum ab omnibus his. Separat enim murus omnia quae dici aut cogitari possunt, a te, quia tu es ab his omnibus absolutus, quae cadere possunt in conceptum cuiuscumque. Unde dum altissime elevor, infinitatem te video. Ob hoc inaccessibilis, incomprehensibilis, innominabilis,

20 immultiplicabilis, et invisibilis.

53   Et ideo oportet ad te accedentem super omnem terminum et finem et finitum ascendere. Sed quomodo ad te perveniet, qui es finis ad quem tendit, si ultra finem ascendere debet? Qui ultra finem ascendit, nonne hic subintrat in indeterminatum et confusum et ita quoad

5 intellectum ignorantiam et obscuritatem, quae sunt confusionis intellectualis? Oportet igitur intellectum ignorantem fieri et in umbra constitui, si te videre velit. Sed quid est, deus meus, intellectus in ignorantia? Nonne docta ignorantia? Non igitur accedi potes, deus, qui es infinitas, nisi per illum cuius intellectus est ignorantia, qui scilicet scit

10 se ignorantem tui. Quomodo potest intellectus te capere, qui es infinitas? Scit se intellectus ignorantem et te capi non posse quia infinitas. Intelligere enim infinitatem est comprehendere incomprehensibile. Scit intellectus se ignorantem te, quia scit te sciri non posse, nisi

conceptum *Z*   11 tuum: tui *p*   quis: aliquis *EN*   12 expresserit: conceptum aliquem quomodo concipi possis s *post* expresserit *scribit et del. J*   secundum illam te: te secundum illam *T*   12-13 similitudinem . . . illam: *in marg. P* (concipientem *pro* concipiendum *habet P*)   14 intellectum tui quis: quis intellectum tui *EN* 15 adhuc: *om. N*   a: ad *N*   a *ex* ad *corr. S*   separaris: speraris *N*   16 separat: seperat *V*   17 a . . . possunt: *om. Pa* (a te quia tu es ab h[-] omnibus absolutus que cadere [-] *in marg. add. Pa²*)   his omnibus: omnibus his *E*   omnibus hiis *GNT* possunt: possum *N*   18 cuiuscumque: *non proprie scribit P*   cuiuslibet *Pa (ad* cuiuscumque *corr. Pa²)*   elevor: in *add. V*   19 video: vide *R*   hoc: es *add. p* 20 immultiplicabilis: *litterae finales non clarae sunt, sed* is *esse videntur, in N*

    53 1 te: ascendentem *post* te *scribit et del. A*   accedentem: ascendentem *T* 2 finitum: finitu *(rasura) N*   quomodo: quo *S*   perveniet: *om. S*   *non proprie abbreviat T*   3 quem: per *post* quem *scribit et del. T*   ultra¹: *clarius supra lin. rescribit Pa²*   finem¹: *non proprie scribit V*   4 nonne: non *AN*   subintrat: subiverat *V*   in: *om. AC (supra lin. add. C²) EGLMNOPQRSTZ (in linea add. Z²)*

cept is not a concept of You; for every concept reaches its limit at the wall of Paradise. Moreover, if anyone expresses any likeness and maintains that You are to be conceived in accordance with it, I know as well that this likeness is not a likeness of You. Similarly, if anyone recounts his understanding of You, intending to offer a means for Your being understood, he is still far away from You. For You are separated by a very high wall from all these |modes of apprehending|. For |this| wall separates from You whatever can be spoken of or thought of, because You are free from all the things that can be captured by any concept. Hence, when I am very highly elevated, I see that You are Infinity. Consequently, You are not approachable, not comprehensible, not nameable, not manifold, and not visible.

53 And so, one who ascends unto You must ascend beyond every limit and every end and |everything| bounded. But how will he attain unto You, who are the End at which he aims,[56] if he is supposed to ascend beyond |every| end? Does not he who ascends beyond ends enter into what is indeterminate and confused and so, with respect to the intellect, into ignorance and darkness, which are characteristic of intellectual confusion? Therefore, the intellect must become ignorant and must be situated in a shadow if it wishes to see You. But how, my God, is the intellect in ignorance? Is it not with respect to learned ignorance? Therefore, O God, You who are Infinity cannot be approached except by him whose intellect is ignorance—i.e., whose intellect knows that it is ignorant of You. How can the intellect apprehend You, who are Infinity? The intellect knows that it is ignorant and that You cannot be apprehended because You are Infinity. For to understand Infinity is to comprehend the Incomprehensible. The intellect knows that it is ignorant of You, because it knows that

---

5 intellectum: in *supra lin. add. I*   ignorantiam: ignorantia *Pa*   confusionis: confusione *G   ad* confusiones *corr. T*   5-6 confusionis intellectualis: confusiones intellectuales *P*   7 videre: videri *N*   meus: haec *add. p*   in: *om. Ap supra lin. GP* et *CV*   8 potes: potest *Pa (ad* potes *in marg. corr. Pa²) S* (potes *in marg. coni. S)*   deus: *om. Z*   es: est *Pa*   9 intellectus est: est intellectus in *I*   est: in *add. EGJNPaTp*   qui: que *EN*   10 se: te *V*   tui: *ex* te *corr. E supra lin. T*   te: *ex ? corr. P*   10-11 infinitas: *ex ? corr. E*   11 scit . . . infinitas: *om. A*   se: *om. I*   infinitas: es *add. p*   12 infinitatem: *ex ? corr. E*   est: *supra lin. J* aut *Jⁿ*   incomprehensibile: incomprehensibilem *ALPQRZ*   13 te²: *ex* se *corr. E*   se *LQ*   sciri: scire *NP*

sciatur non scibile et videatur non visibile et accedatur non accessibile.

54   Tu, deus meus, es ipsa infinitas absoluta, quam video esse finem infinitum. Sed capere nequeo, quomodo finis sit finis sine fine. Tu, deus, es tui ipsius finis, quia es quidquid habes. Si habes finem es finis. Es igitur finis infinitus, quia tui ipsius finis, quia finis tuus est
5 essentia tua. Essentia finis non terminatur seu finitur in alio a fine, sed in se. Finis igitur, qui est sui ipsius finis, est infinitus; et omnis finis, qui non est sui ipsius finis, est finis finitus. Tu, domine, quia es finis omnia finiens, ideo es finis cuius non est finis; et sic finis sine fine seu infinitus. Quod aufugit omnem rationem; implicat enim con-
10 tradictionem. Quando igitur assero esse infinitum, admitto tenebram lucem, ignorantiam scientiam, impossibile necessarium. Et quia admittimus finem finiti esse, necessario infinitum admittimus seu finem ultimum sive finem sine fine. Sed non possumus non admittere entia finita; ita non possumus non admittere infinitum. Admittimus igitur
15 coincidentiam contradictoriorum, super quam est infinitum.

55   Coincidentia autem illa est contradictio sine contradictione, sicut finis sine fine. Et tu mihi dicis, domine, quod sicut alteritas in unitate est sine alteritate, quia unitas, sic contradictio in infinitate est sine contradictione, quia infinitas. Infinitas est ipsa simplicitas; contradic-
5 tio sine alteratione non est. Alteritas autem in simplicitate sine altera-tione est, quia ipsa simplicitas. Omnia enim quae dicuntur de abso-luta simplicitate coincidunt cum ipsa, quia ibi habere est esse. Oppo-sitio oppositorum est oppositio sine oppositione, sicut finis finitorum est finis sine fine. Es igitur tu, deus, oppositio oppositorum,

---

54 2 capere: *non proprie abbreviat Pa*   finis[1]: fine *post* finis[1] *scribit et del. E*
finis[2]: *om. R*   3 quia: qui *Q*   4 tuus: *om. I*   5 essentia[2]: *om. R*   6 finis
igitur: *bis V*   sui ipsius: suiipsins *p*   est[2]: finis *add. GQ*   infinitus: *non clare
scribit J*   infinitus (in *supra lin.*) *Q*   6-7 finis[2]... finis[2]: *om. I*   7 est[2]: es *OP*
quia: qui *ACILMOPQRSVZ*   8 es: est *N*   9 aufugit: *ex* aufigit *corr. J*   implicat: complicat *p*   10 infinitum: *ex* infintum *corr. Z*   finem *add. p*   tenebram:
tenebras *p*   11 necessarium: necessiarium *Q*   11-12 admittimus: admittius *J*
12 necessario: necessiario *Q*   seu: se *N* sive *V*   13 sive: seu *ENp*   entia:
essencia *P*   13-14 entia ... admittere: *om. GI*   14 non[2]: *supra lin. AL*   admittere: encia finita *post* admittere *scribit et del. S*   15 infinitum: *bis M (*infinitum[1]
del. M)

55 1 illa: *om. LR*   2 fine: *non proprie scribit V*   mihi dicis domine: domine
dicis michi *EN*   alteritas: est *post* alteritas *scribit et del. E*   3 sic: sit *Pa*   3-4 est
sine contradictione: sine contradiccione est *Z*   4 simplicitas: omnia enim que

You can be known only if the unknowable is known, the unseeable seen, and the unapproachable approached.

54 You, my God, are Absolute Infinity, which I see to be an Infinite End. But I cannot apprehend how it is that an end is an End without an end. You, O God, are Your own end, because You *are* whatever You *have*. If You have an end, You are an end. Therefore, You are an Infinite End, because You are Your own end, since Your end is Your essence. The essence of end is not limited by, or ended in, something other than end but by and in itself. Therefore, the End which is its own end is infinite; and every end which is not its own end is a finite end. Because, O Lord, You are the End that delimits all things, You are an End of which there is no end; and thus You are an End without an end—i.e., an Infinite End. This |fact| escapes all reasoning, for it implies a contradiction. Therefore, when I assert the existence of the Infinite, I admit that darkness is light, that ignorance is knowledge, and that the impossible is the necessary. And because we admit that there is an end of the finite, necessarily we admit the Infinite—i.e., the Final End, or End without an end. But we cannot fail to admit that there are finite beings. So we cannot fail to admit that there is the Infinite. Hence, we admit the coincidence-of-contradictories, above which the Infinite exists.

55 But this coincidence is Contradiction without contradiction, just as it is End without an end. O Lord, You tell me that just as in oneness otherness is present without otherness, because |in oneness otherness is| oneness, so in Infinity contradiction is present without contradiction, because |in Infinity contradiction is| Infinity. Infinity is simplicity; contradiction does not exist apart from otherness. But in simplicity otherness is present without otherness, because |in simplicity otherness is| simplicity itself. For whatever is predicated of absolute simplicity coincides with absolute simplicity, because in absolute simplicity having is being. The oppositeness of opposites is oppositeness without oppositeness, just as the End of finite things is an End without an end. You, then, O God, are the Oppositeness of opposites,[57] because You are infinite. And because You are infinite, You are Infin-

dicuntur *post* simplicitas *add.* C; omnia *ad* omnium *corr., et* enim que dicuntur *del.,* C   5 alteratione: alteriacione *Pa*   alteritas: *ex* alteriatas *corr.* E   6 est: *om.* N   dicuntur: dicunt *V*   8 est oppositio: oppositio est *R*   oppositio: *ex* oppositione *corr.* L   sine: *non proprie scribit V*   8-11 sicut . . . oppositione: *in*

10 quia es infinitus. Et quia es infinitus, es ipsa infinitas. In infinitate est oppositio oppositorum sine oppositione.

56 Domine deus meus, fortitudo fragilium, video te ipsam infinitatem esse. Ideo nihil est tibi alterum vel diversum vel adversum. Infinitas enim non compatitur secum alteritatem, quia cum sit infinitas, nihil est extra eam. Omnia enim includit et omnia ambit infinitas abso-
5 luta. Ideo quando foret infinitas et aliud extra ipsam, non foret infinitas neque aliud. Infinitas enim non potest esse nec maior nec minor. Nihil igitur est extra eam. Nisi enim omne esse includeret in se infinitas, non esset infinitas. Quod si non foret infinitas, neque tunc foret finis neque tunc aliud nec diversum, quae sine alteritate finium et
10 terminorum non possunt esse. Sublato igitur infinito nihil manet. Est igitur infinitas et complicat omnia, et nihil esse potest extra eam. Hinc nihil ei alterum vel diversum. Infinitas igitur sic omnia est quod nullum omnium. Infinitati nullum nomen convenire potest. Omne enim nomen potest habere contrarium. Infinitati autem innominabili
15 nihil potest esse contrarium. Neque infinitas est totum cui pars opponitur; neque esse potest pars. Neque est magna infinitas neque parva neque quidquam omnium quae sive in caelo sive in terra nominari possunt. Supra omnia illa est infinitas. Infinitas nulli est maior nec minor nec aequalis.

57 Sed dum infinitatem considero non esse maiorem vel minorem cuicumque dabili, dico ipsam esse mensuram omnium, cum nec sit maior nec minor. Et sic concipio eam aequalitatem essendi. Talis autem aequalitas est infinitas. Et ita non est aequalitas modo quo
5 aequalitati opponitur inaequale, sed ibi inaequalitas est aequalitas. Inaequalitas enim in infinitate est sine inaequalitate, quia infinitas. Sic et aequalitas est infinitas in infinitate. Infinita aequalitas est finis

---

marg. P 10 quia¹: qui *R* quia es infinitus et: *om. J* (et *post* oppositorum *(55:9) supra lin. add. J ⁿ*) es³: es (*non* et) *scribit L* est: es *I*

56 1 te ipsam: *om. A* ipsam: ipsum *EN* 2 tibi: *om. G* 4 et: *om. R* 5 foret¹: esset *p* foret²: esset *p* 7 igitur: enim *V* est: *om. R* nisi: *non proprie abbreviat L* 8 quod: quia *Q* foret¹: esset *p* foret²: esset *p* 9 neque: *om. V* nec: neque *AEILMNOPQRZ* sine: sue *L* 10 non possunt esse: esse non possunt *R* manet: *om. E* (erit *in marg. add. E³*) erit *N* 11 complicat: memorie *post* conplicat *scribit et del. G* esse potest: potest esse *p* 12 ei: est *J om. N* igitur: *in marg. A om. J* sic: sit *V* 14-15 infinitati . . . contrarium: *om. V* 16 esse potest: potest esse *Z* pars: *om. V* infinitas neque parva: neque parva infinitas *EN* 17 neque: *ex* nec *corr. R* quidquam: quodquam *J* omnium

ity. In Infinity the oppositeness of opposites is present without oppositeness.

56 Lord my God, Strength of the frail, I see that You are Infinity itself. And so, there is not anything that is other than You or different from You or opposed to You. For Infinity is not compatible with otherness, because there is not anything outside it, since it is Infinity. For Absolute Infinity includes and encompasses all things. And so, if there were "Infinity" and something else outside it, there would be neither Infinity nor anything else. For Infinity cannot be either greater or lesser. Therefore, there is not anything outside it. For unless it included all being in itself, it would not be Infinity. But if Infinity did not exist, then *end* would also not exist. And in that case, what is *other* and *different* would also not exist, for they cannot exist without the otherness of ends and of limits. So if the Infinite is removed, nothing remains. Therefore, Infinity exists and enfolds all things; and no thing can exist outside it. Hence, nothing is other than it or different from it. Therefore, Infinity is all things in such way that it is none of them.[58] No name can befit it. For every name can have a contrary; but to unnameable Infinity nothing can be contrary. Moreover, Infinity is not a whole, to which a part is opposed; nor can Infinity be a part. Furthermore, Infinity is neither great nor small; nor is it any of all the things which—whether in heaven or on earth—can be named. Infinity is beyond all these things. It is not greater than, lesser than, or equal to, anything else.

57 But when I consider that Infinity is not greater or lesser than any positable thing, I say that it is the Measure of all things, because it is neither greater nor lesser. And in this way I conceive it to be Equality of being. But such Equality is Infinity. And so, it is not equality in the way in which what is unequal is opposed to equality. Rather, in Equality inequality is Equality. For in Infinity inequality is present without inequality, because |in Infinity inequality is| Infinity. Similarly, in Infinity Equality is Infinity. Infinite Equality is an End with-

quae: omniumque *N*   18 possunt: $\overline{\overline{pt}}$ *A*   supra: super *ENV*   19 aequalis: nec inequalis *add. EN*

57 1 minorem: minorum *p*   1-2 cuicumque: cuilibet *R*   2 ipsam: eam *R* esse: *supra lin. P*   3 eam: *non proprie scribit V*   aequalitatem: qualitatem *N* 4 ita: *in marg. E*   quo: qua *Q*   5 inaequale: inequalitas *Z*   6 infinitate: esse *post* infinitate *scribit et del. P*   6-7 est . . . infinitate: *om. V*   7 sic: *ex* sit *corr.*

sine fine. Unde licet non sit nec maior nec minor, non tamen propterea est aequalitas modo quo capitur aequalitas contracta, sed est
10 infinita aequalitas, quae non capit magis nec minus. Et ita non est
magis aequalis uni quam alteri, sed ita aequalis uni quod omnibus, ita
omnibus quod nulli omnium. Infinitum enim non est contrahibile,
sed manet absolutum. Si esset contrahibile ab infinitate, non esset
infinitum. Non est igitur contrahibile ad aequalitatem finiti, licet non
15 sit alicui inaequale. Inaequalitas enim quomodo conveniret infinito,
cui non convenit nec magis nec minus? Infinitum ergo nec est dato
quocumque aut maius aut minus aut inaequale. Nec propter hoc est
aequale finito, quia est supra omne finitum per infinitum. Et quia per
infinitum est supra omne finitum, hoc est per se ipsum, tunc infini-
20 tum est absolutum penitus et incontrahibile.

58 O quam excelsus es, domine, supra omnia, et cum hoc humilis,
quia in omnibus! Si infinitas esset contrahibilis ad aliquod nominabile, ut est linea aut superficies aut species, ad se attraheret id ad
quod contraheretur. Et ita implicat [contradictionem,] infinitum esse
5 contrahibile, quia non contraheretur sed attraheret. Si enim dixero
infinitum contrahi ad lineam, ut cum dico infinitam lineam, tunc
linea attrahitur in infinitum. Desinit enim linea esse linea, quando
non habet quantitatem et finem. Infinita linea non est linea, sed linea
in infinitate est infinitas. Et sicut nihil addi potest infinito, ita infini-
10 tum non potest ad aliquid contrahi, ut sit aliud quam infinitum.
Infinita bonitas non est bonitas, sed infinitas. Infinita quantitas non
est quantitas, sed infinitas. Et ita de omnibus.

J aut J^n et: *ex* est *corr. Q*   est infinitas in infinitate: in infinitate est infinitas *p*
infinita: infinitas *N*   8 non^1: *om. R*   nec^1: *om. T*   non^2: *om. T*   10 capit:
nec *add. LRZ*   magis: maius *A*   ita: ideo *V*   11 alteri: e *non clare scribit Pa*
12 omnium: omni *Pa*   contrahibile: contractabile *V*   13-14 ab . . . contrahibile:
om. S   15 conveniret: conveniet *I*   16 cui: cum *Q*   non: nec *R*   nec^1: *om. ENT*
magis: maius *AGQ*   ergo: igitur *EGIJNPaT*   nec^3: non *V*   17 aut^1: *non proprie
abbreviat L*   aut^2: *non proprie abbreviat L*   aut^3: nec *R*   18 supra: super *J*
confuse abbreviat Pa   per^2: *om. GT*   18-19 per^1. . . finitum: *om. CVp in
marg. P*   19 supra: *confuse abbreviat Pa*   finitum: per infinitum *post* finitum
scribit et del. I   20 est: eciam (?) *N*   absolutum: sui ipsius *add. A*   abso'lū *C*
(ad absolutum *corr. C*^{2}*)*   absosu absolutum *Q*   et: *bis S*   incontrahibile: incomprehensibile *A*   incontrahibile *V*
   58 1 supra: super *LV confuse abbreviat Pa*   2 contrahibilis: contrahabilis *V*

out an end. Hence, although it is neither greater nor lesser, nevertheless it is not on this account equality in the way in which contracted equality is apprehended to be. Rather, it is Infinite Equality, which does not admit of more or less. And so, it is not more nearly equal to one thing than to another but is equal to one thing in such way that it is equal to all—and is equal to all in such way that it is equal to none. For the Infinite is not contractible but remains absolute. If the Infinite were contractible away from Infinity,[59] it would not be the Infinite. Therefore, the Infinite is not contractible to equality with the finite, although it is not unequal to anything. For how could inequality befit the Infinite, which *more* and *less* do not befit? Therefore, the Infinite is not greater than or lesser than or unequal to any given thing. Yet, it is not on this account equal to the finite, because it is infinitely above everything finite. And because it is infinitely above everything finite—i.e., because it exists per se—the Infinite is altogether absolute and uncontractible.

58   O how exalted You are above all things, O Lord! And at the same time how lowly You are because You are present in all things! If Infinity were contractible to something nameable (such as a line or a surface or a species), it would attract to itself that to which it would be contracted. And so, for the Infinite to be contractible implies a contradiction, because the Infinite would not be contracted but would attract. For example, if I say that the Infinite is contracted to a line (as when I speak of an infinite line), then the line is attracted into the Infinite. For the line stops being a line when it does not have quantity and an end. An infinite line is not a line; rather, in Infinity a line is Infinity. And just as nothing can be added to the Infinite, so the Infinite cannot be contracted to anything, so that it becomes other than the Infinite. Infinite goodness is not goodness but is Infinity. Infinite quantity is not quantity but is Infinity. And so on.

aliquod: aliquid *AEGN*   2-3 nominabile: nominale *PaQS*   3 se: ad *post* se *scribit et del. S*   4 ita: *om. p*   contradictionem: *supplevi (cf. 54:9-10)*   esse: *bis S* (esse[2] *del. S*)   6 infinitum: *bis P* (infinitum[2] *del. P*)   ad: *om. Q*   7 attrahitur: attrahit *Q*   8 et: in *Pa*   9 nihil: *om. A*   10 aliquid: aliquod *EIJLMOPPaQRTV* ut sit: *om. R*   sit: sic *N*   11-12 infinita[2]... infinitas: *om. I*   12 quantitas: *om. V*   et: est *N*

59   Tu es, deus, magnus, cuius magnitudinis non est finis. Et ideo
video te immensurabilem omnium mensuram, sicut infinitum omnium
finem. Es igitur, domine, quia infinitus, sine principio et fine. Es
principium sine principio et finis sine fine. Es principium sine fine et
5 finis sine principio; et ita principium quod finis et ita finis quod
principium; et neque principium neque finis, sed supra principium et
finem ipsa absoluta infinitas semper benedicta.

60   CAPITULUM XIV

             QUOMODO DEUS OMNIA COMPLICAT SINE ALTERITATE

Video, domine, ex infinitate misericordiae tuae, te infinitatem
omnia ambientem. Non est igitur extra te quidquam. Omnia autem in
5 te non sunt aliud a te. Doces me, domine, quomodo alteritas, quae in
te non est, etiam in se non est nec esse potest. Nec facit alteritas, quae
in te non est, unam creaturam esse alteram ab alia, quamvis una non
sit alia. Caelum enim non est terra, licet verum sit caelum esse caelum et terram terram. Si igitur quaesiero alteritatem, quae neque in te
10 neque extra te est, ubi reperiam? Et si non est, quomodo terra est alia
creatura quam caelum? Nam sine alteritate non potest hoc concipi.

61   Sed loqueris in me, domine, et dicis alteritatis non esse positivum
principium, et ita non est. Nam quomodo alteritas esset sine principio, nisi ipsa foret principium et infinitas? Non est autem principium

---

59 2 immensurabilem: *non proprie abbreviat Pa*   3 fine: *ut* sine *legit, et* fine
add., T³   4 principium¹: principio *V*   et¹: es *Q*   es . . . fine: *om. EN*   4-5 fine¹
. . . sine: *om. I*   5 et¹: es *EGT*   quod¹: *supra lin. E*   ita²: *om. A*   6 et¹: es *EGT*
7 infinitas: infinita *R*   benedicta: amen *add. J*   et cetera *add. P*

60 1 capitulum XIV: capitulum 15 *E³*   2 quomodo . . . alteritate: quomodo
omnia complicantur sine alteritate in deo *R (in 1:1* quomodo omnia complicat sine
alteritate *habet R)*   deus: *om. AGLM³ (in 1:1 om. etiam M) OP³ (in 1:1 om.
etiam P) Pa³Q² (in 1:1 om. etiam Q) TZ*   omnia complicat: complicat omnia *V²*
sine alteritate: *om. E³ (sed in 1:1 habet E³)*   3 video: ideo *Q*   4 ambientem:
ambigentem *GT*   te: *om. CIV*   5 doces: *ex* doce *corr. R*   quomodo: quoniam *I*
quomodo *bis J*   6 te: est *add. A*   esse: in se *S*   potest: *litteram* o *non clare*

59   You, O God, are great, and there is no end of Your greatness. And so, I see that You are the Immeasurable Measure of all things, even as You are the Infinite End of all things. Therefore, O Lord, because You are infinite You are without beginning and end. You are Beginning without a beginning and End without an end. You are Beginning without an end and End without a beginning. You are Beginning in such way that You are End—and End in such way that You are Beginning. And You are neither Beginning nor End but, above beginning and end, are Absolute Infinity, blessed forever.

60   CHAPTER FOURTEEN

                    GOD ENFOLDS, WITHOUT OTHERNESS, ALL THINGS

From the infinity of Your mercy, O Lord, I see that You are all-encompassing Infinity. Therefore, there is not anything outside You. But in You no thing is *other* than You. You teach me, O Lord, that otherness, which is not present in You, does not, and cannot, exist even in itself. Moreover, otherness, which is not present in You, does not make one creature to be *other* than another, even though one creature is not another creature. For the sky is not the earth, even though it is true that the sky is the sky and the earth the earth. If, then, I seek otherness, which is not present either within You or outside You, where shall I find it? And if it does not exist, how is the earth another creature than the sky? For without otherness this |difference| cannot be conceived.

61   But You speak within me, O Lord, and You say that there is not a positive beginning of otherness; and so otherness does not exist. For how could otherness exist without a beginning, unless it itself were Beginning and Infinity? But otherness is not the Beginning of being.

---

format V   6-7 etiam . . . est: *om. P (in marg. add. P²)*   7 te: est *add. A*   non²: *om. IS*   8 enim: autem *p*   caelum²: non *post* celum² *scribit et del. R*   9 terram¹: esse *add. p*   quae: *om. T*   te: est *add. p*   10 te: *om. Q*   reperiam: reperiatur *A*   si: *ex* sic *(?) corr. P aut P²*   terra: celum *R*   11 caelum: terra *R*   sine: *ex ? corr. E²*   hoc concipi: concipi hoc *EN*

    61 1 domine: *om. ALMOPQRZ (in marg. add. Z²)*   alteritatis: *ad* alteritates *corr. G*   alteritas *Pa*   1-2 positivum principium: principium positivum *EN*   3 foret:

essendi alteritas. Alteritas enim dicitur a non esse. Quod enim unum
5 non est aliud, hinc dicitur alterum. Alteritas igitur non potest esse
principium essendi, quia dicitur a non esse. Neque habet principium
essendi, cum sit a non esse. Non est igitur alteritas aliquid.

62   Sed quod caelum non est terra, est quia caelum non est infinitas
ipsa, quae omne esse ambit. Unde quia infinitas est infinitas absoluta,
inde evenit unum non posse esse aliud, sicut essentia Socratis ambit
omne esse socraticum, in quo simplici esse socratico nulla est alteri-
5 tas seu diversitas. Nam omnium quae sunt in Socrate, est esse Socratis unitas individualis, ita quod in eo unico esse complicatur omnium
quae in Socrate sunt esse, in ipsa scilicet individuali simplicitate, ubi
nihil reperiatur alterum seu diversum. Sed in illo esse unico omnia
quae esse habent socraticum, sunt et complicantur, et extra illud nec
10 sunt nec esse possunt—licet cum hoc: in eo esse simplicissimo oculus
non sit auris, et caput non sit cor, et visus non sit auditus, et sensus
non sit ratio. Neque hoc evenit ex aliquo principio alteritatis. Sed
posito simplicissimo esse socratico, evenit caput non esse pedes, quia
caput non est ipsum simplicissimum esse socraticum. Hinc esse eius
15 non ambit omne esse socraticum. Et ita video, te domine illustrante,
quod quia esse simplex socraticum est incommunicabile penitus et
incontrahibile ad esse cuiuscumque membri, inde esse unius membri
non est esse alterius. Sed esse illud simplex socraticum est esse
omnium membrorum Socratis, in quo omnis essendi varietas et alter-

esset *p*   et: finis *(?) post* et *scribit et del. P*   4 essendi: quia dicitur a non esse
neque habet principium essendi *post* essendi *scribit et del. J*   5 est: *bis EN*
6 essendi: *om. T*   6-7 quia . . . essendi: *om. I*   7 essendi: *om. G* quia dicitur a
non esse *post* essendi *scribit et del. S*   aliquid: aliquod *IJPa*
  62 1 quod: cum *Q*   est[2]: *om. V*   3 evenit: evet *(=eve*[t]*=evenit) A*   posse:
om. A   esse: est *A om. V*   essentia: esse *p*   4 socratico: sacratico *TZ*   est:
om. Q   5 in: *om. EN*   Socrate: socrato *A*   6 eo: ea *T*   6-7 omnium quae:
omniumque *N*   7 quae: sunt *add. A*   in Socrate sunt: sunt in socrate *G*   scilicet:
videlicet *G*   individuali: *ex* individuale *corr. G*   individuali simplicitate: simplicitate individuali *EN*   8 reperiatur: reperitur *GIJPaT*   seu: vel *EGIJNPaT* sive *R*
in illo: *bis S*   esse unico: unico esse *EN*   9 esse: sunt *A*   complicantur: explicantur *p*   illud: illud *(?) A*   9-10 nec sunt nec: sunt nec nec *ad* nec sunt nec
transponit T et T[3]   10 hoc: homine *supra* hoc *coni. I*   oculus: *ex* oculis *corr. S*
oculis *Z*   11 sit[1]: fit *N*   visus: *ex* usus *corr. Pa*   12 alteritatis: alteritas *Pa (ad*

For otherness derives its name from not-being. For because one
thing is *not* another thing, it is called *another*. Therefore, otherness
cannot be the Beginning of being, because it derives its name from
not-being. And it does not *have* a beginning of being, since it derives
from not-being. Therefore, it is not the case that otherness is
something.

62   But the reason the sky is not the earth is that the sky is not Infinity itself, which encompasses all being. Hence, because Infinity is
Absolute Infinity, the result is that one thing cannot be another
thing. By comparison, the essence of Socrates encompasses the whole
of Socratic being.[60] In the simple Socratic being there is no otherness
or difference. For the being of Socrates is the individual oneness of
whatever is present in Socrates, so that the being of all that is in
Socrates is enfolded in this one being—i.e., in the individual simplicity, wherein there is nothing other or different. But in this one being
all the things that have Socratic being are present and enfolded, and
apart from it they neither exist nor can exist—although with this
|qualification|: in this most simple being the eye is not the ear, the
head is not the heart, sight is not hearing, and the senses are not
reason. These differences do not result from any beginning of otherness. Rather, when most simple Socratic being is posited, the result
is that the head is not the feet, because the head is not most simple
Socratic being. Hence, the head's being does not encompass the
whole of Socratic being. And in this manner I see, by Your illumination, O Lord, that because simple Socratic being is altogether
incommunicable to, and uncontractible to, the being of any member,
the being of one member is not the being of the other. But the
simple Socratic being is the being of all the members of Socrates; in
it the complete variety-of-being and otherness-of-being that happens

alteritatis *corr. Pa²)*   13 posito simplicissimo esse: simplicissimo esse posito *I*
14 caput: *om. G*   ipsum: *om. LPa*   esse¹: *om. GT*   14-15 hinc . . . socraticum:
om. R   eius non ambit: non ambit eius *V*   15 esse: *om. ST*   esse socraticum:
om. EN   et: *supra lin. P*   ita: *in marg. O*   ideo *T*   domine: domino *A*   16 incommunicabile: incommutabile *EN*   17 cuiuscumque: *ex* cuicumque *corr. Q*   membri¹: non est esse alterius *post* membri¹ *scribit et del. A*   18 est¹: *om. S*   simplex
socraticum: socraticum simplex *ad* simplex socraticum *transponit R*   19 omnis:

20 itas quae membris evenit, est simplex unitas—sicut pluralitas formarum partium, in forma totius, est unitas.

63	Sic se habet aliqualiter, deus, tuum esse, quod est esse infinitatis
absolute, ad omnia quae sunt. Sed absolute dico ut absoluta essendi
forma omnium formarum contractarum. Unde manus Socratis, quando separatur a Socrate, licet post abscisionem non sit amplius manus
5 Socratis, manet tamen adhuc in aliquo esse cadaveris. Hoc ex eo est
quia forma Socratis, quae dat esse, non dat simpliciter esse sed esse
contractum, scilicet socraticum, a quo esse manus est separabilis, et
quod nihilominus sub alia forma maneat. Sed si semel separaretur
manus ab esse incontracto penitus, quod est infinitum et absolutum,
10 totaliter desineret esse, quia ab omni esse foret separata.

64	Gratias tibi ago, domine deus meus, qui te mihi quantum capere
possum largiter ostendis, quomodo tu es ipsa infinitas esse omnium
complicans simplicissima virtute, quae non foret infinita nisi infinite
unita. Virtus enim unita fortior. Quae igitur virtus ita est unita, quod
5 magis uniri nequit, est infinita et omnipotens. Tu es, deus, omnipotens, quia absoluta simplicitas, quae est infinitas absoluta.

omnes *Q*　　varietas: veritas *V*　　20 evenit: *om. G*　　20-21 sicut . . . unitas: *om. V*
21 est: sunt *ACEGIJLMNOPPaQRSTZ*
　　63 1 aliqualiter: equaliter *S*　　aliquo pacto *p*　　deus: *om. I*　　quod est esse:
om. EN　　esse²: *scribit C et del. C²* *om. p*　　infinitatis: infinitas *CVp*　　2 ab-
solute¹: ab te (=abᵗᵉ=absolute*)* *A*　　omnia: ea *add. p*　　absoluta: absolute *V*　　4 sit:
supra lin. Z　　6 dat¹: *om. R*　　dat²: *om. I*　　*ex* datur *corr. R*　　simpliciter esse:
esse simpliciter *Z*　　7 scilicet: esse *add. G*　　esse: est *N* *om. V*　　8 maneat:
manet *Q*　　separaretur: separetur *R*　　9 incontracto: contracto *V*　　penitus:
peitus *Pa*　　est: *om. R*　　10 totaliter: tataliter *P*　　desineret: disineret *p*　　omni:
om. A　　foret: *om. R*　　esset *p*
　　64 1 capere: carpere *OP* *non proprie abbreviat Pa*　　2 quomodo: quoniam *QR*
ipsa: *ex* ipsas *corr. J* *aut Jⁿ om. Pa (in marg. add. Pa²)*　　3 simplicissima:
simplicissime *L*　　virtute: *ex* virtutem *corr. R*　　non: *bis E*　　foret: *in marg. P*
esset *p*　　4 unita²: est *add. ALM²* *(om. M; supra lin. scribit M²) OPQZ*　　fortior:
est *add. EN*　　virtus²: *om. R*　　ita est: est ita *LQZ*　　est unita: unita est *p*　　5 est:
esse *V*　　et omnipotens: *om. V*

to the members is a simple oneness—even as in the form of a *whole* the plurality of the forms of the *parts* is a oneness.

63   In some such way |as the foregoing,| O God, Your being—which is, absolutely, the being of Infinity—is related to all existing things. Now, by "absolutely" I mean "as the Absolute Form-of-being of all contracted forms." Thus, if the hand of Socrates were separated from Socrates, then in spite of its no longer being Socrates' hand after the amputation, it would nevertheless continue on, in a certain respect, as the being of a corpse. This |point| holds true because of the fact that the form of Socrates, which gives being, does not give *being* in an unqualified sense but gives *contracted being*, viz., Socratic being. The hand's being is separable from the Socratic being, and it continues on, though under another form. But if the hand were once separated from altogether uncontracted being, which is infinite and absolute, it would altogether cease to exist, because it would be separated from all being.

64   Lord my God—who generously manifest Yourself to me to the extent of my capability to receive—I thank You that You are Infinity itself, enfolding the being of all things by a most simple power, which would not be infinite were it not infinitely unified. For power that is unified is stronger. Therefore, a power that is so unified that it cannot be more greatly unified is infinite and omnipotent. O God, You are omnipotent, because You are Absolute Simplicity, which is Absolute Infinity.

65   CAPITULUM XV

QUOMODO ACTUALIS INFINITAS EST UNITAS IN QUA FIGURA EST VERITAS

Sustine adhuc servulum utique insipientem nisi quantum conces-
seris ut loquatur ad te deum suum. Video in hac picta facie figuram
5 infinitatis. Nam visus est interminatus ad obiectum vel locum, et ita
infinitus. Non enim plus est conversus ad unum quam alium qui
intuetur eam. Et quamvis visus eius sit in se infinitus, videtur tamen
per quemlibet respicientem terminari, quia ita quemlibet respicit
determinate, qui intuetur eam, quasi solum eum et nihil aliud. Videris
10 igitur mihi, domine, quasi posse esse absolutum et infinitum, formabile et terminabile per omnem formam. Dicimus enim potentiam
materiae formabilem esse infinitam, quia numquam penitus finietur.
Sed respondes in me, lux infinita, absolutam potentiam esse ipsam
infinitatem, quae est ultra murum coincidentiae, ubi posse fieri coin-
15 cidit cum posse facere, ubi potentia coincidit cum actu. Materia
prima, etsi sit in potentia ad infinitas formas, non tamen actu illas
habere potest; sed per unam terminatur potentia, qua sublata, terminatur per aliam. Si igitur posse esse materiae coincideret cum actu,
ipsa esset sic potentia quod actus. Et sicut fuit in potentia ad infini-
20 tas formas, ita actu esset infinities formata. Infinitas autem actu est
sine alteritate, et non potest esse infinitas quin sit unitas. Non possunt igitur esse infinitae formae actu, sed actualis infinitas est unitas.

66   Tu igitur, deus, qui es ipsa infinitas, es ipse unus deus, in quo video
omne posse esse esse actu. Nam absolutum posse ab omni potentia

65 1 capitulum XV: capitulum 16 E^3 3 sustine: ssstine *L*   quantum: inquantum *R*   4 ut: *om. S*   loquatur: loquitur *V*   5 interminatus: indeterminatus *G*
vel: ad *add. I*   et: ut *I*   6 infinitus: infinitas *V*   plus: amplius *S*   quam: ad
add. AENOPQRSV   qui: quia *S*   7 sit in se: in se sit *EN*   8 quia: quod *N*
9 qui: que *J*   eam: et *add. Pa*   eum: *non clare scribit V*   10 igitur: ergo *Q*
10-11 formabile: *ex* formale *corr. A*   11 et: *om. Pa (supra lin. add. Pa²)*   12 materiae: materie *bis E* (materie¹ *del. E*)   formabilem: *ex* formalem *corr. J*   formabile *V*   quia: que *Q*   13 infinita: infinitam *T*   14 quae: qui *IJPa*   est
ultra murum: ultra murum est *CVp* et ultra murum *S*   15 cum¹: *bis V*   cum¹
... coincidit: *om. QS*   16 prima: *om. p*   sit: sic *V*   ad: *bis Q*   17 potentia:
potentiam *I*   qua: absoluta *post* qua *scribit et del. P*   18 coincideret: coin-
cederet *G*   coincidit *Q*   19 esset sic: sic esset *EN*   sic: *ex* sicut *corr. P* sicut *QR*

65

CHAPTER FIFTEEN

ACTUAL INFINITY IS A ONENESS IN WHICH IMAGE IS TRUTH

Continue to sustain Your servant, who surely is foolish except insofar as You grant that he speak to You, his God. In this |icon's| painted face I see an image of Infinity. For the gaze is not confined to an object or a place, and so it is infinite. For it is turned as much toward one beholder of the face as toward another. And although in itself the gaze of this face is infinite, nevertheless it seems to be limited by any given onlooker. For it looks so fixedly upon whoever looks unto it that it seems to look only upon him and not upon anything else. Therefore, O Lord, You seem to me as if You were absolute and infinite possibility-to-be that is formable and determinable by every form; for we say that the formable possibility of matter is infinite, because it will never be fully determined. But You reply within me, O Infinite Light, that Absolute Possibility is Infinity itself, which is beyond the wall of the coincidence in which the possibility-to-be-made coincides with the possibility-to-make and in which possibility coincides with actuality. Although prime matter is in potency to an infinite number of forms, nevertheless it cannot have them actually. Rather, the potency is determined by one form; and if this form is removed, the potency is determined by another form. Therefore, if matter's possibility-to-be coincided with actuality, matter would be possibility in such way that it would be actuality; and just as it would be in potency to an infinite number of forms, so it would be actually formed by an infinity of forms. But Infinity, as it exists actually, is without otherness; and it cannot exist without existing as oneness. Therefore, there cannot be, actually, an infinite number of forms. Instead, Actual Infinity is oneness.

66 You, then, O God, who are Infinity itself, are the one God Himself, in whom I see that all possibility-to-be exists actually.[61] For possibility which is free from all possibility that is contracted to

---

fuit: *om. T* 20 formata: informata *EN* autem: *bis scribit, et* autem[2] *del., J* autem actu: actu autem *ad* autem actu *transponit E* 21 quin: quando *N* 21-22 possunt: *ex* potest *in marg. corr. J*

66 1 deus[1]: *om. EN* es[2]: *ex* est corr. *I* est *M (ad* es *corr. M[2]) OPQS* 2 esse[2]: *om. N* nam: non *I* 3 primam: *om. p* 3-4 passivam potentiam:

contracta ad materiam primam seu quamcumque passivam potentiam, est absolutum esse. Quidquid enim in infinito esse est, est
5 ipsum esse infinitum simplicissimum. Ita posse esse omnia in infinito
esse est ipsum infinitum esse. Similiter et actu esse omnia in infinito
esse est ipsum infinitum esse. Quare posse esse absolutum et actu
esse absolutum in te deo meo non sunt nisi tu deus meus infinitus.
Omne posse esse tu es, deus meus. Posse esse materiae primae non
10 est posse absolutum; ideo non potest cum actu absoluto converti.
Quare materia prima non est actu quod esse potest, sicut tu deus.
Posse esse materiae primae est materiale, et ita contractum et non
absolutum; sic et posse esse sensibile vel rationale contractum est.
Sed penitus incontractum posse cum absoluto simpliciter, hoc est
15 infinito, coincidit.

67   Quando igitur tu, deus meus, occurris mihi quasi prima materia
formabilis, quia recipis formam cuiuslibet te intuentis, tunc me elevas, ut videam quomodo intuens te non dat tibi formam, sed in te
intuetur se, quia a te recipit id quod est. Et ita id quod videris ab
5 intuente recipere, hoc donas, quasi sis speculum aeternitatis vivum,
quod est forma formarum. In quod speculum dum quis respicit,
videt formam suam in forma formarum, quae est speculum. Et iudicat formam quam videt in speculo illo esse figuram formae suae,
quia sic est in speculo materiali polito—licet contrarium illius sit
10 verum, quia id quod videt in illo aeternitatis speculo non est figura
sed veritas, cuius ipse videns est figura. Figura igitur in te, deus
meus, est veritas et exemplar omnium et singulorum quae sunt aut
esse possunt.

potenciam passivam *EN*   4 enim: esse *add. EN*   in infinito esse est: est in
infinito esse *p*   infinito: infinitate *G*   esse est: esse est *Z (ad* est esse *corr. Z²)*
5 esse infinitum: infinitum esse *EN*   6 est: et *V*   infinitum: *? post* infinitum
scribit et del. J   esse²: *om. G*   et: *supra lin. G*   6-7 similiter . . . esse²: *om. T*
(in marg. add. T²)   7 esse¹: *om. Ip*   est: et *add. N* et *V*   actu: et *post* actu
scribit et del. L   8 meo: et *add. N*   nisi: *om. I*   meus: ab *post* meus *scribit et*
del. E   posse esse *post* meus *scribit et del. G*   9 omne: omnia *S*   es: *om. ALMO*
PQRZ (in marg. add. Z²)   esse²: absolutum *post* esse² *scribit et del. G*   primae:
est materiale et ita contractum et non absolutum *post* prime *scribit et del. R*   9-
12 primae . . . primae: *om. p*   non . . . primae: *om. CV*   10 posse: esse *supra lin.*
add. I   absolutum: esse *post* absolutum *scribit et del. P*   12 materiae primae:
materia prima *N*   est: et *V*   non: *supra lin. L*   13 est: *om. L* et non absolutum
post est *scribit et del. Pa*

prime matter or to any passive potency whatsoever is Absolute Being. For whatever exists in Infinite Being is most simple Infinite Being. Thus, in Infinite Being the possibility-to-be-all-things is Infinite Being itself. Likewise, in Infinite Being actually-being-all-things is Infinite Being itself. Therefore, in You my God absolute possibility-to-be and absolute actual being are only You my Infinite God. You, my God, are all possibility-to-be. The possibility-to-be of prime matter is not absolute possibility, and so it is not convertible with absolute actuality. Therefore, prime matter is not actually that which it can be, as are You O God. The possibility-to-be of prime matter is material and, thus, is contracted and not absolute. Likewise, sensible or rational possibility-to-be is contracted. But altogether uncontracted possibility coincides with the altogether Absolute, i.e., with the Infinite.

67   Therefore, my God, when You seem to me as if You were formable prime matter, because You receive the form of each one who looks unto You, You elevate me, so that I discern the following: viz., that the one who looks unto You does not bestow form upon You; rather, he beholds himself in You, because he receives from You that which he is. And so, that which You seem to receive from the one who looks unto You—this You bestow, as if You were a living Mirror-of-eternity, which is the Form of forms. When someone looks into this Mirror, he sees his own form in the Form of forms, which the Mirror is. And he judges the form seen in the Mirror to be the image of his own form, because such would be the case with regard to a polished material mirror. However, the contrary thereof is true, because in the Mirror of eternity that which he sees is not an image but is the Truth, of which the beholder is the image. Therefore, in You, my God, the image is the Truth and Exemplar of each and every thing that exists or can exist.

67 1 prima: *om. p*   2 formam: cuius te *post* formam *scribit et del. Pa*   cuiuslibet: tu in *post* cuiuslibet *scribit et del. A*   cuilibet *S*   2-3 elevas: *ex* eleves *corr. J aut J^n*   3 ut videam: *om. R*   4 id^2: id^2 *scribit, del., et clarius rescribit J* 5 recipere: *non proprie abbreviat Pa*   6 forma: *om. G*   7 in forma: *in marg. A* 8 videt: formam suam *post* videt *scribit et del. A*   formae suae: sue forme *Q* 9 sic: sicut *A*   speculo: illo esse *post* speculo *scribit et del. S*   materiali: materiale *S*   polito: posito *E (ad* polito *corr. E^2) N*   sit: sic *J*   10 id: illud *Q om. p* illo: *om. G*   12 est veritas: *om. I*   et^1: et^1 *ad* est *corr. I*   aut: et *A*

68   O deus omni menti admirandus, videris aliquando quasi sis umbra,
qui es lux. Nam dum video quomodo ad mutationem meam videtur
visus eiconae tuae mutatus et facies tua videtur mutata quia ego
mutatus, occurris mihi quasi sis umbra quae sequitur mutationem
5 ambulantis. Sed quia ego sum viva umbra et tu veritas, iudico ex
mutatione umbrae veritatem mutatam. Es igitur, deus meus, sic
umbra quod veritas; sic es imago mea et cuiuslibet quod exemplar.

69   Domine deus, illustrator cordium, facies mea vera est facies, quia
tu eam mihi dedisti, qui es veritas. Est et facies mea imago, quia non
est ipsa veritas sed veritatis absolutae imago. Complico igitur in conceptu meo veritatem et imaginem faciei meae, et video in ea coinci-
5 dere imaginem cum veritate faciali, ita quod quantum imago intantum vera. Et tunc ostendis mihi, domine, quomodo ad mutationem
faciei meae facies tua est pariter mutata et immutata: mutata quia
non deserit veritatem faciei meae, immutata quia non sequitur mutationem imaginis. Unde sicut facies tua non deserit faciei meae verita-
10 tem, sic etiam non sequitur mutationem alterabilis imaginis. Absoluta
enim veritas est inalterabilitas. Veritas faciei meae est mutabilis, quia
sic veritas quod imago; tua autem immutabilis, quia sic imago quod
veritas. Veritatem faciei meae absoluta veritas deserere non potest. Si
enim desereret eam absoluta veritas, non posset subsistere ipsa facies
15 mea, quae est veritas mutabilis. Sic videris tu, deus, propter bonitatem tuam infinitam mutabilis, quia non deseris creaturas mutabiles;
sed quia es absoluta bonitas, non es mutabilis, quia non sequeris
mutabilitatem.

---

68 1 deus: qui es *add. p*   menti: *ex* mente *corr. P*   2 dum: cum *EN*   quomodo: *ex* quoniam *corr. I*   ad: te *post* ad *scribit et del. L*   3 visus . . . mutatus:
mutatus visus eikone tue *EN* (eicone *scribit N*)   videtur mutata: mutata videtur *ad*
videtur mutata *transponit R*   quia: et *Pa (ad* quia *corr. Pa²)*   ego: *om. p*
3-4 et . . . mutatus: *bis Q*   4 sis: sic *L*   7 quod¹: quid *N*   quod²: *om. Pa (supra
lin. add. Pa²)*

69 1 facies²: *bis S*   2 eam mihi: michi eam *AR*   mihi eam *p*   es: *ex* est
corr. T   et: *om. R*   tu *add. V*   3 veritatis: veritas *SV*   4 ea: eo *EN*   5 veritate: ad mutacionem faciei mee *post* veritate *scribit et del. A*   veritati *S*   6 quomodo: *non proprie scribit L*   7-8 et . . . immutata: *om. A*   8 deserit . . . non:
om. OP   8-9 mutationem: mutacionem *ex* inmutacionem *corr. Pa*   9 faciei: *bis
scribit O* (faciei¹ *del. O*)   meae: mei *C (ad* mee *corr. C aut C²) JPaV*   11 inalterabilitas: inalterabilis *L*   meae: mei *N*   12 sic¹: *ex* sicut *corr. G*   immutabilis:

68 You, O God, worthy of admiration by every mind, You who are Light sometimes seem as if You were a shadow. For when I see that in accordance with my changing, Your icon's gaze seems to be changed and that Your countenance seems to be changed because I am changed, You seem to me as if You were a shadow which follows the changing of the one who is walking. But because I am a living shadow and You are the Truth, I judge from the changing of the shadow that the Truth is changed. Therefore, O my God, You are shadow in such way that You are Truth; You are the image of me and of each one in such way that You are Exemplar.

69 Lord God, Enlightener of hearts, my face is a true face; for You, who are Truth, have given it to me. My face is also an image; for it is not Truth itself but is the image of Absolute Truth. Therefore, in my conception I enfold my face's truth and image; and I see that with regard to my face the image coincides with the facial truth, so that my face is true insofar as it is an image. And subsequently You show me, O Lord, that with respect to the changing of my face Your Face is changed and unchanged, alike: it is changed because it does not desert the truth of my face; it is unchanged because it does not follow the changing of the image. Hence, just as Your Face does not desert the truth of my face, so also it does not follow the changing of the changeable image. For Absolute Truth is Unchangeability. The truth of my face is mutable, because it is truth in such way that it is image; but |the Truth of| Your |Face| is immutable, because it is image in such way that it is Truth. Absolute Truth cannot desert the truth of my face. For if Absolute Truth deserted it, then my face, which is a mutable truth, could not continue to exist. Thus, O God, on account of Your infinite goodness[62] You seem to be mutable, because You do not desert mutable creatures; but because You are Absolute Goodness, You are not mutable, since You do not follow mutability.

---

est *add. R*   quia: quod *V*   sic²: veritas quod *post* sic² *scribit et del. M*   quod²: mutabilis *post* quod *scribit et del. P*   13 veritatem: *ex* veritas *corr. G*   15 mea: *non proprie scribit V*   est: facies *post* est *scribit et del. G om. R*   veritas mutabilis: mutabilis veritas *G*   mutabilis: a *non proprie format E*   sic: si *AS ex* si *corr. G*   15-16 bonitatem: *ex* veritatem *in marg. corr. A*   16 creaturas: creaturos *Pa*   16-17 deseris . . . non²: *om. V*   18 mutabilitatem: mntabilitatem *p*

70　　O altitudo profundissima, deus meus, qui non deseris et simul non sequeris creaturas! O inexplicabilis pietas, offers te intuenti te, quasi recipias ab eo esse; et conformas te ei, ut eo plus te diligat, quo appares magis similis ei. Non enim possumus odire nos ipsos. Hinc
5 diligimus id quod esse nostrum participat et comitatur; et similitudinem nostram amplectimur, quia praesentamur nos in imagine in qua nos ipsos amamus. Ostendis te, deus, quasi creaturam nostram ex infinitae bonitatis tuae humilitate, ut sic nos trahas ad te. Trahis enim nos ad te omni possibili trahendi modo, quo libera rationalis
10 creatura trahi potest. Et coincidit in te, deus, creari cum creare. Similitudo enim quae videtur creari a me, est veritas quae creat me, ut sic saltem capiam quantum tibi astringi debeam, cum in te amari coincidat cum amare. Si ego enim me in te similitudine mea diligere debeo, et tunc maxime ad hoc constringor, quando video te me diligere ut
15 creaturam et imaginem tuam. Quomodo pater non potest diligere filium, qui sic est filius quod pater? Et si multum est diligibilis, qui est aestimatione filius et cognitione pater, nonne tu maxime, qui aestimatione excedis filium et cognitione patrem? Tu, deus, voluisti filialem dilectionem in aestimatione constitui, et vis similior filio aesti-
20 mari et intimior patre cognosci, quia es amor complicans tam filialem quam paternalem dilectionem. Sis ergo dulcissimus amor meus, deus meus, in aeternum benedictus.

70 1 profundissima: profudissima *Pa*　　qui: es *post* qui *scribit et del. P*　　2 inexplicabilis: bonitas *post* inexplicabilis *scribit et del. P*　　3 conformas: *ex* formas *corr. T*　　plus te: te plus *Pa*　　4 magis: in actis *Q*　　odire: odisse *p*　　hinc: *om. Q* 5 diligimus: diligius *Pa*　　diligamus *T*　　comitatur: *ex* communicatur *corr. Pa* 6 quia: et *L*　　praesentamur: repraesentamur *p*　　nos: nobis *A ͵* nos *M* (nobis *supra lin. coni. M²*)　　nos in imagine: in imagine nos *EN* (ymagine *scribit N*) qua: quo *R*　　7 ipsos: *om. V*　　te deus: deus te *ad* te deus *transponit O*　　8 infinitae: infinitate *AN*　　infinite *ex* infinitate *corr. E*　　9 enim: *om. A*　　trahendi: trahendo *P*　　trahendi modo: modo trahendi *ENQ*　　10 in: *om. Pa (supra lin. add. Pa²)*　　deus: meus *add. GT*　　creari cum creare: creare cum creari *L*　　creare: hec *add. EN*　　11 enim: *om. Pa (supra lin. add. Pa²)*　　quae¹: *om. EN*　　videtur: a me *add. Q*　　12 saltem: saltim *GT*　　astringi: constringi *Q*　　in: *om. I*　　amari: amare *N*　　12-13 coincidat: coincidit *I*　　13 amare: similitudo enim que videtur creari a me est veritas que creat me ut sic saltem capiam q *post* amare *repetit et del. C*　　ego enim: enim ego *EINZp*　　enim ego *ad* ego enim *transponit O*　　ego enim me: enim me ego *ad* enim ego me *transponit R*　　14 hoc: *om. I*　　video te:

70   O my God, deepest Depth, You who do not desert creatures and, at the same time, do not follow them! O inexplicable Graciousness, to him who looks unto You You give Yourself as if You received being from him;[63] and You conform Yourself to him, in order that the more You appear to be like him, the more he will love You. For we cannot hate ourselves.[64] Hence, we love that which shares in and accompanies our being; and we embrace our likeness, because we are shown ourselves in an image, and we love ourselves therein. O God, from the humility of Your infinite goodness You manifest Yourself as if You were our creature, in order thus to draw us unto Yourself. For You draw us unto Yourself by every possible means of drawing by which a free rational creature can be drawn. And in You, O God, being created coincides with creating.[65] For the likeness which seems to be created by me is the Truth which creates me, so that in this way, at least, I apprehend how closely I ought to be bound to You, since, in You, being loved coincides with loving. For if in You who are my likeness I ought to love myself, then I am exceedingly bound to do so when I see that You love me as Your creature and image. How can a father not love a son who is son in such way that he is a father? And if someone who is both a son with a good reputation and a father with knowledge is quite lovable, then are not You exceedingly lovable who surpass a son in repute and a father in knowledge? You, O God, willed that filial love be established in repute; and You will to be reputed as one who is of closer likeness than a son and to be known as one who is more intimate than a father. For You are love that enfolds both filial and paternal love. May You, then, my most sweet Love, my God, be blessed forever.

---

te video *Z*   te me: me te *Pa*   15 imaginem: ymaginam *N*   imaginem tuam: tuam ymaginem *Q*   quomodo: quoniam *I*   ex quoniam *corr. R*   pater: pater *Pa (abbreviationem del., et supra lin. explicat, Pa²)*   non potest: potest non *p* 16 filium: *om. S*   qui¹: quia *G*   17 aestimatione: exstimacione *V*   nonne: none *p*   19 aestimatione: extimacione *V*   similior: similis *E*   similis et *N* similiter *T*   filio: fieri *post* filio *scribit et del. G*   filior *S*   19-20 aestimari: extimari *V*   20 intimior: *om. EN*   patre: pater *EN*   amor: *bis I*   21 ergo: tu qui es *add. p*   amor: honor *I*   21-22 deus meus: meus deus *ad* deus meus *transponit A*   22 in aeternum benedictus: benedictus in eternum *R*   benedictus: et cetera *add. IV*

71 CAPITULUM XVI

QUOD NISI DEUS ESSET INFINITUS, NON FORET FINIS DESIDERII

Non cessat ignis ab ardore neque amor desiderii qui fertur ad te, deus, qui es forma omnis desiderabilis et veritas illa quae in omni
5 desiderio desideratur. Unde quia coepi ex tuo mellifluo dono degustare incomprehensibilem suavitatem tuam, quae tanto mihi fit gratior quanto infinitior apparet, video quod ob hoc tu, deus, es omnibus creaturis incognitus, ut habeant in hac sacratissima ignorantia maiorem quietem, quasi in thesauro innumerabili et inexhauribili. Multo
10 enim maiori gaudio perfunditur ille, qui reperit thesaurum talem quem scit penitus innumerabilem et infinitum, quam qui reperit numerabilem et finitum. Hinc haec sacratissima ignorantia magnitudinis tuae est pascentia intellectus mei desiderabilissima, maxime quando talem reperio thesaurum in meo agro, ita quod thesaurus sit
15 meus.
72 O fons divitiarum! vis comprehendi possessione mea et manere incomprehensibilis et infinitus, quia es thesaurus deliciarum, quarum nullus potest finem appetere. Quomodo appetitus posset appetere non esse? Enim sive appetat esse sive appetat non esse voluntas, ipse appe-
5 titus quiescere nequit sed fertur in infinitum. Descendis, domine, ut comprehendaris, et manes innumerabilis et infinitus. Et nisi maneres infinitus, non esses finis desiderii. Es igitur infinitus, ut sis finis omnis

---

71 1 capitulum XVI: capitulum 17 *E⁴*   *numerum capituli om. J*   2 quod . . . desiderii: quod nisi deus infinitus non foret non esset finis desiderii *Z (in 1:1* quod nisi deus infinitus non foret finis desiderii *habet Z)*   deus esset: *om. P³ (in 1:1* deus habet P)*   esset: *om. AC (supra lin. add. C²) E³GJLM³ (in 1:1 om. etiam M) OPa³Q² (in 1:1 om. etiam Q) RTV²*   foret: esset *R (sed in 1:1* foret *habet R) p*
3 qui: que *V*   ad: a *EN*   4 desiderabilis: *ex* desiderii *corr. O*   veritas: unitas *I JPa*   in: *ex* non *(?) corr. C om. V*   5 desiderio: *ex* desidero *corr. Pa*   quia: *om. R*   5-6 dono degustare: degustare dono *N*   6 quae: qua *V*   mihi fit: fit michi *I*   7 ob: ab *V*   hoc: quod *post* hoc *scribit E et del E²* quod *add. N* es: et *add. S*   8 sacratissima: beatissima *R*   8-9 maiorem: *ex* miorem *corr. Z* 9 innumerabili: in mirabili *G*   inenarrabili *Q*   inexhauribili: inexhauribili *N* inexhauribili *ex* inhauribili *corr. Q*   10 enim: *om. GT*   maiori: *ex* maiore *corr. Pa* gaudio: gaudi *S*   reperit: reperiet *S*   11 quem: que *N*   quam: quoniam *V* reperit: reperiet *S*   13 tuae: *om. I*   pascentia: pascenda *ad* pascena *corr. E (ad*

71 ## CHAPTER SIXTEEN

UNLESS GOD WERE INFINITE, HE WOULD NOT BE THE END OF DESIRE

Fire does not cease from its flame and neither does the burning love which is directed toward You, O God. You are the Form of everything desirable; You are the Truth which is desired in every desire. Hence, because from Your mellifluous gift I have begun to taste of Your incomprehensible sweetness, which becomes more pleasing to me the more infinite it appears to be, I see the following: that the reason You, O God, are unknown to all creatures is so that amid this most sacred ignorance creatures may be more content, as if |they were situated| amid a countless and inexhaustible treasure. For one who finds a treasure of such kind that he knows it to be altogether uncountable and infinite is filled with much greater joy than is one who finds a countable and finite treasure. Hence, this most sacred ignorance of Your greatness is a most delectable feast for my intellect—especially since I find such a treasure in my own field,[66] so that it is a treasure which belongs to me.

72   O Fount of riches! You *will* both to be comprehended by my possessing You and to remain incomprehensible and infinite. For You are a treasure of delights, whose termination no one can desire. How could the appetite desire to cease being? For whether the will desires to exist or not to exist, the appetite cannot cease from desiring but is directed toward infinity. You descend, O Lord, in order to be comprehended;[67] and You remain uncountable and infinite. And unless You remained infinite, You would not be the End of desire.[68] You,

---

pascencia *in marg. corr.* E²) pascena N   14 talem reperio: reperio talem *EN* reperio thesaurum: thesaurum reperio *LZ*   meo agro: agro meo *GRT*   sit: est *EN* **72** 1 O fons: sic o fons *EN*   comprehendi: *ex* comprehendendi *(?) corr.* R manere: maius V   2 quia: qui *GT*   3 quomodo . . . appetere: *om.* V   posset: *ex* potes *corr.* T   appetere²: e² *clarius supra lin. rescribit* J   4 enim: etenim *AL* OPQRZ *om.* I   enim M (etenim *in marg. scribit* M²)   enim sive: enim sive E *(ad* sive enim *corr* E²)   sive enim *GTp*   sive¹: si V   appetat¹: appetere N   appetat²: *om.* T *(in marg. add.* T²)   appetat non: non appetat *ad* appetat non *transponit* C *aut* C²   4-5 appetitus: *non proprie scribit* N   5 nequit: nescit A   in: *supra lin.* Pa   6 innumerabilis: in mirabilis G   innumerabiles *Pa*   et infinitus: bis *Pa*   maneres: maneries V   7 esses: *ex* sis *in marg. corr.* G   es: et N   7-

desiderii. Desiderium enim intellectuale non fertur in id quod potest esse maius et desiderabilius sed in id quod non potest maius esse nec
10 desiderabilius. Omne autem citra infinitum potest esse maius. Finis igitur desiderii est infinitus.

73 Tu igitur es, deus, ipsa infinitas, quam solum in omni desiderio desidero; ad cuius quidem infinitatis scientiam non possum propius accedere, quam quod scio eam esse infinitam. Quanto igitur te deum meum comprehendo magis incomprehensibilem, de tanto plus attingo
5 te, quia plus attingo finem desiderii mei. Igitur quidquid mihi occurrit, quod te comprehensibilem ostendere nititur, hoc abicio quia seducit. Desiderium meum, in quo tu reluces, me ad te ducit, quia omne quod finitum et comprehensibile abicit. In his enim quiescere nequit, quia per te ducitur ad te. Tu autem es principium sine princi-
10 pio et finis sine fine. Ducitur igitur desiderium per principium aeternum, a quo habet quod est desiderium, ad finem sine fine; et hic est infinitus.

74 Quod igitur ego homuncio non contentarer de te deo meo si scirem te comprehensibilem, est quia ducor per te ad te incomprehensibilem et infinitum. Video te, domine deus meus, in raptu quodam mentali, quoniam si visus non satiatur visu nec auris auditu, tunc
5 minus intellectus intellectu. Non igitur id quod satiat intellectum, seu est finis eius, est id quod intelligit. Neque id satiare potest quod penitus non intelligit, sed solum illud quod non intelligendo intelligit. Intelligibile enim quod cognoscit non satiat; nec intelligibile satiat

---

8 es ... desiderii: *om. IQ* 8 enim: *supra lin. Pa* 8-9 potest ... quod: *om. OP* 9 et: nec *Pa (ad et corr. Pa²)* et ... esse: *om. CVp* desiderabilius: desiderabilibus *N* non: *om. I* maius esse: esse maius *EIJNR* esse²: *om. GM (supra lin. add. M²) ST (ante* maius² *add. T³)* nec: et *R* aut *p* 9-10 sed ... desiderabilius: *om. Pa (in marg. add. Pa²;* esse maius *pro* maius esse *habet Pa²) Q* 11 igitur: enim *R* est: et *C (ad est corr. C²)*
73 1 igitur es: es igitur *Q* es deus: es deus *ad* deus es *transponit C aut C²* deus es *Vp* quam: qua *P* solum: solam *G* 2 desidero: *om. S* quidem: quidam *GT* possum: *in marg. I* propius: propinquius *I* 4 de: *om. Np* tanto: *non plene legibile C* plus: *non proprie scribit L* 5 te: *om. OP* te ... attingo: *om. NPa (quia plus attingo in marg. add. Pa²)* quidquid: quod quid *Pa* 6 comprehensibilem: *ex* incomprehensibilem *corr. L* 7 desiderium ... ducit: *om. L* 8 quod: quoddam *T* possibile *post* quod *scribit et del. V* comprehensibile: est *add. EN* enim: *om. GT* quiescere: abicit *post* quiescere *scribit et del. M* 9 nequit: nescit sew nequit *A* nescit *Q* 10 igitur: principium per desiderium

then, continue to be infinite in order to be the End of all desire.[69] For intellectual desire does not aim at that which can be greater and more desirable but at that which cannot be greater and more desirable. Now, everything that is less than infinite can be greater. Therefore, the End of desire is infinite.

73   You, then, O God, are Infinity itself, which alone I desire in every desire. I can approach unto a knowledge of Your Infinity no more closely than to know that Your Infinity is infinite.[70] Therefore, the more incomprehensible I comprehend You-my-God to be, the more I attain unto You, because the more I attain the End of my desire. Therefore, I cast aside anything occurring to me that purports to show that You are comprehensible, because it misleads me. My desire, wherein You shine forth, leads me to You, because it casts aside all finite and comprehensible things. For in these things it cannot find rest; for it is led unto You by You Yourself. But You are Beginning without a beginning and End without an end. Therefore, my desire is led by the Eternal Beginning—from which it has the fact that it is desire—unto the End without an end. And this End is infinite.

74   I, an insignificant human being, would not be content with You my God if I knew You to be comprehensible. The reason is that I am led by You unto You Yourself, who are incomprehensible and infinite. Lord my God, I see You by means of a certain mental rapture. For if the capacity of sight is not filled up by seeing nor that of the ear by hearing, then even less that of the intellect by understanding. Therefore, it is not the case that that which the intellect understands is that which fully satisfies the intellect, i.e., is the intellect's end. On the other hand, that which the intellect does not at all understand cannot fully satisfy it, either. Rather, |it is fully satisfied| only |by| that which it understands by not understanding. For an intelligible object

---

eter[num] *post* igitur *scribit et del.* E   11 hic: finis *add.* GT

   74 1 ego: *om.* V   homuncio: humuncio S   te: *om.* A   2 te[1]: deum meum *add.* V   est: esse N   est (?) T *(ad* esse *corr.* T[3])   ducor: ad te *post* ducor *scribit, del., et post* per te *rescribit,* O   3 raptu: captu G   4 satiatur: *om.* CV   visu: viso A   auris: aures S   5 minus: *om.* V   intellectu: intellctum *Pa (cf. 91:15;* e[2] *in* intellectum *saepe om. Pa)*   intellectum S   satiat: facit I   faciat J Pa   saciatur S   seu: quod *add.* Gp   6 est finis: finis est Z   est[2]: sed R   id[1]: illud Q   intelligit: sed solum illud *post* intelligit *scribit et del.* I   id[2]: quod *add.* G   satiare: facere I   sociare Pa   saciare *ut* sanare *scribit* V   7 illud: id p   intelligit[2]: *ex* intelligitur

quod penitus non cognoscit; sed intelligibile quod cognoscit adeo
10 intelligibile, quod numquam possit ad plenum intelligi, hoc solum
satiare potest—sicut habentem insaturabilem famem non satiat cibus
brevis, quem deglutire potest, nec cibus qui ad eum non pervenit, sed
solum ille cibus qui ad eum pervenit et licet continue deglutiatur,
tamen numquam ad plenum potest deglutiri, quoniam talis est quod
15 deglutiendo non imminuitur, quia infinitus.

75

CAPITULUM XVII

QUOD DEUS NON NISI UNITRINUS VIDERI PERFECTE POTEST

Ostendisti, domine, te mihi adeo amabilem, quod magis amabilis
esse nequis. Es enim infinite amabilis, deus meus. Numquam igitur
5 poteris a quoquam amari sicut amabilis es, nisi ab infinito amante.
Nisi enim esset infinite amans, non esses infinite amabilis. Amabilitas
enim tua, quae est posse in infinitum amari, est quia est posse in
infinitum amare. A posse in infinitum amare et posse in infinitum
amari oritur amoris nexus infinitus ipsius infiniti amantis et infiniti
10 amabilis. Non est autem infinitum multiplicabile. Tu igitur, deus
meus, qui es amor, es amor amans et amor amabilis et amoris amantis
et amabilis nexus.

corr. L   8 satiat[1]: faciat *N*   9 cognoscit[2]: *ex* congnoscit *corr. L*   10 possit ad
plenum: ad plenum possit *Pa*   solum: *om. R*   11 insaturabilem: instaurabilem *GT*
12 brevis: *non proprie scribit A*   non: *supra lin. L om. Pa (supra lin. add. Pa[2])*
12-13 sed . . . pervenit: *in marg. E*[n]   13 continue: continuo *L*   14 ad plenum
potest: potest ad plenum *R*   potest: *om. Pa (in marg. add. Pa[2])*   quoniam: qui *V*
est: *om. S*   15 non: *om. LV*   imminuitur: minuitur *AGQS*
    75 1 capitulum XVII: capitulum 18 *E[4]*   2 non: *supra lin. Z*   videri: *in 1:1*
non potest *post* videri *scribit et del. Q*   videri perfecte: perfecte videri *in 1:1*
habet R; videri perfecte (*transpositum ex* perfecte videri) *in 75:2 habet R*   perfecte
videri *Z (in 1:1* videri perfecte *habet Z)*   perfecte: *om. A in 1:1* perfecte *non
proprie abbreviat Q*   perfecte potest: potest perfecte *ad* perfecte potest *transponit G*   potest: *litteram* t[1] *non proprie format L*   3 domine te: te domine *AGL*

that is known by the intellect does not fully satisfy the intellect—and neither does an intelligible object that is not at all known by the intellect. Rather, the intellect can be fully satisfied only by an intelligible object which it knows to be so intelligible that this object can never fully be understood. By comparison, a man who has an insatiable hunger is not fully satisfied by a snack which he can eat. Nor is he fully satisfied by food that does not reach him but only by food which does reach him and, though eaten continually, can never all be eaten up, since it is such that it is not diminished by being eaten, since it is infinite.[71]

75

CHAPTER SEVENTEEN

GOD CAN BE SEEN PERFECTLY ONLY AS TRIUNE

O Lord, You have manifested Yourself to me as so lovable[72] that You cannot be more lovable. For You are infinitely lovable, my God. Therefore, except by one whose love is infinite You can never be loved by anyone as You are lovable. For unless there were someone who loved infinitely, You would not be infinitely lovable.[73] For Your lovability, which is the ability to be loved infinitely, exists because there is the ability to love infinitely. From the ability to love infinitely and the ability to be loved infinitely there arises the infinite union of the love of the infinite loving one and of the infinite lovable one. But the infinite is not multiple. You, then, my God, who are Love, are Loving Love, Lovable Love, and the Union of Loving Love and Lovable Love.

4 esse: non possis et *add. Q*   igitur: enim *Q*   5 a quoquam amari: amari a quoquam *G*   5-6 es . . . amabilitas: *om. J* (es nisi ab infinit[-] amante nisi enim esset infinite amans non esses infinit[-] amabilis *in marg. add. J*[n]; amabili[tas] *post* amabilis *in marg. add. alia manus)*   7 amari: amare *J (ad* amari *corr. J*[n]*)*   amari *ex* amare *corr. Q*   posse[2]: michi *add. V*   in[2]: *supra lin. E*   7-8 est[2]. . . amare[1]: *om. J* (est quia est *in marg. add. J*[n]*)*   8 a: ex *E* et *NV*   in[1]: *supra lin. G*   et: *ex* est *corr. P*   9 amantis: et amoris amabilis nexus infinitus *post* amantis *scribit et del. A*   10 infinitum: *om. p*   11 meus: *om. P*   amor[1]: et *post* amor[1] *scribit et del. L*   et[2]: amor *add. p*   12 et: amoris *add. ALM*[2] *(om. M; in marg. add. M*[2]*)* OPQZ

76   Video in te deo meo amorem amantem; et ex eo quia video in te amorem amantem, video in te amorem amabilem; et quia in te video amorem amantem et amorem amabilem, video utriusque amoris nexum. Et hoc non est aliud quam illud quod video in absoluta uni-
5 tate tua, in qua video unitatem unientem, unitatem unibilem, et utriusque unionem. Quidquid autem in te video, hoc es tu, deus meus. Tu es igitur amor ille infinitus qui sine amante et amabili et utriusque nexu non potest per me naturalis et perfectus amor videri. Quomodo enim possum concipere perfectissimum et naturalissimum amorem
10 sine amante et amabili et unione utriusque? Quod enim amor sit amans et amabilis et nexus utriusque, experior in contracto amore esse de essentia perfecti amoris. Id autem quod est de essentia perfecti amoris contracti, non potest deesse absoluto amori, a quo habet contractus amor quidquid perfectionis habet.

77   Quanto autem amor simplicior, tanto perfectior. Tu autem, deus meus, es amor perfectissimus et simplicissimus. Tu igitur es ipsa essentia perfectissima et simplicissima et naturalissima amoris. Hinc in te amore non est aliud amans et aliud amabile et aliud utriusque
5 nexus, sed idem tu ipse, deus meus. Quia igitur in te coincidit amabile cum amante et amari cum amare, tunc nexus coincidentiae est nexus essentialis. Nihil enim in te est, quod non sit ipsa essentia tua. Illa igitur quae occurrunt mihi tria esse—scilicet amans, amabilis, et nexus—sunt ipsa simplicissima essentia absoluta. Non sunt igitur tria
10 sed unum. Illa essentia tua, deus meus, quae occurrit mihi esse simplicissima et unissima, non est naturalissima et perfectissima sine tribus praenominatis. Est igitur essentia trina, et tamen non sunt tria in

---

76 1 deo meo: deum meum *L*   amantem: et amabilem *add. p*   quia: quod *J QRV*   in te^2: *om. I*   1-2 et . . . amantem: *om. S*   2 in te video: video in te *ARZ* 2-3 video^1. . . amantem: *om. CVp*   et . . . amabilem: *om. QT (in marg. add. T^2)* 3 amorem^2: *om. EN*   5 unientem: *om. L*   quicquid *post* unientem *scribit et del. Q* unitatem^2: *om. Q*   6 quidquid: quid quod *Pa*   in te video: video in te *G*   7 infinitus: infinite *I*   amante: amanti *V*   amabili: *ex* amabilo *corr. J*   utriusque: unio *post* utriusque *scribit et del. O*   9 concipere: *non proprie abbreviat Pa* amorem: *om. IPa (in marg. add. Pa^2)*   10 et^1: *supra lin. E*   et^2: *om. V*   10-11 quod . . . utriusque: *om. IT*   11 et^2: *om. N*   12 perfecti amoris: amoris perfecti *ad* perfecti amoris *transponit R*   amoris: contracti *add. C et del. C aut C^2* id contracti *add., et* id *del., I*   13 deesse: *ex* esse *corr. I*   amori: amoveri *EN* a: de *V*   14 amor: amator *Q*
77 1-2 simplicior . . . amor: *om. S*   2 perfectissimus: perfectissima *N*   igitur

76   In You my God I see Loving Love. And from the fact that I see in
You Loving Love, I see in You Lovable Love. And because I see in
You Loving Love and Lovable Love, I see the Union of each Love.
And this is not other than what I see with regard to Your Absolute
Oneness,[74] wherein I see Uniting Oneness, Unitable Oneness, and the
Union of each. But whatever I see in You, this You are, my God.
Therefore, You are that Infinite Love which without the Loving and
the Lovable and the Union of each cannot be seen by me as natural
and perfect love. For how can I conceive of most perfect and most
natural love apart from the loving one and the lovable one and the
union of each? For in the case of contracted love I experience that it
is of the essence of perfect love that love be loving and lovable and
the union of each. But that which is of the essence of perfect contracted love cannot be absent from Absolute Love, from which contracted love has whatever perfection it has.

77   Now, the simpler love is, the more perfect it is. But You, my God,
are most perfect and most simple Love. Therefore, You are the most
perfect, most simple, and most natural essence of love. Hence, in
You, who are Love, what loves is not one thing, what is lovable
another thing, and the union of each a third thing; rather, they are
the same thing: viz., You Yourself, my God. Therefore, because in
You what is lovable coincides with what is loving, and being loved
coincides with loving, the union of |this| coincidence is an essential
union. For in You nothing is present which is not Your essence itself.
Therefore, those things which appear to me to be three—viz., the
Loving, the Lovable, and the Union—are the absolute, most simple
essence. Therefore, they are not three but one. Your essence, my
God, which appears to me to be most simple and most one, is not
most natural and most perfect apart from the aforementioned three.
Therefore, Your essence is trine. And yet, there are not three things

es: es igitur *R*   4 amore: amor *EGN*   amans et aliud: *om. S*   5 coincidit: coincidat *A*   6 et: *om. Pa (supra lin. add. Pa²)*   amari: vel *post* amari *scribit et del. O*
7 essentialis: essenciabilis *V*   enim in te: in te enim *ad* enim in te *transponit G*   in
te est: est in te *V*   ipsa: *om. L*   ipsa essentia: essencia ipsa *Z (ad* ipsa essencia
corr. Z²)   8 illa igitur: igitur illa *S*   occurrunt: occurrit *A*   9 non: nom *ex*
nam *corr. V*   10 quae: qui *N*   11 et¹: ut sic dicam *add. p*   12 praenominatis:
prenominatis *ex* prenotatis *corr. E*   preprenominatis *G*   prenominatis *ex* nominatis
corr. I   essentia: *om. ALMOPQRZ (in marg. add. Z²)*   trina: *om. T*   sunt:

ea, quia simplicissima. Pluralitas igitur trium praenominatorum est
ita pluralitas quod unitas; et unitas est ita unitas quod pluralitas.
15 Pluralitas trium est pluralitas sine numero plurali. Nam pluralis
numerus non potest esse simplex unitas, quia est numerus pluralis.
Non igitur est trium numeralis distinctio, quia illa est essentialis;
numerus enim a numero essentialiter distinguitur. Et quia unitas est
trina, non est unitas numeri singularis; unitas enim numeri singularis
20 non est trina.

78   O admirabilissimus deus, qui neque es numeri singularis neque
numeri pluralis, sed supra omnem pluralitatem et singularitatem
unitrinus et triunus! Video igitur in muro paradisi, ubi es, deus meus,
pluralitatem coincidere cum singularitate, et te ultra habitare quam
5 remote. Doce me, domine, quomodo possim concipere id possibile,
quod video necessarium. Occurrit enim mihi impossibilitas, quod
trium pluralitas, sine quibus concipere te nequeo perfectum et naturalem amorem, sit pluralitas sine numero—quasi quis dicat unum,
unum, unum. Dicit ter unum; non dicit tria sed unum, et hoc unum
10 ter. Non potest autem dicere unum ter sine tribus, licet non dicat
tria. Nam cum dicit unum ter, replicat idem et non numerat. Numer-
are enim est unum alterare. Sed unum et idem triniter replicare est
plurificare sine numero. Unde pluralitas quae in te deo meo per me
videtur, est alteritas sine alteritate, quia est alteritas quae identitas.
15 Quando enim video amantem non esse amabilem et nexum non esse
nec amantem nec amabilem, non sic video amantem non esse amabilem, quasi amans sit unum et amabilis aliud; sed video distinctionem

trina unitas *post* sunt *scribit et del. A*   13 quia: *bis J in marg. Pa*   15 pluralis:
om. T (in marg. add. T²)   16 potest: *ex* est *corr. I*   est numerus pluralis:
pluralis numerus est *Z*   17 trium: in *add. A*   numeralis: naturalis *GT*   est²:
om. N   18 unitas: *om. I*   19 trina: terna *P*   singularis¹: *ex* singulatis *corr. Pa*
unitas². . . singularis: et quia est unitas numeri singularis *in marg. I*

78 1 admirabilissimus: mirabilissimus *p*   es: *om. A*   est *EN*   2 numeri:
om. R   pluralis: pluraris *Q*   supra: super *CVp confuse abbreviat Pa*   3 triunus: trinus unus *A*   trinus *L*   igitur: enim *Q*   muro: numero *I* (muro *supra
lin. coni. I)*   4 quam: quam *M* (valde *in marg. substituit M²*) valde *add. QR*
perquam *p*   5 possim: possum *L*   concipere id possibile: id concipere inpossibile *R*   possibile: impossibile *ALNOP*   inpossibile *EQ*   possibile M (impossibile
in marg. coni. M²)   6 necessarium: necessiarium *Q*   7 concipere: concipi *EN*
concipere te: te concipere *QZ*   8 pluralitas: pluraritas *Z*   9 hoc: *om. Q*

in it, because it is most simple. Therefore, the plurality of the aforementioned three is a plurality in such way that it is a oneness; and
the oneness is oneness in such way that it is a plurality. The plurality
of the three is a plurality without plural number. For plural number
cannot be simple oneness, because it is more than one number.
Therefore, there is not a numerical distinction of the three,[75] because
a numerical distinction would be an essential distinction (for number
is distinguished from number in an essential way). Now, because the
oneness is trine, it is not the oneness characteristic of a single
number; for the oneness of a single number is not trine.

78   O most wonderful God, who are neither singular in number nor
plural in number but—beyond all plurality and singularity—are one-
in-three and three-in-one! I see, then, my God, that plurality coincides with singularity at the wall of the Paradise in which You dwell;
and I see that You dwell ever so remotely beyond |this wall|. Teach
me, O Lord, how I can conceive to be possible that which I see to be
necessary.[76] For the following appears to me to be an impossibility:
viz., that the plurality of the three (without which I cannot conceive
You to be perfect and natural love) is a plurality without number—as
if someone were to say "one, one, one." He says "one" three times.
He does not say "three" but "one"—and this "one" three times. However, he cannot say "one" three times without three; and yet, he does
not say "three". For when he says "one" three times, he repeats the
same thing and does not number. For to number is to alter one. But
to repeat one and the same thing three times is to plurify apart from
number. Hence, the plurality which I see in You my God is otherness
without otherness, because it is otherness which is identity. For when
I see that the Loving is not the Lovable and that the Union is neither
the Loving nor the Lovable, then it is not in the following manner
that I see the Loving not to be the Lovable: viz., as if the Loving
were one thing and the Lovable another thing. Rather, I see that the

10 potest autem: autem potest *EN*   unum: *om. p*   11 tria: *om. I*   cum: *om. V*
12 enim: unum *add. Q*   unum²: *om. T (supra lin. add. T²)*   triniter: terniter *JN*
est²: *om. N*   13 plurificare: plurifacere *Q*   meo: *om. EN*   per me: *om. J (in marg. add. J")*   14 est¹. . . quia: *om. Pa (in marg. add. Pa²)*   15 enim: igitur *Z*
amabilem: quasi amans sit unum et amabilis aliud sed video distinctionem *post*
amabilem *scribit et del. E*   non²: *om. p*   16 non¹: nec *RV*   16-17 amabilem:

amantis et amabilis intra murum coincidentiae unitatis et alteritatis esse. Unde distinctio illa, quae est intra murum coincidentiae, ubi
20 distinctum et indistinctum coincidunt, praevenit omnem alteritatem et diversitatem quae intelligi potest. Claudit enim murus potentiam omnis intellectus, licet oculus ultra in paradisum respiciat. Id autem quod videt, nec dicere nec intelligere potest. Est enim amor secretus suus et thesaurus absconditus qui, inventus, manet absconditus.
25 Reperitur enim intra murum coincidentiae absconditi et manifesti.

79 Sed non possum retrahi a suavitate visionis, quin adhuc aliquo modo mihi ipsi referam revelationem distinctionis amantis, amabilis, et nexus. Nam dulcissima degustatio eius aliqualiter videtur praegustabilis in figura. Tu enim sic das, domine, quod in me video amo-
5 rem, quia video me amantem. Et quia video me amare me ipsum, video me amabilem, et naturalissimum nexum me esse video utriusque. Ego sum amans; ego sum amabilis; ego sum nexus. Unus est igitur amor, sine quo non posset aliquod trium esse. Ego unus sum qui sum amans; et ille idem qui sum amabilis; et ille idem qui sum
10 nexus exsurgens ex amore quo me amo. Ego sum unus et non sum tria. Esto igitur quod amor meus sit essentia mea, uti in te deo meo. Tunc in unitate essentiae meae esset trium praedictorum pluralitas; et in trinitate trium praedictorum essentiae unitas. Essentque cuncta in mea essentia contracte, modo quo in te video veraciter et absolute
15 existere. Deinde amor amans non foret amor amabilis nec nexus; et hoc experior hac praxi. Nam per amorem amantem quem ad rem aliam extra me extendo, quasi ad amabile extrinsecum essentiae

---

et *add.* V   17 sit: *ex si corr.* P   amabilis: sit *add.* Z   18 amantis et amabilis: amabilis et amantis *T*   intra: inter *A*   coincidentiae: ubi distinctum et indistinctum coincidunt prevenit *post* coincidentie *scribit et del.* R   19 est: *om.* A   intra: ultra *A*   20 praevenit: provenit *I*   21 claudit: *bis I*   23 nec¹: non *V*   23-24 amor . . . thesaurus: amor eius secretus thesaurus et *p*   secretus suus: secretus suus *ad* suus secretus *transponit I*   25 intra: ultra *EN*   intra *ex* ultra *corr. I*

79 1 quin: quoniam *CIV*   quando N   adhuc: referam *post* adhuc, *et non post* ipsi *(79:2), ponit R*   2 mihi ipsi: michipsi *C*   referam: referatur *EN*   reseram *G*   revelationem: revelacionem *ex* revelacionis *corr. T*   distinctionis: distinctione *G*   3 aliqualiter: quantulumcunque *p*   3-4 praegustabilis: degustabilis *LZ* (*ad* pregustabilis *in marg. corr. Z²*)   4 quod: *ex* quid in marg. corr. T   me: te *p*   5 quia¹: quod *A*   me ipsum: meipsum *Pa* (*abbreviationem del., et supra lin. explicat, Pa²*)   6 me amabilem: amabilem me *I*   nexum: video *post* nexum *scribit et del.* A   8 aliquod: aliud *G*   aliquid *I*   unus sum: sum unus *IJPa*   9 ille²: *om.* Pa   10 exsurgens: exurgens *ACEGLMNOPPaQRSTZp*

distinction between the Loving and the Lovable occurs on the inner side of the wall of the coincidence of oneness and otherness. Hence, this distinction—which is inside the wall of coincidence, where the distinct and the ˙indistinct coincide—precedes all comprehensible otherness and diversity. For the wall is the limit of the power of every intellect, although the eye looks beyond the wall into Paradise. But that which the eye sees, it can neither speak of nor understand. For it is the eye's secret love and hidden treasure,[77] which, having been found, remains hidden. For it is found on the inner side of the wall of the coincidence of the hidden and the manifest.

79   But I cannot be drawn away from the sweetness of |this| vision without in some way proceeding to apply to myself the revelation of the distinction between the loving, the lovable, and their union. For the most sweet savoring of this revelation somehow seems to be savorable in advance by means of a befiguring. For in this |befiguring| manner, O Lord, You grant that I see love in myself, because I see myself loving. And because I see myself loving myself, I see myself as lovable and I see myself to be a most natural union of each. I am loving; I am lovable; I am the union |of each|. Therefore, the love, without which there could not be any of the three, is one. I who love am one; and I who am lovable am this same one; and I who am the union arising from the love by which I love myself am this same one. I am one and not three. Therefore, suppose my love were my essence, as is the case with You my God. Then, in the oneness of my essence there would be the plurality of the aforementioned three; and in the trinity of the aforementioned three there would be the oneness of my essence. And all |three| would be in my essence contractedly, in the manner in which I see them all to be in You truly and absolutely. So then, the loving love would not be either the lovable love or the union |of each|. And this |fact| I experience by means of the following practical example. As a result of the loving love which I extend outside myself toward an object other than myself, as if toward a lovable

---

ex: ab *p*   11 te: *om. CVZp*   12 essentiae: essencia *E*   pluralitas: unitas *CEG JNPaRSTVp* unitas *MO* (pluralitas *in marg. coni. M²O*) unitas *add. P*   12-13 pluralitas . . . praedictorum: *om. I*   13 in trinitate: infinitate *N*   trium: *om. P (in marg. add. P²)*   praedictorum: predictorum *non proprie abbreviat Pa (cf. 79:12 in Pa)*   cuncta: *om. L*   14 contracte: contracta *EN* contracto *GRT* quo: que *G*   in te video: video in te *L*   15 non: nec *R*   foret: esset *p*   16 quem:

meae, sequitur nexus quo illi rei astringor quantum ex me est. Quae
res mihi non iungitur eo nexu, quia me non amat. Unde licet eam
20 amem, ita quod amor meus amans se extendat super ipsam, tamen
non trahit secum amor amans meus amorem amabilem meum. Non
enim fio amabilis sibi. De me enim non curat, licet ipsam valde
amem—sicut filius aliquando de matre non curat, quae ipsum tener-
rime diligit. Et ita experior amorem amantem non esse amorem
25 amabilem nec nexum, sed distingui video amantem ab amabili et
nexu. Quae quidem distinctio non est in essentia amoris, quia non
possum amare, sive me sive rem aliam a me, sine amore. Sic amor
est de essentia trium; et sic video trium praedictorum simplicissimam
essentiam, licet inter se distinguantur.

80   Expressi, domine, aliqualem praegustationem naturae tuae in similitudine. Sed parce, misericors, quia nitor infigurabilem gustum
dulcedinis tuae figurare. Si enim dulcedo pomi incogniti manet omni
pictura et figura infigurabilis, et omni verbo inexpressibilis, quis sum
5 ego miser peccator, qui nitor te inostensibilem ostendere et te invisibilem visibilem figurare, et illam infinitam et penitus inexpressibilem dulcedinem tuam sapidam facere praesumo? Quam numquam
adhuc gustare merui; et per ea quae exprimo, eam potius parvam
quam magnam facio. Sed tanta est bonitas tua, deus meus, quod
10 etiam sinis caecos de lumine loqui et eius laudes praeconisare, de quo
nihil sciunt nec scire possunt, nisi eis reveletur. Revelatio autem gustum non attingit. Auris fidei non attingit dulcedinem degustabilem.
Hoc autem tu, deus, revelasti mihi, quia nec auris audivit, nec in cor

per *post* quem *scribit et del.* E   17 aliam: illam *S*   ad: *om.* I   18 est: *om. OP*
19 quia: quo *V*   me: forte *add. p*   licet: *non proprie scribit Q*   20 meus: *om.* I
extendat: extendit *I*   20-21 tamen non: non tamen *G*   tamen non trahit: non
tamen attrahit *Z*   21 secum . . . meum: amor meus amans secum amorem meum
amabilem *R*   amor amans: amans amor *ad* amor amans *transponit A*   22 fio:
fit *R*   sibi: ei *p*   de me enim: enim de me *N*   24 amorem[2]: *om. R*   25 nec:
nex *S*   distingui: distigwi *MPa*   distingui video: distingwendo *I*   25-26 et
nexu: *om. EN*   26 est: distinccio *post* est *scribit et del. A*   in essentia amoris:
amoris in essencia *ad* in essencia amoris *transponit A*   27 sive[1]: sine *T*   sive
me sive: *om. I* (sive[1] [aut2] *scribit et del. I*)   rem aliam: aliam rem *Z*   sine amore:
bis M (sine amore[1] *del. M*)   28 trium[1]: ex tua *corr. A*   et: *om. EGIJNPaT*   et
. . . trium: *om. V*   praedictorum: predictorum *non proprie abbreviat Pa (cf. 79:12
in Pa)*   29 distinguantur: distinguuantur *C*
    80 1 aliqualem: qualemcunque *p*   1-2 similitudine: similitudinem *I*   sili-

object that is the externalization of my essence, there occurs a union by which I am bound to that object as much as I have the power to be. |However,| this object is not bound to me by this union, because it does not love me. Hence, although I love it, so that my loving love extends itself unto it, nevertheless my loving love is not accompanied by my lovable love. For I do not become lovable to the other, since the other is not concerned about me, even though I exceedingly love the other. (By comparison, sometimes a son is unconcerned about his mother, who loves him most tenderly.) And so, I experience loving love to be neither lovable love nor the union |of each|; indeed, I see that the loving is distinguished from the lovable and from the union. This distinction is not present in the essence of love, because I cannot love either myself or something other than myself without love. Thus, love is of the essence of the three; and thus I see that the essence of the aforementioned three is most simple, even though the three are distinguished among themselves.

80   O Lord, by means of a likeness I have expressed a kind of foretasting of Your nature. But indulge, O Merciful One, my attempt to depict the undepictable taste of Your sweetness. For if the sweetness of an unknown fruit remains undepictable by every picture and image, as well as inexpressible by every word, then who am I, a wretched sinner, to attempt to portray You who are unportrayable and to depict as visible You who are invisible? |Who am I| to presume to make tasty that infinite and altogether inexpressible sweetness of Yours? As yet, I have not deserved to taste of it. And by the things I express I render it small rather than great. But so great is Your goodness, O my God, that You even permit the blind to speak of the Light and to sing the praises of Him of whom they do not and cannot know anything unless it is revealed to them. But the revelation falls short of the savoring. The ear of faith does not attain unto Your tastable sweetness. But You, O God, have revealed to me the

tudine *L*   2 parce: per te *GIPa (abbreviationem del., et in marg.* parce *scribit, Pa²)* nitor: *ex* inter *(?) corr. I om. OP*   3 pomi: poni *G*   incogniti: non *post* incongniti *scribit et del. E*   omni: cum *GT*   5 inostensibilem: inostendibilem *N* innoscibilem *T (*vel inostensibilem *in marg. add. T²)*   te²: *om. Pa (supra lin. add. Pa²)*   6-7 inexpressibilem: *non proprie scribit A*   9 quam: quem *QV*   deus: *bis I*   10 sinis: permittis *EN*   12 attingit¹: dulcedinem *add. N*   auris . . .

hominis descendit infinitas dulcedinis tuae, quam praeparasti diligen-
15 tibus te. Revelavit nobis hoc Paulus, magnus apostolus tuus, qui
ultra murum coincidentiae raptus est in paradisum, ubi solum revelate potes videri, qui es fons deliciarum. Conatus sum me subicere
raptui, confisus de infinita bonitate tua, ut viderem te invisibilem et
visionem revelatam irrevelabilem. Quo autem perveni tu scis; ego
20 autem nescio. Et sufficit mihi gratia tua, qua me certum reddis te
incomprehensibilem esse, et erigis in spem firmam, quod ad fruitionem tui te duce perveniam.

81

CAPITULUM XVIII

QUOD NISI DEUS TRINUS ESSET, NON ESSET FELICITAS

Utinam, domine, aperirent oculos mentis omnes qui eos tuo dono
sunt assecuti, et mecum viderent quomodo tu, deus Zelotes, quia
5 amor amans, nihil odire potes! In te enim deo amabili, omnia amabi-
lia complicanti, omne amabile amas, ut sic viderent mecum, quo foe-
dere aut nexu sis omnibus unitus. Diligis tu, deus amans, ita omnia
quod singula; expandis amorem tuum ad omnes. Multi autem te non
diligunt, qui tibi praeferunt aliud a te. Si autem amor amabilis non
10 esset distinctus ab amore amante, esses omnibus adeo amabilis, quod

---

attingit: *om. I* degustabilem: gustabilem *S* 14 descendit: descendit *scribit, et*
as[cendit] *supra lin. coni., I* ascendit *R* infinitas: infinit *L* 15 nobis: *om. L*
nobis hoc: hoc nobis *OPS* hoc nobis *ad* nobis hoc *transponit M aut M²* hoc:
hec *EGIJNPaT* magnus apostolus: apostolus magnus *ad* magnus apostolus *transponit A* apostolus: *om. I* 16 murum: modum *Q* ubi: *om. R* 17 qui:
que *V* es: *ex* est *corr. E* est *V* 18 infinita bonitate tua: tua infinita bonitate *R*
ut: *om. I* 19 quo: quomodo *I* 20 autem: *om. QR* sufficit: suffit *A* qua:
quia *S* 20-21 reddis te incomprehensibilem: incomprehensibilem reddis te *N*
22 tui: tuam *E om. N* perveniam: et cetera *add. P*
   81 1 capitulum XVIII: capitulum 19 *E⁴* 2 quod: quomodo *E³* deus: *om. A*
GLM³ (in 1:1 om. etiam M) OP³ (in 1:1 om. etiam P) Pa³Q² (in 1:1 om. etiam Q)
R (in 1:1 deus *scribit et del. R) TZ (supra lin. hic, sed non in 1:1, add. Z²)* esset¹:

following: that the ear has not heard and that there has not descended into the heart of man the infinity of Your sweetness, which You have prepared for those who love You. This point was revealed to us by Your great apostle Paul, who, beyond the wall of coincidence, was caught up into Paradise.[78] *There* alone can You who are the Fount of delights be seen unveiledly. Trusting in Your infinite goodness, I endeavored to become the subject of a rapture,[79] in order to see You who are invisible and who are the revealed but unrevealable vision. But You, not I, know how far I got. And Your grace is sufficient for me.[80] By it You make me certain that You are incomprehensible, and by it You raise me up in the firm hope that through Your guidance I will attain unto enjoyment of You.

81

CHAPTER EIGHTEEN

UNLESS GOD WERE TRINE, THERE WOULD NOT BE HAPPINESS[81]

O Lord, would that all who by Your gift have obtained mental eyes would open them and, with me, would recognize that You, O Jealous God,[82] cannot hate anything, because You are Loving Love! For every lovable[83] thing is loved by You in Yourself, who are a Lovable God, enfolding all lovable things. Thus, from this consideration all |rational beings| may see, with me, by what covenant or union You are united to all things. O Loving God, You love all things in such way that You love each thing. You shed abroad Your love upon all |rational beings|. Yet, many do not love You, preferring to You something other than You. But if lovable love were not distinct from loving love, then (1) You would be so lovable by all that they would not

om. AC (supra lin. add. C²) GJLM³ (in 1:1 om. etiam M) OP³ (in 1:1 om. etiam P) Pa³Q² (in 1:1 om. etiam Q) RTV²Z supra lin. E³ in titulo qui in indice est esset[1] *non habet p* felicitas: foelicitas *(ut paene semper) p; in titulo qui in indice est* felicitas *habet p* 3 domine: *om. E (supra lin. add. Eⁿ) N* aperirent: aperient *C (ad* aperirent *corr. C²)* eos: *om. Pa (supra lin. add. Pa²)* 4 quomodo: quoniam *R* tu: es *add. S* quia: tu *add. CVp* 5 amor: amator *V* amans: et *add. GT* odire: odisse *p* 6 amabile: amabili *N* amas: *ex* amans *corr. L* amans *Q* 7 deus: meus *add. A* ita: sic *I* 8 quod: *om. N* 9 qui:

nihil praeter te amare possent, et omnes rationales spiritus necessita-
rentur ad tui amorem. Sed tam nobilis es, deus meus, ut velis in
libertate esse rationalium animarum te diligere vel non. Quapropter
ad amare tuum non sequitur quod ameris. Tu igitur, deus meus,
15 amoris nexu omnibus unitus es, quia expandis amorem tuum super
omnem creaturam tuam; sed non omnis rationalis spiritus est unitus
tibi, quia amorem suum non in tuam amabilitatem proicit sed in
aliud, cui unitur et nectitur.

82   Desponsasti omnem animam rationalem amore tuo amante; sed
non omnis sponsa te sponsum amat sed saepissime alium cui ad-
haeret. Sed quomodo posset attingere finem suum sponsa tua, deus
meus, anima humana, nisi tu fores diligibilis, ut sic te diligibilem
5 diligendo ad nexum ac unionem felicissimam pertingere posset? Quis
igitur negare potest te deum trinum, quando videt quod neque tu
nobilis neque naturalis et perfectus deus esses, nec spiritus liberi arbi-
trii esset, nec ipse ad tui fruitionem et felicitatem suam pertingere
posset, si non fores trinus et unus? Nam quia es intellectus intelligens
10 et intellectus intelligibilis et utriusque nexus, tunc intellectus creatus,
in te deo suo intelligibili, unionem tui et felicitatem assequi potest.
Sic cum sis amor amabilis, potest creata voluntas amans in te deo suo
amabili, unionem et felicitatem assequi. Qui enim recipit te deum
lucem receptibilem rationalem, ad talem usque tui unionem pervenire
15 poterit, ut sit tibi unitus ut filius patri. Video, domine, te illustrante,
naturam rationalem non posse unionem tui assequi, nisi quia amabilis
et intelligibilis. Unde natura humana non est unibilis tibi deo amanti,

quia *Z*   qui tibi: que te *N*   tibi: te *E*   11 te: *om. L*   12 meus: *om. EN*   ut:
in *add. G*   in: voluntate et *add. Z*   13 rationalium: racionabilium *ex* nobilium
corr. A   racionabilium *G*   rationabilium *R*   14 amare: amorem *S*   quod: ut *R*
ameris: amicus *V*

82 1 desponsasti: despondisti *L*   omnem animam rationalem: enim animam
racionalem omnem *ad* omnem enim animam racionalem *transponit E et ad* omnem
animam racionalem *corr. E²*   amante: *ex* amantem *corr. T*   2 alium: *ex* aliud
corr. G   aliud *R*   cui: tui *L*   3 quomodo: quo *Q*   posset: possit *P*   suum:
non clare scribit J   tuum *Zp*   sponsa tua: tua sponsa *Q*   4 fores: esses *p*   te:
om. EN   diligibilem: diligem *S*   5 felicissimam: selicissimam *L*   posset: possit
EN   7 et: *supra lin. E*   8 esset: esse *CEGIJM* (esset *sub lin. coni. M²*) *NPaSTV*
felicitatem: feliciter *S*   suam: *om. N*   9 non: *om. C* (*supra lin. add. C²*)   fores:
ternus *post* fores *scribit et del. G*   esses *p*   10 intelligibilis: intellectualis *I*   utrius-

be able to love anything except You and (2) all rational spirits would be constrained to love You. But You, my God, are so noble that You will that whether or not to love You be |placed| within the freedom of rational souls. Accordingly, Your loving is not necessarily followed by Your being loved. Therefore, my God, You are united to all by a union of love, because You shed abroad Your love upon all Your creatures; yet, not every rational spirit is united to You, for not every such spirit directs its love unto Your Lovability but directs it unto something else, to which it is united.

82   You have betrothed every rational soul through Your loving love. But not every betrothed soul loves You, her Betrothed; rather, in most cases a soul loves someone else, to whom she clings. But how could Your betrothed, the human soul, attain her end, my God, unless You were lovable, so that thus, by loving You who are lovable, she could attain unto a most happy union? Who, then, can deny that You who are God are trine?—when he sees that unless You were three and one, You would not be either a noble or a natural and perfect God, nor would the spirit of free choice exist, nor could he himself attain unto the enjoyment of You and unto his own happiness. For since You are Intellect-that-understands, Intellect-that-is-understandable, and the Union of both, created intellect can attain in You—its understandable God—union with You and happiness. Similarly: since You are Lovable Love, the created will that loves can attain, in You its lovable God, union and happiness. For he who receives You, who are God and are rational, receivable Light, can arrive at such a close union with You that he will be united to You as a son to his father. By Your illumination I see, O Lord, that a rational nature can attain unto union with You only because You are lovable and understandable. Hence, human nature is not unitable to

que: *littera* u¹ *supra lin. V*   creatus: increatus *IQ   om. JPa*   11 suo: amabili *post* suo *scribit et del. G*   intelligibili: intelligibile *V*   tui: *om. V*   et felicitatem: felicitatem et *ad* et felicitatem *transponit C aut C²*   felicitatem: suam *add. EN* 11-13 potest . . . assequi: *om. JT (in 82:11* potest *supra lin. add. JⁿT²; sic . . .* assequi *in marg. add. JⁿT²)*   12 sis: sit *CV*   amans: *om. OPPa*   13 recipit: recepit *I*   recipit te: te recipit *V*   13-14 deum lucem: lucem deum *N*   14 tui: uti *S*   tui unionem: triunionem *R*   15 sit: *om. I*   tibi: sibi *I*   domine te: te domine *ENZ*   16 posse: posso *N*   tui: tuam *GV*   17 tibi: ut *add. G*   amanti:

sic enim non es obiectum eius; sed est tibi unibilis ut deo suo amabili, cum amabile sit amantis obiectum. Sic pariformiter intelligibile
20 est obiectum intellectus. Dicimus autem hoc veritatem quod obiectum. Quare tu, deus meus, quoniam es veritas intelligibilis, tibi uniri
potest intellectus creatus.

83   Et sic video humanam rationalem naturam tuae divinae naturae
intelligibili et amabili tantum unibilem et quod homo te deum receptibilem capiens, transit in nexum qui ob sui strictitudinem filiationis
nomen sortiri potest. Nexu enim filiationis non cognoscimus strictio-
5 rem. Quod si hic nexus unionis est maximus, quo maior esse nequit
(hoc evenire necesse erit, quia tu, deus amabilis, plus diligi non potes
ab homine), tunc nexus ille usque ad perfectissimam filiationem pervenit, ut filiatio illa sit perfectio complicans omnem possibilem filiationem, per quam omnes filii ultimam felicitatem et perfectionem
10 assequuntur. In quo altissimo filio, filiatio est ut ars in magistro aut
lux in sole; in aliis vero, ut ars in discipulis aut lux in stellis.

84   CAPITULUM XIX

QUOD IHESUS UNIO DEI ET HOMINIS

Ago ineffabiles gratias tibi deo, vitae et luci animae meae. Nam
video nunc fidem quam revelatione apostolorum tenet catholica
5 ecclesia, quomodo scilicet tu deus amans de te deum generas amabi-

amati *V*   17-18 tibi . . . unibilis: *om. Pa (in marg. add. Pa²)*   18 enim: *om. I*
es: est *A*   ut: cum *Pa (cum del. Pa²)*   18-19 eius . . . obiectum: *om. I*   19-
20 sic . . . obiectum: *om. V*   20 est: es *S*   hoc: id *p*
    83 1 humanam rationalem: racionalem humanam *Pa*   rationalem: creaturam
post racionalem *scribit E et del. E²*   racionalem *ex* racionabilem *corr. P aut P²*   naturam: *ex* creaturam *corr. Q*   divinae: *? post* divine *scribit et del. S*   2 te deum:
bis *OP*   3 capiens: cupiens *Q*   strictitudinem: districtitudinem *R*   filiationis:
filicionis *S*   4 sortiri: sortire *P*   filiationis: filicionis *S*   5 hic: *om. EN*   hec *V*

You qua *loving* God, for You are not in this respect its object; rather, it is unitable to You qua its own *lovable* God, since the lovable is the object of the loving. In like manner, too, what is understandable is the object of the intellect. Now, we call that which is the object |of the intellect| *truth*. Therefore, my God, since You are understandable Truth, the created intellect can be united to You.[84]

83 And in the foregoing manner I see that rational human nature is unitable only to Your understandable and lovable divine nature and that a man who receives You, His receivable God, passes over into a union which, because of its closeness, can be given the name *sonship*. For we know of no closer union than that of sonship.[85] But if this bond of union is a maximum bond, than which there cannot be a greater bond (this will necessarily be the case because You, O Lovable God, cannot be more greatly loved by man), then this union will reach the point of most perfect sonship, so that this sonship will be the perfection that enfolds all possible sonship, whereby all sons will attain unto their ultimate happiness and perfection. In this loftiest Son[86] sonship is present as artistry is present in a master or as light is present in the sun; but sonship is in other sons as artistry is in |the master's| students or as light is in the stars.

84

CHAPTER NINETEEN

JESUS IS THE UNION OF GOD AND MAN

I give ineffable thanks to You-my-God, Life and Light of my soul. For I now see the faith which the Catholic church holds by revelation of the Apostles: viz., that You who are God who is loving beget from

6 hoc: *non proprie abbreviat L*   quia: si *add. p*   plus diligi: diligi plus *EN*
9 per: venit *post* per *scribit et del. E*   ultimam: ulcionem *I (alias* ultimam *in marg.*
notat I) J   filiacionem et *add. Q*   felicitatem: filicitatem *N*   felicitatem et perfectionem: perfeccionem et felicitatem *Z*   10 filiatio: *om. T*   aut: vel *J (ad* aut
corr. J")   11 aliis: alii *Q*   stellis: et cetera *add. E"I*
   84 1 capitulum XIX: capitulum 20 *E⁴*   2 quod: quomodo *CE³JV²p*   Ihesus:
est *add. A³p* sit *add. V²* Iesu *Z (hic, sed non in 1:1, ad* Iesus *corr. Z²)*   3 ago:
ego *AQ*   ineffabiles: ineffabilis *P*   4 revelatione: revelacionem *N*   5 quomodo:

lem, atque quod tu deus genitus amabilis es absolutus mediator. Per
te enim est omne id quod est et esse potest. Tu enim deus volens seu
amans in te deo amabili complicas omnia. Omne enim quod tu deus
volens vis aut concipis, est in te deo amabili complicatum. Non enim

10 esse potest quidquam nisi illud velis esse. Omnia igitur in conceptu
tuo amabili causam seu rationem habent essendi. Neque est alia
rerum omnium causa, nisi quia sic tibi placet. Nihil placet amanti ut
amanti nisi amabile. Tu igitur deus amabilis es filius dei amantis
patris. In te enim est omnis complacentia patris. Ita omne esse crea-

15 bile complicatur in te deo amabili. Tu igitur deus amans, cum ex te
sit amabilis deus, uti filius a patre, in hoc quod es deus pater amans
dei amabilis filii tui, es pater omnium quae sunt. Nam conceptus tuus
est filius, et omnia in ipso.

85   Et unio tui et tui conceptus est actus et operatio exsurgens, in qua
est omnium actus et explicatio. Sicut igitur ex te deo amante generatur deus amabilis—quae generatio est conceptio—ita procedit ex te
deo amante et conceptu tuo amabili a te genito actus tuus et tui

5 conceptus. Qui est nexus nectens et deus uniens te et conceptum
tuum, quemadmodum amare unit amantem et amabile in amore. Et
hic nexus spiritus nominatur. Spiritus enim est ut motus procedens a
movente et mobili. Unde motus est explicatio conceptus moventis.
Explicantur igitur omnia in te deo spiritu sancto, sicut concipiuntur

10 in te deo filio.

86   Video igitur—quia tu, deus, sic me illustras—quomodo omnia in te

quoniam *A*   deum: deus *CV*   generas: generans *A*   6 atque: quotque *J*   8 complicas: complicans A conplicans *Q*   8-9 complicas . . . amabili: *om. Pa (in marg.*
add. Pa[2])   9 volens: *om. CVp*   concipis: cupis *Q*   10 esse potest: potest esse
AEN   illud: id *A*   esse[2]: *supra lin. T*   11 neque: enim *add. Q*   12 rerum
omnium causa: causa rerum omnium *Z*   causa: nichil quod *post* causa *scribit et*
del. J   sic: sicut (?) *A om. J*   sic tibi: tibi sic *Z*   placet: placent *R*   13-
14 amantis patris: patris amantis *ad* amantis patris *transponit R*   14 in te: ita *I*
complacentia: complacencia (*non* complacenciam) *scribit L*   patris[2]: *om. G*   ita:
om. E (in marg. add. E[n]) N   16 sit: *ex* sis *corr. G*   uti: ut *Z*   es: *om. OP*
17 dei: ab *add. T sed del. T[3]*   quae: qui *EN*   tuus: *om. Pa*   18 ipso: *ex* ipsa
corr. Pa
    85 1 tui[1]: tua *p*   tui[2]: tuus *p*   operatio: consurgens *post* operatio *scribit E et*
del. E[2] consurgens *add. N*   exsurgens: exurgens *AGILOPQRSTZp*   2 deo:
domine *A*   2-3 generatur: generantur *N*   3 quae: quem *N*   4 conceptu: concepto *AL*   amabili: ad *post* amabili *scribit et del. P*   tuus: *om. P*   tui: tuus *p*

Yourself God who is lovable, and that You who are God begotten and lovable are the Absolute Mediator. For through You there exists whatever does and can exist. For You who are God who wills and loves enfold all things in Yourself, who are God who is lovable. For whatever is willed or conceived by You who are God who wills is enfolded in You who are God who is lovable. For nothing whatsoever can exist unless You will that it exist. Therefore, in Your Lovable Concept all things have the cause of, or reason for, their being. And the sole cause of all things is that it pleases You |that all be| thus. The one who loves is pleased, qua one who loves, only by what is lovable.[87] You, then, who are God who is lovable are the Son of God the Loving Father. For the Father's entire pleasure is in You.[88] So all creatable being is enfolded in You who are God who is lovable. Therefore, since from You who are God who is loving there exists God who is lovable—as a son exists from a father—then in that You are God the loving Father of God Your lovable Son, you are Father of all existing things. For Your Concept is Your Son, and all things exist in Him.[89]

85 And the Union of You and Your Concept is an activity and a working that arises, wherein is present the activity and unfolding of all things. Therefore, just as from You who are God who loves there is begotten God who is lovable (this begottenness is a conceiving), so from You who are God who loves and from the lovable Concept begotten from You there proceeds the Activity of You and of Your Concept. And this Activity is a uniting Union—is God who unites You and Your Concept (just as the act of loving unites in love the one who loves and that which is lovable). And this Union is called *spirit*. For spirit is as motion, which proceeds from a mover and the movable. Hence, motion is the unfolding of the mover's concept. Therefore, all things are unfolded in You who are God the Holy Spirit, even as they are conceived in You who are God the Son.

86 Therefore, because You, O God, thus enlighten me, I see that in

---

5 nectens: nectans *C*   deus: *om. A*   deus uniens: uniens deus *ad* deus uniens *transponit R*   5-6 et[1]. . . unit: et unit *P (*et unit *del., et* et[1]. . . unit *in marg. add., P*[2])
6 amabile: ama'le *C (ad* amabile *perficit C*[2]) amabile *ex* amabilem *corr. V*   7 nominatur: *ex* vocatur *corr. E*   9 explicantur: explicatur *P*   deo: *ex* domine *in marg. corr. A*   spiritu sancto: spiritusancto *p*
    86 1 quia: quod *ITV*   tu: *ex* tua *corr. G*   es *add. N (*tu es *non proprie scribit N)*

deo filio dei patris sunt ut in ratione, conceptu, causa, seu exemplari et quomodo filius est medium omnium, quia ratio. Mediante enim ratione et sapientia tu deus pater omnia operaris. Et spiritus seu
5 motus ponit conceptum rationis in effectu—sicut experimur arcam in mente artificis poni, mediante virtute motiva quae inest manibus, in effectu. Video deinde, deus meus, filium tuum esse medium unionis omnium, ut cuncta in te, mediante filio tuo, quiescant. Et video Ihesum benedictum hominis filium filio tuo unitum altissime et quod
10 filius hominis non potuit tibi deo patri uniri, nisi mediante filio tuo mediatore absoluto. Quis non altissime rapitur haec attentius prospiciens? Aperis enim tu, deus meus, mihi misero tale occultum, ut intuear hominem non posse te patrem intelligere nisi in filio tuo, qui est intelligibilis et mediator et quod te intelligere est tibi uniri. Potest
15 igitur homo tibi uniri per filium tuum, qui est medium unionis. Et natura humana altissime tibi unita, in quocumque homine hoc fuerit, non potest plus medio uniri quam unita est. Sine enim medio tibi uniri nequit. Unitur igitur medio maxime. Non tamen fit medium. Unde quamvis non possit fieri medium, cum sine medio non possit
20 tibi uniri, sic tamen iungitur medio absoluto, quod inter ipsam et filium tuum, qui est medium absolutum, nihil mediare potest. Si enim aliquid mediare posset inter naturam humanam et medium absolutum, tunc tibi altissime non uniretur.

87   O Ihesu bone, video in te naturam humanam altissime iungi deo

te: filio *post* te *scribit et del.* V   2 filio: video P   dei: *om.* T   ut: et E *(ad* ut *corr.* E²) N *om.* I   4-5 seu motus: semotus I   5 ponit conceptum: *om.* A   effectu: effctu Pa   experimur: in *add.* N   arcam: Abraham S   5-7 sicut . . . effectu: *om.* A   5-6 in². . . poni: poni in mente artificis Z   6 mediante: mediate Pa   motiva: *om.* EN   inest: est in IJ   est in *(?)* Pa *(ad* inest *supra lin. corr.* Pa²) 7 effectu: effctu Pa   deus meus: *om.* EN   tuum: *om.* EN   8 ut: et V   mediante filio tuo: filio tuo mediante A   8-9 quiescant . . . tuo: *om.* J *(in marg. add.* J"; hominis *non plene visibile)*   9 hominis: homines S   hominis filium: filium hominis QRV   filium: tuum *add.* L   unitum altissime: unitum altissime *in linea scribit* J *et post* tuo *in marg. scribit et del.* J"   11 non: absolute *post* non *scribit et del.* O   haec: h^c A *(in* A=hec *aut* hoc) hoc IJ   attentius: altissime LZ 12 tale: *ex* talem *corr.* T   13 intuear: intueatur V   14 uniri: *ex* unire *corr.* V 15 homo tibi: tibi homo N   16 homine: homo T   hoc fuerit: fuerit hoc *ad* hoc fuerit *transponit* G   17 non: *bis* G   enim medio: medio enim I   18 uniri: unire P   maxime: maximo AOPQR   maxime M *(ad* maximo *corr.* M²)   non: *ex* tamen *corr.* N   fit: sit N   19 medio: fieri *post* medio *scribit et del.* V   19-

You who are God-the-Son of God-the-Father all things are present as in their Rational Principle (*ratio*), Concept, Cause, or Exemplar. And |I see| that the Son is the Medium of all things, because He is the Rational Principle |of all things|. For by the medium of Reason (*ratio*) and Wisdom You who are God the Father work all things. And Spirit, or Motion, puts the concept of Reason into effect, just as we witness that a chest in the mind of an artisan is put into effect by the medium of the moving force in his hands. I see, then, my God, that Your Son is the uniting Medium of all things, so that all things may find rest in You by the medium of Your Son. And I see that Blessed Jesus, the son of man, was most closely united to Your Son and that only by the mediation of Your Son, who is Absolute Mediator, could the son of man be united to You who are God the Father. Is there anyone who, upon quite carefully considering these |truths|, is not most highly caught up in rapture? For You, my God, disclose to wretched me such a hidden |truth as this| in order that I may recognize the following: (1) that a man cannot understand You who are Father except in Your Son, who is the Understandable One and the Mediator, and (2) that to understand You is to be united to You. Therefore, man can be united to You through Your Son, who is the uniting Medium. And the human nature that is the most closely united to You—in whichever man this uniting occur—cannot be more closely united to the Medium than it is. For it cannot be immediately united to You. Therefore, it is maximally united to the Medium and yet does not become the Medium. Hence, although the human nature cannot become the Medium (since it cannot be immediately united to You), nevertheless it is joined to the Absolute Medium in such way that nothing can mediate between the human nature and Your Son, who is the Absolute Medium. For if something could mediate between the human nature and the Absolute Medium,[90] then the human nature would not be most closely united to You.

87   O good Jesus, I see that in You the human nature is joined most

20 non possit tibi: tibi non possit *R*   20 sic: si *N*   21 tuum: absolutum *post* tuum *scribit et del. R*   nihil mediare: mediare nichil *GT*   mediare: *non proprie abbreviat S*   22 aliquid: aliquod *JLPaV*   posset: possit *P*   humanam: humana *Pa* 23 tibi: ibi *I*

87 1 in: *supra lin. A*   in te: *ex* inter *corr. E*   naturam humanam: humanam

patri per unionem altissimam, qua iungitur deo filio mediatori absoluto. Filiatio igitur humana—quia tu filius hominis—filiationi divinae
in te Ihesu altissime unita est, ut merito dicaris filius dei et hominis,
5 quoniam in te nihil mediat inter filium hominis et filium dei. In filiatione absoluta, quae est filius dei, omnis complicatur filiatio, cui
filiatio humana tua, Ihesu, est supreme unita. Subsistit igitur humana
filiatio tua in divina, non solum complicite sed ut attractum in attrahente et unitum in uniente et substantiatum in substantiante. Non est
10 igitur possibilis separatio filii hominis a filio dei in te, Ihesu. Nam
separabilitas evenit ex hoc, quod unio potuit esse maior. Ubi autem
unio non potest esse maior, nihil mediare potest. Separatio igitur non
habebit ibi locum, ubi nihil mediare potest inter unita. Ubi autem
unitum non subsistit in uniente, unio non est altissima. Maior est
15 unio ubi unitum subsistit in uniente, quam ubi unitum separatim
subsistit. Separatio enim est remotio ab unione maxima. Sic video in
te Ihesu meo quomodo filiatio humana, qua es filius hominis, subsistit in filiatione divina, qua es filius dei, sicut in maxima unione
unitum in uniente. Tibi gloria, deus, in saecula.

naturam *R*   2 qua: quam *N ex ? corr. P*   iungitur: iungi *Q*   mediatori:
media tori *A* (altissimo *post* media *scribit et del. A*)   mediatore *CEGIJM* (ad
mediatori *corr. M²*) *NPaSTV*   2-3 absoluto: et *add. EN*   4 est: *supra lin.*
P   5 in
te nihil: nichil in te *N*   filium¹: filius *Q*   6 omnis: hominis *P*   6-7 cui filiatio:
in marg. I   7 humana tua Ihesu: tua Ihesu humana *R*   supreme: suprema *OP*
7-8 humana filiatio tua: filiacio tua humana *A*   8 tua: *om. T*   attractum: ad-
tactum *Q*   8-9 attrahente: trahente *EN*   9 uniente: es *post* uniente *scribit et*
del. G   10 filii: filio *Z*   11 potuit: potest *N*   12 mediare potest: potest mediare
ad mediare potest *transponit R*   igitur: enim *A*   12-13 non habebit ibi: ibi non
haberet *N*   13 habebit: habet *A*   haberet *E*   14 non²: *om. Pa (supra lin. add.*
Pa²)   maior: namque *add. p*   14-15 unio . . . uniente: *om. S*   15 separatim:
ex separatum *corr. E (?)* separatum *N*   15-16 separatim subsistit: subsistit
separatim *V*   16 enim: omnium *S*   est: racio *add. N*   video: *om. A*   vides *G*
17 te: deo *add. R*   18 filiatione: filiacio *Q*   qua: *ex* quas *corr. I*   dei sicut:
sicut dei *ad* dei sicut *transponit G*   19 deus: sit *add. I*   in²: seculorum *add. Q*
saecula: amen *add. AN*   et cetera *add. P*

closely to God the Father by means of the exceedingly close union by which it is joined to God the Son, who is Absolute Mediator. Therefore, in You, Jesus, the human sonship (for You are son of man) is most closely united to the Divine Sonship. Hence, You are rightly called *Son of God and of man*, since in You nothing mediates between son of man and Son of God. In Absolute Sonship, which the Son of God is, all sonship is enfolded; and to Absolute Sonship Your human sonship, O Jesus, is supremely united. Therefore, Your human sonship exists in the Divine Sonship not only in an enfolded manner but also as the attracted in the attracting, the united in the uniting, and the substantified in the substantifying. Therefore, in You, O Jesus, separation of the son of man from the Son of God is not possible.[91] For separability results from the fact that a union could have been greater. But where a union cannot be greater, there can be no mediation. Hence, where nothing can mediate between the things united, separation will have no place. Now, where the united does not exist in the uniting, the union is not the closest. Greater is the union where the united exists in the uniting than where the united exists separately. For separation is a remoteness from maximum union. Thus, in You, my Jesus, I see that the human sonship, by which You are son of man, exists in the Divine Sonship, by which You are Son of God—even as in a maximum union the united exists in the uniting. To You, O God, be glory forever.

88   CAPITULUM XX

QUOMODO INTELLIGITUR IHESUS COPULATIO
DIVINAE ET HUMANAE NATURAE

Ostendis mihi, lux indeficiens, maximam unionem qua natura
5 humana in Ihesu meo est tuae divinae naturae unita, non esse quovismodo infinitae unioni similem. Unio enim, qua unione tu deus
pater es unitus deo filio tuo, est deus spiritus sanctus; et ideo est
infinita unio. Pertingit enim in identitatem absolutam et essentialem.
Non sic ubi natura humana unitur divinae. Nam humana natura non
10 potest transire in unionem cum divina essentialem, sicut finitum non
potest infinito infinite uniri. Transiret enim in identitatem infiniti, et
sic desineret esse finitum, quando de eo verificaretur infinitum. Quapropter haec unio, qua natura humana est naturae divinae unita, non
est nisi attractio naturae humanae ad divinam in altissimo gradu, ita
15 quod natura ipsa humana, ut talis, elevatius attrahi nequit. Maxima
igitur est unio eius naturae humanae, ut humanae, ad divinam, quia
maior esse nequit. Sed non est simpliciter maxima et infinita, ut est
unio divina.

89   Video igitur ex benignitate gratiae tuae in te, Ihesu, filio hominis
filium dei, et in te filio dei patrem. In te autem filio hominis filium
dei video quia ita es filius hominis quod filius dei. Et in natura
attracta finita video naturam attrahentem infinitam. Video in filio
5 absoluto patrem absolutum. Filius enim non potest, ut filius, videri
nisi pater videatur. Video in te, Ihesu, filiationem divinam, quae est
veritas omnis filiationis, et pariter altissimam humanam filiationem,

---

88 1 capitulum XX: capitulum 21 *E⁴*   2 intelligitur: intelligatur *G*   3 naturae:
om. A   5 est: et *R*   divinae naturae: naturae divinae *p*   6 unioni: *aut* unioni
ex unione *aut* unione *ex* unioni *corr. E (cf.* existis *in 91:17 et* venire *in 94:2)*
unione *N*   unio: *ex* unione *corr. E*   unione: *om. T*   7 spiritus sanctus:
spiritussanctus *p*   8 identitatem: ydemptitate *V*   9 sic: sicut *R*   natura humana
unitur: unitur natura humana *EN*   11 infinite: finite *Pa (ad* infinite *corr. Pa²)*
uniri: unire *P ex* unire *(?) corr. Pa ex* unire *corr. V*   transiret: transire *R*
enim: *om. E (supra lin. add. E²) N*   12 desineret: sineret *EN*   quando . . .
infinitum: *om. EN*   infinitum: finitum *G*   13 qua: que *N om. S*   naturae:
natura *N*   14 attractio: attracto *A*   humanae: humane *ex* humani *corr. G*   ad:
in *T*   divinam: divina *V*   15 ipsa humana: humana ipsa *R*   nequit: sed non est

88 ## CHAPTER TWENTY

HOW JESUS IS UNDERSTOOD TO BE THE UNITING
OF THE DIVINE NATURE AND THE HUMAN NATURE

You show me, O Light Unfailing, that the maximum union by which, in my Jesus, the human nature is united to Your divine nature is not in any way like an infinite union. For the Union by which You, God the Father, are united to God Your Son is God the Holy Spirit. And so, it is an infinite Union, for it attains unto an absolute and essential identity. But this is not the case when the human nature is united to the divine nature. For the human nature cannot pass over into essential union with the divine nature,[92] even as the finite cannot be infinitely united to the Infinite. For the finite would pass over into an identity with the Infinite and thus would cease to be finite, since *infinite* would be predicated truly of it. Therefore, the union by which the human nature is united to the divine nature is only the attraction—in the highest degree—of the human nature to the divine nature, so that the human nature, qua human nature, cannot be attracted more highly. Therefore, the union of Jesus's human nature, qua human, to the divine nature is maximal, because it cannot be greater. But it is not maximal and infinite in an unqualified sense, as is the Divine Union.[93]

89 Therefore, in You, O Jesus, who are the son of man, I see, through the kindness of Your grace, the Son of God; and in You, the Son of God, I see the Father. Now, in You, the son of man, I see the Son of God because You are son of man in such way that You are Son of God. And in the attracted finite nature I see the attracting infinite nature. In the Absolute Son I see the Absolute Father, for a son cannot be seen as son unless the father is seen. In You, Jesus, I see the Divine Sonship, which is the Truth of all sonship; and, likewise,

simpliciter maximam et infinita *post* nequit *scribit et del. A*   17 nequit: hominis *post* nequit *scribit et del. Q*   est[1]: *om. OP*   et: *om. L*

89 1 benignitate: bonitate *S*   filio: tuo filio *post* filio *scribit et del. O*   2 dei[2]: *om. V*   2-3 et . . . dei[1]: *om. Pa (*et in te filio de[-] in te autem filio h[-] filium dei *in marg. add. Pa²) om. T (*et . . . video *in marg. add. T²)*   3 es: est *IPa (ad* es corr. *Pa²) om. N*   quod: et *add. p*   filius[2]: *om. L*   4 filio: patrem *post* filio *scribit et del. V*   5 videri: *om. Pa (supra lin. add. Pa²)*   7 filiationem: filiacione

quae est propinquissima imago absolutae filiationis. Sicut igitur imago, inter quam et exemplar non potest mediare perfectior imago,
10 propinquissime subsistit in veritate cuius est imago, sic video naturam tuam humanam in divina natura subsistentem. Omnia igitur in natura humana tua video, quae et video in divina; sed humaniter illa esse video in natura humana, quae sunt ipsa divina veritas in natura divina. Quae humaniter video esse in te, Ihesu, similitudo sunt di-
15 vinae naturae. Sed similitudo est sine medio iuncta exemplari, ita quod magis similis nec esse nec cogitari potest.

90   In natura humana seu rationali video spiritum rationalem humanum spiritui divino, qui est absoluta ratio, strictissime unitum—et sic intellectum humanum intellectui divino et omnia in intellectu tuo, Ihesu. Intelligis enim omnia, Ihesu, ut deus, et hoc intelligere est esse
5 omnia; intelligis omnia ut homo, et hoc intelligere est esse similitudinem omnium. Non enim res intelligitur per hominem nisi in similitudine. Lapis non est in intellectu humano ut in causa vel ratione propria eius sed ut in specie et similitudine. Est igitur in te, Ihesu, unitum intelligere humanum ipsi intelligere divino, sicut perfectis-
10 sima imago veritati exemplari—ac si in mente artificis considerarem formam arcae idealem et speciem arcae perfectissimae per magistrum ipsum secundum ideam factae. Quomodo tunc forma idealis est veritas speciei et unita ei, ut veritas imagini, in uno magistro, ita in te, Ihesu, magistro magistrorum, video absolutam ideam rerum omnium
15 pariter et speciem similitudinariam earundem altissime uniri.

EN   8 propinquissima: a *ante* propinquissima *scribit et del.* G   9 mediare: *in marg. scribit* L; esse *ante* perfectior *scribit et del.* L   10 subsistit: subsistet L   est: *om.* N   est imago: imago est R   sic: sicut A   12 humana tua: tua humana *VZ* 13 natura humana: humana natura Q   in²: ipsa *post* in² *scribit et del.* G   13-14 veritas . . . divina: *om.* V   natura divina: divina natura *ad* natura divina *transponit* R 14 humaniter: esse *add.* P   esse in te: in te esse S   esse in te Ihesu: in te Ihesu esse *ad* esse in te Ihesu *transponit* R   15 naturae: sed similitudo sunt divine nature *post* nature *scribit et del.* Pa

90 1-2 humanum: *litteram* u² *clarius supra lin. rescribit* J   2 qui: que *I ex* que *corr.* J   3 in: *om.* AE *(supra lin. add.* E²*)* NQ   intellectu: intellectum N tuo: intelligere est esse omnia *post* tuo *scribit et del.* G   4 intelligere: omnia *post* intelligere *scribit et del.* A   5 intelligis: enim *add.* G   intelligas S   5-6 similitudinem omnium: omnium similitudinem *ad* similitudinem omnium *transponit* R 7 lapis: enim *add.* Q   in¹: *om.* N   causa: propria *post* causa *scribit et del.* E   7-8 propria eius: sua propria *p*   8 et: in *Pa (ad* et *corr.* Pa²*)*   9 unitum: unicum V 10 veritati: *ex* veritate *corr.* M   ac si: acsi *p*   considerarem: *ex* consideralem *in*

|I see| the closest human sonship, which is the closest image of Absolute Sonship. Therefore, just as an image between which and its exemplar a more perfect image cannot mediate exists most closely in the truth of which it is the image, so Your human nature, I see, exists in the divine nature. Therefore, in Your human nature I see whatever I also see in Your divine nature. But all this, which in the divine nature is the Divine Truth, I see to be in the human nature in a human way. Whatever I see to exist in a human way in You, Jesus, is a likeness of the divine nature. But the likeness is joined to its Exemplar[94] without a medium, so that there can neither be nor be thought to be a greater likeness.

90   In Your human, or rational, nature I see the rational human spirit to be united most closely to the Divine Spirit, which is Absolute Reason; and in like manner |I see| Your human intellect—and in Your intellect, Jesus, all things—|to be united| to the divine intellect. For You, O Jesus, understand all things according as You are God, and this understanding is Your being all things;[95] You understand all things according as You are a man, and this understanding is Your being the likeness of all things. For a thing is understood by a man only by means of a likeness. A stone is not present in the human intellect as it is present in its cause or its own rational principle but as it is present in its image and likeness. Therefore, in You, Jesus, human understanding is united to divine understanding as a most perfect image is united to its truth and exemplar—as if I were to consider in the mind of an artisan the ideal form of a chest and the image of a most perfect chest made by the master artisan in accordance with his idea.[96] As, then, the ideal form is the truth of the image and is united to it (as truth to image) in the one master, so in You, Jesus, Master of masters, I see that the Absolute Idea of all things and the resembling image of these things are likewise most closely united.

---

marg. corr. E   considerare *S*   11 formam: *om. Z (in marg. add. Z²)*   arcae¹: arte *Q*   perfectissimae: perfectissime *p*   12 ipsum secundum ideam: secundum ideam ipsum *E (*eam *post* secundum *scribit et del. E) N (*ydeam *pro* ideam *scribit N)* factae: facte *ex* factam *corr. I*   factam *V*   13 speciei . . . veritas: *om. E (in marg. add. E") N*   13-14 ita . . . magistro: *in marg. Pa*   14 Ihesu magistro magistrorum: magistro magistrorum scilicet yhesu *V*   rerum omnium: omnium rerum *ENR* 15 altissime: altissimi *EN*

91　Video, Ihesu bone, te intra murum paradisi, quoniam intellectus
tuus est veritas pariter et imago; et tu es deus pariter et creatura,
infinitus pariter et finitus. Et non est possibile quod citra murum
videaris. Es enim copulatio divinae creatricis naturae et humanae crea-
5 tae naturae. Hoc autem inter tuum humanum intellectum et alterius
cuiuslibet hominis interesse video: quia nemo hominum scit omnia
quae per hominem sciri possunt, quia nullius hominis intellectus est
ita coniunctus exemplari rerum omnium, ut similitudo veritati, quin
possit propinquius coniungi et magis in actu constitui. Et ideo non
10 tot intelligit quin plura intelligere posset per accessum ad exemplar
rerum, a quo habet actualitatem omne actu existens. Tuus autem
intellectus actu omnia per hominem intelligibilia intelligit, quia in te
natura humana est perfectissima et exemplari suo coniunctissima. Ob
quam quidem unionem intellectus tuus humanus omnem creatum
15 excedit intellectum in perfectione intelligendi. Omnes igitur rationales
spiritus longe sunt infra te, quorum omnium tu, Ihesu, magister et
lux existis. Et tu es perfectio et plenitudo omnium; et per te ad
absolutam veritatem, tamquam per mediatorem, accedunt. Tu enim
es via ad veritatem pariter et ipsa veritas. Tu es via ad vitam intellec-
20 tus pariter et vita ipsa. Tu es odor cibi laetitiae pariter et gustus
laetificans. Sis igitur, dulcissime Ihesu, semper benedictus.

91 1 murum: *non proprie scribit S* quoniam: *non proprie abbreviat S* quando *V* 2 tu es: *in marg. E* es: *supra lin. Pa* creatura: *ex* creaturam *corr. Pa*
aut *Pa²* 3 et¹: *supra lin. P* finitus: *ex* infinitus *corr. E* quod: ut *EN* 4 creatricis: creantis *(ex ? correctum) C* humane *post* creatricis *scribit et del. R* creaturis
V creantis p et: nature *add. EN* 5 intellectum: et alterius cuiuslibet intellectui
post intellectum *add. et del. V* 6 quia: quod *Pa (ad* quia *corr. Pa²) Sp* 7 sciri:
ex scire *corr. E (?)* scire *N* nullius: *non proprie scribit A Pa* nullus *ENV* hominis: *om. EN* 8 rerum: verum *N* ut: *in marg. R* quin: quando *N* 9 possit: posset *G Pa T* 10 quin: quando *N* plura: *om. P (in marg. add. P²)* posset:
possit *P* per: pro *N* ad: ut *V* 11 a: quasi *L* quo habet: qualibet *V*
omne: esse *A* omnem *ad* omne *corr. C* omne *O (*esse *in marg. coni. O)* omne
esse *P* 12-13 in te natura humana: natura humana in te *ad* in te natura humana
transponit R 13 humana: huna *G* 14 quidem: quidam *Pa* 15 excedit:
cedit *A* intellectum: *ad* intellectui *corr. V* omnes: ommes *Q* 16 Ihesu
magister: magister Ihesu *ad* Ihesu magister *transponit E* 17 existis: *ex* existes
corr. E ad: *om. A L* 18 per: ad *(non clare scribit) V* 20 cibi: tibi *CJ Pa V*
21 sis: *om. G* Ihesu: Ihesus *C*

91   I see You, O good Jesus, on the inner side of the wall of Paradise, since Your intellect is both truth and image. And You are God and, likewise, creature—infinite and, likewise, finite. You cannot possibly be seen on this side of the wall. For You are the uniting of the creating divine nature and the created human nature. But I see the following difference between Your human intellect and the intellect of any other man: viz., that no other man knows all that can be known by men; for no other man's intellect is so conjoined to the Exemplar of all things (as a likeness is conjoined to its truth) that it could not be more closely conjoined and could not be made more actual. And so, it is not the case that another man's intellect understands so many things that it could not understand many more by closer access to the Exemplar of all things, from which every actually existing thing has its actuality. But Your intellect *actually* understands all that *can be* understood by man, because in You the human nature is most perfect and is most closely conjoined to its Exemplar. Indeed, on account of this union Your human intellect excels every other created intellect with respect to its perfection of understanding.[97] Therefore, all rational spirits are far beneath You; and You, Jesus, are the Teacher and Light of them all. You are the Perfection and Fulness of them all; and through You, as through a mediator, they approach unto Absolute Truth. For You are the Way unto the Truth and, likewise, are Truth itself. You are the Way unto the life of the intellect and, likewise, are Life itself. You are the Fragrance of the food of delight and, likewise, are the delighting Flavor. Therefore, most sweet Jesus, may You be blessed forever.

92 CAPITULUM XXI

QUOD SINE IHESU NON SIT POSSIBILIS FELICITAS

Ihesu, finis universi, in quo quiescit, tamquam in ultimitate perfectionis, omnis creatura! Tu es omnibus huius mundi sapientibus penitus ignotus, quia de te contradictoria verissima affirmamus, cum sis creator pariter et creatura, attrahens pariter et attractum, finitum pariter et infinitum. Stultitiam asserunt id credere possibile. Fugiunt igitur nomen tuum; et lucem tuam, qua nos illuminasti, non capiunt. Sed cum se putent sapientes, stulti et ignorantes et caeci manent in aeternum. Si autem crederent quia tu es Christus, deus et homo, et verba evangelii ut tanti magistri reciperent et tractarent, clarissime tandem conspicerent omnia, in comparatione illius lucis in simplicitate verborum tuorum ibi occultatae, penitus esse densissima tenebra et ignorantia. Solum igitur parvuli creduli hanc consequuntur gratiosissimam et vivificam revelationem. Est enim in tuo sacratissimo evangelio, qui cibus est caelestis, uti in manna, omnis dulcedo desiderii abscondita, quae non potest degustari nisi per credentem et manducantem. Si quis vero credit et accipit, experitur verissime quia tu de caelo descendisti et solus es magister veritatis.

93   O Ihesu bone, tu es arbor vitae in paradiso deliciarum. Nemo enim poterit cibari vita desiderabili nisi ex fructu tuo. Es cibus prohibitus, Ihesu, omnibus filiis Adae, qui de paradiso expulsi, in terra, in qua

---

92 1 capitulum XXI: capitulum 22 *E⁴*   2 felicitas: foelicitas (*ut paene semper*) *p; in titulo qui in indice est* felicitas *habet p*   3 Ihesu: Ihesus *QS*   ultimitate: *ex* ultimitate *corr. A*   ultima *CV*   ultimate *E (ad* ultimitate *in marg. corr. E²) JM* (in ultimate *ad* in ultimitate *in marg. corr. M²) NPaQSZ (ad* ultimitate *corr. Z²)* ultimo *p*   3-4 perfectionis omnis: omnis perfectionis *GT*   4 es: *bis E*   huius mundi: huiusmodi *S*   huius mundi sapientibus: sapientibus huius mundi *E*   sapientibus: sapientissimus *V*   4-5 huius ... ignotus: sapientibus ignotus penitus huius mundi *N*   penitus: *om. S*   5 de: ad *V*   contradictoria: conttadictoria *p* verissima: veissima *A*   verissime *EGIJNPaST*   verissima affirmamus: *ex* verissime affirmanus *corr. L*   affirmamus: affirmatur *EN*   affirmantur *GT*   6 et²: *om. OP* 8 tuum: *litteram* n *aut* u *post* tuum *scribit et del. G*   qua: quia *V*   non: *om. S* 9 se putent: putent se *R*   putent: putant *GTZ*   et²: *supra lin. A*   10 si: sed *G* quia: quod *p*   et²: *om. N*   11 ut: et *P om. Q*   12 conspicerent: conspiceret *A* 13 verborum tuorum: tuorum verborum *P*   occultatae: a *in* occultate *clarius*

92   CHAPTER TWENTY-ONE

WITHOUT JESUS HAPPINESS IS NOT POSSIBLE

O Jesus, End[98] of the universe, in whom every creature finds rest,
as in the Finality of perfection! You are altogether unknown to all the
wise of this world,[99] because we affirm of You most true contradictories. For You are Creator and likewise creature, the Attracting and
likewise the attracted, the Infinite and likewise the finite. To believe
that this is possible is foolishness, say |the wise of this world|. Hence,
they flee from Your name; and they do not receive Your light, by
which You have enlightened us. But although they consider themselves wise, they will remain forever foolish, ignorant, and blind.[100]
But were they to believe that You are the Christ, God and man, and
were they to accept and ponder the words of the Gospel, as |words|
of so great a Teacher, then they would come to see the following
most clearly: that in comparison to the light hidden in the Gospel in
the simplicity of Your words, all else is in every respect ignorance and
deepest darkness. Therefore, only humble believers obtain this enlivening and most pleasing revelation. For as in manna, so in Your most
sacred Gospel, which is food from Heaven, there is hidden all desired
sweetness—which can be tasted only by one who believes and par-
takes. But if anyone believes and accepts, he will most truly find that
You descended from Heaven and that You alone are the Teacher of
truth.

93   O good Jesus, You are the Tree of Life in the Paradise of delights.
For no one can be nourished by the desirable Life except from Your
fruit. You, O Jesus, are the food forbidden to all the sons of
Adam,[101] who, expelled from Paradise, seek in the earth, wherein

supra lin. rescribit G   occulte *S*   13-14 densissima . . . ignorantia: densissimas
tenebras et ignorantiam *p*   14 solum: soli *p*   14-15 gratiosissimam: gracio-
sissima *Pa*   15 et: *om. T*   enim: igitur *A*   16 uti: ut *N*   17 quae: qui *EN*
degustari: *ex* degustare *corr. G*   18 vero: non *P* enim *p*   tu: *supra lin. G*
93 1 bone: *om. L*   2 poterit: potest *V*   cibari: ex *add. N*   tuo: tu *add. Q*
prohibitus: prohitus *C (ad* prohibitus *corr. C²)*   3 terra: terram *L*   in²: *om. A*

laborant, quaerunt unde vivant. Oportet igitur omnem hominem
5 exuere veterem praesumptionis hominem et induere novum humilita-
tis hominem, qui secundum te est, si intra paradisum deliciarum vitae
cibum sperat degustare. Una est natura novi et veteris hominis; sed
est in veteri Adam animalis, in te, novo Adam, spiritualis, quia in te,
Ihesu, est unita deo, qui spiritus est. Oportet igitur omnem hominem,
10 sicut per communem naturam humanam ipsius et tui, ita et in uno
spiritu tibi, Ihesu, uniri, ut sic in sua natura tibi, Ihesu, communi
accedere possit ad deum patrem, qui est in paradiso. Videre igitur
deum patrem et te Ihesum filium eius est esse in paradiso et gloria
sempiterna—quia extra paradisum constitutus, non potest talem
15 habere visionem, cum nec deus pater nec tu, Ihesu, sis extra paradisum reperibilis.

94   Omnis igitur felicitatem assecutus, est tibi, Ihesu, ut membrum
capiti suo unitus. Nemo potest venire ad patrem, nisi per patrem
attractus. Tuam, Ihesu, humanitatem per filium suum pater attraxit,
et per te, Ihesu, omnes attrahit pater homines. Sicut igitur humanitas
5 tua, Ihesu, est filio dei patris unita, tamquam medio per quod pater
ipsam attraxit, ita cuiuslibet hominis humanitas tibi, Ihesu, tamquam
unico medio per quod pater omnes attrahit homines, est unita. Es
igitur, Ihesu, sine quo impossibile est quemquam felicitatem assequi.
Es, Ihesu, revelatio patris. Nam pater est omnibus hominibus invisi-
10 bilis, et tibi filio eius solum visibilis, et illi post te, qui per te et tua
revelatione ipsum videre merebitur. Tu es igitur uniens omnem feli-

---

4 vivant: vivunt *EN   non proprie scribit S*   5 exuere: *om. L*   praesumptionis:
presumpcconis *Pa*   6 intra: inter *L*   7 natura: materia *LZ (ad* natura *in marg.
corr. Z²)*   veteris: veteri *CPa (ad* veteris *in marg. corr. Pa²)*   hominis: Adam *p*
8 est: *om. IJPa*   9 est¹: *om. I*   spiritus est: est spiritus *R*   10 humanam: sui
add. p   tui: Ihesu *add. E*   Ihesu et *add. N*   11 ut: et *AQ*   sic: sicut *Q*   sua:
tua *V*   sui *Z*   tibi²: *om. V*   12 possit: *ex* possint *corr. C aut C²*   possint *V*   est:
es *J*   videre: *ex* videtur *corr. I*   igitur: te *add. T*   12-13 videre . . . paradiso:
om. V   14-15 talem habere: habere talem *AL*
  94 1 igitur: *om. L*   homo *post* igitur *add. supra lin. C² et in marg. Z² et in
textu p*   est: qui *post* est *add. supra lin. C² et in textu p*   Ihesu: *om. L*   2 capiti
suo: suo capiti *N*   suo: *om. Rp*   unitus: est *post* unitus *add. supra lin. C² et in
textu p*   venire: *ex* veniri *corr. E*   3 attractus: tractus *R*   pater: patris *IJ*   pater
attraxit: attraxit pater *G*   4 omnes: *om. I*   attrahit: attrahit *I*   attrahit pater:
pater attrahit *Z*   5 est: in *add. IJ* et *NV*   dei: *non proprie abbreviat A*   patris:

they labor, their means of life. Therefore, if any man hopes to taste of the food of life within the Paradise of delights, he must put off the old man of presumption and put on the new man of humility,[102] who conforms to ·You. The nature of the new man and of the old man is one nature. But in the old Adam this nature is fleshly, whereas in You, the new Adam, it is spiritual; for in You, Jesus, it is united to God, who is spirit. Therefore, just as every man is united to You, Jesus, by the human nature common to himself and to You, so every man need also be united to You in one spirit, so that in this way he can—in his nature, which is common to You, Jesus—approach unto God the Father, who is in Paradise. Therefore, to see God the Father and You who are Jesus, His Son, is to be present in Paradise and in everlasting glory. For if any man is situated outside of Paradise, he cannot have such a vision, since neither God the Father nor You, Jesus, dwell outside of Paradise.

94   Therefore, everyone who has attained unto happiness is united to You, O Jesus, as a member |of the body| is united to its head. No one can come to the Father unless he is drawn by the Father.[103] The Father attracts Your humanity, O Jesus, through His Son; and through You, Jesus, the Father attracts all men. Therefore, O Jesus, just as Your humanity is united to the Son of God-the-Father, as to the Medium through which the Father attracted it, so the humanity of each man is united to You, Jesus, as to the one Medium through which the Father attracts all men. Therefore, You, Jesus, are the one without whom no one can possibly attain unto happiness. You, Jesus, are the Revelation of the Father.[104] For the Father is invisible to all men; He is visible only to You, His Son, and, subsequent to You, to one who will merit to see Him through You and by Your revelation. Therefore, You unite everyone who is happy; and everyone who is

om. R   unita: quam *post* unita *scribit et del. P aut P²*   tamquam: filio *post* tamquam *scribit et del. G*   quod: *ex* quem *corr. E*   pater: *scribit et del. C   om. V*   5-6 tamquam . . . humanitas: *om. P (in marg. add. P²)*   6 ipsam: ipsum *V*   cuiuslibet: habet *I*   7 unico: unito *N*   pater: ipsam attraxit *post* pater *scribit et del. M*   pater omnes: omnes pater *Z*   attrahit: attraxit *V*   8 felicitatem: filicitatem *C*   9-10 invisibilis: *non proprie scribit P*   10 tibi: soli *add. A*   eius: suo *p*   solum: *om. A (in marg. add. A²)*   post: *ex* potest *corr. L*   10-11 tua revelatione: tuam revelationem *p*   11 igitur: unicus *post* igitur *scribit et del. L*   omnem: omnium *R*

cem; et omnis felix in te subsistit sicut unitum in uniente. Nullus
sapientum huius mundi felicitatem veram capere potest, quando te
ignorat. Nemo felicem videre potest, nisi tecum, Ihesu, intra paradi-
15 sum. De felice verificantur contradictoria, sicut de te, Ihesu, cum tibi
in rationali natura et uno spiritu sit unitus. Subsistit enim omnis spiritus felicis in tuo, sicut vivificatus in vivificante. Videt omnis spiritus
felix invisibilem deum, et unitur in te, Ihesu, inaccessibili et immor-
tali deo. Et sic finitum in te unitur infinito et inunibili; et capitur
20 incomprehensibilis fruitione aeterna, quae est felicitas gaudiosissima
numquam consumptibilis. Miserere, Ihesu, miserere, et da mihi revelate videre te, et salva facta est anima mea.

95

CAPITULUM XXII

QUOMODO IHESUS VIDEAT ET OPERATUS SIT

Non potest oculus mentis satiari videndo te, Ihesu, quia es complementum omnis mentalis pulchritudinis; et in hac eicona conicio
5 mirabilem valde ac stupidum visum tuum, Ihesu superbenedicte.
Nam tu, Ihesu, dum in hoc sensibili mundo ambulares, carneis nobis
similibus oculis utebaris. Cum illis enim, non secus quam nos homines, unum et unum videbas. Erat enim in oculis tuis spiritus quidam, qui erat organi forma, quasi sensibilis anima in corpore anima-
10 lis. In eo spiritu erat vis nobilis discretiva, per quam videbas, domine,

11-12 felicem: felicitatem *Q*   12 in²: *supra lin. I*   nullus: nullum *G*   14 felicem:
felicitatem *Q*   foelix *p*   potest: pater *C (*potest *in marg. coni. C²) SV*   patrem *in
marg. add. Z²*   patrem *add. p*   14-15 paradisum: padisum *E*   15 verificantur:
verificatur *R*   16 natura: naturali *CVp*   natura *ex* creatura *corr. ER*   omnis: *ex*
unus *corr. N*   17 felicis: *non proprie scribit P*   foelix *p*   vivificatus: vivificatus
L (litteras ur *pro* us *supra lin. coni. L)*   vivificatus in vivificante: unificatus in
unificante *CV*   in²: tuo *add. S*   vivificante: unificante *p*   18 inaccessibili:
inaccessabili *S*   19 deo: *om. R*   inunibili: invisibili *T*   20 gaudiosissima: iocun-
dissima *p*   21 numquam: numque *I*   consumptibilis: consuptibilis *V*   miserere²:
misereri *V*   mihi: *om. V*   22 videre te: te videre *Z*
   95 1 capitulum XXII: capitulum 23 *E⁴*   2 *titulum scribit E⁴*   Ihesus: deus *V²*
videat: vidit *ALM³ (in 1:1 habet etiam M) OP³ (in 1:1 habet etiam P) Q² (in 1:1*

happy exists in You, as the united exists in the uniting. None of the wise of this world can obtain true happiness, since they are ignorant of You. No one can see anyone happy, except inside Paradise with You, Jesus. Contradictories are predicated truly of anyone happy, even as of You, Jesus; for one who is happy is united to You in rational nature and in one spirit. For everyone of happy spirit exists in Your spirit, as the enlivened in the enlivening. Every happy spirit sees the invisible God and is united, in You, Jesus, to the unapproachable and immortal God. And thus, in You, the finite is united to the Infinite and Ununitable; and the Incomprehensible is apprehended with eternal enjoyment, which is a most joyous and everinexhaustible happiness. Have mercy, O Jesus; have mercy. Grant that I may see You unveiledly, and my soul shall be saved.[105]

95

CHAPTER TWENTY-TWO

HOW JESUS SEES AND HOW HE WORKED

The eye of the mind cannot get enough of seeing You, O Jesus, because You are the fulfillment of all mental beauty. And by means of this icon I will conjecture about Your exceedingly marvelous and amazing gaze, O Superblessed Jesus. For while You, Jesus, walked amid this sensible world, You used fleshly eyes that were like ours. For with these eyes You perceived in no other way than do we men: viz., one thing and another. For in Your eyes there was a certain spirit, which was the form of the organ—as is the sensible soul in the body of an animal. In this spirit there was a noble discriminating power through which, O Lord, You saw distinctly and discretely *this*

---

habet etiam Q) RZ   3 oculus: oculis *S*   Ihesu: *habent Rp* Ihesum *aut* Iesum *alii omnes codices*   quia: tu *add. p*   es: est *A*   5 mirabilem: mirabiliter *Q*   mirabilem valde: valde mirabilem *G*   valde ac: *om. T*   Ihesu: *ex* Ihesum *corr. E* superbenedicte: semper benedicte *V*   6 sensibili: visibili *EN*   7 oculis: *bis L* quam: quod *Pa*   7-8 secus . . . homines: quasi nos *I*   homines: *ex* hominis *corr. G*   9 organi: origini *V*   9-10 animalis: et *add. EGIJNPaT*   10 spiritu: spiritum *Pa*   erat: *om. AC (supra lin. add. C²) EGIJLMNOPPaQRSTVZ (in marg. add. Z²)*   vis: animalis *post* vis *scribit et del. Q*   domine: *non proprie*

distincte et discrete hoc coloratum sic et aliud aliter. Atque adhuc
altius: ex figuris faciei et oculorum hominum, quos videbas, verus
eras iudex passionum animae—irae, laetitiae, et tristitiae. Atque
adhuc subtilius: ex paucis signis comprehendebas id quod in hominis
15 mente latebat. Nihil enim in mente concipitur, quod non in facie et
maxime in oculis aliquo modo signetur, cum sit cordis nuntius.
Multo enim in his omnibus iudiciis verius attingebas interiora animae
quam quisque creatus spiritus. Ex uno enim aliquo, licet parvo valde,
signo totum videbas hominis conceptum, uti intelligentes ex paucis
20 verbis omnem longum praevident explicandum sermonem praeconceptum. Et bene docti, dum parvo tempore iniciunt oculos in librum,
totum ac si legissent recitant scriptoris intentum. Excellebas, Ihesu,
in hoc visionis genere omnes omnium hominum praeteritorum, prae-
sentium, et futurorum perfectiones, velocitates, et acuties.

96   Et haec visio humana erat, quae sine carnali oculo non perficie-
batur; fuit tamen stupenda et admirabilis. Nam si homines reperiuntur, qui longa et subtili discussione mentem scribentis sub tunc nov-
iter fictis characteribus et invisis signis legunt, tu, Ihesu, sub omni
5 signo et figura omnia videbas! Si aliquando homo repertus legitur,
qui cogitationem interrogantis eum vidit ex quibuscumque oculi signis, etiam si metrum aliquod mente cantabat, melius omnibus tu,
Ihesu, ex omni nutu oculorum omnem conceptum deprehendebas.
Vidi ego mulierem surdam, quae ex motu labiorum filiae suae, quem
10 vidit, omnia ac si audivisset intellexit. Si hoc ex consuetudine longa

---

scribit A   11 et discrete: *om. p*   coloratum: coleratum *J*   12 figuris: fuguris *CT*
(ad figuris (?) *corr. T³)*   hominum: *non proprie abbreviat S*   quos: quas *EN*
verus: verax *R*   13 animae: anime *om. P (in marg. add. P²)*   et: *supra lin. E*
14 subtilius: subtilibus *Pa*   15 latebat: letebat *N*   non: *supra lin. clarius*
rescribit Q   in²: *om. I*   et: *om. T*   16 aliquo modo: aliquomodo non *ex* aliquomodo *corr. G*   modo: non *add. omnes codices* non *non habet p*   nuntius:
nunctius *J* nunccius *NS*   17 multo enim: *bis O* (multo enim¹ *del. O*)   his:
om. EN   iudiciis: indiciis *p*   18 quisque: quis *Pa (ad* quisque *in marg. corr.*
Pa²) quisquam *Q*   19 intelligentes: intelligens *G*   20 praevident: provident *V*
sermonem: *non proprie scribit Pa*   20-21 praeconceptum: pre *supra lin. R (*conceptum *in linea R)*   21 dum: *om. Q*   iniciunt: inicint *V*   22 ac si: acsi *p*
23 omnium: *om. Pa (supra lin. add. Pa²)* non proprie abbreviat V*   24 velocitates: velocitatis *N*
    96 2 stupenda: stupienda *S*   2-3 reperiuntur: reperintur *Q*   3 scribentis: *non*
proprie scribit P   4 fictis: fictis *E* (factis *supra lin. coni. E²*)   et *add. p*   charac-

object to be colored in this way and *that* object to be colored in another way. And still more deeply: on the basis of the poses of the face and eyes of the men upon whom You looked, You were a true judge of the passions of the soul—viz., of anger, of joy, and of sorrow. And more subtly still: from merely a few signs You comprehended that which lay hidden in a man's mind. For whatever is conceived in the mind is signaled in some way in the face (and especially in the eyes), since the face is the messenger of the heart. For in all these judgments You attained much more truly unto the inner recesses of the soul than does any created spirit. For from some one sign, be it ever so small, You saw a man's entire conception, even as from a few words those with discernment foresee the whole, lengthy preconceived sermon that is to be unfolded. And when those who are very learned look briefly at a book, they recount the intent of the author as if they had read the entire book. With regard to this kind of vision, O Jesus, You excelled all the perfection, swiftness, and acuteness of all past, present, and future men.

96   And this seeing, which was not accomplished without fleshly eyes, was human; nevertheless, it was amazing and wonderful. For if there are men who through long and meticulous examination read the mind of a writer beneath what to them are newly devised characters and previously unseen signs, You, O Jesus, saw everything beneath every sign and figure! If at times we read of there having been a man who, from whatever signals of the eye, discerned the thought of the one who queried him |about it|—discerned it even if the questioner was mentally singing a certain meter—then You, Jesus, better than all others, discerned every concept from every signaling movement of the eyes. I saw a deaf woman who from observing the movement of her daughter's lips understood everything as if she had heard it. If

teribus: caractibus *A* catharacteribus *T*   legunt: legium *V* et *post* legunt *scribit et del. Z*   4-5 omni . . . figura: *bis V*   5 si: sed *L* sibi *T*   repertus legitur: legitur repertus *V*   6 cogitationem: interrogacionem *A*   vidit: videt *P*   oculi: ocultis *I* oculi *ex* oculis *corr. R*   7 aliquod: in *add. C*   et *add. V*   cantabat: cantabant *J*   omnibus tu: tu omnibus *ad* omnibus tu *transponit G*   8 omni: motu *post* omni *scribit et del. E*   nutu: muto *S*   nutu oculorum: oculorum nutu *E*   deprehendebas: comprehendebas *N*   9 ego: *om. L*   motu: oculorum *post* motu *scribit et del. I*   mutu *Q*   labiorum: *om. V*   filiae suae: filii sui *ex ? corr. E* filii sui *N*   suae: fue (=sue) *I*   quem: quam *Q* *om. V*   10 vidit: videt *P*   ac si: acsi *p*   si¹: intellexisset *post* si¹ *scribit et del. Pa*   audivisset:

sic possibile est in surdis, mutis, et religiosis qui per signa sibi loquuntur, perfectius tu, Ihesu, qui omne scibile actu sciebas quasi magister magistrorum, in minimis et nobis invisibilibus mutationibus et signis verum de corde et eius conceptu faciebas iudicium. Sed erat
15 huic tuae humanae perfectissimae licet finitae visioni, ad organum contractae, absoluta et infinita visio unita; per quam quidem visionem omnia pariter et singula, ut deus, videbas, tam absentia quam praesentia, tam praeterita quam futura. Videbas igitur, Ihesu, oculo humano accidentia visibilia, sed visu divino absoluto rerum substan-
20 tiam. Nemo umquam in carne constitutus, praeter te, Ihesu, substantiam vidit aut rerum quidditatem. Tu solus animam et spiritum et quidquid in homine erat vidisti verissime. Nam sicut vis intellectiva in homine unita est virtuti animali visivae, ut homo non solum videat ut animal sed etiam discernat et iudicet ut homo, ita visus absolutus
25 unitus est in te, Ihesu, virtuti humanae intellectuali, quae est discretio in visu animali. Vis visiva animalis in homine non in se sed in anima rationali, tamquam in forma totius, subsistit. Sic vis visiva intellectualis non in se in te, Ihesu, sed in virtute visiva absoluta subsistit.

97   O admirabilis visus tuus, Ihesu dulcissime! Experimur aliquotiens quomodo praetereuntem in oculo deprehendimus; sed quia non fuimus intenti, ut discerneremus quis esset, nescimus interrogati nomen noti praetereuntis, licet sciamus aliquem praeterisse. Vidimus igitur

---

audisset *AEGIJLMNOPPaQRSTZ*   hoc: homo *S*   longa: longe *G*   11 sic:
om. Z   possibile est: est possibile *Zp*   surdis: et *add. p*   sibi: *om. Pa*; sibi (*ex*
? correctum) *in marg. add. Pa²*   12 loquuntur: *ex* locuntur *corr. S*   omne scibile
actu: omnem actum scibilem *Q* (scibilem *post* omnem *etiam scribit, sed del., Q*)
scibile: subtile *A*   scibili *G*   stabilo *N*   13 magister: magistrum *P*   magistrorum:
et *add. V*   in: omnibus *add. V*   invisibilibus: invisibibus *Z*   mutationibus:
nucibus *E*   mutacionibus *I* (nutationibus *supra lin. coni. I*)   mutis *N*   nutibus *p*
14 verum: veris *P*   15 huic: *om. A*   humanae: licet *post* humane *scribit et del. I*
perfectissimae: *om. EN*   finitae: infinite *LOPQR* *ex* infinite *?* (*rasura ante*
finite) *corr. Z*   ad: et *N*   16 absoluta: a² *non clare scribit G*   et: *om. N*
18 quam: et *A*   preterita *post* quam *scribit et del. G*   19 humano: humana *Q*
visu: viso *AC*   20 nemo: nemo *S* (nemo *clarius esse facit S³*)   carne: *non clare*
scribit N   21 quidditatem: quodditatem *J*   quidtitatem *S*   23 unita est: est
unita *Z*   virtuti: humane *post* virtuti *scribit et del. J*   visivae: visivi *G*   23 ff.:
necesse est transponere folia 39 et 40 in J   24 animal: *ex* animalis *corr. I*   animalis *J*   discernat: decernat *V*   et: *ex* ut *corr. J*   ita: si *add. EN*   24-

from a long period of familiarization this |kind of communication| is thus possible among the deaf and the mute and among the religious who speak to one another through signs, then by means of the slightest movements and signs, as well as by movements and signs invisible to us, You, Jesus (who as Teacher of teachers knew *actually* everything that *can be* known), more perfectly made a true judgment about the heart and its concept. But to this most perfect, though finite, human vision of Yours—a vision contracted to a |bodily| organ—there was united absolute and infinite Vision. Indeed, through this Vision You, qua God, saw each and every thing—things absent as well as things present, things past as well as things future. Therefore, O Jesus, with Your human eye You saw the visible accidents; but with Your absolute, divine gaze You saw the substance of things. Except for You, O Jesus, no one constituted of flesh has ever seen the substance of things or the quiddity of things. You alone have seen most truly the soul and the spirit and whatever else is in man. For just as in man the intellectual power is united to the seeing power that is animal (so that a man not only *sees* as an animal but also *discerns* and *judges* as a man),[106] so in You, Jesus, Absolute Sight is united to the human intellectual power, which, in |man's| animal sight, is |the power of| discernment. In man the seeing power that is animal exists not in itself but in the rational soul, as in the form of the whole soul. Similarly, in You, Jesus, the intellectual seeing power exists not in itself but in the absolute seeing power.

97   O wonderful is Your sight, sweetest Jesus! Occasionally, we have the experience of glimpsing a passer-by. Yet, because we were not intent upon discerning who he was, we do not know, when asked, the name of this known passer-by, though we know that someone did pass by. Therefore, we saw him in an animal way; but we did not see

25 absolutus unitus: unitus absolutus *N*   25 unitus est: est unitus *SZ*   virtuti: veritati *A* *ex* virtute *corr. P*   est²: *ex* es *corr. I*   26 visu: *om. EN*   animalis in homine: in homine animalis *EN*   27 in: *om. G*   subsistit: consistit *Q*   sic: sed *A*

97 1 Ihesu: *ex* Ihesus *corr. E*   aliquotiens: aliquoties *p*   2 praetereuntem: preteriuntem *P*   in: *om. p*   deprehendimus: comprehendimus *T*   2-3 fuimus: sumus *G*   3 discerneremus: discernerencius *N*   discernemus *R*   nescimus: indicare

5 illum animaliter, sed non vidimus humaniter, quia vim discretivam
non applicavimus. Ex quo comperimus naturas virium, etsi sint uni-
tae in una forma hominis, manent tamen distinctae et distinctas
habent operationes. Sic in te uno, Ihesu, video simili quodam modo
humanam intellectualem naturam divinae naturae unitam, et quod
10 pariformiter ut homo operatus es plurima atque ut deus mirabilia
multa supra hominem. Video, Ihesu piissime, intellectualem naturam
esse, in respectu sensibilis, absolutam et nequaquam uti sensibilis fin-
itam et ad organum alligatam, quemadmodum vis visiva sensibilis est
oculo alligata. Sed improportionabiliter absolutior est vis divina
15 supra intellectualem. Nam intellectus humanus ut ponatur in actu,
opus habet phantasmatibus. Et phantasmata sine sensibus haberi
nequeunt; et sensus sine corpore non subsistunt. Ob hoc vis humani
intellectus est contracta et parva, indigens praenarratis. Divinus vero
intellectus est ipsa necessitas, non dependens neque indigens aliquo;
20 sed omnia eo indigent, sine quo non possunt esse.

98 Attentius considero quomodo alia est vis discursiva quae ratioci-
nando discurrit et quaerit, alia quae iudicat et intelligit. Videmus
enim canem discurrere et quaerere dominum suum et discernere illum
et audire vocationem eius. Hic quidem discursus est in natura animal-
5 itatis in gradu specificae perfectionis caninae. Adhuc alia reperiuntur
animalia lucidioris discursus, secundum perfectiorem speciem. Et hic
discursus in homine proxime accedit ad virtutem intellectualem, ut
sit supremitas perfectionis sensibilis virtutis et infimum intellectualis.

add. p   interrogati: interroganti *p*   5 illum: *in marg. O om. R*   vidimus:
om. R   6 etsi: ut si *V* et si *p*   sint: sunt *N*   7 in: *bis Pa*   8 sic: sicut *G*
uno: vero *I*   10 es: est *EN*   12 esse: *supra lin. scribit, et in marg. clarius
rescribit, L*   uti: ut *R*   sensibilis²: est *add. p*   13 et: *om. SV*   alligatam:
illigatam *EGIJNT*   14 improportionabiliter: inproporcionabiliter *ex* inpropor-
cionaliter *corr. G*   improportionaliter *(sed non proprie scriptum) L*   absolutior
est: est absolutior *ad* absolutior est *transponit R*   vis: visiva *add. V*   15 supra:
super *V*   nam: ut *add. et del. T*   ponatur: *ex* ponatus *corr. S*   16 phantasmata:
fantasma *Q*   haberi: *ex* heberi *corr. O*   habere *S*   17 nequeunt: nequiunt *CJM
NPaQSZ aut* nequeunt *ex* nequiunt *aut* nequiunt *ex* nequeunt *corr. E*   et: sed *A*
subsistunt: subsistant *T*   18 indigens: indigens (e *supra lin.*) *G*   divinus: divinus
Pa (abbreviationem del., et supra lin. explicat, Pa²)   19 dependens: deprehendens *V*
neque: nec *CNQVp   om. P (in marg. add. P²)*   aliquo: aliqua *N*
    98 1 est: es *EGNQ*   1-2 ratiocinando: racionando *GNPa (ad* raciocinando
corr. Pa²) TV   raciocionando *Q*   3 canem: *abbreviationem del., et in marg. corr.*

him in a human way, because we did not use our discriminating power. From this example we ascertain that even though the natures of these powers are united in the one form of man, nevertheless they remain distinct and have distinct functions. So then, I see that in You, Jesus, who are one, the human intellectual nature is united, in a certain similar way, to the divine nature and that You did very many things as a man and likewise did many marvelous and superhuman things as God. O most gracious Jesus, I see that the intellectual nature, in contrast to the sensible nature, is free from, and not at all limited to, or restricted to, bodily organs, as is the sensible nature (e.g., the sensible seeing power is restricted to the eye). But the divine power is incomparably more elevated and unrestricted than is the intellectual power. For the human intellect, in order to be actualized, needs images. But images cannot exist without the senses; and the senses do not exist without a body. Consequently, the power of the human intellect is contracted and small and is in need of the aforementioned things. But the divine intellect is Necessity itself and does not depend on or need anything. Instead, all else needs it and cannot exist without it.

98   I will consider more closely how the power of inference which, by reasoning discursively, makes inferences and investigates is distinct from the power of inference which judges and understands. For we see that a dog makes inferences and seeks out his master and recognizes him and responds to his call.[107] Indeed, in the nature of animality this |power of| inference is present in the degree[108] of perfection of the canine species. There are still other animals who have a keener |power of| inference, in accordance with their more perfect species. And in man |the power of| inference approaches very closely to the intellectual power, so that it is the highest degree of perfection of sensible power and the lowest degree of |perfection of| intellectual

*aut explicat, Pa*² 4 audire vocationem eius: vocem eius audire *Q* quidem: quidam *P* 5 caninae: canime *G* alia: *om. P* (alia *post* animalia *in marg. add. P²)* 6 animalia: *non proprie abbreviat S* discursus: in homine proxime *post* discursus *scribit et del. C* discrursus *L* discursis *V* secundum: sed *A* perfectiorem: perfecciorem *ex* perfeccionem *corr. Pa*; discursum *post* perfecciorem *scribit et del. Pa* speciem: *non proprie scribit Pa* hic: hec *V* 7 proxime: proprie *T* accedit: *ex ? corr. Q* virtutem: [ ]tutem *(rasura) correctum est ex* [ ]tatem *Z* 8 supremitas: summitas *G* et: *om. S* 8-9 virtutis . . . sensibilis: *om. CVp*

Habet igitur vis animalis sensibilis multos gradus perfectionis, et
10 innumerabiles, sub intellectuali—prout species animalium nobis patefaciunt. Nulla enim species est quin gradum perfectionis proprium
sibi non sortiatur. Est etiam quisque graduum latitudinem habens,
intra quam videmus individua speciei varie speciem participare. Intellectualis vero natura pariformiter sub divina gradus habet innumera-
15 biles. Unde sicut in intellectuali complicantur omnes gradus sensibilis
perfectionis, sic in divina omnes gradus intellectualis perfectionis, sic
et sensibilis et omnium.

99 Ita in te Ihesu meo video perfectionem omnem. Nam cum sis
homo perfectissimus, in te video intellectum virtuti rationali seu discursivae, quae est supremitas sensitivae, uniri. Et sic video intellectum in ratione, quasi in loco suo, ut locatum in loco quasi candela in
5 camera, quae illuminat cameram et omnes parietes et totum aedificium, secundum tamen gradus distantiae plus et minus. Video deinde
intellectui in sua supremitate uniri divinum verbum, atque intellectum ipsum locum esse ubi verbum capitur, uti in nobis experimur
intellectum locum esse ubi verbum magistri capitur, quasi lux solis
10 iungatur candelae praelibatae. Illuminat enim verbum dei intellectum, sicut lumen solis hunc mundum. In te igitur Ihesu meo video
vitam sensibilem illuminatam lumine intellectuali, vitam intellectualem lumen illuminans atque illuminatum, et vitam divinam illuminantem tantum. Nam et fontem luminis in lumine illo intellectuali

9 gradus: grados *G*   gradus perfectionis: perfeccionis gradus *Z*   10 intellectuali:
continens *add. p*   species animalium: animalium species *Q*   10-11 patefaciunt:
patefiunt *I*   11 quin: qui *CV*   quae *p*   quin gradum: que in gradu *EN*   gradum:
om. I   12 non: *(cf.* quin *usum sine* non *in 10:12-13 et 91:10 supra) om. LZ*
sortiatur: sociatur *S*   etiam: igitur *A*   enim *OP*   13 quam: *om. OP*   individua:
individuam *Q*   13-14 intellectualis: intualis *IPa (ad* intellectualis *in marg. corr.*
Pa²) abbreviationem in marg. explicat Jⁿ   15 sicut: *om. R*   in: *om. CNPaV*
16 sic¹: *ex* sicut *corr. I*   in . . . sic: *om. S*   sic²: sicut *A*   17 et²: *bis S*
   99 1 omnem: omnium *N*   2 perfectissimus: *non proprie scribit Q*   te: deo
add. V   virtuti: virtute *G*   seu: sive *Z*   2-3 discursivae: discrursive *L*   3 supremitas: summitas *G*   et sic: sic et *P*   4 candela: candelam *p*   5 camera: *non*
proprie scribit J   parietes: parietas *N*   5-6 aedificium: edificium *non clare scri-*
bit V   6 plus: *non proprie scribit N*   et: vel *Pa*   7 intellectui: intellectum *GN*
sua: sui *EN*   supremitate: presumitate *CV*   summitate *G*   uniri: unire *G*   8 ip-

|power|. Therefore, sensible animal power has many—indeed, countless—degrees of perfection below the level of intellectual |power|, as the species of animals make obvious to us. For there is no species that does not receive unto itself its own degree of perfection. Moreover, each species has a range of gradations, and within this range we see that individuals of a species participate in that species in varying degrees. Similarly, intellectual nature has countless degrees |of perfection| below the level of the divine |nature|. Hence, just as in the intellectual |nature| there are enfolded all the gradations of sensible perfection, so in the divine |nature are enfolded| all the gradations of intellectual perfection—and thus all the gradations of sensible perfection and of the perfection of all things.

99   And so in You, my Jesus, I see all perfection. For since You are the most perfect man, I see that in You the intellect is united to the rational power, or power of inference, which is the highest degree of sensible power. And in this way I see that the intellect is present in reason, as in its own location, so that the intellect is located in a place as a candle |is located| in a room, illumining the room and all the walls and the entire building—according, nevertheless, to its greater or lesser degree of distance |from them|. Next, I see that to the intellect, in its highest degree, the Divine Word is united[109] and that Your intellect is the place where the Word is received (even as we know by reference to ourselves that the intellect is the place where the word of a teacher is received)—as if the light of the sun were joined to the aforementioned candle, for the Word of God enlightens the intellect, just as the light of the sun illumines the earth. Therefore, I see that in You my Jesus the sensible life is illumined by the intellectual light, that the intellectual life is both an illumining and an illumined light, and that the divine life is only an illumining light. For in Your intellectual light I see the Fount of

sum locum esse ubi: locum esse ubi ipsum *EN*   verbum: *om. T*   experimur: *bis Pa* (experimur¹ *del. Pa*)   8-9 capitur . . . verbum: *om. ALMOPQRZ (in marg. add. Z²)*   10 candelae: condele *A*   12 illuminatam: illuminantem *P*   illumitatam *S*   12-13 intellectualem: esse *add. EN* et *add. GT*   13 illuminatum: illuminatam *N*   et vitam: *bis L*   vitam divinam: divinam vitam *ad* vitam divinam *transponit O*   14 illo: *non proprie scribit V*   illo intellectuali: intellectuali illo

15 video, verbum scilicet dei, quod est veritas illuminans omnem intellectum. Tu igitur solus altissimus omnium creaturarum, quia ita creatura quod creator benedictus.

100   CAPITULUM XXIII

QUOMODO IHESUS MORTUUS FUIT UNIONE CUM VITA MANENTE

O Ihesu, mentis sapidissimus cibus, quando intra paradisi murum te intueor, admirabilis mihi occurris. Verbum enim dei es human-
5 atum, et homo es deificatus. Non es tamen quasi compositus ex deo et homine. Inter componentia proportio est necessaria, sine qua non potest esse compositio. Finiti ad infinitum nulla est proportio. Neque es coincidentia creaturae et creatoris modo quo coincidentia facit unum esse aliud. Nam natura humana non est divina aut e converso.
10 Divina enim natura non est mutabilis aut alterabilis in aliam naturam, cum sit ipsa aeternitas. Neque natura quaecumque propter unionem ad divinam transit in aliam naturam, sicut cum imago unitur suae veritati. Ipsa enim non potest dici tunc alterari sed potius recedere ab alteritate, quia unitur veritati suae propriae, quae est ipsa
15 inalterabilitas. Neque, Ihesu dulcissime, dici potes copula media inter naturam divinam et humanam, cum inter illas non possit poni quae-

---

EN   15 dei: ei *N*   15-16 omnem intellectum: intellectum omnem *Q*   17 quod: et *add. p*   benedictus: et cetera *add. V*

100 1 capitulum: *in rubeis litteris in marg. scribit J^n*   capitulum XXIII: capitulum 24 *E⁴*   2 Ihesus: deus *V²*   fuit: sit *Z (in 1:1* fuit habet *Z)*   vita: *ex* unita *corr. L*   3 O Ihesu: I Ihesu *Q*   Ihesu *S*   dulcissime *add. R*   paradisi: padisi, *ut videtur, G*   paradisi murum: murum paradisi *A*   4-5 humanatum: humanitatum *A*   5 deificatus: edificatus *P*   deificus *Pa*   deficiatus *V*   es²: est *I* 6 necessaria: necessa *N*   7 potest esse: est *A*   ad infinitum: et infiniti *R*   infinitum: infiniti *EN*   finitum *S*   est: es *I*   8 es: est *I*   creaturae et creatoris: creatoris et creature *Q*   quo: iam *post* quo *scribit et del. P*   coincidentia²: incidencia *N*   9 natura: est *post* natura *scribit et del. V*   natura humana: humana natura *ENZ*   est: *om. OP*   10 in: alteram seu *add. T*   aliam: alium *V*   11 quaecumque: ad *post* quecumque *scribit et del. E*   11-12 cum . . . naturam: *om. T*

light, viz., the Word of God, which is the Truth that enlightens every
intellect. Therefore, You alone are the highest of all creatures,
because You are creature in such way that You are the Blessed
Creator.

100   CHAPTER TWENTY-THREE

O Jesus, most delectable Food for the mind, when I behold You
on the inner side of the wall of Paradise, You appear to me to be
wonderful. For You are the humanified Word of God; and You are
the deified man. (1) Nevertheless, You are not "composed," as it
were, of God and man.[110] Between components a comparative relation is necessary; without it there can be no composition. But there is
no comparative relation of the finite to the Infinite.[111] (2) Furthermore, You are not the coincidence of creature and Creator in the way
in which a coincidence causes one thing to be another thing. For the
human nature is not divine, nor vice versa. For the divine nature is
not changeable or alterable into another nature, since it is Eternity
itself. Nor would any nature on account of its union to the divine
nature pass over into *another* nature (as when an image is united to
its truth). For in the case of that passing over, the nature could
|rightly be said| to recede from otherness but could not |rightly| be
said to be altered, because it would be united to its own Truth,
which is Unalterability itself. (3) O most sweet Jesus, You cannot be
said, either, to be the uniting medium between the divine nature and
the human nature, since between the two natures there cannot be

12 divinam: divina *CV*   aliam: alia *Pa*   unitur: uni *Q*   13 enim: tunc *post*
enim, *et non post* dici, *ponit R*   15 neque: enim *add. p*   Ihesu dulcissime:
dulcissime Ihesu *Q*   Ihesu . . . potes: dici potes Ihesu dulcissime *EN*   dici: *om. Q*
copula: *om. CVp*   copuli *N*   15-16 inter naturam divinam: natura inter divinam *p*
16 naturam divinam: divinam naturam *EN*   naturam divinam et humanam: di-

dam media natura participans utramque. Natura enim divina non est participabilis, quia penitus absolute simplicissima. Nec tunc tu, Ihesu benedicte, fores vel deus vel homo.

101   Sed video te, domine Ihesu, super omnem intellectum unum suppositum, quia unus Christus es, modo quo video unam tuam humanam animam, in qua, uti in cuiuslibet hominis anima, video corruptibilem sensibilem fuisse naturam et in intellectuali incorruptibili natura
5 subsistere. Neque anima illa composita fuit ex corruptibili et incorruptibili, neque coincidit sensibilis cum intellectuali. Video autem animam intellectualem uniri corpori per virtutem sensibilem vivificantem corpus. Et quando anima intellectiva cessaret a vivificatione corporis, sine eo quod a corpore separaretur, tunc homo ille mortuus
10 foret, quia vita cessaret. Nec tamen a vita esset corpus separatum, cum intellectus sit vita eius. Sicut cum homo qui intente inquisivit medio visus discernere venientem et tamen, aliis considerationibus raptus, cessat postea attentio circa illam inquisitionem, oculis non minus in ipsum coniectis, tunc non separatur oculus ab anima, licet
15 ab attentione discretiva animae separatus existat. Quod si raptus ille non solum cessaret a vivificatione discretiva, sed etiam a vivificatione sensitiva, oculus ille mortuus foret, quia non vivificaretur. Nec tamen propterea esset a forma intellectiva separatus, quae est forma dans esse, sicut manus arida manet unita formae quae unit corpus totum.

102   Reperiuntur homines qui sciunt retrahere spiritum vivificantem, et apparent mortui et non sentientes, ut beatus recitat Augustinus. Eo

vinam et humanam naturam *IJPa*   possit: posset *Pa*   17 natura[1]: natuta *p* utramque: naturam *add. EN*   natura[2]: nam *S*   18 participabilis: participalis *S* absolute: *ex* absoluta *corr. Pa*   18-19 tunc . . . benedicte: tu Ihesu benedicte tunc *Q*   19 fores: esses *p*

101 2 es: quomodo *post* es *scribit et del. P*   2-3 humanam: naturam *post* humanam *scribit et del. Q*   3 uti: ut *add. V*   in[2]: *supra lin. A Pa*   4 sensibilem: sensibile *P*   fuisse naturam: naturam fuisse *EN*   in: *om. IJRSV supra lin. L* 5 subsistere: subsistimus *V*   composita fuit: fuit composita *R*   8 a: in *p*   vivificatione: vificacione *Q*   8-9 corporis: *non proprie abbreviat Pa*   9 a corpore: *om. T*   corpore: *non proprie abbreviat Pa*; vivificaretur *post* corpore *scribit et del. Pa*   separaretur: separetur *G*   separeretur *Q*   *ex* separetur *corr. S et S[3]* 10 foret: esset *p*   esset corpus: corpus esset *ENTZ*   11 qui: *om. EN*   11-12 inquisivit medio visus: medio visus inquisivit *EN*   12 tamen: cum *V*   eo *add. p* considerationibus: considerantibus *G*   13 raptus: rapto *p*   attentio: intencio *Z* *(ad* attencio *in marg. corr. Z[2])*   oculis: *ex* oculus *corr. G*   13-14 non minus in ipsum: in ipsum non minus *EN*   14 ipsum: separatus *post* ipsum *scribit et del. A*

posited a middle nature that participates in both. For the divine nature cannot be participated in, because it is completely and absolutely most simple. Moreover, in such case, Blessed Jesus, You would not be either God or man.

101   But I see You, Lord Jesus, to be, beyond all understanding, one person (*suppositum*),[112] because You are one Christ. |I see this| in the way in which I see Your human soul to be one—in which soul, as in each man's, I see there to have been a corruptible sensible nature and |see this nature| to exist in an incorruptible intellectual nature. But Your soul was not *composed* of the corruptible and the incorruptible; nor did the sensible |nature| *coincide* with the intellectual |nature|. Yet, I see that the intellectual soul is united to the body by a sensible power that enlivens the body. And when the intellectual soul would cease enlivening the body, without being separated from the body, then the man |Jesus| would be dead, because His life would have ceased. Nevertheless, His body would not be separated from life, since the intellect is the life of the body.[113] By comparison, suppose that a man were to seek intently to discern by means of sight someone approaching him. And suppose that he were seized by other thoughts and that his attention subsequently ceased with regard to his seeking, though his eyes were no less directed toward the on-comer. In this case his eye would not be separated from his soul, although it would be separated from the discerning attention of his soul. However, if when seized |by other thoughts| he not only ceased enlivening |the eye| with the power of discernment but also ceased enlivening |it| with the power of sensation, then the eye would be dead, because it would not be enlivened. Nevertheless, it would not on this account be separated from the intellectual form, which is the form that gives being—just as a withered hand remains united to the form that unites the whole body.

102   There are men who know how to retract their enlivening spirit and who appear dead and insentient, as Blessed Augustine recounts.[114]

---

separatur: sepatur *Q*   oculus: oculus *(?) E*   15 ab: in *post* ab *scribit et del. G*
attentione: intencione *IQ*   animae separatus: *om. Z (in marg. add. Z²)*   existat:
sit *EN*   ille: *ex* illi *corr. V*   16 solum: non *add. E*   17 ille: iste *V*   mortuus:
oculus *G*   foret: esset *p*   quia: et *L*   vivificaretur: vivificareretur *Q*   nec:
non *G*   nec tamen: tamen nec *S*   18 propterea: *in marg. Pa*   perpetua *T*   quae
est: quia es *T*   19 manet: remanet *TV*   unita: unita (*non* unica) *habet J*   unica *V*
     102 1 sciunt: solum *V*   retrahere: *ex* attrahere *corr. R*   2 ut: et *N*   recitat

enim casu, intellectualis natura unita maneret corpori, quod quidem corpus non esset sub alia forma quam prius, immo haberet eandem
5 formam et maneret idem corpus. Neque vis vivificandi desineret esse sed maneret in unione cum intellectuali natura, licet actu non extenderet se in corpus. Video hominem illum veraciter mortuum, quia caret vita vivificante; mors enim est carentia vitae vivificantis. Et tamen non foret corpus illud mortuum a vita sua, quae est anima
10 eius, separatum. Eo modo, Ihesu clementissime, intueor absolutam vitam, quae deus est, humano intellectui tuo et per illum corpori tuo inseparabiliter unitam. Nam unio illa talis est quod maior esse nequit. Separabilis igitur unio multo inferior est unioni quae maior esse nequit. Numquam igitur fuit verum neque erit umquam divinam
15 naturam ab humana tua separatam—ita nec ab anima nec a corpore, quae sunt sine quibus natura humana non potest esse, quamvis verissimum sit animam tuam desisse corpus vivificare, et te veraciter mortem subisse, et tamen numquam a veritate vitae separatum.

103 Si sacerdos ille, de quo meminit Augustinus, aliqualem habuit potestatem tollere vivificationem de corpore attrahendo eam in animam, quasi candela cameram illuminans, foret viva et attraheret radios, per quos cameram illuminavit, ad centrum lucis suae, sine eo
5 quod separetur a camera (et hoc attrahere non est nisi desinere influere), quid mirum si tu, Ihesu, potestatem habuisti, cum sis lux viva liberrima, vivificantem animam ponendi et tollendi? Et quando tollere voluisti, passus es mortem; et quando ponere voluisti, propria virtute resurrexisti. Dicitur autem intellectualis natura humana anima,

---

Augustinus: Augustinus recitat *Vp*   3 unita maneret: maneret unita *EN*   maneret: maret *S (ad* maneret *corr. S²)*   quidem: *ex* quidam *corr. G*   4 corpus: *non proprie scribit V*   6 maneret: manent *V*   8 vita vivificante: vivificante vita *I* mors: *ex* mor *corr. I*   est: *om. S*   vitae: *om. CVp*   9 foret: fores *N* esset *p* 10 separatum: *ex* separatus *corr. G*   Ihesu: dulcissime *post* Ihesu *scribit et del. E* 11 deus: *supra lin. S*   tuo²: *om. I*   12 inseparabiliter unitam: unitam inseparabiliter *EN*   unitam: unita *R*   unio illa: illa unio *G*   quod: ut *EN*   13 est: *om. N*   unioni: unione *p*   13-14 separabilis . . . nequit: *om. A*   14 nequit: num *add. S*   numquam: numquid *S*   15 naturam: tuam *add. GTZ* tuam *post* naturam *scribit et del. R om. V*   tua: *supra lin. R*   corpore: *non proprie abbreviat Pa*   16 sine: *om. Pa (in marg. add. Pa²)*   natura humana: humana natura *GRT*   16-17 verissimum: verum *R*   18 tamen: *om. I*   numquam: nunque *I*
103 1 si: sed *L*   meminit: beatus *add. ENR*   aliqualem: qualemcunque *p*

For in this case the intellectual nature would remain united to the body, which, indeed, would not be a body under another form than previously but rather would have the same form and would remain the same body. And the enlivening power would not cease to exist but would remain in union with the intellectual nature, even though this power would not extend itself, actually, unto the body. I see that this man would be truly dead, because he would lack enlivening life; for death is the lack of enlivening life. But nevertheless, this dead body would not be separated from its life, which is its soul. In this way I see, most merciful Jesus, that Absolute Life, which is God, is inseparably united to Your human intellect and, by means of Your intellect, to Your body. For this union is such that it cannot be greater. Therefore, a separable union is far inferior to a union which cannot be greater. Therefore, it never was true and never will be true that the divine nature is separated from Your human |nature|; and, thus, it is never separated, either, from Your soul or from Your body, which are necessary constituents of human nature. And nevertheless, it is most true that Your soul ceased enlivening Your body and that You truly underwent death and that, nevertheless, You were never separated from true Life.

103   That priest whom Augustine tells of had a power to withdraw vitality from his body by attracting it into his soul—as if the candle illuminating the room[115] were alive and, without being removed from the room, were to attract to the center of its flame the rays by which it illumined the room. (This attracting is only the candle's ceasing to radiate.) If so, then what wonder if You, Jesus, since You are most free Living Light, had the power to send forth and to withdraw Your enlivening soul? When You willed to withdraw it |from the body|, You underwent death; and when You willed to send it forth |into the body|, You arose by Your own power. Now, when the intellectual

2 potestatem: potest autem *N*   tollere: tollerem *V*   de: a *Q*   corpore: *non proprie abbreviat Pa*   2-3 animam: anima *P*   3 quasi: si *add. p*   candela: condela *A*   foret: esset *p*   5 separetur: separaretur *AEGLNOPPaQRTZ* seperetur *J*   separetur *M (ad* separaretur *corr. M²)*   a: *ex* in *corr. Pa*   6 quid: quod *N* tu: domine *add. R*   cum: *supra lin. scribit Pa aut Pa² (in marg. clarius rescribit Pa²)*   sis: si *post* sis *scribit et del. L*   7 ponendi et tollendi: tollendi et ponendi *Z (ad* ponendi et tollendi *corr. Z²)*   8 es: *om. T*   quando: animam *add. S* ponere: tollere *A*   resumere *p*   9 resurrexisti: surrexisti *GZ*   autem: *non clare*

10 quando vivificat seu animat corpus; et dicitur anima tolli, quando
cessat intellectus humanus vivificare. Quando enim intellectus ab
officio vivificandi cessat, et quoad hoc se separat a corpore, propterea
simpliciter non est separatus.

104 Haec inspiras, Ihesu, ut te mihi indignissimo, quantum capere possum, ostendas et in te contempler humanam naturam mortalem
induisse immortalitatem, ut omnes homines, eiusdem humanae naturae, in te resurrectionem et divinam vitam assequi possint. Quid igitur
5 dulcius, quid iocundius quam hoc cognoscere, quoniam in te, Ihesu,
omnia in nostra natura reperimus, qui solus omnia potes et das liber-
alissime et non improperas? O pietas et misericordia inexpressibilis!
Tu, deus, qui es ipsa bonitas, non potuisti satisfacere infinitae clemen-
tiae et largitati tuae, nisi te nobis donares. Nec hoc convenientius et
10 nobis recipientibus possibilius fieri potuit, quam quod nostram assu-
meres naturam, qui tuam accedere non potuimus. Ita venisti ad nos,
et nominaris Ihesus, salvator semper benedictus.

105 CAPITULUM XXIV

QUOMODO IHESUS SIT VERBUM VITAE

Contemplor tuo dono utique optimo atque maximo te Ihesum
meum praedicantem verba vitae et largiter divinum semen in corda
5 audientium seminantem. Et video eos abire, qui non perceperunt ea
quae spiritus sunt; sed manentes video discipulos, qui iam gustare

---

scribit A   anima: *om. L*   11 intellectus[2]: humanus *add. Z*   12 se: *om. P (in
marg. add. P[2])*   corpore: *non proprie abbreviat Pa*   13 simpliciter: *om. G*
simpliciter non est: non est simpliciter *Z*

104 1 haec: hoc *IJ*   ut: et *Q*   tu *R*   2 contempler: conpler *G*   contemplar *N*
exemplar *R*   3 ut: et *G*   3-4 humanae naturae: nature humane *EGN*   5 hoc:
hac *L*   te: domine *add. R*   7 improperas: inperas *Pa*   misericordia: *non
proprie abbreviat L*   8 potuisti: potuisse *V*   9 et largitati tuae: tue et largitati *EN*
largitati: *ex* largitate *corr. JO*   donares: dares *G*   et[2]: *om. CVp*   10 recipien-

nature enlivens, or animates, the body, it is called the human soul; and when the human intellect ceases to enliven |the body|, the soul is said to be withdrawn. For when the intellect ceases its function of enlivening and when, accordingly, it separates itself from the body, it is not therefore separated in an unqualified sense.

104   You inspire these |thoughts|, O Jesus, so that You may reveal Yourself to most unworthy me, insofar as I am capable of receiving |this revelation|, and so that in You I may contemplate the following: that mortal human nature put on immortality in order that in You all men, who are of this same human nature, can attain unto resurrection and divine life. Therefore, what is sweeter, what more delightful than to know that in You, Jesus—who alone are all-powerful and who give most generously and do not reproach[116]—all things are present in our nature? O inexpressible Graciousness and Mercy! You, O God, who are goodness itself,[117] were not able to satisfy Your infinite mercy and generosity without giving us Yourself. This |giving| could not be done more suitably and more conducively to our receiving than by Your assuming our nature, given that we could not approach unto Yours. And so, You came to us; and You are named Jesus, the Ever-blessed Savior.

105   ## CHAPTER TWENTY-FOUR

JESUS IS THE WORD OF LIFE

By Your gift, assuredly best and greatest, I contemplate You my Jesus preaching the words of life[118] and generously sowing the divine seed in the hearts of those who hear.[119] And I see that those who did not perceive the things that are of the Spirit go away,[120] whereas those who have already begun to taste of the sweetness of

tibus: experientibus *EN*   quam: *ex* quoniam *corr. S*   nostram: naturam *P*
11 qui: quia *I*   12 benedictus: amen *add. A*   et cetera *add. V*
  105 1 capitulum XXIV: capitulum 25 *E⁴*   2 *titulum scribit E⁴*   sit: *om. AC*
(*supra lin. add. C²*) *E⁴GJLM³ (in 1:1 om. etiam M) OP³ (in 1:1 om. etiam P)*
Pa³Q² (in 1:1 totum titulum om. Q) RTV²Z   3 contemplor: *ex* contemplacio
corr. G   te: deum *add. R*   4 verba: *non proprie abbreviat G*   divinum: *non*

coeperunt dulcedinem doctrinae animam vivificantis. Pro quibus omnibus princeps ille atque summus omnium apostolorum Petrus confessus est quomodo tu, Ihesu, haberes verba vitae; et vitam quae-
10 rentes admiratus est a te abire. Paulus a te, Ihesu, verba vitae in raptu audivit; et tunc neque persecutio neque gladius neque fames corporis eum a te separare potuit. Nemo omnium umquam te deserere potuit, qui verba vitae gustavit. Quis potest ursum separare a melle, postquam dulcedinem eius degustavit? Quanta est dulcedo
15 veritatis, quae vitam praestat delectabilissimam, ultra omnem corporalem dulcedinem! Absoluta enim dulcedo est; unde manat omne quod omni gustu appetitur. Quid fortius amore ex quo omne amabile habet quod ametur? Si contracti amoris nexus aliquando tantus est quod timor mortis eum rumpere nequit, qualis tunc est nexus gustati
20 illius amoris a quo omnis amor? Nihil miror ego crudelitatem poenarum pro nihilo habitam ab his militibus tuis, Ihesu, quibus te vitam praegustabilem praebuisti. O Ihesu, amor meus, seminasti semen vitae in agro credentium et testimonio sanguinis irrigasti. Morte corporali ostendisti veritatem esse vitam spiritus rationalis. Crevit semen
25 in terra bona et fecit fructum.

106   Ostende mihi, domine, quomodo anima mea est spiraculum vitae quoad corpus, in quod vitam spirat et influit, et non est vita quoad te deum sed quasi potentia ad vitam. Et quia non potes non concedere quae petuntur si attentissima fide petantur, influis mihi in puero esse
5 animam quae habet vim vegetativam in actu; crescit enim puer. Habet et vim sensitivam in actu; sentit enim puer. Habet et vim

---

proprie scribit Pa   5 et: *om. EN*   6 spiritus sunt: sunt spiritus dei *R*   7 animam: animarum *G*   quibus: *ex* qui *corr. C aut C²*   8 ille: *om. Z*   atque summus omnium: omnium atque summus *Z*   omnium apostolorum: apostolorum omnium *V*   9 est: *om. T*   tu: in *V*   haberes: habens *IJ*   vitam: vita *T*   9-10 et . . . vitae: *om. I*   10 abire: et cetera *add. P*   11 tunc: *supra lin. L*   neque¹: nec *V*   neque²: nec *C*   neque gladius: neglectus (?) *V*   12 eum a te: a te eum *R* nemo: enim *add. R*   omnium: enim *P*   omnium umquam: unquam omnium *ad* omnium unquam *transponit J aut J^n*   12-13 nemo . . . gustavit: *om. L*   te deserere: deserere te *ad* te deserere *transponit S*   13 ursum: visum *V*   separare: *ex* sapere *in marg. corr. O*   14 dulcedinem eius degustavit: semel gustaverit dulcedinem eius *A*   gustavit eius dulcedinem *R*   16 unde: *supra lin. clarius rescribit J^n*   manat: manet *N*   17 omni: omnium *N non proprie scribit V* gustu: u² *non plene videtur in R (lacuna)*   quid: quid *aut* quod *(non proprie abbreviatum) L*   omne: omni *S*   18 tantus est: talis est et tantus *Q*   19 rumpere:

the learning that enlivens the soul remain as disciples. Peter, that leader and head of the Apostles, confessed on behalf of all Your disciples that You, Jesus, had the words of life;[121] and he marveled that those who were seeking life went away from You. Paul, in a rapture,[122] heard from You, Jesus, the words of life; and thereafter neither persecution nor sword nor bodily hunger was able to separate him from You.[123] None of all those who have tasted the words of life were ever able to forsake You. Who can separate a bear from honey after it has tasted honey's sweetness? How great the sweetness of Truth, which furnishes a most delectable life, beyond all corporeal sweetness! For it is Absolute Sweetness; hence, it remains all that is desired by any sense of taste. What is stronger than the Love from which whatever is lovable[124] has the fact that it is loved? If at times the bond of contracted love is so great that the fear of death cannot sever it, then of what sort is the bond of that tasted Love from which all love derives? I am not at all surprised, O Jesus, at the punishing cruelty which is esteemed as nothing by these soldiers of Yours, to whom You have given Yourself as a foretaste of life. O Jesus, my Love, You have sown the seed of life in the field of those who believe; and You have irrigated it with the testimony of Your blood. By Your bodily death You showed that truth is the life of the rational spirit. The seed has grown in good earth and has brought forth fruit.

106   Disclose to me, O Lord, how it is that my soul is the breath of life with respect to a body (into which it breathes, and infuses, life) but with respect to You who are God is not life but, as it were, a "potency for life." Because You cannot fail to grant our petitions if they are made in most earnest faith, You infuse into me |the following disclosure|: in a boy there is a soul which has an actualized vegetative power, for the boy grows. This soul also has an actualized sensible power, for the boy senses. It also has an imaginative power,

non proprie abbreviat Pa   est nexus: nexus est *V*   20 miror ego: ego miror *EN*
21 his: aliis *CVp   om. EN*   22 praegustabilem: *ut* pregustalem *scribit A   om. S*
23 sanguinis: sagwnis *I*   saguinis *M*   24 crevit: cernit *Pa (ad* crevit *corr. Pa²)*
25 fructum: centuplum *add. I*
   106 1 ostende: ostendis *p*   mea: *om. GT*   2 te: *om. A*   3 et: *supra lin. P*
non¹: *in marg. A*   potes: potest *AI*   5 quae habet vim: *om. R*   6 habet¹:
om. J (in marg. add. Jⁿ)   enim *post* habet¹ *scribit et del. O*   sensitivam . . . vim:
om. EN   et²: *om. V*   vim²: se *post* vim² *scribit et del. Pa*   6-8 habet². . . actu
(106:6-7) et habet . . . distantior *(106: 7-8): transponit Q (sed nondum in actu post*

imaginativam, sed nondum in actu. Habet et vim ratiocinativam,
cuius actus est adhuc distantior. Habet et vim intellectivam, sed in
remotiori potentia. Ita animam unam experimur quoad potentias in-
10 feriores esse in actu prius, et postea quoad superiores, ut prius sit
animalis homo quam spiritualis. Sic experimur vim quandam mineralem, quae et spiritus dici potest, in visceribus terrae esse, et illum in
potentia esse, ut fiat minera lapidis; aut in potentia esse, ut fiat minera salis; et alius, ut fiat minera metalli; et varios esse tales spiritus
15 secundum varietatem lapidum, salium, et metallorum. Unum tamen
esse spiritum minerae auri, qui, ex influentia solari seu caeli continue
plus et plus depuratus, tandem figitur in aurum tale quod non est per
aliquod elementum corruptibile. Et in eo plurimum caelestis incorruptibilis lucis resplendet. Multum enim corporali luci solis assimilatur.

107   Sic quidem de spiritu vegetabili et sensibili experimur. Nam sensibilis in homine multum se conformat virtuti caelesti motivae et
influentiali, et sub caeli influentia capit successive augmentum, usque
quo ponatur in perfecto actu. Educitur autem de potentia corporis;
5 ideo cessat perfectio eius, deficiente perfectione corporis a qua
dependet. Est deinde spiritus intellectualis, qui in actu perfectionis
non dependet a corpore sed unitur ei mediante virtute sensitiva. Hic
spiritus, quia non dependet a corpore, non subest influentiae corpor-
um caelestium nec dependet a spiritu sensibili. Sic non dependet a
10 virtute motiva caeli; sed sicut motores orbium caelestium subsunt
primo motori, sic et hic motor, qui est intellectus. Sed quia unitus est

raciocinativam *scribit, del., et post* ymaginativam *rescribit, Q)*   7 sed . . . ratiocinativam: *om. Z (in marg. add.* Z^2; rationativam *pro* ratiocinativam *scribit* Z^2)
nondum: nundum *CM (ad* nondum *in marg. corr.* M^2)   ratiocinativam: racionativam *ANV* racinativam *G* raciocionativam *P* racionativa *Pa*   8 cuius: cuus *Q*
est adhuc: adhuc est *ad* est adhuc *transponit R*   9 animam: *non proprie scribit Pa*
potentias: potencias *ex* potenciam *corr. A*   10 prius[1]: *supra lin. E*   ut: et *S*
11-12 mineralem: *litteram* e[1] *in linea perfecit, et* e *supra lin. scribit* T^3 12 quae:
quem *V*   potest: *om. V*   terrae: terra *E*   esse et: et esse *N*   illum: illim *S*
13-14 lapidis . . . minera[1]: *om. EGN*   14 alius: aut *add. EN* aluminis
aut *G* alunis aut *T* alium *p*   metalli: *in marg. I*   15 varietatem: *ex* varietatam
corr. E   lapidum: salis *post* lapidum *scribit et del. G*   lapidum salium: salium
lapidum *EN*   et: *om. EN*   16 minerae: mineri *N* minere *ex* minerum *corr. Q*
om. *R*   auri: *ex* aurei *corr. P* aut P^2 qui: que *V*   influentia: influencia *ex*
fluencia *corr. Pa* inconfluencia *V*   17 depuratus: depuraturus *A* deputatus *SV*
18 aliquod elementum: elementum aliquod *T*   elementum: elimentum *V*   18-
19 incorruptibilis: *ex* corruptibilis *corr. A*   19 lucis: licis *C (ad* lucis *corr.* C^2)

though not yet actualized. Moreover, it has a rational power, whose actuality is still more distant. And it has, as well, an intellectual power, though in quite remote potency. So we find that the one soul is actual first with respect to its lower powers and later with respect to its higher powers, so that a man is animal before he is spiritual. Similarly, we find that there is in the interior of the earth a certain mineral power—which can also be called a spirit—and that this spirit is potentially the source of stone or potentially the source of salt; and there is another spirit that is |potentially| the source of metal. And, |as we find|, there are various such spirits, in accordance with the variety of stones, salts, and metals. Nevertheless, |we know| that there is a single spirit of the source of gold. As a result of the influence of the sun or the heavens this spirit is more and more purified until at last it is fashioned into gold which is such that it is not corruptible by any other element. And in this gold a great degree of incorruptible celestial light shines forth. For the gold becomes quite like the corporeal light of the sun.

107 We find a similar thing regarding the vegetative spirit and the sensible spirit. For in man the sensible |spirit| makes itself quite like the motive and influencing celestial power; and under the influence of the heavens it becomes successively increased—to the point where it is posited in perfect actuality. But it is educed from the potency of the body; and so, its perfection ceases when the body's perfection, on which it depends, fails. Next, there is the intellectual spirit, which, with regard to its actual perfection, does not depend on the body but is united to the body by the medium of the sensible power. Because this spirit does not depend on the body, it is not subject to the influence of the heavenly bodies and does not depend on the sensible spirit. Likewise, it does not depend on the motive power of the heavens; yet, just as the movers of the celestial orbits are subject to the First Mover,[125] so too is this mover, which is the intellect. But

enim corporali: corporali enim *I*   luci: *ex* luce *corr. V*   solis: comparatur et *add. A litteram* o *non clare scribit M*   assimilatur: assimulatur *S* assimiliatur *Z*
  107 1 nam: spiritus *post* nam *add. C² (supra lin.) et p*   2 et: *om. P*   3 influentia: influentiali *T*   successive: sensitive *Pa (ad* successive *corr. Pa²)*   4 autem: aut *Pa*   de: in *R*   8 corpore: *non proprie abbreviat Pa*   non²: nec *ALOPQRZ* nec *ex? supra lin. corr. M²*   9 a²: spiritu sen *post* a² *scribit et del. E*   10 motores:

corpori per medium sensitivae, tunc sine sensibus non perficitur. Omne enim quod ad eum pervenit, de mundo sensibili per medium sensuum ad ipsum pergit. Unde nihil tale potest esse in intellectu
15 quod prius non fuit in sensu. Quanto autem sensus fuerit purior et perfectior, et imaginatio clarior, et discursus melior, tanto intellectus, in suis intellectualibus operationibus minus impeditus, promptior existit.

108 Pascitur autem intellectus per verbum vitae—sub cuius influentia constituitur, sicut motores orbium. Differenter tamen, uti etiam spiritus qui subsunt influentiis caeli differenter perficiuntur. Et non perficitur nisi per accidens a sensibili spiritu, sicut imago non perficit,
5 licet excitet ad inquirendum veritatem exemplaris. Velut imago crucifixi non influit devotionem sed excitat memoriam, ut influatur devotio. Et quoniam non necessitatur per influentiam caeli spiritus intellectualis sed est penitus liber, tunc nisi se influentiae verbi dei per fidem subiciat, non perficitur. Sicut discipulus liber qui sui iuris est,
10 nisi se verbo magistri subiciat per fidem, non perficitur; oportet enim quod confidat et audiat magistrum. Perficitur autem intellectus per verbum dei, et crescit, et fit continue capacior et aptior atque verbo similior. Et haec perfectio, quae venit sic a verbo, a quo habuit esse, non est perfectio corruptibilis sed est deiformis—sicut perfectio auri
15 non est corruptibilis sed caelestiformis. Oportet autem omnem intellectum per fidem verbo dei se subicere, et attentissime internam illam summi magistri doctrinam audire; et audiendo quid in eo loquatur dominus, perficietur. Quapropter tu, Ihesu, magister unice, praedicasti fidem esse omni accedenti ad vitae fontem necessariam. Et

motrices *L*   caelestium: *om. I*   11 est[2]: *om. E (supra lin. add. E²) N*   12 non: *supra lin. E*   14 ipsum: eum *A*   in intellectu: intellectivum *E (ad* in intellectu *corr. E²) N*   15 non fuit: *bis G*   fuit: fuerit *p*   sensu: censu *V*   quanto: quando *P*   17 impeditus: impetitus *S*   promptior: perspicacior *p*

108 2 differenter: differentur *Q*   etiam: eciam *supra lin. Pa*   3 subsunt: subsut *Pa*   caeli: *om. L*   perficiuntur: perfiuntur *Z*   3-4 perficitur: intellectus *add. EN*   4 accidens: accides *Pa*   a: et *A*   sensibili: sensibi *O*   sicut: sed *Pa*   perficit: perficitur *G*   5 excitet: extitet *Pa*   inquirendum: inquirendam *p*   veritatem: virtutem *L*   velut: sicut *EGINPaT* sicud *J* velud[1] *O*   6 excitat: devocionem *post* excitat *scribit et del. Q*   influatur: inflatur *S*   7 quoniam: quomodo *R*   spiritus *om. P* (spiritus *post* intellectualis [*108:7-8*] *in marg. add. P²*)   8 est: et *V*   9 subiciat: subiciant *Q*   liber: non perficitur *post* liber *scribit et del. E*   9-10 sicut . . . perficitur: *om. Pa* (sicud discipulus liber qui [-] iuris est nisi

because the intellect is united to the body through the medium of the sensible |power|, it is not perfected apart from the senses. For whatever comes to it proceeds to it from the sensible world through the medium of the senses. Hence, there cannot be in the intellect anything which is such that it was not first in the senses.[126]. But the purer and more perfect the senses and the clearer the imagination and the better the power of rational inference, the quicker will be the intellect, since it will be less hampered in its intellectual operations.

108   But the intellect is nourished by the Word of Life—under whose influence it is placed, as are the movers of the orbits. However, |the intellect and these movers| are perfected in different ways, just as also the spirits which are subject to the influences of the heavens are perfected in different ways. Moreover, the intellect is perfected by the sensible spirit only accidentally, just as an image does not perfect |its exemplar| but serves as a stimulus for seeking out the exemplar's truth. For example, an image of the Crucified One does not inspire devotion but stimulates the memory, in order that devotion may be inspired. And since the intellectual spirit is not constrained by the influence of the heavens but is altogether free, it is not perfected unless it subjects itself by faith to the influence of the Word of God. (By comparison, a free student, who is under his own guidance, is not perfected unless he subjects himself by faith to the word of a teacher; for he needs to trust and hearken unto a teacher.[127]) Now, through the Word of God the intellect is perfected and grows and is made progressively more capable of receiving the Word and progressively more conformed, and similar, to the Word. And this perfection, which comes in this way from the Word, from which the intellect has being, is not a corruptible perfection but is Godlike—just as the perfection of gold is not corruptible but is like the heavens. But every intellect needs to subject itself by faith to the Word of God and to listen most attentively to the inner teaching of the Supreme Teacher. And by hearkening unto what the Lord says in His Word, the intellect will be perfected. Wherefore You, O Jesus, sole Teacher,[128] proclaimed that faith is necessary for anyone coming unto the Fount

se ve[-] magistri subiciat per f[-] non perficitur *in marg. add. Pa²)*   10 verbo: sui *post* verbo *scribit et del. L*   11 autem: enim *N*   per: *bis G*   12 et crescit: *om. V*   13 venit sic: sic venit *EN*   esse: et *add. P*   15 omnem: felicem *post* omnem *scribit et del. L*   17 et: in *add. I*   quid in eo: in eo quid *V*   19 esse: in *add. A*

20 secundum gradum fidei adesse influxum virtutis divinae ostendisti.

109 Duo tantum docuisti, Christe salvator: fidem et dilectionem. Per fidem accedit intellectus ad verbum; per dilectionem unitur ei. Quantum accedit, tantum in virtute augetur; et quantum diligit, tantum figitur in luce eius. Verbum autem dei intra ipsum est; et non est opus 5 ut quaerat extra se, quia intus reperiet, et accedere poterit per fidem. Et ut propius accedere possit, poterit precibus obtinere. Nam verbum adaugebit fidem per communicationem luminis sui. Tibi, Ihesu, gratias ago, quoniam ad hoc tuo lumine perveni. In lumine enim tuo video, lumen vitae meae, quomodo tu verbum influis omnibus creden- 10 tibus vitam et perficis omnes te diligentes. Quae umquam brevior et efficacior doctrina tua, Ihesu bone? Non persuades nisi credere, et non praecipis nisi amare. Quid facilius quam credere deo? Quid dulcius quam ipsum amare? Quam suave iugum est iugum tuum, et quam leve est onus tuum, praeceptor unice! Promittis hanc doctrinam 15 servantibus omne desideratum. Nihil enim astruis credenti difficile et nihil amanti denegabile. Talia sunt promissa, quae tuis discipulis spondes. Et verissima sunt, quia tu es veritas, quae non nisi vera promittere potes. Immo non nisi te ipsum promittis, qui es perfectio omnis perfectibilis. Tibi laus, tibi gloria, tibi gratiarum actio per 20 aeterna saecula.

omni: *bis J* (omni¹ *del. J aut J ⁿ*)   accedenti: accidenti *IN Pa*   vitae fontem: fontem vite *N*   fontem vite *ad* vite fontem (vite *ex* vitem *correctum*) *transponit Pa aut Pa²*   20 gradum: gradus *EN*   influxum: *ex* influencie *corr. E*

109 1 dilectionem: dulcedinem *V*   2 accedit: *om. V*   ei: *supra lin. P*   2-3 quantum: ad *post* quantum *scribit et del. O*   3 virtute: *non proprie scribit R* tantum²: in virtute *post* tantum² *scribit et del. T, etiam del. T³*   4 figitur: *ex* vigitur *corr. J*   est¹: *om. R*   et: *om. S*   5 quia: *ex* quod *corr. T*   6 propius: proprius *V*   obtinere: optinere *J*   7-8 Ihesu gratias ago: gracias ago yhesu *V*   9 video: videbo *I* quomodo: quoniam *AEIJNQZ*   quo modo *p*   10 vitam: vita *Pa*   11 tua: *om. P (in marg. add. P²)*   Ihesu bone: bone Ihesu *Q*   persuades: suades *p*   12 non: *om. EN*   quid¹: quam *V*   quam: *om. V*   12-13 quid². . . amare: *bis V* (quam: *semel* quem *semel* quam *scribit V; cf. abbreviationem pro quemadmodum, 97:13*) 13 quam²: quoniam *N* O quam *R*   iugum¹: *om. Jp*   iugum tuum: tuum iugum *S*   14 est: *om. Z*   unice: unite *S*   15 servantibus: servantum *L*   astruis: aservis *S (ad* aseris *corr. S²) non clare scribit V*   credenti: credentibus *N* 16 denegabile: negabile *T*   sunt: sut *Pa*   17 quae: qui *p*   17-18 vera . . . nisi: *om. G*   19 omnis: omnibus *N*   tibi²: et *ENQ*   tibi gloria: *om. I*   tibi³: *om. S* 20 saecula: amen *add. A Rp*   et cetera *add. P*   seculorum. Amen *add. Q*

of life. And You disclosed that the infusing of divine power is proportional to the degree of faith.

109   O Christ, our Savior, You taught only two things: faith and love. Through faith the intellect approaches unto the Word; through love it is united therewith. The closer the intellect approaches, the more it is increased in power; and the more it loves |the Word|, the more it is fashioned in the Word's light. But the Word of God is within the intellect, which need not search outside itself. For it will find the Word within, and it will be able to approach the Word by faith. And through prayer the intellect will be able to obtain the capability of approaching more closely. For the Word will increase the |intellect's| faith by imparting its own light. I thank You, Jesus, because I have arrived at this |discernment| by means of Your light. For by means of Your light, O Light of my life, I see that You who are the Word infuse life to all believers and perfect all who love You. What teaching was ever more concise and more effective than Yours, good Jesus? You urge us only to believe, and You command us only to love. What is easier than to believe God?[129] What is sweeter than to love Him? How pleasant a yoke is Your yoke, and how light is Your burden, O sole Teacher![130] To those who heed this teaching You promise all that is desired. For Your teaching is not difficult for one who believes[131] and is not refusable for one who loves. Such are the promises which You make to Your disciples. And these promises are most true, because You are Truth, which can make only true promises. Indeed, You promise only Yourself, who are the Perfection of everything perfectible. To You be praise, to You be glory, to You be thanksgiving forever and ever.

110

CAPITULUM XXV

QUOMODO IHESUS SIT CONSUMMATIO

Sed quid est hoc, domine, quod immittis in spiritum hominis quem perficis? Nonne spiritum tuum bonum, qui penitus est in actu virtus
5 omnium virtutum et perfectio perfectorum, quoniam ille est qui omnia operatur? Sicut enim vis solaris, descendens in spiritum vegetabilem, movet ipsum ut perficiatur et fit, gratissima et naturalissima decoctione caelestialis caloris, fructus bonus medio boni arboris, ita spiritus tuus, deus, venit in spiritum intellectualem boni hominis, et
10 calore divinae charitatis decoquit virtualem potentiam, ut perficiatur et fiat sibi gratissimus fructus. Experimur, domine, simplicem spiritum tuum, virtute infinitum, capi multipliciter. Capitur enim aliter in uno, ubi efficit spiritum propheticum; aliter in alio, ubi peritum efficit interpretem; et in alio docet scientiam; ita in aliis aliter. Varia
15 enim sunt dona eius; et illae sunt perfectiones intellectualis spiritus, sicut idem calor solaris in variis arboribus varios perficit fructus.

111 Video, domine, spiritum tuum nulli spiritui deesse posse, quia spiritus spirituum et motus motuum; et est replens omnem orbem. Sed disponit omnia quae non habent spiritum intellectualem, per naturam intellectualem quae movet caelum et, per eius motum, omnia quae ei
5 subsunt. Dispositionem vero atque dispensationem in natura intellectuali non nisi sibi ipsi reservavit. Desponsavit enim sibi hanc naturam, in qua elegit quiescere tamquam in domo mansionis et caelo

---

110 1 capitulum XXV: capitulum 26 *E⁴   numerum capituli om. CJ   2 titulum
scribit E⁴   Ihesus sit: om. AGLM³ (in 1:1 om. etiam M) OP³ (in 1:1 om. etiam
P) Pa³Q² (in 1:1 om. etiam Q) Z   Ihesus sit consummatio: consummacio Ihesus T
(sit om. T)   sit: om. C (supra lin. add. C²) E⁴JRTV²   3 quod: om. JPa (supra
lin. add. Pa²)   promittis post quod scribit et del. M   4 nonne: none S   spiritum
tuum: tuum spiritum Z   qui: quia N   5 est: om. EN   6-7 vegetabilem: ille
add. Q   7 gratissima et naturalissima: naturalissima et gratissima EN   8 caloris:
coloris PS   medio: om. P   medio boni arboris: arboris boni medio S (medio ad
medii corr. S²)   boni: bone AELNPZ   boni O (bone supra lin. coni. O²)   bonae
p   9 boni: boni O (bone supra lin. scribit et del. O²)   10 calore: caloris N
divinae: bonitatis post divine scribit et del. R   decoquit: in tua add. S (ad in
natura in marg. corr. S²)   11 sibi: tibi ALMOPQRZ   ei p   experimur: ex
expermur corr. S   12 tuum: om. I   virtute: virtutum A   om. OP   14 efficit:
ex perficit corr. L   in¹: om. p   alio: ubi add. p   15 illae: illa EN   intel-*

110   CHAPTER TWENTY-FIVE

But what, O Lord, is that which You send forth into the spirit of the man whom You perfect? Is it not Your good Spirit, which is fully and actually the Power of all powers and the Perfection of all perfect things, since it is that which works all things? The power of the sun descends into the vegetative spirit and moves it, so that it is perfected; and by the most pleasing and most natural warming from the celestial heat, good fruit is produced by means of a good tree. Similarly, O God, Your Spirit comes into the intellectual spirit of a good man and warms the potential power by the heat of divine love, so that the intellectual spirit is perfected and so that there is produced fruit that is most pleasing to the Spirit. We observe, O Lord, that Your simple Spirit, infinite in power, is received in multiple ways. For it is received in one way in an intellectual spirit in which it produces the spirit of prophecy; it is received in another way in an intellectual spirit in which it produces a skilled interpreter; and in another intellectual spirit it imparts knowledge; and so on, in different ways in different spirits. For the Spirit's gifts are various; and they are perfections of the intellectual spirit, just as |one and| the same solar heat perfects various fruits in various trees.

111   O Lord, I see that Your Spirit cannot be lacking to any spirit, because it is the Spirit of spirits and the Motion of motions; and it fills the whole world.[132] But whatever things do not have an intellectual spirit Your Spirit governs by means of the intellectual nature that moves the heavens—and by means of the motion of the heavens Your Spirit governs whatever things are subject to their motion. But in the case of the intellectual nature Your Spirit has reserved exclusively for itself the governance and ordering. For it has betrothed this nature, in which it chooses to rest as in a house of lodging and a heaven of

lectualis: intellectuales *ALMOPQRVZ*   16 perficit: perfecit *A*   fructus: *non proprie scribit Pa*

111 1 spiritui: *om. GT*   posse: pos *Pa*   1-2 spiritus: est *add. p*   2 orbem: *om. ALMOPQRZ (in marg. add. Z²)*   4 motum: celum *post* motum *scribit et del. T*   5 vero: . . . que *Q*   6 nisi: *in marg. A*   sibi¹: *om. S*   sibi ipsi: sibipsi *(ut semper) C*   desponsavit : dispensavit *I*   enim sibi: sibi enim *GIJPaT*   7 ele-

veritatis. Nullibi enim capi potest veritas per se, nisi in intellectuali
natura. Tu, domine, qui omnia propter temet ipsum operaris, univer-
10 sum hunc mundum creasti propter intellectualem naturam—quasi
pictor, qui diversos temperat colores, ut demum se ipsum depingere
possit, ad finem ut habeat sui ipsius imaginem, in qua delicietur et
quiescat ars sua. Cum ipse unus sit immultiplicabilis, saltem modo
quo fieri potest, in propinquissima similitudine, multiplicetur. Multas
15 autem figuras facit, quia virtutis suae infinitae similitudo non potest
nisi in multis perfectiori modo explicari. Et sunt omnes intellectuales
spiritus cuilibet spiritui opportuni. Nam nisi forent innumerabiles,
non posses tu, deus infinitus, meliori modo cognosci. Quisque enim
intellectualis spiritus videt in te deo meo aliquid quod, nisi aliis reve-
20 laretur, non attingerent te deum suum meliori quo fieri posset modo.
Revelant sibi mutuo secreta sua amoris pleni spiritus, et augetur ex
hoc cognitio amati et desiderium ad ipsum, et gaudii dulcedo inardescit.

112   Neque adhuc, domine deus, sine Ihesu filio tuo, quem prae consor-
tibus suis unxisti, qui Christus est, complementum operis tui perfe-
cisses. In cuius intellectu quiescit perfectio creabilis naturae. Nam est
ultima et perfectissima immultiplicabilis dei similitudo. Et non potest
5 esse nisi una suprema talis. Omnes autem alii spiritus intellectuales
sunt, illo spiritu mediante, similitudines; et quanto perfectiores, tanto
huic similiores. Et quiescunt omnes in illo spiritu, ut in ultimitate
perfectionis imaginis dei, cuius imaginis assecuti sunt similitudinem
et gradum aliquem perfectionis.

git: eligt *Q*   8 capi potest: potest capi *V*   potest veritas: veritas potest *R*   in:
om. S   10 intellectualem naturam: naturam intellectualem *Q*   quasi: qui *V*   11 ut:
et *P*   12 delicietur: deliciatur *G*   et: ac *p*   13 sua: eius *p*   cum: *del., et supra*
lin. clarius rescribit, E   ut cum *p*   sit: sic *(?) L (saepe* t *non proprie format L)*
saltem: saltim *AEGIJMPaQST ex* saltim *corr. O   om. N*   13-14 modo quo: quo
modo *OP*   15 autem: enim *R*   suae: tue *R*   similitudo: simulitudo *Q*   17 cuilibet: *ex* cuiuslibet *corr. E aut E²* cuiuslibet *J*   opportuni: oportune *P*   nisi:
si *S*   forent: essent *p*   innumerabiles: innumerales *C (ad* innumerabiles *corr. C²)*
18 infinitus: deus *add. EN*   quisque: *ad unum verbum corr. T*   19 aliquid: aliquod *MOPQR*   quod: quodam *T*   nisi: aliquis *post* nisi *scribit et del. J*   19-
20 revelaretur: reveletur *J*   20 attingerent: attingeret *IQR*   te: *om. EN*   quo: sibi
post quo *scribit et del. Pa*   posset: possit *P*   21 revelant: igitur *add. p*   mutuo:
mutua *Pa* motuo *Q*   sua: sui *N*   22 amati: amanti *Q*

112 2 suis: tuis *AIQ*   unxisti: unxit *V*   est: et *add. S*   3 quiescit perfectio:
perfeccio quiescit *A*   est: *om. I*   4 ultima et: *om. R*   dei: creatura *post* dei
scribit et del. E   dei similitudo: similitudo dei *G*   et²: *scribit et del. I*   5 su-

truth. For nowhere other than in the intellectual nature can Truth itself be received. You, O Lord, who work all things for Your own sake, created this whole world on account of the intellectual nature. |You created| as if You were a Painter who mixes different colors in order, at length, to be able to paint Himself—to the end that He may have an image of Himself wherein He Himself may take delight and His artistry may find rest. Although the Divine Painter is one and is not multipliable, He can nevertheless be multiplied in the way in which this is possible: viz., in a very close likeness.[133] However, He makes many figures, because the likeness of His infinite power can be unfolded in the most perfect way only in many figures. And *all* intellectual spirits are useful to *each* |intellectual| spirit. Now, unless they were countless, You, O Infinite God, could not be known in the best way possible. For each intellectual spirit sees in You-my-God something |without| which the others—unless it were revealed to them—could not in the best possible manner attain unto You-their-God. Full of love, the spirits reveal to one another their respective secrets; and, as a result, their knowledge of the one who is loved and their desire for Him is increased; and the sweetness of their joy is aflame.

112   O Lord God, without Your Son, Jesus—whom You anointed more than his fellow-men[134] and who is the Christ[135]—You would not yet have brought about the completion of Your work.[136] In His intellect the perfection of creatable nature finds rest. For He is the ultimate and most perfect unmultipliable Likeness of God.[137] And there can be only one such supreme |Likeness|. Yet, all other intellectual spirits, by the mediation of this Spirit, are also likenesses. And the more perfect they are, the more like unto this Spirit they are. In this Spirit they all find rest, as in the ultimate perfection of the Image of God. And they have attained unto a likeness of this Image and unto a certain degree of its perfection.

prema talis: talis suprema *EN*   omnes: omnis *V*   autem: t *non proprie format (ut saepe) L*   7 huic: *om. A R*   ut: et *Q*   ultimitate: ultima *C V*   ultimate *E G M (ad ultimitate corr. M²) N P a S T*   ultimo *p*   7-8 ultimitate perfectionis: ultimate perfecciores *S (post* perfecciores *repetit* tanto . . . ultimate *[112:6-7] et procedit* perfeccionis ymaginis dei *etc. S)*   8 imaginis¹: imagine *E* ymagine *N* ymagines *P* imaginis dei: dei ymaginis *ad* ymaginis dei *transponit I*   9 aliquem: modo *post* aliquem *scribit et del. L*

113   Habeo igitur dono tuo, deus meus, totum hunc visibilem mundum
et omnem scripturam et omnes administratorios spiritus in adiutor-
ium, ut proficiam in cognitione tui. Omnia me excitant ut ad te
convertar. Non aliud scripturae omnes facere nituntur, nisi te osten-
5 dere; neque omnes intellectuales spiritus aliud habent exercitii, nisi ut
te quaerant et, quantum de te repererint, revelent. Dedisti mihi super
omnia Ihesum magistrum, viam, vitam, et veritatem, ut penitus mihi
nihil deesse possit. Confortas me spiritu sancto tuo; inspiras per eum
electiones vitae, desideria sancta. Allicis per praegustationem dulce-
10 dinis vitae gloriosae, ut te bonum infinitum amem. Rapis me, ut sim
supra me ipsum et praevideam locum gloriae ad quem me invitas.
Multa mihi saporosissima fercula, odore suo optimo me attrahentia,
ostendis. Thesaurum divitiarum, vitae, gaudii, et pulchritudinis videre
sinis. Fontem ex quo effluit omne desiderabile, tam in natura quam
15 arte discooperis. Nihil secreti tenes. Venam amoris non occultas,
neque pacis, neque quietis. Omnia offers mihi miserrimo, quem de
nihilo creasti.

114   Quid igitur moror? Cur non curro in odore unguentorum Christi
mei? Cur non intro in gaudium domini mei? Quid me tenet? Si tenuit
me ignorantia tui, domine, et vacua sensibilis mundi delectatio,
amplius non tenebit. Volo enim, domine, quia tu das ut velim, ista
5 linquere quae huius mundi sunt, quia me linquere vult mundus.

---

113 2 scripturam: figuram *EN*   administratorios: administratores *V*   4 convertar: nisi *post* convertar *scribit A* (nisi *del., et in marg.* quid *scribit, A²*)   non:
om. A   scripturae: scrutetur *I*   facere nituntur: nituntur facere *G*   5 exercitii:
exercicii *ex* exercii *corr. E*   exercii *N*   exercicium *Z*   ut: *ex? corr. Pa*   6 et . . .
revelent: *om. S*   6-7 super omnia: *om. I*   7 ut: *supra lin. P   om. V*   mihi: de
post michi *scribit et del. T, etiam del. T³*   7-8 mihi nihil: nichil michi *AG*   nihil mihi *L*
8 nihil: *om. V*   confortas: spiritu *post* confortas *scribit et del. Pa*   me: in *add. Z*
spiritu sancto: spiritusancto *p*   9 electiones: elecciones *Pa (ut abbreviationem
explanet, litteram e supra lin. scribit Pa²)*   sancta: *om. N*   10 vitae gloriosae:
gloriose vite *Q*   amem: amen *N*   11 praevideam: provideam *A   in* prevideam
litteras ea *non proprie format V*   12 saporosissima: saporissima *CGJM (ad
saporosissima corr. M²) PaSTV*   odore: ordine *I*   13 thesaurum: *hic om., et
post* pulchritudinis *(113:13) scribunt EN*   thesauris *P*   divitiarum vitae: vite
divitiarum *ad* divitiarum vite *transponit R*   et: *om. p*   14 sinis: finis *J*   si
vis (?) *V*   fontem: *in marg. L*   effluit: fluit *AR*   quam: in *add. EN*   15 discooperis: discoperis *ACEJLMOPaQSTVZp*   nihil: michi *S (in marg.* nihil *coni.*

113 Therefore, by Your gift, my God, I have—as an aid for advancing in knowledge of You—this whole visible world and all Scripture and all administering spirits. All things induce me to turn toward You. All Scripture attempts to do nothing other than to disclose You. And all intellectual spirits have no other duty than to seek You and to reveal as much of You as they discover. Above all, You have given me Jesus as Teacher and Way and Life and Truth,[138] so that nothing at all can be lacking to me. You comfort me with Your Holy Spirit, through whom You inspire holy desires and the decisions of life. Through a foretaste of the sweetness of a glorious life You draw |me unto Yourself|, so that I may love You, who are infinite good. You enrapture me, in order that I may transcend myself and foresee the glorious place to which You invite me. You show me many exceedingly appetizing repasts that attract me by their most appealing aroma. You permit |me| to see the treasure of riches, of life, of joy, and of beauty. You disclose, in nature as well as by art, the Fount from which flows everything desirable. You keep nothing secret. You do not hide the source of love, of peace, and of rest. To wretched me, whom You created from nothing, You offer all things.

114 Why, then, do I delay? Why do I not hasten to the fragrance of the ointments of my Christ? Why do I not enter into the joy of my Lord?[139] What holds me back? If ignorance of You, O Lord, as well as the empty delight characteristic of the sensible world has held me back, it shall do so no longer. For since You grant me to will, O Lord, I will to forsake the things of this world, because the world

S²) 16 pacis: paucis *I*   offers mihi: mihi offers *Z*   mihi: in *post* michi *scribit et del. I*   17 nihilo: limo *EN*

114 1 odore: odorem *V*   unguentorum: ungentorum *ACEIJLMNOPPaQT (ex* ungwentorum *(?) corr. T) Z* ungwentorum *G om. R*   2 quid: quod *J*   2-3 tenuit me: me tenuit *NR*   3 vacua: vana *Jp*   sensibilis mundi: mundi sensibilis *A*   4 amplius: me *add. Q*   tu: *ex* tui *corr. L*   5 linquere¹: *ex* relinquere *corr. J* quia: *om. IJPa (in marg. add. Pa²)*   me linquere vult: linquere wlt me *R*

Propero ad finem; cursum paene consummavi; praevenio licentiare ipsum, quia anhelo ad coronam. Trahe me, domine—quia nemo pervenire poterit ad te nisi a te tractus—ut attractus absolvar ab hoc mundo et iungar tibi deo absoluto in aeternitate vitae gloriosae.
10 Amen.

6 paene: bene *J*   licentiare: licenciari *P*   6-7 licentiare ipsum: vale facere ipsi *p*
7 trahe: traho *V*   7-8 pervenire: pervevenire *C* prevenire *Pa* venire *R*   pervenire poterit: potest pervenire *EN*   8 a: ad *IT*   10 amen: Reverendissimi patris domini Nicolai cardinalis sancti Petri ad vincula Brixnensis episcopi liber de visione dei ad fratres in Tegrinsee anno domini M°CCCC°LIIII° *add. A*   Reverendissimi domini Nicolai cardinalis sancti Petri ad vincula Brixinensis episcopi liber de visione dei explicit *add. C*   Explicit tractatus N. cardinalis de praxi seu manuductione in misticam theologiam, alias de visione dei. Anno domini M°CCCC°LXI *add. E* Finivit Brixne 1453. 8 Novembris. Nycolaus cardinalis *add. G*   Explicit mistica theologia pro contemplatione utilis. N. Cusa *add. I*   Reverendissimi patris domini Nicolai cardinalis sancti Petri ad vincula Brixinensis episcopi liber de visione dei explicit ad fratres et priorem in Tegernsee *add. L*   Reverendissimi patris domini Nicolai cardinalis sancti Petri ad vincula Brixinensis episcopi liber de visione dei anno 1454, infra octavam Epiphanie, ad fratres in Tegernsee *add. M*   Explicit de visione dei, et cetera, N.C.C. [=Nicolay de Cusa cardinalis] *add. N*   Reverendissimi patris domini Nicolai cardinalis sancti Petri ad vincula Brixinensis episcopi liber de visione dei ad fratres in Tegernsee. Explicit anno 1455, in vigilia assumptionis gloriose virginis Marie *add. O*   Reverendissimi patris domini Nicolai cardinalis sancti Petri ad vincula Brixinensis episcopi liber de visione dei ad fratres in Tegernsee etc. *add. P*   Finis eykone dei. Finis librorum reverendissimi patris domini Nicolai de Cusa cardinalis sancti Petri ad vincula et episcopi Brixinensis *add. R* Finis *add. T*   Explicit. Reverendissimi domini Nicolai cardinalis sancti Petri ad vincula Brixinensis episcopi liber de visione dei finit *add. V*   Finit theoria *manu alia⁴ additur in Z*   Libri de visione dei sive de icona R[everendissimi] P[atris] Nicolai de Cusa Finis *add. p*

wills to forsake me. I hasten toward the goal; I have almost finished the course; I anticipate being finished with it, because I aspire to the crown.[140] Draw me, O Lord, because no one can come unto You unless he be drawn by You.[141] |Draw me| so that, being drawn, I may be freed from this world and be joined unto You, the Absolute God, in an eternity of glorious life. Amen.

aBBReVIaTIONS

Ap.   *Apologia Doctae Ignorantiae (Nicolai de Cusa Opera Omnia,*
           Vol. II, edited by Raymond Klibansky; published by Felix
           Meiner Verlag, 1932).

DC   *De Coniecturis (Nicolai de Cusa Opera Omnia,* Vol. III,
           edited by Joseph Koch and Karl Bormann; published by
           Felix Meiner Verlag, 1972).

DD   *De Dato Patris Luminum (Nicolai de Cusa Opera Omnia,*
           Vol. IV (*Opuscula I*), edited by Paul Wilpert; published by
           Felix Meiner Verlag, 1959).

DI   *De Docta Ignorantia* (Latin-German edition: *Schriften des
           Nikolaus von Kues in deutscher Übersetzung,* published by
           Felix Meiner Verlag. Book I (Vol. 264a), edited and trans-
           lated by Paul Wilpert; 3rd edition with minor improvements
           by Hans G. Senger, 1979. Book II (Vol. 264b), edited and
           translated by Paul Wilpert; 2nd edition with minor improve-
           ments by Hans G. Senger, 1977. Book III (Vol. 264c), Latin
           text edited by Raymond Klibansky, introduction and transla-
           tion by Hans G. Senger, 1977).

DP   *De Possest* (Latin-German edition: *Schriften des Nikolaus
           von Kues in deutscher Übersetzung,* Vol. 285, edited and
           translated by Renate Steiger; published by Felix Meiner Ver-
           lag, 1973. Latin text reprinted—with J. Hopkins's trans-
           lation—by the University of Minnesota Press as a compo-
           nent of *A Concise Introduction to the Philosophy of Nicholas
           of Cusa,* 2nd edition, 1980).

IL   *De Ignota Litteratura* by John Wenck (Latin text edited by
           J. Hopkins and published in 1981 by The Arthur J. Banning
           Press as a component of *Nicholas of Cusa's Debate with
           John Wenck: A Translation and an Appraisal of De Ignota
           Litteratura,* 2nd edition, 1984).

MFCG   *Mitteilungen und Forschungsbeiträge der Cusanus-Gesell-
           schaft,* edited by Rudolf Haubst. A continuing series pub-
           lished in Mainz, Germany by Matthias-Grünewald Verlag.

NA   *Directio Speculantis seu De Non Aliud (Nicolai de Cusa Opera Omnia*, Vol. XIII, edited by Ludwig Baur and Paul Wilpert; published by Felix Meiner Verlag, 1944. Latin text reprinted—with J. Hopkins's English translation—by The Arthur J. Banning Press under the title *Nicholas of Cusa on God as Not-other: A Translation and an Appraisal of De Li Non Aliud*, 2nd ed., 1983).

PL   *Patrologia Latina*, edited by J.-P. Migne. Series published in Paris.

SHAW   *Sitzungsberichte der Heidelberger Akademie der Wissenschaften. Philosophisch-historische Klasse*; series published by Carl Winter Verlag.

VS   *De Venatione Sapientiae (Nicolai de Cusa Opera Omnia*, Vol. XII, edited by Raymond Klibansky and Hans G. Senger; published in the same volume with *De Apice Theoriae* by Felix Meiner Verlag, 1982).

The abbreviations for the books of the Bible are the standard ones.

BiblioGraphy

[Nicholas of Cusa]. *The Single Eye, Entituled the Vision of God*. Translated by Giles Randall. London: J. Streater, 1646.

[Nicholas of Cusa]. *La vision de Dieu*. Translated by Edmond Vansteenberghe. Louvain: Editions du Museum Lessianum, 1925.

[Nicholas of Cusa]. "De visione Dei. Die Gottes-Schau," pp. 93-219 of Vol. III of *Philosophisch-theologische Schriften* [*des Nikolaus von Kues*]. Translated by Dietlind and Wilhelm Dupré. Vienna: Herder, 1967.

[Nicholas of Cusa]. *The Vision of God*. Translated by Emma G. Salter. New York: Ungar, paper edition, 1978 (reprint of the 1928 London hardcover edition).

[Nicholas of Cusa]. *Scritti Filosofici*. Translated by Giovanni Santinello. Bologna: Zanichelli. Vol. I, 1965 (*Idiota; De Possest; Compendium; De Apice Theoriae*); Vol. II, 1980 (*Opuscula; Apologia Doctae Ignorantiae; De Visione Dei; De Beryllo*). Includes Santinello's edition of the Latin text of *De Visione Dei*.

[Nicholas of Cusa]. *Nicolai de Cusa Opera Omnia*. Vol. V: *Idiota. De Sapientia, De Mente, De Staticis Experimentis*. Edited by Renate Steiger and Ludwig Baur. Hamburg: F. Meiner, 1983. Vol. 12: *De Venatione Sapientiae. De Apice Theoriae*. Edited by Raymond Klibansky and Hans G. Senger. Hamburg: F. Meiner, 1982. Vol. 17: *Sermones II (1443-1452)*. Fascicle 1: *Sermones XXVII-XXXIX*. Edited by Rudolf Haubst and Hermann Schnarr. Hamburg: F. Meiner, 1983.

[Nicholas of Cusa]. *Acta Cusana. Quellen zur Lebensgeschichte des Nikolaus von Kues*. Vol. I, Issue 2: *1437 Mai 17 - 1450 Dezember 31*, edited by Erich Meuthen. Hamburg: F. Meiner, 1983.

Alcorta, José I. "Intuitividad y racionalidad en Nicolás de Cusa," *Crisis*, 14 (1967), 63-73.

Alvarez-Gómez, Mariano. "'Coincidentia oppositorum' e infinitud, codeterminantes de la idea de Dios según Nicolás de Cusa," *La Ciudad de Dios*, 176 (July-December 1963), 666-698.

————. "Peculiaridad de la pregunta sobre Dios según Nicolás de Cusa," *La Ciudad de Dios*, 177 (July-September 1964), 409-434.

————. "Añoranza y conocimiento de Dios en la obra de Nicolás de Cusa," pp. 651-685 of *Wahrheit und Verkündigung*. Edited by Leo Scheffczyk et al. (Festschrift for Michael Schmaus). Munich: F. Schöningh, 1967.

————. "Zur Metaphysik der Macht bei Nikolaus von Kues," *MFCG*, 14 (1980), 104-112.

Biechler, James E. "Nicholas of Cusa and the End of the Conciliar Movement: A Humanist Crisis of Identity," *Church History*, 44 (March 1975), 5-21.

————. "Christian Humanism Confronts Islam: Sifting the Qur'an with Nicholas of Cusa," *Journal of Ecumenical Studies*, 13 (Winter 1976), 1-14.

————. "Nicholas of Cusa and Muhammad: A Fifteenth-Century Encounter," *Downside Review*, 101 (January 1983), 50-59.

Biser, Eugen. "Nikolaus von Kues als Denker der unendlichen Einheit," *Tübinger Theologische Quartalschrift*, 146 (1966), 305-328.

Blumenberg, Hans. "The Cusan: The World as God's Self-Restriction," pp. 483-547 and 652-661 of his *The Legitimacy of the Modern Age*. Translated by Robert M. Wallace. Cambridge, Massachusetts: MIT Press, 1983.

Bodewig, Martin. "Zur Tugendlehre des jungen Cusanus," *MFCG*, 13 (1978), 214-224.

Bredow, Gerda von. "Der Gedanke der *singularitas* in der Altersphilosophie des Nikolaus von Kues," *MFCG*, 4 (1964), 375-383.

————. "Figura Mundi. Die Symbolik des Globusspieles von Nikolaus von Kues," pp. 193-199 of *Urbild und Abglanz. Beiträge zu einer Synopse von Weltgestalt und Glaubenswirklichkeit*. Edited by Johannes Tenzler. Regensburg: Verlag J. Habbel, 1972.

————. "Der Punkt als Symbol. Aufstieg von der Metaphysik zu Anschauung und Einung," *MFCG*, 12 (1977), 103-115.

————. "Die personale Existenz der Geistseele," *MFCG*, 14 (1980), 123-145.

Colomer, Eusebio. "Heimeric van den Velde entre Ramón Llull y Nicolás de Cusa," pp. 216-232 of *Joseph Vives zum goldenen Priesterjubiläum 20. Oktober 1963*. By Baudouin de Gaiffier *et al.* (Vol. 21 of Gesammelte Aufsätze zur Kulturgeschichte Spaniens). Münster: Aschendorff Verlag, 1963.

————. "Nicolás de Cusa: un pensamiento entre tradición y modernidad," *Pensamiento*, 20 (October-December 1964), 391-416.

Dangelmayr, Siegfried. "Vernunft und Glaube bei Nikolaus von Kues," *Tübinger Theologische Quartalschrift*, 148 (1968), 429-462.

Doyon, Jacques. "La christologie de Nicolas de Cues," pp. 171-189 of *Le Christ hier, aujourd'hui et demain* [Colloque de christologie tenu à l'Université Laval (21 et 22 mars 1975)]. Edited by Raymond Laflamme et Michel Gervais. Québec: Les Presses de l'Université Laval, 1976.

Duclow, Donald F. "The Dynamics of Analogy in Nicholas of Cusa," *International Philosophical Quarterly*, 21 (September 1981), 294-301.

————. "Anselm's Proslogion and Nicholas of Cusa's Wall of Paradise," *Downside Review*, 100 (January 1982), 22-30.

Flasch, Kurt. "Nikolaus von Kues und Pico della Mirandola," *MFCG*, 14 (1980), 113-120.

Floss, Pavel. "Cusanus und Comenius (†1670)," *MFCG*, 10 (1973), 172-190.

Frankl, Victor. "Metafísica catolica y matemática infinitesmal (Nicolás de Cues y Blaise Pascal)," *Ideas y Valores* (Bogata), 2 (1952), 445-471.

Fuehrer, Mark L. "Purgation, Illumination and Perfection in Nicholas of Cusa," *Downside Review*, 98 (July 1980), 169-189.

Gamberoni, Paul. "Cusanus und der italienische Humanismus," *Bijdragen. Tijdschrift voor Filosofie en Theologie*, 25 (1964), 398-417.

Gandillac, Maurice de. "Platonisme et aristotélisme chez Nicolas de Cues," pp. 7-23 of *Platon et Aristote à la Renaissance* (XVIᵉ Colloque international de Tours). Paris: J. Vrin, 1976.

Garin, Eugenio. "Vico e Cusano," *Bollettino del Centro di Studi Vichiani*, 7 (1977), 138-141.

Gebel, Doris. "Die 'Sapientes Nationum' bei Nikolaus von Kues, *Jahrbuch der Gesellschaft für niedersächsische Kirchengeschichte*, 76 (1978), 139-154.

Gómez Nogales, Salvador, editor. *Nicolás de Cusa en el V centenario de su muerte (1464-1964)*. Madrid: Instituto 'Luis Vives' de filosofia, 1967.

Haubst, Rudolf. "Schöpfer und Schöpfung. Zur spekulativ-mystischen Gotteserkenntnis des Nikolaus von Kues," *Wissenschaft und Weisheit*, 13 (1950), 167-172.

―――. "Die Bedeutung des Trinitätsgedankens bei Nikolaus von Kues," *Trierer Theologische Zeitschrift*, 61 (January-February 1952), 21-29.

―――. "Nikolaus von Kues vor dem verborgenen Gott," *Wissenschaft und Weisheit*, 23 (1960), 174-186.

―――. "Nikolaus von Kues ueber die Gotteskindschaft," pp. 29-46 of *Nicolò da Cusa. Relazioni tenute al Convegno Interuniversitario di Bressanone nel 1960*. Florence: G. Sansoni, 1962.

―――. "Die Thomas- und Proklos-Exzerpte des 'Nicolaus Treverensis' in Codicillus Strassburg 84," *MFCG*, 1 (1961), 17-51.

―――. *Nikolaus von Kues und die moderne Wissenschaft* (Kleine Schriften der Cusanus-Gesellschaft, 4). Trier: Paulinus-Verlag, 1963 (16 pp.).

―――. "Nikolaus von Kues und der Evolutionsgedanke," *Scholastik*, 39 (1964), 481-494.

―――. "Wort und Leitidee der 'repraesentatio' bei Nikolaus v. Kues," pp. 139-162 of *Der Begriff der Repraesentatio im Mittelalter. Stellvertretung, Symbol, Zeichen, Bild*. Edited by Albert Zimmermann with the assistance of Gudrun Vuillemin-Diem. Berlin: W. de Gruyter, 1971.

―――. "Gottes Wirken und die menschliche Freiheit," *Trierer Theologische Zeitschrift*, 88 (1979), 175-193.

―――. "Marginalien des Nikolaus von Kues zu Abaelard (oder: Abaelard, wie Cusanus ihn sah)," pp. 287-296 of *Petrus Abaelardus (1079-1142). Person, Werk und Wirkung* (Trierer Theologische Studien, Vol. 38). Edited by Rudolf Thomas *et al.* Trier: Paulinus-Verlag, 1980.

―――. "Nikolaus von Kues als Interpret und Verteidiger Meister Eckharts," pp. 75-96 of *Freiheit und Gelassenheit. Meister Eckhart heute*. Edited by Udo Kern. Mainz: Kaiser Verlag, 1980.

Hedtke, Ulrich. "Coincidentia oppositorum oder die verweltlichte Unendlichkeit—Dialektik und Systemdenken bei Nikolaus von Kues," pp. 19-54 of *Dialektik und Systemdenken. Historische Aspekte. Nikolaus von Kues. Französische Aufklärung, Schelling*. Edited by Helga Bergmann *et al.* Berlin: Akademie-Verlag, 1977.

Hedwig, Klaus. "Cusanus: Pyramis lucis et tenebrarum," Chap. 9 of his *Sphaera Lucis. Studien zur Intelligibilität des Seienden im Kontext der mittelalterlichen Lichtspekulation* (Beiträge zur Geschichte der Philosophie und Theologie des Mittelalters, New Series, Vol. 18). Münster: Aschendorff, 1980.

Heinz-Mohr, Gerd. *Nikolaus von Kues und die Konzilsbewegung* (Kleine Schriften der Cusanus-Gesellschaft, 3). Trier: Paulinus-Verlag, 1963.

Heller, Henry. "Nicholas of Cusa and Early French Evangelism," *Archiv für Reformationsgeschichte*, 63 (1972), 6-21.

Herold, Norbert. "'Subjektivität' als Problem der Cusanusinterpretation," *MFCG*, 14 (1980), 146-166.

Hirschberger, Johannes. "Gegenstand und Geist bei Nikolaus von Cues," *Studium Generale* (Berlin), 21 (1968), 274-284.

————. *Die Stellung des Nikolaus von Kues in der Entwicklung der deutschen Philosophie* (Sitzungsberichte der wissenschaftlichen Gesellschaft an der Johann Wolfgang Goethe-Universität Frankfurt am Main, Vol. 15, Number 3). Wiesbasden: F. Steiner, 1978.

Hoffmann, Ernst. "Gottesschau bei Meister Eckehart und Nikolaus von Cues," pp. 1033-1045 of Vol. II, *Festschrift. Heinrich Zangger*. Edited by Max Huber *et al.* Zurich: Rascher & Cie, 1935.

Hoffmann, Fritz. "'Entwicklung' und 'Harmonisierung'. Zur Stellung des Nikolaus von Kues in der Geschichte des Erkenntnisproblems," *MFCG*, 12 (1977), 72-102.

Hopkins, Jasper. "A Detailed Critique of Pauline Watts' *Nicolaus Cusanus: A Fifteenth-Century Vision of Man*," *Philosophy Research Archives*, 9 (1983), Microfiche Supplement, pp. 26-61.

Kaiser, Alfred. "Cusanus-Bibliographie, 4. Fortsetzung (1972 bis 1982) mit Ergänzungen," *MFCG*, 15 (1982), 121-147; 166-169. Also see the bibliographies in Vols. 1, 3, 6, and 10.

Koch, Josef. *Cusanus-Texte. 1. Predigten. 7. Untersuchungen über Datierung, Form, Sprache und Quellen. Kritisches Verzeichnis sämtlicher Predigten. SHAW*, 1942 (Jahrgang 1941/42).

————, editor. *Cusanus-Texte. IV. Briefwechsel des Nikolaus von Cues. Erste Sammlung. SHAW*, 1944 (Jahrgang 1942/43).

————. *Nikolaus von Cues und seine Umwelt. Untersuchungen zu Cusanus-Texte. IV. Briefe. Erste Sammlung. SHAW*, 1948 (Jahrgang 1944/48).

Koenigsberger, Dorothy. "The Infectious Imagination of Nicholas of Cusa," pp. 100-147 of her *Renaissance Man and Creative Thinking: A History of Concepts of Harmony 1400-1700*. Atlantic Highlands, N. J.: Humanities Press, 1979.

Laufner, Richard. "Eine Kurzbiographie des Nikolaus von Kues um 1550," *MFCG*, 15 (1982), 81-85.

Lohr, Charles. "Die Exzerptensammlung des Nikolaus von Kues aus den Werken Ramón Lulls," *Freiburger Zeitschrift für Philosophie und Theologie*, 30 (1983), 373-384.

Martínez Gomez, Luis. "El hombre 'Mensura rerum' en Nicolás de Cusa," *Pensamiento*, 21, (January-March 1965), 41-63.

Meinhardt, Helmut. "Nikolaus von Kues und der Nominalismus," pp. 177-193 of *Theologie und Menschenbild* (Festschrift for Ewald Link). Edited by Gerhard Dautzenberg *et al.* Frankfurt am Main: Peter Lang, 1978.

Miller, Clyde Lee, "Nicholas of Cusa and Philosophic Knowledge," *Proceedings of the American Catholic Philosophical Association*, 54 (1980), 155-163.

―――. "Nicholas of Cusa's *The Vision of God*," pp. 293-312 of *An Introduction to the Medieval Mystics of Europe*, edited by Paul E. Szarmach. Albany: State University of New York Press, 1984.

Muraro Vaiani, Luisa. "Congettura e precisione matematica in Nicolò Cusano," *Rivista di filosofia Neo-Scolastica*, 62 (January-April 1970), 163-172.

Norman, Julie C. "Nicholas of Cusa, Apostolate of Unity," *Downside Review*, 99 (January 1981), 59-74.

Oehl, Wilhelm, editor. *Deutsche Mystikerbriefe des Mittelalters 1100-1550*. Darmstadt: Wissenschaftliche Buchgesellschaft, 1972 (reprint of the 1931 edition). [Pp. 531-569 contain German translations of some of Nicholas's Latin letters.]

Oppenheimer, Oscar. "Der Wahrheitsgehalt mystischer Erfahrung. Oder: Mit Cusanus über Cusanus hinaus," *Zeitschrift für philosophische Forschung*, 26 (1972), 29-41.

Otto, Stephan. "Langage dialectique et silence hiérophanique. L'horizon de la métaphysique chez Proclus, Cusanus et Hegel," pp. 105-114 of *Prospettive sul sacro*. By Enrico Castelli *et al.* (Archivio di filosofia). Padova: Cedam, 1975.

Pätzold, Detlev. *Einheit und Andersheit. Die Bedeutung kategorialer neubildungen in der Philosophie des Nikolaus Cusanus*. Cologne: Pahl-Rugenstein, 1981.

Pralle, Ludwig. *Die Wiederentdeckung des Tacitus. Ein Beitrag zur Geistesgeschichte Fuldas und zur Biographie des jungen Cusanus*. Fulda: Verlag Parzeller, 1952.

Raeder, Siegfried. "Der Christus des Korans in der Sicht des Nikolaus von Kues," pp. 71-93 of *Toleranz und Absolutheitsanspruch*. Edited by Willi Höpfner. Wiesbaden: Breklumer Verlag, 1975.

Rescher, Nicholas. "Nicholas of Cusa on the Qur'ān: A Fifteenth-Century Encounter with Islam," *Muslim World*, 55 (July 1965), 195-202.

Röhricht, Rainer. "Die Vielfalt der einen Wahrheit," pp. 23-38 of *Ärger mit der Wahrheit. Denken - Leben - Glauben*. Edited by Gerd Heinz-Mohr. Cologne: Wienand, 1972.

Rossmann, Heribert. "Der Magister Marquard Sprenger in München und seine Kontroversschriften zum Konzil von Basel und zur mystischen Theologie," pp. 350-411 in *Mysterium der Gnade* (Festschrift for Johann Auer). Edited by Heribert Rossmann and Joseph Ratzinger. Regensburg: F. Pustet, 1975.

Saitta, Giuseppe. *Nicolò Cusano e l'umanesimo italiano*. Bologna: Editrice Tamari, 1957.

Santinello, Giovanni. "Mittelalterliche Quellen der ästhetischen Weltanschauung des Nikolaus von Kues," pp. 679-685 of *Die Metaphysik im Mittelalter. Ihr Ursprung und ihre Bedeutung*. Edited by Paul Wilpert. Berlin: W. de Gruyter, 1963.

―――. "Nikolaus von Kues und Petrarca," *MFCG*, 4 (1964), 174-197.

―――. *Introduzione a Niccolò Cusano*. Bari: Laterza, 1971.

―――. "Cusano e Vico: a proposito di una tesi di K. O. Apel," *Bollettino del Centro di Studi Vichiani*, 7 (1977), 141-150.

Schär, Hans R. "Spiel und Denken beim späten Cusanus," *Theologische Zeitschrift* (Basel), 26 (November/December 1970), 410-418.

Schneider, Stefan. *Die "kosmische" Grösse Christi als Ermöglichung seiner universalen Heilswirksamkeit an Hand des kosmogenetischen Entwurfes Teilhard de Chardins und der Christologie des Nikolaus von Kues.* Münster: Aschendorff Verlag, 1979.

Schramm, Michael-Angelo. "Zur Lehre vom Zeichen innerhalb des Compendiums des Nikolaus von Kues," *Zeitschrift für philosophische Forschung*, 33 (1979), 616-620.

Schultz, Rudolf. *Die Staatsphilosophie des Nikolaus von Kues.* Meisenheim: A. Hain, 1948.

Senger, Hans G. "Die Nikolaus von Kues-Ausgabe als Beispiel einer historisch-kritischen Edition," *Zeitschrift für philosophische Forschung*, 38 (1984), 73-83.

Sommer, Wolfgang. "Cusanus und Schleiermacher," *Neue Zeitschrift für systematische Theologie und Religionsphilosophie*, 12 (1970), 85-102.

Stachel, Günter. "Schweigen vor Gott. Bemerkungen zur mystischen Theologie der Schrift *De visione Dei*," *MFCG*, 14 (1980), 167-181.

Stallmach, Josef. "Auspicios del moderno filosofar en el pensamiento cusánico," *Folia humanistica*, 2 (November 1964), 963-975.

―――. "Zum Charakter der cusanischen Metaphysik," *MFCG*, 14 (1980), 87-103.

Sullivan, Donald. "Nicholas of Cusa as Reformer: the Papal Legation to the Germanies, 1451-1452," *Mediaeval Studies*, 36 (1974), 382-428.

Ullman, B. L. "Manuscripts of Nicholas of Cues," pp. 357-364 of his *Studies in the Italian Renaissance*. Rome: Edizioni di Storia e Letteratura, 2nd edition, 1973.

Vansteenberghe, Edmond. "Quelques lectures de jeunesse de Nicolas de Cues d'après un manuscrit inconnu de sa bibliothèque," *Archives d'histoire doctrinale et littéraire du Moyen Age*, 3 (1928), 275-284.

Verd, Gabriel M. "Ser y nombre de Dios en Nicolás de Cusa," *Miscelánea Comillas*, 52 (1969), 29-59.

―――. "Dios transcendente e inmanente en Nicolás de Cusa," *Miscelánea Comillas*, 53 (January-June 1970), 163-195.

Volkmann-Schluck, Karl-Heinz. "La filosofía de Nicolás de Cusa. Una forma previa de la metafísica moderna," *Revista de Filosofía*, 17 (1958), 437-458.

―――. "Nicolás de Cusa. Idea de un humanismo cristiano," *Folia humanistica*, 2 (November 1964), 919-927.

Walsh, James J. "Cardinal Nicholas of Cusa," pp. 85-114 of his *Catholic Churchmen in Science* (Freeport, N.Y.: Books for Libraries Press, 1966; reprint of the 1917 edition).

Wentzlaff-Eggebert, Friedrich-Wilhelm. "Die Wandlung der Mystik in der Philosophie des Nikolaus Cusanus," pp. 150-160 of his *Deutsche Mystik zwischen Mittelalter und Neuzeit. Einheit und Wandlung ihrer Erscheinungsformen.* Berlin: W. de Gruyter, 3rd edition, 1969.

Wisser, Richard. "Nikolaus Cusanus im 'lebendigen Spiegel' der Philosophie von Karl Jaspers," *Zeitschrift für philosophische Forschung*, 19 (1965), 528-540.

Wyller, Egil A. "Identität und Kontradiktion. Ein Weg zu Cusanus' Unendlichkeitsidee," *MFCG*, 15 (1982), 104-120.

select Related works

[Anselm of Canterbury]. *Anselm of Canterbury: Volumes One - Three.* Edited and translated by Jasper Hopkins and Herbert Richardson. New York: The Edwin Mellen Press, Vol. I, 1974 (2nd edition, 1975); Vols. II and III, 1976.

Blumenberg, Hans. "Neoplatonismen und Pseudoplatonismen in der Kosmologie und Mechanik der frühen Neuzeit," pp. 447-471 (with discussion on pp. 472-474) of *Le Néoplatonisme* by Cornelia de Vogel *et al.* Paris: Editions du Centre National de la Recherche Scientifique, 1971.

Bonaventure (Saint). *The Soul's Journey into God. The Tree of Life. The Life of St. Francis.* Translated by Ewert Cousins. New York: Paulist Press, 1978.

Caputo, John D. "Fundamental Themes in Meister Eckhart's Mysticism," *The Thomist,* 42 (April 1978), 197-225.

Clark, James M. *The Great German Mystics: Eckhart, Tauler, and Suso.* Oxford: Blackwell's, 1949.

————. *Meister Eckhart: An Introduction to the Study of His Works, with an Anthology of His Sermons.* London: T. Nelson, 1957.

Combes, André. *Essai sur la critique de Ruysbroeck par Gerson.* Paris: J. Vrin, Vol. I, 1945; Vol. II, 1948.

————. *La théologie mystique de Gerson. Profil de son évolution.* Paris: Desclée et Socii Editores Pontificii, 1963 (Vol. I) and 1964 (Vol. II).

Copleston, Frederick. *A History of Philosophy.* Westminster, Maryland: The Newman Press, Vol. II (1950); Vol. III (1953).

Courtenay, William J. "Nominalism and Late Medieval Religion," pp. 26-59 of *The Pursuit of Holiness in Late Medieval and Renaissance Religion.* Edited by Charles Trinkhaus and Heiko A. Oberman. Leiden: E. J. Brill, 1974.

Cousins, Ewert. *Bonaventure and the Coincidence of Opposites.* Chicago: Franciscan Herald Press, 1978.

Dan, Joseph and Frank Talmage, editors. *Studies in Jewish Mysticism: Proceedings of Regional Conferences Held at the University of California, Los Angeles and McGill University in April, 1978.* Cambridge, Massachusetts: Association for Jewish Studies, 1982.

Denifle, Heinrich S. *Die deutschen Mystiker des 14. Jahrhunderts. Beitrag zur Deutung ihrer Lehre.* Fribourg: Paulusverlag, 1951.

Dionysius (Pseudo-). *Dionysiaca.* Paris: Desclée de Brouwer et Cie, 1937 (Vol. I) and 1950 (Vol. II).

————. *The Divine Names and Mystical Theology.* Translated and introduced by John D. Jones. Milwaukee: Marquette University Press, 1980.

Ebeling, Heinrich. *Meister Eckharts Mystik.* Stuttgart: W. Kohlhammer, 1941 (reprinted 1966 by Scientia Verlag in Aalen).

Emery, Kent. "Mysticism and the Coincidence of Opposites in Sixteenth- and Seventeenth-Century France," *Journal of the History of Ideas*, 45 (January-March 1984), 3-23.

Erigena, John Scotus. *Iohannis Scotti Erivgenae Periphyseon (De Divisione Naturae)*. Edited and translated by I. P. Sheldon-Williams, with the collaboration of Ludwig Bieler. Dublin: The Dublin Institute for Advanced Studies, Vol. I, 1968; Vol. II, 1972; Vol. III, 1981.

Gabriel, Astrik L. " 'Via Antiqua' and 'Via Moderna' and the Migration of Paris Students and Masters to the German Universities in the Fifteenth Century," pp. 439-483 of Vol. 8 of *Miscellania Mediaevalia*. Berlin: W. de Gruyter, 1974.

[Gerson, Jean]. *Ioannis Carlerii de Gerson de Mystica Theologia*. Edited by André Combes. Lucani, Italy: Thesaurus Mundi, 1958.

[Gerson, Jean]. *Selections from* A Deo exivit, Contra curiositatem studentium *and* De mystica theologia speculativa. Introduced, edited, and translated by Steven E. Ozment. Leiden: E. J. Brill, 1969.

[_____]. *Oeuvres Complètes*. Edited by Palémon Glorieux. Paris: Desclée & Cie, 1960-1973 (10 vols.).

[_____]. *Collectorium super Magnificat*, pp. 163-534 of Vol. 8 of *Oeuvres complètes*. Edited by Palémon Glorieux. Paris: Desclée & Cie, 1971.

Haas, Alois M. "Meister Eckharts mystische Bildlehre," pp. 113-138 of *Der Begriff der Repraesentatio im Mittelalter. Stellvertretung, Symbol, Zeichen, Bild.* Edited by Albert Zimmermann with the assistance of Gudrun Vuillemin-Diem. Berlin: W. de Gruyter, 1971.

Hall, Roland. "Dialectic," *Encyclopedia of Philosophy*, Vol. II, pp. 385-389. New York: Macmillan, 1967.

Happold, Frederick C. *Mysticism: A Study and an Anthology*. Baltimore: Penguin Books, 1971.

Hartig, Michael. *Die Benediktinerabtei Tegernsee 746-1803. Kurzer Überblick über ihre Geschichte und ihre Verdienste um Wissenschaft und Kunst*. Munich: Schnell and Steiner, 1946.

Heimsoeth, Heinz. *Die Sechs Grossen Themen der abendländischen Metaphysik und der Ausgang des Mittelalters*. Mainz: W. Kohlhammer, 1965 (5th edition).

Hopkins, Jasper. "Augustine on Foreknowledge and Free Will," *International Journal for Philosophy of Religion*, 8 (1977), 111-126.

_____. "On Understanding and Preunderstanding St. Anselm," *The New Scholasticism*, 52 (Spring 1978), 243-260.

_____. "Anselm on Freedom and the Will: A Discussion of G. Stanley Kane's Interpretation of Anselm," *Philosophy Research Archives*, 9 (1983), 471-493.

_____. "On an Alleged Definitive Interpretation of *Proslogion* 2-4: A Discussion of G. Schufreider's *An Introduction to Anselm's Argument*," *Southern Journal of Philosophy*, 19 (Spring 1981), 129-139.

Hugh, of Balma. *Mystica Theologia* [pp. 699-730 of *Sancti Bonaventurae ex ordine minorum, S. R. E. episcopi card. albanen. eximii ecclesiae doctoris operum tomus septimus* (Rome: Vatican Press, 1596; pp. 699-730 are reprinted from the Strasburg edition of 1495)]. A copy is located in the British Museum, Department of Printed Books, shelfmark L.19 f.3 vol. 7.

Katz, Steven T., editor. *Mysticism and Philosophical Analysis.* London: Sheldon Press, 1978.

Kelley, Carl F. *Meister Eckhart on Divine Knowledge.* New Haven: Yale University Press, 1977.

Kertz. Karl G. "Meister Eckhart's Teaching on the Birth of the Divine Word in the Soul," *Traditio,* 15 (1959), 327-363.

Kieckhefer, Richard. "Meister Eckhart's Conception of Union with God," *Harvard Theological Review,* 71 (July-October 1978), 203-225.

Lossky, Vladimir. *Théologie négative et connaissance de Dieu chez Maître Eckhart.* Paris: J. Vrin, 1960.

Martin, C. B. "A Religious Way of Knowing," *Mind,* 61 (October 1952), 497-512.

Matthews, Gareth B. "Paradoxical Statements," *American Philosophical Quarterly,* 11 (April 1974), 133-139.

Mavrodes, George I. "The Experience of God," Chap. 3 of his *Belief in God: A Study in the Epistemology of Religion.* New York: Random House, 1970.

————. "Real v. Deceptive Mystical Experiences," pp. 235-258 of *Mysticism and Philosophical Analysis.* Edited by Steven Katz. London: Sheldon Press, 1978.

McGinn, Bernard. "Meister Eckhart on God as Absolute Unity," pp. 128-139 of *Neoplatonism and Christian Thought.* Edited by Dominic J. O'Meara. Albany: State University of New York Press, 1982.

————. "Theological Summary," pp. 24-61 of *Meister Eckhart: The Essential Sermons, Commentaries, Treatises, and Defense.* Translated and introduced by Edmund Colledge and Bernard McGinn. New York: Paulist Press, 1981.

Meuthen, Erich. "Peter von Erkelenz (ca. 1430-1494)," *Zeitschrift für Aachener Geschichtsvereins,* 84-85 (1977-1978), 701-744.

Mieth, Dietmar. *Die Einheit von vita activa und vita contemplativa in den deutschen Predigten und Traktaten Meister Eckharts und bei Johannes Tauler. Untersuchungen zur Struktur des christlichen Lebens.* Regensburg: F. Pustet, 1969.

Oberman, Heiko A. "Some Notes on the Theology of Nominalism. With Attention to its Relation to the Renaissance," *Harvard Theological Review,* 53 (1960), 47-76.

————. *The Harvest of Medieval Theology: Gabriel Biel and Late Medieval Nominalism.* Cambridge, Massachusetts: Harvard University Press, 1963.

Osment, Steven E. *Homo Spiritualis: A Comparative Study of the Anthropology of Johannes Tauler, Jean Gerson and Martin Luther (1509-16) in the Context of their Theological Thought.* Leiden: E. J. Brill, 1969.

————. *Mysticism and Dissent: Religious Ideology and Social Protest in the Sixteenth Century.* New Haven: Yale University Press, 1973.

Plantinga, Alvin. *Does God Have a Nature?* Milwaukee: Marquette University Press, 1980.

Quint, Josef. "Mystik und Sprache. Ihr Verhältnis zueinander insbesondere in der spekulativen Mystik Meister Eckharts," *Deutsche Vierteljahrsschrift für Literaturwissenschaft und Geistesgeschichte,* 27 (1953), 48-76.

————, editor and translator. *Meister Eckehart. Deutsche Predigten und Traktate.* Munich: Carl Hanser Verlag, 1955. [See "Einleitung," pp. 9-50.]

Rice, Eugene F. "Jacques Lefèvre d'Étaples and the Medieval Christian Mystics," pp. 89-124 of *Florilegium Historiale: Essays Presented to Wallace K. Ferguson.* Edited by J. G. Rowe and W. H. Stockdale. Toronto: University of Toronto Press, 1971.

Rowe, William L. "Religious Experience and the Principle of Credulity," *International Journal for Philosophy of Religion,* 13 (1982), 85-92.

Schwab, Johann B. *Johannes Gerson. Professor der Theologie und Kanzler der Universität Paris.* Würzburg, 2 vols., 1858.

Smart, Ninian. "Interpretation and Mystical Experience," *Religious Studies,* 1 (1965), 75-87 [also printed, with minor emendations, as pp. 133-143 of *Art, Mind, and Religion: Proceedings of the 1965 Oberlin Colloquium in Philosophy.* Edited by W. H. Capitan and D. D. Merrill (Pittsburgh: University of Pittsburgh Press, n. d.)].

————. "Mystical Experience," pp. 133-143 and 156-158 of *Art, Mind, and Religion: Proceedings of the 1965 Oberlin Colloquium in Philosophy.* Edited by W. H. Capitan and D. D. Merrill. Pittsburgh: University of Pittsburgh Press, n.d.

Staal, Frits. *Exploring Mysticism: A Methodological Essay.* Berkeley: University of California Press, 1975.

Stace. Walter T. *The Teachings of the Mystics.* New York: The New American Library, 1960.

————. *Mysticism and Philosophy.* New York: Macmillan, 1960.

Théry, G., editor. "Edition critique des pièces relatives au procès d'Eckhart contenues dans le manuscrit 33^b de la Bibliothèque de Soest," *Archives d'histoire doctrinale et littéraire du moyen âge,* 1 (1926-1927), 129-207.

Wentzlaff-Eggebert, Friedrich-Wilhelm. *Deutsche Mystik zwischen Mittelalter und Neuzeit. Einheit und Wandlung ihrer Erscheinungsformen.* Berlin: W. de Gruyter, 3rd edition, 1969.

Yandell, Keith E. "Religious Experience and Rational Appraisal," *Religious Studies,* 10 (June 1974), 173-187.

————. "The Ineffability Theme," *International Journal for Philosophy of Religion,* 10 (1979), 209-231.

pRaenotanòa

1. In the English translation strokes are used in place of brackets in order to conduce to readability. Words and phrases thus "bracketed" are supplied by the translator to fill out the meaning implied by the Latin text.

2. In the Interpretive Study commas and periods are occasionally placed outside of quotation marks in order to emphasize that they are not included in what is being cited or mentioned.

3. In the Notes to the Interpretive Study longer Latin passages that stand by themselves are not italicized.

4. All translations are mine, unless otherwise indicated. Many of these translations are taken verbatim from my previous works; sometimes, however, italics are added or various emendations made. E.g., most translations of Anselm are taken from *Anselm of Canterbury: Volumes I-III* (New York: The Edwin Mellen Press, 1974-76). These volumes contain, in translation, Anselm's complete treatises, and they are more literal and more accurate than the earlier Harper and Row Torchbooks *Truth, Freedom, and Evil* and *Trinity, Incarnation, and Redemption*, which should no longer be regarded.

5. The present bibliography is supplementary to the bibliographies contained in my previous works *A Concise Introduction to the Philosophy of Nicholas of Cusa* and *Nicholas of Cusa on Learned Ignorance: A Translation and an Appraisal of De Docta Ignorantia*. Accordingly, not all the entries in the present bibliography are directly relevant to the present topics and themes; and some entries that are directly relevant occur in the earlier bibliographies. Moreover, practical considerations have necessitated keeping short the number of entries listed under "Select Related Works."

6. All references to Nicholas of Cusa's works are to the Latin texts—specifically to the following texts in the following editions (unless explicitly indicated otherwise):

    A. Heidelberg Academy edition of the *Opera Omnia Cusana: De Concordantia Catholica; Sermones; De Coniecturis; De Deo Abscondito; De Quaerendo Deum; De Filiatione Dei; De Dato Patris Luminum; Coniectura de Ultimis Diebus; De Genesi; Apologia Doctae Ignorantiae; Idiota* (1983 edition) *de Sapientia, de Mente, de Staticis Experimentis; De Pace Fidei; De Li Non Aliud* (Banning reprint); *De Venatione Sapientiae; Compendium; De Apice Theoriae.*

    B. Texts authorized by the Heidelberg Academy and published in the Latin-German editions of Felix Meiner Verlag's Philosophische Bibliothek: *De Docta Ignorantia, De Beryllo, De Possest* (Minnesota reprint).

285

C. Paris edition (1514) of the *Opera Cusana: Complementum Theologicum, De Aequalitate, De Principio* (=Paris edition, Vol. II, Part I, fol. 7ʳ-11ᵛ).

D. Strasburg edition (1488) of the *Opera Cusana* as edited by Paul Wilpert and republished by W. de Gruyter (Berlin, 1967, 2 vols.): *Cribratio Alkoran, De Ludo Globi*.

The references given for some of these treatises indicate book and chapter, for others margin number and line, and for still others page and line. Readers should have no difficulty determining which is which when they consult the particular Latin text. E.g., "*DI* II, 6 (125:19-20)" indicates *De Docta Ignorantia*, Book II, Chap. 6, margin number 125, lines 19-20. And "*Ap.* 8:14-16" indicates *Apologia Doctae Ignorantiae*, p. 8, lines 14-16.

notes

NOTES TO THE PREFACE

1. For a brief explanation of the meaning of the term "dialectical" see n. 264 of the Notes to the Interpretive Study.

2. In n. 334 of the present study I seek also to correct certain misjudgments about Anselm of Canterbury. As a supplement to that note see the articles by me that are listed in the bibliography. Also see my *Anselm of Canterbury: Volume Four: Hermeneutical and Textual Problems in the Complete Treatises of St. Anselm* (New York: The Edwin Mellen Press, 1976). In these works I modify various points that were made in my earlier *Companion to the Study of St. Anselm* (1972).

NOTES TO THE INTERPRETIVE STUDY

1. The former Austrian city of Brixen is today the Italian city of Bressanone.

2. Edmond Vansteenberghe, *Autour de la Docte Ignorance. Une controverse sur la Théologie mystique au XVᵉ siècle* [Vol. 14 of Beiträge zur Geschichte der Philosophie des Mittelalters (Münster: Aschendorff, 1915)], p. 108n. Cited hereafter as "Vansteenberghe, *Autour*". [N.B. Ludwig Baur's and Josef Koch's corrections for Vansteenberghe's edition: pp. 107-110 of Koch's *Cusanus-Texte. IV. Briefwechsel des Nikolaus von Cues. Erste Sammlung, SHAW,* 1944 (Jahrgang 1942/43). My quotations and translations from Vansteenberghe's edition *include* the corrections made by Baur and Koch.] Also see Josef Koch, *Nikolaus von Cues und seine Umwelt. Untersuchungen zu Cusanus-Texte. IV. Briefe. Erste Sammlung, SHAW,* 1948 (Jahrgang 1944/48), pp. 111-152. Erich Meuthen, *Nikolaus von Kues 1401-1464. Skizze einer Biographie* (Münster: Aschendorff, 4th edition, 1979), pp. 85-86.

3. Vansteenberge, *Autour*, pp. 126 and 129. (In Letter 11 Nicholas accepts the counsel of Bernard, Prior at Tegernsee; and in Letter 14 he indicates that he is counting on the arrival of the Tegernsee delegation that visited the nunnery at Sonnenberg.)

4. *Ibid.*, p. 122 (Letter 9).

5. *Ibid.*, p. 110 (Letter 3, from Caspar to Nicholas, Sept. 22, 1452): "Est autem hec quaestio utrum anima devota sine intellectus cognicione, vel etiam sine cogitacione previa vel concomitante, solo affectu seu per mentis apicem quam vocant synderesim Deum attingere possit, et in ipsum immediate moveri aut ferri."

6. Hereafter Pseudo-Dionysius will be referred to without the prefix "Pseudo." Nicholas, like his contemporaries, believed that the author of *De Caelestis Hierarchia, De Nominibus Divinis, De Mystica Theologia*, etc., was Dionysius the Areopagite, converted in Athens by St. Paul (Acts 17:34). In fact, however, these works did not appear until the beginning of the sixth century and are the product

of an unknown writer who assumed Dionysius's name.

7. Dionysius, *De Mystica Theologia*, Chap. 1, Sec. 3 [*Dionysiaca* (Paris: Desclée de Brouwer et Cie), Vol. I (1937), p. 575].

8. Dionysius, *De Nominibus Divinis*, Chap. 7, Sec. 1 (*Dionysiaca, op. cit.*, Vol. I, p. 386).

9. John Gerson (1363-1429) became Chancellor of the University of Paris in 1395.

10. "Theologia mistica est extensio animi in Deum per amoris desiderium." "Theologia mistica est motio anagogica, hoc est sursum ductiva in Deum, per amorem fervidum et purum." "Theologia mistica est cognitio experimentalis habita de Deo per amoris unitivi complexum." "Theologia mistica est sapientia, id est sapida notitia habita de Deo, dum ei supremus apex affective potentie rationalis per amorem coniungitur et unitur." "Mistica theologia est cognitio experimentalis habita de Deo per coniunctionem affectus spiritualis cum eodem . . . ."

11. The foregoing quotations are translated from Gerson's 28th consideration in his *De Mystica Theologia. Tractatus Primus Speculativus*, edited by André Combes [in his *Ioannis Carlerii de Gerson de Mystica Theologia*] (Lucani, Italy: Thesaurus Mundi, 1958), p. 72. According to Combes [*Essai sur la critique de Ruysbroeck par Gerson* (Paris: J. Vrin, Vol. I, 1945), p. 566] the *Tractatus Primus Speculativus* dates from 1402-1403 and formed Gerson's lectures during that academic year. The *Tractatus Secundus Practicus* was finished in 1407. Both parts were published in 1408 as a complete work. Combes' publication of 1958 also includes Gerson's *Annotatio doctorum aliquorum qui de contemplatione locuti sunt* (1402-1403) and his *Elucidatio Scolastica Theologiae Mysticae* (1424). The entire volume will be referred to hereafter as "Combes". And the following abbreviations will be used: "*Mys. Theol. Spec.,*" "*Mys. Theol. Prac.,*" and "*Elucidatio Scolastica.*"

12. Gerson, *Mys. Theol. Spec.*, 43rd consideration (Combes, p. 117). Also note Gerson's *Collectorium super Magnificat*, 7th tractate [in Vol. 8 (1971) of Gerson's *Oeuvres complètes*, ed. by Palémon Glorieux (Paris: Desclée et Cie), p. 308]: "Multi multa locuti sunt, et nos multotiens iam inter multos, de et super verbis Dionysii dum tractat de mystica theologia et divina sapientia christianorum. Dixerunt aliqui quod consistit haec theologia in abnegatione omnium a Deo; alii quod in affectu et dilectione; nonnulli quod in intelligentiae puritate; alii quod in mentis ad Deum collectione vel unione; alii quod in devotione seu mentis elevatione; alii quod in raptu vel extasi vel mentis alienatione." The *Oeuvres complètes* will be cited hereafter as "Glorieux". The abbreviated title "*Super Magnificat*" will also be used.

13. Latin quoted from Gerson's *Mys. Theol. Spec.*, 28th consideration (Combes, pp. 72-73). "Mystical theology is irrational, mindless, foolish wisdom . . . ." See n. 8 above. Cf. Gerson, *Mys. Theol. Spec.*, 43rd consideration (Combes, p. 117, lines 9-10 from top).

14. Gerson, opening section of *Elucidatio Scolastica* (Combes, p. 222).

15. Gerson, *Mys. Theol. Spec.*, 41st consideration (Combes, pp. 105-112).

16. Gerson, *ibid.*, 29th consideration (Combes, pp. 73-74).

17. Gerson, *ibid.*, 29th and 30th considerations (Combes, pp. 74 and 77).

18. Gerson, *Elucidatio Scolastica*, 9th consideration (Combes, p. 229). Cf. *Super Magnificat*, 7th tractate (Glorieux, Vol. 8, p. 316, lines 8-9).

19. Gerson, *Mys. Theol. Spec.*, 30th consideration (Combes, p. 79).

20. Gerson, *ibid.* (Combes, p. 78).

21. Note Gerson, *Elucidatio Scolastica*, 11th consideration (Combes, p. 230): "Stare nequit ut theologia mistica sit in hominis mente sine qualicumque Dei cognitione."

22. Gerson, *Elucidatio Scolastica*, 8th consideration (Combes, p. 229). Gerson borrows this formulation of Augustine's idea from Hugh of Balma's *Mystica Theologia*. N.B. Hugh's response to Augustine.

23. Gerson, *Mys. Theol. Spec.*, 30th consideration (Combes, p. 78).

24. Gerson, *ibid.*, 2nd consideration (Combes, p. 10).

25. Gerson, *ibid.*, 28th consideration (Combes, p. 70): "Cognitio Dei per theologiam misticam melius acquiritur per penitentem affectum, quam per investigantem intellectum . . . ." N.B.: Gerson uses the term "*intellectus*" in several senses. Sometimes, as in the present instance, it refers to the intellectual generally, in contrast to the affectional; at these times it is not being distinguished from *ratio*, or reason. At other times, however, it *is* contrasted with, and distinguished from, *ratio*—which is regarded as inferior to *intellectus*; at these times it is often called "*intelligentia simplex*" and is described as "the cognitive power of soul which receives immediately from God a natural light in which and through which—when we grasp terms—first principles are known to be true and altogether certain" [*Mys. Theol. Spec.*, 10th consideration (Combes, p. 26)]. By contrast, *ratio* is "the cognitive power of soul which deduces conclusions from premises, which derives the nonperceived from the perceived, and which abstracts quiddities—without needing any bodily organ for its own operation" [*ibid.*, 11th consideration (Combes, p. 29)]. Finally, the expressions "*intelligentia simplex*" and "*intelligentia pura*" should not be confused. Gerson uses the former to indicate a faculty—or, perhaps better, an operation—of the rational soul. By contrast, he uses the latter to indicate a state of mind that is free of all images and concepts of whatever is other than God; *intelligentia pura* is not *spiritus* but belongs to *spiritus*. The expression "*intelligentia simplex*" occurs, e.g., in *Mys. Theol. Spec.*, 10th consideration (Combes, p. 26). The expression "*pura intelligentia*" occurs in *Mys. Theol. Prac.*, 12th consideration (Combes, p. 208); cf. *Mys. Theol. Spec.*, 25th consideration (Combes, p. 65, next to last line); this expression also occurs in *Super Magnificat*, 7th tractate (Glorieux, Vol. 8, p. 316, line 4; cf. the expression "*intelligentiae depuratio*" on p. 315, lines 5-6 from bottom).

26. Gerson, *Super Magnificat*, 7th tractate (cf. Glorieux, Vol. 8, p. 311, line 7 with p. 318, lines 12-13). Also note *ibid.*, pp. 308-309: "Relinquitur tandem haec depurata et expolita seu colata theologiae mysticae descriptio, dicendo quod est experimentalis Dei perceptio. Ponitur autem perceptio potius quam cognitio, quia generalis est terminus ad omnem vim mentis, scilicet rationalem, concupiscibilem et irascibilem, vel ad vim apprehensivam et affectivam, quamvis nihil vere videatur percipi quin vis apprehensiva concurrat; alioquin vis affectiva ferri posset in incog-

nitum, quod aliqui nedum concedunt, sed hoc probare contendunt."

27. E.g., the experience is said to be nonspeculative, joyous, ecstatic, uniting, transforming, fulfilling. It is an experience of that which is ineffable and indescribable, except symbolically.

28. Gerson, *Mys. Theol. Spec.*, 42nd consideration (Combes, p. 113). Cf. *Super Magnificat*, 7th tractate (Glorieux, Vol. 8, p. 307, lines 5-6). Also note *Super Magnificat*, 7th tractate (Glorieux, Vol. 8, p. 314): ". . . quemadmodum devotissima mens laicorum simplicium pertingere potest ad experimentalem Dei perceptionem seu theologiam mysticam quae in unione consistit mentis ad Deum . . . ."

29. Gerson, *Mys. Theol. Spec.*, 41st consideration (Combes, p. 105). Gerson also uses the expression "*theologia mystica*" in several other less common senses, as when he writes: "in anima contemplativa amor et mistica theologia aut oratio perfecta, aut idem sunt aut se invicem presupponunt" [*ibid.*, 43rd consideration (Combes, pp. 116-117)].

30. Gerson, *ibid.*, 41st consideration (Combes, p. 105). See *ibid.* (Combes, p. 107) for the expression "*spiritualis transformatio.*"

31. Gerson, *Super Magnificat*, 7th tractate (Glorieux, Vol. 8, p. 311, lines 2-5).

32. I.e., the pathway of pure understanding and the pathway of devotion. Note *Super Magnificat*, 7th tractate (Glorieux, Vol. 8, p. 315, last paragraph). Also note *ibid.*, p. 301: "Describitur autem devotio secundum doctores, nominatim Hugonem in suo De oratione: devotio est elevatio mentis in Deum per pium et humilem affectum, fide, spe et caritate subnixum. Nihil hac descriptione verius, nihil lucidius, nihil proposito nostro simplicium documento accommodatius tradi potuerat."

33. E.g., Johann Schwab, "Gersons mystische Theologie," Chap. 7 of his *Johannes Gerson. Professor der Theologie und Kanzler der Universität Paris* (Würzburg, 2 vols., 1858), Vol. I, p. 329. Schwab speaks of a *scheinbarer Widerspruch*.

34. "Posuimus itaque theologiam misticam esse amorem extaticum, qui consequitur ad intelligentiam ipsius spiritus, que intelligentia utique caret nubibus fantasmatum. Propterea necesse est eum, qui vult mistice theologie se tradere conari ad hanc puram intelligentiam; alioquin amorem inde subsequentem qua ratione compararet?" *Mys. Theol. Prac.*, 12th consideration (Combes, p. 208).

35. *Super Magnificat*, 7th tractate (Glorieux, Vol. 8, p. 316): "Experimentalis Dei perceptio cognitionem intelligentiae purae praecedentem non requirit nec sequentem." Gerson also calls this form of *perceptio*, or *notitia*, "*theologia mystica.*" N.B. the Latin quotation in n. 26 above.

36. André Combes judges that Gerson radically changed his mind about *theologia mystica*—that after Oct. 1, 1425 he moved closer to Dionysius. Thus, maintains Combes, Gerson abandoned some of his views expressed in *De Mystica Theologia* in favor of the views put forth in *Super Magnificat* and elsewhere. In particular, he is purported to have rejected his earlier view that mystical theology has to do with the operation of an affective faculty. At the same time, continues

Combes, Gerson moved closer to Dionysius's account of mystical theology as a supermental union. "Sans revenir jamais à ses convictions antérieures, Gerson tient l'expérience mystique pour l'avant-goût de la vision béatifique, lui accorde une grande portée cognitive dans l'ordre intellectuel même, et adopte tous les termes qui signifient non seulement union, mais unité, voire identité." See A. Combes, *La théologie mystique de Gerson. Profil de son évolution* (cited in the bibliography), Vol. II, pp. 671-672 and 567. N.B. Gerson's letter to Jean Le Célestin, pp. 259-263 (especially from the bottom of 261 to the end) in Vol. II of Gerson's *Oeuvres complètes*, edited by Palémon Glorieux.

I myself do not deem this change on Gerson's part to be radical in the way that Combes supposes: "Il serait impossible de concevoir rupture plus profonde, discontinuité plus radicale, contradiction plus consciente et plus formelle. Tout ce qu'a vécu et enseigné, en ce qui touche à l'essence de la théologie mystique, le Gerson de 1402 à 1425, le Gerson de 1425 à 1429 le condamne et le renie" (Combes, *ibid.*, Vol. II, p. 671). Yet, even in *Super Magnificat*, 7th tractate (Glorieux, Vol. 8, p. 302) Gerson is still saying such things as: "Certissimum quidem est quod amor omnis cognitionem praesupponit aut unam aut alteram. Habemus ecce tria principaliter in descriptione devotionis. Primo, quod est elevatio mentis in Deum; secundo, quod haec elevatio fit per pium et humilem affectum; tertio, quod hujusmodi affectus debet esse fide, spe et caritate subnixus seu formatus." Moreover, in *Mys. Theol.*, as much as in *Super Magnificat*, Gerson emphasizes the *via purae intelligentiae* of Dionysius. [See *Mys. Theol. Spec.*, 36th-39th considerations (Combes, pp. 95-102) and *Mys. Theol. Prac.*, 12th consideration (Combes, pp. 208-216). Also note *Mys. Theol. Spec.*, 25th consideration (Combes, pp. 64-65).] He regards this route as leading upward unto *mentis excessus* [*Mys. Theol. Spec.*, 39th consideration (Combes, p. 102); cf. *Mys. Theol. Prac.*, 12th consideration (Combes, p. 213)]. Finally, even in *Super Magnificat* [7th tractate (Glorieux, Vol. 8, p. 298)] Gerson is still using the term "*synderesis*" [cf. *Mys. Theol. Spec.*, 14th consideration (Combes, p. 33)].

37. Gerson, *Super Magnificat*, 7th tractate (Glorieux, Vol. 8, p. 307): "Est igitur commune studium omnium qui de theologia mystica, quae consistit in unione, locuti sunt, inducere ad tria quae requiruntur et sufficiunt, videlicet desiderium divini objecti, remotio impedimenti, imploratio divini beneplaciti. Primum fit insinuando pulchritudinem et valorem; secundum fit aperiendo defectum nostrum et languorem; tertium fit per orationis vehementiam et ardorem. Haec autem tria complectitur ipsa devotio quae est elevatio mentis in Deum sicut in objectum proprium; et hoc per pium et humilem affectum, in quo semper est Deo beneplacitum."

38. Gerson, *ibid.* (Glorieux, Vol. 8, p. 309): "Experimentalis perceptio Dei facialis et immediata non habetur hic in via, de lege communi; sed exspectatur pro praemio in gloria consummata.—Conceditur haec ab omnibus, nec oportet probationibus immorari; immo sic concessa est haec propositio ut in errorem aliqui prolapsi sint dicentes quod nec in patria Deus immediate videbitur, sed in theophaniis quibusdam contemperantibus inaccessibilem lucem Dei imbecilli menti."

39. "*Via abnegationis*" is another name for the *via negativa*. Both *via negativa* and *via superexcellentia* (or *via supereminentia*) belong to the *via purae intelli-*

gentiae, according to Gerson. In contrast to the *via purae intelligentiae* is the *via devotionis*, which has its own kind of *via abnegationis*: viz., the denial-of-the-world referred to by St. Paul as "being crucified with Christ" (Gal. 2:20). However, just as Scripture speaks of our "understanding by faith" (Heb. 11:3) and Anselm speaks of "faith's certainty" (*Monologion* 64), so too does Gerson [*Mys. Theol. Spec.*, 30th consideration (Combes, p. 78, line 3)]. Accordingly, Gerson sometimes regards the *via devotionis* as a form of *cognoscere* (e.g., *Super Magnificat*, Glorieux, Vol. 8, p. 315, last paragraph). Both the *via devotionis* and the *via purae intelligentiae* belong to *theologia mystica* (i.e., the *via purae intelligentiae* does not belong to *theologia speculativa seu scolastica*, which, says Gerson, can never effect mystical union) [*Anagogicum de Verbo et Hymno Gloriae* I.8.a (Glorieux, Vol. 8, p. 543, lines 1-2)].

40. Gerson, *Super Magnificat*, 7th tractate (Glorieux, Vol. 8, p. 310). Cf. Gerson, *Mys. Theol. Spec.*, 36th consideration (Combes, p. 97).

41. Gerson, *Super Magnificat*, 7th tractate (Glorieux, Vol. 8, p. 319): ". . . quando mens ab omnibus aliis recedens postea etiam seipsam dimittens. Hoc quomodo fieri possit, pluries ostensum est, etiam naturalibus industriis, maxime praesupposita fide summi Dei."

42. Gerson, *ibid.* (Glorieux, Vol. 8, pp. 310-311): "Primo deseritur operatio sensitiva, quia non oportet de vegetativa deseratur; secundo operatio intellectiva, secundum omne ens et non ens; et hoc plane accipiendum est de ente vel non ente creato vel creabili, non de ente primo et puro. Tertio deseritur mens ipsa; non utique quin maneat essentialiter in se, alioquin esset et non esset, nisi velimus insanire cum Almarico et similibus haereticis dicentibus mentem contemplativi vel beati perdere suum esse in proprio suo genere et redire in illud esse ideale quod habuit essentialiter in arte divina. Et hoc prorsus esset mentem annihilari, aut nihil omnino posset annihilare Deus. Et hoc aliqui volunt; sed male; quia similiter ipse creare non posset. Quid est igitur mentem seipsam deserere? Hoc est ipsam in actu primo suo essentiali manentem, nullum actum secundum circa seipsam aut circa quodlibet aliud ens praeter Deum exercere . . . ." Cf. *Mys. Theol. Spec.*, 36th-39th considerations (especially Combes, p. 102, first two lines).

43. Gerson, *ibid.* (Glorieux, Vol. 8, p. 310): "Necesse est mentem ab omni actu cognitivo vel affectivo circa creaturam omnem, etiam circa seipsam tunc vacare et in silentio summo esse . . . ." Cf. *Analogicum de Verbo et Hymno Gloriae* II.4.d (Glorieux, Vol. 8, p. 546): "Si fiat inquisitio quid est illa caligo, quid quaeso habent respondere nisi quod est cognitionis privatio et amoris defectio." *Ibid.*, II.6.c (Glorieux, Vol. 8, p. 547): "Sic fit tandem ut deficiat a seipsa per cognitionis defectum et suscipiatur a spiritu Christi per dilectionis illapsum."

44. Gerson, *Super Magnificat*, 7th tractate (Glorieux, Vol. 8, p. 310). Cf. Rom. 6:11.

45. Gerson, *Mys. Theol. Spec.*, 36th consideration (Combes, p. 97). This ecstatic experience is granted by grace. It is not achieved by human efforts alone. *Super Magnificat*, 7th tractate (Glorieux, Vol. 8, p. 319): "Sed quod sequitur prorsus est supernaturale, prorsus gratuitum, ad quod nec natura sufficit nec attingit industria . . . ."

46. Gerson, *Super Magnificat*, 7th tractate (Glorieux, Vol. 8, p. 311).

47. Gerson, *Elucidatio Scolastica*, 6th consideration (Combes, p. 226, first four lines and p. 227). Also note *Super Magnificat*, 7th tractate (Glorieux, Vol. 8, p. 320, last paragraph).

48. Gerson, *Mys. Theol. Spec.*, 2nd consideration (Combes, p. 9): "Quis autem diceret quod theologia mistica solam abnegationem consectetur, nihil relinquens de Deo positive cognitum vel expertum?" *Super Magnificat*, 7th tractate (Glorieux, Vol. 8, pp. 312-313): "Experimentalis Dei perceptio non fit per solam abnegationem . . . . Sed accipiuntur affirmatio et negatio respectu diversorum quia negatur a Deo quidquid est imperfectionis in creatura, sicut omnis creatura est imperfecta, quantumcumque perfecta sit in suo genere; et ponitur per superexcellentiam affirmatio de Deo. Propterea dicit saepe Dionysius quod Deus non est ens sed superens, superbonus, superdominus et similia." Also note *Elucidatio Scolastica*, first part of 11th consideration (Combes, pp. 230-231).

49. Gerson, *Super Magnificat*, 7th tractate (Glorieux, Vol. 8, p. 316, lines 3-7).

50. Gerson, *ibid.* (Glorieux, Vol. 8, p. 314).

51. Gerson, *ibid.* (Glorieux, Vol. 8, bottom of p. 315 and top of p. 316).

52. Gerson, *Mys. Theol. Spec.*, 36th consideration (Combes, pp. 97-98): "Cum igitur amor sit radix aliarum qualiumcumque affectionum, si ostenderimus quod affectio potius quam cognitio raptum agat, patebit sufficienter quod intendimus."

53. Gerson, *Super Magnificat*, 7th tractate (Glorieux, Vol. 8, pp. 312-313): "Experimentalis Dei perceptio non fit per solam abnegationem. Ratio: quia pura negatio nihil ponit . . . . Quidquid affirmative de Deo dicimus, includit negationem aliquam et e converso negatio relinquit affirmationem, non quidem ad idem et secundum idem et pro eodem; alioquin esset contradictio manifesta; sed accipiuntur affirmatio et negatio respectu diversorum quia negatur a Deo quidquid est imperfectionis in creatura, sicut omnis creatura est imperfecta, quantumcumque perfecta sit in suo genere; et ponitur per superexcellentiam affirmatio de Deo. Propterea dicit saepe Dionysius quod Deus non est ens sed superens, superbonus, superdominus et similia." Also note the entire succeeding paragraph (on p. 313 of Glorieux).

54. Gerson, *Mys. Theol. Spec.*, 36th consideration (Combes, p. 96): "Porro extasim dicimus speciem quamdam raptus, que fit appropriatius in superiori portione anime rationalis, que spiritus vel mens vel intelligentia nominatur, dum mens ita in suo actu suspensa est quod potentie inferiores cessant ab actibus, sic quod nec ratio nec ymaginatio nec sensus exteriores, ymmo quandoque nec potentie naturales nutritive ⟨et⟩ augmentative et motive possint exire in suas proprias operationes." Also note *ibid.*, 39th consideration (Combes, p. 101): "Raptus mentis supra potentias inferiores fit per affectionis scintillam menti cognatam vel appropriatam, que amor extaticus vel excessus mentis nominatur."

55. Gerson, *Elucidatio Scolastica*, 9th consideration (Combes, p. 229). Cf. *Super Magnificat*, 7th tractate (Glorieux, Vol. 8, p. 316, lines 8-9).

56. Gerson, *Super Magnificat*, 7th tractate (Glorieux, Vol. 8, pp. 316-317).

Cf. *Anagogicum de Verbo et Hymno Gloriae*, II.6.a-c (Glorieux, Vol. 8, p. 547).

57. Gerson, *Super Magnificat*, 7th tractate (Glorieux, Vol. 8, p. 317).

58. Gerson, *Mys. Theol. Spec.*, 36th consideration (Combes, pp. 97-98): "Cum igitur amor sit radix aliarum qualiumcumque affectionum . . . ."

59. Gerson, *ibid.*, 28th consideration (Combes, p. 70): "Cognitio Dei per theologiam misticam melius acquiritur per penitentem affectum, quam per investigantem intellectum, ipsa quoque ceteris paribus eligibilior est et perfectior quam theologia symbolica vel propria⟨de⟩qua est contemplatio, sicut dilectio perfectior est cognitione, et voluntas intellectu, et caritas fide."

60. Gerson, *Super Magnificat*, 7th tractate (Glorieux, Vol. 8, p. 307).

61. Gerson, *ibid.* (Glorieux, Vol. 8, p. 307, lines 31-32).

62. Gerson, *Mys. Theol. Spec.*, 30th consideration (Combes, pp. 77-78): "Sed quoniam plerumque venit, etiam in brutis, ut ibi sit maior affectio ubi parum est cognitionis, sequitur quod ad comparandam huius theologie mistice doctrinam non est magna scientia opus, presertim acquisita. Nam cognito ex fide quod Deus est totus desiderabilis, totus amabilis, affectiva portio, si purgata, ⟨si illuminata⟩, si disposita, si exercitata sit, cur non in illum totaliter desiderabilem et totum amabilem, sine plurimo librorum studio, tota feretur totaque rapietur?"

63. Gerson, *Super Magnificat* (Glorieux, Vol. 8, p. 307): "Superest ostendere quod doctrinalis traditio theologiae mysticae se extendit ad theologiam scolasticam, nec ab eadem diversa est vel seclusa, immo nec a vera philosophia."

64. I.e., Pseudo-Dionysius. See n. 6 above.

65. Vincent of Aggsbach, in his treatise against Gerson (Vansteenberghe, *Autour*, p. 195): "Gerson vero habet nomen iuxta nomen magnorum in terra, et scripsit multa que deferuntur in omnem locum, cui ex fama celebri maxime apud litteratos fides adhibetur."

66. See Vansteenberghe, *Autour*, pp. 189-201. In Codex Latinus Monacensis 19114, Vansteenberghe tells us, this treatise has as title simply "*Tractatus cuiusdam Carthusiensis de Mystica Theologia.*"

67. Vincent of Aggsbach, treatise against Gerson (Vansteenberghe, *Autour*, p. 193).

68. Vincent of Aggsbach, *ibid.* (Vansteenberghe, *Autour*, pp. 196-197). Cf. Gerson, *Mys. Theol. Spec.*, 43rd consideration (Combes, bottom of p. 116 and top of p. 117).

69. Vincent of Aggsbach, *ibid.* (Vansteenberghe, *Autour*, p. 197). Cf. John 4:24, to which Vincent subsequently alludes.

70. Vincent of Aggsbach, *ibid.* (Vansteenberghe, *Autour*, p. 193). In the exposition above I have reconstructed the order of Vincent's objections.

71. Vincent of Aggsbach, *ibid.* (Vansteenberghe, *Autour*, p. 197).

72. Vincent of Aggsbach, *ibid.* (Vansteenberghe, *Autour*, p. 191).

73. Vincent of Aggsbach, *ibid.* (Vansteenberghe, *Autour*, pp. 197-198).

74. Vincent of Aggsbach, *ibid.* (Vansteenberghe, *Autour*, p. 195).

75. Vincent of Aggsbach, *ibid.* (Vansteenberghe, *Autour*, p. 196). Vincent is quoting Dionysius, *De Mystica Theologia*, Chap. 1, Sec. 2 (*Dionysiaca, op. cit.*, Vol. I, pp. 569-570). Cf. II Chron. 6:1 (Old Testament).

76. Vincent of Aggsbach, *ibid.* (Vansteenberghe, *Autour*, p. 196).

77. Vincent of Aggsbach, *ibid.* (Vansteenberghe, *Autour*, p. 195).

78. Gerson, *Super Magnificat*, 7th tractate (Glorieux, Vol. 8, p. 318, lines 30-31). *Elucidatio Scolastica*, 7th consideration (Combes, p. 227, opening lines).

79. When Vincent here (Vansteenberghe, *Autour*, p. 198) mentions Gerson's *De 12 Industriis*, he is referring to *Mys. Theol. Prac.* In the present instance he is citing the 12th consideration (Combes, p. 211).

80. Gerson, *Anagogicum de Verbo et Hymno Gloriae* III.9.a (Glorieux, Vol. 8, p. 555, lines 21-25).

81. Vincent of Aggsbach, *op. cit..* (Vansteenberghe, *Autour*, p. 198).

82. Vincent of Aggsbach, *op. cit.* (Vansteenberghe, *Autour*, p. 198, last paragraph). See Gerson's *Mys. Theol. Spec.*, considerations 21-24 and 27.

83. Vincent of Aggsbach, *op. cit.* (Vansteenberghe, *Autour*, p. 199).

84. Vincent of Aggsbach, *op. cit.* (Vansteenberghe, *Autour*, p. 199).

85. Vincent of Aggsbach, *op. cit.* (Vansteenberghe, *Autour*, p. 200). See Gerson's *Mys. Theol. Prac.*, 12th consideration (Combes, p. 213).

86. Vincent of Aggsbach, *op. cit.* (Vansteenberghe, *Autour*, pp. 200-201).

87. John Wenck, *De Ignota Litteratura* (1442-1443). Wenck was a professor of theology at the University of Heidelberg. For further details see J. Hopkins, *Nicholas of Cusa's Debate with John Wenck: A Translation and an Appraisal of De Ignota Litteratura and Apologia Doctae Ignorantiae* (Minneapolis: The Arthur J. Banning Press, 2nd edition 1984).

88. Vincent's letter to John of Weilheim, Dec. 19, 1454 (Vansteenberghe, *Autour*, p. 208).

89. *Ibid.*, p. 206 and p. 209, lines 3-4.

90. *Ibid.*, p. 208.

91. *Ibid.*, p. 206. Vincent is referring to the work *De Visione Dei*.

92. Vincent here draws upon Hugh of Balma's distinction between *via purgativa, via illuminativa,* and *via unitiva.*

93. See Rudolf Haubst, "Die Thomas- und Proklos-Exzerpte des 'Nicolaus Treverensis' in Codicillus Strassburg 84," *MFCG* 1 (1961), p. 18. See also Nicholas's Sermon 16 ("*Gloria in excelsis Deo*"), *Opera Omnia* XVI, p. 268. Edmond Vansteenberghe, "Quelques lectures de jeunesse de Nicolas de Cues d'après un manuscrit inconnu de sa bibliothèque," *Archives d'histoire doctrinale et littéraire du Moyen Age*, 3 (1928), 275-284. Codex Latinus Strassburg 84 also contains Bonaventura's *Itinerarium Mentis in Deum*.

94. Nicholas of Cusa, Letters 4 and 5 in Vansteenberghe's *Autour*, pp. 111-117 (especially 112 and 115).

95. See Nicholas, Letter 5 (Vansteenberghe, *Autour*, p. 114). Nicholas declares that Dionysius, in his treatise on mystical theology, was of this same opinion. Cf. Dionysius's *De Mystica Theologia*, Chap. 1, Sec. 2 (*Dionysiaca, op. cit.*, Vol. I, pp. 571-572).

96. II Cor. 11:14. Vansteenberghe, *Autour*, p. 115. Regarding the point made in the text marked by the present note, Nicholas and Gerson are in disagreement.

97. Letter 5 (Vansteenberghe, *Autour*, p. 115). Cf. Letter 9 (*Autour*, p. 122):

"Nichil enim incognitum amatur." Also note Letter 16 from Nicholas to Bernard of Waging (*Autour*, pp. 134-135): "Qui attendit Deum esse obiectum anime racionalis, et tam intellectus quam voluntatis, ille ad coincidencias se convertit, et dicit: Deus qui est superbonum et superverum, vis boni et veri, non attingitur uti est, nisi supra omne id quod intelligitur pariter et amatur, quamvis dum nos ad ipsum accedimus non possimus nisi querendo accedere. Querere autem sine intelligere et amare non est. Amamus bonum et querimus quid sit quod amamus, et tamen, ut ait Augustinus, neque quereremus si penitus ignoraremus quia et inventum ignoraremus. Amor igitur boni sine omni boni notitia non est; et notitia sine amore non est."

98. Letter 4, Sept. 22, 1452 (Vansteenberghe, *Autour*, pp. 111-113). Also see the sermon excerpt ("*Suscepimus deus misericordiam tuam*") at the bottom of fol. 91^v and the top of 92^r in Vol. II of the Paris edition of Nicholas's works.

99. Nicholas, Letter 4 (Vansteenberghe, *Autour*, pp. 111-112).

100. Gerson, *Elucidatio Scolastica*, 11th consideration (Combes, p. 231): "Sed aliunde deducitur consideratio presens, notando quod omnis apprehensio vel motio intellectualis, sive de Deo sive de aliis, dici potest cognitio, ymmo et visio per illum modum loquendi quo utimur de sensibus exterioribus, ubi omnis sensatio visio nominatur . . . ."

During the penultimate stage of mystical ascent, just prior to the possible experience of union, the soul entertains the concept of God as *Inconceivable Infinity*, according to Nicholas's version of *theologia mystica*. This conception Nicholas considers to be a "cognitive" element. But during the experience-of-union itself there is, Nicholas professes, a further cognitive element: viz., the soul's knowledge that it is united with God (whose nature remains, however, unknowable and— positively—inconceivable to it). Mystical experience is never regarded by Nicholas as evidence either establishing or confirming the existence of God. For the degree of belief prerequisite to mystical experience is supposedly so great and so commitment-filled that the idea of regarding the subsequent experience as *evidential* is totally foreign to him. Similarly, he nowhere aims to set forth criteria for distinguishing veridical from nonveridical experience of God. Nor, for that matter, do any of the major mystics—whether speculative or nonspeculative—propose "adequate" criteria. Regarding St. Teresa, for example, see George Mavrodes' important article "Real v. Deceptive Mystical Experiences," pp. 235-258 of *Mysticism and Philosophical Analysis*, edited by Steven Katz (London: Sheldon Press, 1978).

101. N.B. Letter 4, Sept. 22, 1452 (Vansteenberghe, *Autour*, p. 112): "Inest igitur in omni tali dilectione qua quis vehitur in Deum, cognicio, licet quid sit id quod diligit ignoret. Est igitur coincidencia sciencie et ignorancie, seu docta ignorancia." Letter 5, Sept. 14, 1453 (Vansteenberghe, *Autour*, pp. 115-116): "Et michi visum fuit quod tota ista mistica theologia sit intrare ipsam infinitatem absolutam, dicit enim infinitas contradictoriorum coincidenciam, scilicet finem sine fine; et nemo potest Deum mistice videre nisi in caligine coincidencie, que est infinitas." Also note *Ap.* 19-20, and 24. Note especially *DVD* 13 (52-53). Cf. Gerson's use of Dionysius at *Anagogicum de Verbo et Hymno Gloriae* I.10.b and II.4.e (Glorieux, Vol. 8, pp. 544 and 546).

In *DI* Nicholas was not yet deeply influenced by Dionysius's views on mystical theology. This fact is evidenced by *DI* III, 11, where a believer's mystical ascent unto God is characterized in less radical terms than it is in *Ap.*, in *DVD*, in the correspondence with the Tegernsee monks, and in *DP*. *Ap.* 12 indicates that at the time of writing *DI* Nicholas had just become familiar with Dionysius's writings. Also testifying to such familiarity is Sermon 20 (*"Nomen eius Jesus"*), delivered on Jan. 1, 1439.

102. Letter 5 (Vansteenberghe, *Autour*, p. 116): "Nec quiescam quousque perficiam."

103. That is, the copying was finished on this date.

104. Letter 9, Nicholas to Caspar, Feb. 12, 1454 (Vansteenberghe, *Autour*, pp. 121-122).

105. Letter 7, Nicholas to Caspar, Oct. 23, 1453 (Vansteenberghe, *Autour*, p. 118). This letter intervenes between Nicholas's letter of Sept. 14 and his actual communication of *DVD* to Caspar.

106. *DVD* 10 (41:9).

107. *DVD* 8 (32:1-2).

108. *DVD* 8 (32:10-18). Cf. *DVD* 12 (49:5-8); 15 (67:4-11).

109. N.B. Karsten Harries' excellent article "The Infinite Sphere: Comments on the History of a Metaphor," *Journal of the History of Philosophy*, 13 (January 1975), 5-15.

110. I.e., "I see." Note *NA* 23 (104:12-13). *DVD* 1 (6:6); 5 (18:3); 8 (33:1).

111. *NA* 23 (104:15-17).

112. II Chron. 16:9 (King James version).

113. Ps. 138:7-10 (Douay version).

114. *DVD* 5 and *DVD* 8 (33:2-3). Cf. the critique of Walter Schulz in my *Nicholas of Cusa's Metaphysic of Contraction* (Minneapolis: The Arthur J. Banning Press, 1983), pp. 30-31.

115. Note the *incipit*, for *DVD*, in Codex Latinus Monacensis 14213 and in the Paris edition (1514).

116. Cf. *DP* 41:19-20: "For, assuredly, God is not able to be conceived unless all that is able to be conceived is actually conceived."

117. Faith, teaches Nicholas, is a prerequisite to enrapturing love: "Non est amor Dei qui rapiat in Deum amantem, nisi credatur Christo qui revelavit ea que apud patrem vidit . . . ." Letter 4, Nicholas to Caspar (Vansteenberghe, *Autour*, p. 112).

118. Ps. 27:4 (King James version).

119. *DVD* 6 (21:17-18).

120. See the references to *pulchritudo* in *Dionysiaca, op. cit.*, Vol. I (1937) and Vol. II (1950). Note especially Dionysius's *De Mystica Theologia*, Chap. 1, Sec. 1.

121. *DVD* 6 (21:10-13).

122. *DVD* 6 (21:16-17).

123. See n. 116 above. Also note the crucial opening passage in *DVD* 13 (52-53). See *DI* I, 26 (88:16-20) and *Cribratio Alkoran* II, 1 (p. 463 of Vol. II of P.

Wilpert's reissue of the Strasburg edition), where Nicholas says that God is knowable only to Himself. It follows that He is conceivable to Himself.

124. *DVD* 13 (58:11).

125. *DVD* 6 (22:1).

126. *DVD* 6 (22:8-14).

127. *DVD* 6 (22:20-22). The italics that are added here are not present in the translation facing the Latin text, in Part II of the present work.

128. Gerson, *Super Magnificat*, 7th tractate (Glorieux, Vol. 8, p. 312). Gerson appears to endorse the example. In effect, Nicholas himself endorses it in *DI* III, 11 but not in his later accounts of mystical theology. See n. 101 above and n. 521 below.

129. Gerson, *loc. cit.*: "Constat quod oculus satagens inspicere solem, non intuebitur nisi caliginem, quamvis inde suscipiat obliquam solis irradiationem. Alioquin non videret oculus illam caliginem, radiatione hujusmodi non extante."

130. Nicholas never abandons the principle that between the finite and the infinite no comparative relationship is possible. See Sermon 4 ("*Fides autem catholica*"), 34:39-40. *DI* I, 1 (3:2-3); I, 3 (9:4-5); II, 2 (102:4-5). *Ap.* 32:7-8. *De Filiatione Dei* 2 (61:6-8). *De Pace Fidei* 1 (5). *DVD* 23 (100:7). *Complementum Theologicum* 13 (Paris edition, Vol. II, 2nd Part, fol. 99ᵛ, line 2 from bottom). *Epistola ad Ioannem de Segobia* 98:10-11 (*Opera Omnia*, Vol. 7). *DP* 10:12-17. *Cribratio Alkoran* II, 1 (p. 463 of Vol. II of Wilpert's reissue of the Strasburg edition). This same principle also occurs in the sermon "*Dies Sanctificatus*" (*SHAW*, 1929, p. 30, line 20)—dated by Haubst as 1440.

131. Cf. *DVD* 1 (7:1-3): "But God, insofar as He is true Uncontracted Sight, is not sight that is *less* than the intellect can conceive abstract sight to be; rather, He is incomparably more perfect Sight." Also note *DVD* 12 (51:8-9): "You are not creator but are infinitely more than creator." Finally, see *DI* I, 18 (54:10-12). The *via superexcellentiae* is, for Nicholas, an extension of the *via negativa*, since terms such as "supersubstantial" and "supergood" are regarded as *negations*.

132. *DP* 74.

133. *DP* 74: 20-21.

134. Nonetheless, Nicholas maintains that "by *negation* we pursue the truer way, since He whom we seek is incomprehensible and infinite" (*DP* 66:2-4). Cf. *De Beryllo* 11 (12:13-16): "Recte igitur . . . Plato omnia de ipso principio negat. Sic et Dionysius noster negativam praefert theologiam affirmativae." *De Filiatione Dei* 6 (84:12-15): "Nec verius hic dicit, qui ait deum omnia esse, quam ille, qui ait ipsum nihil esse aut non esse, cum sciat deum super omnem affirmationem et negationem ineffabilem . . . ."

135. Gerson, *Super Magnificat*, 7th tractate (Glorieux, Vol. 8, p. 310).

136. Note *Cribratio Alkoran* II, 1 (p. 463 of Vol. II of Wilpert's reissue of the Strasburg edition): "Illud autem principium [i.e., deus] potest considerari sine respectu ad principiata, ut non plus sit principium quam non principium ea consideratione est penitus infinitum et interminum, incomprehensibile et ineffabile, tunc certe cum excedat omnem sensum et omnem intellectum et omne nomen et omne nominabile, nec dicitur unus nec trinus nec bonus nec sapiens nec pater nec

filius nec spiritussanctus, et ita de omnibus que dici aut cogitari possunt, ut dyonisius ariopagita hoc astruit, quoniam omnia talia nomina excellit et antecedit in infinitum, sic manet absconditus ab oculis omnium sapientum, et nulli creature sed sibi tantum cognitus, et hoc tantum de ipso cognoscimus quod ipse est ipsa infinitas excedens omnem creatum intellectum infinite, eo modo cum de ipso nihil proprie dici et affirmari possit quod non excedat, in silentio tantum admiramur et contemplamur et colimus . . . ."

137. Erigena [*De Divisione Naturae* IV.7 (*PL* 122:771)] denies that God has a nature: not even God knows *what He is*, because there is no quiddity in God. Nicholas does not subscribe to Erigena's doctrine. Instead, he maintains that God defines Himself and all things [*NA* 1 (5:6-9); also Prop. 12], and that God is known only to Himself [*DI* I, 26 (88:19-20). *Cribratio Alkoran* II, 1. *DP* 30:2-3]. So when he states that what God is is incomprehensible (Sermon 1, "*Fides autem catholica*," Sec. 32, *Opera Omnia* XVI, p. 70), he means that it is incomprehensible to finite minds, not that it is incomprehensible to God. Nicholas speaks of God as the Divine Nature [*VS* 21 (62:5)]. Moreover, in *VS* 29 (87:25-26), he also speaks of Him as the Divine Essence: "Divina enim essentia cum sit incognita, consequens est nullam rerum essentiam cognitione posse comprehendi." The Divine Essence, which is the Essence of all essences, is nonetheless not *essence* in any sense analogous to what is meant in speaking of finite essences. "Essence of all essences" is thus a symbolic expression that signifies God's superessentiality [Dionysius, *De Mystica Theologia*, Chap. 1, Sec. 3 (*Dionysiaca, op. cit.*, Vol. I, p. 573); cf. *NA* 14 (71:7); 10 (39); 8 (27)].

Even Meister Eckhart spoke of God as having a nature: "Hätte Sankt Peter Gott unmittelbar in seiner Natur geschaut, wie er es späterhin tat und wie Sankt Paulus, als er in den dritten Himmel verzückt ward . . . " [German Sermon 28 ("*Intravit Jesus in quoddam castellum*," Luke 10:38), p. 284 of *Meister Eckehart. Deutsche Predigten und Traktate*, edited and translated into high German by Josef Quint (Munich: C. Hanser, 1955)]. In a contemporary vein, see Alvin Plantinga's *Does God Have a Nature?* (Milwaukee: Marquette University Press, 1980).

138. *DVD* 12 (51:4-6).

139. *DVD* 13 (52:3-5).

140. *DVD* 13 (54:11-14). Cf. the reasoning in *DP* 3: "When in seeing what is perceptible I understand that it exists from a higher power (since it is finite, and a finite thing cannot exist from itself; for how could what is finite have set its own limit?), then I can only regard as invisible and eternal this Power from which it exists."

141. Rev. 22:13.

142. *DVD* 13 (54:7-10). Nicholas uses "end" in a twofold sense: God is *delimitor* of all finite beings and God is, ultimately, the *goal* of every intellect's desire. Cf. *DVD* 16 (72-73).

143. *DI* II, 11 (157:23-26).

144. Cf. the dialogue *NA*, where Nicholas attempts to understand how God, as Not-other, is the definition of all things.

145. *DVD* 13 (58:11).

146. We can imagine what it might be like to transcend our own limited perspective or what it would be like to behold a thing from several perspectives at once. But we cannot imagine what it would be like to behold a thing from all possible perspectives at once and with all possible "instruments" (e.g., through the eye of a bee, an owl, a dog, etc.). Nicholas's point is that there is no comparative relationship between the several imaginable perspectives and the infinity of perspectives. Strictly speaking, according to Nicholas, God's infinity of perspective is identical with His transcendence of all perspective.

147. *DVD* 8 (32:16-18).

148. *DVD* 1. Cf. *DVD* 24 (109:18-19), where Jesus is said to be the Perfection of everything perfectible.

149. *DP* 75:5-6. Also note *DP* 31:11-12. *DVD* 24 (108:18; 109:14). Cf. *DVD* 19 (86:12-13). Note *DVD* 21 (94:9-11): "You, Jesus, are the Revelation of the Father. For the Father is invisible to all men; He is visible only to You, His Son, and, subsequent to You, to one who will merit to see Him through You and by Your revelation."

150. *DVD* 4 (12:6-8).

151. *DVD* 24 (108:12-13).

152. *DP* 34:8-10: "Purity of heart is the preparation which is necessarily required of the believer who wills to see God."

153. *DVD* 19 (86).

154. *DVD* 19 (86:11-12). Cf. *DVD* 25 (113:10-11): "You enrapture me, in order that I may transcend myself and foresee the glorious place to which You invite me." This rapture is purported to accompany *speculation* and *discernment*. It is not the rapture of mystical *experience*, of mystical *union*—a rapture which comes when one actually transcends himself. Note Gerson's distinction between kinds of rapture [*Mys. Theol. Spec.*, 37th-39th considerations (Combes, pp. 99-102)]. And see Sec. 7.1 of Part I of the present work.

155. Douay version.

156. *De Filiatione Dei* 1 (52:2-5): "Ego autem, ut in summa dicam, non aliud filiationem dei quam deificationem, quae et theosis graece dicitur, aestimandum iudico. Theosim vero tu ipse nosti ultimatem perfectionis exsistere, quae et notitia dei et verbi seu visio intuitiva vocitatur." N.B. Rudolf Haubst's fine article "Nikolaus von Kues ueber die Gotteskindschaft," pp. 29-46 of *Nicolò da Cusa. Relazioni tenute al Convegno Interuniversitario di Bressanone nel 1960* (Florence: G. Sansoni, 1962).

157. *De Filiatione Dei* 3 (62:3).

158. *Ibid.* 1 (53:1).

159. *Ibid.*, 1 (54).

160. *Ibid.*, 2 (56:1-3): "Non arbitror nos fieri sic filios dei, quod aliquid aliud tunc simus quam modo. Sed modo alio id tunc erimus, quod nunc suo modo sumus."

161. John 1:12. *De Filiatione Dei* 1 (54:22-26).

162. Regarding the identity of Truth itself with the Word, see *DVD* 22 (99:15); *De Filiatione Dei* 3 (67:13-14); *DP* 75:10. Also note *De Filiatione Dei* 3

(65:2-5), where "altissima resplendentia . . . dei gloriosi" refers to Christ.

163. That *De Filiatione Dei* deals with the eschatological state is clear from many considerations. Note, for example, 2 (61:20-21): "Tali quadam licet remotissima similitudine gaudium est filiis dei absque intermissione . . . ." Similarly, the mastery (*magisterium*) that Nicholas discusses in 2 (56-61) can be eternally possessed (cf. 60:3-4) only in the future state.

164. *De Filiatione Dei* 3 (62:4-8): "Arbitror te satis intellexisse veritatem in alio non nisi aliter posse comprehendi. Sed cum illi modi theophanici sint intellectuales, tunc deus etsi non uti ipse est attingitur, intuebitur tamen sine omni aenigmatico phantasmate in puritate spiritus intellectualis, et haec ipsi intellectui clara est atque facialis visio." That Nicholas distinguishes Christ, who is Truth itself, from God as He is in Himself is evident from the following passage in *De Filiatione Dei* 3 (63:5-9): "Veritas ipsa non est deus ut in se triumphat, sed est modus quidem dei, quo intellectui in aeterna vita communicabilis exsistit. Nam deus in se triumphans nec est intelligibilis aut scibilis, nec est veritas nec vita, nec est, sed omne intelligibile antecedit ut unum simplicissimum principium" (punctuation slightly modified by me).

165. *DP* 15:1-10. Cf. *DP* 75.

166. *De Filiatione Dei* 3 (65-67).

167. Col. 3:11.

168. *De Filiatione Dei* 3 (69:21-22); cf. 3 (69:5).

169. *Ibid.*, 3 (69:1-5). See n. 173 below.

170. *Ibid.*, 3 (70:6).

171. *Ibid.*, 3 (71:5-6). N.B.: Nicholas distinguishes intellect (*intellectus*) from reason (*ratio*). Accordingly, rational considerations and intellectual considerations are not the same thing.

172. *Ibid.*, 6 (86:5-9).

173. *Ibid.*, 6 (87). Note that Nicholas is appropriating for his own purposes the Aristotelian doctrine that the intellect must become like an object if it is to know it.

174. *DP* 38:6-15. Also note *DVD* 7 (26:5).

175. *DI* III, 11 (252:11-14). In *DI* Nicholas concentrates his discussion more upon the pilgrim's pathway. In *De Filiatione Dei* he concentrates more upon the future state. Nicholas seems to allow that even on this earthly pathway there is the possibility of attaining, through mystical theology, a vision of the risen Christ—a vision which would illuminate the pilgrim's intellectual darkness (cf. *DP* 75). But such a vision is generally reserved for the heavenly state. When Nicholas says that in the heavenly state God will be seen *as He is*, he means that the believer will see God as He is in Christ, not as He is in Himself. And when he states that Christ, or Truth, will be seen *as He is*, He means that Christ, who is God, will be seen by the human intellect apart from sensible images and sensible symbols, though the essence of His deity will, necessarily, remain hidden. Cf. n. 164 above. By contrast, Aquinas teaches that in the next life the believer's intellect will behold (but not comprehend) the essence of God (*Summa Theologiae* Ia.12,1).

These distinctions help elucidate an apparent contradiction. For in a sermon delivered in 1431 (Sermon 4, "*Fides autem catholica*," Sec. 32, p. 70 of *Opera Omnia* XVI) we find: "Hold fast to the following: that in the earthly state we can know *that God is*; in the heavenly state we can know Him *as He is*; but neither here nor there can we ever know *what He is*, because He is incomprehensible." By contrast, we find in *De Filiatione Dei* 3 (62:6): " . . . although God is not attained as He is . . . ." Also cf. Sermon 32, "*In nomine Jesu*," Sec. 1, lines 7-16, on p. 52 of *Opera Omnia* XVII, with Sermon 29, "*Accepistis*," Sec. 11, lines 22-24, on p. 39 of *Opera Omnia* XVII.

    Complementum Theologicum 2 (Paris edition, 2nd half of Vol. II, fol. 93ʳ) states: "The mind sees only the existence, not the essence, of Truth itself, through which Truth it sees itself and all other things." According to *De Filiatione Dei* 3 (63:5-8) Truth is not God as He is in Himself but is an intelligible mode of God. In apprehending Christ as God, the believer does not thereby either know or conceive God as He is in Himself. The believer's face-to-face vision of God—a vision that Nicholas calls *immediate*—is the nonsensory, intellectual vision of God-in-Christ: "In this rapture . . . the believer sees Christ in his own self apart from a symbolism" (*DP* 39:10-11).

    176. *DI* III, 8 (228:23-26).

    177. *Letter to Cardinal Julian* [*DI* III (264:16)].

    178. *DI* III, 12 (260:13).

    179. Gerson, *Mys. Theol. Spec.*, 41st consideration (Combes, pp. 105-112). Cf. *Super Magnificat*, 9th tractate (Glorieux, Vol. 8, p. 435).

    180. *DI* III, 11 (253:2). At the time of writing *DVD* Nicholas found the term "*transformatio*" dispensable, for it nowhere appears there.

    181. *DI* III, 8 (228:22-24).

    182. *DI* III, 12 (260:12-13).

    183. *De Filiatione Dei* 6 (86:4).

    184. *Ibid.*, 1 (54:22-26).

    185. *Ibid.*, 1 (52:5).

    186. *Ibid.*, 3 (71:5-6).

    187. *DVD* 19 (86:13-14).

    188. *De Filiatione Dei* 4 (78:1-5): "Ineffabilis igitur nec nominari nec attingi quovis modo potest. Nomen igitur absolutum sive entitas sive deitas sive bonitas sive veritas sive etiam virtus aut aliud quodcumque nequaquam deum nominat innominabilem, sed innominabilem ipsum deum variis intellectualibus modis exprimit."

    189. *Ap.* 25.

    190. Herbert Wackerzapp, *Der Einfluss Meister Eckharts auf die ersten philosophischen Schriften des Nikolaus von Kues (1440-1450)* [Vol. 39 of Beiträge zur Geschichte der Philosophie und Theologie des Mittelalters (Münster: Aschendorff, 1962)]. Rudolf Haubst, "Nikolaus von Kues als Interpret und Verteidiger Meister Eckharts," pp. 75-96 of *Freiheit und Gelassenheit. Meister Eckhart heute*, edited by Udo Kern (Mainz: Kaiser Verlag, 1980). Note Josef Koch's conclusion [*Vier Predigten im Geiste Eckharts, SHAW*, 1937 (Jahrgang 1936/37), p. 55]: "Damit können wir diese Untersuchung abschliessen. Es ergibt sich aus ihr vor

allem, dass Eckharts lateinische Schriften keineswegs zu den primären Quellen Cusanischen Denkens gehören. Ihre Benutzung lässt sich mit Sicherheit erst seit der Mitte der vierziger Jahre nachweisen; insbesondere üben sie erst in den fünfziger Jahren einen tiefergehenden Einfluss auf die Predigten des Cusanus aus."

191. Nicholas of Cusa, *De Ludo Globi* II (Paris edition, Vol. I, fol. 164^r, my revised punctuation). Cf. *DVD* 4 (10:9-11).

192. Eckhart, German Sermon 2 ("*Intravit Jesus in quoddam castellum*," Luke 10:38), p. 163 of *Meister Eckehart. Deutsche Predigten und Traktate*, edited and translated into high German by Josef Quint (Munich: C. Hanser, 1955).

193. Eckhart, German Sermon 7 ("*Iusti vivent in aeternum*," Wisd. 5:16). See Quint, *ibid.*, p. 185.

194. Eckhart, German Sermon 2, *op. cit.* See Quint, *ibid.*, p. 161.

195. See Quint, *ibid.*, "*Einleitung*," p. 33.

196. *Loc. cit.*

197. Nicholas goes as far as to say that in the state of sonship the intellect is so Christlike that it is both God and all things insofar as it has become perfect [*De Filiatione Dei* 2 (58:6-12)]. Moreover, he adds that in this state God is present in the intellect *as* the intellect [*De Filiatione Dei* 6 (86:6-9)]. Both of these declarations echo Meister Eckhart.

198. *DVD* 7 (25).

199. Eckhart, German Sermon 32 ("*Beati pauperes spiritu, quia ipsorum est regnum coelorum*," Matt. 5:3). See Quint, *op. cit.* p. 308.

200. Eckhart, *loc. cit.*

201. Cf. Herbert Wackerzapp, *Einfluss Meister Eckharts, op. cit.*, pp. 140-144. See also Karsten Harries' comparison between Nicholas and Eckhart in his "The Infinite Sphere: Comments on the History of a Metaphor," *op. cit.*

202. This point is not defeated by a citing of Nicholas's *Cribratio Alkoran* II, 10 (Vol. II, p. 471 of the reissue of the Strasburg edition by P. Wilpert): "Adhuc attende non ita dicimus esse plures humanitates sicut plures homines, sic non est idem humanitas et homo, sed idem est deitas et deus propter simplicissimam essentiam divinam. Unde sicut non sunt plures deitates, ita nec plures dii . . . ." For even Eckhart admits that *idem est deitas et deus* in the sense in which 'there is only one *deitas*' entails 'there is only one *deus*.' Nicholas himself affirms, in *De Pace Fidei* 7 (21:1-2): "Deus, ut creator, est trinus et unus; ut infinitus, nec trinus nec unus nec quicquam eorum quae dici possunt."

203. I have modified slightly the punctuation of the text as found in the Heidelberg Academy's critical edition.

204. Note Alois M. Haas's "Meister Eckharts mystische Bildlehre," pp. 113-138 of *Der Begriff der Repraesentatio im Mittelalter. Stellvertretung, Symbol, Zeichen, Bild*, edited by Albert Zimmermann with the assistance of Gudrun Vuillemin-Diem (Berlin: W. de Gruyter, 1971).

205. *DVD* 10 (42:1-5). At *DVD* 41:10-11 Nicholas writes: "If they [i.e., creatures] were not to see You, who see [them], they would not receive being from You."

206. *DVD* 7 (24:13-20).

207. Nicholas's example has too often been misinterpreted as indicating that in created objects the human intellect can apprehend God as God. Because the example occurs in *De Visione Dei*, it has been construed as a constitutive part of his speculative *mystical* theology rather than of his nonmystical *speculative* theology. Ernst Hoffmann (p. 1044 of his "Gottesschau bei Meister Eckehart und Nikolaus von Cues," cited in the bibliography) understands the example to teach at least three points: (1) that the one who speculates can see, in the tree, God as tree; (2) that in the tree, which is an image of the Exemplar, the Exemplar as Exemplar can be seen; (3) that the tree derives from God in accordance with a Spinozisticlike logical necessity. Yet, contrary to Hoffmann's interpretation, none of these points are present in, or elicitable from, *DVD* 7. Hoffmann also misconstrues Eckhart's conception of God and creation when he interprets Eckhart as meaning: "Gott der Schöpfer und das, was er geschaffen hat, sind so untrennbar von einander, dass es im Grunde dasselbe ist, ob Gott der Schöpfer des Geschaffenen oder ob das Geschaffene der Schöpfer Gottes heisst. Der christlich-dogmatische Radikalschnitt zwischen Creator und Creatura wird aufgehoben" (*ibid.*, p. 1035). Cf. Nicholas of Cusa, *Ap.* 25.

208. *DVD* 19 (86:8-11).

209. Similarly, Nicholas conveys the impression that the person of Jesus is distinct from the person of God the Son, when he writes: "The Father attracts Your humanity, O Jesus, through His Son . . . ." *DVD* 21 (94:3).

210. In *DVD* 23 (101:1-2) Nicholas states unequivocally that Jesus is one person (*suppositum*). Cf. *DI* III, 7 (223:1-3).

211. *Cribratio Alkoran*, Alius Prologus (11 and 14) [Vol. II of the Strasburg edition as reissued by P. Wilpert]. In *Cribratio Alkoran, ibid.*, III, 20 (234) Nicholas also states unequivocally: "Haec si recte advertis, vides in Christo non esse nisi unam divinam ypostasim in qua radicatur humana natura. Ypostasis vero divinae et immortalis naturae humanam in se colligit naturam, ob quam ypostasim Christus est una divina persona, licet sit divinae pariter et humanae naturae, et de ipso dicuntur communicatione idiomatum quae divinae naturae pariter et humanae tribuimus . . . " (punctuation and spelling revised by me).

212. *DVD* 23 (100:4-5).

213. Or, if the indefinite article is excluded, the sentence will sound as if Nicholas meant that human nature as such was deified and that Jesus is unindividuated Man. See Emma Salter's translation as signaled by n. 296 below. Cf. n. 463 below, regarding Hans Blumenberg's corresponding mistake.

214. Cf. Anselm of Canterbury, *De Incarnatione Verbi* 11. Anselm calls Jesus "the assumed man" ("*homo assumptus*").

215. See J. Hopkins, *Nicholas of Cusa on Learned Ignorance: A Translation and an Appraisal of De Docta Ignorantia* (Minneapolis: The Arthur J. Banning Press, 1981), Introduction, pp. 36-40.

216. *DVD* 19 (86).

217. *DVD* 19 (86:16-23).

218. Cf. *DVD* 19 (87) with 20 (89).

219. *DVD* 23 (100:15-18): "O most sweet Jesus, You cannot be said, either, to

be the uniting medium between the divine nature and the human nature, since between the two natures there cannot be posited a middle nature that participates in both. For the divine nature cannot be participated in, because it is completely and absolutely most simple."

220. *DVD* 20 (90:1-3).

221. *DVD* 20 (90:4-6). At *DVD* 22 (96:12) Nicholas repeats his claim that Jesus qua a perfect man knew everything knowable. But at 20 (91:5-7) he qualifies this assertion: Jesus knew everything that can be known *by men*. At 20 (91:11-12) he makes the same qualification with regard to Jesus's understanding.

222. *DVD* 21 (94:3-7).

223. *DVD* 21 (93:9-11). In another sense, God's Spirit is not lacking to any spirit, says Nicholas, because it is the Spirit of spirits [*DVD* 25 (111:1-2)].

224. Cf. *DI* III, 8 (228:23-26): "Therefore, all shall arise through Christ, but not all shall arise as Christ and in Christ through union; rather, only those who are Christ's through faith, hope, and love [shall so arise]."

225. *DVD* 20 (89:6-8).

226. *DVD* 20 (89:8-16). Cf. *DVD* 20 (90:8-10).

227. *DVD* 23 (102:14-18). Cf. *DI* III, 7 (223-224). *DI* III, 3 (202).

228. See n. 130 above.

229. *DI* I, 11 (30:14-17).

230. The Maximal Image is God the Son, i.e., the Word of God, who is called in Scripture "the image of the invisible God" (Col. 1:15). Cf. *DVD* 25 (112:3-4 and 7-9). Regarding the finitude of Jesus' humanity, note *DI* III, 3 (202:11-12), where this humanity is spoken of as created.

231. *DVD* 20 (89:11-16).

232. Regarding this incoherence, see the reference cited in n. 215 above.

We know that Nicholas uses "*absolutus*" in many different senses. (Cf. p. 103 of my *Nicholas of Cusa's Metaphysic of Contraction.*) Sometimes that which he labels as absolute is understood by him to be only qualifiedly absolute, whereas at other times he means unqualifiedly absolute. In *De Genesi* 4 (173:7), for example, the expression "*absoluta quiditas*" does *not* refer to God, even though in *Ap.* 33:21-22 it does refer to Him. With this complexity of terminology in mind, we might want to construe "*humanitas plurimum absoluta*" to mean, in *DI* III, 7, *humanity insofar as it is uncontracted to any individual of the species.* But even on this construal Nicholas's argument in *DI* III, 7 remains incoherent. For given this construal, *humanitas plurimum absoluta* would not be *Jesus's* humanity, and thus *Jesus's* humanity would not be as a medium between what is purely absolute and what is purely contracted. But suppose Nicholas had said: '*In Christ* humanity is both contracted and fully absolute. It is contracted insofar as it is *Christ's* humanity; and it is fully absolute *humanity* insofar as it is uncontracted to any individual of the species. Therefore, in Christ humanity is as a medium between the purely absolute and the purely contracted.' Even putting this most charitable of all interpretations upon the passage in *DI* III, 7 (125), we still cannot free Nicholas's thought from an incoherence. For since in Christ the humanity, or human nature, in question is always subsumed in the divinity, or divine nature, either it is Christ's human nature or it is not. It cannot at once be both human nature that is Christ's and human nature that is no one's (though it could at once be both Christ's human nature and, qua in God, God—i.e., qua in God, not be human nature at all). And so, it cannot be as a medium between the purely absolute and the purely contracted.

The four criticisms of Nicholas's Christology made by Jacques Doyon are indefensible. (See his "La christologie de Nicolas de Cues," cited in the bibliography.) Doyon begins by impugning what he takes to be one of the key points in Nicholas's Christology: viz., its alleged espousal of exaggerated realism. In particular, Doyon alludes to Nicholas's "Platonistic thesis regarding the requirement of a maximum in a species and regarding the participation of all the individuals in this maximum, which is not an abstract idea but a very real individual that hypostatizes the species—a thesis which has been called 'exaggerated realism'" (pp. 185-186). Doyon should explain carefully just what doctrine exaggerated realists propound; then he should state accurately what Nicholas's position on this issue is; and, finally, he should indicate what exactly is objectionable in Nicholas's view. To dismiss a view simply on the basis of assigning it the vague label "exaggerated realism" is unacceptable. Now, Nicholas's doctrine of universals in Book III of *DI* should be interpreted in the light of his explicit statements in *DI* II, 6 (126)— statements which show that, in general, he is a moderate realist. Nicholas obviously regards the case of Jesus as an exception. But even with respect to this exception he holds that the maximum individual exists *above the species* as the essence of all the perfection that is possible within the species, so that it is *actually* all this perfection [*DI* III, 2 (190-191)]. Thus, this maximum individual which is the fulness-of-perfection of the species is the *final goal of the species*. Now, Nicholas maintains that species and genera exist actually only in individuals [*DI* III, 1 (184:5-6); see also III, 5 (208:5-7)]. So in every existing substance a genus and a species are actually present—in the sense that these individual things have individuated natures that belong to one and the same species and, therefore, to one and the same genus. Yet, no one of these individuated natures *is* the species to which it belongs. In Christ, the maximum individual, there is present the entire perfection of the species to which Christ belongs and to which, at the same time, He is transcendent. Thus, although human nature is present in Christ, Christ's human nature is numerically distinct from the human natures of other members of the human species [*DI* III, 3 (199:1-3): "Now, humanity is present only contractedly in this or that. Therefore, it would not be possible that more than one true human being could ascend to union with Maximality." III, 7 (225:1-4): "Assist your smallness of intellect and your ignorance by Christ's example about the grain of wheat. In this example the numerical distinctness of the grain is destroyed, while the specific essence remains intact; by this means nature raises up many grains." III, 8 (227:12-16): "But there is only one indivisible humanity and specific essence of all human beings. Through *it* all individual human beings are numerically distinct human beings, so that Christ and all human beings have the same humanity, though the numerical distinctness of the individuals remains unconfused." III, 8 (228:1-5 and 12-13): "And although there is a single humanity of all human beings, there are various individuating principles which contract it to this or that person—so that in Jesus Christ there were only the most perfect and powerful principles and those nearest to the essence of the humanity that was united with the divinity . . . . Christ is the one through whom, according to the nature of His humanity, our human nature has contracted immortality . . ."]. Accordingly, although all human beings are one in species, it would be incorrect to ascribe to Nicholas the doctrine that human nature is *hypostatized* in Christ, if "hypostatized" has a meaning that is at odds with the position of moderate realism. For according to Nicholas, Jesus assumed a contracted human nature, not an uncontracted human nature [*DI* III, 3 (202:6-17)]. In *DI* he goes on to add the qualification that Jesus's human nature is as a medium between what is purely contracted and what is purely absolute, so that Jesus's human nature is "the universal contraction of all things" (*loc. cit.*), not just of human beings. This is the point at which the incoherence of his position— which is not a variant of exaggerated realism—begins. [The doctrine of exaggerated realism, not defined by Doyon, is usually regarded as entailing that there is one universal human nature, which is wholly identical with the species, or essence, and which, though present in each human being, is numerically one in them all. (The same point applies, mutatis mutandis, with respect to the other species besides the human species.) But Nicholas holds that Jesus's human nature—of which, necessarily, his rational soul and his body are components—is distinct from the human natures of other men. Cf. *DVD* 23 (101:1-10 and 102:14-16)—with which *DI* III, 3 (302:14-17) is not at odds. In the *Apologia* Nicholas rightly repudiates Wenck's accusation that he "universalizes." Doyon, whether wittingly or unwittingly, aligns himself with Wenck.]

In his second criticism Doyon states: "The other thesis—that of the coincidence of opposites in the absolute because the maxima can no longer exclude one another—seems clear when one takes the mathematical examples which Nicholas favors. But it becomes debatable if one generalizes it. Reason is something other than a maximal sensibility, and the most intelligent blind man would remain deprived of sight" (Doyon, p. 186). Here Doyon misconstrues the doctrine of *coincidentia oppositorum*. According to Nicholas the doctrine does not apply to contracted things—no one of which is absolutely maximal—but applies only to Absolute Maximality itself. (But note the qualification expressed in n. 19 of the Notes to Book Three, in my *Nicholas of Cusa on Learned Ignorance*.) Absolutely maximal sensibility would no longer be sensibility; for in God, who is Absolute Maximality, everything is God. Opposites coincide only in God, says Nicholas. And a blind man—be he ever so intelligent—is not God.

Thirdly, Doyon misconceives the structure of Nicholas's reasoning in *DI* III: "in the logic of the [Cusan] system, 'it is necessary' that Jesus be born of a virgin mother, that He die amid sufferings, that He be resurrected, that He be the Universal Judge and the Mediator-of-salvation of all. This 'it is necessary' dispenses with the need to investigate by means of positive proofs whether the facts of the matter have been such. Or if the facts *are* of interest to us, it is uniquely as 'a posteriori' confirmation of an 'a priori' argument" (Doyon, p. 186). Doyon detects here a danger: viz., "that of giving, within the faith, greater importance to systematic thought and to human logic than to tradition and to the Word of God"—the danger of "an insensitivity to history" (*loc. cit.*). Yet, in *DI* III Nicholas allows adequate room for historical factors. Indeed, his *hypothetical* line of reasoning ("If a maximum which is contracted to a species could be posited as actually existing, then . . . ") is only complete when it takes account of the historical evidence ("On the basis of what Jesus, who was a man, divinely and suprahumanly wrought and on the basis of other things which He, who is found to be true in all respects, affirmed about Himself—[things to which] those who lived with Him bore witness with their own blood and with an unalterable steadfastness that was formerly attested to by countless infallible considerations—we justifiably assert that . . . "). To elaborate upon these historical considerations is not a part of Nicholas's purpose in *DI* III, any more than it was a part of Anselm of Canterbury's purpose to present such an elaboration in the *Cur Deus Homo*. Like Anselm, Nicholas regards these considerations as important; but unlike Anselm he does not consider his line of reasoning to prove the truth of "whatever is contained in the Old and in the New Testament" (*Cur Deus Homo* II, 22). Nor does he adhere to the method of proof *rationibus necessariis.*

Fourthly, in alluding to works other than *DI* Doyon complains: "It is this infinite wisdom itself, possessed by Jesus, which serves as Nicholas's usual argument for establishing the divinity of Christ. Because Christ is Infinite Wisdom, He is both the equal of God and the Son of God. This Neoplatonic Christology has the obvious disadvantage of neglecting almost completely Jesus the prophet and public man who—in the name of a kingdom of justice and love, and in the tradition of the prophets of Israel—takes the side of the poor, the weak, and the exploited" (Doyon, pp. 186-187). In fact, however, Nicholas does *not* attempt to *establish* the divinity of Christ by arguing from Jesus's *infinite* wisdom. Indeed, within Nicholas's system, Jesus's wisdom is deemed to be infinite *because* Jesus is deemed to be divine, so that there can be no question of arguing *from* the infinity of the wisdom *to* the deity and sonship of Christ. [Cf. the selection from the sermon "*Qui manducat hunc panem*" in Vol. II of the Paris edition of Nicholas's works—in particular, all the lines on fol. 108ʳ that precede the new paragraph. Even in *De Sapientia* I Jesus is not *proven* to be divine by appeal to the infinity of His wisdom; instead, God's Infinite Wisdom is simply *asserted* to be the Son. Finally, there is no such proof in *De Pace Fidei* either.] Moreover, Nicholas does not neglect Jesus's mission as prophet and as defender of the poor. (See "*Qui manducat* . . . ," *ibid.*, fol. 106ᵛ-110ʳ.) But the place to look for his concern is not in *De Concordantia, De Docta Ignorantia, De Pace Fidei*, or *De Visione Dei* but in the sermons, which Doyon, in his article, roundly ignores.

233. *DVD* 23 (101:1-2).

234. Just as Nicholas does not claim to understand *how* Jesus can be one person with two natures, so he does not claim to understand *how* from Absolute Perfection there could originate a world of mere contingent perfection (*DI* II, 2) or *how* the Maximum can enfold and unfold all things (*DI* II, 3)—and so on. Yet, on the basis of the diverse considerations that he offers, he supposes himself to understand *that* these doctrines are true. Unlike Kierkegaard he does not expatiate upon

the theme of paradox. He is content to affirm that the Incarnation is a mystery, *super omnem intellectum*. His use of paradoxical *expression* does not center upon the mystery of trinity, creation, and incarnation. Yet, the kinds of paradoxical utterances that he employs are such that when translated into nonparadoxical discourse, the mysteries remain mysteries (i.e., remain paradoxes in Kierkegaard's sense). For example, when a statement such as "God is all in all and nothing in nothing" is translated into an equivalent nonparadoxical expression or set of expressions, the mystery of *how* God can be both transcendent and immanent will remain. N.B. *DVD* 21 (92:4-7).

235. *Proslogion* 14-22.

236. One of the interpreters of Eckhart who call attention to Eckhart's use of dialectic is Bernard McGinn. See his "Meister Eckhart on God as Absolute Unity," pp. 128-139 of *Neoplatonism and Christian Thought*, edited by Dominic J. O'Meara (Albany: State University of New York Press, 1982).

237. *DVD* 6 (20:4-10).

238. *DVD* 15 (67:7-13).

239. Cf. *Ap.* 16:21-22. *DVD* 19 (84:17-18).

240. Cf. *DI* I, 24 (77:1-7).

241. Cf. *DVD* 7 (25:6).

242. *DVD* 15 (68:1-7).

243. *DVD* 15 (69:6-18).

244. This point has sometimes been misunderstood. See the critique of Walter Schulz in Chapter One of my *Nicholas of Cusa's Metaphysic of Contraction* (Minneapolis: The Arthur J. Banning Press, 1983).

245. *DVD* 15 (70:1-2).

246. *DVD* 6 (20:14-19).

247. *DVD* 13 (58:11).

248. *DVD* 4 (12:1).

249. *DVD* 25 (113:10).

250. *DVD* 23 (104:8).

251. *DVD* 9 (37).

252. *DVD* 12 (50).

253. *DVD* 12 (50:15-16).

254. *DVD* 13 (57:11-12).

255. *DVD* 17 (77:15).

256. *DVD* 17 (80:19).

257. E.g., *DVD* 9 (39:8).

258. *De Deo Abscondito* 15. Indeed, God is not even being, insofar as being is conceivable by us and is contrasted with not-being. *De Deo Abscondito* 11:1-5. *DP* 74:1-2.

259. Nicholas is here defending his preceding assertion: "Suppose we say that God is sun. If, as is correct, we construe this [statement] as [a statement] about a sun which is actually all it is able to be, then we see clearly that this sun is not at all like the sensible sun."

260. Sometimes Nicholas says that contradictories coincide in God (*Letter to*

Cardinal Julian, at the end of *DI* III) and sometimes he says that God is beyond the coincidence of contradictories [*DVD* 13 (54:14-15)]. These expressions are meant to be interchangeable. Note *DP* 74, which states both that in God opposites coincide and that God is above duality and otherness. Similarly in *DVD* 10 (43-44) Nicholas remarks both that all temporal succession coincides in one and the same *now* of eternity, in which God conceives, and that God exists beyond *now* and *then*. Note p. 219 of Kurt Flasch's *Die Metaphysik des Einen bei Nikolaus von Kues. Problemgeschichtliche Stellung und systematische Bedeutung* (Leiden: E. J. Brill, 1973).

261. By contrast, mathematical objects are such that they can be conceived of as they are in themselves, for they can be conceived of in accordance with their respective definitions (*DP* 63:10-12).

262. *DVD* 12 (50:5-9). The translation above adds italics to the translation that appears later in Part II.

263. *DVD* 7 (26:13-14).

264. The word "dialectic" has many different uses. Socratic dialectic proceeds by asking questions and eliciting answers, toward the end of arriving at definitions of ethical terms. Since Socrates often trapped the Sophists into answering his questions in such way that, in answering, they contradicted the very thesis they had begun by propounding, dialectic became associated with the notion of contradiction. This association became accentuated by Plato's reasoning in the *Parmenides*, where a series of inconsistent conclusions are "demonstrated" to be true (e.g., that if the One is existent then it is a plurality and that if it is existent then it is not a plurality). In *Topics* I, 11 Aristotle construes the subject-matter of a dialectical problem as something (1) about which most people have no special opinion one way or the other, or else (2) about which they have an opinion that is at odds with the opinion of the wise, or else (3) about which, though there are opinions, there is no general agreement of opinion within either class (i.e., the class of *polloi* and the class of *sophoi*). By way of example he offers the puzzle about whether or not the universe is eternal. In the eighteenth century this very puzzle is one that Kant deals with in the section of his *Critique of Pure Reason* called "Transcendental Dialectic." He regards as *dialectical* reasoning any reasoning that infers, by "valid" logical deductions, two inconsistent conclusions—eliciting one of them from a given assumption and the other from the contradictory of the given assumption. On the one hand, for example, he postulates that the world is without a beginning in time; and herefrom he deduces an impossibility, thereby warranting the conclusion that the world has a beginning in time. On the other hand, he postulates that the world has a beginning in time, and herefrom he deduces an impossibility, thereby warranting the conclusion that the world is without a beginning in time. Hegelian dialectic builds upon the notion of contradictoriness by regarding the triad of thesis-antithesis-synthesis in such way that the antithesis is the negation of the thesis and that the synthesis (which is the negation of a negation) somehow resolves the contradiction, thereby becoming a new thesis that generates a new antithesis, and so on. With Kierkegaard, dialectical reasoning emphasizes conceptual theses and antitheses for which, purportedly, there can be no resolution. For

example, even when the believer receives "eternal life," he does not thereby become timeless; time and eternity are irreducible to each other—though, paradoxically, the eternal can be present in time. Whereas Kierkegaard stresses the irreducibility of certain conceptual opposites, Hegel stresses the dynamic impulses generated by the opposition. Thus, Kierkegaard emphasizes the *incomprehensibility* of the Incarnation, whereas Hegel emphasizes the *manifestation* of the Infinite through the finitude of the historical Jesus.

N.B.: There are, of course, other senses of "dialectic" that have nothing special to do with the notion of opposition. E.g., sometimes the word is used merely to indicate various rules for the art of arguing or simply to indicate the branch of learning that deals with disputing well. This last sense is the one operative in Augustine's (?) *De Dialectica*: "*Dialectica est bene disputandi scientia.*"

265. See n. 234 above.

266. Kierkegaard's anti-Hegelianism should not be mistaken for anti-speculativeness in an unqualified sense. Likewise Nicholas's dialectic must not be confused with his doctrine of *coincidentia oppositorum in deo*. The latter teaches that, e.g., necessity and impossibility coincide in God [see *DVD* 9 (39) and n. 260 above], who is, absolutely speaking, without modal differentiation. However, Nicholas *reasons dialectically* when he speaks of God by means of opposing metaphors, as when he calls God both his Exemplar and his image.

267. *DVD* 2 (8:14-15).

268. *DVD* 9 (35:13).

269. *DVD* 9 (36:4).

270. *DVD* 13 (58:9-10).

271. *DVD* 13 (55:1).

272. *DVD* 21 (93:1-4).

273. Although Ms. Metz 355 was destroyed in Sept. 1944 as a result of World War II, the Heidelberg Academy possesses a photocopy of the portion that had contained *DVD* and other of Cusa's texts. Since the scribe for this portion of Metz 355 used Munich 18570, there was no special need, in the preparation of the present edition of *DVD*, to consult this photocopy. (See R. Klibansky's note on p. XIX of Vol. VII of *Nicolai de Cusa Opera Omnia*.) Using a photocopy or a microfilm is a *pis-aller* that is not without risk when uncheckable against the original.

274. In some instances a redactor might be the original scribe himself, using a different pen or a different texture of ink.

275. Giovanni Santinello considers C² to be Nicholas himself: "Le correzioni autografe del Cusano su C, da noi segnate con la sigla C², sono avvenute in due momenti successivi. Il microfilm del manoscritto non permette di distinguere dal colore dell'inchiostro tali due momenti." See p. 50, Vol. II of his edition of Cusa's *Scritti filosofici* (Bologne: Zanichelli, 1980).

276. Some mss. indicate in their *incipit* that the *Prologus* begins in 1:1 with "Pandam nunc . . . ."

277. Cf. R. Klibansky's appraisal of the text of *DI* contained in Codex Cusanus 218—an appraisal that is found on pp. 222-225 in the appendix to Vol. III of

the Latin-German edition of *DI* (Hamburg: F. Meiner, 1977).

278. According to its *explicit* it was copied on Nov. 8, 1453 at Brixen. It was not, however, the copy that was sent to Abbot Caspar at Tegernsee. For as we know from the Abbot's letter [Letter 8 in Vansteenberghe, *Autour, op. cit.*, p. 119], the copy received by him referred to the brothers as "*devoti*"—a word not found in the *incipit* of the text in *G* but found only in *E*, which was not copied until 1461, so that it too was not the copy received by the Abbot.

279. Certain relationships are, however, obvious. Codex *O* depends upon *M*; and *P* depends upon *O*. Codex *N* follows a ms. that depends upon *E*. Codices *C* and *V* are cognates, *V* perhaps having been copied from a lost ms. that resulted from *C*—as Santinello judges. And *p* depends upon the Strasburg edition (1488), which depends upon *C*.

280. Note Giovanni Santinello's valiant attempt to introduce viable rules of this rigid sort. See p. 52, Vol. II of his edition of Cusa's *Scritti filosofici* (Bologna: Zanichelli, 1980).

281. Other examples can be taken from other mss. For example, at 72:6 *G* has "*in mirabilis*" in place of "*innumerabilis*". In the variant readings for the present edition of the Latin text even simple errors of orthography are recorded. Accordingly, "*igitus*" is noted for *S* at 35:1, even though the copyist obviously intended to write "*igitur*"; similarly, "*fue*" is recorded for *I* at 96:9, even though "*sue*" was obviously intended.

282. Nicholas of Cusa, *The Vision of God*, translated by Emma G. Salter (New York: E. P. Dutton, 1928). Reprinted in paperback in 1978 by F. Ungar Publishing Company of New York City. Cited hereafter as "Salter".

283. The Basel edition itself is based upon the Paris edition (1514).

284. The reference "47:15-16" and all such subsequent references to *DVD* are to the margin and line numbers in the Latin text contained in Part II of this present work.

285. Another example occurs at *DVD* 15 (66:9-11), where the Basel and the Paris editions omit two sentences: "Posse esse materiae primae non est posse absolutum; ideo non potest cum actu absoluto converti. Quare materia prima non est actu quod esse potest, sicut tu deus."

286. On p. 17 Salter has "With Thee, to behold is to give life; 'tis unceasingly to impart . . . ." The word "only" is missing.

287. The editor of the Paris edition makes this decision for the reader by deviating from Codex Latinus Cusanus 219 in the following way: instead of "quando non nisi omnis conatus meus est . . . ," the Paris editor has "quando omnis conatus meus non est nisi . . . ." This reading is then repeated by the Basel editor. Salter has simply taken liberties here with the Basel text. These liberties do not result from a text-critical decision on her part but from a lack of precision in rendering the Basel text.

288. See n. 89 on p. 196 of J. Hopkins, *Nicholas of Cusa on Learned Ignorance, op. cit.*

289. "There cannot, then, be an infinite number of forms in act, for actual infinity is unity" (p. 71 of Salter's translation).

290. Salter, p. 82. Basel text: "Est igitur essentia trina, et tamen non sunt tria in ea, quia simplicissima."

291. Salter, p. 82. Basel text: "Non igitur est trium numeralis distinctio, quia illa est essentialis . . . ."

292. Salter's translation fails to take account of the crucial word "*igitur*".

293. Salter, p. 97. Basel text: "Ostendis mihi lux indeficiens, maximam unionem, qua natura humana in Iesu meo, est tuae naturae divinae unita, non esse quovismodo, infinitae unioni similem."

294. *DVD* 23 (100:15-17).

295. Salter, p. 98. Basel text: "Maxima igitur est unio, eius naturae humanae ut humanae, ad divinam . . . ."

296. Salter, p. 113. *DVD* 23 (100:4-5). See n. 213 above. Also note *Cribratio Alkoran* (Vol. II of the Strasburg edition, reissued by Paul Wilpert), Alius Prologus (14:1-15).

297. Salter, p. 99.

298. "So" here sounds as if it were a term of inference equivalent to "therefore"; in fact, however, Nicholas's Latin word "*ita*" is here a term of comparison.

299. Salter, p. 100.

300. *DVD* 20 (90:13-15).

301. Salter, pp. 113-114.

302. In other contexts other inaccuracies on Salter's part could be readily indicated: e.g., (1) the incorrect translation of (Basel) " . . . ut prius sit animalis homo, quam spiritualis" [*DVD* 24 (106:10-11)] by the words " . . . as if man were animal before he is spiritual" (Salter, p. 121); (2) the incorrect references to St. Austin instead of, correctly, to St. Augustine (Salter, pp. 115-116); the mistranslation of "*discurrit*" as "runneth hither and thither" rather than as "makes inferences" (*DVD* 22; Salter pp. 110-111).

303. Frederick Copleston, *A History of Philosophy* (Westminster, Maryland: The Newman Press, Vol. III, 1953), p. 231.

304. Heinrich Rombach, *Substanz, System, Struktur. Die Ontologie des Funktionalismus und der philosophische Hintergrund der modernen Wissenschaft* (Freiburg: K. Alber, Vol. I, 1965), p. 150n.

305. Hans Blumenberg, *The Legitimacy of the Modern Age*, translated by Robert M. Wallace (Cambridge, Massachusetts: MIT Press, 1983), p. 483. Cited hereafter as "Blumenberg".

306. Blumenberg, p. 483. Also note p. 540 ("For precisely in the implications of this concept of freedom, the Cusan's acute concern regarding the disintegration of the Middle Ages becomes tangible"), p. 541 ("the Cusan's conservative effort"), and n. 77 on p. 659 ("The authentic sense of the text is more 'conservative,' . . . ").

307. Blumenberg, p. 485.

308. See the critique of Rombach in my *Nicholas of Cusa's Metaphysic of Contraction, op. cit.*, Chap. 3.

309. See n. 305 above.

310. Vol. I: *Säkularisierung und Selbstbehauptung*, 1974. Vol. II: *Der Prozess der theoretischen Neugierde*, 1973. Vol. III: *Aspekte der Epochenschwelle:*

Cusaner und Nolaner, 1976 (2nd edition 1982). All three volumes published in Frankfurt, West Germany by Suhrkamp Verlag.

311. In accordance with correct English grammar the words "much disputed" should be hyphenated when they modify a noun.

312. "Et sic concipis mundum, quo nulla quantitas maior, in puncto, quo nihil minus, contineri, et centrum atque circumferentiam eius non posse videri."

313. *DI* II, 1 (96:1-8; 97:13-17). See the references in n. 35 on p. 200 of my translation *Nicholas of Cusa on Learned Ignorance, op. cit.*

314. There are also certain infelicities—as, for example, the following three: "the stars shine in order not to give light to man or to other beings but rather to fulfill their own nature", p. 516 (instead of "the stars shine not in order to . . . "). In line 3 of n. 59 on p. 657 "*infinita*" is misprinted as "*infinitia*", and in line 7 of n. 69 on p. 658 "*erat*" is misprinted as "*erate*"—though in each case the German edition has the correct spelling.

315. "Diese Art der Transzendenz ist also ein innergeschichtlicher Vorbehalt, ist eschatologisch aufhebbar und damit nicht 'substantiell'" (German edition, p. 38). A less opaque translation would be "This sort of transcendence is thus a restricting condition within history . . . ."

316. "An dieser Stelle stösst sich ein platonisierender Exemplarismus mit dem der Souveränität der Gottheit vermeintlich geschuldeten Absolutismus des Willens . . . " (German edition, p. 76). A more accurate translation would render "*geschuldet*" more freely: "In this passage, a Platonizing exemplarism conflicts with the absolutism-of-will that presumably belongs to the sovereignty of the Divinity . . . ."

317. The corresponding German text reads: "Gerade weil und wenn Gott solcher Selbstbezogenheit hingegeben war, musste sein Werk in höchstem Masse jedem Wesen das Seine geben" (German edition, p. 72). The English phrase "Precisely because and if it was the case that . . . " is linguistically and conceptually bizarre. A better rendering would be "Precisely if it was the case—and it was—that . . . ." Better still would be, *simpliciter*: "Precisely because God . . . ." Moreover, "indulged . . . in behavior" has, as applied to deity, a pejorative resonance that is not present in the German; and God's *creating* is not a *behaving*. Finally, "His work had in the highest degree to give to each being what belonged to it" reads as if "in the highest degree" modifed "had": God was in the highest degree obliged to give. But, actually, "in the highest degree" goes with "to give": God had to give in the highest degree. In last analysis, then, the entire German sentence would be more accurately and intelligibly rendered into English as: "Precisely because God was given to such self-relatedness, His work had to bestow upon each being—and to do so in the highest degree—that which was proper to each."

318. This passage is translated on p. 533 of the English edition.

319. The Paris edition—which is, presumably, the one used by Blumenberg—has: "Necessitares enim libertatem, cum tu non possis esse meus nisi et ego sim meiipsius; et quia hoc posuisti in libertate mea, non me necessitas sed expectas ut ego eligam meiipsius esse." (Vol. I, folio 102^r; I have modernized the punctuation.) In line 2 of n. 112 on p. 175 Blumenberg mistakenly has "*respondens*" instead of

"*respondes*".

320. Similarly, n. 28 on p. 654 of the English edition corrects n. 49 on p. 168 of the German edition. But nowhere does Wallace, the English translator, ever state that *improvements* have been undertaken in his edition.

321. *De Beryllo* 29 in the Paris edition is *De Beryllo* 30 in the Latin-German text edited by Karl Bormann and published by F. Meiner Verlag, 1977.

322. All subsequent references à propos of Blumenberg will be to the English translation unless otherwise indicated.

323. Blumenberg, p. 355 (=Vol. II, p. 160 of the German paperback edition). The correct dates, 1401-1464, are printed in the first German edition (1966).

324. Blumenberg, p. 485.

325. Blumenberg, p. 523.

326. Blumenberg, p. 489.

327. *Proslogion* 15 must be read in connection with *Proslogion* 14, *Monologion* 65-66, and *Reply to Gaunilo* 8.

328. See *On Behalf of the Fool* 4 and *Reply to Gaunilo* 8, as found in *Anselm of Canterbury. Volume One*, edited and translated by J. Hopkins and H. Richardson (New York: The Edwin Mellen Press, 2nd edition 1975). Cf. the distinction between *secundum te* and *secundum nos* in *Proslogion* 8. Also note *Monologion* 65-66.

329. Blumenberg, p. 100.

330. Blumenberg, p. 489.

331. Blumenberg, pp. 488-489.

332. Re the predicate "omnipotent" see William E. Mann, "The Divine Attributes," *American Philosophical Quarterly*, 12 (April 1975), 151-159.

333. Blumenberg, p. 489.

334. Another striking example of a miscast comparison between Anselm and Nicholas of Cusa is Donald F. Duclow's "Anselm's Proslogion and Nicholas of Cusa's Wall of Paradise," the *Downside Review*, 100 (January 1982), 22-30. Duclow's principal point is, *passez-moi l'expression*, puerile: "The analogy between Cusanus and Anselm is now complete: Anselm's argument parallels Cusanus's wall of paradise in overcoming finite distinctions, and in insisting on the limit of thinking and on divine infinity. Cusanus's threefold pattern of finite, limit and infinite thus expresses the implicit structure of the *Proslogion*" (p. 26). To be sure, there are certain similarities between Anselm's *Proslogion* and Nicholas's *DVD*. Indeed, some of these similarities Duclow himself disregards; and, on the other hand, certain features which he regards as differences are really similarities. For example, he disregards the following consideration: in *DVD* (Chap. 17) Nicholas makes a point of affirming that God can be seen perfectly only as triune; similarly, in the *Proslogion* (Chap. 23), as also in the *Monologion*, Anselm includes triunity among the points that he is aiming to elucidate. On the other hand, Duclow attempts to mark a difference between Anselm's and Nicholas's view of human sinfulness as it relates to the vision of God: "Concerning the *via negativa* and divine transcendence, Cusanus claims that the divine nature is *essentially* hidden and unknowable. For Anselm, however, it is not only the excessive brilliance of God's light that renders

it inaccessible, but also and *primarily* man's fallen state which has weakened our vision of God . . . " (p. 26, final italics mine). But this comparison between Anselm and Nicholas is partly miscast—a fact that is easily recognizable once Duclow's word "primarily" is deleted, a word whose presence is not justified on the basis of *Proslogion* 14-17, the section educed by Duclow as documentation. For Nicholas himself maintains that man's vision of God is weakened because of the human condition of sin. In *DVD* 21 (93) Nicholas indicates the need to "put off the old man of presumption and put on the new man of humility" if one is to partake of the food of life within the Paradise of delights. And he adds: "To see God the Father and You who are Jesus, His Son, is to be present in Paradise and in everlasting glory. For if any man is situated outside of Paradise, he cannot have such a vision, since neither God the Father nor You, Jesus, dwell outside of Paradise." The one who is situated outside of Paradise is the sinner who strays from God [*DVD* 5 (16:7)]; the one who has put off the old man and put on the new is the repentant and obedient believer. "If I hearken unto Your Word, which does not cease to speak within me and which continually shines forth in my reason, I shall be my own—free and not a servant of sin—and You will be mine and will grant me to see Your Face and then I shall be saved" [*DVD* 7 (28:5-8)]. Indeed, according to Nicholas, one must merit to see the Father in the Son [*DVD* 21 (94:10-11)], and one's approach unto God's light is proportional to the degree of one's faith [*DVD* 24 (108-109)].

Yet, even though there are similarities between Anselm's *Proslogion* and certain of Nicholas's works such as *DVD,* and even though these similarities are in certain respects *stronger* than Duclow recognizes, the end result is that the differences vastly outweigh the similarities and that the *essential* structure of the *Proslogion* is not significantly illuminable by appeal to Nicholas's metaphor of the wall of absurdity. There are many reasons for this inilluminability, but perhaps the configuration of three overlapping reasons will suffice: (1) In the *Proslogion*, just as in *Monologion* 28, 31, and 34, Anselm subscribes to a doctrine of degrees of being and degrees of proportionality between created things and the Supreme Being. Accordingly, he calls God "the highest of all things" (*Proslogion* 5 and 14), "that which alone is greater than all others" (*Reply to Gaunilo* 6) and is "whatever it is better to be than not to be" (*Proslogion* 5). It follows that there is some remote but real analogy between divine goodness and human goodness, even if the difference between God and creatures is so great that creatures, by comparison with God, do not exist in the proper sense of "existing" (*Proslogion* 22). By contrast, in *DVD* 23 (100) and elsewhere Nicholas subscribes to the doctrine of *nulla proportio finiti ad infinitum*. (2) The structure of the *Proslogion* involves a series of interconnecting *reductio ad absurdum* arguments; by contrast, the structure of *DVD* is wholly different. (3) In the *Proslogion* and elsewhere Anselm does not propound a doctrine of *coincidentia oppositorum* in the sense that Nicholas does in *DVD*; for Nicholas's view, but not Anselm's, is to be interpreted as meaning that God is undifferentiated being itself. Thus, according to Anselm, for example, but not according to Nicholas, the three persons of the Trinity are *numerically* three. (Cf. Anselm's *De Incarnatione Verbi* 2 and 9 with Nicholas's *Ap.* 24:1-9, *De Pace Fidei*

8 (23), and *DP* 46.) Moreover, Anselm could never be rightly envisioned as agreeing with Nicholas's statement: "God as Creator is three and one; as infinite, however, He is neither three nor one . . . " [*De Pace Fidei* 7 (21)]. Anselm considers God *a being*—to be sure, a supreme being, an infinite being, a being greater than can be comprehended. By contrast, Nicholas regards God as *beyond being*, insofar as being is conceivable by us or significant to us, i.e., insofar as being is differentiated from not-being [*De Deo Abscondito* 11:1-5. *Ap.* 9. *DP* 74:1-2. *NA* 2 (7:12-17)]. Yet, if God is not *a* (nonfinite) *being*, it is difficult to discern in what sense Nicholas could consistently ascribe to Him *a* (nonfinite) *nature*. (See n. 137 above.) In last analysis, then, Infinite Being, according to Nicholas, is not *a* being; and Infinite Nature is not *a* nature. God is Quiddity, not a quiddity. His "having" quiddity is His being Quiddity. (The major problem that faces Nicholas's doctrine of God is what sense can be made out of such claims.) Many of Nicholas's points are already germinally present in Anselm—as when Anselm says, at the end of *Monologion* 65, that even the word "being" ("*essentia*") cannot express God's unique loftiness. But Anselm does not draw from his germinal ideas consequences as unqualifiedly radical as Nicholas's.

These foregoing three differences between Anselm and Nicholas can be summarized in the following sentence: the wall of absurdity is, for Nicholas, an *absolute* cognitive barrier separating the finite from the Infinite, not only in this era but also in the eschatological age; for Anselm, however, there is no wall of absurdity, since there is no *absolute* cognitive barrier. *Monologion* 66 and 31 indicate that the likeness that exists between the human mind and the Divine Mind is a real likeness, whereas for Nicholas it is only a symbolic likeness. [The "whereas" statement holds true even for *DVD* 25 (111:14-15), *DI* II, 2 (104:9), and *De Mente* 3 (73:2-11). N.B. *Ap.* 24:19-22: " 'All the [symbolic] likenesses proposed by the saints (including the most divine Dionysius) are altogether disproportional [to God]; and to all who do not have learned ignorance (i.e., a knowledge of the fact that [the likenesses] are altogether disproportional), [the likenesses] are useless rather than useful.' "] Now, the *Monologion's* doctrine of greater and lesser approximative likenesses is not abandoned in the *Proslogion* but rather is presupposed. Duclow, we have seen, cites *Proslogion* 14-17 (on his p. 26); but he should also have cited *Proslogion* 18, where Anselm's dialectical meditation moves to the opposite polarity when he prays: "Cleanse, heal, focus, illumine the eye of my mind so that it may behold You. Let my soul muster all its strength and with all its understanding stretch forth once more unto You, O Lord. What are You, what are You, O Lord? What shall my heart understand You to be? Certainly You are life, wisdom, truth, goodness, blessedness, eternity—You are every true good. These are many things; and my limited understanding cannot in a single view behold so many at once in order to delight in all at once. How then, O Lord, are You all these things?" In both *Monologion* 65 and *Proslogion* 17 Anselm alludes to God's ineffability; and in both *Monologion* 66 and *Proslogion* 14 he indicates that we do not know God as He is in Himself. And, yet, these assertions do not prevent him from consistently maintaining, in accordance with his dialectical style, that God can be truly, though obliquely, conceived and known by us. Our understanding of God's nature is limited, says Anselm in *Proslogion* 18; and yet, it is a limited *understanding*. This is the kind of understanding for which Anselm prays at the outset of the *Proslogion*: "Lord, I do not attempt to comprehend Your sublimity, because my intellect is not at all equal to such a task. But I yearn to understand some measure of Your truth, which my heart believes and loves." Duclow claims that, on Anselm's view, the expressions "something than which nothing greater can be thought" and "that than which a greater cannot be thought" "lack the determinacy of a positive concept; they rather indicate the boundary of all finite conceptions and contingent being . . . " (p. 25). But Duclow should point out that for Anselm these expressions, together with certain other premises, are taken to imply that God is omnipotent, just, living, omnipresent, truthful, etc., and that these entailed concepts, as Anselm applies them to God, do not lack all positive determinacy. Even in the *Monologion* (Chap. 49) Anselm wrote: "*Quam enim absurde negetur summus spiritus se amare, sicut sui memor est et se intelligit, cum et mens rationalis se et illum amare posse convincatur, ex eo quia sui et illius memor esse et se et illum intelligere potest?*": "For would it not be very absurd to deny that the Supreme Spirit loves itself as well as remembering and understanding itself—since even a rational [human] mind, from the fact that it can remember and understand both itself and this Spirit, is proved to be able to love both itself and this Spirit?" Anselm could never be rightly imagined to assert what Nicholas asserts in *DVD* 6: "As regards whoever sets out to see Your Face: as long as he conceives of something, he is far removed from Your Face."

Other parts of Duclow's article are equally undiscerning. On pp. 24 and 28 he speaks of Anselm's "one single argument" in the *Proslogion*; and in n. 9 he refers to Gillian Evans' *Anselm and Talking about God* for further elucidation. To translate "*unum argumentum*" as "one single argument" would not be wrong, provided the rendering were understood in the sense of "one single argument-form" or "one single line of reasoning." But by appealing to Evans' book, Duclow shows that he does not understand the phrase in this correct manner. [See p. 390 of my review of Evans' book in *The New Scholasticism*, 55 (Summer 1981), 387-396.] Furthermore, Duclow does not realize (see his p. 27) that Gaunilo's expression "*aliquid omnibus maius*" is a shorthand for '*aliquid omnibus maius quae cogitari possunt.*' (See the beginning and the end of *On Behalf of the Fool* 4. Also note pp. 98-100 of my *Anselm of Canterbury: Volume Four: Hermeneutical and Textual Problems in the Complete Treatises of St. Anselm.*) And he should call attention to the following contrast: that whereas Anselm uses "*aliquid quo nihil maius cogitari potest*" to formulate an admittedly imperfect positive conception of God, Gaunilo denies that the formula is at all useful in conceiving of God *secundum rem*.

On p. 27 Duclow displays a further unclarity when he writes: "But if we consider the argument of chapters II-IV [of the *Proslogion*] in relation to the entire *Proslogion* and to Cusanus, we may acknowledge its validity. For then *Proslogion* II-IV marks but one phase of a meditation which discloses a previously hidden presence, and the argument's truth hinges upon the success of this disclosure. The *Proslogion's* devotional character, its boundary language, and Anselm's doctrine of truth support this interpretation. Throughout the *Proslogion* Anselm seeks a progressive disclosure of God's concealed presence . . . ." Here Duclow professes that the argument of *Proslogion* 2-4 is valid because it is a phase of a meditation which (successfully) discloses God's hidden presence—a disclosing upon which the argument's truth "hinges." Now, Duclow is confused about the notion of validity. For the argument's *validity* depends not upon the argument's *successful disclosure* but upon its *logical form*. (Of course, its logical form must be related to truth in such way that any interpretation that makes the premises true will not also make the conclusion false.) Moreover, what is the meaning of the phrase "the argument's truth"? Does it mean the truth of the argument's conclusion? the truth of its premises? the truth of both premises and conclusion? But an argument might have false premises and a false conclusion and still be valid. Furthermore, the *Proslogion's* devotional character has nothing to do with the argument's validity.

Also objectionable is Duclow's statement that Anselm's *Proslogion* is a colloquy (p. 23). For a colloquy is a conversation; and a conversation is, minimally, a two-directional exchange. But in the *Proslogion* Anselm does not converse with God. Rather, throughout the text, he addresses God in prayer: "*tu, domine deus meus* . . . ." So when in the preface he terms his work an *alloquium*, he means *alloquium* in the sense of an address, not in the sense of a *colloquium*.

Even when Anselm of Canterbury is not being compared with Nicholas of Cusa, his ideas are frequently expounded in fundamentally objectionable ways. Two recent and noteworthy instances hereof are Richard Campbell's article "Anselm's Background Metaphysics" [*Scottish Journal of Theology*, 33 (August 1980), 317-343] and Marcia Colish's "Anselm: The Definition of the Word," pp. 55-109 and 240-252 of her book *The Mirror of Language: A Study in the Medieval Theory of Knowledge* [Lincoln, Nebraska: University of Nebraska Press, 1983 (revised edition; first edition published by Yale University Press, 1968)]. Campbell's article is beset by incoherence of exposition. For example, on p. 320 we are told that according to the perplexity expressed in *De Veritate* 2 by the Student "a proposition has the proper function (*accepit*) of signifying to be what is and what is not . . . ." And on p. 321 we are told that Anselm deals with the perplexity by maintaining that "the proper function of a proposition, its correct end, is to signify to be what is." (That is, Anselm, through the Teacher, denies one of the conjuncts allegedly expressed by the Student: viz., that a proposition has the proper function of signifying to be what is not.) Now, with respect to the relevant speech by the Student and the subsequent response of the Teacher there is no Latin expression that can rightly be translated as "proper function." What the Student says is, in part: "*Sed doce me quid respondere possim, si quis dicat quia, etiam cum oratio significat esse quod non est, significat quod debet. Pariter namque accepit significare esse, et quod est et quod non est*": "But teach me how to reply, if someone should maintain that even when a statement signifies that what-is-not is, it signifies what it ought to. For the statement has received the capability of signifying both that what is is and that what-is-not is." Campbell, in his attribution to the Student, apparently takes the Latin phrase "*accepit significare*" to indicate *having the proper function of signifying*. But not only is this construal linguistically inaccurate, so that Campbell has made a mistake, but it also renders his exposition inconsistent. For although Campbell (wrongly) adheres to this construal in the case of the Student's speech, he (rightly) does not do so in the case of the Teacher's speech—as when the Teacher says: "*Alia igitur est rectitudo et veritas enuntiationis, quia significat ad quod significandum facta est; alia vero, quia significat quod accepit significare.*" At the same time, Campbell shows no awareness either of this linguistic discrepancy or of the leap that is introduced into the Student's speech by representing his initial perplexity as perplexity about proper function.

A second incoherence of exposition occurs on the very next set of pages. For on p. 322 Campbell writes: "The curious thing about language is that, whereas in general any sentence may be either true or false, the point (the *ad quod*, as Anselm calls it) of language-use is truth." This assertion is wrong, because it is not the case that "in general any sentence may be either true or false." The sentence "Please close the door," as well as thousands of sentences like it, is neither true nor false and cannot become either true or false while remaining the same sentence. Here Campbell has simply blundered and has pushed the blunder off on Anselm. Yet, on p. 323 Campbell asserts inconsistently, but this time correctly: "Some well-formed sentences neither affirm nor deny anything, for example, a prayer. Since such sentences are neither true nor false, Anselm, following Boethius, will not call them propositions." But there is really a further inconsistency here. For having now admitted, vis-à-vis Anselm, that prayers are sentences but not propositions, Campbell will have to withdraw his ascription to Anselm of the view that "the point (the *ad quod*, as Anselm calls it) of language-use is truth." Indeed, there is for Anselm no such thing as *the* point of language-use. Anselm sees that one point of language-use is truth, another point is not. When Anselm prays "*Pater noster, qui es in caelis: sanctificetur nomen tuum. Adveniat regnum tuum. Fiat voluntas tua, sicut in caelo, et in terra. Panem nostrum supersubstantialem da nobis hodie. Et dimitte nobis debita nostra, sicut et nos dimittimus debitoribus nostris. Et ne nos inducas in tentationem. Sed libera nos a malo. Amen*" there is not a single true sentence in the entire prayer!

A third incoherence of exposition begins on p. 325, where Campbell concludes: "It emerges from all this that for Anselm truth, that is, correctness, is something which is *done*." But at the top of the next page (i.e., p. 326) Campbell implies that Anselm held the view that truth is *something to be done*. Once again, Campbell shows no awareness either of the discrepancy or of its importance. Does Anselm, according to Campbell, think that truth is something which is done or that it is something which is to be done? And does "which is to be done" mean "which is supposed to be done" or "which is able to be done" or something else? Campbell will have to clarify his point. And when he does so, he will have to restrict his unqualified claim. For in *De Veritate* 10 Anselm alludes to the truth that is in the existence (*existentia*) of things, just as in *De Veritate* 7 he speaks of the truth that is in the being (*essentia*) of all that exists. So there is truth in a stone, because the stone has the nature that God gave it: it is a true stone. But as the stone lies there on the ground it is not doing anything, in the proper sense of "doing." That is, its truth of being is not a doing, in the proper sense of "doing."

(See *Anselm of Canterbury: Volume Two*, p. 6.) Anselm makes plain that any verb can replace the verb "to do," so that in a less than proper sense the verbs "sitting," "lying," "enduring," etc., signify a doing. (Cf. *Proslogion* 7.) But Campbell, in his sweeping claim that for Anselm "truth, that is, correctness, is something which is *done*," does not distinguish between proper and improper uses of language, proper and improper senses of "which is *done*." Accordingly, he oversimplifies, in a way that Anselm does not. In last analysis, it is not the case that truth, according to Anselm, is *tout simplement* something which is done. That there is truth in the being, or existence, of things may *involve* a doing—a creating—on God's part. But it is not the case that this truth *is* a doing. (When in *De Veritate* 12 Anselm speaks of a stone as *acting* by nature, he has in mind situations such as a stone's hitting a window and breaking it. Whoever threw the stone acted on the stone; and in accordance with its nature the stone acted on the window.)

A fourth incoherence of exposition occurs on p. 333, where Campbell alludes to a passage in *De Grammatico* 17 (erroneously identified by him as *De Grammatico* 8): "Since sounds (*voces*) do not signify unless they signify things, in order to say what the words signify, it is necessary to say what the things are." Now, this translation, which is an intrinsic part of Campbell's exposition, contains a misleading inconsistency of rendering. For Campbell translates the first occurrence of "*voces*" as "sounds" and puts the Latin word in parentheses; but the second occurrence he translates as "words," without putting "*voces*" in parentheses. Campbell's translation misleads because it suggests that Anselm is making a distinction between sounds and words in the context at hand—whereas, in reality, "*voces*" means *words* in both instances. Furthermore, in place of "it is necessary" Campbell should have "it was necessary" (*necesse fuit*); and the phrase "in order to say" is not the most suitable translation of "*dicendo*" in the sentence in which it occurs. (See my translation of *De Grammatico* in *Anselm of Canterbury: Volume Two*.)

A fifth incoherence of exposition is the following: Campbell expounds the correspondence theory of truth as if it were necessarily coupled with a "post-Cartesian" theory of representation. On Anselm's view, he tells us, "words re-present things, not in the sense in which post-Cartesian philosophers understood representation as the occurrence of some mental or linguistic entity which stood as some surrogate for a thing, but in the sense that words point the mind towards the reality they signify, thus enabling the mind to think the things themselves, to have them *in intellectu*" (p. 334). Although this much of Campbell's interpretation of Anselm is close enough to being correct, it does not entail that Anselm repudiates a correspondence theory of truth. Campbell understands (post-Cartesian) correspondence theories to teach that a proposition expresses a "relation amongst *ideas* which might or might not correspond to what is the case" (p. 332)—i.e., to teach that words signify ideas or meanings *rather than* things (p. 333). But Campbell seems never to realize that according to Anselm words signify things *by means of* their meanings (*sensus*). Thus, in *Reply to Gaunilo* 7, Anselm concedes that the Fool might not at all think the meaning of "God" (" . . . *deum, cuius sensum nullo modo cogitat*"), hereby implying that realities can be thought through thinking meanings. In *Monologion* 10 Anselm maintains that one way in which someone can "speak of" a man is by silently thinking [the meaning of] the name "man"—that is, by thinking the name "man" insofar as it is significative. And in *Monologion* 65 Anselm is even plainer, when discussing God's ineffability: "*Nam quaecumque nomina de illa natura dici posse videntur: non tam mihi eam ostendunt per proprietatem, quam per aliquam innunt similitudinem. Etenim cum earundem vocum significationes cogito, familiarius concipio mente quod in rebus factis conspicio, quam id quod omnem humanum intellectum transcendere intelligo. Nam valde minus aliquid, immo longe aliud in mente mea sua significatione constituunt, quam sit illud ad quod intelligendum per hanc tenuem significationem mens ipsa mea conatur proficere*": "For whatever words seem to be predicable of this Nature do not so much reveal it to me in its reality as hint at it through a likeness. For when I think the significations of these words, I more readily conceive of what I observe in created things than of that [Being] which I understand to transcend all human understanding. By their respective significations these words form in my mind something much less than—indeed, something vastly other than—that toward which my mind, by means of these inadequate significations, tries to advance in order to understand." Likewise, in *De Grammatico* 4 Anselm alludes to the *meanings* of words: "The common term of a syllogism must be common not so much in verbal form as in meaning. For just as no conclusion follows if it is common in verbal form but not in meaning, so no harm is done if it is common in meaning but not in verbal form. Indeed, the meaning—rather than the words—determines a syllogism." (See my brief discussion in *Anselm of Canterbury: Volume Four*, pp. 9-11.) Campbell ignores these passages, thereby overlooking the fact that, for Anselm, the mind thinks meanings *and* things—thinking the latter by means of the former. Words, through their meanings, signify things. These meanings are *mental words*, or concepts. For this reason, I can signify a man, can mentally speak of a man, by means of conceiving his universal being, viz., *rational, mortal animal* (*Monologion* 10). (In *Monologion* 10 each of the three kinds of speaking is significative, not just the first kind. Anselm states explicitly that natural words *signify*.) But even forgetting about Anselm for a moment, why should all correspondence theorists of truth be saddled by Campbell with the view that words refer exclusively to ideas (or meanings) and that these ideas (or meanings) are what *correspond to* things or states of affairs? Campbell owes us a more penetrating exposition both of Anselm's position and of the basic issues.

In the end, Campbell not only ignores important Anselmian texts, he even expounds certain texts in ways which distort their meanings. Thus, on p. 333 he quotes a passage from *Monologion* 10—a quotation that begins (according to Campbell's translation) with the words "Without absurdity words can be said to be truer the more they are like the things of which they are words and the more expressly they signify them." Campbell then proceeds to expound this passage, in the light of *Monologion* 32 and 33, by talking about how for Anselm "words are likenesses of things": "The view that words are likenesses of things sounds rather bizarre, although it might call to a modern reader's mind Wittgenstein's picture theory of language in his *Tractatus*" (p. 334). With respect to *Monologion* 32 Campbell earlier (p. 333) introduced the following direct quotation (in translation): "Every word is a word of something . . . [*sic* 3 dots instead of 4.] Of what has not been, and is not, and will not be there can be no word." Taking all of the immediately foregoing data together creates the strong impression that Campbell thinks Anselm is talking about words in the usual sense of "words." Indeed, recourse to this usual sense is what leads Campbell to suggest that Anselm's view might sound bizarre to some readers. But, in truth, Campbell has given a distorted translation of the passage in *Monologion* 10; and he misinterprets Anselm's point in *Monologion* 32. In *Monologion* 10 Anselm does not state: "Without absurdity words can be said to be truer the more they are like the things of which they are words . . . ." The subject of the verb *"possunt"* (Schmitt text, Vol. I, p. 25, line 15) is not *"verba"* but *"haec verba,"* i.e., *"verba naturalia."* So Anselm is maintaining that natural words—i.e., images, concepts, and definitions of things—can without absurdity be said to be truer the more they are like that for which they are words. The image that I form of a man when I think of him, says Anselm, is a word (*verbum*) for him. In *Monologion* 10 Anselm distinguishes three different kinds of words. The first kind of word is word in the usual sense of spoken (or written) word. But it is of the third kind of word, viz., natural words, that he says: they can be called truer the more they are like the things for which they are words. That is, some images are truer images than others, some concepts are more precise concepts than others, some definitions are more adequate definitions than others—as judged against the reality with which they are correlated. In *Monologion* 10 Anselm allows for such possibilities as onomatapoetic words. But he is not making the absurd claim that Campbell misrepresents him as making: viz., that ordinary *spoken and written words are likenesses of things.* Instead, his central assertion is that *mental likenesses are natural words for things.* How could the vocalization of "dog" be like a dog? Such a view would not only *sound* rather bizarre, as Campbell says; it would simply *be* bizarre. And it would have nothing to do with Wittgenstein's *Tractatus*, either. (To repeat, onomatapoetic words such as the French word *"glouglou"* in the expression *"le glouglou du vin"*—or even the simple English word "hiss"—would, when vocalized, be similar to that of which they are words. Such instances are tacitly allowed for by Anselm, when he gives his example about sounds which serve as names for themselves—in particular, the vowel "a".) Similarly, Campbell misrepresents the quotation from *Monologion* 32. For there too Anselm is not referring to spoken and written words when he says (my translation): "Every word [or image] is a word [or image] of some thing . . . . There can be no word [or image] of that which neither was, is, nor will be." Anselm is talking about "words by which an object is *thus* mentally spoken"—i.e., about thoughts which "depict" what they are thoughts of. (Cf. the second sentence of *Monologion* 31.) Hence, what he means by "Every word is a word of some thing" is: Every mental image is the image of some thing. And when he declares, "There can be no word of that which neither was, is, nor will be," he is not suggesting the absurd theory that our language can have no words for nonexistent things such as unicorns. Rather, he is stating that an image is not rightly said to be the *image* of some thing unless that thing at some time exists. (See *Anselm of Canterbury: Volume One*, p. 150, n. 71, from which the foregoing sentences are taken verbatim.) Anselm does not require—in the *Monologion*, the *Proslogion, De Veritate*, or anywhere else—that there be some existing (past, present, or future) referent for a spoken or a written word in order for this word to be significative of that thing. This point is already evident in *Reply to Gaunilo* 8, where Anselm takes the expression "[*id*] *quo maius cogitari nequit*" to be significative of a good which is without beginning and without end, etc., whether or not such a good is believed to exist. (Moreover, he is aware of the fact that if it does not exist, then it has never existed in the past and will never exist in the future.) Once again, then, we come across a central passage that Campbell altogether ignores.

However, Campbell's errors run even deeper, thereby doing violence to the core of the *Monologion's* reasoning. For on p. 335 he interpretively infers: "So, if things are what they are only through the Divine Word, and depend upon nothing else than the utterance of a word or separate words, they are, as it were, a kind of language." Campbell also speaks of "the inner expressions of the Creator." Tragically, Campbell has neglected to take account of *Monologion* 30: "Why, then, should I continue to doubt what I earlier left in doubt, viz., whether this Expression is many words or only one? For if [the Expression of the Supreme Nature] is so consubstantial with it that there is one Spirit rather than two, then surely just as the Supreme Nature is supremely simple, so too is this Expression. Therefore, it is not many words but is one word, through which all things have been made." Even the chapter title of *Monologion* 33 tells us much the same thing: "The Supreme Spirit speaks both itself and its creation by means of one word." Moreover, since Anselm goes on to identify this Word with God the Son, he could not possibly, qua orthodox Christian and qua Prior of the Benedictine Abbey of Bec, have concluded that there are two or more words in the Supreme Nature or that created things are, as it were, God's "language." Moreover, according to *Monologion* 63 the Father, the Son, and the Holy Spirit speak themselves and one another by one and the same word.

Just as Campbell totally misses a point that lies at the core of the *Monologion*, so he totally misses a point that is central to *De Veritate*: viz., that Anselm subscribes to a version of the correspondence theory of truth, that Anselm is of the Student's opinion when the Student says: a statement is true "when what it states, whether affirmatively or negatively, is the case. I mean what it states even when it denies that what-is-not is; for even then it expresses what is the case (*quemadmodum res est*)." A few speeches later Anselm repeats the gist of this view by putting it once again into the mouth of the Student, thereby exhibiting that it is still operative in the dialogue: "All I know is that when the statement signifies that what is is, then it is true and truth is in it." Accordingly, still a few more speeches later the Teacher himself can infer: "Therefore, when it [i.e., a statement] signifies that what is is, its signification is true." And he can add: "This conclusion [viz., that a statement's truth is its rightness] also applies when the statement signifies that what-is-not is not." Moreover, in *De Veritate* 3, where the topic is the parallel topic of the truth of thought, Anselm shows that he has not abandoned the view that a true statement, in the customary sense of "true statement," is one which signifies that what is is (or that what-is-not is not). For now the Student says: "*In accordance with the reasoning evidenced in the case of statements*, the truth of thought is best called its rightness, or correctness. For to the end that we might think that what is is and that what-is-not is not, we have been given the capability of thinking that something is or is not. Thus, whoever thinks that what is is thinks what he ought to; and so his thinking is correct. Accordingly, if our thought is correct and true simply because we think that what is is, or that what-is-not is not, then the truth of thought is simply its rightness, or correctness." And the Teacher's endorsement of this verdict is unambiguous: "Your thinking is correct."

The task for an interpreter of *De Veritate* is not the task of deciding whether or not Anselm, with respect to factual propositions, subscribes to the correspondence theory of truth; for unquestionably he does. The task is that of determining and explicating just what Anselm's own version of correspondence was. In last analysis, then, Campbell has misunderstood Anselm's "background metaphysics," even as earlier [*From Belief to Understanding*] he misunderstood the notion of *vere esse* in Anselm's *Proslogion* argument for God's existence.

Marcia Colish's chapter on Anselm ("Anselm: The Definition of the Word") is an irredeemable failure. Let us focus upon the treatises that are so roundly misinterpreted by her.

(1) *De Grammatico.* According to Colish (p. 76) the main question dealt with in this dialogue is "whether a grammarian is a substance or a quality." This construal shows that all of Desmond P. Henry's perceptive and pathbreaking labor on this dialogue has made no impact upon Colish. Though she cites Henry's books, the contents thereof have not gotten through to her. For one of the things most strongly denounced by Henry is the foregoing construal. Indeed, on p. 90 of his *The De Grammatico of St. Anselm* he writes: "Only a crass disregard of the elucidatory method of the dialogue can have led critics like Maurice to assume that Anselm was unconscious of the ambiguities and incongruities, both explicit and implicit, lurking in that opening question as to whether *grammaticus* is a substance or a quality—a question which becomes even more unintelligible than it is intended to be if, with Maurice, one insists on translating '*grammaticus*' as 'a grammarian,' and so makes the problem read, 'Is a grammarian a substance or a quality?'" Henry goes to great lengths to explain why this translation is objectionable, why it obscures and distorts the problem of the dialogue. But Colish seems to have taken neither the dialogue nor Henry's study of it seriously. Thus, she proceeds from bad to worse, when on p. 77 she informs us: "This grammarian, according to Anselm, is a quality . . . ." Now, such a statement expresses precisely the kind of nonsense that Henry takes pains to show not to be Anselm's and not to enter into the argumentation of the dialogue. So already, right at the outset, Colish has miscast Anselm's reasoning so badly that she has rendered it nonsensical. In much the same nonsensical tone, she remarks (p. 76): "But it is equally true [according to Anselm] that grammarians are chronologically and logically derived from the human race, since it is necessary to be a man before one can be a gram-

marian, and *grammaticus* is a species of the genus *homo*." Now, a grammarian, who is an individual man, is not *logically* derivable from the human race; nor does Anselm make such a claim. Moreover, even if we granted that *grammaticus* is included in the genus *homo*, it would not follow herefrom that a grammarian is logically derivable from the human race. And furthermore, even if we assumed that "grammarians are . . . logically derived from the human race" were a *sensible* utterance, Colish's reason for believing it to be a *true* utterance, (viz., "since . . . *grammaticus* is a species of the genus *homo*") would not be a good reason. For inasmuch as not every *homo* is *grammaticus*, *grammaticus* is not logically derivable from *homo*. Finally, Colish's supporting remark is also mistaken: "Sensing that the discipulus will have difficulty understanding this logical relationship, [!] the magister has recourse to a grammatical example in order to clarify it. The genus *homo*, and the species *grammaticus*, he points out, are related in logic the way that the adjective *hodiernum*, and the adverb *hodie* are related in grammar" (p. 76). But what Anselm teaches in *De Grammatico* 13 is that just as "*hodiernum*" does not signify *hodie*, so "*grammaticus*" does not signify *homo*. Hence, his point is that *homo* and "*grammaticus*" are related in the way that *hodie* and "*hodiernum*" are related—i.e., Colish has *reversed* the correct order of comparison. Moreover, in accordance with standard philosophical convention she should use quotation marks to indicate when she is *mentioning* a word; and she should drop her misplaced distinction here between *related in logic* and *related in grammar*, because no such distinction is operative. Anselm is simply pointing out two parallel *grammatical* (i.e., semantical) considerations.

The following cryptic statement (p. 77) is neither documentable from, nor explicable by reference to, *De Grammatico* 18—the text cited by Colish: "Substance is to accident as a word which can either stand alone or be modified is to a word which is grammatically dependent on the word it modifies." Here Colish fails to provide any clarification whatsoever. Some words—e.g., "*grammaticus*"—can both stand alone and modify. But it is not clear in what respect something which is a substance could be an accident. Vis-à-vis a cognate issue Colish writes: "For Anselm, thus, grammatical relationships are prior to, and more comprehensible than, logical and chronological relationships" (p. 77). But what kind of priority is Colish talking about? Are grammatical relationships *chronologically* prior to logical relationships? What sense would this make? On the other hand, grammatical relationships cannot be *logically* prior to logical relationships, since logical priority is a logical relationship. And who would be foolish enough to say that grammatical relationships are *grammatically* prior to logical relationships?

"Now words, Anselm states, *represent* things" (Colish, p. 77, my italics). However, what Anselm says—e.g., in *De Grammatico* 17—is that "*voces non significant nisi res*": "words signify only things." But the notion of signifying and the notion of representing are not identical notions, so that usually "*significare*" should not be translated as "to represent." And where it is thus translated, some accompanying justification needs to be given by the translator. In *De Grammatico* 14 the Student indicates ("*Nempe nomen equi . . . significat mihi equi substantiam per se, et non per aliud*") that "*equus*" *significat equum*. Now, although the word "horse" *signifies* (a) horse, it would not ordinarily be said to *represent* (a) horse. So it behooves a translator and an interpreter to exercise caution with regard to understanding what Anselm means by "*significare*." In Colish's exposition and interpretation, however, caution is thrown to the wind, as the saying goes. Accordingly, on p. 69 Colish jumps from citing the definitions of *noun* given by Donatus, Priscian, Remigius of Auxerre, and Alcuin to concluding: "The grammarians, in short, assert that a noun *defines* a thing both substantially and accidentally, both generically and specifically. They lump these two types of *designation* together, without providing any insights into what changes nominal *signification* undergoes, if any, when it moves from the one to the other" (my italics). That is, she moves from the definitions of *noun* given by the grammarians to the summarizing assertion that, according to these grammarians, nouns define. But this inference is a non sequitur. And fast upon its heels comes the misequating of two ways in which a noun defines with two types of designation. And thereafter comes the unmediated switch to the topic of signification. Colish seems not to realize that a noun (e.g., the noun "man") does not define anything, though its meaning may be defined or though "man" may be used in a definition. Similarly, she seems unaware of any possible distinction between designation and signification. In the end, then, she gives us only a garbled account of Anselm's line of reasoning, and of the interrelationship between grammar and logic, in the dialogue *De Grammatico*.

(2) *Philosophical Fragments*. Colish's discussion of these fragments [*Ein neues unvollendetes Werk des hl. Anselm von Canterbury*] is much too brief, given their direct bearing upon her overall theme. And yet, even this brief discussion is far too imprecise. For example, on p. 78, lines 5-9, she needs to make clear that Anselm is not speaking of cause and effect in the usual sense in such passages as *Philosophical Fragments* 27:26 (wrongly cited by Colish as 27:6): "If we say 'A man is an animal,' *man* is a cause of there being, and being said to be, an animal. I do not mean that *man* is a cause of the existence of *animal*; rather, I mean that *man* is a cause of man's being, and being said to be, an animal." That is, Colish creates the impression that Anselm regards all causation as a logical relationship. For what she says is (p. 78): "Anselm's taste for explaining logical relationships in terms of grammatical relationships is also visible in the *De potestate et impotentia* [i.e., in the *Philosophical Fragments*], particularly with respect to causality. He compares causes to effects by analogizing them to nouns and predicate nominatives." But in the passage from the *Fragments* Anselm is not explaining logical relationships in terms of grammatical relationships; on the contrary, he is explaining grammatical relationships in terms of such logical considerations as the following: "the part here follows from the whole, because it is necessary that the part be where the whole is." And in doing so, he nowhere adopts the position that all causal relations are logical relations.

A few lines later, on p. 78, Colish makes another direct attribution to Anselm: "In the case of efficient causality Anselm's illustrative example is drawn from metaphorical signification. The efficient cause, although it is not the effect, can still be affirmed of it, just as the foot, although it is not the eye, is, figuratively speaking, the eye of a blind man." But with his illustration Anselm is elucidating not some mode of efficient causation but a mode of the verb "to be" ("*esse*"), which, he says, imitates the verb "*facere*" ("to do" or "to cause"). That is, he is illustrating a grammatical point, and he does so by appealing to an empirical linguistic consideration, which is misread by Colish. For Anselm does not make the odd statement that "the foot . . . is, figuratively speaking, the eye of a blind man." Rather, he remarks: "Someone is said to be a foot for the lame and an eye for the blind—not because he is what he is said to be [viz., a foot, an eye], but because he is something else which serves the lame man in place of a foot and serves the blind man in place of an eye." And a little later, when illustrating the verb "to have" ("*habere*"), he notes: "Someone bereft of eyes is said to have eyes—not because he really has eyes but because he has someone else who does for him what eyes do. And he who does not have feet is said to have feet simply because he has something else which serves him in place of feet."

Colish does not know the following a priori truth: viz., that what is logically paradoxical is likewise, by definition, logically absurd and, a fortiori, logically implausible. Consequently, she unjustifiably imputes to Anselm an inconsistent admission: "Anselm admits that this conclusion [viz., that what does not exist is both necessarily nonexistent and necessarily existent] is absurd even though it is logically plausible" (p. 77). This is a misstatement of the outset of the *Philosophical Fragments*, where the Student finds this paradoxical *conclusion* (along with two others) to be "very absurd"; yet, he admits to not knowing how to fault the reasoning by which the logically paradoxical conclusion was reached: "But all these [results] are very absurd. For 'It is impossible to be' and 'It is impossible not to be' are never true [of something] at the same time; nor are, 'It is necessary to be' and 'It is necessary not to be'. . . . Hence, if these [pairs of statements] are inconsistent, then the *premise* from which they follow is also inconsistent: viz., 'What does not in any respect exist both cannot exist and cannot not exist, since it has no ability.' But I cannot at all discern that this premise is false." So the Student never claims that the *conclusion* is both (logically) absurd and logically plausible. And he knows that something is wrong with the premise (because otherwise the conclusion would not be logically absurd, i.e., inconsistent), even though he does not know exactly what is wrong and therefore asks the Teacher for guidance.

Still other imprecisions occur on p. 77. For in interpreting Anselm, Colish speaks of God as serving truth and as serving justice. But this mode of discourse misconstrues Anselm's phrases "*servat veritatem*" and "[*non*] *violentia iustus est.*" According to Anselm, God *keeps to* the truth and is *just* [not] because of compulsion. God does not *serve* truth and does not *serve* justice, as if each were something set independently over against Him. Finally, when Colish writes "so far as God is concerned, necessity and impossibility signify perfections . . . ," she needs quotation marks around the mentioned words "necessity" and "impossibility." Moreover, the Student does not puzzle over whether these words signify perfections; rather, he puzzles over whether they signify an insuperable strength, which is a perfection.

(3) *De Veritate*. In interpreting this dialogue, Colish writes: "There is, according to Anselm, an intrinsic, natural truth in speech, a *veritas enuntiationis*, in

virtue of the fact that a statement signifies truly what its speaker means. The natural significative function pertains to all statements, whether or not they are factually accurate. If they are in fact accurate in addition to expressing the intention of their speakers, they are acidentally true. It is this latter type of truth that Anselm dignifies with the name 'rectitude.' Statements that are intrinsically erroneous may yet be naturally true, but only statements which signify that what is, is, and that what is not, is not, possess both truth and rectitude. Rectitude, the correct relation of the sign to the thing it signifies, is the real criterion of its epistemological validity. This being the case, it is clear that the hearer can perceive the rectitude of a sign only if he knows both the sign and the object it signifies" (p. 79). This interpretive exposition shows how far Colish is from understanding Anselm's *De Veritate*. In the first place, the natural truth of a statement is not said by Anselm to depend upon speaker-meaning, and statements are not said by him to be naturally true *because* they *express the intention* of the respective statement-utterer. Rather, for Anselm, a statement has a natural truth by virtue of its having an established meaning within a language (e.g., Hebrew, Greek, Latin) and because of signifying in accordance with its given nature (*De Veritate* 5): "*That* truth of a statement which . . . cannot be separated from it must be classified as natural. For just as when fire heats it does the truth because it has received [the power to heat] from Him from whom it has its being, so also the statement 'It is day' does the truth when it signifies that it is day (whether it is daytime or not) since it has received the nature to do this." Anselm is, then, not making a claim about subjective speaker-meaning; instead, he is dealing with signification insofar as it is regarded as belonging naturally to a statement. The natural truth of a statement has to do with whether the *statement has a meaning* within the language to which it belongs; it does not concern what *I mean* by the statement. Colish's further interpretation, "Statements that are intrinsically erroneous may yet be naturally true . . . , " is confused. For on Anselm's view a statement's *intrinsic* truth is its natural truth, as Colish herself affirms in the opening sentence of the passage presently under discussion. Accordingly, no statement can be both intrinsically erroneous and naturally true. Thirdly, Colish egregiously misinterprets *De Veritate* 2 when she claims that "only statements which signify that what is, is, and that what is not, is not, possess both truth and rectitude." For in *De Veritate* 2 nothing is clearer than the following: "Admittedly, we are not accustomed to call the statement true when it signifies that what-is-not is; nevertheless it has a truth and a correctness [*rectitudo*] because it does what it ought." Finally, here (p. 79) and elsewhere (p. 101) Colish switches from talking about the rectitude of a statement to talking about the rectitude of a sign. This switch leads to her interpretive claim that "the hearer can perceive the rectitude of a sign *only if* he knows both the sign and the object it signifies" (my italics). This claim is misleading because it obscures the fact that, according to Anselm, not all "signs" signify *objects*, whether actually existing or only possibly existing. Thus, in *De Casu Diaboli* 11 Anselm maintains: "Therefore, in this way, 'evil' and 'nothing' signify something; and what is signified is something not according to fact but according to a form of speaking. For 'nothing' signifies only not-something, or the absence of things which are something. And evil is only not-good, or the absence of good where good either ought to be or is advantageous to be. But that which is only the absence of what is something is surely not something. Therefore, evil truly is nothing, and nothing is not something. And yet, in a certain sense, evil and nothing *are* something because we speak about them as if they were something, when we say 'Nothing caused it' or 'Evil caused it' . . . ." Colish *does* later (p. 96) discuss Anselm's treatment of *nihil* in *Monologion* 8; however, she does not proceed to relate it to the more elaborate treatment in *De Casu Diaboli*. Nevertheless, even her limited exposition of *Monologion* 8 should have brought to her attention the misleading character of her "only if" statement above.

Colish is imprecise when she ascribes to Anselm the view that "discourse, and by extension other kinds of signification, would have no rectitude unless its objects existed . . . " (p. 80). Presumably, she means "at some time existed." And presumably she intends for the reader to supply the prefacing words "in general." For we have no reason to believe that Anselm would deny the truth and the correctness of the statement "Unicorns do not exist" ("existence" here meaning, as on Colish's p. 80, existence in reality). Other imprecisions abound. On pp. 79 and 80 Colish speaks, on Anselm's behalf, of the "truth of the essences of things." Yet, in *De Veritate* 7 Anselm speaks singularly of truth "*in omnium quae sunt essentia.*" And in *De Veritate* 9 and 10 he substitutes "*in rerum existentia*" for "*in rerum essentia.*" Accordingly, it would be more precise to construe "*in rerum essentia*" as "in the being of things" than as "in the essences of things"—more precise to speak of the truth which is in the being of all things than to speak of the truth of the essences of things. However, even more *imprecise* is Colish's substitution of the expression (mutatis mutandis) "truth of fact" (p. 81, line 3) for the expression "truth of essence." And on p. 80 even Anselm's notions of truth and of justice are stated by Colish imprecisely: "For Anselm, thus, truth is rectitude perceived with the reason; justice is rectitude sought consciously by the will and expressed in right action for the sake of, and by means of, justice itself." Yet, Anselm affirms that truth is rightness, or rectitude, perceptible only to the mind (*De Veritate* 11). And justice, he says in *De Veritate* 12, is "uprightness (*rectitudo*)-of-will kept for its own sake." In the case of the notion of truth, Colish's omission of the word "only" and her choice of "perceived" instead of "perceivable" are of momentous import. Equally grave is her apparent implication that justice is (always?) expressed in right action and her mistaken phrase "for the sake of . . . justice itself" instead of "for the sake of . . . uprightness itself." With regard to a different issue, what sense can be made of the following sentence on p. 92?: "That equipollency is a sure path to the rectitude on which truth depends is underlined in the *De veritate*, where the discipulus at the beginning of the dialogue insists that the magister demonstrate his conclusions with a 'definition of truth,' as he had in the *Monologion*." How can anyone demonstrate his conclusions with a definition of truth? For a *definition* does not *demonstrate* (i.e., *prove*) anything. Nor does the Student make any such odd request of the Teacher in *De Veritate* 1.

(4) *Epistolae de Incarnatione Verbi Prior Recensio.* We have already seen that Colish does not understand *De Grammatico*. Her incomprehension of *Episto-*

lae de Incarnatione Verbi Prior Recensio follows suit: "When it comes to the actual content of Roscellinus's teachings, Anselm presents an objection derived bodily from the eleventh-century grammar with which, as we have seen, he was so deeply concerned. In fact, his argument is quite reminiscent of the *De grammatico*. He holds Roscellinus to be in error because his attribution of the names 'Father,' 'Son,' and 'Holy Spirit' to the Persons of the Trinity, as Anselm understands them, is grammatically inaccurate. In Roscellinus's mouth, he states, these names are *flatus vocis*, because they are applied to God in the way that such terms as 'white,' 'just,' 'king,' and 'grammarian' are applied to an individual man" (p. 84). However, neither in *Epistolae de Incarnatione Verbi Prior Recensio* 2 nor 4 nor 11—the citation given by Colish—nor anywhere else does Anselm allege that in Roscelin's mouth the names "Father," "Son," and "Holy Spirit" are *flatus vocis*. Moreover, in making the comparison between "Father," "Son," "Holy Spirit" and the terms "white," "just" and "*grammaticus*," Anselm is not alluding to the opinion of Roscelin but rather to the opinion of a Frankish friend of his, who, reportedly, claimed to have heard this comparison being used by Anselm himself. Furthermore, "certain dialecticians"—among whom Anselm does not explicitly place Roscelin—are said by Anselm to consider [the names of] universal substances to be mere vocal sounds [*flatus vocis*]. But, of course, the words "Father," "Son," and "Holy Spirit" signify relations, not universal substances, so that it does not follow that they are among the words considered by these dialecticians to be *flatus vocis*. Moreover, qua signifying *relations*, they are not like the terms "white," "just," and "*grammaticus*," which properly signify *qualities*. Colish owes us an unmuddled account of *Epistolae de Incarnatione Verbi Prior Recensio*. Symptomatic of her textual misapprehension is her muddled translation of the following portion of Section 4 of the *Prior Recensio*: "*Deo protegente numqam de hac fide disputabo quomodo non sit; deo dante semper credendo, amando, vivendo de illa disputabo quomodo sit.*" These words she renders as "By no means does God protect me if I dispute against the faith on how he does not exist. Through God's continual grace I believe, I love, I live for the disputation on how he does exist" (p. 85), instead of as (something like) "God safeguarding, I will never, with respect to this faith, discuss the [alleged] reasons why it is not true. God granting, I will—while ever believing, loving, and living [this faith]—discuss, with respect to it, the reasons why it *is* true." A smoother but equally acceptable rendering would be: "God safeguarding, I will never enter into dispute about the [alleged] reasons why this faith is not true. God granting, I will—while ever believing, loving, and living [this faith]—enter into dispute about the reasons why it *is* true." (Likewise erroneous is her translation, on pp. 91-92, of a portion of *Epistola* 77, "*Ea enim ipsa sic beatus AUGUSTINUS in libro* De trinitate *suis magnis disputationibus probat, ut eadem quasi mea breviori ratiocinatione inveniens eius confisus auctoritate dicerem*" as "For since this is how blessed Augustine proved his great disputations in his book *De trinitate*, I may argue in the same way, finding, as it were, my brief arguments in his sure authority.")

(5) *Cur Deus Homo*. In n. 78 on p. 245 Colish indicates that "all Anselm quotations in English, unless otherwise indicated, will be taken from this translation"

[i.e., from my translation in *Anselm of Canterbury*]. Yet, in a way that belies her scholarly credentials as an historian, Colish amends many of these Anselm quotations without always giving an indication thereof. At no place is this practice more unpardonable than on p. 83 (where she silently alters the translation "You prove the necessity of God's becoming a man . . . " *to* "You prove the necessity of God's becoming man . . . ") and p. 87 (where she unacknowledgedly changes "For what reason and on the basis of what necessity did God become a man?" to "For what reason and on the basis of what necessity did God become man?"). Moreover, vis-à-vis the latter translation she once writes "that" for "which," writes "elegance" instead of "the elegance," and excises a series of eight words without using ellipsis marks. (Other tampered-with quotations, unacknowledged as such, occur on pp. 85, 91, and 92. Furthermore, Colish should refer readers to the revised translations of *Monologion* 1-5, found in Appendix I of *Anselm of Canterbury: Volume Four*; and she herself should quote from this revision—something she fails to do at the top of p. 96.) No doubt Colish prefers, for the title "*Cur Deus Homo*," the translation "*Why God Became Man*." But this preference does not justify her imputation of this translation to me, the translator. Nor does it excuse her failure to state her reasons for *her* preference and to show in exactly what respects the *translator's* reasons in support of the translation "*Why God Became a Man*" (i.e., "*Why God Became a Human Being*") are unacceptable. (These reasons are presented in the notes to the translation, and they are discussed at greater length in Volume Four. N.B.: the title on the cover of the *paperback* edition entitled "*Why God Became Man*" was placed there by the Editor of The Edwin Mellen Press without my advance knowledge or consent.) All translations of extended medieval philosophical and theological texts are destined to need revisions of one kind or another. Indeed, all translators are to some extent dependent upon others to find and to make whatever emendations and corrections seem necessary. But no translator should brook the misrepresentation that results from the unacknowledged and undefended substantive altering of a translation that is imputed to him. Especially he should not do so when the alteration produces a substantial error.

Turning to another topic, we see that much of Colish's discussion of *rationes necessariae* (i.e., compelling reasons, compelling considerations, necessary reasons, rational necessity) is misguided. In particular, there is no attempt to distinguish between, or else to call into question the alleged distinction between, *rationes necessariae* and *rationes congruentes*. In general, no serious analysis is ever given of the many different kinds of reasoning that Anselm includes under the label "*rationes necessariae*." On p. 83 Colish writes: "According to Anselm, an argument may be considered to have been proved by necessary reasons when it states that things are the way they really are, without invoking the support of a higher authority." But how can an *argument* be *proved* by merely *stating* that things are the way they *really* are? On the same page Colish remarks: "All kinds of statements may be verified by means of necessary reasons . . . . Apparently, their major practical limitation as epistemological tools seems to be the fact that they are usually grammatical in structure." But how can Colish speak generally of *verification* by necessary reasons if necessary reasons are usually *grammatical*? Elsewhere (viz., p. 88) we are told that "according to Anselm, necessary reasons have several epistemological advantages. Like all signs possessing rectitude, they are accurate representations of their objects, so far as they go; and they are more useful than authoritative statements, which are not decisive for the nonbeliever." But in what sense are necessary reasons *signs*? And in virtue of what are they said to *represent*? (Would anyone ordinarily say that "compelling" considerations are signs or that they *represent*? On p. 83 Colish says, inconsistently, not that *rationes necessariae* are signs, but that they are "a mode of explaining the rectitude that exists between a sign and the object it signifies.") Moreover, Colish makes it sound as if necessary reasons differed from authoritative statements in that they *are* decisive for the nonbeliever. However, on the very next page (viz., p. 89) she conveys exactly the opposite impression when she tells us that "the most they [i.e., necessary reasons] can do for a nonbeliever is to show him that Christian beliefs are not entirely incoherent." And this conveyed impression is also at odds with Boso's conclusion in the *Cur Deus Homo*: "All the statements you make seem to me to be reasonable and to be statements which cannot at all be contradicted. And I recognize that whatever is contained in the Old and in the New Testament has been proved by the solution of the single problem which we have set forth. For you prove the necessity of God's becoming a man, and you do so in such way that even if the few things you have introduced from our books are removed (e.g., what you mentioned about the three persons of God and about Adam), you would satisfy not only the Jews but also the pagans by reason alone."

(6) *Monologion*. "Just as a man has interior *locutiones mentis* before expressing himself in externally perceptible signs," claims Colish on behalf of Anselm, " . . . so the Creator has *locutiones* about the universe before he reifies it externally" (p. 97). But as we learned in the foregoing examination of Richard Campbell, such a claim is flatly and pivotally wrong, so that Colish's overall interpretation of the *Monologion's* trinitarianism collapses. Her extended misinterpretation of *Monologion* 1-4 has equally disastrous consequences. To begin with, she wrongly views *Monologion* 1-4 as constituting a single proof (pp. 95-96: "By the time Anselm has reached the end of chapter 4, which terminates the proof of God's existence in the *Monologion* . . . "). Then she misleadingly claims that Anselm *assumes* at the outset that the various goods which men desire have a single cause (p. 96). Anselm himself, however, does not *assume* this conclusion; rather, he attempts to infer it. And so, he commences deliberately: "Although the good things whose very great variety we perceive by the body's senses and distinguish by the mind's reason are so numerous, are we to believe that there is one thing through which all good things are good, or are we to believe that different goods are good through different things?" Obviously, there are difficulties with Anselm's subsequent inferential reasoning. Yet, the reasoning should not mistakenly be termed an assumption. How logically confused Colish is is evident from her statement that "Anselm has more or less inferred the proof *that* a Supreme Being exists" (p. 96). Now, in a proof the *conclusion* is inferable from the premises; but what is it to infer a *proof*? And does Anselm do it? Elsewhere Colish remarks that Anselm "establishes the proof of God's existence" (p. 95), when she should say that he purportedly estab-

lishes God's existence, not the proof thereof. Colish sees Anselm as inferring, from the assertion that all men naturally desire the things which they judge to be good, that all men *should* want to know the ultimate cause of the goods which they desire (p. 95, my italics). However, Anselm makes no such inference that includes (the Latin equivalent of) the deontic operator "should." According to Colish, Anselm's proof "is based on a theory of participation and proportionality" and is, in part, "reminiscent of Platonic idealism" (p. 95). She begs the question against F. S. Schmitt by interpreting the *Monologion's* "*per aliud*" terminology to be tantamount to the language of participation. [She should refer the reader to F. S. Schmitt's provocative discussion in his article "Anselm und der (Neu-)Platonismus."] In addition to begging an important question Colish, in effect, travesties Anselm's reasoning, at the outset of the *Monologion*, when she expounds it along the following lines: "The first shift in definition is the almost imperceptible conversion of this *supreme good* into a being. Next, since this being is indubitably very good, and since all other goods exist through it and in relation to it, it must therefore be self-existent, assuming the absurdity of infinite regress. As self-existent, it is not merely very good, but *supremely good*" (p. 95, my italics). At times, in dealing with the *Monologion*, Colish makes undisciplined overstatements, as when she writes: "Anselm insists that his intention as a theologian is *purely* utilitarian. He formulates his speculations, he says, with an eye to their practicality" (p. 93, my italics). At times, she incautiously ascribes to Anselm that which she does not recognize to be unintelligible: "Anselm holds that nonrelative expressions, such as infinitive statements, may be properly and truly applied to the Creator, so long as the characteristics which these statements attribute to him *are better than they are not*" (p. 98, my italics).

   Colish also misconstrues Anselm's argument regarding truth. For à propos of *Monologion* 18 she remarks: "truth must be eternal in order for any statement about eternity to be true" (p. 98). Anselm's argument, however, does not have recourse to statements about eternity. Other sections of the *Monologion* are likewise badly misrepresented. "It is even more difficult," writes Colish, "for man to grasp precisely how the Creator and his Word can be two and yet one, although, he [i.e., Anselm] thinks, the terms 'Father' and 'Son' have a high degree of rectitude" (p. 99). Yet, Anselm does not say that the terms "Father" and "Son" have *rectitude*; he says that they are *suitable*, or *fitting* (*Monologion* 42). "Anselm," notes Colish on p. 99, "attempts to provide some consolation by elaborating some of the positive features of human nature, on the basis of his definition of the human mind as the best *speculum* of the Trinity." Contrary to this verdict, however, Anselm does not *define* the human mind as the best mirror of the Trinity; rather, through reflective meditation, he arrives at this conclusion.

   (7) *Proslogion* and *Debate with Gaunilo.* Colish's treatment of these three works is riddled with as many errors and imprecisions as is her treatment of the *Monologion*. On p. 90, for example, we find the claim that "nowhere in Anselm's work does he refer to the *Monologion* and *Proslogion* as proofs of God's existence." But this claim does not hold true of the *Proslogion*. For in the preface thereto Anselm indicates that he was looking for a single consideration which

"would suffice by itself to demonstrate that God truly exists . . . ." Moreover, in *Reply to Gaunilo* 10 he recapitulates: "I have now showed, I believe, that in the aforementioned work I proved—not by inconclusive reasoning but by quite compelling reasoning—that something than which a greater cannot be thought exists in reality."

At the beginning of *Proslogion* 2 Anselm prays: "Lord, Giver of understanding to faith, grant me to understand—to the degree You deem best—that You exist, as we believe, and that You are what we believe [You to be]." But Colish construes Anselm's Latin to mean that God is *what* we believe Him to be and *as* we believe Him to be (p. 100)—thereby misconstruing the role of "*sicut*" in "*quia es sicut credimus* . . . ." Similarly, the expression "*aliquid quo maius nihil cogitari potest*" is wrongly translated as "that than which nothing greater can be conceived" (p. 100). At various times these words are called by Colish the "name of God," a "formula" (p. 100), a name that is "a self-evident definition," a name that is "an accurate designation of God," "a sign" (p. 101). How the words can be all these things—e.g., both a name and a definition—is never explained ["From Anselm's point of view, the beauty of the name lies in the fact that it is a self-evident definition; it virtually proves itself" (pp. 100-101)]. Colish goes on to allege that "the name proves the existence of the being which it defines" (p. 101), so that, apparently, according to her, it is not only a name and a definition but also a proof. So, then, Colish has made two quite different claims: viz., that the name or definition virtually proves *itself* and that the name proves the existence of *the being* it defines. Previously she asserted that "by putting the definition in the negative, Anselm gains the advantage of being able to develop the first stage of his argument without having to prove that God is a being . . . " (p. 100). So we are being told by Colish that although the name proves the existence of the being it defines, the first stage of Anselm's argument is developed without his having to prove that God is a being! Confusion increases when she maintains: "It is not Anselm, but the fool, who makes an unwarranted leap from thought to being. What Anselm does, on the other hand, is to move from being to thought in the formulation of a name of God that does not contradict the nature of God as he is" (p. 101). So even though Colish has told us that the name of God proves the existence of the being which it defines, she now tells us that Anselm moves from being to thought in formulating this name, which does not contradict the nature of God as He is. Thus defying all logic, Colish's reasoning somehow culminates in the conclusion that Anselm, in the first chapters of the *Proslogion*, has "established the rectitude of the definition of God as *aliquid quo maius nihil cogitari potest*" (p. 101). In the jumbled process of reaching this (erroneous) point she has managed to contend that "according to Anselm, the reason why the fool is wrong is that he fails to make this distinction between *esse in solo intellectu* and *esse et in intellectu et in re*" (p. 101). Hereby she confirms her own utter failure to comprehend Anselm's reasoning in *Proslogion* 2. For not only does Anselm not charge the Fool with failing to make this distinction, but also his entire approach is based upon the conviction that the Fool is not so foolish as to fail to make it.

Colish's misapprehension of Gaunilo is likewise total—as is her misrepresentation of Anselm's responses. On p. 104 she singles out "four major objections" (p. 103) raised by Gaunilo on behalf of the Fool. "Gaunilo," she says, "finds it impossible to follow Anselm's distinction between *esse in solo intellectu* and *esse et in intellectu et in re*. They are both in the mind; and if we begin with the mind, he asks, what grounds have we for claiming that the latter is extramentally real while the former is not?" (p. 104). Now, this alleged objection is a case of pure invention on Colish's part. Gaunilo's text makes clear that the Fool does not find it impossible to follow Anselm's distinction; and there is nothing in the text that corresponds to the remainder of the alleged objection. Colish is also mistaken in her representation of Anselm's response: "Taking up next the difficulty found by Gaunilo in the distinction between *esse in solo intellectu* and *esse et in intellectu et in re*, he [viz., Anselm] points out that the intellect and reality cannot be thought of as locations where God may be found sometimes but not always" (p. 105). But Anselm does not say that once a given intellect has conceived of God, God remains continually in that intellect, even when it is no longer conceiving of Him; nor does he say that that intellect cannot stop conceiving of God.

Gaunilo's second objection, according to Colish, is that if the distinction between *esse in solo intellectu* and *esse et in intellectu et in re* "were so obvious as Anselm makes it, there would be no fools" (p. 104). However, what Gaunilo says is that if a nature than which a greater cannot be thought could not, when spoken of or heard of, be thought not to exist, then "why was your entire argument enjoined against one who doubts or denies that there is any such nature as this?" Anselm's response, says Colish among other things, maintains that "words are intrinsically meaningful, in one way or another" and that "statements, even if defective, resemble the things they signify, and they therefore provide some positive knowledge about them" (p. 105). However, Anselm does not say, unqualifiedly, that spoken and written words are intrinsically meaningful, in one way or another. Nor does he teach that statements *resemble* the things they signify.

Gaunilo's third objection, affirms Colish, states that "the name ['God'] is meaningless unless one knows what it signifies. Even if we assume that the name of God is *in intellectu*, this does not prove the existence of God *in re* . . . " (p. 104). Yet, Gaunilo does not make the vacuous (?) assertion that the name "God" is meaningless unless one (someone?) knows what it means; rather, he maintains that one simply does not know what is signified by the *word* "God" (the implication being that "God" is not a *name*). Colish needs to analyze Gaunilo's distinction between "*cogitare secundum vocem*" and "*cogitare secundum rem*." Then, perhaps, she will see that Gaunilo does not say "if we assume that the name of God is *in intellectu* . . . ." Rather, he says "if that which cannot even be properly conceived [i.e., the thing, not the word] must nonetheless be said to be in the understanding, then . . . . " To this alleged third objection, supported by Gaunilo's appeal to the counterexample about a perfect island, Anselm is alleged to respond by pointing out that all islands (a) are created things and (b) are contingent and (c) come into being and (d) pass away and (e) can be conceived not to exist (p. 105). None of these five responses, however, can be found in Anselm's *Reply*. Perhaps instead of inventing responses to put into Anselm's mouth, Colish might want simply to claim that the logic of Anselm's reasoning commits him to such responses, while admitting that he does not actually make any of them. But if so, she would have to revise her list of points *a-e*. For Anselm's logic does not necessarily commit him to invoking the view that all islands are created things which pass away.

Gaunilo's fourth objection, notes Colish, "argues that it is possible to conceive hypothetically of the nonexistence of God, just as it is possible to conceive of the nonexistence of the self or of anything else" (p. 104). But Gaunilo does not *argue* that it is possible to conceive of the nonexistence of the self or of anything else. Rather, he indicates perplexity ("I do not know whether, during the time when I know most certainly that I exist, I can think that I do not exist"), and by way of argument he poses an ingenious dilemma ("If I can, why [can I] not [think not to exist] whatever else I know as certainly [as I know my own existence]? On the other hand, if I cannot [think that I do not exist], then this [property of not being able to be thought not to exist] will no longer be uniquely God's"). According to Colish, Anselm responds by maintaining that "the self and all other beings that are not God are contingent . . . and thus eminently conceivable as nonexistent" (p. 105). However, Colish's representation of Anselm misses the point. For Anselm does not say that *because* all things other than God are contingent they can be conceived not to exist. Indeed, if he were to have said something close to this, then he would have said it the other way around: viz., that because all things other than that-than-which-a-greater-cannot-be-thought can be thought not to exist, they are contingent. But instead of saying this, he distinguishes two different senses of "to think" ("*cogitare*") and indicates that in one sense a thing (other than God) can be thought not to exist, even while it is known to exist, but that in another sense it cannot then be thought not to exist.

Colish's distortion of Anselm's debate with Gaunilo is not limited to the foregoing objections and responses. For she also views Gaunilo as having recast Anselm's *formula* ("*aliquid quo maius nihil cogitari potest*") *into a hypothetical syllogism* (p. 104). But how such a recasting would be possible once again defies all logic. Furthermore, she regards Anselm as making "the trechant observation that Gaunilo has misquoted him by understanding him to say that *if* something exists in the mind it *therefore* exists in reality" (p. 105). Here again Colish fails to be precise. For Anselm does not reproach Gaunilo for imputing to him the view "if *something* . . . , it therefore . . . ." Instead, he reproaches him for imputing the view "if *that which is greater than all others* . . . , it . . . ." This difference is critical—something Colish fails to realize. Colish likewise says of Anselm: "He also slices through Gaunilo's query of how, from a purely formal perspective, one would differentiate *esse in solo intellectu* from *esse et in intellectu et in re*. It is an irrelevant question, he says, that 'is not my concern'" (p. 105). But in *Reply to Gaunilo* 6 Anselm is not talking about Gaunilo's alleged query regarding the foregoing distinction. He is talking about Gaunilo's notion of understanding, and he (wrongly) charges Gaunilo with contradicting himself. This contradiction, he says, "is not my concern; you attend to it." So he does not dismiss the matter as irrelevant; he dismisses it as incoherent. Colish also purports to find, in *Reply to Gaunilo* 1, Anselm observing that "no fool . . . could have constructed objections as good as Gaunilo's" (p. 104). But here again she is inventing.

In the publisher's blurb on p. i—a blurb approved by Colish and incorporated by the editor directly into the volume—we read the simplistic claim that "Augustine stressed rhetoric, Anselm shifted to grammar (including grammatical proofs of God's existence), and Thomas Aquinas stressed dialectic." Since we are presently focusing attention exclusively upon Anselm, let us merely remind ourselves that in Anselm's corpus of works *there are no grammatical proofs of God's existence*. Indeed, only a judgment as wrongheaded as the judgment that the *Monologion* or the *Proslogion* contains a grammatical proof of God's existence could lend credence to the oversimplified differentiation that is made between Augustine, Anselm, and Aquinas. On p. 92 Colish tones down her judgment slightly: "The specific kind of necessary reasons which Anselm employs in the *Monologion, Proslogion*, and *Contra Gaunilonem* tend [*sic*] to be grammatical in nature. His principal methods for implementing necessary reasoning in these three works are equipollent proofs and explanations turning on the grammatical relationships among words." But even as thus stated, the claim is tendentiously exaggerated—as are the following cognate claims: (1) "the verbal medium in which Anselm himself thinks and works is grammar" (p. 58); (2) "Anselm's major epistemological concern is the theological problem of speaking about God" (p. 59); (3) "where [*sic*] Augustine sees the task of theology as the eloquent expression of the Word, Anselm sees it as the conscientious and faithful definition of the Word" (p. 59); (4) "Anselm's primary mode of thought is grammar" (p. 63); (5) "Anselm's whole approach to this problem [of the persons of the Trinity] is verbal rather than logical" (p. 84). But we have already seen how Colish's tendentious approach distorts not only Anselm's debate with Gaunilo but also the structure of Anselm's *Proslogion*, the structure of his *Monologion*, his actual criticisms of Roscelin in *De Incarnatione Verbi (Prior Recensio)*, his doctrine of signification in *De Grammatico*, his notions of truth, rectitude, and justice in *De Veritate*, his notion of *rationes necessariae* in the *Cur Deus Homo*, and the relation between grammar and logic in the *Philosophical Fragments*.

Also noteworthy is Colish's misrepresentation of Anselm's solution—in *Proslogion* 7—to his perplexity regarding God's omnipotence: "How, he asks, can we say that God is omnipotent when there are some things, namely evil things, which he cannot do? Are his inabilities in this respect a real curtailment of his power? Anselm answers that God's inability to do evil in no way qualifies his omnipotence, because *not* to be able to do evil is better than *to* be able to do evil, and is consequently true of God" (p. 102). Here Colish's representation of the supporting reason ("because *not* to be able to do evil is better than *to* be able to do evil") is wrong. For Anselm's answer is not in terms of an inability's being *better* than a corresponding ability. Rather, he explains that God's "inability" to do evil is improperly called an inability. For it is a power, not a powerlessness. "Therefore, Lord God, You are more truly omnipotent because none of Your abilities are really inabilities and because nothing has any power over You." With respect to *Proslogion* 9-11 Colish travesties Anselm's reasoning when she expounds: "His [i.e., God's] compassion extends to all, even to the wicked, because it operates in accordance with God's nature rather than being proportioned to our own just deserts. This idea may seem difficult for men to understand, says Anselm, but it is true, because the reverse would be impious. In any case, he points out, justice can be redefined as the will of God, which effectively takes care of the problem" (p. 102). Once again Colish misrepresents a supporting reason ("it is true, because the reverse would be impious"). And nowhere does Anselm redefine justice as the will of God.

With regard to secondary literature Colish erroneously speaks of Immanuel Kant's "reading of the *Proslogion* proof as an ontological argument" (p. 56). Her statement is objectionable because Kant, in his *Critique of Pure Reason*, had in mind Descartes' and Leibniz's versions of a priori proofs for God's existence. Colish's brief treatment of Charles Hartshorne, on p. 62, is totally inadequate, since it fails to mention Hartshorne's distinction between *actuality* and *existence*—a distinction that is central to Hartshorne's attempt to clarify "Anselm's discovery." And there should be some mention of William Rowe's significant article "The Ontological Argument and Question-Begging" (1976).

Finally, Colish should be more cautious in her claim (p. 106) about the number of extant manuscripts of the *Monologion* and the *Proslogion*. She does not entertain the possibility that new manuscripts have been located (as in fact has occurred) since the publication of F. S. Schmitt's critical edition in 1938.

(8) *Concluding Observations*. Ironically, Colish belongs to the group of interpreters who regard what Anselm says as simple and as easily comprehensible (p. 63)—so unaware is she of her own extensive incomprehension. Moreover, given her theme, it is surprising that she takes no account of Helmut Kohlenberger's *Similitudo et Ratio. Überlegungen zur Methode bei Anselm von Canterbury* (1972). As for philosophical terminology, she alludes to tautology, denotation, logical untenability, question-begging, logical necessity, a priori thought, new ontological idealism, Hegelianism in its modern Italianate form, Whiteheadean metaphysics, static absolutes (p. 62). And yet, in the name of what is "fully self-evident to the historian" (p. xvi) she presumes to make a virtue of having "expressly avoided using philosophical and literary terms with the technical meanings and connotations that contemporary thought attributes to them" (p. xv). In the end, much of her distortion of Anselm's views is directly attributable to her impoverished understanding both of the contemporary and of the Anselmian notions of word, name, definition, proof, designation, signification, representation, rational necessity, logical priority, necessary truth, logical demonstration, rational consistency. Her shortcomings in philosophy are combined with a lack of facility in textual interpretation (as epitomized by the inability to portray accurately the debate between Anselm and Gaunilo), a defective historical sense (as evidenced by the inventing of views to put into Anselm's mouth and by the substantive, rather than merely heuristic, utilization of the oversimplified organizing categories *rhetorical-grammatical-dialectical*), a disrespect for scholarly procedure (as betrayed by the unacknowledged alteration of translations and, in the case of *Monologion* 1-5, by neglect in calling attention to the more accurate of two different renderings by the same translator), and, finally, a superficiality in surveying the relevant secondary

literature (as manifested, on the one hand, by the repetition of egregious errors that were long ago exposed as such in the very literature cited by her in her bibliography— e.g., the errors regarding "*grammaticus*" and regarding "*locutio spiritus summi*"— and, on the other hand, by an oversight of some of the most important literature in the field). The final result, sad to say, is an interpretation of Anselm that must be altogether discounted.

[The following are additional corrigenda for Colish's Chapter Two: (1) Change the reference in n. 79 to '27.26'. (2) Change the reference in n. 98 to '*Proslogion 23*'. (3) Re n. 162: there is no *Proslogion* 27. (4) Change the reference in n. 164 to '*Monologion* 65'. (5) In line 3 on p. 59 and in line 11 on p. 103 change 'where' and 'Where' to 'whereas' and 'Whereas' respectively. (6) In lines 14-15 on p. 83 change 'seems to be' to 'is'. (7) In line 16 on p. 95 change 'as if . . . is' to 'as if . . . were'. (8) In line 16 on p. 102 change 'God, which' to 'God—something which'. (9) In line 7 on p. 104 *et passim* change 'so . . . as' to 'as . . . as'.]

Were the present footnote not already too long, it could easily have included a detailed discussion of Gregory Schufreider's article "Reunderstanding Anselm's Argument," *The New Scholasticism*, (Summer 1983), 384-409. For the many confusions in this article also need to be patiently untangled. Perhaps such a discussion will be possible in the notes to my new translation of the *Monologion* and the *Proslogion*—a translation that is currently in preparation.

335. Blumenberg, pp. 489-490.

336. Blumenberg, n. 7, p. 653 (italics mine).

337. Blumenberg, p. 495 (italics mine).

338. Note Anselm's own claims in *De Incarnatione Verbi* 6 [*Anselm of Canterbury: Volume Three*, edited and translated by J. Hopkins and H. Richardson (New York: The Edwin Mellen Press, 1976), p. 23]: " . . . the *Monologion* and the *Proslogion* (which I wrote especially in order [to show] that what we hold by faith regarding the divine nature and its persons—excluding the topic of incarnation— can be proven by compelling reasons apart from [appeal to] the authority of Scripture . . . ." Also note *Cur Deus Homo* II, 22 (*ibid.*, p. 137), Boso speaking: "For You prove the necessity of God's becoming a man, and you do so in such way that even if the few things you have introduced from our books are removed (e.g., what you mentioned about the three persons of God and about Adam), you would satisfy not only the Jews but also the pagans by reason alone."

339. Blumenberg, p. 495.

340. P. 483. The German edition reads (p. 34): "Der Cusaner: Die Welt als Selbstbeschränkung Gottes."

341. *DI* II, 8 (140:7-8); II, 9 (148:8; 150:9-10); II, 13 (177:9-10); III, 1 (182:5-6). *DVD* 6 (19:10-11); 13 (57:12-13). N. B.: The phrase "*secundum contractiorem*," as it appears on p. 14, lines 19-20 of Hoffmann and Klibansky's edition of the sermon "*Dies Sanctificatus*" (*SHAW*, 1929), is mistaken. According to Rudolf Haubst the correct reading is "*secundum contractum modum*."

342. Cf. *DI* III, 1 (183:10 - 184:3) and n. 341 above.

343. *DI* III, 1 (182:5-6). Here the Latin word "*immersibile*" means "not able

to be commingled (with)." (See my list of corrections in the appendix to *Nicholas of Cusa's Metaphysic of Contraction, op. cit.*)

344. See my discussion of this point on pp. 18-25 of *Nicholas of Cusa on Learned Ignorance, op. cit.* Also note Chap. 2 of *Nicholas of Cusa's Metaphysic of Contraction, op. cit.*

345. Blumenberg, p. 518.

346. At other times, as in the first full paragraph on p. 508, Blumenberg seems rightly to grasp Nicholas's view. In repeating Nicholas's statement that the world is neither finite nor infinite, he should add that it can likewise be called both finite and infinite, depending upon the respects.

347. The German edition reads (p. 89): "Wille ist der Weltaspekt des Unendlichen . . . ."

348. The German edition reads (p. 80): " . . . die 'Naturen', aus denen die Welt besteht, sind ihrerseits Einfaltungen der Unendlichkeit von Merkmalen, die sich in den Individuen einer Art realisieren."

349. Cf. *DI* II, 1 (96) and III, 1 (183:3-9; 187) with *DVD* 15 (65:21-22).

350. *DI* I, 22 (69:10-11).

351. Blumenberg, p. 486. The German edition reads (p. 37): "Während die aus dem Platonismus stammende Konzeption von Transzendenz sich auf ein *räumliches* Schema zurückführen lässt, in dem primär von den Ideen behauptet wird, dass sie nichts in dieser Welt und an dieser Welt sind, sondern sich ausserhalb und getrennt davon finden . . . ."

352. *VS* 28 (84:9-14). Cf. *DVD* 3 (9:15-16) and 9 (36). *DP* 22.

353. *DI* I, 24 (77:1-7). Cf. *Ap.* 27:3-8.

354. *DI* II, 9 (148:11-13).

355. *DI* II, 9 (149:8-10).

356. *DI* II, 3 (108:4-11). This same idea is repeated in *De Mente* 6 (94:9-10).

357. *DI* III, 3 (201:10): " . . . sicut ipse est maximus, ita et opus eius . . . ."

358. Cf. *De Ludo Globi* I (Paris edition, Vol. I, fol. 154ʳ): "For the world was not so perfectly created that in creating it God created everything that He was able to create, even though the world was created as perfect as it was able to be created. Accordingly, God was able to create a more perfect and more circular world and likewise a less perfect and less circular world, even though the world was created as perfect as it was able to be."

359. See n. 313 above.

360. My italics.

361. Blumenberg, p. 520 (italics mine).

362. Cf. *DI* II, 13 (180:2-6), where created things are depicted as saying: "Of ourselves [we are] nothing, and of our own ability we cannot tell you anything other than nothing. For we do not even know ourselves; rather, God alone— through whose understanding *we are that which He wills, commands, and knows in us*—[has knowledge of us]." Also note *DI* II, 4 (116:9-13): "just as in a craftsman's design the whole (e.g., a house) is prior to a part (e.g., a wall), so because *all things sprang into existence from God's design*, we say that first there appeared the universe and thereafter all things . . . ."

363. Even the word "emanation," as Nicholas uses it in *DI* [e.g., at II, 4 (116:3)], does not have a meaning opposed to "*creatio ex nihilo.*" That the universe is said to emanate from God does not mean that it is not freely created by God.

Blumenberg, on p. 531, ascribes a related inconsistency to Nicholas with respect to the doctrine of creation. This ascription is also unjustifiable, and it arises from Blumenberg's misunderstanding of Nicholas's teachings on *complicatio* and *explicatio*.

364. Italics mine.

365. *DI* III, 1 (185:14-19). Blumenberg himself recognizes (p. 544) that Nicholas subscribes to this kind of hierarchy.

366. *DI* III, 1 (187:13-15).

367. *DI* III, 3 (197-198). Cf. the mention of higher and lower species and genera in *DI* III, 1 (185-186) and of higher and lower forms in *DI* II, 12 (174).

368. Cf. *DI* II, 6 (124).

369. *DI* II, 12 (170:3-7).

370. *DI* II, 10 (153:6-13).

371. *DI* II, 11 (156:5-6): "Of all things there is none which is not *one* from possibility, actuality, and uniting motion."

372. *DI* II, 8 (138), together with the title of II, 8. N. B.: Although Nicholas endorses this section of Chap. 8, he does not endorse everything that is earlier stated in this chapter. Also note the reference to matter in *DI* I, 22 (68:13).

373. *DI* II, 3 (110:13-24).

374. *DI* II, 12 (171:15-18): "Thus, [we surmise], these intellectual solar natures are mostly in a state of actuality and scarcely in a state of potentiality; but the terrestrial [natures] are mostly in potentiality and scarcely in actuality; lunar [natures] fluctuate between [solar and terrestrial natures]." In *DVD* 24 (107:1-6) Nicholas indicates that in human beings the sensible spirit is brought to actuality by the influence of the heavens.

375. *DI* II, 13 (178:12-13).

376. *DI* II, 12 (173:1-3). Cf. the concluding sentence in n. 374 above.

377. *DI* II, 12 (162:15-17). Cf. II, 11 (157:23-26). In the text above, the formula in single quotation marks is a paraphrase of Nicholas's words.

378. The phrase "in order not to" should be corrected to "not in order to".

379. Here Wallace's translation should be corrected by replacing "its light" either with "it" or with "light". Moreover, the punctuation in this sentence should be corrected.

380. *DI* II, 12 (166:10-12).

381. Nicholas calls the earth and the other planets *stars*.

382. *DI* II, 12 (168:11-12).

383. *DI* II, 13 (178:5-8).

384. *DI* II, 12 (174:15). Cf. *DVD* 25 (111:9).

385. *DI* II, 13 (177:12-13).

386. *DI* II, 13 (179:9).

387. *DI* II, 12 (170:4).

388. My translation. Blumenberg, German edition, p. 79: "Wenn Gott die Zusammenfaltung von allem—also auch des Gegensätzlichen—sei, bleibe nichts,

was sich seiner Vorsehung entziehen könne. Diese Universalität könne weder vermehrt noch vermindert werden, auch wenn sie anderes vorgesehen hätte, als sie tatsächlich vorgesehen hat oder vorsehen wird, und obwohl sie vieles vorgesehen hat, was sie nicht vorzusehen brauchte." Cf. English edition, p. 522. N.B.: "*Vorsehung*" must be taken primarily in the sense of *Vorhersehen*. Otherwise, Blumenberg has erroneously rendered Nicholas's word "*providentia*" in Nicholas's context.

389. My translation. Blumenberg, German edition, p. 79. Cf. English edition, p. 522.

390. " . . . obwohl sie vieles vorgesehen hat, was sie nicht vorzusehen brauchte."

391. *DI* I, 22 (68:2-3). The proper subject of the Latin clause is *God*, not (à la Blumenberg) *universality*.

392. *DI* II, 13 (176:7-9): "And when Eternal Wisdom ordained the elements, He used an inexpressible proportion, so that He foreknew to what extent each element should precede the other . . . ."

393. *DI* I, 22 (68:1-4). My translation, from the Latin.

394. This is my translation, but it retains much of Wallace's phrasing, while correcting other parts thereof. Blumenberg, German edition, pp. 35-36. English edition, pp. 484-485.

395. N. B. Anselm's *Monologion* 15-17, Augustine's *De Trinitate* 5.8.9 (*PL* 42:917), and Dionysius's *De Mystica Theologia*, Chap. 4 (*Dionysiaca*, Vol. I, p. 595). Each of these passages teach explicitly that there is no quality in God.

396. Blumenberg, p. 526. Cf. n. 492 below.

397. *DVD* 24 (107:14-15). Also note *De Mente* 2 (64:10-11) and 4 (77:22-25). For a further discussion of Nicholas's alleged nominalism, see my article "A Detailed Critique of Pauline Watts' *Nicolaus Cusanus: A Fifteenth-Century Vision of Man*," *Philosophy Research Archives*, 9 (1983), Microfiche Supplement, pp. 43-47.

398. See Nicholas of Cusa, *Compendium* 8. This illustration is discussed by Blumenberg on his p. 536.

399. Cf. *DVD* 12 (51:8-9). *DI* I, 24 (78-79).

400. In *Compendium* 10 (34:17-18) Nicholas indicates that his conception of truth is "adaequatio rei ad intellectum aut aequatio rei et intellectus."

401. My translation. German edition, p. 95. Cf. English edition, p. 536.

402. Blumenberg, p. 485. By "nominalism" Blumenberg seems to be referring, *at least in part*, to the view that (1) empirical concepts of the human mind are not merely *abstracted* from images initially furnished by the senses and reproduced by the imagination and (2) that therefore these concepts are not merely descriptive universal constructs but are reworked and partially transformed reconstructions, so that their correspondence to reality comes more into question. However, Blumenberg nowhere makes clear just what he understands nominalism to be. For various other meanings see (1) Heiko Oberman, "Some Notes on the Theology of Nominalism. With Attention to its Relation to the Renaissance," *Harvard Theological Review*, 53 (1960), 47-76. (2) Frederick Copleston, *A History of Philosophy* (Westminster, Maryland: The Newman Press, Vol. II (1950), pp. 136-155, and Vol. III (1953), pp. 49-61. (3) William J. Courtenay, "Nominalism and Late Medieval

Religion," pp. 26-59 of *The Pursuit of Holiness in Late Medieval and Renaissance Religion*, edited by Charles Trinkhaus and Heiko Oberman (Leiden: E. J. Brill, 1974). It is crucially important to distinguish philosophical nominalism (e.g., in the sense of Copleston) from theological nominalism (e.g., in the sense of Oberman). For if a nominalist were primarily someone who subscribed to the doctrine that there is no comparative relation between the finite and the infinite, then Nicholas would have to be labelled a nominalist. But most philosophers, even in Europe, do not adhere to this construal of "nominalism."

403. J. Hopkins, "A Detailed Critique of Pauline Watts' *Nicolaus Cusanus: A Fifteenth-Century Vision of Man,"* *op. cit.*, Microfiche Supplement, pp. 34-35.

404. Blumenberg, pp. 498-499.

405. *Ap.* 11:23-24. Cf. *DI* II, 3 (111:14-15): "In all things He is that which they are, just as in an image the reality itself (*veritas*) is present."

406. *Ap.* 11:15. Precise truth, says Nicholas, is inapprehensible by us [*DI* I, 2 (8:9-10)].

407. The only exception, says Nicholas, obtains in the case of God the Son, who is the Perfect Image of God the Father. See *DI* I, 11 (30:13-17). Cf. *DI* I, 3 (9-10).

408. *Ap.* 11:14.

409. *Ap.* 26:8-10: " 'The form of the image is a formed form, and whatever truth [the image] has, it has it only from [that] form which is its truth and exemplar . . . .' " *Ap.* 11:20-23: " 'Just as the being of an image does not at all have any perfection from itself, so its every perfection is from that of which it is an image; for the exemplar is the measure and the form (*ratio*) of the image.' " *DI* I, 11 (30:13-17): "Although every image seems to be like its exemplar, nevertheless except for the Maximal Image (which is, in oneness of nature, the very thing which its Exemplar is) no image is so similar or equal to its exemplar that it cannot be infinitely more similar and equal." [This statement implies that images of real objects are likenesses, in some degree, of the respective real object they image.] *DI* II, 6 (126:12-16): "Now, with respect to the things understood: the intellect's understanding follows, through a likeness, being and living and the intelligibility of nature. Therefore, universals, which it makes from comparison, are a likeness of the universals contracted in things." *DI* I, 1 (2:7-14): "[All things] have an innate sense of judgment which serves the purpose of knowing. [They have this] in order that their desire not be in vain but be able to attain rest in that [respective] object which is desired by the propensity of each thing's own nature. But if perchance affairs turn out otherwise, this [outcome] must happen by accident—as when sickness misleads taste or an opinion misleads reason. Wherefore, we say that a sound, free intellect knows to be true that which is apprehended by its affectionate embrace. (The intellect insatiably desires to attain unto the true through scrutinizing all things by means of its innate faculty of inference.)" *Ap.* 11:27-28: " ' . . . this infinite Being which in all comprehensible things is present as in a mirror and in a symbolism . . . .' " [This clause implies that some things—including, in the context, empirical objects—are comprehensible, i.e., knowable.]

410. *Ap.* 11:24-26 and 11:28 - 12:1: " 'If anyone sees that the very great variety

of things is an image of the one God, then when he leaves behind all the variety of all the images, he proceeds incomprehensibly to the Incomprehensible . . . . He sees clearly that this Form, of which every creature is an image, is not comprehensible on the basis of any created thing.' "

411. I.e., n. 23 on p. 654 of the English edition.

412. See n. 101 above.

413. See Erich Meuthen, *Nikolaus von Kues 1401-1464. Skizze einer Biographie* (Münster: Aschendorff, 4th edition, 1979), pp. 9-12.

414. Regarding the *Compendium* Rudolf Haubst is certainly right: "Dabei denkt Nikolaus auch keineswegs etwa nominalistisch. Er ist ja gerade davon überzeugt, dass sich uns die Dinge in den je entsprechenden Zeichen—und letztlich Gott und seine Schöpferideen in den Dingen—nicht adäquat, aber doch 'wahrheitsgemäss (vere) repräsentieren' " (p. 160 of "Wort und Leitidee der 'repraesentatio' bei Nikolaus v. Kues," cited in the bibliography). Similarly, Helmut Meinhardt's general conclusion on p. 192 of his "Nikolaus von Kues und der Nominalismus" (cited in the bibliography) is correct: "Ich sehe keinen *besonderen* nominalistischen *Einbruch*, auch nicht im Compendium"—though his exposition of *De Mente* a few pages earlier needs to be stated more precisely.

415. Blumenberg refers to *De Genesi* (Paris edition, Vol. I, fol. 73^v). This reference corresponds to *De Genesi* 5 (175:7-12) on p. 124 of Vol. IV of the critical edition: "Nicolaus: Experientia didici auctoritatem maxime studio conferre. Qui enim recipit dictum aliquod quasi divina revelatione propalatum et id quaerit omni conatu intellectualiter videre quod credit, qualecumque dictum illud fuerit, thesaurus undique latens se inapprehensibiliter ibi reperibilem ostendit. Hinc altissima fide ad altissima ducimur . . . ." The word "*quasi*" here means *as*, not *as if*. [Cf. the use of "*quasi*" at *De Genesi* 5 (176:1), *Opera Omnia*, Vol. IV.] In Blumenberg, English edition, p. 654, line 2 of n. 29 the word "*aliquod*" is misprinted.

416. Blumenberg, p. 502 (my italics).

417. Douay version.

418. *DVD* 21 (92:18-19).

419. This metaphor is used in *DVD* 16 (71).

420. Rom. 8:28 (Douay version). Cf. *Letter to Cardinal Julian. DI* III (264:13-14): "Taliter intranti in Iesum omnia cedunt . . . ."

421. Matt. 7:7.

422. Deut. 4:29: "And when thou shalt seek there the Lord thy God, thou shalt find him: yet so, if thou seek him with all thy heart, and all the affliction of thy soul" (Douay version).

423. My translation. Blumenberg, German edition, p. 54. Cf. English edition, p. 501.

424. This statement and the immediately succeeding ones are drawn from *DI* III, 11.

425. Blumenberg, p. 501.

426. See Sec. 2.2 above.

427. N.B. the different senses of "*videre deum*" that I have discussed above. Blumenberg makes no effort at all to distinguish different senses of "*visio*" on

behalf of Nicholas.

428. See Blumenberg, p. 654, n. 27. The reference is to *Excitationes* IX (in particular, to Vol. II, fol. 167ᵛ of the Paris edition of Nicholas's works). Blumenberg, elides a portion of this quotation; in the absence of this portion Nicholas's point will not be fully intelligible to the reader.

429. Blumenberg, p. 501. I have added the German words. See the German edition, p. 55.

430. *DI* III, 11 (245:1-8 and 10-14). My italics.

431. Blumenberg, pp. 501-502.

432. See *DI* III, 12 (259), and cf. the *Letter to Cardinal Julian* [*DI* III (263-264)]. Also see *DVD* 16 (74:1-7): "I, an insignificant human being, would not be content with You my God if I knew You to be comprehensible . . . . Therefore, it is not the case that that which the intellect understands is that which fully satisfies the intellect, i.e., is the intellect's end. On the other hand, that which the intellect does not at all understand cannot fully satisfy it, either. Rather, [it is fully satisfied] only [by] that which it understands by not understanding." Cf. *DVD* 16 (71:7-15).

433. Nicholas of Cusa, Letter 5 (Vansteenberge, *Autour*, p. 115, line 4). *DVD* 25 (113:10-11). *DP* 15:4-5; 17:19-20.

434. *Ap.* 20:3-4.

435. Blumenberg, pp. 538-539.

436. *DVD* 5 (15:5-9). Cf. *DVD* 8 (30:11-12): "You do not, for all that, altogether desert us." Note *DVD* 5 (16:10-12): "Hence, wherever any man goes Your mercy follows him for as long as he is alive, just as Your gaze, too, does not desert anyone." *DVD* 5 (15:11-12): "Notwithstanding, You still do not turn altogether away from me, but Your mercy follows me . . . ."

437. *DVD* 4 (11:11-13).

438. *DVD* 8 (32:15-18).

439. Cf. my critique of Walter Schulz in Chap. 1 of *Nicholas of Cusa's Metaphysic of Contraction, op. cit.*

440. *DVD* 5 (15:9). Also note the expression "*pietatis oculo*" at 15:1. Cf. *DVD* 8 (30:13-14): "And You are always ready to look upon us with Your earlier paternal eye (*paterno oculo*) if we turn back and turn unto You."

441. *DVD* 8 (33:1-4): "To all who examine it, my God, how admirable is Your sight, which is *theos*! How beautiful and lovable it is to all who love You! How terrifying it is to all who forsake You, O Lord my God!"

442. *DVD* 5 (17:1): "Tu, domine, es socius peregrinationis meae . . . ."

443. Note Blumenberg's actual words (German edition, p. 98): "Vielheit und Individualität der Betrachter sind der Identität des Bildes nicht entgegen, sondern die ihm angemessene, seine geheimnisvolle Potentialität erst entfaltende Partnerschaft."

444. *DP* 14. *DI* I, 4 (11:14).

445. My translation, German edition, p. 100: "Wenn ich so im Schweigen der Betrachtung zur Ruhe komme, antwortest du, Herr, mir in meiner eigenen Brust, indem du sprichst: Sei du dein eigen, so werde ich dir zu eigen sein. Du, Herr, hast es meiner Freiheit anheimgestellt, dass ich mir selbst gehöre, wenn ich nur will.

Wenn ich mir selbst nicht zu eigen geworden bin, so bist auch du mir nicht zu eigen. Du nötigst insofern meine Freiheit, als du nicht mein Eigentum sein kannst, wenn ich mir nicht selbst zu eigen bin. Du nötigst mich nicht, insofern du dies meiner Freiheit anheimgegeben hast, sondern du erwartest, dass ich selbst mich dafür entscheide, mir zu eigen zu sein." Cf. English edition, p. 540.

446. See the correct version of the argument in the translation in Part II of the present work.

447. My translation. Blumenberg, German edition, p. 102. Cf. English edition, p. 542.

448. Another example of a wild interpretation is the following: "This disintegration [of the Middle Ages] had led at first to the position of nominalism, *which had deprived human freedom of any significance over against God's absolute demand* for justification . . . ." Blumenberg, p. 540. My italics.

449. *DVD* 25 (111:5-6).

450. Cf. *DI* III, 6 (217).

451. *DVD* 7 (28:1-8).

452. My translation. Blumenberg, German edition, p. 103: "Der Cusaner hat aus der Freilassung einen Akt der Selbstfreisprechung gemacht, der aber zugleich Inbegriff des Gehorsams ist und der die 'Familienbindung' nicht auflöst, sondern in der Selbstüberlassung Gottes an den freien Menschen erst begründet wird." Cf. English edition, p. 542.

453. My translation. Blumenberg, German edition, p. 105. Cf. English edition, p. 544.

454. Cf. *DI* III, 1 (189:1-3).

455. Cf. *DI* III, 3 (201:10-15).

456. *DI* II, 1 (97).

457. *DI* III, 3 (201:10).

458. Blumenberg follows Raymond Klibansky in mistakenly believing that *"Dies Sanctificatus"* was preached on Christmas Day, 1439 (and therefore prior to the completion of *DI*). N. B.: Nicholas also has several other, later, sermons entitled *"Dies Sanctificatus."* These sermons should not be confused.

459. My translation. Blumenberg, German edition, p. 105: "Es muss unter den Wirklichkeiten der Welt, unter dem Inbegriff der Einschränkungen, ein Wirkliches geben, das die Möglichkeit der Art, in der es existiert, erschöpft." Cf. English edition, p. 545.

460. My translation, from the Latin.

461. *DI* III, 4 (203).

462. Cf. *DI* III, 3 (199:12-17).

463. But even in his later section on Bruno, Blumenberg continues to misrepresent Nicholas's Christology. On p. 593 we read: "The great symmetry of man becoming God and God becoming man, which the Cusan had set up against the conflict that was breaking out between the medieval consciousness of God and the new consciousness of self, had been destroyed by the third element of the system . . . ." Nowhere, however, does Nicholas maintain that man becomes God. In the Incarnation the Word of God assumed a human nature. But Nicholas states

unequivocally that this human nature does not pass over into the divine nature, does not become identical to the divine nature [*DI* III, 2 (194)]. And even when he says "Verbum enim dei es humanatum, et homo es deificatus" [*DVD* 23 (100:4-5)], the word "*deificatus*" indicates not that the human nature has become God but rather that it has become Godlike. [Note the use of "*deificatio*" in *De Filiatione Dei*. Cf. the use in *Cribratio Alkoran* (Vol. II of the Strasburg edition, reissued by P. Wilpert), Alius Prologus (14:10-11).]

464. Blumenberg, p. 547. In the present context Blumenberg's verb "*genötigt habe*" would be better translated as "required" than as "compelled".

465. *DI* III, 7 (221:14-21). Also note *DVD* 23 (104).

466. *Cur Deus Homo* II, 11.

467. *DI* III, 4 (205:10-17): "In that species which is actually supreme within the genus *animal*, viz., the human species, the senses give rise to an animal such that it is so animal that it is also intellect. For a man is his own intellect. In the intellect the perceptual contractedness is somehow subsumed in (*suppositatur*) the intellectual nature, which exists as a certain divine, separate, abstract being, while the perceptual remains temporal and corruptible in accordance with its own nature." *DI* III, 6 (215:4-9): "There is no doubt that a human being consists of senses, intellect, and reason (which is in between and which connects the other two) . . . . The intellect is not temporal and mundane but is free of time and of the world. The senses are temporally subject to the motions of the world." *DI* III, 10 (240:1-2): "The intellectual nature, which is beyond time and is not subject to temporal corruption, . . ." N. B. *VS* 32.

468. Cf. I Cor. 15:52-53.

469. *DI* III, 7 (221:18-19). Also the following passages from *Cribratio Alkoran* [Strasburg edition, Vol. II, as reissued by P. Wilpert]: III, 20 (232:5-7): "Unde sicut ipse secundum ypostasim divinam [Christus] fuit naturaliter immortalis, ita in assumpta humana natura meruit ut esset immortalis." III, 19 (231:4-5): "Oportet igitur fateri quoniam Christus homo mortalis meruit immortalitatem in humana natura . . . ." III, 20 (232:9-10): "Meruit enim, deposita mortalitate per mortem, quam ob obedientem dei passus est, fieri amplius immortalis." II, 16 (137:14): " . . . ipse qui esse potuit immortalis si voluisset, mortus est." Spelling and punctuation revised by me.

470. *DI* III, 8 (228:20-26). Cf. *DI* III, 10 (239:12-13), which speaks of "the securing of the respective end (viz., glorification with regard to the translation of the sons of God and damnation with regard to the exclusion of the unconverted) . . . ."

471. Cf. *De Filiatione Dei* 2 (56:1-3). When Nicholas says that each thing is perfect in the way it can be [*DI* III, 1 (189:1-3)], he is referring to its status in the present order of creation, without thereby excluding the possibility of its having a different degree of perfection in the world to come. Moreover, he does not exclude its having been rendered, as a result of the Fall, less perfect than it otherwise would have been. Qua *created* thing, it is, in a given degree, a perfect individual thing of its kind; and its kind is, in a given degree, a perfect specimen of its genus; and the genus is, in a given degree, a perfect contraction of the universe; and the universe

exists in the best way in which the condition of its nature allows.

472. Note the phrase "intellectual and eternal desires" [*"intellectuales et aeterni affectus"*] at *DI* III, 6 (217:3-4).

473. *DI* III, 10 (241:15-16).

474. *DI* III, 6 (218:11-15): "But Christ the Lord willed to mortify completely—and in mortifying to purge—by means of His own human body all the sins of human nature which draw us toward earthly things . . . ."

475. *DI* III, 6 (218:19-20).

476. *DI* III, 4 (203:22-25).

477. *DI* III, 6 (220:1-5).

478. *DI* III, 6 (219:10-12).

479. *DI* III, 6 (219:1-2).

480. Similarly, in *"Dies Sanctificatus"* (*SHAW*, 1929, p. 36) he writes: " . . . quisque Christo adherens et unitus non in alio, sed in sua humanitate, que est et Christi, satisfecit debito, iustificatur, vivificatur, quia ipsa sua humanitas, que est una in eo et Christo, Deo Verbo unita est."

481. These accounts are supplementary to each other, as is evident from *DI* III, 7 (221:6-11): "How could what is mortal have put on immortality otherwise than by being stripped of mortality? How would it be free of mortality except by having paid the debt of death? Therefore, Truth itself says that those who do not understand that Christ had to die and in this way enter into glory are foolish and of slow mind."

482. In Sermon 3 (6:7-21) [*"Hoc facite . . . ,"* *Opera Omnia*, Vol. XVI, pp. 44-45] he subscribes to Anselm's theory of atonement. But he does not revert to it—or to any other elaborate theory—in *Cribratio Alkoran*.

483. Blumenberg, pp. 483 and 469.

484. Blumenberg, p. 540.

485. Blumenberg, pp. 484 and 485.

486. Blumenberg, p. 485.

487. Blumenberg, p. 483.

488. Blumenberg, p. 483. My italics.

489. Blumenberg, p. 483.

490. Blumenberg, German edition, p. 34. My translation: "Our hermeneutical task here, as always, consists in the following: to relate statements, doctrines and dogmas, speculations and postulates as answers to questions whose projection onto the background of what is documented [viz., the documented statements, doctrines, etc.] constitutes our understanding." Cf. English edition, p. 483.

491. Blumenberg, p. 485.

492. Blumenberg, p. 526: "I will not make what I believe would have to be a futile attempt at a unitary interpretation of the Cusan's theory of knowledge. Here in particular the inner consistency of his philosophical accomplishment is doubtful." But not only does Blumenberg make no attempt to give a *unitary* account of Nicholas's theory of knowledge, he also makes no attempt to give *any* detailed account of it, even one that points out the alleged strands of inconsistency. Note Helmut Meinhardt's correct opinion: "Gegen Blumenberg bin ich sehr wohl der

Meinung, dass sich die kusanische Erkenntnislehre einheitlich interpretieren lässt . . . " [p. 193 of "Nikolaus von Kues und der Nominalismus" (cited in the bibliography)]. N. B.: It is difficult to reconcile Blumenberg's judgment that Nicholas's epistemology contains an inner inconsistency (an inconsistency so grave that *no unitary account of Nicholas's epistemology* is worth attempting) with Blumenberg's other claim that the *unity of Nicholas's thought* can be understood only on the basis of a concern to preserve the medieval world. Given Blumenberg's judgment, should he not have claimed that the *disunity* of Nicholas's thought can be understood only on the basis of a concern to preserve the medieval world?

493. Blumenberg never specifies exactly what questions he is projecting back. This failure further undermines his attempt to give an account of his own hermeneutic.

494. Blumenberg, p. 526.

495. Blumenberg himself, on p. 356, does cite this passage. But he makes little of it.

496. *Letter to Cardinal Julian* [*DI* III (264:4-5)].

497. *Ap.* 1:14-15.

498. *Ap.* 36:8-9. Many of these philosophers belong to the "Aristotelian sect," which Nicholas says "now prevails" (*Ap.* 6:7). In the quotation above, from *Ap.* 36, Nicholas views the philosopher in much the same way as he does in the *Idiota* dialogues.

499. By contrast, he does make a concerted effort to maintain *unitas ecclesiae*.

500. *Ap.* 34:15-21: " 'What was written in *Learned Ignorance* about Jesus was written in accordance with Holy Scripture and in a manner which befits the goal that Christ increase in us. For in its own way *Learned Ignorance* endeavors to lead us to those [teachings] about Christ which were left to us by John the Evangelist, Paul the Apostle, Hierotheus, Dionysius, Pope Leo, Ambrose in his letters to Herennius, Fulgentius, and the other loftiest holy intellects . . . .' "

501. Blumenberg, p. 483.

502. Blumenberg, p. 520. My italics.

503. *DVD* 18 (82-83).

504. *DVD* 17 (80:7-8 and 17-20).

505. *DVD*, prologue (1:7-8).

506. *DVD* 16 (74:3-4).

507. *DVD* 25 (113:9-14).

508. *DI* III, 11 (245:13-14).

509. *DVD* 21 (92:15 - 93:1). Also note *DVD* 17 (80:1-2): "O Lord, by means of a likeness I have expressed a kind of foretasting of Your nature."

510. *DVD* 21 (92:18-19).

511. Cf. *DVD*, prologue (1:8-15). *DI* III, 11 (245:14-23). *Ap.* 14:17-18 and 20:1-2.

512. *DP* 15.

513. *De Genesi* 1 (147:1-2).

514. *NA* 5 (17).

515. *De Apice Theoriae* 5:1-6.

516. Letter 9, Nicholas to Caspar, Feb. 12, 1454 (Vansteenberghe, *Autour*, p. 122).

517. Letter 5, Nicholas to the abbot and monks of Tegernsee (Vansteenberghe, *Autour*, p. 115, lines 3-4). In *Ap.* 31 Nicholas makes the following reply vis-à-vis Wenck: " 'How astounding that he writes such puerile foolishness!—especially when he construes learned ignorance as a life of detachment [*abstracta vita*].' " The words "*abstracta vita*" are used by Nicholas in place of Wenck's "*abgescheiden leben*". Nicholas is protesting against reducing the notion of learned ignorance to the notion of detachment. He is not denying that detachment is an essential part of mystical theology.

518. *Ap.* 7:27.

519. *DVD* 16 (71:3-4).

520. *DVD* 16 (71:7-12).

521. *DVD* 6 (22:16-22). When the mystical theologian reaches the "end to the ascent of all cognitive power" (*DP* 15:3), he has entered into total darkness, having transcended all that is sensory, imaginative, rational, and intellectual.

522. Letter 4, Nicholas to Caspar (Vansteenberghe, *Autour*, p. 112, lines 6-8). Also note the account of Nicholas's view given by Hans G. Senger on pp. 180-186 of his book *Die Philosophie des Nikolaus von Kues vor dem Jahre 1440. Untersuchungen zur Entwicklung einer Philosophie in der Frühzeit des Nikolaus (1430-1440)* [Vol. 3 (New Series), Beiträge zur Geschichte der Philosophie und Theologie des Mittelalters (Münster: Aschendorff, 1971)].

523. *DVD* 13 (58:11).

524. *DVD* 24 (109:18-19).

525. Letter 8, Caspar to Nicholas (Vansteenberghe, *Autour*, p. 120, lines 9-10).

526. *DVD* 24 (109:1-2).

527. That is, faith formed (or in-formed) by love. *DI* III, 11 (248:9-10 and 250:13-14).

528. *Complementum Theologicum* XI (Paris edition, Vol. II, 2nd Part, fol. 98ᵛ): "Una enim substantia non est magis substantia quam alia, quia non est quantitas substantia. Hinc substantia non recipit magis nec minus, sicut quantitas. Tamen ob hoc etiam non omnes substantiae sunt aequales. Una enim est perfectior alia" (punctuation modified by me). Also note *DI* III, 1 (189:4-6): "In each species—e.g., the human species—we find that at a given time some individuals are more perfect and more excellent than others in certain respects."

529. *DI* II, 12 (169:8-12). Human nature, says Nicholas [*DI* III, 3 (198:2-4)], "enfolds intellectual and sensible nature and encloses all things within itself . . . ."

530. *DI* II, 13 (177:12-13).

531. Augustine, *Confessions* 10.27.38.

532. Gerson, *Super Magnificat*, 7th tractate (Glorieux, Vol. 8, p. 316).

533. Johann Schwab makes this point quite forcefully on p. 375 of his *Johannes Gerson. Professor der Theologie und Kanzler der Universität Paris* (Würzburg, Vol. I, 1858).

NOTES TO THE TRANSLATION

1. Rogier van der Weyden (1400-1464).

2. These considerations are presented in Chapters 1-3 respectively.

3. Literally: "With regard to the icon-of-God's sight nothing can be apparent that is not truer with regard to God's true sight."

4. Cf. Chapter 15 of Anselm of Canterbury's *Proslogion.*

5. Note *DVD* 5 (18:2-3); 8 (33:1); and *NA* 23 (104:12-14).

6. "Free" translates both "*abstractus*" and "*absolutus*". N.B.: Although abstract sight is *absolutus ab his conditionibus,* it is distinguished by Nicholas from Absolute Sight, which is God. At the beginning of Chapter 2 Nicholas further explains that in human beings sight is conditioned by the dispositions (*passiones*) of the body and the affections (*passiones*) of the mind. Cf. *De Ludo Globi* I (26:1-6), Strasburg edition, reprinted in two volumes by de Gruyter, 1967, under the title *Nikolaus von Kues: Werke,* edited by Paul Wilpert.

7. Nicholas later makes clear that God, who is infinite, is not Sight—even as He is also not Goodness (Chapter 13). But just as, in accordance with the *via negativa,* He is called Goodness, so Nicholas here calls Him Sight, as well. Note *DVD* 12 (51:8-9).

8. *DI* I, 16 (46:9-12). *DP* 13:11-12. *DVD* 6 (19:13-15); 9 (36).

9. In calling God the "Contraction [i.e., the Contractedness] of contractions," "Uncontractible Contraction," and "most simple Contraction" Nicholas does not mean to imply that either God or His Sight is contracted. These are *modi loquendi.* Indeed, just a few lines earlier Nicholas spoke of God's Sight as "free from all contractedness" (8:7); and in Chapter 13 (57:12-13) he goes on to state flatly that the Infinite is not contractible. Also note *DVD* 6 (19:10-11).

10. *DI* I, 23 (70:23-24). *DD* 2 (98). *Ap.* 8-9 and 26.

11. *DI* I, 21 (66:3-8).

12. *DI* I, 8 (22:7-8); I, 23 (73:3); II, 2 (98:6). *Ap.* 17:17-18.

13. *DI* II, 2 (104:10-20); II, 5 (121:1-7). *DD* 1 (93:4-11). *DVD* 15 (70:4-5); 17 (79:5-7).

14. Heb. 13:5.

15. I John 4:8.

16. I Cor. 13:12.

17. Ps. 30:20 (31:19).

18. Isa. 45:15. *DP* 74:21.

19. In the corresponding Latin text for this English sentence (16:5-7) I regard "*igitur*" as a mistake on Nicholas's part. Hence, I render the text as if Nicholas had written "*enim*".

20. Ps. 113B:1 (115:1).

21. Note *DVD* 1 (6:6). *NA* 23 (104:12-14).

22. Literally: ". . . by the contracted shadow here."

23. See the references in n. 8 above.

24. *DI* III, 11 (245-246).

25. *Ap.* 2:16-22.

26. Ps. 79:20 (80:19).

27. Cf. Augustine, *Confessions*, opening sentence.

28. Luke 15:16-17.

29. *DP* 18-19.

30. Cf. *De Ludo Globi* II (84), Strasburg ed. *DI* II, 11 (157:23-26). Note the title of *DI* I, 23.

31. See the references in n. 5 above.

32. *DI* II, 6 (125:2-5; 12-13).

33. "Uncontracted Humanity," "Absolute Humanity," and "Human Nature per se" are names for God. They are *modi loquendi*, since Nicholas does not believe that God is Humanity in any sense that can be conceived by us. See notes 7 and 9 above.

34. *Ap.* 26:3-6.

35. *De Mente* 5 (65:13-14). See the references in n. 8 above.

36. *DI* I, 16 (45:4). *Ap.* 33:21-22.

37. *DI* II, 3 (110:4-6).

38. *DP* 21.

39. *DP* 21.

40. *DVD* 10. Note the title of *DI* I, 22.

41. *DVD* 21 (92: 4-5). Also note *Complementum Theologicum* 12 (Paris ed., Vol. II, fol. 99^r, lines 22-24).

42. Heb. 5:14. In the remainder of the Latin sentence—specifically at 39:6-7—I take the future tense of "*coincidere*" to express a present meaning.

43. Gen. 3:24.

44. Cf. the discussion in Chapter 12. Also note *Complementum Theologicum* 14 (Paris ed., Vol. II, fol. 100^v, lines 11-13).

45. Heb. 5:12.

46. II Cor. 4:7.

47. The beginning of Chapter 13 makes clear what kind of "seeing" this is. Also note *Complementum Theologicum* 2 (Paris ed., Vol. II, fol. 93^r, lines 18-21).

48. Chapter 5. See n. 18 above.

49. Chapter 10.

50. This English sentence is a correct translation of the corresponding Latin text (49:17-19). Skeptics are referred to *Gildersleeve's Latin Grammar*, 3rd ed. (London: St. Martin's Press, 1980), p. 149, Remark 1c. Cf. the syntax in *DVD* 16 (74:5-6). Cf. *DI* II, 11 (156:26-27) with II, 12 (162:16-17).

51. This view belongs to earlier medieval philosophy as well. Cf. Anselm of Canterbury, *Monologion* 14 and 23. The formula "in all things You are all things" is from I Cor. 15:28 but is mediated to Nicholas from Pseudo-Dionysius. Note *NA* 14 (59:9). *DP* 74:6. *DI* III, 4 (206:12).

52. Rom. 11:33.

53. In the corresponding Latin text (51:6) "*ortum*" is from "*ortus,-us*". (Cf. 13:14.) At 52:3 "*horto*" is from "*hortus,-i*"; I have added the "*h*" for clarity. As for God's being a *creatable* Creator, see *Complementum Theologicum* 14 (Paris ed.,

Vol. II, fol. 100^v, lines 16-19). N. B.: In *DVD* 17 (80:17) God is called *fons deliciarum*.

54. See n. 7 above.

55. See n. 53 above.

56. "End" (*"finis"*) here has the sense of *goal*; but in the next paragraph it has more the sense of *limit*.

57. *NA* 19 (89:13-14).

58. *DI* I, 16 (43:15-16). *Ap.* 31:25-27.

59. With regard to the idiom *"contrahibile a"* note *DC* II, 16 (170:11-14) and *Complementum Theologicum* 12 (Paris ed., Vol. II, fol. 99^v, lines 23-26).

60. *DD* 2 (100:13-20).

61. *DI* I, 5 (14:11-12). *DP* 14.

62. In Chapter 13 (58:11) Nicholas states that infinite goodness is not goodness but is Infinity. [Cf. *Complementum Theologicum* 12 (Paris ed., Vol. II, fol. 99^v, lines 20-22).] Nevertheless, he continues to refer to God as Absolute Goodness— a *modus loquendi* associated with his conviction that God is *not less than* goodness.

63. *DVD* 6 (20:14-19); 15 (67:1-2).

64. See the references in n. 13 above.

65. *DVD* 12 (50:14-16).

66. Matt. 13:44. Nicholas also uses the example of an inexhaustible treasure at the end of *De Beryllo* (Latin-German edition, edited by Karl Bormann, 1977), Chapter 31.

67. See n. 63 above.

68. "End" (*"finis"*) here has the sense of *goal*, more than of *limit*.

69. This point is made in reference to the Incarnation. The incarnated Son of God continues to be infinite.

70. Nicholas does not hesitate to predicate "infinite" of "Infinity".

71. *DI* III, 12 (259).

72. As this chapter makes clear, *"amabilis"* means "able to be loved." But Nicholas, like the Ancients, tends to regard only certain kinds of things as able to be loved by us. Human nature is not able, for example, to love the ugly (qua ugly). What is able to be loved by human nature is what has worth or value. Hence, *"amabilis"* has the connotation of being worthy of love. Cf. *DI* III, 12 (255:5-8).

73. Nicholas is not here drawing the mistaken inference that nothing could be lovable (i.e., able to be loved) unless someone actually loved it. Rather, he is discussing the Trinity; and he goes on to indicate in the next sentence that the Son (Infinite Lovability) exists from the Father (Infinite Loving) and could neither exist nor be infinite apart from the Father. Cf. *DI* I, 20 (59). *De Mente* 11 (95:6-14).

74. *DI* I, 5 (14:9-12).

75. *DI* I, 19 (57:10-11). *DP* 46:1-6. Contrast Anselm of Canterbury, *De Incarnatione Verbi* 2 (Schmitt Latin text, p. 13, lines 17-21).

76. *DVD* 9 (38:7-9).

77. Matt. 13:44.

78. I Cor. 2:9. II Cor. 12:3-4.

79. See Edmond Vansteenberghe's *Autour de la Docte Ignorance. Une controverse sur la Théologie mystique au XVe siècle* [Vol. 14 of Beiträge zur Geschichte der Philosophie des Mittelalters (Münster: Aschendorff, 1915)], p. 113, lines 4-7, where Nicholas appears to be declaring—in his letter to the abbot of the Monastery at Tegernsee—that he has not yet had any mystical experience.

80. II Cor. 12:9.

81. See Chapter 21.

82. Ex. 34:14.

83. See n. 72 above.

84. God is understandable only to Himself. But just as in seeking truth the intellect (whether wittingly or unwittingly) is seeking God, who is Truth, so in understanding any truth the intellect aims to understand Truth itself, which is beyond all finite comprehension. Thus, the union of Jesus's human intellect with the divine nature is not a *cognitive* union—i.e., is not a union in which the human intellect acquires either knowledge, or a correct concept, of what God is in Himself. In Chapter 19 Nicholas makes clear that human nature can understand God the Father only in God the Son and can understand God the Son only in Jesus.

85. This statement reflects the values of Nicholas's day. But it is also a consequence of his orthodox doctrine of the Trinity.

86. Viz., Jesus.

87. See n. 72 above.

88. Mark 1:11.

89. *DP* 38:11-12.

90. Cf. *DI* III, 7 (225:15-17).

91. *DI* III, 7 (224).

92. *DI* III, 2 (194:7).

93. Cf. *DI* III, 12 (261:6-17).

94. Jesus's divine nature is the Exemplar; thus, Jesus is the Medium. Cf. the previous chapter.

95. *DI* II, 3 (108:8-11).

96. I.e., in accordance with the ideal form.

97. *DI* III, 4 (206).

98. I.e., End in the sense of *Goal*.

99. *DVD* 9 (39:1-5).

100. I Cor. 1:20-21.

101. Cf. Gen. 3:22-24.

102. Eph. 4:22-24.

103. John 6:44.

104. John 1:18. John 14:8-9.

105. Ps. 79:20 (80:19).

106. *De Mente*, Chapter 5.

107. *Ap.* 14:25 - 15:2.

108. In this chapter "*gradus*" is translated by both "degree" and "gradation".

109. *DI* III, 4 (206). *DVD* 20 (91).

110. *DI* III, 2 (194).

111. *DI* I, 3 (9:4-5); II, 2 (102:4-5). *Ap.* 32:7-8.

112. Cf. the use of *"suppositum"* at *DI* III, 8 (228:1-3). Also note Sermon 17 (*"Gloria in excelsis Deo"*), *Nicolai de Cusa Opera Omnia,* Vol. XVI, Fascicle 3, ed. Rudolf Haubst and Martin Bodewig, 1977, Sections 6-7 (pp. 274-276). Sermon 19 (*"Verbum caro factum est"*), *Ibid.,* Sec. 9 (p. 297).

113. *DI* III, 7 (224).

114. *City of God* 14.24.2 (*PL* 41:433).

115. *DVD* 22 (99).

116. James 1:5.

117. See n. 7 above.

118. John 6:64 (6:63).

119. Mark 4:14-20.

120. I Cor. 2:14.

121. John 6:68-69 (6:67-68).

122. II Cor. 12:2-4.

123. II Cor. 12:10. Rom. 8:38-39.

124. See n. 72 above.

125. The First Mover is God.

126. This well-known slogan was also Thomas Aquinas's. Cf. Nicholas's use of it in *De Mente* 2 (53:7) and 4 (61:8-11).

127. Cf. p. 48, lines 6-12 of *Das Vermächtnis des Nikolaus von Kues. Der Brief an Nikolaus Albergati nebst der Predigt in Montoliveto (1463),* ed. and trans. by Gerda von Bredow (*SHAW*, 1955).

128. Matt. 23:10.

129. On the distinction between believing God (*deo credere*) and believing in God (*in deum credere*) see Sermon 4 (*"Fides autem catholica"*), *Nicolai de Cusa Opera Omnia,* Vol. XVI, Fascicle 1, ed. Rudolf Haubst, Martin Bodewig, and Werner Krämer, 1970, Sec. 25 (p. 67).

130. Matt. 11:29-30.

131. Cf. p. 50, line 3 of *Das Vermächtnis des Nikolaus von Kues, op. cit., SHAW* 1955. Cf. Nicholas's use of *"astruebat"* at *DI* I, 7 (18:8).

132. Wisdom 1:7.

133. *DI* II, 2 (99 and 104). *DD* 2 (99).

134. Hebrews 1:9.

135. Christus—i.e., the Anointed One.

136. *DVD* 22 (99).

137. Col. 1:15.

138. John 14:6.

139. Matt. 25:21.

140. II Tim. 4:7-8.

141. John 6:44.

index of persons

Abraham, 42, 82
Adam, 44, 89, 233, 235, 333
Alcuin, 327
Ambrose (St.), 350n500
Anselm (of Canterbury), 37, 52, 57-61, 88,
  287n2, 292n39, 304n214, 308, 315n334-
  340n334, 340n338
Aquinas, see 'Thomas (St.)'
Aristotle, 13, 51, 310n264
Augustine, Aurelius, 6, 60, 78, 92, 97, 249,
  251, 289n22, 311n264, 313n302, 331, 338
Baur, Ludwig, 56, 287n2
Bernard (Chancellor), 41
Bernard (of Waging), 95, 287n3, 296n97
Blumenberg, Hans, vii, 51-93, 304n213,
  313n306, 341n346, 342n363n365, 343n391
  n402, 345n415n427, 346n428n443, 347
  n448n458n463, 348n464, 349n490n492, 350
  n492n493n495
Boethius, Anicius, 320
Bormann, Karl, 56
Boso, 333, 340n338
Bruno, Giordano, 347n463
Campbell, Richard, 319-325, 333
Caspar (Ayndorffer), 3, 16, 17, 96, 287n5,
  297n105n117, 312n278
Colish, Marcia, 319, 325-340n334
Combes, André, 288n11, 290n36, 291n36
Copleston, Frederick, 50
Courtenay, William, 343n402
Descartes, 93, 339
Dickens, Charles, 36
Dionysius (Pseudo-), 4, 9, 11-15, 19, 21,
  29, 37, 43, 63, 92, 96, 287n6, 288n12,
  291n36, 293n53, 294n75, 295n95, 296n101,
  297n101n120, 298n134, 317, 350n500, 353
  n51
Donatus, 327
Doyon, Jacques, 306-308
Duclow, Donald, 315 (n334)-319
Eckhart, Meister, vii, 5, 29, 30, 34, 37, 43,
  44, 92, 299n137, 303n190n197n202, 304
  n207, 309n236
Erigena, John Scotus, 60, 299n137
Evans, Gillian, 318

Eve, 44
Flasch, Kurt, 310n260
Frederick III (King), 3
Fulgentius, 350n500
Gabriel, Leo, 56
Gaunilo (of Marmoutier), 57, 318, 335-338,
  339
Gerson, John, 5-16, 20, 21, 28, 96, 97, 288
  n9n11n12n13, 289n21n22n25n26, 290n28
  n29n30n35n36, 291n36n37n38, 292n39n41
  n42n43n45, 293n48n52n53n54, 294n58n59
  n62n63n65, 295n79n96, 296n100n101, 298
  n128n129, 300n154
Glorieux, Palémon, 288n12
Grabmann, Martin, 60
Haas, Alois, 303n204
Harries, Karsten, 297n109, 303n201
Hartshorne, Charles, 339
Haubst, Rudolf, viii, 66, 295n93, 298n130,
  300n156, 345n414
Hegel, 43, 311n264
Henry, Desmond, 325
Herennius, 350n500
Hierotheus, 350n500
Hoffmann, Ernst, 54, 55, 304n207
Hugh (of Balma), 12, 13, 289n22, 290n32,
  295n92
Isaac, 42
Isaiah, 80
Jesus (Christ), *ubique*
John (St.), 350n500
John (Le Célestin), 291n36
John (of Weilheim), 295n88
Kant, Immanuel, 310n264, 339
Kierkegaard, Sören, 42-44, 308n234,
  309n234, 310n264, 311n264n266
Klibansky, Raymond, 54, 55, 311n273n277,
  347n458
Koch, Josef, 287n2, 302n190
Kohlenberger, Helmut, 339
Leibniz, Gottfried, 339
Leo (Pope), 350n500
McGinn, Bernard, 309n236
Mann, William, 315n332
Maurice, Frederick, 325

357

appendix 1

ADDENDA TO THE VARIANT READINGS
OF THE LATIN TEXT OF *DE VISIONE DEI*

After correcting the final page proofs for the present book, I learned to my distress—of two additional manuscripts containing the text of *De Visione Dei*: viz., Manchester 459 and Eichstätt Staat Hs. 528. Both were listed in the third volume of Paul Kristeller's *Iter Italicum*. Already in 1982 I had written to the Benedictine monastery at Melk, Austria, requesting a microfilm of their Codex Latinus 862, which contained a copy of *De Visione Dei* on folios 74^r - 96^v. I was told that manuscript 862 had been divided and sold (or sold and divided) sometime during the period of the World Wars and that the middle section (folios 73 - 173) was of unknown location. Unbeknowns to the present-day librarians at Melk, the John Rylands Library (University of Manchester) had acquired the middle section of their manuscript from Ernst P. Goldschmidt in 1938.

Neither the Rylands manuscript nor the Eichstätt manuscript (which is cognate with Salzburg b.IV.11) afford grounds for revising any of the critical readings that I have already determined. In this present appendix, then, I simply record the variants. And I add thereto the variants from the Strasburg printed edition of 1488, even though this edition is wholly dependent upon Mss. Cusanus 218 and 219. (My adoption of the spelling "Strasburg," here and elsewhere, is deliberate.) I regret that these appended variant readings cannot be placed together with the previous ones, in proximity with the printed Latin text. Yet, their presence qua items appended will witness to the fact that scholarship advances only by means of cumulative efforts and findings. A further witness to this fact occurs vis-à-vis Volume V of *Nicolai de Cusa Opera Omnia*, published on behalf of the Heidelberg Academy by Felix Meiner Verlag in 1937. When this volume was revised and was republished in 1983, the critical apparatus of the Latin texts of *De Sapientia*, etc., was left *incomplete*—by "failing" to record the variant readings of *De Sapientia* as found in Latin Codex Mainz 166 (Bibliothek des Bischöflichen Priesterseminars), pp. 370-393 and Augsburg 8° Cod. 35 (Staats- und Stadtbibliothek), fol. 237^v - 265^v. Such "failures" are inevitable, so that no one dare expect of a scholar what no scholar can possibly deliver—viz., finality and perfection. Thus, the revised Volume V of *Nicolai de Cusa Opera Omnia* is a distinct achievement.

I have been helped through the expertise of H. Jurcic of the Universitätsbibliothek in Eichstätt and Glenise Matheson of the John Rylands University Library in Manchester. In a more general way I wish also to acknowledge the friendly assistance of John Jenson in the Wilson Library, University of Minnesota, and Liselotte Renner of the Handschriftenabteilung in the Bavarian Staatsbibliothek.

ADDITIONAL MANUSCRIPTS AND PRINTED EDITION COMPARED

H   Eichstätt Staat Hs. 528, fol. 142^r - 183^r.
       Location: Universitätsbibliothek, Eichstätt, Germany.
       Previous location: Augustiner Chorherrenstift, Rebdorf (outside Eichstätt)
       Date *DVD* was copied: 2nd half of 15th c.
       Described: paper; trim size 10.5 cm. wide by 15.2 cm. long; body of text of *DVD* is 6.4 cm. wide by 11.4 cm. long; top margin line is used as a base line; 28-30 lines per page; incipit and chapter-titles in red; single copyist of *DVD* , with glosses and emendations by other hands; *DVD* is the sole Cusan work in this collection.

Y   Manchester 459, fol. 1^r - 23^v.
       Location: John Rylands University Library, University of Manchester, England.
       Previous location: Benedictine Monastery at Melk, Austria.
       Date *DVD* was copied: 2nd half of 15th c.
       Described: Neil R. Ker, *Medieval Manuscripts in British Libraries. Vol. III: Lampeter - Oxford.* Oxford: Clarendon Press, 1983.

s   Strasburg printed edition of 1488.

1 1 *H*: Tractatulus reverendissimi in Christo patris domini Nicolai cardinalis tituli sancti Petri ad vincula necnon Brixinensis episcopi ad venerabilem patrem dominum Caspar abbatem et fratres in Tegernse de visione dei. Incipit prologus [Incipit prologus *del. H*[n]]. *Capitulorum tituli in tractatu distribuuntur. Capitulorum numeri omittuntur. (Vide notam pro 5:3).* *Y*: Tractatus reverendissimi in Christo patris domini Nicolai cardinalis sancte Romane ecclesie tituli sancti Petri ad vincula necnon episcopi Brixinensis ad venerabilem patrem dominum Caspar abbatem et fratres in Tegernsee de visione dei incipit feliciter. Prohemium. *Capitulorum tituli in tractatu distribuuntur. Capitulorum numeros ex 6 ad 25 in marg. add. Y (numeros 1-3 in linea habet Y; numeros 4 et 5 om. Y)* *s*: Tractatus Reverendissimi in christo patris et domini domini Nicolai de Cusa tituli sancti Petri ad vincula presbiteri Cardinalis Episcopi Brixinensis ad abbatem et fratres in Tegernsee De visione dei.

1 2 pandam: *Litteram initialem magnam ornatam semper om. s* 5 dari: dare *s* 10 sacratissimam: sanctissimam *H* (*ad* sacratissimam *in marg. corr. H*[2]) 14 sumus: per *post* sumus *scribit et del. Y* 15 benedicti: apparencia qua vos fratres amantissimos per quandam praxim devocionis in misticam propono elevare theologiam premittendo tria ad hoc oportuna *add. Y*

2 1 si: *divisionem novam faciunt H Ys* (Prefatio *ante* si *non add. H Y sed add. s*) 4 facies: *ex ? corr. Y* 5 sagittarii: sagittarie *s* 6 Nurembergensi: Nürmbergensi *H* Nurnbergensi *Y* Nurenbergensi *s*

3 2 intuebiminique: intuebitisque *HYs* 10 experietur: experitur *s*

4 1 et si: etsi *s* 2 comperiet: comperit *s* et si: etsi *s* 4 moveatur: movebatur *s* 6 confratrem: suum *post* confratrem *scribit H et del. H*[2] (?) 8 si: et *ante* si *scribit H et del. H*[2](?) 9 credet: credet *scribit et* e[2] *supra lin. clarius rescribit H* et[2]: si *post* et[2] *scribit et del. H* 10 crederet: *ex* crediderit *corr. Y* 12 igitur: ? *ante* igitur *scribit et del. Y*

5 3 opportuna: scilicet per tria capitula *in marg. add. H*[2]; ad titulos trium *sequentium capitulorum, numeros* 1, 2, *et* 3 *in marg. add. H*[2]

6 2 perfectissimo: perfectissime *HY* 3 praesupponendum... apparere: presuppo *in linea, et* nendum . . . apparere *in antecedente linea, scribit Y, ut lineam tituli compleat* 5 ipsa: *om. Y* 7 inspiciens: respiciens *Y* 11 attingit: *ex* affigit *in marg. corr. H* 13 omnem[1]: *om. Y* omnem[3]: *om. Y* 17 tempus et: *in marg. Y* 19 ac quod: *scribit, del., et recte rescribit H*

7 1 quam: per *post* quam *scribit et del. Y* 2-3 improportionaliter: improportionabiliter *s* 5 esse absoluto: absoluto esse *H*

8 1 II: *numerum* 2 *in marg. add. H*[2] (*vide notam pro 5:3*) 4 sequitur: sequetur *H* 8 visuum omnium: omnium visuum *ad* visuum omnium *transponit Y* 14 contractio[2]: *om. H* enim est: est enim *HY*

9 1 III: *numerum* 3 *in marg. add. H*[2] (*vide notam pro 5:3*) 2 quod: *om. s* 6 formabilium: formalium *s* 7 omnium: omnes *s* 8 odoratum: *ex* odor *corr. H* 14 attribuamus: *in abbreviatione* us *plus elevare debet Y; cf. 9:9* 15 ipse: ipsa *s* est: *supra lin. H*

10 7 quadam: quodam *s* 12 quocumque: quoquam *s* ob: *om. s* quin: que *s* 13 suum[1]: non *add. s* 18 esse potest: potest esse *s*

11 1 domine: dūe *s*   me: *om. HY*   3 ibi amor ubi oculus: *habent HY*   ibi oculus ubi amor *s*   te: *in marg. Y*   4 super: supra *s*   attentissime: attentissimi *HY*   6 sic et: et sic *s*   8 domine: et *post* domine *scribit et del. H*   10 diligentissimam: diligentissime *H*

12 1 sed: *abbreviationem pro* sed *scribit, del., et in marg. explicat H*   2-3 poteris me: me poteris *HY*   5 est: aliud *add. Y*   7 bonitati tuae: tui bonitati *Y*   8 quod: *abbreviationem pro* quod *scribit H et alio modo supra lin. rescribit H*   9 gratiae et bonitatis: bonitatis et gracie *ad* gracie et bonitatis *transponit Y*   tuae: *om. Y*   10 quam: *abbreviationem pro* quam *scribit, del., et alio modo rescribit H*   virtutis: tue *post* virtutis *scribit et del. Y*   17 oculos mentis: mentis oculos *H*   19 charitas: es *add. HYs (supra lin. H, in marg. Y)*   es conversus: conversus es *s*

13 1 tua: *ad* tue *corr. H(?)Y*   4 visio: visio *ex* vita *in marg. corr. Y*   7 tui[1]: t *non proprie format (ut saepe) H*   9 potare: perfundere *Y*   atque: at *s*   13 filii: dei *add. Y*   14 desiderari: desiderare *s*

14 2 quod . . . operari: *titulum capituli IV hic repetit s*   3-4 abscondisti timentibus: abscon ti *H*   6 contactu: contractu *s*   7 tua: sua *Y*

15 1 domine est: est domine *ad* domine est *transponit Y*   pietatis: pletatis *s*   9 est mea: mea est *Hs*   11 adhuc: non *add. s*   13 tuae: *om. s*

16 3 non vocasses ipsum: ipsum non vocasses *Y*   10 misereri: miserere *Y*   13 monitione: mocione *HY*

17 1 tu: autem *add. Y*   8-9 convertar: convertor *HY*   10 te: *supra lin. H*

18 2 nobis igitur domine: igitur domine nobis *ad* nobis igitur domine *transponit H*   4 habeo: haheo *s*   6 pius: atque *post* pius *scribit et del. Y*   qui[2]: quia *H*   7 conservator: *ex* conversator *corr. Y*   uno: atque *post* uno *scribit et del. Y*

19 2 faciali visione: visione faciali *s*   13 et: est *Hs*   est *ad* et *in marg. corr. Y*   15 veritas: facies *Y*   16-17 quacumque . . . minor: *om. s*   21 ac: at *s*   23 intueri: intuere *HY*   nihil: uihil *s*   25 et: aut *s*

20 2 sic: *in marg. Y*   6 se amorose: amorose se *ad* se amorose *transponit Y*   8-9 amorosiorem . . . tuam: *om. HY*   15 tibi faciem: faciem tibi *ad* tibi faciem *transponit H*   17 naturam humanam: humanam naturam *s*   18 faciem tibi: tibi faciem *Y*

21 2 quis: qui *Y*   4 quod: *om. s*   5 illum: eum *H*   7 quando: que *Y*   14 sunt: *om. Y*   18 omnia: omnibus *Y*

22 7 esse faciem: faciem esse *ad* esse faciem *transponit H*   8 sicuti: sicut *Y* (*ad* sicuti *in marg. corr. Y*)   9 respicit: inspicit *s*   10-11 intueri ipsam: ipsam intueri *Ys*   17 se[1]: esse *post* se[1] *scribit et del. Y*   21 splendorem: e[1] *non proprie format Y*

23 3 domine: *supra lin. H*   5 tu[2]: *om. s*   7 omnes: *ex* omnia *corr. Y*   8 quaero videre: videre quero *H*   10 deinde: inde *s*   oculo: oculis *s*

24 1 omnem: domine *s*   5 me: *om. HY*   7 nihil penitus: penitus nihil *s*   aut: et *H* [*sub lin. ad* aut *corr. H²(?)*]   8 stupidissimam: stupendissimam *Y*   10 dans: das *s*   quae: *abbreviationem pro* que *del., et* que *ut verbum initiale in marg. scribit, H²*   16 speciei: faciei *s*

25 2 explicatur: *ex* conplicatur *corr. Y*   5 deo: *ex* domine *corr. Y*

26 4 sibi manet: manet sibi *s*   5 omnia³: videt q *post* omnia³ *scribit et del. Y*
8 habebo: habeo *s*   9 tuo: eius *H (ad* tuo *supra lin. corr. H²)*   9-10 omni modo:
omnino *H (ad* omni modo *in marg. corr. H²) Y*   15 intra: *ex* in te *corr. H*

27 3 possis: *ex* posses *corr. Y*   ego: non *post* ego *scribit et del. H*   5 sed: *in
marg. recte rescribit Y*

28 2 me: *om. H (supra lin. add. H²)*   domine *post* me *add. H*   7 mihi: *om. s*
9 ut speret: *om. Y*

29 2 causare: creare *ad* causare *sub lin. corr. H*   3 in se omnia: omnia in se *HY*
habere: tenere *s*   9 pariter: *om. s*   12 filium: filiorum *s*

30 3 non: *ex* nos *corr. Y*   8 qui²: *ex* quia *corr. H*   10 libertatem: nostram *post*
libertatem *scribit et del. H*   14 et: *om. s*   ad te conversi: conversi ad te *Y*
15 qui: *ad* quia *corr. H*   17 doce: me *add. H*   20 exsurgens: exurgens *HYs*

31 1 omnia: *om. s*   3 volo: voluero *Y*   8 legunt: simul *post* legunt *scribit et
del. Y*   9 et: *habet H (ad* sed *supra lin. corr. H²)*   16 tempore: videri v *post*
tempore *scribit et del. Y*

32 5 recipiat: respiciat *s*   7 quia: *ex* que *corr. H*   13 quod: *abbreviationem
pro* quod *del., et alio modo supra lin. rescribit, H²*   14 se ad obiectum: ad
obiectum se *Y*   quia: quod *Ys*   18 omnia: omuia *s*

34 4 admiror: diutor *s (litteram initialem ornatam* a *om. s)*   5 haec etiam:
eciam hec *ad* hec eciam *transponit H*   6 singulari: sngulari *s*

35 3 nec: *om. Y*   neque *s*   5 occidentalibus: est *add. s*   16 numquam: nuquam *Y*

36 12 igitur te: te igitur *s*

37 4 simul: *om. H (supra lin. add. H²)*   6 quae: qui *HYs*   8 reperitur simul
tempore: simul tempore reperitur *ad* reperitur simul tempore *corr. Y*   contracte:
contractum *s*   12 concipi: possunt *post* concipi *scribit et del. Y*   18 est: es *H
(ad* est *sub lin. corr. H²)*

38 2 super: supra *Y*   6 absoluta: abscondita *Y*

39 2 hominibus: *om. H*   5 impossibilitas occurrit: occurrit impossibilitas *ad*
impossibilitas occurrit *transponit Y*   6-7 coincidet: coincidet *H (ad* coincidat
corr. H²) coincidit *s*   8 et: *ex* ut *corr. H*   10 nisi: *abbreviationem pro* nisi *ex
abbreviatione pro* non *corr. H; abbreviationem del., et* nisi *in marg. explicat, H²*

40 5 intueri: videre *H*   7-8 et . . . loqui tuum: *om. s*   9 simul omnia: omnia
simul *Y*   11 loquor: *om. Y*   12 est: in *post* est *scribit et del. H*   18 itaque:
igitur *Y*   19 omnes: *in marg. H*   21 si: *in marg. H*   22 coincideret: coinciderent *s*   23 uti: *ex* sic *supra lin. corr. Y*   virtus: veritas *ante* virtus *scribit et
del. Y*   et: *supra lin. Y*   26 audirem: et sicut singulis simul loquerer *post* audirem
scribit et del. Y

41 1 ostio: hostio *Y*   3 et: *in marg. Y*   6 si: *ex* sic *corr. H*

42 2 audiunt te: te audiunt *s*   3 loqueris¹: tunc *post* loqueris¹ *scribit et del. Y*
9 et³: *om. H*

43 3 ostii: hostii *Y*   5 est autem possibile: autem possibile est *Y*   14 tuum
verbum: verbum tuum *s*   15 concepisti: *ex* concepit *in marg. corr. Y*

44 1 secundum: *ex* sed *corr. H*   2 tu: *? post* tu *scribit et del. Y*   enim: *om. s*
4-6 ille . . . aliud: *om. s*   5 prius unum: unum prius *Y*   6 es¹: *om. Y*   9 o:

omega habet Y   11 natum: fuisse *post* natum *scribit et del. H*   13 quod: *in marg.* Y   prius: *om.* Y   16 qui: *confuse abbreviat, et deinde del. et rescribit,* Y
   45 1 XI: II *s*   12 est prius: prius est *H*
   46 1 conceptu: *ex* conceptus *corr. H*   5 evenit: eveniet *HY*   8 sit: sic *s*   9 in: *om.* Y   horologio: horologii *Y*
   47 1 benedictus: igitur *add. s*   2 tribuas: mihi *add. s*   me: *om. H* [*supra lin. add.* H²(?)] *om.* Y   3 nisi: me *add. s*   subsistere in via: in via subsistere *ad* subsistere in via *transponit* Y   4 fictilis: victilis *H*   futilis *s*   7 ostium: hostium *Y*   12 creatore: ad creaturas *add. H*   ad creaturam *add.* Y   13 numerat: *ex ? in marg. corr.* Y   15 in te: *om. s*
   48 9 visibilis: vifibilis *s*   12 visionis: visio (*aut* visioe ?) *post* visionis *scribit et del.* Y
   49 1 domine: deus *Y*   3 sis omnia: omnia sis *ad* sis omnia *transponit* Y   8 scientia: scieutia *s*   10 arborem videret: videret arborem *s*   14 ultra: omnem *post* ultra *scribit et del.* Y
   50 1 adhuc: aduc *Y*   3 obiectum: visionis tue *post* obiectum *scribit et del.* Y   13 creare: et *add. H*
   51 3 creabilem: creabilis *Y*   nondum: *ex* mundum *in marg. corr.* Y   6 aliquid: aliquod *HY*
   52 3 horto: orto *HY*   ortu *s*   7 quia: quod *s*   9 et si: etsi *s*   10 quo modo: quo *s*   11 et si: etsi *s*   13 tuam: sed si quis in *post* tuam *scribit et del.* Y   17 ab: *supra lin. H*
   53 1 ad te accedentem: accedentem ad te *H*   4 in: *om. HY*   7 in: et *s*   9 infinitas: *ex* infinitus *corr. H*   11 se: in *add.* Y   12 incomprehensibile: incomprehensibilem *HY*   13 te²: *ex* se *in marg. corr.* Y
   54 4 finis¹: fnis *aut* fins *ante* finis¹ *scribit et del.* Y   7 quia: qui *HY*   11 impossibile: impos *scribit*, pos *del., et* possibile *continuit* Y   14 infinitum: ita *post* infinitum *scribit et del. H*
   55 10 infinitate: autem *add.* Y   est: *ad* et *in marg. corr.* H³(?)
   56 1 ipsam: *om. H*   3 compatitur: patitur *H* (p, *non abbreviationem pro* com, *scribit H; cf. 96:16 et 100:3*)   5 aliud: *in marg.* Y   9 nec: neque *HY*   10 non possunt esse: esse non possunt *Y*   possunt: possuut *s*   11 esse potest: potest esse *s*   15 pars: *om.* Y   16 esse potest: potest esse *Y*   17 quidquam: quoddam *s*
   57 8 non²: est *post* non² *scribit et del. H*   18 per²: omne *post* per² *scribit et del. H*   18-19 per¹ . . . finitum: *om. s*
   58 4 ita: *om. s*   7 desinit: *habet H* (de *retinet, sed abbreviationem pro* sinit *in marg. explicat, H*)   10 aliquid: aliquod *Y*
   59 4 principio: prinpio *s*   5 ita²: *om. H*
   60 2 deus: *om. HY*   8 enim: autem *s*   licet: sit *H*   9 terram¹: esse *add. s*   te: est *add. s*   10 et si: etsi *s*
   61 1 loqueris: loqueueris *s*   domine: *om. HY*
   62 3 essentia: esse *s*   8 reperiatur: reperitur *Y*   9 complicantur: explicantur *s*   21 est: sunt *HYs*

63 1 esse[2]: *om. s*   infinitatis: infinitas *s*   2 omnia: ea *add. s*   8 sub alia: substancia *H*

64 2 quomodo: quoniam *H*   4 unita[2]: est *add. HY*   est unita: unita est *s*

65 7 visus eius: eius visus *ad* visus eius *transponit H*   infinitus: finitus *s*   14 est ultra murum: ultra murum est *s*

66 4 esse est: est esse *s*   6 in: ipso *add. Y*   7 esse[1]: *om. s*   8 infinitus: infiuitus *s*   9 esse[1]: *? post* esse[1] *scribit et del. Y*   es: *om. HY*   9-12 non . . . primae: *om. s*   13 sic: sicut *Y*

67 2 formabilis: formalis *s*   10 id: *om. s*   12 aut: et *H*

68 1 menti: mente *s*   2 video: ad *post* video *scribit et del. H*   3 ego: *om. s*   7 mea: quod *post* mea *scribit et del. Y*

69 2 eam mihi: mihi eam *s*   4 faciei: tue *post* faciei *scribit et del. Y*   12 tua: *ex* tu *corr. H*   17 sed: *in marg. Y*

70 1 altitudo: *ex* altissima *corr. H*   3 recipias: *om. H*   6 nos: nobis *H*[nos(?) *supra* nobis *scribit et del. H aut H*[n]] o *non proprie format Y*   13 ego enim: enim ego *H*   19 aestimatione: estimatioue *s*   21 dulcissimus: *ex* dilectissimus *in marg. corr. H*   22 benedictus: amen *add. H*

71 2 esset: *om. HY*   7 hoc: o *non proprie format Y*   11 penitus innumerabilem: innumerabilem penitus *Y*   14 reperio thesaurum: thesaurum reperio *H*

72 1 vis: in *post* vis *scribit et del. H*   4 enim: etenim *HY*   enim sive: sive enim *s*   9 et . . . esse: *om. s*   10 infinitum: *ex* infinitus *corr. Y*

73 1 es deus: deus es *s*   7 seducit: quia omne quod finitum et comprehensibile abycit *post* seducit *scribit et del. Y*   8 comprehensibile: est *supra lin. add. H*   9 sine: fine *s*

74 4 satiatur: *om. s*   tunc: multo *post* tunc *in marg. add. H*[4]   5 intellectu: intelectu *s*   id: *om. Y*   5-6 seu . . . intelligit: *habet H*; seu *del., et* seu id quod intelligit *in marg. scribit, H*[4]; est finis eius *sequitur in linea*; est id quod intelligit *in linea del. H*[4]   7 illud: id *Y*   8 cognoscit: *ex* intelligit *supra lin. corr. Y*   10 possit ad plenum: possit *scribit, del., et* ad plenum possit *continuit Y*   15 deglutiendo: de *in* degluciendo *supra lin. Y*

75 2 videri perfecte: perfecte videri *Y*   3 domine te: te domine *ad* domine te *transponit Y*   domine te mihi: te michi domine *H*   5 quoquam: *ex* quocumque *corr. Y*   amabilis es: es amabilis *Y*   7 infinitum: infitum *s*   9 infiniti[2]: inifiniti *s*   10 infinitum: in (?) *post* infinitum *scribit et del. Y   om. s*   12 et: amoris *add. HY*

76 2 in te video: video in te *H*   2-3 video[1] . . . amantem: *om. s*   et . . . amabilem: *om. Y*   4 illud: id *H*   10 unione utriusque: utriusque unione *ad* unione utriusque *transponit Y*

77 2 igitur es: es igitur *Y*   10 illa: *abbreviationem del., et* illa *ut verbum initiale in marg. scribit, H*   essentia tua: tua essencia *ad* essencia tua *transponit H*   12 igitur: te *post* igitur *scribit et del. H*   essentia: *om. HY*   17 igitur est: est igitur *Y*   18 numero: nunumero *s*

78 1 admirabilissimus: mirabilissimus *s*   neque[1]: *abbreviationem scribit, del., et alio modo clarius rescribit Y*   2 supra: super *s*   omnem: *om. Y*   5 id: *om. Y* possibile: impossibile *HY*   7 concipere te: te concipere *ad* concipere te *trans-*

ponit Y   te: *om.* H   9 ter: t ter *s*   10 unum: *om. s*   12 idem: *?* triniter alterare *post* idem *scribit et del.* Y   13-14 per me videtur: videtur per me *ad* per me videtur *transponit* Y   15 video: *bis* H   19 intra: ultra H   20 indistinctum: habet H (in *supra lin.* H)   23 est: *abbreviationem scribit, del., et* est *ut verbum initiale in marg. rescribit* H

79 1 possum: *ex* possunt *in marg. corr.* H   4 me: te *s*   5 quia[1]: *om.* Y 8 esse: et *add.* H   10 exsurgens: exurgens HYs   ex: ab *s*   11 quod: *abbreviationem scribit, del., et in marg. proprie rescribit* H   te: *om. s*   12 pluralitas: trinitas Y unitas *s*   17 ad: *supra lin.* H   amabile: *ex* amabilem *corr.* H (?) 18 illi: *ex* ille *corr.* H   23 aliquando de matre: de matre aliquando H

80 7 numquam: nuquam Y   15 magnus apostolus: apostolus magnus *ad* magnus apostolus *transponit* H   20 autem: *supra lin.* Y

81 2 deus: *om.* HY   esset[1]: *om.* HY   3 oculos mentis: mentis oculos Y   eos: o *non proprie format* (*ut saepe*) Y   4 quia: tu *add. s*   16 est unitus: unitus est Y

82 3 attingere: te *post* attingere *scribit et del.* Y   suum: tuum *s*   7 et: neque *ante* et *scribit et del.* Y   8 esset: esse *s*   tui fruitionem: tui fruitionem *ad* fruitionem tui *transponit* H   12 sis: sit *s*   potest: postet *s*   17 tibi: ut *add.* H   21 deus: deus H (u *supra lin.* H)

83 7 perfectissimam: perfectissiam Y

84 2 quod: quomodo *s*   5 deum: deus *s*   6 mediator: meditator *s*   9 volens: *om. s*   12 sic tibi: tibi sic *ad* sic tibi *transponit* Y

85 1 exsurgens: exurgens HYs   4 conceptu: concepto H   5 est: es Y   deus: *om.* H   6 et[2]: *supra lin.* H   9 omnia: *in marg.* H

86 5 ponit conceptum: *om.* H   conceptum: seu *post* conceptum *scribit et del.* Y   5-7 sicut . . . effectu: *om.* H   7 tuum: *om.* H   16 altissime: adverbum est *in marg. notat* H[3]   18 igitur: tibi *post* igitur *scribit et del.* H   maxime: maximo HY   20 iungitur medio: medio iungitur *ad* iungitur medio *transponit* H

87 2 mediatori: mediatore *s*   7 tua: *om.* Y   12 mediare: madiare *scribit* H, *et* a[1] *ad* e *supra lin. corr.* H[3] (?)   15 separatim: separatum H   16 video: *om.* H 18 qua: *ex* quas *corr.* Y

88 5 divinae naturae: nature divine H*s*   9 sic: sicut Y   12 verificaretur: verificatur H

89 2 et: te *post* et *scribit et del.* H   7 humanam filiationem: filiacionem humanam Y   14 esse in te: in te esse *ad* esse in te *transponit* Y

90 1 in: *ex* si *in marg. corr.* H   humana: hnmana *s*   7 lapis: enim *add.* Y 8 eius: *om.* Y   9 intelligere: intelllgere *s*   10 exemplari: adiectivum est *in marg. notat* H[3]   ac si: acsi *s*   11 arcae[1]: arce H (*ad* arche *corr.* H[3]; arce[2] *non corr.* H[3])   13 unita: est *add.* Y

91 4 creatricis: creantis *s*   11 omne: cause H   omnem *s*   15 excedit: ezcedit *s* 16 sunt: sint *s*   17 ad: *om.* H (*in marg. add.* H[3])

92 3 ultimitate: ultimate H (*ad* ultimitate *in marg. corr.* H) ultimita *in linea et* te *supra lin. scribit* Y; te *del., et in subsequente linea rescribit,* Y ultima *s* 4 huius mundi sapientibus: sapientibus huius mundi Y   5 verissima: verissime Y 9 putent: putant H   11 ut: *ex* et *corr.* H   15 enim: igitur H   17 degustari: degustare *s*   18 vero: enim *s*

93 1 arbor: arbor *H (ad* lignum *in marg. corr. H⁵)* 3 qua: *bis* Y (qua¹ *del.* Y) 4 vivant: vivunt Y 5 exuere veterem: veterem exuere *ad* exuere veterem *transponit H* veterem: hominis *post* veterem *scribit et del.* Y 10 tui: tue *(?)* Y 14 non potest: *bis* Y (non potest¹ *del.* Y)

94 1 igitur: homo *add. s* est: qui *add. s* 2 suo: *om. s* unitus: est *add. s* 6 ipsam: *ex* ipsum *corr. H* 8 felicitatem: posse *post* felicitatem *scribit et del.* Y 14 potest: pater *add. s* 16 natura: naturali *s* 17 vivificatus in vivificante: unificatus in unificante *s* 21-22 revelate: t *non proprie format* Y

95 2 videat: vidit *HY* sit: est Y 3 Ihesu:Ihesum *HY* iesum *s* 3-4 complementum: complemeutum *s* 5 ac: et Y 8 enim: euim *s* 9 organi: oculi Y 10 erat: *om. HY* nobilis: *abbreviationem (non proprie scriptam) del., et* nobilis *in marg. recte rescribit, H⁵* 11 et discrete: *om. s* 16 modo: non *add. H et del. H aut Hⁿ* non *add. Ys* 17 his omnibus: omnibus hiis *H* iudiciis: indicijs *s* 22 ac si: acsi *s*

96 1 carnali: r *non proprie format H* 3 et: *scribit et del. H* discussione : discussionem *s* 6 oculi: oculis Y 10 ac si: acsi *s* audivisset: audisset *H* audysset Y 11 possibile est: est possibile *s* surdis: et *add. s* 12 scibile: subtile *H* sciebas: *ex* videbas *corr. H* 15 finitae: finite *ex* infinite *corr.* Y 18 Ihesu: in *(?) post* Ihesu *scribit et del.* Y 22 vidisti verissime: verissime vidisti Y 23 ut²: homo *post* ut² *scribit et del.* Y 27 visiva: *om.* Y 28 subsistit: a *ante* subsistit *scribit et del. H*

97 2 quomodo: de *post* quomodo *scribit et del.* Y 3 interrogati: interroganti *s* nomen: *habet H; abbreviationem del., et* nomen *alio modo in marg. abbreviat, H² (?)* 6 virium: que *in marg. add. H⁵* etsi: et si *s* 8 simili: simul Y 13 visiva sensibilis: sensibilis visiva *ad* visiva sensibilis *transponit* Y 14 vis: visiva *post* vis *scribit et del.* Y 16 sensibus: sensu Y 17 subsistunt: substunt *s* 19 neque: nec *s*

98 2 quae: *ex . . .* que *corr. H* videmus: videus Y 3 dominum: *in abbreviatione* m *non proprie format* Y 4 in: *om.* Y 5 adhuc: aduc Y 8-9 virtutis . . . sensibilis: *om. s* 9 animalis: *abbreviationem scribit, del., et alio modo rescribit H* 11 quin: que *s* 12 non: *scribit H et del. H aut Hⁿ* 15 in: *om. s*

99 3 uniri: *ex* unire *corr. H* 4 in². . . ut: *scribit H et del. H aut Hⁿ* candela: candelam *H* 7 supremitate: presumitate *s* 8 locum esse: esse locum Y 8-9 capitur . . . verbum: *om. HY* 11 lumen: lux Y 17 quod: et *supra lin. add. H³* creator: creaator *s*

100 1 XXIII: XXII *in marg.* Y 3 paradisi murum: murum paradisi Y 5 compositus: quasi *post* compositus *scribit et del. H* 9 aut: nec *ante* aut *scribit et del.* Y 12 divinam: divina *s* 13 enim: tunc *post* enim *scribit et del. H* 15 neque: enim *add. s* copula: *om. s* 18 absolute: absoluta *H*

101 2-3 humanam: naturam *post* humanam *scribit et del. H* 4 in: *supra lin. H* 8 a: in *s* 10 foret: esset *s* 18 propterea esset: esset propterea Y 19 arida: que *post* arida *scribit et del. H*

102 2 recitat Augustinus: augustinus recitat *s* 8 vitae: *om. s* 11 intellectui tuo: tuo intellectui *ad* intellectui tuo *transponit* Y et: unitam *ante* et *scribit et del.* Y 15 naturam: tuam *add.* Y tua: *in marg.* Y 17 corpus: tuum *post*

corpus *scribit et del. H* 18 tamen: *om. H*

103 5 separetur: separaretur *HY* 9 intellectualis: intellectus *ante* intellectualis *scribit et del. H*

104 9 et[2]: *om. s*

105 2 sit: *om. HY* 3 atque: et *Y* 4 vitae: vite *ex* vita *corr. H*[n] 5 perceperunt: perceperut *aut* percepernt *H* 9 quomodo: *ex* quoniam *corr. H* 11 neque[2]: nec *s* gladius neque fames: fames neque gladius *H* 12 corporis: *om. H* omnium umquam: umquam omnium *ad* omnium umquam *transponit H* 15-16 corporalem dulcedinem: dulcedinem corporalem *Y* 17 quid: *abbreviationem scribit, del., et alio modo rescribit H* amore: o *non proprie format Y (cf.* amare *in 109:13)* 18 quod: *abbreviationem scribit, del., et alio modo in marg. rescribit H* 21 his: alijs *s*

106 6 vim[1]: ymaginativam sed nondum *post* vim[1] *scribit et del. Y* sensitivam: *in marg. Y* 11 vim: *om. Y* 12 illum: illam *H* 14 metalli: *ex* metallorum *corr. Y* 17 depuratus: *ex* depuraturus *corr. H* 18 aliquod: *om. Y*

107 3 capit: continue *post* capit *scribit et del. Y* 8 quia: *abbreviationem pro* quia *(?) scribit, del., et* quia *in marg. explicat H* non[2]: nec *Y* 11 hic: *om. Y* 13 pervenit: peurenit *s* 14 ipsum: eum *H* tale: *scribit et del. Y* 17 impeditus: et *post* impeditus *supra lin. add. H*[3] *(?)* promptior: pronior *s*

108 1 cuius: *ex* eius *(?) in marg. corr. H* 15 caelestiformis: celestiformis *ex* celiformis *in marg. corr. Y*

109 5 quia: penitus *post* quia *scribit et del. Y* 6 verbum: dei *post* verbum *scribit et del. Y* 9 quomodo: quoniam *HY* 13 iugum[1]: *om. s* 19 tibi[3]: et *H*

110 2 Ihesus sit: *om. HY* 3 quod: *abbreviationem pro* quod *del., et alio modo in marg. abbreviat, H*[3] *(?)* 5 omnium: omni *aut* enim *ante* omnium *scribit et del. Y* 8 boni: bone *HYs* 11 sibi: tibi *HY* 15 intellectualis: intellectuales *HY*

111 2 et est: *scribit H (ad* est et *transponit H aut H*[n]*)* orbem: *om. HY* 6 enim sibi: sibi enim *ad* enim sibi *transponit H* 8 capi potest: potest capi *H* 12 et: ac *s* 18 quisque: quisquis *Y* 19 spiritus: *om. Y* aliquid: aliquod *Y* 20 meliori: modo *post* meliori *scribit et del. H* fieri posset: posset fieri *Y* 21 revelant: revelavit *s*

112 1 neque: Christus *post* neque *scribit et del. H* 2 suis: tuis *H* 7 huic: *om. H* ultimitate: *abbreviationem pro* ultimitate *del., et* ultimitate *plene scribit, H* ultima *s*

113 8 spiritu sancto: sancto spiritu *ad* spiritu sancto *transponit Y* 12 saporosissima: saporissima *s* 13 vitae: et *post* vite *scribit et del. H* et: *om. s* 15 discooperis: discoperis *HYs*

114 1 unguentorum: ungentorum *HY* 2-3 tenuit me: me tenuit *Y* 3 sensibilis mundi: mundi sensibilis *H* 10 amen: Explicit *add. H* Explicit de visione dei *add. Y* Reverendissimi domini Nicolai Cardinalis sancti Petri ad vincula Brixinensis episcopi Liber de visione dei Explicit *add. s*

appendix II

HUGH OF BALMA'S *DE MYSTICA THEOLOGIA*[1]

(an excerpt, in translation)

PROLOGUS

"The ways of Zion mourn because there is no one who goes to the solemn feast."[2] Although these words were uttered by the Prophet Jeremiah, deploring the captivity of his people, they can also be uttered by each comprehending observer when he discerns, throughout the entire world, the very extensive captivity of souls and the vast deviation from the paths of justice and the ways of equity. For "ways" signifies the longings of loving souls—|longings| by means of which even souls that inhabit earthly bodies are elevated, beyond all reason and intellect, unto God and the Heavenly City, Jerusalem. Moreover, these ways are said to mourn because there is no one who has regard for so solemn a feast. For having cast aside true wisdom, the clerics as well as the laity immerse themselves in worldly delights and in useless curiosities. But more to be deplored and to be lamented unceasingly with tears of the heart is |the following|: that just as formerly the Israelites (having abandoned[3] worship of their Creator), bowed down to handmade idols, so |nowadays| many of the religious and also many of the well-known and the well-reputed (having abandoned true wisdom, by which God alone is inwardly and perfectly worshiped and adored solely by those who love |Him|) have wretchedly filled their minds with various forms of knowledge and with mind-made edifices |constructed| of multiple arguments—|i.e., filled their minds| with certain idols, as it were.[4] Being urged on by the Devil, they are so absorbed with these matters, and their minds are so completely prepossessed therewith, that in their minds true wisdom finds no place. For by this very harmful activity—|an activity| which God has granted to the sons of men—they are miserably encaptivated, so that there is no opening whereby their souls may attain unto their Creator through fiery affections of love. For |God| did not create the soul to the end that, counter to its nobility, it would be filled with multitudinous quires of parchment; rather, |He created it| to the end that it would be the seat of wisdom and that in it would reside the peace-loving King of the Heavenly City, viz., the Most High God. For this wisdom, which is called mystical theology, was taught by the Apostle Paul and was written down by his disciple Dionysius the Areopagite. It is the same thing as the extension of love unto God, by means of the |soul's| longing love. As far as the east is from the west,[5] |so far does this wisdom| incomparably excel all creatures' knowledge. For other forms of knowledge are taught |to us| by mundane teachers. But regarding this |form of knowledge, viz., mystical wisdom|: the |human| spirit is taught immediately by God alone, not by mortal men. This |knowledge| is written on the heart by divine illuminations and heavenly infusions; but that |worldly knowledge| is written on parchment with ink and the quill of a goose. This |knowledge| says "It is sufficient." For through this |knowledge| the mind discovers its Cause, viz., God, its Creator; and in Him, who is the Fount of all goodness and of most immediate beauty, it finds rest. But the other |form of knowledge| never says "It is sufficient." For |the following| is a just judgment: |viz.,| that one who deviates from the supreme truth, as a result of being unconcerned about supreme wisdom, is enveloped in darkness, as is a blind man; and, thus, his soul runs to and fro, stultified by vain and erroneous matters and frenzied with human contrivances.

Furthermore, |mystical| knowledge kindles the affection[6] and illumines the intellect; but the other |form of knowledge|, very often finding a heart devoid of true wisdom, inflates |it|; and very often it bedarkens the intellect with various opinions and diverse errors. Therefore, once the religious soul has relinquished human wisdom, together with both the curiosity for useless knowledge and the pitfalls of arguments and opinions, it mounts upward, through longing and by means of an upward movement of love, unto the Fount of all things. Only in this Fount does it find truth. But because this supreme wisdom cannot be taught by men, |Dionysius| adds that each |attainer|, no matter how much of a layman he is in the school of God, receives this wisdom immediately from God—|receives it| beyond all intellect and through the affection of love. No philosopher and no other scholar or secular teacher apprehends it by any human understanding, regardless of how great his striving.

Accordingly, this way to God is threefold: |The first is| the purgative |way|, by which the mind becomes disposed to learn true wisdom. The second is called the illuminative |way|, by which the mind, through reflecting,[7] is aroused for the kindling of love. The third |is| the unitive |way|, by which—beyond all intellect, reason, and understanding—the mind is actually directed upward by God alone. By means of illustration: In the case of bridges, when they are being erected, we see that at the outset wooden beams are used as supports, so that the rigid layers of stone may be extended more highly. But after the |stone| structure is finished, the supporting wooden beams are completely removed. Something similar holds true of the mind. For at first it is imperfect in love. Subsequently, it ascends toward the perfection of love by meditating. But when as a result of much exercise it is confirmed in unitive love, and when on account of many fiery affections, or aspirations, of love it is elevated beyond itself by the power of its Creator, then sooner than can be conceived and without any guiding or accompanying reflection and as often as it will—whether one hundred times or one thousand times, whether during the daytime or at night—it is aroused by God, in order that it may possess Him alone, by aspiring with innumerable longings. For in this way each new disciple mounts upward, by degrees, unto the perfection of this knowledge. Thus, he first most diligently exercises himself in the purgative way, which is a childish way and the way for beginners. It commences with the following |consideration|: "Justice and judgment are the preparation of Your throne."[8] But next,[9] after a brief period of time—viz., a month or two, according as will seem to him expedient, on the basis of the divine light radiating from on high—he ascends, by means of reflecting, unto love. But perhaps to someone it may seem presumptuous that the soul, becloaked with numerous sins, would dare to seek from Christ a union of love. If so, let him realize that there is no danger, provided he kiss Christ first on the feet through the recalling of sins, and then on the hand, through the recognition of the benefits bestowed upon himself. And, thirdly, let him mount upward unto the kiss of love,[10] by desiring Christ alone and by cleaving through fiery affections only unto Him, so that (as will be seen subsequently) by praying the Lord's Prayer he mounts upward by stages, according as through the Lord's Prayer the mind ascends by reflecting. Fourthly, the soul, by exercising itself in accordance with this way (which is called the illuminative |way| and which begins with the following |consideration|: "Night |shall be| my illumination in my pleasures"[11]) ascends unto a much more excellent stage and state.[12] There the soul—as often as it will, and apart from any guiding knowledge—is immediately aroused by God. The soul cannot be fully taught by any |purely| human skill. But by exercising itself through the purgative and the illuminative ways, the soul—being inwardly directed and taught by God alone—experientially perceives that which cannot be disclosed by any mortal power or eloquence. |The content of this disclosure is such that| neither Aristotle nor Plato nor any other mortal |ever| is able, was able, or will be able to understand it by means of any philosophy or |worldly| knowledge. The Lord alone, or Love, teaches it inwardly, in order that every rational soul may learn to obtain knowledge from the supreme and eternal Teacher. All reason and all intellect fall short of this knowledge. And the affection, disposed by love, soars transcendently above all human understanding, with only the norm of unitive love directing |it| unto the Spirit, who is the Fount of all goodness.

So the foregoing is mystical theology, i.e., a hidden divine word by which the mind, disposed through ardor, speaks secretly with tongues of affection unto its beloved Christ. The present mystical treatise proceeds as follows: First, the purgative way is presented. With regard to this way I expound three |topics|: (a) how the soul ought to be purified; (b) how by means of true prayer an abundance of grace is obtained; (c) how a sinner obtains full remission of sins. Secondly, I present two |additional topics|: regarding the illuminative way I append a section in which I explain (a) how it is that, usually, the mind ascends unto love through meditating by means of the Lord's Prayer and (b) how it is that through this same procedure, |illustrated| by means of interpreting the Lord's Prayer, all Scripture can be interpreted spiritually, by referring everything anagogically[13] unto God. Thirdly, I specify the unitive way, which begins with the following |consideration|: "O wisdom, which from the mouth of the Most High . . .," etc.[14] In this section |on the unitive way| I first of all show how great a sublimity of life there is through mystical wisdom and how great a consummation of strength. |I show this| to the end that |mystical wisdom| may be desired more intensely and may be obtained by its practicants. But perhaps to some reader |the unitive way| may seem especially difficult because of the profundity of the knowledge or the obscure meanings of the words. Since this |difficulty| would apply to the third way,[15] which is beyond all understanding, let him exercise himself in the purgative way and in the subsequent illuminative way; and immediately he will experience and will understand in his own case, solely through God's inward working, whatever he will find written about the third way or whatever he will be told |about it| by anyone. For with regard to this wisdom he must first—in his own case and experientially—perceive the truth; and thereafter he will deem the meaning of all the words which pertain to mystical wisdom to be |comparatively| easy, in proportion to |the degree of difficulty of| each doctrine. For this wisdom differs from all other forms of knowledge in the following way: that with respect thereto (1) one must have the use in his own case before understanding the words and (2) practice precedes theory. With regard to other forms of knowledge one must understand the words before he has the knowledge that is gained. |But| knowledge is possessed more quickly in proportion to the excellence of the teacher from whom it is acquired. And thus it happens that with regard to mystical wisdom a disciple, being taught |directly| by God, is more perfect than with regard to any of the liberal arts is a teacher who understands perfectly, or than is a good artisan with regard to a mechanical art.

Secondly,[16] in the passage |that says|[17] "Come unto Him and be illumined," etc.,[18] I teach how it is that by reference to all creatures—higher ones as well as lower ones—the rational soul receives perfect instruction for attaining unto love of the Creator. Thirdly, I plainly expound[19] the text of |Dionysius's| *Mystical Theology*, in which, although there are few words, there is "infinite" meaning, as it were. When this meaning is fully understood, not only the difficulty of Blessed Dionysius's books but also the mystical meaning of the entire Old and New Testaments becomes cleared up for true lovers |of God|. For from one fount many streams are derived, and these are formed into an "infinite" number of rivers, as it were; likewise, from one central point proceed an "infinite" number of lines, as it were. A similar thing holds true with regard to understanding those few words which are interpreted in that section of mine. By those words the |human| spirit, being disposed in its own summit, is taught how it should be united to God; and in this union it will find, experientially, the origin of all wisdom. As a result of this union the faithful disciple is, to be sure, manifoldly and most affluently instructed regarding a very clear understanding of lower forms of knowledge, regarding interpretations of Sacred Scripture, and regarding words which are suitable, in preaching, to kindle the hearts of listeners.[20] Fourthly, I add eight spiritual counsels (*industriae*) by which the soul is wisely taught how to obtain this wisdom and how to preserve it, once obtained.[21] Lastly, I append a disputation against certain self-styled intellectuals who impugn this supreme wisdom and who maintain that the affection never ascends except by premeditating and by reflecting.[22] Their error is refuted by |the marshalling of| authorities and |of| rational considerations. And the truth about this wisdom is quite effectively explained—viz., that the soul, apart from the medium of prevening |rational| discrimination and solely by means of the conveyance of love, is experientially elevated beyond itself, as often as it wills to be. This elevation is not understood by reason and is not beheld by the intellect—just as in that section is said: "Taste and see."[23]

. . . .

QUESTIO UNICA[24]

In order to manifest the mysteries and hidden matters which I have stated about the truth, I will pose a difficult question—one in which the truth concerning this |hidden| wisdom shines forth quite brightly to whoever has understanding. Accordingly, I ask whether by aspiring and by longing, the soul, in accordance with its affection, can be moved unto God without any guiding or accompanying reflecting on the part of the intellect.

It seems that reflecting must always precede the affection's movement unto God through its extending forth its love.

|1.| First of all, |this is proven| in the following way on the basis of authorities: In the Psalms are the words "in my meditation a fire is kindled."[26] Therefore, the mind must meditate, through reflecting, before the affection, as a result of yearning, is inwardly set aglow while it ascends—by the fire of love—unto its Beloved. |2.| Furthermore, Augustine |writes|: "We are able to love things that are unseen, but we cannot at all love things that are unknown."[27] Therefore, before something is loved by means of the affection of love, it must be known through reasoning or through intellectually reflecting. Necessarily, then, reflecting precedes the affection of love. |3.| The same |point| is proven by rational considerations—first of all, by the following consideration elicited with respect to God: The soul which through the longing of love actually extends itself unto God, whom it loves, is called "deified" in |Chapter| Seven of *The Divine Names*.[28] For insofar as is possible for a creature: |the loving soul|, through extending its love, is conformed to the most superexcellent Trinity. But in the Trinity the following is the case: that according to the order of the |divine| nature the Father, who is Supreme Power, is first; the Son, who is the Knowledge, or Supreme Wisdom, of the Father, is second; and the Holy Spirit, who is True Love, is third. Therefore, a similar |order| will obtain in the soul, which through extending its love endeavors to imitate the most blessed Trinity insofar as is possible in accordance with the mode of its smallness: by means of reflecting or understanding, the soul will have knowledge of Him-unto-whom-it-tends *before* it is able to ascend unto Him by aspiring with longing love. Therefore, reflective knowing always precedes the affection of love. |4.| Furthermore, in accordance with the statement of Blessed Dionysius,[29] the church militant imitates, insofar as possible, the church triumphant. Therefore, the faithful soul that wills to ascend by degrees, through love, ascends in conformity with the orders of angels. And the minds of those who love most greatly are comparable to the final hierarchy, in which there are three orders, viz., the Thrones, the Cherubims, and the Seraphims.[30] Hence, in the soul that actually wills to ascend, the three offices or distinguishing properties of these three orders must be imitated. First, there must be "the Thrones"—i.e., |the soul must| altogether leave behind other things (viz., the worldly honors, carnal cravings, and earthly pleasures) in order that God alone may dwell in it, once a throne has been prepared |for Him|. Secondly, there must be "the Cherubims," i.e., by interpretation, fulness of knowledge. This |state| occurs by means of divinely infused light, by which the mind, reflecting supraintel-

lectually, knows and grasps divine and heavenly things in accordance with human understanding. Thirdly, there must be "the Seraphims," which are the highest order; that is, the affection—by desiring Him alone, whom the cherubic mind already knows—must now be set aglow for Him through fiery affections. And at that moment there will be "the Seraphims," for "Seraphim" means *ardent*. Now, the order of Cherubims, to whom is assigned reflective knowledge, precedes the order of Seraphims, which is interpreted as the ardor of love. Hence, in the soul, which endeavors to imitate this threefold angelic office, it will likewise be the case that reflective knowing precedes actual ardor, so that without guiding reflection the affection of love will not at all ascend. |5.| Furthermore, the soul, in ascending through love, endeavors to be conformed to the blessed minds of the saints, who contemplate God face to face. But, for those saints, beholding precedes cleaving-by-love. For unless that ineffable Fulness were perceived by them intellectually, they would not at all cleave steadfastly unto it with kindled affections—by the delightful satisfying of which affections their happiness is made perfect. And so, unless we reflected or cognized prior to our affection of love, we would not be conformed in glory to the minds of the saints, since they behold the divine beauty in such way that beyond all understanding they inwardly delight in it through love by means of their affections. In these saints, therefore, understanding precedes loving. |6.| Furthermore, with respect to the fact that the soul is endowed with its own powers, it seems likewise to be moved naturally and in accordance with its endowment. But I see that from the very beginning of its creation the soul has three naturally distinct powers—viz., memory, understanding, and will. Our memory is nothing other than the representation of God's likeness. Our understanding is that through which each soul by nature (not by investigating or by reasoning out) knows its Creator. Will is the power through which the soul loves its Creator and tends by nature unto Him; and because of this tendency human affection cannot be fully satisfied by earthly riches and honors. For it tends unto God alone, so that it finds complete rest |only| in Him. Therefore, since the power of the intellect (in which there is reflective thinking) precedes by nature the power of the will (in which there is ardor, or the affection of love), the movement of the understanding (viz., reflective thinking) precedes the movement of the will (i.e., loving). Hence, without guiding reflection no intellect—regardless of how much its affections are kindled—can ascend by means of the affection of love, so that it becomes elevated unto God. |7.| Furthermore, this same |point| is manifest with regard to |the power of| apprehension and with regard to the sensible stimulus. For insofar as I am moved toward relishing something imaginatively, I must first have perceived it through the senses. Hence, I must apprehend a given delectable object with the outer eye or with some other sense before taking delight in it, thereby desiring to have it. Accordingly, vis-à-vis |the power of| cognition and the stimulus with respect to higher things, the case will be similar: viz., that I must reflect upon God (or some other delectable object) before I can inwardly aspire unto Him, or can at all delight in Him, by means of my affections. Therefore, reflection always precedes ascent-by-love. |8.| Furthermore, according to what Blessed Dionysius says at the beginning of his *Mystical Theology*, in the ascent of love one must leave behind all intellect and all reflection not only upon sensible creatures but also upon both God and the angels.[31] But this assertion seems very foolish. For what would the mind be doing if it is not to reflect upon God or the Trinity or the angels? In that case, |the mind| seems beclouded or at sea, as it were, since the intellect's knowledge always directs its love. For otherwise mystical *wisdom* seems not to be wisdom but a misnomer or foolishness. |9.| Furthermore, whatever is apprehended is apprehended under a certain representation of being—e.g., |apprehended| either as true or as good. Therefore, in whatever way God is apprehended He is apprehended under the aspect of being—either insofar as He is Supreme Oneness or insofar as He is Supreme Truth or insofar as He is Supreme Goodness. Therefore, since only through cognition can God be apprehended in any of these ways (for example, if I were to apprehend |Him| as one, I would have to reflect upon oneness; and if as true, |I would have to reflect upon| truth; and if as good, upon goodness), then since love's apprehending apprehends God insofar as He is good, necessarily there would have to be a guiding reflection upon goodness prior to |the mind's| actually being moved unto goodness through the affection of love. Therefore, etc.

|B.| CONTRA[32]

It seems that the affection, being disposed through love, is freely moved unto God without any guiding or accompanying reflection.

|1.| First of all, |this opinion seems to be warranted| on the basis of the authority of the great hierarch Dionysius, who at the beginning of his *Mystical Theology* speaks in the following manner to Timothy: "But as concerns mystical visions, O Friend Timothy: in deep contrition leave behind the senses, intellectual operations, all things sensible and intelligible, and all existent or nonexistent things; and insofar as possible ascend unknowingly unto the union with that which is above all substance and all cognition," etc.[33] Therefore, since according to this |instruction| one must, in the mystical ascent of love, leave behind every intellectual operation and

all cognition and must ascend only in accordance with the union of affectionate love—|a union| which is beyond all intellect and cognition—then the one who truly loves ascends by means of the affection of love without any guiding reflection. |2.| In the third translation of Dionysius[34] we find in *Mystical Theology* the statement: "through the union of love, which is effective of true knowledge, one is intellectually united unto God by an unknown knowledge,[35] which is nobler than intellectual reflection; and with respect to the fact that one leaves behind intellectual reflecting, he knows God beyond intellect and mind," etc. Since, then, as is said in the same place, God cannot be known through intellectual reflecting, He is known most truly through the contact of love. Therefore, as is clearly stated, one must leave behind all intellect and ascend unto God only by means of the affection of love. |3.| Furthermore, in |Chapter| 7 of *The Divine Names* is stated: "We need to see (1) that our mind has the power to understand (through which power it beholds intelligible objects) but (2) that the union through which our mind is conjoined to those things that are above it transcends the mind's nature. Therefore, we must understand divine things in accordance with this |union|, not in accordance with ourselves; but . . . " etc.[36] Therefore, although in human |matters| understanding must precede being affected, nevertheless in the case of true, experiential knowledge of God sensing through love must precede the intellectual reflection upon the God who is sensed. Therefore, we must ascend through love, so that from *this* state of knowing |i.e., experiential knowing|, true knowledge may be reposited in the mind. For that which the affection senses about God experientially, the intellect also truly understands. |4.| Furthermore, in the same chapter the following is stated regarding mystical wisdom: "In exceedingly high praise of this irrational, foolish, and mindless wisdom I say that it is the cause of every mind and of all reason, wisdom, and prudence. In it all counsel is present; and from it comes all knowledge and prudence. In it are hidden the treasures of wisdom and of knowledge," etc.[37] Therefore, since Dionysius calls it irrational, it does not proceed through rational investigation. And since he calls it foolish, it does not proceed as does other, scholastic, knowledge; for when we proceed by stages, we first *know* whatever we |subsequently| *love*. Therefore, if mystical theology were to proceed first of all by reflecting or meditating in terms of rational considerations (as we observe in other |approaches|), then Blessed Dionysius would not have called it foolish or mindless (i.e., without mind); for |in mystical theology| the affection of love is kindled without any mental reflecting or meditating. Therefore, knowledge is reposited in the mind as a result of the affection of love, not vice versa, etc. |5.| Furthermore, the Psalmist |writes|: "Taste and see," etc.[38] Therefore, inasmuch as tasting relates to the affection of love but seeing relates to reflecting, or meditating, on the part of the intellect, then ascending by the movement of love must precede knowing the most hidden God by intellectually reflecting. For in mystical theology the following general rule obtains: viz., that practice must precede theory—i.e., the practical application in the heart must precede possessing the |theoretical| knowledge of the thing or things spoken of. |6.| Furthermore, this same |point| is evident on the basis of the authority of the commentator on *Mystical Theology*—|the commentator| from Vercelli |viz., Thomas Gallus|, who says: "The activity of |mystical| wisdom suspends the use and services of the senses, of the imagination, of reason, of the intellect, and of both the practical and the theoretical; and it excludes every intellect and all that is intelligible. |It excludes| *being* and *one* and *true*; and it transcends symbolisms and mirrors. And to the Divine Spirit it unites, in divine honor, the summit of the principal affection," etc.[39] Therefore, with regard to mystical affection no reflection or knowledge, on the part of the intellect, is required. |7.| Furthermore, this same |point| is proven on the basis of a rational consideration elicited with respect to God. For the mind is perfected by reason, in conformity with the fact that in mounting upward by degrees the mind ascends unto divine things by stages. But I see that in the divinity there are three persons—viz., Father, Son, and Holy Spirit. The Father is Supreme Power; the Son, Supreme Wisdom; the Holy Spirit, Uniting Love. But the Holy Spirit, who is True Love, is the last person in God—last according to nature and also according to our understanding, but not according to time. For we understand the Begetting Father to be first, the Begotten Son to be second, and the Holy Spirit proceeding from both to be third. Therefore, the Holy Spirit is last and is nearer to us. Hence, since the soul proceeds by stages when it mounts upward by degrees, it will have to have love (which is distinctively ascribed to the Holy Spirit, who is closer to us) before it has reflective understanding or wisdom (which is distinctively ascribed to the Son). Therefore, the affection of love precedes knowing, and not vice versa. |8.| Furthermore, with respect to the fact that the soul receives an infusion from God, the Fount of all happiness, it is perfected after the fashion of the church triumphant. Now, in accordance with Dionysius, it is evident that the order of the Seraphims ("Seraphim" signifies *ardent*) earlier and more fully and more perfectly receives an infusion from God than does the order of the Cherubims ("Cherubim" signifies *fulness of knowledge*).[40] Therefore, the affection, by means of the ardor-of-love (which corresponds to the Seraphims) is primarily and principally affected and moved unto God, before the intellect reflectively understands (this understanding corresponds to the Cherubims) that which the affection desires. Therefore, the affection is first of all moved unto God without any guiding reflection on the part of the intellect, which, rather |than guiding|, follows the affection. |9.| Furthermore, the rational spirit receives an infusion from God primarily and principally, insofar as it is closer to Him. But the affection, being especially disposed by love, is supreme within the rational spirit; and, consequently, it is nearer to the Uncreated Spirit. Therefore, the summit of the affection, as being nearer to God, is touched by God through an infusion of kindled[41] love within the |rational| spirit; |this touching occurs| before the intellect, which is a power much more distant from the Supreme Creator than is the affection, is able to apprehend God. Therefore, the affection is always moved unto God before the intellect understands |Him| by means of reflecting. |10.| Furthermore, God is distant from each creature as if by infinite degrees. Therefore, in order that He be known to some extent in this unhappy state |of ours|, the soul must draw near unto Him in such way that He is somehow attained by it. Therefore, since only love, through extending itself, causes the soul to draw near unto God: the more intently the mind loves, the nearer it approaches unto the Fount of light. And, consequently, the nearer the mind draws unto the Fount of light through love, the more the intellect is illumined by the Fount of light through cognition. Therefore, with respect to |approaching unto| God, ardent loving precedes intellectual cognizing.

|C.| SOLUTIO

We must agree with Blessed Dionysius at the beginning of his *Mystical Theology*: this |mystical| wisdom is predicated only of Christians.[42] Hence, it presupposes the knowledge-of-faith and the foundation of love. Accordingly, no mortal man, however great a philosopher or however knowledgeable he may be, |ever| was able or |ever| will be able to apprehend, by rational investigation or by the exercise of his understanding, this wisdom which is present in supreme affection and which transcends the faculty of the human mind. Rather, it is communicated mercifully and with paternal affection only unto the sons, as they await consolation only from the eternal Father. And it is called mystical—i.e., concealed or hidden—because it is known by few. Hence, we must note that there is a twofold mode of apprehending, in accordance with the twofold natural power of attaining unto God. For each soul has the power of *understanding* (this is the power of the intellect) and the power of *loving* (which is called the affection). By these two powers we apprehend God, who is Supreme Truth and Supreme Goodness. Hence, we apprehend truth by means of the intellect, and we attain unto goodness by means of the affection. In accordance with these two |powers| there is a twofold way of excellence. The one way,

which is called contemplation and is befigured by Rachel, who is said to
be attractive in appearance,[43] |occurs| when the mind, by a light divinely
infused from on high, receives the power to contemplate, through meditation and reflection, heavenly things alone. The other way is in terms of the
affection and is called the ardor of love; |it occurs| when by the fire-of-the-
Holy Spirit sent from on high the soul, with flaming affections and aspir-
ing unto God alone, desires only Him, in order that it may be more inti-
mately united unto Him through a closer bond of love. And this is called
the perfect part of Mary,[44] who was ardent with desire, as is told of in |the
Gospel of| John.[45] Hence, just as the New Testament is more excellent
than the Old, so the way of love, or of the perfection that there is in the
ardor of love—|a way| which is befigured through Mary—is more noble
than all meditation or intellectual striving, which is befigured through
Rachel. But in order that truth may be seen more perspicuously, we must
note |the following|: that in the intellect contemplation is twofold; and,
likewise, in the affection the ardor of love is acquired in a twofold manner.
For there is a certain meditation or contemplation from lower things to
higher things; and, conversely, |there is| a certain |meditation| that des-
cends from higher things to lower things. Concerning the former, Richard
of St. Victor makes a determination in his |work on the| mystical arc,
showing through 42 meditations, or considerations, regarding created things
how it is that the mind, adorned with the light of understanding, is supposed to attain unto knowledge of the Supreme Creator.[46] And just as the
Israelites came from Egypt unto the land of the promise by means of 42
dwelling places, so through those 42 considerations, ordered in 6 grades,
the faithful soul attains unto a knowledge of the Supreme Truth—|a
knowledge| transmitted to the entire rational spirit.[47] But the other |kind
of| contemplation proceeds conversely. For the mind, by means of light
infused from on high, judges about lower creatures in accordance with
standards of truth and eternal rational principles, which, in accordance
with divine illuminations, it perceives within itself through meditating.
And according as the soul is infused with fuller light by a radiating from
on high, so much the more infallibly does the mind examine—in accordance with these causes and rational principles, which are identical with
God, from whom every exemplified and conceived creature originally went
forth—the truth in created things and in all affections. |And this mode of
examination is| much better than is rational scrutiny. Nevertheless, we
must not deem that this |mode of| contemplation does not conclude in
affection, |for| otherwise it would not be contemplation.

But at present |let us say| nothing about these |immediately foregoing
issues|. For the ardor of love is much more excellent, much more lovable,

and much easier to achieve. But there is a twofold mode of attaining unto this ardor of love: one mode is scholastic and common; the other is mystical and hidden. For the scholastic mode occurs by way of inquiry and of elevation, and it is originated from lower things and mounts upward to the Supreme |Being| through prolonged practice. For example, this mode of loving God occurs through the guidance of meditation. For, first of all, the faithful student beholds outer creatures with his outer sense, i.e., with his outer eye. Next, mounting upward a little higher, he preserves, reposited in his imagination, that which he has just seen with his outer eye. Thereupon, rising still higher, by reasoning and comparing, he finds the one necessary, creative Cause of all things. In such way, the philosophers have arrived at a knowledge of God. For through beholding such a magnitude of creatures, so lovely an ordering of them, and their very great usefulness, the philosophers and all others know infallibly the one most powerful, most wise, most excellent Creator. And this |knowing| comes through a power of the soul that is higher than the outer senses and the imagination—|a power| which is called reason. Thereupon, from the foregoing consideration of creatures and by means of the aforesaid |occurrences| a certain disposition is left in the intellect, where the primordial foundation of created things is reposited. And the mind, being infused not only through the viewing of created things but also through radiation and illumination, is somehow elevated by God unto contemplating divine things more clearly. And this power is called the intellectual power, or the intellect, which engages only in pure meditation. Finally, all meditation or contemplation is of little or no use without the subsequent affection of love. Hence, Augustine says that it is possible always to flit hither and thither in reflection but |not always possible| to cling steadfastly in love.[48] Thus, knowledge or meditation always precedes the affection of love. Moreover, the faithful soul is aroused by God apart from all other creatures and by means only of the knowledge that is infused by God.

But the other |i.e., the mystical| mode of ascending unto God is much nobler than all the foregoing |steps| and is also easier to achieve. And this |kind of| wisdom is unitive |wisdom|, which is present in the longing of love when through kindled affections |the soul| aspires to ascend higher. In Book 7 of *The Divine Names* this wisdom is defined by Blessed Dionysius as follows: "Wisdom is most divine knowledge-of-God, acquired through ignorance and acquired in accordance with a supermental union |that occurs| when the mind, leaving behind all other things, and subsequently taking leave even of itself, is united with superbrilliant rays unto the Inscrutable and is illuminated with a depth of wisdom."[49] Hence, conformably with what is stated at the beginning of *Mystical Theology*: |proceeding| in this wisdom, leave behind the senses and sensible things, intelligible and nonintelligible things, etc.[50] Thus, this wisdom draws the affection of the lover upward without any guiding investigation or meditation. Accordingly, *there* there is no need to reflect either about creatures or about angels or about the Trinity. For this wisdom is able to ascend, not through a guiding meditation but by |the soul's| aspiring through the longing of its affection.

But we must note that this wisdom is understood in one way in those who are progressing, and in another way in those who have been perfected. For, necessarily, those who are progressing have to purge themselves, through the pathway that has been discussed—viz., through humility, through knowledge, and through illumination by the method of prayer. And, thereafter, by reflecting somewhat, |they must| go forth toward God Himself, who kindles |them| from on high. However, |they progress| not by meditating about God or the angels, as was said, but by ascending in accordance with the pathway[51] which immediately follows the purgative way in my shorter exposition of the *Pater noster*, which is a prayer in spirit and in truth. But after |the one who is ascending| has more diligently elevated himself through the affection's exercising itself or through reflecting in accordance with what was said in that earlier section of mine, then all reflection or meditation is dismissed, and the mind of the one who ascends is elevated only through the longing of love—|elevated| each time he wills, whether during the day or at night, whether indoors or outdoors, as he aspires only for union with his Beloved. And in this case the affection of love precedes reflection. For, that which the affection senses the intellect truly understands. And just as was stated regarding contemplation—viz., that it is twofold, one |type| which ascends, another which descends—such is also the case regarding the affection of love. For according to the previously-mentioned scholastic way, |the soul| ascends from lower creatures unto the affection of love; but with regard to mystical wisdom, the opposite obtains.[52] For that True Love, which is the Holy Spirit, the third person in God, last with respect to the order of the persons, is nearer to us and is first with respect to our affective ascent unto God. Hence, through the fire of love the Holy Spirit touches and kindles the summit of our affective |power| and draws |us| ineffably unto Himself, without any reflection or any rational discrimination. Accordingly, just as a stone is drawn by its weight and is naturally borne downward toward its center, so the summit of the affection—by its own weight and by a straight path, without deviation to the right or to the left, and without any guiding or accompanying reflection—is immediately borne upward unto God. Hence, this power—which is the affection and is what is supreme in the human spirit—is immediately unitable to the Holy Spirit by the bond of love. And this power, insofar as it is what is supreme in the |human| spirit, is unrecognized by all, as it were, except those in whom the affection is touched and moved immediately[53] by the fire of the Holy Spirit. Hence, Dionysius calls this a power that is immediately moved by the Holy Spirit; and his entire mystical theology proceeds in accordance with it. And |of it| he says: "Now we have a predetermined law. It teaches us to assert the truth about God, not with persuasive words of supreme wisdom but with a demonstration of the power[54] of theologians—|a power that is| moved by the |Holy| Spirit.[55] According to this power we are, in an ineffably fiery manner, ineffably and unknowingly conjoined, in accordance with a better union of our intellectual power and operation," etc.[56] Hence, in accordance with this power, which is immediately moved by the Holy Spirit, there is a much greater knowledge of God than |comes| by investigation through any intellect or reason. Thus, the summit of the affection is touched first of all. In accordance with the affection |the soul| is moved unto God through ardor; and from this contact a most true intellectual knowledge is reposited in the mind. For only that which |the affection| senses about God does the intellect apprehend most truly, as is said at the conclusion to the beginning of *Mystical Theology*: "through the union of love, which is effective[57] of true knowledge, one is intellectually united unto the unknown God," etc.[58] As a result of this union the intelligence is wonderfully illumined for investigating hidden |truths|. As a further result of this |union| the imaginative components[59] are removed |from the intellect|. Moreover, as a result of this |union| the disorder of the outer senses is restrained, as if by an inner rein. And in a fiery manner the affection overflows, extending even unto the sensuality of the flesh, where the affection mortifies the corruption of noxious material objects. For the more the mind is elevated through aspiring, the more the corruption of its evilly inflaming flesh is weakened. Hereby is evident, in greater part, the difference between the scholastic and the mystical teacher. For their arguments proceed conformably with their different understandings.

Now I must reply to the considerations previously advanced:[60]

|1.| To the first |argument| it must be said that the verse "In my meditation a fire will be kindled," etc.,[61] is understood with respect to those who are progressing; for in such |individuals| the ardor of love does not yet abound. Hence, by |the soul's| meditating a little in accordance with that way which was mentioned in my shorter exposition of the Lord's Prayer[62] (not, however, by reflecting upon the angels, supercelestial things, God, or the Trinity), the affection must be aroused more effectively. However, in the third stage—|viz.| on the pathway of unitive love, |at which stage| the one who is perfected is already aroused—guiding reflection is dismissed. By way of illustration, with regard to bridges: we see that in the construc-

tion of a bridge wooden beams are used as supports for the stones: once the edifice has been constructed, with the perfect stability of the stone layers, all the wooden beams are removed, for the structure of the stone layers can remain rigid without the assistance of the wooden supports. Similarly, in those who are progressing, reflection in the aforesaid manner is premised. Then follows the affection of love. Once the perfection has been established, the assistance of all guiding or accompanying reflection or meditation is removed, as was said above. |2.| To the second |argument| it must be said that I well concede the following: we *are* able to love things that are unseen, but we cannot at all love things that are unknown.[63] For mystical wisdom *presupposes* reflection upon God; hence, at the beginning of *Mystical Theology* |reflective thought| is referred to as the wisdom of Christians.[64] And |the second argument must be conceded| for another reason—viz., because knowledge is twofold, and one |kind of knowledge| does precede the affection of love. For with regard to the first |kind of| affection or progression in accordance with the scholastic, common way, there is a knowledge of God through created things or through the intellect *before* the affection of love is kindled in the one |who ascends|. And Augustine's statement is understood in terms of this |fact|. But according to Dionysius: in mystical progression the affection of love precedes reflection on the part of the intellect, as was said. Now, the Prophet David speaks of both |kinds of knowledge|. Accordingly, with respect to the first |kind| he says: "In my meditation a fire is kindled."[65] And about the other |kind he says|: "Come unto Him and be illumined"[66]—|illumined|, namely, through knowledge of truth; and this knowledge is more certain and more infallible than the former |kind|. By way of illustration: oftentimes, by means of certain features which are observed in something, it is known to be delicious to eat. From this knowledge the appetite of the viewer, in very many instances, is stimulated to partake. After the food has been tasted, there remains a fuller and more certain knowledge of the taste than was the knowledge which preceded the tasting. By comparison, something similar is understood regarding those |of whom David is speaking|.[67] |3.| To the third |argument|—" . . . with respect to God . . . ," etc.—it must be said that |this argument| is sound as regards the common, |scholastic| mode, if the soul is actually ascending. But as regards mystical progression the opposite[68] is the case. Thus, the objection on the other side |i.e., in the *Contra* section| still holds good—|a fact| which is evident in the development of the arguments. |4.| Thereby it is evident that the other argument |viz., the fourth| regarding the Cherubims and the Seraphims is sound with respect to |the order of| ascending more highly from lower things; and, thus, knowledge precedes love, even as the Cherubims precede the

Seraphims. But the opposite holds good with respect to |the order of| descending. For the Seraphim primarily and principally receives an infusion from God, *before* the Cherubim does. And so, by comparison: in |the order of| descending, the affection is moved unto God through love before the intellect perceives that which the affection senses. And, thus, the second part of the *Contra* section holds good. |5.| To the fifth |argument| it must be said that the case is dissimilar regarding the blessed and the pilgrims. For the blessed behold the brightness of the eternal light face to face; and they contemplate without any component imagery, without any bodily corruption, any obscuring mist, or any intermediary. And so, *there* there is the supreme degree of ordinance, because *there* there is no hindrance; and, thus, the intellect naturally apprehends the divine beauty before the affection delights in it by an indissoluble union. But with regard to pilgrims: although while existing in the bodily state they love, nevertheless (as says the Philosopher)[69] the human intellect is mingled with the imagination; and so, it apprehends in conjunction with images whatever is intelligible— especially the supreme intelligible |being|, viz., God. But even if through divinely infused love and illumination the component imagery were separated out of the intellect, nevertheless no matter how much the intellect were illumined from on high, it would always apprehend God in a finite and delimited manner, even though He is immense and infinite. And so, every intellectual reflection is always impure and unclean. And, hence, if there is to be true mystical ascent in the present |lifetime|, Dionysius commands that reflection be completely separated out from the affection of love and that |the soul| ascend only through ardent love. For even if |God| is all-desirable, as is said in the Canticles,[70] He is not all-comprehensible— neither in the present |lifetime| nor in the future |age|. And the more effectively all intellectual knowledge is removed during this ascent, the sooner |the mind|, by ardent affection and as if free-soaring, apprehends what it desires. And we must especially beware of the following: viz., that any intellectual knowledge be commingled with the ascent of unitive love. |6. & 7.| To the sixth |argument| it must be said that it is refuted in accordance with |the distinction between| the twofold mode of ascending through a love that is neither of the Trinity nor of the angels, as was said. Through this same |distinction| the seventh |argument| is refuted. |8.| To the eighth |argument| it must be said that although the manner of ascending mystically seems foolish and irrational to those who are ignorant of this |mystical| wisdom, nevertheless it proceeds most wisely and with a wonderful ordering. For the affection, by its weight alone and by discernment of love is borne unto Him whom it loves—|borne| more truly and certainly and infallibly than the corporeal eye sees any sensible object or than the intellect can apprehend, through reflection, any truth about God. If I am asked what, then, I will be reflecting upon, since I ought not to be reflecting upon God or the angels, then it must be said that |my mind| will only aspire and that it will not be reflecting.[71] So, then, suppose that the mind, having been prepared to some extent according to the purgative way, |becomes| free of any reflecting upon God or upon other things. And suppose that it knows only how to ascend by praying "O Lord, when shall I love You? When shall I embrace You?" and does not know how to pray any other prayer. Then if it were to repeat this |prayer| very frequently, it would experience itself to be inflamed, sooner than |it would| if it were to reflect a thousand times upon most hidden heavenly things and upon eternal generation or eternal procession. Accordingly, this |pathway| is most excellent foolishness, of which Blessed Dionysius says: "Thus, in exceedingly high praise of this foolish, irrational, and mindless wisdom, I say that it is the cause of every mind and of all reason and prudence" (as was cited earlier in the *Contra* section[72]). |9.| To the ninth |argument the following| must be said: in accordance with the ascent of that wisdom God is apprehended through the mode-of-being neither as one nor as true nor as good. But when the supreme power of the soul—viz., the summit of the affection— is touched by the fire of love, then because of this motion and this touching the affection gleams brilliantly as it aspires unto God. And so, Blessed Dionysius refutes those scholastic and speculative teachers. For they think they know all things, although they know little or nothing (except perhaps by conjecturing or surmising) about true wisdom, by which the mind is drawn unto God. And Dionysius, writing to Timothy, says in the following words that this true wisdom ought not at all to be disclosed to such |scholastic teachers|: "But see that none of the unlearned hear these things— I mean the unlearned who are established in existing things," etc.[73] And ridiculing such |teachers|, he immediately thereafter makes the following inference: "They esteem themselves to perceive divine things by their intelligence and with fulness of knowledge. Likewise, I mean the unlearned . . . ," etc.[74] And subsequently: " . . . truly believing that by means of what according to them constitutes knowledge, they know Him who has made darkness His hiding place," etc.[75] And this |mistakenness| occurs because this |mystical| knowledge is completely supramental and is present where every intellect fails, for the intellect apprehends only under the aspect of the true or the good. But mystical theology teaches that through the summit of the affection students of truth ascend by means of love. And what's more, the mind could never actually ascend by means of these movements if during the ascent it were reflecting upon something; indeed, the affection would |thereby| be wretchedly forced downward from its own elevated height. But, instead, the affection leaves behind, on a lower level and as a withdrawn attendant, the intellectual |power|; and without assistance therefrom, it ascends, by active movements upward, unto union with its Beloved. And, elevated more highly away from the intellectual |power|, it becomes more distant from it than the midday is distant from the sunrise. And this |occurs|, provided the body can stand it, as often as |the soul| wills—whether during daytime or at night, whether one hundred times or one thousand times. And |as an indication| that this is the case, I presently employ an example from the physical world, so that you may understand. I consider the movement of a stone which, naturally and by its weight, is descending toward its center. By comparison, the affection, disposed through the weight of love, ascends unto God apart from all reflection or deliberation—extending itself as if unto its own center. And by these movements (except in cases where briefly, as in a rapture, it is raised beyond itself—not by nature but by grace—through a divine lifting up), it elevates itself with continual longing; and it will obtain, in eternal happiness, fulfillment of its longing and satisfaction for its gaze. But if a speculative teacher or a scholastic student cannot discern this |doctrine|, let him listen to the Apostle, who was the principal hierarch of this wisdom, which none of the wise among the Greeks were able to understand, since this wisdom is known only by spiritual examination. Regarding this wisdom |the Apostle| says to the Corinthians: "Our spirit, united unto the Divine Spirit, senses the things of God";[76] and this is the wisdom which |the Apostle| spoke among those who are perfect.[77] Thus, this is |the gift| which the Lord promised to the apostles, when he said: "Be endued with power from on high."[78] Hence, just as the priest puts on his vestment |commencing| from his head, so the soul is endued |commencing| from the summit of the affection. Accordingly, the soul is touched by the fire of the Holy Spirit before the advent of any reflection. Therefore, it is quite evident that the soul which truly loves can ascend unto God through the affection—the longing of love having been kindled—apart from any guiding reflection, etc.

NOTES TO APPENDIX II

1. Hugh of Balma, whose exact dates are unknown, flourished during the second half of the thirteenth century. Balma, or Balmey, was his family name; his place of birth was the château of Dorche(s) (*Dorchiae* in Latin), which was located in the canton of Seyssel, Département of Ain, Province of La Bresse. (This canton is generally north of the Lac du Bourget and west of the Rhône river.) Accordingly, he is sometimes referred to as Hugh of Balma of Dorche(s). From 1289 to 1304 he was prior of the Carthusian monastery at Meyriat, also in La Bresse and about 16 kilometers north of the village of Dorche(s). Sometime during his *floruit* he wrote his insightful *Mystica Theologia*, alternatively referred to by its *incipit* "*Viae Sion lugent*" or by the rubric "*De Triplici Via.*" There is no critical edition of this work, since the edition announced for the series *Sources Chrétiennes* (Paris: Les Editions du Cerf) was never completed. The earliest printed edition (1495) appeared in Strasburg among the works of St. Bonaventure. It was republished, among other places, in Rome in Vol. 7 (1596) of St. Bonaventure's works. (See my bibliography section, p. 282 *supra*, under "Hugh, of Balma.") Of special importance are the following articles: (1) Anselme Stoelen, "Hugues de Balma," Columns 859-873 of Vol. 7, fascicles 46-47, of *Dictionnaire de spiritualité ascétique et mystique* (Paris: Beauchesne, 1969). (2) Artaud-M. Sochay, "Hugues, de Balma," Columns 1028-1030 of Vol. 5 of *Catholicisme hier aujourd'hui demain* (Paris: Letouzey et Ané, 1959). (3) S. Autore, "Hugues de Balma," Columns 215-220 of Vol. 7 of *Dictionnaire de Théologie Catholique* (Paris: Letouzey et Ané, 1922). (4) Jacques Dubois, "Le domaine de la chartreuse de Meyriat," Chap. 10 of his *Histoire monastique en France au XIIe siècle: Les institutions monastiques et leur évolution* (London: Variorum Reprints, 1982) [Chap. 10 is reprinted from *Le Moyen Age*, 74 (1968), 459-493, published in Brussels].

Hugh of Balma's *Mystica Theologia* is not contained among the books in Nicholas of Cusa's personal library in the hospice at Bernkastel-Kues. In *De Visione Dei* and in the letters to the Tegernsee monks, he exhibits no detailed knowledge of its contents.

The present English translation has been made from the edition published in Rome in 1596. This printed edition is an uncritical one. Therefore, the present translation should be regarded as more tentative than the ordinary tentativeness of all translations, even those made from critical editions. In the subsequent notes I correct several egregious mistakes in the Rome edition.

2. Lamentations 1:4.

3. I have examined microfilms of five manuscripts of *De Mystica Theologia*: (1) Graz 1068 (Universitätsbibliothek, Graz, Austria), fol. 1^r - 54^v, copied ca. 1400; (2) Melk 1719 (Stiftsbibliothek, Benedictine Monastery of Melk, Austria), fol. 112^r -204^r, copied during the 15th c.; (3) Salzburg b.XII.27 (St. Peter Archabbey, Salzburg, Austria), fol. 316^r - 346^r, copied during the 15th c.; (4) Trier 158/1254 8° (Stadtbibliothek, Trier, Germany), fol. 52^r - 96^v, copied during the 15th c.; (5) Vienna 1727 (Nationalbibliothek), fol. 1^r -72^v, copied 1424. All five mss. have

"relicto cultu" in place of *"recto cultu"*. Accordingly, my translation here follows these mss. rather than the printed edition.

4. Cf. Francis Bacon's use of the term *"idola"* in his *Novum Organum*.

5. Ps. 102:12 (103:12).

6. Hugh uses *"affectus"* and *"affectio"* interchangeably—even as he also interchanges *"unio"* and *"unitio,"* *"influentia"* and *"immissio,"* *"imaginaria"* and *"phantastica."* At the beginning of Section C *affectus* is referred to as *"potentia amandi"* ("power of loving"), an expression indicative of a general operation of the soul. But Hugh also uses *"affectus"* to signify a particular act of this operation, or power. Similarly, he uses *"affectio"* sometimes to signify an act, sometimes to signify a power. Thus, he writes not only " . . . *ista vis animae suprema, quae est apex affectus* . . . " but also " . . . *per apicem affectionis* . . . ." I translate both *"affectus"* and *"affectio"* as "affection"; and I leave to the reader, as does Hugh, the task of determining when the power, and when the act of the power, is being referred to.

7. The Latin word *"cogitatio"* has a plethora of meanings and nuances. But Hugh uses it, in the present work, primarily in the sense of reflecting or meditating or conceptualizing—as when one reflects upon the doctrine of the eternal generation of the Son from the Father, meditates upon the Lord's Prayer, or conceives of the oneness or the goodness or the truth of God's being. Such reflecting, meditating, or conceptualizing he also sometimes calls *knowledge* (*cognitio*; note Hugh's expression *"cogitando cognoscere."*) Thus, in these senses, *"cogitatio"* is used in a restricted way, which is narrower in meaning than are the English words "awareness," "consciousness," "thinking." Thus, in Hugh of Balma's *Mystica Theologia* *"cogitatio"* has a different meaning from its meaning in Richard of St. Victor's *Benjamin Maior*, Book I, Chap. 4, where we read: *"cogitatio autem est improvidus animi respectus ad evagationem pronus"* (*PL* 196:67D). Accordingly, for clarity and emphasis, Hugh at times uses *"cogitare"* in combination with *"intelligere"*—as in the expression *"cogitando intelligit."*

8. Ps. 88:15 (89:14).

9. I.e., "next" alludes to the *via illuminativa*.

10. Canticle of Canticles (Song of Songs) 1:1 (1:2).

11. Ps. 138:11 (139:11).

12. Viz., ascends unto the unitive stage.

13. "Anagogically" means *upwardly* and has special connotations within mystical contexts. Hugh here uses it in order to allude to a form of allegorical interpretation which seeks out the *higher* (i.e., deeper) spiritual and mystical meaning of Scriptural texts. For example, David's triumph over Goliath is interpreted allegorically as Christ's overcoming of the Devil. See Hugh's discussion of the three methods of anagogic interpretation (p. 704, Cols. 1-2 of the Rome edition of his *Mystica Theologia*). But Hugh concedes that *"proprie dicitur anagogia, idem quod sursum actio."*

14. Ecclesiasticus 24:5.

15. Here I follow the manuscripts cited in n. 3 above and read *"cum id tangat tertiam viam quae* . . . " in place of *"iam illud tangat tertia via, quae"* in the Rome edition. (The Salzburg ms. has *"illud,"* whereas the other four have *"id".*)

16. "*Secundo*" seems to be correlated with "*primo*" on p. 700, Col. 2, Section C, line 4 of the Rome edition of *Mystica Theologia*. This reference corresponds, in the present translation, to the sentence immediately after the numeral for footnote 14.

17. The passage being referred to can be found in the Rome edition, p. 715, Col. 1.

18. Ps. 33:6 (34:5).

19. This exposition begins on p. 715, Col. 1 of the Rome edition.

20. In this sentence I follow Mss. Melk, Salzburg, and Vienna (see n. 3 above) and read "*nimirum*" in place of "*mens*".

21. This exposition begins on p. 718, Col. 2 of the Rome edition.

22. This disputation begins with the "*Questio Unica*" and is here translated in its entirety. See n. 7 above.

23. Ps. 33:9 (34:8).

24. This is the very last section of Hugh's text.

25. The arguments in this section are rejected by Hugh in Section C.

26. Ps. 38:4 (39:3).

27. Augustine, it seems, nowhere uses these exact words. See his *De Trinitate* 10.1.2 through 10.2.4 (*PL* 42:973-975; *Corpus Christianorum Series Latina* 50:312-316).

28. Dionysius, *The Divine Names*, Chap. 7, Section 1 (*Dionysiaca* I, 386). Hugh makes use of the Latin translation (ca. 1167) by John the Saracen. This translation employs an inflected form of the word "*deificatus*," whereas Hugh's text has an inflected form of "*deificus*." In general Hugh does not so much quote from his sources as he does merely allude to, and paraphrase, their statements; this practice is followed especially with regard to Dionysius. But it also characterizes his citations of Scripture.

29. Viz., the statement, cited in n. 28 above, from *The Divine Names*, Chap. 7, Section 1.

30. See Dionysius, *The Heavenly Hierarchy*, Chap. 6 through Chap. 7, Section 1 (*Dionysiaca* II, 828-842, John the Saracen's translation).

31. Dionysius, *Mystical Theology*, Chap. 1, Section 1 (*Dionysiaca* I, 567-568, John the Saracen's translation).

32. The arguments in this section are endorsed by Hugh in Section C.

33. See the reference in n. 31 above.

34. I.e., the translation made by Thomas Gallus, Abbot of Vercelli, in 1238.

35. See the pericope in *Dionysiaca* I, 710, margin number 578. Whereas, according to the edition printed in Rome (1596), Hugh writes "*affectiva verae cognitionis*," the words as recorded in *Dionysiaca* are "*effectiva verae cognitionis*." Mss. Melk, Salzburg, Trier, and Vienna (see n. 3 above) have "*effectiva*".

36. Dionysius, *The Divine Names*, Chap. 7, Section 1 (*Dionysiaca* I, 385, John the Saracen's translation). Although Hugh's citations of Dionysius are allusions rather than exact quotations, the present citation ends in a corrupt manner. Cf. with the Rome edition of Hugh's text the words from John the Saracen's translation, as it continues onto *Dionysiaca* I, 386.

37. Dionysius, *The Divine Names*, Chap. 7, Section 1 (*Dionysiaca* I, 386-

387, John the Saracen's translation). Cf. Colossians 2:3.

38. Ps. 33:9 (34:8).

39. Thomas Gallus, abbot of Vercelli, presumably in his *Glossae super Theologiam Mysticam.*

40. See n. 30 above.

41. Here I follow the five mss. cited in n. 3 above and read "*igniti*" in place of "*igni*".

42. Dionysius, *Mystical Theology*, Chap. 1, Section 1 (*Dionysiaca* I, 565, John the Saracen's translation).

43. Gen. 29:17.

44. Luke 10:42.

45. John 12:3.

46. Hugh of Balma here confuses Hugh of St. Victor with Richard of St. Victor. See Hugh of St. Victor's *De Arca Noe Mystica* (*PL* 176:682-704). Cf. Richard of St. Victor, *Benjamin Maior*, Book I, Chaps. 1 and 2 (*PL* 196:63-66). Hugh of St. Victor alludes to Noah's ark; Richard alludes to the Mosaic ark of the covenant.

47. I.e., transmitted to the *ingenium*, the *imaginatio*, the *sensus*. See the section below, immediately prior to the rebuttal passages.

48. I have not been able to locate this passage in the writings of St. Augustine. Accordingly, I am uncertain that I have understood it correctly. Mss. Graz, Melk, Trier, and Vienna have "*non licet*" in place of "*licet*" and "*sed*" in place of "*et*". In Mss. Graz and Melk "*non*" is written above the line. My intuition is that "*non*" should be supplied before "*amando*" rather than before "*licet*". Thus, instead of the Rome edition's "*Unde dicit Augustinus quod licet semper volitando cogitare, et amando inhaerere, ut . . .* ", I am reading "*Unde dicit Augustinus quod licet semper volitando cogitare sed* [*non*] *amando inhaerere, ut . . . .* "

49. Dionysius, *The Divine Names*, Chap. 7, Section 3 (*Dionysiaca* I, 406, John the Saracen's translation). N.B.: There are significant differences between the Saracen's translation and Hugh's paraphrase of it.

50. Dionysius, *Mystical Theology*, Chap. 1, Section 1 (*Dionysiaca* I, 567-568, John the Saracen's translation).

51. Viz., the *via illuminativa*, discussed by Hugh in a portion of *Mystica Theologia* that is not translated here. See pp. 710-711 of the text published in Rome in 1596.

52. I.e., the affection of love precedes the ascent.

53. Here I follow the five mss. cited in n. 3 above and read the Latin word "*immediate*" in place of the Latin word "*mediate*".

54. Cf. I Cor. 2:4.

55. In place of "*more theoricarum virtutum*" Mss. Melk, Salzburg, and Vienna have "*mote theologorum virtutis*"; Ms. Graz has "*motu theologicorum virtutis*"; and the Trier ms. has "*mote theoricarum virtutis*". I follow the Melk-Salzburg-Vienna reading.

56. Dionysius, *The Divine Names*, Chap. 1, Section 1 (*Dionysiaca* I, 5-7, John the Saracen's translation). The paraphrase by Hugh of Balma is partly corrupt.

57. See n. 35 above.

58. Hugh here makes use of the translation by Thomas Gallus. See n. 35 above. Hugh's paraphrase of Thomas's translation here differs from his earlier paraphrase.

59. I use "imaginative components" to translate "*imaginaria et phantastica,*" both of which terms, as here used by Hugh, have the same signification.

60. These are replies to the arguments set out in the *Pro* section.

61. In the *Pro* section, argument 1, Hugh used the present tense of "*exardescere*" in his quotation of Ps. 38:4 (39:3). He also uses the present tense later. See the passage (in the text) where n. 65 occurs.

62. See n. 51 above.

63. See n. 27 above.

64. See the reference in n. 42 above.

65. Ps. 38:4 (39:3).

66. Ps. 33:6 (34:5).

67. I.e., in Ps. 33:6 (34:5).

68. Viz., that love will precede knowledge.

69. See, e.g., *De Anima* III, 7 (431^a 17-18), Loeb Library edition, 1935.

70. Canticle of Canticles (Song of Songs) 5:16.

71. Here I follow the five mss. cited in n. 3 above and read "*aspirabit non cogitabit*" in place of "*aspirat et cogitabit*". (The Trier ms. adds "*et*" after "*aspirabit*").

72. The *Contra* Section, Number 4.

73. Dionysius, *Mystical Theology*, Chap. 1, Section 2 (*Dionysiaca* I, 569, John the Saracen's translation). Hugh says "*firmati*" where *Dionysiaca* has "*formati*".

74. These words are not in *Dionysiaca*.

75. Dionysius, *Mystical Theology*, Chap. 1, Section 2 (*Dionysiaca* I, 569-570, John the Saracen's translation). Cf. Ps. 17:12 (18:11).

76. Not an exact quote. Cf. I Cor. 2:12-14.

77. I Cor. 2:6.

78. Luke 24:49.

appenòix III

ADDENDA TO THE VARIANT READINGS
OF THE LATIN TEXT OF *DE VISIONE DEI*

The following two manuscripts also contain copies of *De Visione Dei*:

K   Augsburg 99, fol. 167^r - 227^r.
        Location: Staats- und Stadtbibliothek, Augsburg, Germany.
        Previous location: Benedictine monastery of St. Ulrich and Afra
        (Augsburg).
        Date *DVD* was copied: 1472.
        Described: *Notitia Historico-Literaria de Codicibus Manuscriptis
        in Bibliotheca Liberi ac Imperialis Monasterii Ordinis S. Bene-
        dicti ad SS. Udalricum et Afram Augustae Existantibus*,
        Vol. 5 (1794), p. 108. Paper; trim size 11 cm. wide by 14.5 cm.
        long; body of text of *DVD* is 7 cm. wide by 11 cm. long; 23-28
        lines per page; incipit and chapter-titles in red; single copyist of
        DVD, which is the sole Cusan work in this miscellany.

U   Toledo 19 - 26, fol. 17^r - 41^r.
        Location: Cathedral Library, Toledo, Spain.
        Previous location: Rome; private library of Cardinal Francisco
        Xavier Zelada (18th c.).
        Date *DVD* was copied: 2nd half of 15th c.
        Described: Klaus Reinhardt, *Mitteilungen und Forschungsbeiträge
        der Cusanus-Gesellschaft*, 17 (1986), 96-141.

Only the variant readings of the Augsburg manuscript are recorded below.
The Toledo manuscript is of no importance vis-à-vis the text of *De Visione
Dei*.

1 1 *K*: Tractatus de visione dei incipit feliciter (Veni sancte spiritus *ante* Tractatus
scribit K). *Capitulorum tituli cum numeris post textum adduntur. Tituli 1-15 et 17
et 22, cum numeris, etiam in tractatu distribuuntur.*
    2 1 *ante* si: *divisionem novam facit K*   2 imaginem: ymagine *K*   5 uti: ut *K*
sagittarii: *ex* sagittaria *(?) corr. K*   6 Nurembergensi: Nuerenburgensi *K*   Bruxellis: Brurellis *K*   Rogeri: *habet K* (*ad* rudigheri *in marg. corr. K*²)
    3 2 intuebiminique: intuebitisque *K*   9 visum: eicone *ante* visum *scribit, del.,
et post* visum *rescribit, K*   scilicet: *om. K*

4 6 hoc: *om. K*   10-11 perveniet: proveniet *K*   16 dum attenderit: cum *(?)* attenderit *scribit, del., et* dum attenderit *rescribit, K*   quomodo: quoniam *K* 20 creaturae: creature *ex* creatura *corr. K*

6 2 perfectissimo: perfectissime *K*   10 propinqua: propinquinqua *K*   19 quod: quid *K*

8 7 ab: *bis K* (ab¹ *del. K*)   12 contractionum modi: contracti omnimodi *K* 14 enim est: est enim *K*   16 sic: si *K*

9 2 quod: *om. K*   7 omnium rationes complicat: omnem raciones complicat *scribit, del., et* omnium raciones complicat *rescribit, K*

10 6 provocaberisque: provocabisque *K*   17 ut: id *ante* ut *scribit, del., et post* ut *rescribit, K*

11 1 me: *om. K*   4 oculi: celi *K*   attentissime: attentissimi *K*   5 attente me: me attente *K*   13 subtraxeris: *ex* retraxeris *corr. K*

12 2-3 poteris me: me poteris *K*   3 ad: a *ante* ad *scribit et del. K*

13 8 amoris: *bis K* (amoris¹ *del. K*)

16 10 misereri: miserere *K*   13 monitione: mocione *K*

17 8 adsis: assis *K*   8-9 convertar: convertor *K*

18 4-5 nisi . . . conservares: nisi tu conservares *scribit, del., et* nisi tuipse conservares *rescribit, K*   6 qui²: quia *K*

19 6-7 non potuit facies: facies non potuit *K*   10 facies: faciens *K*   tua: *om. K* 12 enim est: est enim *K*   23 intueri: intuere *K*

20 2 ipsa me: ipsamet *K*   3 muto: mitto *K*   8-9 amorosiorem . . . tuam: *om. K*   10 faciem: a *post* faciem *scribit et del. K*   19 iudicaret: indicaret *K*

21 13 est: *bis K* (est¹ *del. K*)

22 4 faciei: feciei *K*   10-11 intueri ipsam: ipsam intueri *K*   12 quaerit²: queri *K* 14 quaerit: queri *K*   16 careat: carea *K*

23 5 sis: si *K*   7 sunt²: *om. K*   11 hic: nunc *K*   inspicio: inspicie *K*

24 4 sit: *bis K*   5 me: *om. K*   8 stupidissimam: *habet K* (*litteras* st *ut* sc *saepe scribit K; cf.* scriptoris *in 95:22 et* stupidum *in 95:5*   12 quae: *om. K*   15 video: vide *K*   17 et: *bis K*

25 2-3 reperibile: *bis K* (reperibile¹ *del. K*)   6 semen: a *post* semen *scribit et del. K*

26 15 quiesco: *om. K*

28 3 mei ipsius: meipsius *K*   5 video: vide *K*

29 7 amare: a *ante* amare *scribit et del. K*   8 est: *habet K, sed non clare scriptum*

30 7 nos: no *K*   20 exsurgens: exurgens *K*

31 10 et: *bis K*

32 12 causa: *bis K* (causa¹ *del. K*)   13 videt: ob *post* videt *scribit et del. K*

34 8 virtute: sui *post* virtute *scribit et del. K*

35 6 non: nec *K*   12 uni homini adest: adest uni homini *K*   14 formae: humana *post* forme *scribit et del. K*   15 humanitatem: contra *post* humanitatem *scribit et del. K*

36 8 compositus: *ex* compositum *corr. K*

37 6 quae: qui *K*

38 3 occurrit: occurra *K*   6 es²: *ex* est *corr. K*   8 obscura: obscur *K*

39 7 necessitate: *ex* necessitatem *corr. K*   9-10 qui nisi vincatur: qui non vincatur *scribit, del., et* qui nisi vincatur *rescribit, K*

40 3 videre: videtur *K*   9 simul omnia: omnia simul *ad* simul omnia *transponit K*   20 simul: *om. K*

41 8 omnibus: *abbreviat, del., et in alio modo reabbreviat, K*   11-12 tuum pariter: pariter tuum *K*

42 2 vocas: voca *K*

43 12 nihil: nichil *ex* michi *corr. K*

44 9 ut sint: ubi sint *scribit, del., et* ut sint *rescribit, K*   10 ante: *bis K* (ante[1] *del. K*)   18 aeternitas: eternitas *bis K* (eternitas[1] *del. K*)

45 8 et: *om. K*   9 esto: est *K*   15 iubet: *om. K*

46 5 evenit: eveniet *K*

47 2 me: *supra lin. K*   3 duxeris: in via *post* duxeris *scribit et del. K*   subsistere: sustinere *K*   in via: nequeo *ante* in via *scribit, del., et post* in via *rescribit, K*   7 ostium: hostium *K*   9 virtutem: virtute *K*

48 9 es[2]: deus *K*   es[3]: *ex* est *corr. K*

50 11 communicare: creare *ante* communicare *scribit et del. K*   13 nihilo: nichilo *ex* nichilum *corr. K*   14 es: *bis K* (es[1] *del. K*)   15 et infinitus: *bis K* neque[2]: nec *K*

51 3 creabilem: creabilis *K*   10 saecula infinita: infinita secula *K*

52 3 horto: orto *K*   7 quod: *abbreviat, et alio modo supra lin. reabbreviat, K*   14 intellectum: *bis K* (intellectum[1] *del. K*)   15 longe: a te *post* longe *scribit, del., et ante* abest *rescribit, K*   adhuc: est *post* adhuc *scribit et del. K*   20 immultiplicabilis: immutabilis *K*

53 4 in: *om. K*   12 incomprehensibile: incomprehensibilem *K*   13 te[2]: se *K* sciri non posse: *ex* scire non posse *corr. K*   14 scibile: *ex* scibili *corr. K*

54 7 quia: qui *K*

55 3 alteritate: *ex* alteritatem *corr. K*   5 alteratione: alteracio *K*

56 6 enim: *om. K*

57 17 inaequale: equale *K*

59 3 igitur: *om. K*

60 2 *Titulum capituli XIII hic repetit, del., et titulum novum scribit, K*   deus: *om. K*

61 1 domine: *om. K*

62 8 diversum: divisum *K*   15 et: id *post* et *scribit et del. K*   16 quod: quia *ante* quod *scribit, del., et post* quod *rescribit, K*   21 est: sunt *K*

63 2 sunt: *om. K*   9 incontracto: incontractus *K*

64 4 unita[2]: est *add. K*   ita est: est ita *K*

65 3 servulum: tuum *add. K*   4 picta: eicona *post* picta *scribit et del. K*

66 6-7 similiter . . . esse[2]: *om. K*   9 es: *om. K*   11 tu: *om. K*

67 1 prima materia: materia prima *K*   4 videris: vederis *K*

69 2 qui: *ex* quis *corr. K*

70 10 creare: si *post* creare *scribit et del. K*   17 nonne: nonno *K*

71 1-2 *Capituli titulum et numerum, atque litteram initialem rubram, om. K; in titulis post textum additis,* esset *om. K*   14 reperio thesaurum: thesaurum reperio *K*

72 3 finem: fine *K*   4 enim: etenim *K*

74 1 quod: quid *K*   5 intellectum: est finis eius *post* intellectum *scribit, del., et post* seu *rescribit, K*   7 illud: id *K*

75 2 non: *hic, sed non in titulis post textum additis,* non *post* perfecte *ponitur in K*   12 et: amoris *add. K*

76 4 illud: hoc *K*   5 unientem: uniente *K*   13 amoris: *supra lin. K (lacuna +* oris *deletum in linea habet K)*

77 10 occurrit: occurri *K*   12 essentia: *om. K*   19 unitas[1]: unita *K*

78 4 coincidere: coincedere *K*   5 possibile: impossibile *K*   8 sit: sint *K*   25 intra: ultra *K*

79 2 distinctionis: a *post* distinctionis *scribit et del. K*   3-4 praegustabilis: degustabilis *K*   10 exsurgens: exurgens *K*   16 hac: *om. K*   22 valde: a *post* valde *scribit et del. K*   26 quae: quem *K*   28 video: vide *K*

80 6 figurare: figurarare *K*   6-7 penitus inexpressibilem: *ex* prenitus inexpressibilem *corr. K*   11-12 gustum: tuum *post* gustum *scribit et del. K*   17 qui es: quies *aut* qui es *scribit, del., et* qui es *clarius rescribit, K*

81 1-2 *Capituli titulum et numerum, atque litteram initialem rubram, om. K; in titulis post textum additis,* deus *et* esset[1] *om. K*   3 eos: *ex* es *corr. K*   7 aut: autem *K*

82 19 amantis: a *post* amantis *scribit et del. K*   22 creatus: creatur *K*

83 4 nomen: se *post* nomen *scribit et del. K*   9 perfectionem: *ex* perfectus *corr. K*

84 1-2 *Capituli titulum et numerum, atque litteram initialem rubram, om. K*   6 es: *ex* est *corr. K*   9 est: et *K*   10 conceptu: conspectu *K*

85 1 exsurgens: exurgens *K*   2-3 generatur: *ex* generato *(?) corr. K*   4 conceptu: concepto *K*   6 amabile: amabilem *K*

86 11 attentius: altissime *K*

87 11 separabilitas: separbilitas *K*

88 1-3 *Capituli titulum et numerum, atque litteram initialem rubram, om. K*

90 3 in: *om. K*

91 3 quod: *bis K (*quod[2] *del. K)*   17 ad: *om. K*   19-20 via[2] . . . es: *om. K*

92 1-2 *Capituli titulum et numerum, atque litteram initialem rubram, om. K*   3 Ihesu: Ihesus *K*   11 magistri: *scribit improprie, del., et proprie rescribit, K*   13 verborum: verbo *K*

93 7 natura: materia *K*   11 ut: *bis K (*ut[1] *del. K)*   communi: commune *K*

94 16 natura: creatura *K*

95 2 videat: vidit *K*   3 Ihesu: Ihesum *K*   10 erat: *om. K*   12 videbas: *ex* vides *corr. K*   16 modo: non *add. K*   24 velocitates: folocitates *K*

96 10 audivisset: audisset *K*   15 finitae: infinite *K*   24 animal: et *post* animal *scribit et del. K*   etiam: et *K*

97 2 praetereuntem: pretereunte *K*   3 nescimus: *scribit improprie, del., et proprie rescribit K*

98 7 proxime: maxime *K*   12 non: *om. K*

99 8-9 capitur . . . verbum: *om. K*   10 iungatur: iugatur *K*

100 1-2 *Capituli titulum et numerum, atque litteram initialem rubram, om. K*

102 1 qui: *om. K*

103 1 meminit: sanctus *add. K*   4 cameram: camerant *K*   5 separetur: separaretur *K*   8 es: *ex* est *corr. K*   10 seu: *non proprie scribit K*

105 1-2 *Capituli titulum et numerum, atque litteram initialem rubram, om. K; in titulis post textum additis,* sit *om. K*   13 gustavit: gustavi *K*   15 delectabilissimam: delectissimam *K*   24 crevit: crevi *K*

106 1 ostende: ostendisti *K*   7 ratiocinativam: racionativam *K*   12 visceribus: vesceribus *K*

107 8 non[2]: nec *K*   11 motori: *ex ? corr. K*

108 12 et aptior: *om. K*

109 9 quomodo: quoniam *K*   14 onus: unus *K*

110 1-2 *Capituli titulum et numerum, atque litteram initialem rubram, om. K; in titulis post textum additis,* Ihesus sit *om. K*   3 quod immittis in spiritum: quod immittis in spiritum *scribit* (quod *non proprie scriptum*), *del., et* quod immittis in spiritum *rescribit, K*   11 sibi: tibi *K*   13 ubi[2]: ub *K*   15 intellectualis: intellectuales *K*

111 2 orbem: *om. K*   13 saltem: saltim *K*   18 quisque: quique *K*

112 2 Christus est: est Christus *K*

114 1 unguentorum: ungentorum *K*   10 amen: 1472. tercio kalendas februarii desero hora sexta *add. K; et continuat, sed in rubro:*Reverendissimi patris domini Nicolai cardinalis sancti Petri ad vincula Brixinensis episcopi liber de visione dei explicit ad priorem et fratres in Tegernsee. Incipiunt capitula in librum de visione dei. *Capitulorum tituli, non in rubro, sequuntur. In fine* 1472 *add. K*